# Contents

# THE GEOGRAPHY OF THE WORLD ECONOMY

**Fifth Edition**

Paul Knox, John Agnew and Linda McCarthy

**HODDER**
EDUCATION
AN HACHETTE UK COMF

First published in Great Britain in 2008 by
Hodder Education, an Hachette UK company,
338 Euston Road, London NW1 3BH

**www.hoddereducation.com**

© 2008 Paul Knox, John Agnew and Linda McCarthy

The advice and information in this book are believed to be true and accurate at
the date of going to press, but neither the authors nor the publisher can accept
any legal responsibility or liability for any errors or omissions.

*British Library Cataloguing in Publication Data*
A catalogue record for this book is available from the British Library

*Library of Congress Cataloging-in-Publication Data*
A catalog record for this book is available from the Library of Congress

ISBN 978 0 340 94835 4

2 3 4 5 6 7 8 9 10

Typeset in 10/12.5 Sabon by Pantek Arts Ltd
Printed and bound in Italy

What do you think about this book? Or any other Hodder
Education title? Please send your comments to the feedback
section on www.hoddereducation.com.

# Acknowledgements

The authors would like to thank the following organizations for permission to use the material listed below:

**Figure 1.4** from 'Shifting governance structures in global commodity chains, with special reference to the Internet', by Gereffi, published in *American Behavioral Scientist* 44, 2001, with permission of Sage Publications.

**Figure 2.3** from *Human Development Report*, 2005, by United Nations Development Programme (UNDP), with permission from the United Nations.

**Figure 2.8** from *World Trade Report*, 2006, by World Trade Organization (WTO), permission requested from the WTO.

**Figure 2.12** from *World Economic Outlook*, 2001, by the World Bank, with permission from the World Bank.

**Figure 3.1** from 'Shifts in economic geography and their causes', by Venables, published in *Economic Review* 31, 2006, with permission from Federal Reserve Bank of Kansas City.

**Figure 4.1** from *An Introduction to Urban Historical Geography*, 1983, by Carter, with permission from Edward Arnold.

**Figure 4.2** from the *Historical Atlas*, 1923, by Shepherd, with permission from the Perry-Castañeda Library Map Collection, The University of Texas at Austin.

**Figure 5.1** from 'Population, technology, and growth: From Malthusian stagnation to the Demographic Transition and beyond', by Galor and Weil, published in *American Economic Review* 90, 2000, with permission of the American Economic Association.

**Figure 5.2** from *Peaceful Conquest: The Industrialization of Europe*, 1760–1970, 1981, by Pollard, with permission of Oxford University Press.

**Figure 5.4** from *The US: A Contemporary Human Geography*, 1988, by Knox *et al.*, with permission of the Longman Group UK.

**Figure 6.1** from 'Industrial restructuring: an international problem', by Hamilton, published in *Geoforum* 15, 1984, with permission of Pergamon Press.

**Tables 6.2, 7.1** and **7.2** from Albrechts and Swyngedouw in Albrechts *et al.* (eds) *Regional Policy at the Crossroads*, 1989, with permission of Jessica Kingsley Publishers.

**Figure 7.2** from *Globalizing Industrial Research and Development*, 1999, by Dalton and Serapio, permission requested from US Department of Commerce.

**Figures 8.1** and **8.2** from *Political Geography: World-Economy, Nation-State and Locality*, 1985, by Taylor, with permission of the Longman Group UK.

**Figure 8.4** from *Industry and Empire*, by Hobsbawn, 1969 © E.J. Hobsbawn, 1968, 1969, with permission of Penguin Books Ltd.

**Figure 8.8** from 'The River Plate countries', by Crossley, published in Blakemoor and Smith (eds) *Latin America: Geographical Perspectives*, 2nd edition, 1983, with permission of Methuen & Co.

**Figure 8.11** from O'Loughlin, in Johnston and Taylor (eds) *A World in Crisis?*, 1986, with permission from Basil Blackwell.

**Figure 10.4** from Crow and Thomas, *The Third World Atlas*, 1985, with permission of the Open University Press.

**Figure 10.6** from 'Networks, keiretsu, and locations of the Japanese electronics industry in Asia', by Aoyama, published in *Environment and Planning* A 32, 2000, with permission of Pion Limited, London.

**Figure 13.1** from Martin, in Martin and Rowthorn (eds) *The Geography of De-Industrialization*, 1986, with permission of Macmillan Publishers Ltd.

Every effort has been made to trace copyright holders of material reproduced in this book. Any rights not acknowledged here will be acknowledged in subsequent printings if notice is given to the publisher.

We are indebted to many of our colleagues for their advice at various stages in the conception and preparation of this book, and in its current revision. We would particularly like to recognize Stuart Corbridge, Raymundo Cota, Bob Dyck, Richard Grant, Larry Grossman, Naeem Inayatullah, D. Michael Kirchoff, Chase Langford, Soo-Seong Lee, Andrew Leyshon, Ragnhild Lund, Sallie Marston, Ezzeddine Moudoud, Pritti Ramamurthy, Bon Richardson, Susan Roberts, David J. Robinson, Freddy Robles, Mark Rupert, David Short, Barney Warf and Colin Warren for their contributions.

# Part 1

# Economic Patterns and the Search for Explanation

In the first part of this book, we introduce the scope and complexity of our subject matter, establish the salient patterns in the world's economic landscapes and review alternative theoretical approaches to understanding the development of these patterns. Chapter 1 provides the orientation for the whole book by outlining the relationships between the organization of the global economy and spatial change. In Chapter 2, the major dimensions of the world's contemporary landscapes are described. The objective here is to identify dominant and recurring patterns and to note the major exceptions to these patterns. Both the patterns and the exceptions raise a number of critical questions about process and theory in economic geography. For example: 'How should the development process be conceptualized?' and 'What are the processes that initiate and sustain spatial inequalities?' and 'Why are economic activity and prosperity spread so unevenly?' Such questions are pursued in Chapter 3, where we outline a broad theoretical framework that enables us to understand the interdependence of the entire world economy and its spatial components.

Picture credit: Linda McCarthy

# Chapter 1

# The changing world economy

As its title suggests, the perspective of this book is global. There is a very compelling reason for this. The rapidly increasing interdependence of the world economy means that the economic and social well-being of countries, regions and cities everywhere depends increasingly on complex interactions that are framed at the global scale. The various processes responsible for the growing interdependence of the world economy are often collectively referred to by the term 'globalization'. Although local, regional and national circumstances remain very important, what happens in any given country or locality is broadly determined by its role in systems of production, trade and consumption, which have become global in scope. Most of the world's 6.2 billion inhabitants now live in countries that are either integrated into global markets for goods and finance or are rapidly becoming so. As recently as the late 1970s only a few less developed countries (LDCs) had opened their borders to flows of trade and investment capital. About one-third of the world's labour force lived in countries like the Soviet Union and China with centrally planned economies and at least another third lived in countries insulated from international markets by prohibitive trade barriers and currency controls. Today three giant population blocs – China, the republics of the former Soviet Union and India – with nearly half the world's labour force among them, have been drawn into the global market. Many other countries, from Brazil in Latin America to newly industrializing countries (NICs) in Southeast Asia such as Taiwan, have already become involved in deep linkages.

Robert Reich, former US Secretary of Labor, was unequivocal in his estimation of the significance of economic globalization:

> We are living through a transformation that will rearrange the politics and economics of the coming century. There will be no national products or technologies, no national corporations, no national industries. There will no longer be national economies, at least as we have come to understand that concept ... As almost every factor of production – money, technology, factories, and equipment – moves effortlessly across borders, the very idea of an American economy is becoming meaningless, as are the notions of an American corporation, American capital, American products, and American technology.
>
> Reich (1991: 3, 8)

All sorts of people in different places are affected by globalization. Take, for example, these three, documented by the World Bank:

> Joe lives in a small town in southern Texas. His old job as an accounts clerk in a textile firm, where he had worked for many years, was not very secure. He earned $50 a day, but promises of promotion never came through, and the firm eventually went out of business as cheap imports from Mexico forced textile prices down. Joe went back to college to study business administration and was recently hired by one of the new banks in the area. He enjoys a comfortable living even after making the monthly payments on his government-subsidized student loan.

> Maria recently moved from her central Mexican village and now works in a US-owned firm in Mexico's maquiladora sector. Her husband, Juan, runs a small car upholstery business and sometimes crosses the border during the harvest season to work illegally on farms in California. Maria, Juan, and their son have improved their standard of living since moving out of subsistence agriculture, but Maria's wage has not increased in years: she still earns about $10 a day.

> Xiao Zhi is an industrial worker in Shenzhen, a Special Economic Zone in China. After three difficult years on the road as part of China's floating population, fleeing the poverty of nearby Sichuan province, he has finally settled with a new firm from Hong Kong that produces garments for the US market. He can now afford more than a bowl of rice for his daily meal. He makes $2 a day and is hopeful for the future.

These examples begin to reveal a complex and volatile interdependence that would have been unthinkable just 25 or 30 years ago. Joe lost his job because of competition from poor Mexicans like Maria and now her wage is held down by cheaper exports from China. But Joe now has a better job and the American economy has gained from expanding exports to Mexico. Maria's standard of living has improved and her son can hope for a better future. Joe's pension fund is earning higher returns through investments in growing enterprises around the world; and Xiao Zhi is looking forward to higher wages and the chance to buy consumer goods. But not everyone has benefited, and economic globalization has come under attack by some in industrial countries where rising unemployment and wage inequality are making people feel less secure about the future. In particular, production line workers in affluent countries are fearful of losing their jobs because of cheap exports from lower cost producers. Others worry about their employers relocating abroad in search of low wages and lax labour laws.

## 1.1 STUDYING ECONOMIC GEOGRAPHY

The task of the student of economic geography is to make sense of the world – the real world – and the ways in which its economic landscapes are changing. But how can we cope, intellectually, with what is happening to the likes of Joe, Maria and Xiao Zhi? How can we cope with the local, regional and national implications of a succession of what are literally headline-making events? Bitter trade disputes between developed and underdeveloped countries, between the United States and Europe and between Japan and nearly every other trading economy; street protests against the drawbacks for LDCs of World Bank policies, high inflation in parts of Africa; weakness and restructuring of Japan's economy, violent labour disputes in Cambodia and Indonesia; the economic impacts of the AIDS epidemic in parts of Africa; and so on.

Furthermore, how should we approach the local, regional and national implications of less newsworthy but equally profound changes in the world economy, such as the remarkable developments that have taken place in international finance and banking? Most of all, how should we interpret the significance of specific changes that have been occurring in the world's economic landscapes: the deindustrialization of traditional manufacturing regions (e.g. the 'Rust Belt' around the Great Lakes in the United States, northern England, the Ruhrgebiet in Germany), the economic revival of formerly 'lagging' regions (e.g. New England, Bavaria), the spread of branch factories in the towns and cities of some newly industrializing countries (e.g. Taipei, Seoul), the emergence of high-technology complexes (e.g. Silicon Valley in California, the Research Triangle in North Carolina or the high-tech corridor along Route 128 in Massachusetts), the consolidation of global financial and corporate control functions in a few cities (London, New York, Tokyo), and the unprecedented rates of urbanization in China's coastal regions?

Our task is to develop an understanding both of the general economic forces and socioeconomic relationships within the world economy and of the unique features that represent local and historical variability. First, we should clarify the use of 'general' and 'unique'. By 'general' we mean something that is universally applicable. By 'unique' we mean something that is distinctive, because there is no other instance of it, but whose distinctiveness *can be accounted for* by a particular combination of general processes and individual responses. (For phenomena that cannot be accounted for in this way, we can use the term 'singular'.) From this perspective we can begin to establish some of the central interrelationships surrounding economic organization and spatial change. Figure 1.1 shows that economic organization, while critical to spatial change, is itself implicated with demographic, political, cultural, social and technological change, as both cause and effect.

The figure also shows that there are many interactions between, for example, political change and cultural change and between locally contingent factors and spatial

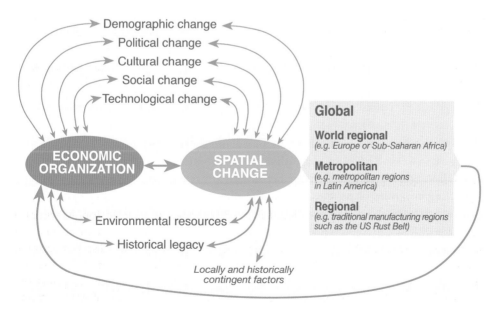

Fig 1.1: Interrelationships surrounding economic organization and spatial change

change. The point to emphasize at the moment is that all these direct, indirect and interaction effects are important to an understanding of spatial change. *They are all implicated, in other words, in accounting for both the general and the unique.* The task of the economic geographer is to unravel these relationships within a coherent and comprehensive framework. In order to do this, we must have a clear perspective on the central relationship between economic organization and spatial change. In the next section, we outline the most important aspects of this relationship, introducing several important concepts that we will refer to throughout the book.

## 1.2 ECONOMIC ORGANIZATION AND SPATIAL CHANGE

At the most fundamental level of abstraction, the idea of 'economic organization' approximates to the concept of mode of production: the way in which human societies organize their productive activities and thereby reproduce their socioeconomic life. The theoretical and historical identification of different modes of production is a difficult and controversial matter, but there are five major modes of production, or forms of economic organization, that are commonly recognized:

1 subsistence
2 slavery
3 feudalism
4 capitalism
5 socialism.

These are all broad categories, however, and each can be broken down into more specific forms of economic organization. It is often useful, for example, to differentiate between merchant capitalism (or mercantilism), competitive capitalism (early phase of industrial capitalism), organized capitalism (later phase of industrial capitalism) and the later advanced (also known as globalized or disorganized) capitalism.

What most distinguishes one mode of production from another are differences in the relations between the factors of production (land and other natural resources, labour, physical and human capital). With the slave mode of production, for example, the labourer is bought and sold, along with other instruments of production, by the slave owner. Under feudalism (or rank redistribution), the peasant labourer may own some of the instruments of production, but the land and a certain amount of the product is the property of the feudal lord and the peasant is legally tied to a specific tract of land. Under capitalism, the labourer owns no instruments of production but is free to sell his or her labour power. It should be noted, however, that different modes of production are also characterized by different *forces of production* (technology, machinery, means of transportation) and by different *social formations* (made up of specific proportions of different social classes).

The significance of all this to spatial change is that the economic 'logic' of different modes of production results in substantially different forms of spatial organization. Thus, for example, whereas feudalism brings a patchwork of self-sufficient domains with little trade and, therefore, few market centres, merchant capitalism requires a highly developed system of market towns and brings a built-in tendency for the colonization of new territories (in order to furnish new resources and bigger markets). Industrial capitalism requires spatial restructuring in order to exploit new energy sources, new production techniques and new forms of corporate organization. New mining and manufacturing towns appear and whole regions, such as the manufacturing cities around the Great Lakes or the Ruhrgebiet in Germany, become specialized in certain kinds of industrial production.

The 'classic' sequence of transformation from one mode of production to another, as experienced in much of western Europe, runs from subsistence economies through slavery, feudalism, merchant capitalism and industrial capitalism to advanced (globalized) capitalism. Because capitalism first developed in Europe and because the 'logic' of capitalism requires ever expanding markets, the sequence elsewhere has been different. In North America, capitalism was imposed directly on subsistence economies (i.e., Native American). In Japan, feudalism was displaced very suddenly by state-sponsored industrial capitalism. In Russia, an embryonic industrial capitalism was displaced by a socialism that soon gave way to state capitalism and so on. As a result of these variations, important regional differences have come about within the world economy.

More spatial change, and further regional differentiation, occurs with the evolution of a particular mode of production. Thus a particular regional agricultural landscape must be seen as *just one of a number of possible realizations*, not as a straightforward reflection of a particular mode of production. Each economic landscape should be interpreted, therefore, as the product of the combination of broad economic forces interacting with local social, cultural, political and environmental factors: a product of both the 'general' and the 'unique'.

## EVOLUTION OF CAPITALISM

The evolution of the capitalist mode of development within the world's developed countries has been a particularly important influence on the development of the world's economic landscapes. There have already been two broad phases in the nature of capitalism and we are now in the beginning of a third phase.

### Competitive capitalism

The earliest phase, which took place in the United Kingdom and spread to much of the rest of northwestern Europe and North America, lasted from the late 1700s until the end of the 19th century. It was a phase of competitive capitalism: the heyday of free enterprise, *laissez-faire* economic development, with markets characterized by competition between small family businesses and with few constraints or controls imposed by governments or public authorities. In the earlier years of this phase, the dynamism of the whole system rested on the profitability of agriculture and, increasingly, manufacture and 'machinofacture' (industrial production that was based less on handicraft and direct labour power than on mechanization, automation and intensively used skilled labour). It was toward the end of this phase that the United States took over from the United Kingdom as the leading industrial economy.

The collective prosperity of the industrial countries was, meanwhile, consolidated by their imperialism, which ensured both supplies of raw materials and markets for their manufactures. Gradually, the most successful family businesses within the industrial economies grew bigger and began to take over their competitors. Business became more organized as companies set out to serve regional or national consumer markets rather than local ones. Labour markets became more organized as wage norms spread and governments began to be more organized as the need for *regulation* in public affairs became increasingly apparent.

## Organized capitalism

By the early 1900s these trends had reached the point where the nature of capitalist enterprise had changed significantly: it had entered its second phase. It could now be characterized as organized capitalism – a label that came to be increasingly appropriate with the evolution of the economy over the next 75 years or so. In the early decades of the 20th century, the basis of profitability came to depend more on a new labour process. This process was Fordism, named after Henry Ford, the automobile manufacturer who was a pioneer of the principles involved: mass production, based on assembly-line techniques and 'scientific' management (known as **Taylorism**), together with mass consumption of durable goods, based on higher wages and sophisticated advertising techniques.

The success of Fordism was associated with the emergence of a workable relationship between business interests and the labour unions, whose new strength was in itself another important element of 'organization'. The role of government, meanwhile, also expanded – partly to regulate the unwanted side-effects of free enterprise capitalism and partly to mediate the relationship between organized business and organized labour. The market failures that had triggered the Great Depression of 1929–34 undermined the legitimacy of classical, *laissez-faire,* free enterprise economic liberalism and led to its eclipse by an egalitarian liberalism that relied on the state to manage economic development and soften the unwanted side-effects of free market capitalism. The role of government expanded dramatically to include responsibility for full employment, the management of the national economy and the organization of various dimensions of social well-being. This type of economic policy, which looks to stimulate aggregate demand in order to reduce unemployment, is known as Keynesianism.

## Globalized (or advanced) capitalism

After the Second World War, another important transformation in the nature of capitalism began to take place, leading to a third major phase. (This is denoted in Figure 1.2 as an evolution from industrial capitalism to advanced capitalism.) First, there was a shift away from industrial production and toward services, particularly sophisticated financial and business services, as the basis for profitability within the more developed economies. With this shift, the decline in manufacturing jobs (but not in manufacturing *production*) and an increasing globalization of the economy (in which huge transnational corporations (TNCs) were able to outmanoeuvre the national scope of both governments and labour unions) contributed to a destabilization of the 'organized' relationship between business, labour and government. By the mid-1990s, two-thirds of international trade were accounted for by the world's largest TNCs, the largest 10 of which have a total income that exceeds that of the world's 100 poorest countries.

Meanwhile, Fordism had begun to be a victim of its own success, with mass markets for many products having become saturated. As it became increasingly difficult

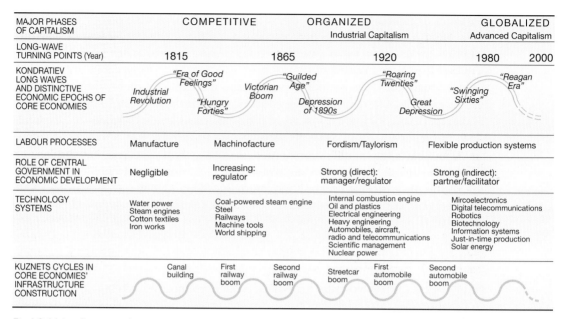

| MAJOR PHASES OF CAPITALISM | COMPETITIVE | | ORGANIZED Industrial Capitalism | | GLOBALIZED Advanced Capitalism |
|---|---|---|---|---|---|
| LONG-WAVE TURNING POINTS (Year) | 1815 | 1865 | 1920 | 1980 | 2000 |
| KONDRATIEV LONG WAVES AND DISTINCTIVE ECONOMIC EPOCHS OF CORE ECONOMIES | Industrial Revolution "Era of Good Feelings" "Hungry Forties" | Victorian Boom "Guilded Age" | Depression of 1890s "Roaring Twenties" | Great Depression "Swinging Sixties" | "Reagan Era" |
| LABOUR PROCESSES | Manufacture | Machinofacture | Fordism/Taylorism | Flexible production systems | |
| ROLE OF CENTRAL GOVERNMENT IN ECONOMIC DEVELOPMENT | Negligible | Increasing: regulator | Strong (direct): manager/regulator | Strong (indirect): partner/facilitator | |
| TECHNOLOGY SYSTEMS | Water power Steam engines Cotton textiles Iron works | Coal-powered steam engine Steel Railways Machine tools World shipping | Internal combustion engine Oil and plastics Electrical engineering Heavy engineering Automobiles, aircraft, radio and telecommunications Scientific management Nuclear power | Mircoelectronics Digital telecommunications Robotics Biotechnology Information systems Just-in-time production Solar energy | |
| KUZNETS CYCLES IN CORE ECONOMIES' INFRASTRUCTURE CONSTRUCTION | Canal building | First railway boom | Second railway boom | Streetcar boom | First automobile boom | Second automobile boom |

Fig 1.2: Major features of economic change in the world's developed economies, 1790–present

to extract profits from mass production and mass consumption, many enterprises sought profitability through serving specialized market niches. Such specialization required flexible production systems. The overall result has sometimes been labelled disorganized capitalism, not so much because of the lack of organization or purpose in business, government or labour but because of the contrast with the orderly interdependence of all three during the previous phase of organized capitalism. The driving force behind economic growth in this latest phase of capitalism is a global informational economy, a new mode of economic production and management in which productivity and competitiveness rely heavily on the generation of new knowledge and on the access to, and processing of, appropriate information. The most important economic sectors in this informational economy are:

• high-technology manufacturing
• design-intensive consumer goods, ranging from high-fashion footwear to entertainment products, selling in market niches around the world
• financial and business services.

## TECHNOLOGY AND ECONOMIC DEVELOPMENT

Changes in technology are crucial to exploring in detail the geographical path dependence of economic activities as the capitalist world economy has evolved: how, over time, patterns of economic activities meet with changing organizational and technological conditions to produce new patterns of economic activities. As new technologies eclipse old ones, 'old' industries – and sometimes entire old industrial regions – have to be 'dismantled' (or, at least, neglected) in order to provide the capital to fund the creation of new centres of profitability and employment. This process is often referred to as creative destruction, something that is inherent to the dynamics of capitalism. Creative destruction provides us with a powerful image to understand entrepreneurs' need, from time to time, to withdraw investments from activities (and regions) that yield low rates of profit, in order to reinvest in new activities (and, often, in new places).

Also important is the periodic development and exploitation of distinctive technology systems, clusters of energy sources, transportation technologies and key industries (Table 1.1). Each system requires different kinds of resource, different kinds of labour force and different socio-institutional frameworks that can harness the technologies for capital accumulation. As one system is eclipsed by another, so different regions are favoured or disadvantaged. Once dominant technologies emerge in a region, they become progressively more 'locked in'. Small initial advantages in the use of the critical new technologies and subsequent refinements in them bring much larger or increasing returns to those firms (and places) that have them. At a later date, however, this can become a disadvantage. Locked in to older technologies, firms (and places) find greater difficulty in adopting and adapting to new technological systems. Small initial differences, therefore, can be seen as producing new technological systems that then get locked in and produce competitive advantage for those who have early access to them. After a certain point, however, diminishing returns set in and the ground is set for a new round of technological innovation.

The so-called knowledge-based industries that are particularly important in today's economy are subject to increasing returns to scale because the businesses involved share three features. First, they have high fixed costs, particularly in research and development (R&D), but very low variable costs. For instance, the cost of writing computer software is the same regardless of the number of copies that are sold. As a result, the higher the sales, the greater the profit margin. Second, once in

**Table 1.1** Technology systems and the evolution of the world economy

**I Water style (around 1785 in England)**

Early mechanization based on water power and steam engines, the development of cotton textiles, pottery and iron working, and the development of river systems, canals and turnpike roads for the assembly of raw materials and the distribution of finished products

**II Steam transport style (late 1820s)**

Development of coal-powered steam engines, steel products, railroads, world shipping and machine tools

**III Steel and electricity style (late 1870s)**

Development of the internal combustion engine, oil and plastics, electrical and heavy engineering, automobiles, aircraft, radio and telecommunications

**IV Fordist style (around 1915 in the United States)**

Exploitation of nuclear power, development of limited-access highways, durable goods consumer industries, aerospace industries, electronics and petrochemicals

**V Microelectronics and biotechnology style (late 1970s)**

Most recent (and still incomplete) technology system is based on microelectronics, digital telecommunications, biotechnology, robotics, fine chemicals and information systems

place with a large number of users the software can become a standard for all users (think of Windows XP® or Adobe Acrobat®) because others will want to produce new software that is compatible with the standard. This gives the 'market leader' an initial and continuing advantage. Third, customers get locked in to established standards, largely because they must learn how to use them. Customer loyalty guarantees future sales when the software is upgraded. It is hard to say when these competitive advantages will be exhausted. In the past they always have been – eventually.

## 1.3 SPATIAL DIVISIONS OF LABOUR

The evolution of capitalism and its accompanying long waves have brought about a changing spatial division of labour. The division of labour within and between firms and over space is not fixed but responds to changes in the historical–structural context in which firms must operate. In the Fordist period in countries such as Britain and the United States, the basic division of labour was organized within the national economy or, even more typically, within regional parts of the national economy. In terms of production, plant, firm and industry were national phenomena, organized around national markets and industries and creating national social (class) divisions. Although capital, labour and technology were often imported and exported, they were subject to intensive regulation by national governments.

The internal geography of a national economy such as Britain's reflected its position in the international division of labour. For example, in the 1930s a small group of industries – coalmining, iron and steel manufacture, shipbuilding – owed their significance to the role of Britain in an international division of labour in which Britain specialized in certain key manufacturing industries. British trading patterns were shaped by the economic implications of previous investment and the increasing returns to scale and external economies of scale that this produced. Elsewhere, different industries, often newer, mass production ones based on larger firms, took root. Trade was a result of cumulative competitive advantage in sectors where each had come to have a 'headstart'.

The locational consequences in the British case are laid out by Massey (1984: 28–9) as follows:

> It was the United Kingdom's position as an imperial power, its early lead in the growth of modern industry, and its consequent commitment to free trade and its own specialization in manufacturing *within* this international division of labour, which enabled the rapid growth, up to the first World War, of these major exporting industries. The spatial structures that were established by those industries were those where all the stages of production of the commodity are concentrated within single geographical areas. The comparatively low level of separation of functions within the process of production, and the relatively small variation in locational requirements between such potentially separable functions, were not sufficient to make geographical differentiation a major attraction.

In other words, the spatial division of labour of key industries within national economies was based on different regional industrial specializations. National economies were regionally differentiated. Agglomeration was a major feature of economic organization across a large number of manufacturing industries. For example, within the United States during this period the northeast contained a vast array of specialized manufacturing clusters – steel in Pittsburgh and vicinity, automobiles in Detroit, chemicals in Wilmington, photographic equipment in Rochester, NY – and regions of agricultural and raw materials specialization elsewhere. Places and regions could readily be associated with specific products.

## GLOBALIZATION AND CHANGING SPATIAL DIVISIONS OF LABOUR

Under the new conditions of **neo-Fordist,** globalized capitalism, however, such regional specialization has been challenged and, to a considerable degree, undermined. Spatial divisions of labour are now structured in a variety of ways depending on the needs and characteristics of particular industries. In addition to *regional specialization* and *regional dispersal* (which has long characterized consumer services – stores, restaurants, hospitals, etc., and some manufacturing industries such as shoe production and food processing), four other spatial divisions of labour can be identified:

1  *functional separation* with management/research activities in major metropolitan regions, skilled labour used in 'old' manufacturing areas and unskilled labour used in regional peripheries to take advantage of lower wages and/or a disorganized (non-union) labour force
2  *functional separation* with management/research in major metropolitan regions, and semi-skilled and unskilled labour used in regional peripheries
3  *functional separation* with management/research and skilled labour in more advanced industrial regions and unskilled labour in the global periphery
4  *division* between areas with investment, technical change and job expansion, and other areas with stagnant and progressively less competitive production and job loss.

These new spatial divisions of labour have been possible because transportation and communications technologies have provided a 'permissive' environment in which firms could decentralize manufacturing and primary production activities yet maintain central control. There is now the possibility of intensive interaction and diffusion without geographical proximity. Firms can remain headquartered in, or relocate to, New York, Zurich or Hamburg, but locate manufacturing facilities in places with isolated and non-union labour forces, with particular combinations of labour force skills, costs and mobility, or close to highly concentrated regional markets.

Under this new international division of labour (NIDL), investment and production are no longer organized primarily around national economies. The actual process of production, most obviously perhaps in the examples of automobile, electronics and software industries, is now global. Components or specific services are 'sourced' or obtained from multiple suppliers in different countries (outsourcing) and assembled in several (see Box 1.1). Increasing numbers of products have no obvious nationality; it is difficult to distinguish some 'American' from some 'Japanese' cars, for example, now that American car companies import vehicles under 'their' names from Japan and Japanese companies now manufacture cars in the United States (e.g., Honda in Marysville, OH). The Barbie doll, an American icon, is made in China (Box 1.2). For many transnational corporations, national markets for capital, labour and plant and office location exist only as part of a global commodity chain. Even small firms have now acquired the propensity and capability to operate globally. So the 'new' conditions cannot be solely identified with giant transnational or global corporations.

## Box 1.1  Outsourcing and global commodity chains

Offshoring affects millions of people and is a sensitive and controversial topic. Neoclassical economics sees it as a healthy and natural consequence of free trade:

> In February 2004, when N. Gregory Mankiw, a Harvard professor then serving as chairman of the White House Council of Economic Advisers, caused a national uproar with a 'textbook' statement about trade, economists rushed to his defense. Mankiw was commenting on the phenomenon that has been clumsily dubbed 'offshoring' (or 'offshore outsourcing') – the migration of jobs, but not the people who perform them, from rich countries to poor ones. Offshoring, Mankiw said, is only 'the latest manifestation of the gains from trade that economists have talked about at least since Adam Smith. ... More things are tradable than were tradable in the past, and that's a good thing.' Although Democratic and Republican politicians alike excoriated Mankiw for his callous attitude toward American jobs, economists lined up to support his claim that offshoring is simply international business as usual.
>
> Blinder (2006: 1)

Figure 1.3 shows employment in **captive outsourcing**, where the work is done by foreign affiliates of US corporations. It excludes **offshore outsourcing**, where the work is done by unaffiliated companies, like independent foreign subcontractors.

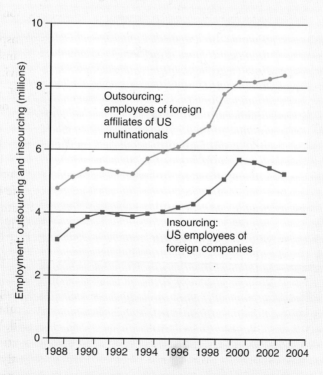

Fig 1.3: Employment outsourcing and insourcing, United States, 1988–2003

*Source:* Adapted from Mankiw and Swagel (2006: 27, Figure 2)

The contemporary world economy is constituted through myriad commodity chains (see Figure 1.4) that criss-cross global space as a result of this global reach of transnational corporations. In *producer-driven* commodity chains, large, often transnational, corporations coordinate production networks; in *consumer-driven* commodity chains, large retailers, brand-name merchandisers and trading companies influence decentralized production networks in a variety of exporting countries, often in the LDCs. Commodity chains link the production and supply of raw materials, the processing of raw materials, the production of components, the assembly of finished products and the distribution of finished products into vast global assembly systems. As we will see in subsequent chapters, these global assembly systems are increasingly important in shaping economic landscapes everywhere.

The advantages to manufacturers of a global assembly system are several. First, a global assembly system for standardized global products for the global market can maximize economies of scale. Second, a global assembly system allows production and assembly to take greater advantage of the full range of geographical variations in costs. Basic wages in manufacturing industries, for example, are between 25 and 75 times higher in advanced industrial countries than in some LDCs. With a global assembly system, labour-intensive work can be done where labour is cheap, raw materials can be processed near their

**Producer-driven commodity chains**

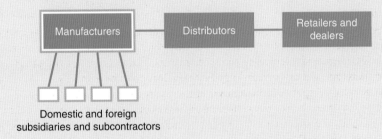

**Buyer-driven commodity chains**

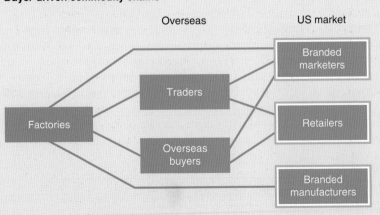

Fig 1.4: Basic elements of commodity chains
*Source*: Gereffi (2001: 1619, Figure 1)

source of supply, final assembly can be done close to major markets, and so on. Third, a global assembly system means that a company is no longer dependent on a single source of supply for a specific component, thus reducing its vulnerability to industrial troubles and other disturbances.

## Box 1.2  Barbie: American icon and global product

The famous (and impossible) physique of the Barbie doll says 'Made in America' but the box it comes in says 'Made in China'. Tracing the doll's production path raises questions about how its place of origin can be identified and how the globalization of production ties together disparate locations in the core and the periphery. Barbie is made from plastic injected into moulds at two factories in south China adjacent to Hong Kong, two in Indonesia and one in Malaysia. Barbie has *never* been made in the USA. The first doll was produced in Japan in 1959. As costs rose in Japan, production was moved to other sites in Asia. At one time the producer, Mattel, had Barbie factories in Taiwan, Hong Kong and the Philippines. In 1988, after a strike, Mattel closed its two Philippine factories with a loss of 4000 jobs. The plastic is made from ethylene, refined from Saudi Arabian oil, which is turned into pellets by a firm in Taiwan. Barbie's nylon hair comes from Japan. Her cardboard packaging is made in the United States. The manufacturing and packaging is managed from Hong Kong. The production story begins, however, in the 'commodity management centre' of the Mattel Corporation, one of the world's largest toy companies, in El Segundo, California, near Los Angeles International Airport. That is where information about commodity prices and wage rates is used to decide on the best locations to buy the plastic resins, the cloth, the paper and other materials and bring them together at a final point of assembly.

At one time, Japan and Taiwan were the main toy makers to the world economy. As their economies diversified into more capital-intensive production, they became the suppliers of the plastics that hitherto had come from the USA and western Europe. Production shifted to lower wage sites, and particularly to China, where Mattel manufactures most of the world's Barbie dolls. Making Barbie is extremely labour intensive. Workers must operate plastic moulds, sew clothing and paint the details on the dolls. A typical Barbie requires 15 separate paint stations. Machines cannot perform these tasks. Thus, the two Barbie plants in China employ about 11,000 workers, mainly unmarried women aged between 18 and 23 from poor regions of interior China brought to work at the factories for two to five years (Tempest, 1996).

So, Barbie is made in China. In the trade ledgers – where country trade deficits and surpluses are defined – Barbie is one of its exports. In fact, a number of firms in different countries contributed to its production and reaped their profits from the final product. The Chinese firms and workers obtain only about 35 cents out of the US$2 export value placed on each Barbie when she leaves Hong Kong. Barbie retails in the USA for around US$15. In recent years, Barbie sales in the USA have been declining. Nevertheless, Barbie accounted for US$1.5 billion in sales for Mattel in 2006. She is sold in 150 countries at the rate of three dolls per second. Over 40 per cent of the dolls are sold in Europe and Japan.

The pace of this economic globalization has accelerated since the late 1960s. Between 1961 and 1976, for example, the number of employees of German firms outside Germany increased tenfold. The number of firms with foreign operations doubled during the same period of time. Today, the 30 largest globally operating Finnish companies employ more than 50 per cent of their employees outside Finland. German and Finnish firms have generally been less willing to expand foreign operations compared to American and British firms, so these figures indicate something of a lower bound among countries with long histories of industrialization.

Paralleling and stimulating this trend has been the emergence of international devices for coordinating and steering capital beyond national control (e.g. the eurodollars in circulation outside the USA, see p. 48) and the offshore financial centres (see p. 348) that, rather like some old city states did in their day, now service the new international division of labour. Table 1.2 highlights the rapid growth in the size and depth the global foreign exchange market, where daily volumes are now close to 10 per cent of US GDP. Some small states such as Switzerland have successfully cashed in on the new world economy to the extent that they now have median income levels higher than those of the 'old' national manufacturing economies such as Britain and the United States.

Table 1.2 Global foreign exchange market turnover (daily averages, US$ billions)

|  | 1989 | 1992 | 1995 | 1998 | 2001 | 2004 |
|---|---|---|---|---|---|---|
| Spot transactions[1] | 317 | 394 | 494 | 568 | 387 | 621 |
| Outright forwards[2] | 27 | 58 | 97 | 128 | 131 | 208 |
| Foreign exchange swaps[3] | 190 | 324 | 546 | 734 | 656 | 944 |
| Estimated gaps in reporting | 56 | 44 | 53 | 60 | 26 | 107 |
| Total 'traditional' turnover | 590 | 820 | 1190 | 1490 | 1200 | 1880 |

[1] Single outright transactions involving the exchange of two currencies at a rate agreed on the date of the contract for value or delivery (cash settlement) within two business days.
[2] Transactions involving the exchange of two currencies at a rate agreed on the date of the contract for value or delivery at some time (more than two business days) in the future.
[3] Transactions involving the actual exchange of two currencies on a specific date at a rate agreed at the time of conclusion of the contract (the short leg), and a reverse exchange of the same two currencies at a date further in the future and at a rate agreed at the time of the contract (the long leg).

Source: Bank for International Settlements (2005: 74)

National economies, therefore, are no longer the sole building blocks of the world economy. For an increasing proportion of agricultural and manufactured commodities and for some services, production and markets have become worldwide. This shift has had important consequences for the spatial distribution of economic activities both globally and within countries. Globally, it has given rise to the growth of NICs such as Brazil, Hong Kong, Mexico, Singapore, South Korea and Taiwan. It has also contributed to a significant polarization of income and wealth. According to the World Bank (2000), the average per capita income in the richest 20 countries is 37 times that of the poorest 20 – a gap that has doubled in the past 40 years. Within the 'core' of advanced industrial national economies, the new international division of labour has led to both a reorientation in employment away from manufacturing to services and massive restructuring of regional economies. In Britain, for example, three sorts of local area have fallen victim to the loss of 'traditional' manufacturing industries and the failure of new ones to replace them:

1  the centres of 19th-century industrialization in the north of England, South Wales and central Scotland
2  the 'inner cities' of London and other large metropolitan areas with concentrations of poor people and few of the unskilled jobs that they used to fill
3  the centres of the growth industries of the 1950s and 1960s (vehicles and engineering) in the West Midlands and northwest of England.

We will draw on this broad framework throughout the remainder of this book as we analyze and describe the geography of the world economy. We begin, in Chapter 2, by establishing the major dimensions of the contemporary economic landscapes within the world economy. In Chapter 3 we establish a comprehensive global historical framework, which serves as the context for the rest of the book. In Part 2, we trace the emergence of three of the world's core economies – Europe, North America and Japan – and follow their different paths towards increasing scale and complexity. Part 3 deals with the spatial transformation of the core and periphery of the world economy, paying special attention to the changes in the periphery that have occurred as a consequence of the colonialism and global capitalism emanating from the core economies, and to the role of agriculture, manufacturing, and services in economic development and spatial change. Finally, in Part 4, we examine some of the reactions to the emergence of ever larger and more powerful economic forces that have come to characterize the world economy, describing the spatial consequences of transnational political and economic integration and of decentralist reactions: nationalism, regionalism and grassroots movements towards economic democracy.

## KEY SOURCES AND SUGGESTED READING

Blinder, A.S. 2006. Offshoring: the next Industrial Revolution?, *Foreign Affairs*, March/April.

Bryson, J., Henry, N., Keeble, D. and Martin, R. (eds) 1999. *The Economic Geography Reader*. New York: John Wiley & Sons.

Clark, G., Feldman, M. and Gertler, M.S. (eds) 2000. *The Oxford Handbook of Economic Geography*. New York: Oxford University Press.

Hughes, A. and Reimer, S. (eds) 2004. *Geographies of Commodity Chains*. New York: Routledge.

Johnston, R.J., Taylor, P.J. and Watts, M. (eds) 2002. *Geographies of Global Change: Remapping the World*. Cambridge, MA: Blackwell.

Lee, R. and Wills, J. (eds) 1997. *Geographies of Economies*. London: Arnold.

Mankiw, N.G. and Swagel, P. 2006. The politics and economics of outsourcing, *Working Paper* 12398, National Bureau of Economic Research.

Massey, D. 1984. *Spatial Divisions of Labour*. London: Methuen.

O'Loughlin, J., Staeheli, L. and Greenburg, E. (eds) 2004. *Globalization and its Outcomes*. New York: Guilford Press.

Venables, A.J. 2006. Shifts in economic geography and their causes, *Federal Reserve Bank of Kansas City Economic Review*, 31, 61–85.

Wallerstein, I. 1991. *Geopolitics and Geoculture. Essays on the Changing World-System.* Cambridge: Cambridge University Press.

## RELATED WEBSITES

Association of American Geographers: http://www.aag.org/
the AAG's website for the subject and discipline of geography has many useful hyperlinks including ones to the websites of specialty groups, such as the Economic Geography Specialty Group

Central Intelligence Agency of the United States: http://www.odci.gov/
website contains publications and maps produced by the CIA, including the latest edition of the *World Factbook*, which has detailed information and a map of every country of the world

Global Trade Watch: http://www.citizen.org/trade/
Global Trade Watch (GTW) is a division of Public Citizen, the consumer and environmental group founded in the United States in 1971. GTW was created in 1995 to promote government and corporate accountability in the globalization and trade arena. This website offers materials and hyperlinks to organizations that include opposition voices to globalization

Globalization: http://www.emory.edu/SOC/globalization/
this Emory University website offers a wealth of information on globalization and includes a glossary of terms related to globalization

Royal Geographical Society with the Institute of British Geographers: http://www.rgs.org/RGS/
the RGS/IBG website for the subject and discipline of geography offers many useful hyperlinks to other websites of interest to economic geographers

Picture credit: Paul Knox

# Chapter 2

# Global patterns and trends

Geography is about local variability within a general context.

Johnston (1984: 444)

In this chapter, we describe the major dimensions of the contemporary economic landscape. Space does not permit anything like a full coverage of patterns of economic activity or of the quilt of economic development, let alone a systematic review, resource by resource, industry by industry, flow by flow of commodities, services and capital. Such a catalogue, in any case, is not our purpose. Rather, our objective is to identify dominant and recurring patterns and to note the major exceptions to these patterns. We are, in other words, concerned primarily with characterizing the *general context* referred to by Johnston in the opening quotation. To the extent that we identify exceptions and contradictions, we are also concerned to some degree with *local variability*. In subsequent chapters our objective will be to uncover the processes that have contributed to these patterns – both the general and the locally distinctive or unique. As we shall see, *it is the interaction of the unique with the general that produces distinctive economic regions.*

It has been widely recognized for several decades that the dominant components of economic geography at the global scale are cast in terms of core–periphery differences. Meier and Baldwin (1957) were perhaps the earliest writers to attempt a conceptual description of this core–periphery structure on a global scale. According to them, a country is at the centre of the world economy:

> [I]f it plays a dominant, active role in world trade. Usually such a country is a rich, market-type economy of the primarily industrial or agricultural-industrial variety. Foreign trade revolves around it: it is a large exporter and importer, and the international movement of capital normally occurs from it to other countries.

In contrast, they argued, a country could be considered peripheral:

> [I]f it plays a secondary or passive role in world trade. In terms of their domestic characteristics, peripheral countries may be market-type economies or subsistence-type

economies. The common feature of a peripheral economy is its external dependence
on the centre as the source of a large proportion of imports, as the destination for a
large proportion of exports, and as a lender of capital.

Meier and Baldwin (1957: 147)

By the 1960s it was clear that international socioeconomic inequalities were
becoming more rather than less pronounced. A virtual avalanche of critical writings appeared, claiming that the prosperity of the developed countries in the
world economy (the USA, Europe and Japan, in particular) was based on *underdevelopment* and squalor in LDCs. The latter could not 'follow' the previous
historical experience of developed countries, it was argued, because their underdevelopment was a structural requirement for development elsewhere. The
development of Europe and North America, in other words, *depended* on the systematic underdevelopment of LDCs. By means of unequal trade, the exploitation
of labour, and profit extraction, the underdeveloped countries were becoming
*increasingly* rather than decreasingly impoverished.

Immanuel Wallerstein's world-system theory (1984) took this kind of disequilibrium into account. According to this perspective, the entire world economy is to be
seen as an evolving market system in which an economic hierarchy of states – a
*core*, a *semi-periphery* and a *periphery* – is a product of the long-wave economic
rhythms that dominate the dynamics of the system. Because of the dynamics of these
economic long waves, the composition of each category is variable: countries can
move from periphery to semi-periphery, core to periphery and so on. The labels
'core' and 'periphery' are used by Wallerstein to refer to the dominant *processes*
operating at particular levels in the hierarchy. Core processes are characterized by
economic relations that incorporate relatively high wages, advanced technology and
a diversified production mix, whereas periphery processes involve low wages, more
rudimentary technology and a simple production mix. The label 'semi-periphery'
refers to places where there is, at present, a mix of both sets of processes. In essence,
semi-peripheral countries are seen as exploiting peripheral countries while being
exploited by core countries.

Figure 2.1 represents an attempt to capture the current composition of the three
categories, based on countries' total gross domestic product (GDP) and GDP per
capita. GDP is an estimate of the total value of all materials, foodstuffs, goods and
services that are produced by a country in a particular year. To standardize for countries' varying sizes, the statistic is normally divided by total population, which gives an
indicator, per capita GDP, that provides a good yardstick of relative levels of economic
development (gross national income (GNI), a similar measure, includes the value of
income from abroad – flows of profits or losses from overseas investments, for example). Countries with high scores on total GDP and GDP per capita are likely to have
politically strong states, large internal markets and predominantly high-wage, capital-
intensive production – all, theoretically, defining characteristics of core status.
Conversely, countries with a low national economic output and a low GDP per capita
are likely to have weak states, and predominantly low-wage, labour-intensive production. These are rather sweeping assumptions; and the allocation of individual
countries to particular categories is inevitably somewhat arbitrary. Additionally, the
category of countries with intermediate scores for total GDP and GDP per capita
comprises quite a diverse group. Semi-peripheral countries include resource-exporting

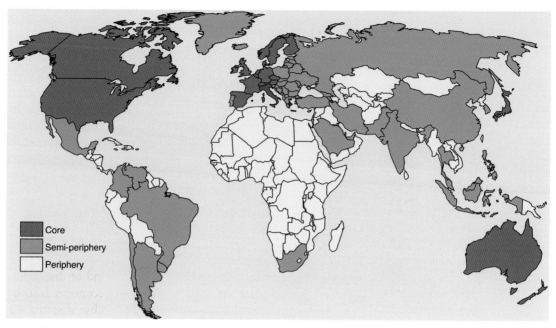

Fig 2.1: The world-system: core, semi-periphery and periphery

countries such as Saudi Arabia and South Africa, recently industrialized countries like Mexico, Brazil, Hong Kong and Singapore, as well as newly industrializing countries such as Malaysia and Thailand. The semi-periphery also includes China, India, poorer European countries like Greece and Portugal, the formerly socialist countries of eastern Europe and Russia. What is important in the present context is to recognize that the division of the world into a core, a semi-periphery and a periphery in this way represents more than an alternative classification of countries: it is a reflection of a particular conception of the dynamics of the world economy.

In making international comparisons, GDP and GNI can be problematic, because they are based on each country's currency. Recently, it has become possible to compare national currencies based on purchasing power parity (PPP). In effect, PPP measures how much of a common 'market basket' of goods and services each currency can purchase locally, including goods and services that are not traded internationally. Using PPP-based currency values instead of market-based exchange rates to compare levels of prosperity usually produces lower GDP figures in wealthy countries and higher GDP figures in poorer ones. Nevertheless, even with this compression between rich and poor, economic prosperity is very unevenly distributed across countries. Indeed, the absolute gap in income between the world's rich and poor is also getting wider rather than narrower. Consider the differences between China and India, the largest LDCs, and the United States, Japan and Germany, the largest developed economies (Figure 2.2). Between 1975 and 2005 the absolute difference in per capita GDP between China and Japan (measured in constant 2000 dollars) grew by more than 50 per cent, while the gap between China and the United States increased by almost two-thirds. India, meanwhile, fell even further behind as the absolute difference in per capita GDP between India and both Japan and the USA increased by over 80 per cent.

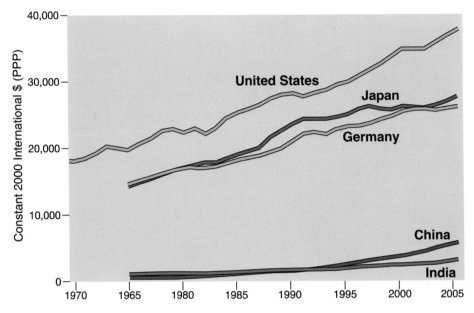

Fig 2.2: Gross domestic product (GDP) per capita (PPP) in constant 2000 dollars

*Source*: Based on data from World Bank's online *World Development Indicators* (WDI) database

## Box 2.1 HIV/AIDS and the threat to development in Sub-Saharan Africa

The weakening of economic performance in many African countries as a result of HIV/AIDS will contribute to increasing the gap between the world's rich and poor. Of the more than 39.5 million people worldwide that were estimated to be living with HIV/AIDS in 2006, 24.7 million were in Sub-Saharan Africa. So despite having only about 12 per cent of the world's population, this region is home to about 63 per cent of the infected people. This pandemic has already claimed 15 million lives and orphaned more than 11 million children there. In the worst hit southern and southeastern Sub-Saharan African countries, HIV/AIDS is expected to wipe out half the teenagers and plunge life expectancy to age 30 by 2010.

This overwhelming human tragedy is magnified by the societal and economic impacts of HIV/AIDS. The ILO has identified a number of ways in which HIV/AIDS weakens economic performance.

- Productivity is reduced because AIDS deaths decrease the number of experienced workers, especially those in their most productive years.
- International competitiveness is hurt by the higher production costs because of a shortage of skilled workers.
- Employment creation is slower due to lower government revenues and reduced private savings.
- Higher expenditures are needed for monitoring, prevention and healthcare.
- Increased pressures are placed on the social security system, including life insurance and pension funds, which are significant sources of capital for the government and private sector.

## 2.1 WHAT 'ECONOMIC DEVELOPMENT' MEANS

Major international economic cleavages not only reflect differences in prosperity but also reflect different forms of economic organization, different kinds of resource base, different demographic characteristics, different political systems and different roles in the system of international specialization and trade. Defining and measuring 'economic development' is therefore problematic. As we have seen, there are strong grounds for thinking in terms of *under*development rather than development as far as the LDCs are concerned, since the term 'development' implies a trajectory of improvement, in both relative and absolute terms. In addition, it is now widely accepted that 'development' must be conceived in broad terms of social well-being. Narrow economic definitions, while admirably precise, provide only part of the picture. They encompass changes in the amount, composition, rate of growth, distribution and consumption of resources, but they do not extend to the effects these changes have on people's lives. This is clearly reflected in the UN's Millennium Development Goals:

1 eradicate extreme hunger and poverty
2 achieve universal primary education
3 promote gender equality and empower women
4 reduce child mortality
5 improve maternal health
6 combat HIV/AIDS, malaria and other diseases
7 ensure environmental sustainability
8 develop a global partnership for development.

Development, then, should really be thought of not only in terms of income and consumption but also in terms of people's health, education, housing conditions, security, civil rights and so on. Seen in this light, development is clearly a 'normative' concept – that is, it involves values, goals and standards that make it possible to compare a particular situation against a preferred one. Development can properly be evaluated only in the context of the human needs and values as perceived by the very societies undergoing change. It also follows that although 'development' implies economic, social, political and cultural transformations, these should be seen not as ends in themselves but as means for enhancing social well-being and the quality of human life.

Recognizing the limitations of measures of national income (i.e. GNI and GDP), the United Nations Development Programme (UNDP) has established a Human Development Index (UNDP, 2005), which is a composite indicator. It covers three dimensions of human welfare: income, education and health. More specifically, the HDI combines countries' scores on three basic components of development:

1 physical well-being, as measured by life expectancy
2 education, as measured by a combination of adult literacy rates (two-thirds weight) and mean years of schooling (one-third weight)
3 standard of living, as measured by GDP per capita, adjusted to PPP.

Its purpose is not to give a complete picture of human development but to provide a measure that goes beyond income. The HDI is a barometer for changes in human well-being and for comparing progress in different regions.

Over the last decade the HDI has been rising across all developing regions, albeit at variable rates and with the obvious exception of Sub-Saharan Africa (Figure 2.3). Amid the overall progress, however, many countries suffered unprecedented reversals. Eighteen countries with a combined population of 460 million people – including many countries in Sub-Saharan Africa and the former Soviet Union – registered lower scores on the HDI in 2005 than in 1990. Figure 2.4 shows the global pattern of development in 2005 according to this index. Many countries in Latin America and East Asia have clearly moved beyond the basic threshold of development. In contrast, most countries in south Asia and Sub-Saharan Africa still have very low levels of development.

In this book, we shall be concerned with both the means and the ends, addressing our subject matter from a broad perspective that sees economic geography as the dynamic core of human geography. In the present context, this brings us first to an examination of some of the international patterns that reflect the 'means' of transformation: global patterns of resources, population, manufacturing, trade, investment, aid and debt. We shall then summarize the 'ends', or net outcomes, in terms of an overall typology of socioeconomic development.

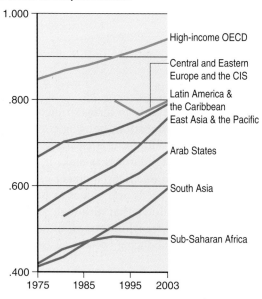

Fig 2.3: Regional change in levels of human development
*Source:* Adapted from UNDP (2005: 21, Figure 1.4)

## 2.2 INTERNATIONAL PATTERNS OF RESOURCES AND POPULATION

The distribution of natural resources has a very important influence on patterns of international economic activity and development. Not only are key resources – energy, minerals, cultivable land – unevenly distributed, but the *combination* of particular resources in particular countries and regions makes for a complex mosaic of opportunities and constraints. A lack of resources can, of course, be remedied

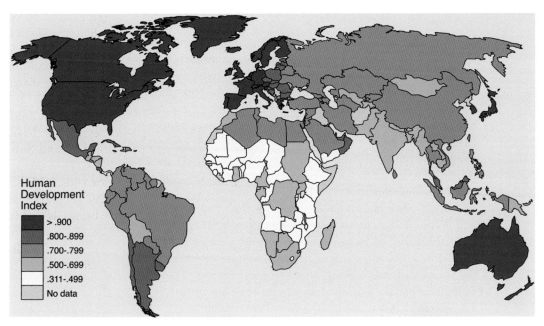

Fig 2.4: UNDP Human Development Index, 2004

*Source:* Based on UNDP online data

through international trade (Japan is the prime example here, see p. 130); but for most countries, the resource base is an important determinant of development.

In overall terms, a very high proportion of the world's key non-renewable natural resources are concentrated in Russia, the USA, Canada, South Africa and Australia. The United States, for example, has 44 per cent of the world's known resources of hydrocarbons (oil, natural gas, oil shales, etc.), 38 per cent of the lignite, 38 per cent of the molybdenum, 21 per cent of the lead, 19 per cent of the copper, 18 per cent of the bituminous coal and 15 per cent of the zinc. Russia has 75 per cent of the vanadium, 50 per cent of the lignite, 40 per cent of the bituminous coal, 38 per cent of the manganese, 30 per cent of the iron, 20 per cent of the cultivable land and 18 per cent of the hydrocarbons. This concentration is largely a function of geology and physical geography; but it is also partly a function of political instability in much of ex-colonial Africa, Asia and Latin America – instability that has been a serious hindrance to resource exploration and exploitation. Current estimates of the distribution of resources will inevitably understate, therefore, the relative size of the resource base of many LDCs.

It should also be noted that the significance of particular resources is sometimes very much a function of prevailing technologies. As technologies change, so resource requirements change. This also means that regions and countries that are heavily dependent on one particular resource are very exposed to the consequences of technological change. This is particularly important for countries such as Bolivia, Chile, Guinea, Guyana, Liberia, Mauritania, Sierra Leone, Surinam and Zambia, whose economies are heavily dependent on non-fuel minerals.

## ECONOMIC DEVELOPMENT AND THE ENVIRONMENT

Meanwhile, the rate of exploitation of some of the world's natural resources can also be a cause for concern. The sheer scale and capacity of the world economy means that humans are now capable of altering the environment at the global scale. The 'footprint' of humankind extends to more than four-fifths of the Earth's surface and many of the important issues facing modern society are the consequences – intended and unintended – of human modifications of the physical environment. For example, clearing land for settlement, mining and agriculture provides livelihoods and homes for some but alters physical systems and transforms human populations, wildlife and vegetation. The inevitable by-products of economic development – garbage, air and water pollution, hazardous wastes and so forth – place enormous demands on the capacity of physical systems to absorb and accommodate them. Large-scale commercial agriculture has contributed to the 'desertification' of marginal environments such as the Sahel, for example. But the most dramatic consequences are to be found in relation to commercial forestry and the indiscriminate logging of subtropical forests. The World Resources Institute estimates that the current rate of global deforestation removes about 183 square kilometres of forest around the world every *hour* – equivalent to the loss of an area of forest exceeding the size of Washington, DC, every hour and amounting to four times the area of Norway every year. Apart from the overall loss of timber resources, this has also resulted in other economic and ecological problems: the loss of livelihood of local inhabitants, as well as the silting of reservoirs, damage to hydroelectric plant and an increase in flash floods with the consequent damage to property, crops and livestock that results from soil erosion from bare hillsides after the trees are cut down. In addition, deforestation results in a serious loss of genetic diversity. Tropical forests support millions of plant, insect and animal species, some of which may prove invaluable to human welfare. The Madagascan Rosy Periwinkle, for example, has been discovered to be the source of two powerful drugs that can be successfully used to treat leukaemia and Hodgkin's disease.

Human activity can also change the climate through altering the composition of the atmosphere. Of greatest concern is the role that human activity is playing in causing global warming, an increase in world temperatures and change in climate associated with increasing levels of carbon dioxide and other gases resulting from human activities such as deforestation and fossil fuel burning. Global warming is associated with the greenhouse effect, the trapping of heat within the atmosphere by water vapour and gases, such as carbon dioxide, resulting in the warming of the atmosphere and surface. Carbon dioxide is produced from burning fossil fuels, from cement production and from deforestation and the level of carbon dioxide in the atmosphere has increased dramatically with increases in human population and consumption over the last 100 years. Earth system scientists suggest that human-caused increases in carbon dioxide may result in an overall global temperature increase of about 3°C (5.5°F) over the next 50 years, as well as regional changes in the amount and distribution of precipitation.

In addition to the destruction of tropical rainforests and the consequent loss of biodiversity and the spectre of global warming, the world currently faces a daunting list of environmental threats: widespread, health-threatening pollution; the degradation of soil, water and marine resources essential to food production; acid rain and so on. Most of these threats are greatest in the world's periphery, where daily environmental pollution and degradation amounts to a catastrophe that will continue to unfold, in slow motion, in the coming years. These trends are intensifying the contrasts between rich and poor regions. Environmental problems are inseparable from processes of demographic change, economic development and human welfare. In addition, it is becoming clear that environmental problems are going to be increasingly enmeshed in matters of national security and regional conflict. The spatial interdependence of economic, environmental and social problems means that some parts of the world are ecological time bombs. The prospect of civil unrest and mass migrations resulting from the pressures of rapidly growing populations, deforestation, soil erosion, water depletion, air pollution, disease epidemics and intractable poverty is real. These issues are alarming not only for the peoples of the affected regions but also for the peoples of DCs, whose continued prosperity will depend on processes of globalization that are not disrupted by large-scale environmental disasters, unmanageable mass migrations or the breakdown of stability in the world-system as a whole.

## SUSTAINABLE DEVELOPMENT

The environmental and economic implications of global warming and environmental despoliation have added a great deal of weight to the importance of **sustainable development** – economic development that seeks to meet the needs and aspirations of the present without compromising the ability to meet those of the future. In 1987, the World Commission on Environment and Development, chaired by former Norwegian Prime Minister Gro Harlem Brundtland, issued an influential report, *Our Common Future* (the 'Brundtland Report', 1987), which stressed the intensification and interdependence of ecological and economic crises, and made a strong plea for the principle of sustainable development. Sustainable development means using renewable natural resources in a manner that does not eliminate or degrade them – by making greater use, for example, of solar and geothermal energy and by greater use of recycled materials. It means managing economic systems so that all resources – physical and human – are used optimally. It means regulating economic systems so that the benefits of development are distributed more equitably (if only to prevent poverty from causing environmental degradation). It also means organizing societies so that improved education, healthcare and social welfare can contribute to environmental awareness and sensitivity and an improved quality of life. A final and more radical aspect of sustainable development is to move away from wholesale globalization toward increased 'localization': a desire to return to a more locally based economy where production, consumption and decision making can be oriented to local needs and conditions.

Put this way, sustainable development sounds eminently sensible yet impossibly Utopian. A widespread discussion of sustainability took place in the early 1990s, and focused on the 'Earth Summit' (the United Nations Conference on Environment and Development) meeting in Rio de Janeiro in 1992. Attended by 128 heads of state, it attracted intense media attention. At the conference, many examples were described of successful sustainable development programmes at the local level. Most of these centred on sustainable agricultural practices for LDCs, including the use of intensive agricultural features such as raised fields and terraces in Peru's Titicaca Basin: techniques that had been used successfully in this difficult agricultural environment for centuries, before European colonization. After the United Nations conference, however, many observers commented bitterly on the deep conflict of interest between core countries and peripheral countries that was exposed by the summit.

One of the most serious obstacles to prospects for sustainable development is continued heavy reliance on fossil fuels as the fundamental source of energy for economic development. This not only perpetuates international inequalities but also leads to transnational problems such as acid rain, global warming, climatic changes, deforestation and health hazards. Sustainable alternatives – renewable energy resources such as solar energy, tides, waves, winds, geothermal and hydro-electric energy – have been pursued half-heartedly because of the vested interests of the powerful corporations and governments that control fossil fuel resources.

Demographic growth in LDCs is a second important challenge to sustainable development. Sustainable development is feasible only if population size and growth are in harmony with the changing productive capacity of the ecosystem. Nearly 800 million people still do not have enough to eat (United Nations, 2001a). The complexity of the interactions between demographic change and economic development, education, culture and resources makes achieving sustainable development extremely difficult. But the greatest obstacle to sustainable development, according to many experts, is the inadequacy of institutional frameworks. Sustainable development requires economic, financial and fiscal decisions to be fully integrated with environmental and ecological decisions. In practice, national and local governments everywhere have evolved institutional structures that tend to separate decision making about what is economically rational and what is environmentally desirable. Supranational organizations, while better placed to integrate policy across these sectors and better able to address economic and environmental 'spillovers' from one country to another, have (with the notable exception of the European Union) never acquired sufficient power to promote integrated, harmonized policies. Without radical and widespread changes in value systems and unprecedented changes in political will, 'sustainable development' will remain an embarrassing contradiction in terms.

## THREE KEY RESOURCES: ENERGY, CULTIVABLE LAND AND WATER

Three particularly important resources in terms of shaping the world's economic geography are energy, cultivable land and water. The major sources of commercial energy are oil, natural gas and coal, all of which are very unevenly distributed across the globe. Most of the world's developed economies are reasonably well off in terms of energy *production*, the major exceptions being Japan and parts of Europe. Most LDCs, by the same token, are energy poor. The major exceptions are Algeria, Ecuador, Gabon, Indonesia, Libya, Nigeria, Venezuela and the Persian Gulf states – all major oil producers. Because of this unevenness, energy has come to be an important component of world trade. Oil is in fact the most important single commodity in world trade, making up around 12 per cent of the total by value in 2005.

For many LDCs, the costs of energy imports represent a huge burden. Consider, for example, the predicament of countries such as Armenia, Egypt, Ghana, India and Paraguay, where in 2005 the cost of energy imports amounted to more than one-quarter of the total value of exported merchandise. Nevertheless, few LDCs can afford to consume energy on the scale of the developed economies, so that patterns of commercial energy *consumption* tend to mirror the fundamental core–periphery cleavage of the world economy (Table 2.1). In 2005, energy consumption in North America was nearly eight times higher than in Sub-Saharan Africa. The World Bank has calculated that high-income countries, with 15 per cent of the world's population, use half its commercial energy and 10 times as much per capita as low-income countries.

Table 2.1 Energy consumption and emissions: a comparison of selected DCs and LDCs

| | Unit | Year | EU25 | USA | China | India | World |
|---|---|---|---|---|---|---|---|
| Total area | Million km$^2$ | | 4.0 | 9.3 | 9.6 | 3.3 | 149.0 |
| Population | Million | 2006 | 461 | 298 | 1314 | 1095 | 6600 |
| GDP | US$ billion | 2005 | 13,927 | 12,439 | 2279 | 749 | 44,168 |
| GDP/capita | US$/capita | 2005 | 30,473 | 41,917 | 1411 | 678 | 6851 |
| Economic growth | %/year | 2004 | 2.4 | 4.4 | 9.5 | 6.5 | 4.8 |
| Primary energy demand | Mio. T oil-eq | 2004 | 1719 | 2332 | 1386 | 376 | 10,224 |
| Primary energy demand per capita | GJ/capita and year | 2004 | 158 | 333 | 44.7 | 14.8 | 67.2 |
| Primary energy demand, coal | Mio. T oil-eq | 2004 | 307 | 564 | 957 | 205 | 2778 |
| Share of coal in primary energy demand | % | 2004 | 17.9 | 24.2 | 69.0 | 54.5 | 27.2 |
| Installed generation capacity | GW$_{el}$ | 2004 | 660 | 942 | 391 | 131 | 3736 |
| Electricity produced | TWh/year | 2004 | 2980 | 3979 | 2080 | 631 | 16,599 |
| Growth in electricity use | %/year | 2004 | 1.7 | 1.6 | 15.2 | 5.3 | 4.3 |
| $CO_2$ emissions, total | Mio. t/year | 2004 | 3789 | 5912 | 4707 | 1113 | 27,044 |
| $CO_2$ emissions/capita | t/capita and year | 2004 | 8.3 | 20.2 | 3.6 | 1.0 | 4.2 |
| $SO_2$ emissions, total | Mio. t/year | 2000 | 8.7 | 16.5 | 20.0 | 5.0 | 98.0 |
| $SO_2$ emissions/capita | Kg/capita and year | 2000 | 19.2 | 58.5 | 15.8 | 5.0 | 16.1 |

Source: Based on *Energie-Spiegel* No. 17 (2006: 2)

It should be noted that these figures do not reflect the use of firewood and other traditional fuels for cooking, lighting, heating and, sometimes, industrial needs. In total, such forms of energy probably account for around 20 per cent of total world energy consumption. In parts of Africa and Asia they account for up to 80 per cent of energy consumption. This points us to yet another DC–LDC contrast. Whereas massive investments in exploration and exploitation are enabling more of the developed, energy-consuming countries to become self-sufficient through various combinations of coal, oil, natural gas, hydroelectric power and nuclear power, *1.5 billion people in the*

*LDCs depend on collecting fuelwood as their principal source of energy.* Although it has been assumed that the collection of fuelwood causes considerable deforestation, recent studies have shown that up to two-thirds of all fuelwood is gathered from non-forest sources such as dispersed woodlands and roadsides. While there are insufficient data to assess the sustainability of fuelwood use, it is expected that many of the world's people will continue to rely on wood energy in the immediate future and that demand will increase substantially as the population grows. The problem is most serious in densely populated locations, arid and semi-arid places, and in cooler mountainous areas, where the regeneration of shrubs, woodlands and forests is particularly slow. Nearly 100 million people in 22 countries (16 of them in Africa) cannot meet their minimum needs even by overcutting remaining forests.

The distribution of cultivable land represents another important environmental influence on international economic differentiation. Much more than half of the Earth's land surface is unsuitable for any productive form of arable farming, either currently or if improved, as suggested by Figure 2.5. This map gives an approximation of the world's cultivable land by excluding regions that have poor soils, too short a growing season, are too dry, too mountainous or are not available for conversion to arable farming because of other uses including grazing, forestry or conservation. This does not mean that agriculture is absent from the unshaded areas of the map – rather, that arable farming in these regions is likely to be marginal. By this measure, we should note, the distribution of the world's cultivable land is highly uneven, being concentrated in Europe, west-central Russia, eastern North America, the Australian littoral, Latin America, parts of India, eastern China and parts of Sub-Saharan Africa. In detail, of course, some of these regions may be marginal for arable farming because of marshy soils or other adverse conditions; while irrigation, for example, sometimes extends the local frontier of productive agriculture. However,

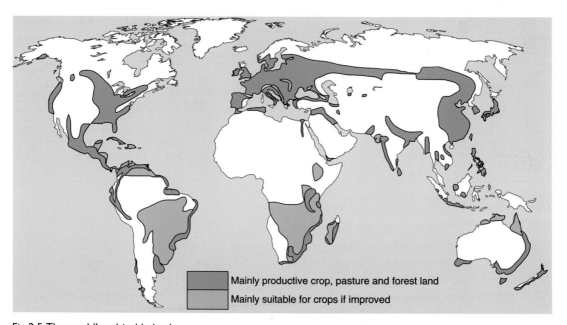

Fig 2.5: The world's cultivable land

*Source:* Adapted from FAO (1995), available at http://www.fao.org/inpho/vlibrary/u8480e/U8480E0e.htm

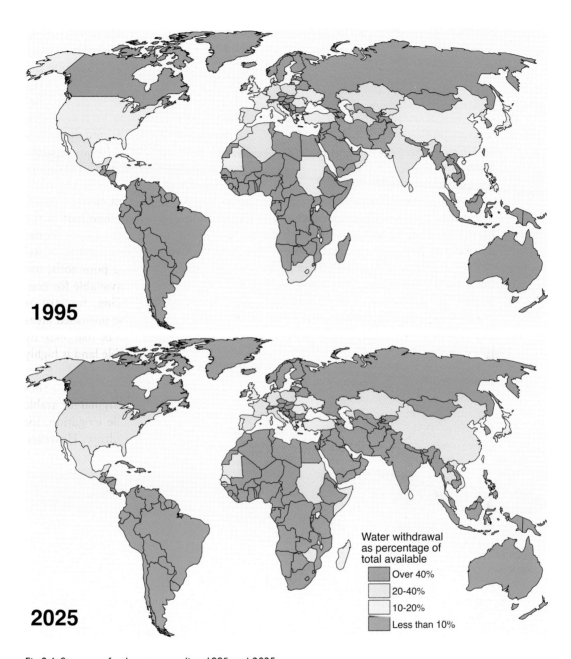

Fig 2.6: Stress on freshwater supplies, 1995 and 2025

*Source*: Based on UNEP (2002: 21b), available at http://www.unep.org/vitalwater

water shortages and the uneven distribution of fresh water supplies are increasingly imposing limits to intensive agriculture. The United Nations Development Human Development Report for 2006 warns of a 'global water crisis', with large parts of the middle latitudes of the northern hemisphere experiencing significant levels of stress on fresh water supplies by 2025 (Figure 2.6):

Ultimately, human development is about the realization of potential. It is about what people can do and what they can become – their capabilities – and about the freedom they have to exercise real choices in their lives. Water pervades all aspects of human development. When people are denied access to clean water at home or when they lack access to water as a productive resource their choices and freedoms are constrained by ill health, poverty and vulnerability. Water gives life to everything, including human development and human freedom.

UNDP (2006: 2)

We also have to bear in mind that not all cultivable land is of the same quality. This leads us to the concept of the carrying capacity of agricultural land: the maximum population that could be fed a minimum daily diet, given the particular soils and climate of a region. More specifically, carrying capacity is defined as the maximum population that can be maintained in a place with rates of resource use and waste production that are sustainable in the long term without damaging the overall productivity of that or other places elsewhere. Another useful concept is that of the ecological footprint of a population, which is a measure of the human pressures on the natural environment from the consumption of renewable resources and the production of pollution. The ecological footprint indicates how much space a population needs compared to what is available. It changes in proportion to population size, average consumption per person and the resource intensity of the technology being used. The ecological footprint is measured in 'area units', where one area unit is equivalent to one hectare of biologically productive land with world average productivity. As land varies in productivity, a hectare of highly productive cropland would represent more 'area units' than the same amount of less productive grazing land. Figure 2.7 shows the intensity of the ecological footprint across the world in 2001. Intensity increases with greater population densities, higher per capita resource consumption, and lower resource efficiencies. The World Wildlife

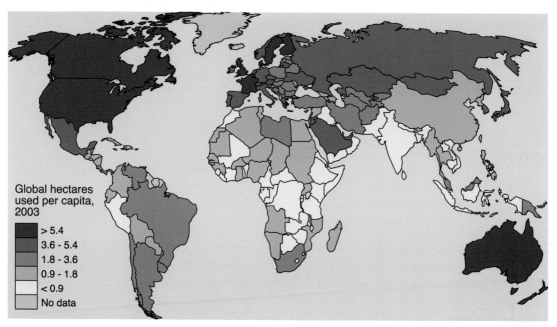

Global hectares used per capita, 2003

> 5.4
3.6 - 5.4
1.8 - 3.6
0.9 - 1.8
< 0.9
No data

Fig 2.7: Resource consumption: ecological footprint

*Source:* Adapted from WWF (2006: 16, Map 5)

Fund has found that the ecological footprint of the world's population has been increasing steadily since the 1970s. By 2000 it was at least 30 per cent greater than the Earth's biologically productive capacity to sustain. This overshoot depletes the Earth's natural capital and is therefore possible only for a limited period of time.

## AGRICULTURAL PATTERNS AND THE FOOD QUESTION

These issues shift our attention from the abstract to reality and to a consideration of the world agricultural map and the world food situation. Both of these are rather different in configuration from the patterns of cultivable land and carrying capacity just described. *The actual pattern of world agriculture is just one of a vast number of possible realizations of the world's agricultural resources.* It is the product of a variety of interpretations, at different times, of environmental possibilities, desirable products and marketable opportunities – all influenced, in turn, by prevailing land tenure systems, levels of technology and global power politics. It is, in short, a legacy of the world's economic history.

In detail, the mosaic of world agricultural regions shows a very high degree of specialization. At the same time, the broader international division of labour means that some countries depend much more on agriculture for employment and income than others. In low-income developing countries, agriculture employs roughly 70 to 80 per cent of the labour force and accounts for 35 to 45 per cent of GDP; in developed economies, agriculture employs around 7 per cent of the labour force and accounts for about 3 per cent of GDP.

One consequence of this specialization is of course a large volume of *trade* in agricultural produce. The biggest exporters of food, however, are not developing countries but a few of the more developed countries – Argentina, Australia, Canada, France and the USA – with highly productive agricultural sectors specializing in cereal production. In recent years, world trade in food has grown rapidly and there have been some significant changes in the pattern of trade. Until the 1950s the dominant flows were those of food grains into western Europe. These have now declined significantly, with the major flows currently originating in Canada and the United States with destinations in Russia, Japan and, increasingly, middle-income developing countries. Over the last 50 years, however, the share of agricultural products in global exports has shrunk dramatically, from almost 40 per cent to under 10 per cent (Figure 2.8).

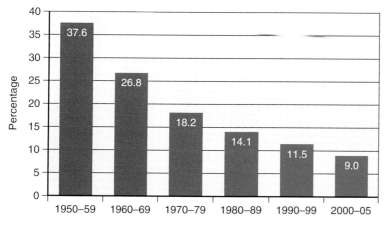

Fig 2.8: Share of agricultural products in world merchandise exports, 1950–2005
*Source:* Based on World Trade Organization (WTO) (2006: 7, Chart 4)

Gross inequalities in the consumption of food, one of the most basic of all human needs, are an important corollary of these patterns and flows. About 815 million people around the world are undernourished, 777 million in the LDCs, 27 million in the 'transition' countries that comprised the former Soviet Union and 11 million in the DCs. Over half of young child mortality in LDCs (6.6 million of the 12.2 million deaths of children under 5) is associated with malnutrition (FAO, 2001). The fact that many of them are from countries that are net *exporters* (by value) of foods is a telling indictment of the world economic system.

## Box 2.2  Agribusiness and the developed countries

Direct corporate involvement in agriculture – agribusiness – has been an inevitable outcome of the logic of specialization and economies of scale. With greater specialization, farms become less autonomous and self-contained as productive units, making for the penetration of an integrated, corporate system of food production, processing and distribution: Agriculture has become increasingly drawn into a food-producing complex whose limits lie:

> [Well] beyond farming itself, a complex of agro-chemical, engineering, processing, marketing and distribution industries which are involved both in the supply of farming inputs and in the forward marketing of farm produce.
>
> Newby (1980: 61)

It is in the actions of food-processing conglomerates like Associated British Foods (ABF), Nestlé and Rank-Hovis-McDougall (RHM Group), Newby suggests, 'that the shape of agriculture and ultimately of rural society in virtually all advanced industrial societies is decided' (1980: 62). The most common form of corporate involvement in agriculture has to do with the forward contracting of produce at a fixed price. This not only weakens the independence of farmers, but also tends to transfer income from farmers and rural communities to the processing industry. Forward-contracting arrangements also reinforce the overall structural changes affecting agriculture:

> They encourage both fewer, larger holdings and increased specialization so that the size of individual enterprises can be enlarged to fully achieve the prevailing scale economies. This trend ... is likely to lead to both a reduction in the numbers employed in agriculture, and a decline in the managerial role of those farmers remaining ... leaving them caretaker functions.
>
> Metcalf (1969: 104)

Rural landscapes have also been affected as the logic of industrial production and centralization has been applied to agriculture. In northwestern Europe, for example, field systems have been rationalized, hedgerows and dykes removed, and mechanization has virtually eliminated the need for gang labour, leaving the fields of most farms devoid of human life for most of the year. Factory farming has brought poultry and pigs indoors permanently, while many cattle spend their winter months indoors, and there are now 'zero-grazing' techniques that may see them inside year round. Only the sheep steadfastly refuse to acknowledge the laws of industrial production, stubbornly refusing to prosper in regimented and sanitized conditions.

## INTERNATIONAL DEMOGRAPHIC PATTERNS

The geography of population and the dynamics of population change are closely interrelated with patterns of economic development. Population density, fertility, mortality and migration are often a direct reflection of economic, social and political conditions. At the same time, they can be important determinants of economic change and social well-being. Human resources are vital to economic development in terms of both production and consumption; but at the wrong time and in the wrong place they can be more of a liability than an asset. Although it is not always easy to unravel cause and effect, it is important to understand the broad context.

In global terms, this broad context is currently dominated by the sheer growth of population. Over 1 million people are added to the population of the world every five days. According to UN estimates, the current population of just over 6.5 billion is likely to grow to 9.3 billion by the year 2050. The population of the LDCs, which has been growing by on average between 2 and 3 per cent each year, is expected to increase from 4.9 to 8.2 billion. In contrast, the population of the advanced industrial countries, which has been growing at an annual rate of about 0.5 per cent, with some western European countries having virtually stagnant populations, is expected to hold at 1.2 billion.

### The Demographic Transition

These core–periphery contrasts are the product of differences in fertility and mortality rates that are, in turn, related to differentials in the demographic transition that is associated with the broad sweep of economic development and social change. This transition is conventionally portrayed as involving three stages (Figure 2.9). In the first, populations exhibit high birth rates and high, fluctuating death rates, with net growth rates of around 1 per cent. In the second stage, death rates fall sharply (largely because of improved diets, improved public health and the availability of scientific medicine). Birth rates also fall, but the decrease in fertility is lagged (largely because it takes time for social and cultural practices concerning family size to respond to changing circumstances). The result is an explosive increase in population. Most western industrial countries experienced this stage during the 19th century. In the third stage, death rates even off at a low level; while birth rates are low but fluctuating, with net growth rates once again around 1 per cent.

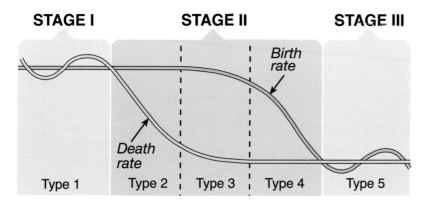

Fig 2.9: The Demographic Transition

While not all countries should be expected to follow this demographic path, it is useful to identify whether a country may be entering the critical second stage of rapid population expansion and thus has the major part of its population growth ahead of it, whether it is in the middle of the population 'explosion' or whether it is on the verge of completing the growth stage. Accordingly, the UN has suggested a threefold division of the second stage, giving five categories of population growth type (Figure 2.9). Figure 2.10 shows how the countries of the world fit into this classification system. The DCs, of course, but also many of the NICs (including Latin American countries such as Argentina, Brazil and Chile, as well as East Asian countries such as Hong Kong, Singapore, South Korea, Taiwan and Thailand) are all already in the final, fifth, slow-growth stage, while a number of other Latin American and Asian countries (such as Colombia, Mexico, Peru and Venezuela, and India, Indonesia and Malaysia) seem to be in the final phase of the growth stage. Much of Africa is experiencing the most explosive phase of the growth stage, while the central and western regions of Africa seem poised to enter this explosive phase. A few African countries, meanwhile – including Angola, Niger and Rwanda – are at the very beginning of the demographic transition, with relatively high death rates that are suppressing the rate of natural increase. Of enormous concern are the southern and southeastern Sub-Saharan African countries, particularly Botswana and Zimbabwe, which slipped back from the most explosive phase of the growth stage to the beginning of the demographic transition during the 1990s as their deaths rates skyrocketed due to the ravages of having more than 20 per cent of their population infected with HIV/AIDS.

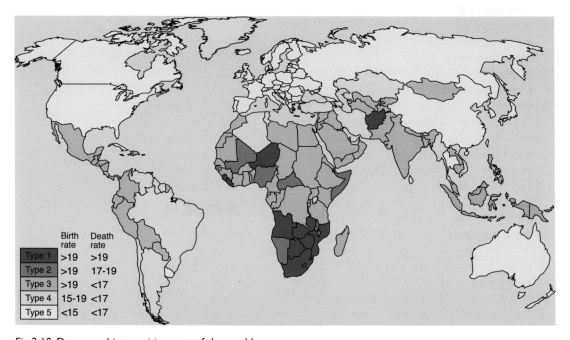

| | Birth rate | Death rate |
|---|---|---|
| Type 1 | >19 | >19 |
| Type 2 | >19 | 17-19 |
| Type 3 | >19 | <17 |
| Type 4 | 15-19 | <17 |
| Type 5 | <15 | <17 |

Fig 2.10: Demographic transition map of the world

*Source*: Based on data from US Census Bureau (2007), International Data Base, Table 008

## Migration

Another important aspect of population change is *migration*. International labour migration has been an important part of the world economic system ever since the industrial revolution of the 19th century. Current estimates of the total number of international migrant workers stand at around 25 million, with a comparable number of dependants accompanying them. About 14 million of these, including 7 or 8 million illegal immigrants, are working in the United States, which now draws most of its immigrants from Mexico. Northwestern Europe has about 5 million migrant workers, most of them from nearby countries such as Portugal, Spain or Turkey or from ex-colonial countries such as Algeria and Jamaica. Since the early 1970s large numbers of workers have also been attracted to the oil-rich countries of southwestern Asia: about 4 million at present, two-thirds of them from the region itself and the rest from south and Southeast Asia. South Africa draws about 500,000 migrant workers from neighbouring countries; and there are also important flows of migrant labour between developing countries in parts of Latin America and in West Africa.

## Box 2.3 Migrant workers' remittances

An increasingly important aspect of globalization is the flow of funds from international migrant workers to their home countries. These remittances are usually to family members in LDCs and, as unilateral transfers, they do not create any future liabilities such as debt servicing or profit transfers. Workers' remittances also have a tendency to move countercyclically with the economy in recipient countries, as migrant workers increase their support to family members during down cycles of economic activity back home so as to help them compensate for lost family income due to unemployment or other crisis-induced reasons. This enables remittances to serve as a stabilizer that helps smooth out large fluctuations in the national income over different phases of the business cycle. Official figures of recorded remittances to LDCs show that they have increased dramatically since the late 1980s, now amounting to around US$100 billion. This is almost as much as the total amount of foreign direct investment (FDI) in LDCs, and is much more significant than official economic aid from developed to less developed countries (see Figure 2.11). The United States is by far the largest single source of remittances. On the receiving end, the bulk of the inflows are recorded by LDCs in the western hemisphere and 'developing Asia' (most of South, Southeast and East Asia – excluding Japan, South Korea, Hong Kong, Singapore and Taiwan). Unrecorded remittances probably increase the real inflow of funds by 10 or 20 per cent, especially in many Asian and Arab economies. In addition to family support, workers' remittances are increasingly important as a source of micro-credit, financing very small enterprises for friends or family members, or providing start-up funds for self-employment for the migrant workers themselves on their return.

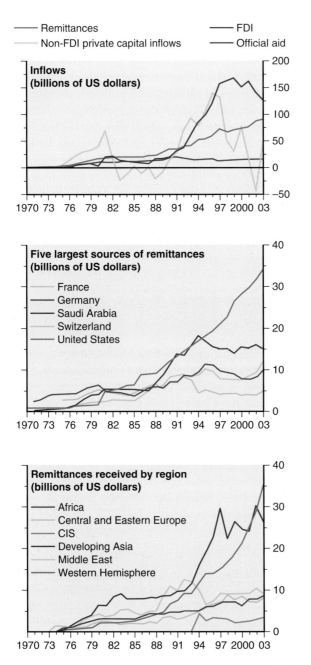

Fig 2.11: Workers' remittances to developing countries, 1970–2003
*Source:* Adapted from IMF (2001, 90, Figure 2.13)

Mention should also be made of the distinctive streams of highly skilled labour – physicians, engineers, scientists, etc. – the so-called '*brain drain*'. The principal recipients of these streams have been the United States, Canada, Britain and Australia. The principal countries of origin have been India, Pakistan, the Philippines, Sri Lanka and, more recently, the former Soviet Union and its satellites. Typically, the brain drain is a result of students and professionals choosing not to return home after the completion of educational courses or training programmes in developed countries. These streams are significant not because of the absolute numbers of people involved but because of the economic implications of the relative gains and losses of highly skilled personnel. The brain drain from the former Soviet Union has had added significance because of the sudden availability of scientists with key skills relevant to military technology and nuclear and biological weapons. This has added a geopolitical dimension to the issue, raising fears of a brain drain of ex-Soviet experts to LDCs. In response, the United States, Japan and the European Union established a scientific centre in Russia in 1992 with the express purpose of stemming the nuclear brain drain.

Meanwhile, the demographic transition continues to flood the labour markets of most LDCs. Without the option of migration or emigration to unsettled territories – an option that represents a crucial difference in the current experience of LDCs compared to the historical experience of developed countries – the increases in population resulting from the demographic transition in LDCs have been channelled into internal, *rural-to-urban migration* streams. Young, reproductively active rural populations are being pushed out by shortages of land and pulled to larger cities by a combination of real and perceived advantages: employment opportunities, wages and modern amenities. As a result, the rate and scale of urbanization in developing countries represents yet another dimension of core–periphery contrasts. The United Nations Centre for Human Settlements estimates that 1 billion urban dwellers occupy inadequate housing, mostly in the slums and squatter settlements of LDCs.

## 2.3 INTERNATIONAL PATTERNS OF INDUSTRY AND FINANCE

As with the agricultural map of the world, the international mosaic of industrial production and employment is highly complex, with a great deal of specialization in particular activities. Once again, what we want to stress here is the overall framework. First, the core economies account for almost 70 per cent of world manufacturing value added (MVA), with continuing steady but modest average annual growth rates for MVA. In terms of individual countries, the United States remains by far the most important source of manufactured goods, accounting for 21.1 per cent of global MVA in 2005 (Table 2.2). Just five countries – China, France, Germany, Japan and the United States – produce 59.8 per cent of the world total. Another important feature that is evident in Table 2.2 concerns *productivity*. In general, the highly capitalized manufacturing industries of the developed countries have been able to maintain high levels of worker productivity, with the result that their share of manufacturing in GDP has remained relatively high even as the size of their manufacturing labour forces has tended to shrink.

Within the framework of this continuing dominance of the advanced industrial economies there are several important trends. Although the United States has retained its leadership as the world's major producer of manufactured goods over the postwar period, its dominance has been significantly reduced. In 1963, for example, its share of world manufacturing output had been 40 per cent, compared to less than 25 per cent by the early 2000s. The United Kingdom, meanwhile, has lost ground in both relative and absolute terms. In contrast, Japan has moved from fifth place with a share of 5.5 per cent in 1963 to second place and a share of about

Table 2.2  World manufacturing data

| Rank | Country | Total manufacturing value added (MVA), 2003 (US$ bn) | Average annual growth in manufacturing | | | | Share of world total MVA | Manufacturing as share of GDP | | Value added per worker in manufacturing (US$ per year) | |
|---|---|---|---|---|---|---|---|---|---|---|---|
| | | | 1970–80 | 1980–90 | 1995–2000 | 2000–2005 | 2005 | 1990 | 2004 | 1980–84 | 1995–99 |
| 1 | USA | 1463.3 | 2.6 | 3.1 | 4.4 | 1.8 | 21.1 | 19 | 15 | 47,276 | 81,353 |
| 2 | Japan | 811.8 | 3.9 | 4.8 | 1.2 | 2.6 | 19.0 | 27 | 21 | 34,456 | 92,582 |
| 3 | Germany | 410.6 | 2.4 | 1.8 | 1.2 | 1.0 | 7.5 | 28 | 23 | 34,945 | 79,616 |
| 4 | China | 410.0 | 7.9 | 10.7 | 9.2 | 10.4 | 8.0 | 33 | 36 | 3061 | 2885 |
| 5 | UK | 220.4 | 0.4 | 1.8 | 1.2 | 0.4 | 3.1 | 23 | 16 | 24,716 | 55,060 |
| 6 | Italy | 216.2 | 5.7 | 2.3 | 1.2 | –1.0 | 2.9 | 25 | 20 | 24,580 | 50,760 |
| 7 | France | 192.3 | 3.5 | 0.8 | 3.4 | 1.0 | 4.2 | 21 | 14 | 26,751 | 61,019 |
| 8 | South Korea | 129.4 | 16.9 | 7.1 | 6.8 | 7.2 | 3.4 | 27 | 32 | – | – |
| 9 | Canada | 118.6 | 3.5 | 3.3 | 6.2 | 1.6 | 1.9 | 17 | 18 | 36,903 | 60,712 |
| 10 | Mexico | 110.7 | 7.0 | 1.5 | 7.6 | 1.0 | 1.1 | 21 | 18 | 17,448 | 25,931 |
| 11 | Spain | 108.4 | 2.5 | 2.1 | 4.4 | 2.4 | 1.9 | 21 | 19 | 18,936 | 47,016 |
| 12 | Russian Fed. | 91.7 | – | – | 0.8 | 9.0 | 1.8 | – | 30 | – | – |
| 13 | Taiwan | 76.0 | 12.2 | 8.4 | 5.6 | 4.8 | 1.4 | – | 27 | 12,829 (85) | 74,202 (99) |
| 14 | India | 72.7 | 4.6 | 7.4 | 4.4 | 6.6 | 1.3 | 17 | 15 | 2108 | 3118 |
| 15 | Indonesia | 59.5 | 14.5 | 12.6 | 1.4 | 5.8 | 1.0 | 21 | 26 | 3807 | 5139 |
| 18 | Brazil | 53.0 | 9.0 | 1.6 | 0.4 | 3.4 | 2.2 | 25 | 23 | 43,232 | 61,595 |
| 19 | Australia | 44.8 | 1.6 | 1.9 | 2.2 | 2.0 | 0.7 | 14 | 13 | 27,801 | 57,857 |
| 21 | Thailand | 42.7 | 10.5 | 9.5 | 1.8 | 7.4 | 1.0 | 27 | 32 | 11,072 | 19,946 |
| 26 | Malaysia | 29.1 | 12.0 | 8.9 | 6.0 | 5.6 | 0.6 | 24 | 31 | 8454 | 12,661 |
| 30 | Singapore | 22.9 | 9.7 | 6.6 | 7.2 | 5.0 | 0.5 | – | 23 | 16,442 | 40,674 |
| 54 | Hong Kong | 7.0 | 7.1 | 4.7 | – | –6.9 | 0.2(98–99) | 17 | 4 | 7886 | 19,533 |

*Source:* Based on World Bank (2001c: 60–63, Table 2.5; 194–7, Table 4.1; 198–201, Table 4.2; 202–205, Table 4.3); UNIDO (2002: *Reference Information* at http://www.unido.org/Regions.cmf?area5GLO)

20 per cent by the late 1990s despite its recession. We shall examine the reasons for these shifts in Chapters 5 to 7, where we discuss in detail the evolution and transition of the world's developed economies. As we shall see, this has involved an *increasing degree of international interdependence* throughout the world economy.

A second important feature is the rapid growth of manufacturing employment and productivity in China and the newly industrializing economies of East Asia. China has experienced a dramatic increase in manufacturing production, achieving annual average growth rates during the 1970s, 1980s and 1990s of about 8 per cent, 11 per cent and 14 per cent respectively. The four Asian 'Tigers' – Hong Kong, Singapore, South Korea and Taiwan – have made remarkable progress up the world league table of exporters, with South Korea recording the most spectacular increase in manufacturing production.

These shifts are part of a globalization of economic activity that has emerged as the overarching component of the world's economic geography. As we shall see in Chapters 6, 10 and 11, it has been corporate strategies, particularly the strategies of large transnational corporations (TNCs), which have created this globalization of economic activity. For the moment, however, it will be sufficient to take note of the magnitude of the phenomenon. One striking measure of the importance of transnational corporations in the world economy is given by the size of their annual turnover in comparison with the GNI of entire countries. By this yardstick, all of the top 50 global TNCs – including the likes of ExxonMobil, General Motors, Ford Motor Company, General Electric, Mitsubishi, IBM, Nestlé, Unilever, BP, Royal Dutch/Shell, Citigroup, Siemens and Toyota Motor Corporation – carry more economic clout than many of the world's smaller LDCs; while the very biggest TNCs are comparable in size with the national economies of countries like Greece, Ireland, Portugal and New Zealand (Table 2.3). Collectively, the 500 largest US corporations now employ an overseas labour force as big as their domestic labour force. Similar statistics apply to the largest Japanese corporations.

These overseas labour forces are spread among different parts of the world, but it is in LDCs and, in particular, the NICs where the most rapid growth has been taking place. Thus two-thirds of the radios made by Japanese manufacturing companies are produced abroad, together with half the stereos and televisions – mostly in South Korea and other nearby East Asian locations. This, clearly, has had much to do with the rise of the NICs. Over 90 per cent of South Korean exports of electronic equipment, for example, are produced by affiliates of Japanese companies.

The governments of LDCs have sought to take advantage of transnational corporation needs for cheap labour by setting up export processing zones (EPZs) – see also Chapters 10 and 11 – adaptations of free trade zones in which favourable investment and trade conditions are created by waiving excise duties on components, providing factory space and warehousing at subsidized rates, allowing tax 'holidays' of up to five years and suspending foreign exchange controls. For example, the resource-poor island of Mauritius had more than 500 companies operating within its EPZ in 2000, employing over 90,000 workers. Many of these firms were foreign owned, or owned jointly with foreigners, and about 250 were engaged in the manufacture of textiles and garments. Other EPZ goods include footwear, watches and toys as well as some higher value-added products such as software, electronics, light engineering, pharmaceuticals and publishing. In 2000 the aggregate exports from these firms exceeded US$1.2 billion, representing 75 per cent of the country's exports by value.

**Table 2.3** World's top non-financial TNCs, 2004

| Rank 2004 | Corporation (home economy) | Industry | Foreign assets (US$m) | Total assets (US$m) | Total sales (US$m) | Total employees |
|---|---|---|---|---|---|---|
| 1 | General Electric (US) | Electrical & electronic components | 448,901 | 750,507 | 152,866 | 307,000 |
| 2 | Vodafone Group plc (UK) | Telecommunications | 247,850 | 258,626 | 62,494 | 57,378 |
| 3 | Ford Motor Company (US) | Motor vehicles | 179,856 | 305,341 | 171,652 | 225,626 |
| 4 | General Motors (US) | Motor vehicles | 173,690 | 479,603 | 193,517 | 324,000 |
| 5 | British Petroleum Company plc (UK) | Petroleum | 154,513 | 193,213 | 285,059 | 102,900 |
| 6 | ExxonMobil (US) | Petroleum | 134,923 | 195,256 | 291,252 | 105,200 |
| 7 | Royal Dutch/Shell Group (UK/NL) | Petroleum | 129,939 | 192,811 | 265,190 | 114,000 |
| 8 | Toyota Motor Corporation (JP) | Motor vehicles | 122,967 | 233,721 | 171,467 | 265,753 |
| 9 | Total (FR) | Petroleum | 98,719 | 114,636 | 152,353 | 111,401 |
| 10 | France Télécom (FR) | Telecommunications | 85,669 | 131,204 | 58,554 | 206,524 |
| 11 | Volkswagen AG (GE) | Motor vehicles | 84,042 | 172,949 | 110,463 | 342,502 |
| 12 | Sanofi-Aventis (FR) | Pharmaceuticals | 82,612 | 104,548 | 18,678 | 96,439 |
| 13 | Deutsche Telekom AG (GE) | Telecommunications | 79,654 | 146,834 | 71,868 | 244,645 |
| 14 | RWE Group (GE) | Electricity, gas and water | 78,728 | 127,179 | 52,320 | 97,777 |
| 15 | Suez (FR) | Electricity, gas and water | 74,051 | 85,788 | 50,585 | 160,712 |
| 16 | E.on (GE) | Electricity, gas and water | 72,726 | 155,364 | 60,970 | 72,484 |
| 17 | Hutchinson Whampoa (HK) | Diversified | 67,638 | 84,162 | 23,037 | 180,000 |
| 18 | Siemens AG (GE) | Electrical and electronic equipment | 65,830 | 108,312 | 93,333 | 430,000 |
| 19 | Nestlé SA (SZ) | Food and beverages | 65,396 | 76,965 | 69,778 | 247,000 |
| 20 | Electricite De France (FR) | Electricity, gas and water | 65,365 | 200,093 | 55,775 | 156,152 |

*Source:* UNCTAD (2006: 280, Annex Table A.1.11)

At a more general level, governments everywhere have responded to the 'global reach' of transnational corporations by intensifying their involvement with supranational economic and political organizations such as the European Union (EU), the Association of South East Asian Nations (ASEAN) and the North American Free Trade Agreement (NAFTA). We shall be reviewing the changing role of the state in the context of the internationalization of the world economy in Parts 2 and 3 of this book. In Part 4, we shall explore supranational reactions to the internationalization of the world economy.

## PATTERNS OF INTERNATIONAL TRADE

The fundamental structure of international trade is based on a few trading blocs, with most of the world's trade taking place *within* these blocs. Membership of these trading blocs is principally the result of the effects of (1) distance, (2) the legacy of colonial relationships and (3) geopolitical alliances. For most of the period 1950–90, for example, four trading blocs dominated international trade:

1 western Europe, together with some former European colonies in Africa, south Asia, the Caribbean and Australasia
2 North America, together with some Latin American countries
3 the countries of the former Soviet world empire
4 Japan, together with other East Asian countries and the oil-exporting countries of Saudi Arabia and Bahrain.

Meanwhile, we should note that a significant number of countries have always exhibited a high degree of autarky from the world economy. That is, they do not contribute significantly to the flows of imports and exports that constitute the geography of trade. Typically, these are smaller LDCs (examples include Burundi, Central African Republic, the Gambia, Guinea-Bissau and Samoa).

The geography of trade has been changing rapidly, however, in response to the several factors:

1 Innovations in transport, communications and manufacturing technology. These innovations have diminished the importance of the 'classical' distance-based factors that have underpinned traditional trading blocs.
2 Shifts in global politics. The most important shift has of course been the break-up of the former Soviet world empire. Other important changes include the trend toward political as well as economic integration in Europe, the increasing participation of China in the world economy and the continuing trend away from isolationism on the part of the United States.
3 The increasing internationalization and flexibility of production processes. As we have seen, the globalization of economic activity has created new flows of materials, components, information and finished products. TNCs account for about two-thirds of world trade and as much as one-third of *all* trade (or half of TNC trade) now takes place within the 'internal markets' of TNCs.

Since 1990 the dissolution of the trading bloc of the former Soviet world empire has left a tripolar framework for international trade: North America, the European Union and Japan and the Asian NICs. It is no coincidence, of course, that this tripolar framework is focused on the countries that constitute the core regions of the world economy. Over the past 20 years the volume of world trade grew twice as fast as world real GDP

(6 per cent versus 3 per cent), deepening economic integration and global interdependency. Developing countries as a group achieved the fastest expansion of trade and, as a result, have become more important players in world trade, including as markets for each other's products. They now account for one-third of world trade, up from about one-quarter in the early 1970s; and 40 per cent of their exports now go to other developing countries. Developing countries have also contributed to a shift in world trade toward manufactures (Figure 2.12). As a global system of manufacturing has emerged, significant quantities of manufactured goods are now imported *and* exported across much of the world; no longer do developed economies export manufactures and LDCs import them. African countries are an important exception, many of them barely participating in world trade in manufactures.

The most striking aspect of commodity flows and the regionalization of trade is the persistence of the *dependence of LDCs on trade with developed countries that are geographically or geopolitically close*. Thus, for example, the United States is the central focus for the exports and the origin of the bulk of the imports of most

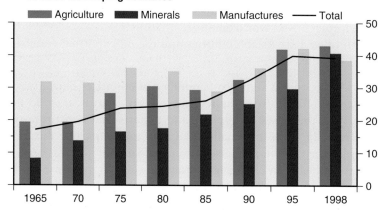

**A    Share of developing countries' exports destined to other developing countries**

**B    Product composition of world merchandise exports**

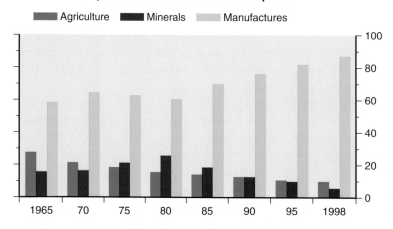

Fig 2.12: World trade and developing countries
*Source:* IMF (2001: 90, Figure 2.13)

**C   Manufactures' share in total exports**

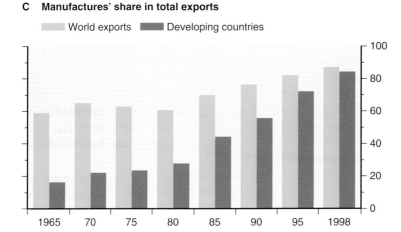

Fig 2.12: *Continued*

Central American countries, while France is the focus for commodity flows to and from French ex-colonies such as Algeria, Cambodia and Côte d'Ivoire. These flows, however, represent only part of the action for the developed economies, whose trading patterns are dominated by flows to and from other developed countries.

One of the implications of this situation is that the smaller, peripheral partners in these trading relationships are highly dependent on levels of demand and the overall economic climate in developed economies. This is an issue that has found expression in the 'fair trade' movement (see Box 2.4). Another aspect of dependency is the degree to which a country's export base is diversified. Figure 2.13 shows one measure of this: the index of commodity concentration of exports. Countries with low values on this index have diversified export bases. They include Argentina, Brazil, China, India and South Korea, as well as most of the developed countries. At the other extreme are LDCs where the manufacturing sector is poorly developed and the balancing of national accounts and the generation of foreign exchange is dependent on the export of one or two agricultural or mineral resources: Angola, Chad, the Dominican Republic, Iran, Iraq, Libya and Nigeria, for example.

## Box 2.4 From free trade to fair trade?

Developed countries such as the United States and those in the European Union (EU) continue to provide billions of dollars in agricultural subsidies to their own growers while limiting access to their markets by poor farmers in the LDCs. Oxfam has developed an index of these 'double standards' using 10 measures of trade policies in the DCs, including average tariffs, the size of tariffs on agricultural imports and restrictions on imports from the LDCs. The index scores for the EU and the United States were at the top of the list of DCs who call for free trade but limit access by the LDCs to their markets. Compounding this situation has been the decline in world prices during the last few decades for the sale of primary products such as tropical beverages and food that farmers in LDCs depend on for income.

Believing that aid alone is not the answer to poverty in the LDCs, Oxfam and other aid organizations have worked to establish a fair trade model. Seeking to set up alternative trading links between producers and consumers, people like Michael Barratt Brown founded organizations such as the Third World Information Network and Twin Trading Ltd. Influenced by ideas of sustainable development, unequal exchange and dependency, Barratt Brown, in his seminal book *Fair Trade*, pointed to the deteriorating trading position of many LDCs due to the decline in basic commodity prices for their exported food and raw materials relative to the prices of their imported manufactured goods.

The fair trade model recognizes the weak bargaining position of many small producers at the beginning of the commodity chains that underpin the global economy. This model is an attempt to directly connect consumers in the DCs with producers in the LDCs through a network that includes features such as long-term trading contracts that offer price stability for farmers. Fair Trade Labelling Organizations International (FLO), an umbrella organization of 17 national labelling groups, maintains the standards for the 'Fairtrade' label and certifies cooperatives that meet these standards. Goods displaying the 'Fairtrade' label are sold with a guaranteed minimum price that includes a social premium paid by the consumer to the democratically organized cooperatives to be spent on infrastructure investments – processing facilities, schools and hospitals – for the benefit of members. 'Fairtrade' goods meet environmental sustainability standards and ILO conventions covering labour practices.

The 'Fairtrade' label applies to a variety of goods, including coffee, tea, cocoa, bananas and honey. The first fair trade coffee was imported in 1973 into the Netherlands from a small-farmer cooperative in Guatemala. In 2003, the United States overtook the Netherlands as the largest destination for fair trade coffee. Today, over 230 coffee cooperatives representing more than over 700,000 farmers across more than two dozen countries in Latin America, Africa and Asia are certified by the FLO. Annual sales of all fair trade products are growing at double-digit rates and now estimated to be worth well over US$1 billion. At the same time, however, the total value of fair trade products – accounting for 0.5–5.0 per cent of all sales in their product categories in Europe, the United States and Canada – is minor in relation to the overall flows of international trade.

Gavin Fridell has identified three emerging perspectives on the fair-trade network. The 'decommodification' perspective incorporates notions of 'ethical trade' and depicts fair trade as a challenge to the commodification of goods under global capitalism. Jeff Popke sees the ethical trade movement as the reincarnation of the traditional Marxist concept of 'defetishizing' the commodity in order to expose its underlying unequal social relations of production. Although challenging the core values of global capitalism – competition, accumulation and profit maximization – this approach has limited potential to change the global trading system because it depends completely on revealing the conditions of global inequity to consumers in the DCs.

The 'alternative' perspective offers a rights-based approach to development that 'makes trade fair' as a replacement for free trade and the consequent dominance of DCs and TNCs. This perspective not only highlights the plight of farmers in the LDCs, but also confronts organizations such as the WTO about the structural causes of poverty, such as the trade barriers and subsidies of the

DCs. The main criticism of this approach, however, is that its successes have only been possible because it has remained part of the dominant paradigm, and as such is limited by the constraints of consumer demand, limits on the price of fair-trade goods imposed by the market, and the growth potential of fair-trade niche markets.

As a result, the 'shaped-advantage' perspective is seen as most accurately reflecting the overall impact of fair trade so far. This more moderate approach seeks to help poor farmers to improve their position in the existing global market through the help of non-governmental organizations (NGOs). The more market-oriented approach of this 'microeconomic tinkering' is seen as accounting for its recent success in assisting certain groups of poor farmers to enter the global capitalism market on better terms. Of concern, however, are the dangers of 'mainstreaming' that require the farmers to deal with TNCs such as Starbucks® in order to get fair trade products more widely into the hands of DC consumers and the lack of an explicit component that directly confronts the structural causes of poverty.

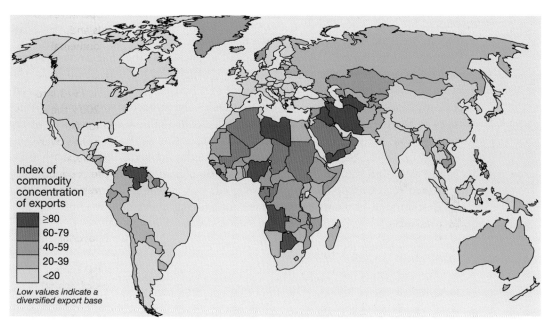

Fig 2.13: Index of commodity concentration of exports, 2003–2004

*Source:* Based on UNCTAD online data: *Trade and Commodity Price Indices,* Table 8.2

## PATTERNS OF INTERNATIONAL FINANCE AND BUSINESS SERVICES

The spatial organization of world production and trade is closely mirrored by patterns of international finance and business services. Once again, therefore, we find a tripolar framework: By the beginning of the 21st century, the United States, the EU and Japan accounted for close to three-quarters of global foreign direct investment (FDI) inflows and 85 per cent of outflows. The longstanding dominance of flows of foreign direct investment between these developed countries, however, is being heavily modified by the globalization of economic activity.

Until the early 1970s US-based transnational corporations accounted for about two-thirds of the total outflows of foreign direct investment and about four-fifths of this was directed towards Canada and the more advanced industrial national economies of western Europe. By the 1990s US transnational corporations' share of the total had dropped to less than half, while foreign direct investment by Japanese, Canadian and German corporations had increased significantly. Meanwhile, another source of foreign direct investment had begun to show up: transnational corporations based in the NICs. More than 25 of the top 100 corporations in the world are now based in NICs. Hyundai, the South Korean shipbuilding, heavy machinery and logistics firm, is bigger than Michelin or 3M (Minnesota Mining and Manufacturing); and Malaysia's Petroliam Nasional Berhad (Petronas) (an oil exploration and production conglomerate) is bigger than Anheuser-Busch or Eastman Kodak.

Along with these changes in the *sources* of investment have been changes in *destination*. The advanced industrial countries still absorb most of the inflows but, as we have seen, the globalization of economic activity has brought significant flows of capital into the NICs. Almost three-quarters of the total inflows to LDCs are accounted for by just seven NICs: Argentina, Brazil, China (including Hong Kong), Malaysia, Mexico, Singapore and South Korea.

Changes in international investment – and in particular the shift away from the United States and the LDCs as the two main destinations for foreign direct investment in the 1970s to a circular movement of FDI between North America, western Europe and Japan, at the expense of the LDCs – have been contingent on other changes in the pattern of international finance. Throughout the first part of the postwar period, the pattern of international finance was set by the Bretton Woods agreement of 1944. This created what was virtually a US-run system, with fixed exchange rates and the US dollar serving as the convertible medium of currency with a fixed relationship to the price of gold. But, as the position of the United States deteriorated in terms of world manufacturing and trade, the system came under pressure.

> The result was that the Bretton Woods system crumbled. In particular, by the late 1960s fixed exchange rates effectively disappeared and every domestic currency became convertible into every other. Exchange rates 'floated' and, as a result, all domestic currencies became a medium that could be bought and sold and out of which a profit could be made.
>
> Thrift (1989: 34)

Meanwhile, there had developed a pool of eurodollars – US dollars held in banks located outside the United States (not to be confused with the European Union currency, the euro) – that was boosted after 1971 as the US government began to finance its budget deficit by paying in its own currency, flooding the world with dollars and fuelling worldwide inflation. Two years later, in 1973, the eurodollar market was swollen still further as oil-producing countries rapidly acquired huge reserves of US dollars as a result of the quadrupling of petroleum prices in the wake of the embargo by the Organization of Petroleum Exporting Countries (OPEC). The combined result of the floating of currencies and the creation of a large market in eurodollars was that a new, more sophisticated system of international finance emerged. Consequently, new patterns of investment were accompanied by an expansion and internationalization of key business services such as stock exchanges, futures markets, banks, advertising agencies and business hotels. As developed economies have lost competitiveness in industrial production, they have come to rely increasingly on these services to earn foreign currency and to balance national accounts. This new system of international finance has produced giant financial conglomerates like Citigroup, UBS, HSBC and Deutsche Bank that dominate world financial affairs (Table 2.4). Indeed, it has been suggested that the internationalization of banking has contributed to an 'electronic colonialism' whereby large European and American banks now exercise a great deal of control over the world economy.

**Table 2.4** World's largest financial TNCs, 2004

| Rank 2004 | Corporation | Home economy | Total assets (US$m) | Total employees | Number of affiliates Total | Foreign |
|---|---|---|---|---|---|---|
| 1 | GE Capital Services | United States | 566,708 | 76,300 | 1425 | 1085 |
| 2 | Citigroup | United States | 1,484,101 | 294,000 | 612 | 347 |
| 3 | UBS | Switzerland | 1,732,121 | 67,424 | 426 | 363 |
| 4 | Allianz Group | Germany | 1,302,894 | 162,180 | 778 | 569 |
| 5 | BNP Paribas | France | 1,230,071 | 94,892 | 622 | 403 |
| 6 | Gruppo Assicurazioni Generali | Italy | 372,996 | 58,354 | 368 | 323 |
| 7 | Zurich Financial Services | Switzerland | 346,083 | 53,246 | 356 | 345 |
| 8 | Unicredito | Italy | 359,903 | 68,571 | 1044 | 998 |
| 9 | HSBC Bank | United Kingdom | 1,274,557 | 243,333 | 1076 | 658 |
| 10 | Société Générale | France | 816,735 | 93,359 | 430 | 253 |
| 11 | Deutsche Bank | Germany | 836,368 | 65,417 | 698 | 493 |
| 12 | AXA Group | France | 642,988 | 76,339 | 481 | 387 |
| 13 | Crédit Suisse | Switzerland | 953,967 | 60,532 | 334 | 280 |
| 14 | ABN AMRO | Netherlands | 825,388 | 99,271 | 851 | 432 |
| 15 | Grupo Santander | Spain | 774,462 | 126,488 | 455 | 311 |
| 16 | Bayerishe HVB Group | Germany | 629,981 | 57,806 | 935 | 572 |
| 17 | Crédit Agricole | France | 1,107,272 | 62,000 | 382 | 172 |
| 18 | Merrill Lynch | United States | 648,059 | 50,600 | 227 | 167 |
| 19 | AIG Group | United States | 798,660 | 92,000 | 368 | 147 |
| 20 | ING Group | Netherlands | 1,177,335 | 113,000 | 856 | 403 |

*Source:* UNCTAD (2006: 287, Annex Table A.1.14)

In large part, of course, the internationalization of financial services and related business services is the result of the tremendous increase in trade, the internationalization of manufacturing and the emergence of transnational corporate empires. And, just as technological changes have facilitated world trade, the internationalization of manufacturing and the emergence of transnational corporations, so advances in telecommunications and data processing have fostered the internationalization of financial and business services. Satellite communications systems and the internet have made it possible for firms to operate key financial and business services 24 hours a day, around the globe.

The growth of the global financial network has created a significant new dimension to the world economy. As Barnet and Cavanagh (1994: 17) put it:

> Twenty-four hours a day, trillions of dollars flow through the world's foreign-exchange markets as bits of data traveling at split-second speed. No more than 10 per cent of this staggering sum has anything to do with trade in goods and services. International traffic in money has become an end in itself, a highly profitable game.

## INTERNATIONAL TRADE AND THE DEBT TRAP

The structured inequality of the world economy has led to a chronic problem of international debt. The role inherited by most LDCs within the international division of labour has been one of producing primary commodities for which both the elasticity of demand and price elasticity are low. That is, demand for their products in their principal markets (the more developed countries) tends to increase by relatively small amounts in response to significant increases in incomes within their principal markets. Similarly, significant reductions in the cost of their products tend to result in only a relatively small increase in demand. In contrast, the elasticity of demand and price elasticity of manufactured goods and high-order services (the specialities of developed economies) are both high. As a result, the terms of trade are stacked against the producers of primary commodities. No matter how efficient primary producers may become, or how affluent their customers, the balance of trade will be tilted against them. Quite simply, they must run in order to stand still.

An obvious counterstrategy is to attempt to establish a new role in the international division of labour, moving away from a specialization in primary commodities towards a diversified manufacturing base. This strategy is known as import substitution. It is a difficult strategy to pursue, however, because establishing a diversified manufacturing base requires vast amounts of startup capital. With the terms of trade running against them, it is extremely difficult for them to accumulate this capital. The only alternative, short of striving for self-sufficiency – for example, Tanzania, Myanmar (Burma) – or opting out of the capitalist world economy altogether – for example, Cuba – is to raise the capital as loans. If the capital is invested in economic development projects that do not yield sufficient returns, further loans have to be undertaken in order to service the original debt and/or in order to finance new development projects. Hence, the evolution of international debt. The syndrome of having constantly to borrow in order to fund 'development' has come to be known as the debt trap.

Servicing long-term debts (i.e., meeting costs of both interest charges and repayments) has become a significant burden for some countries (Figure 2.14). In the likes of Belize, Brazil, Burundi, Ecuador, the Gambia and Pakistan, for example,

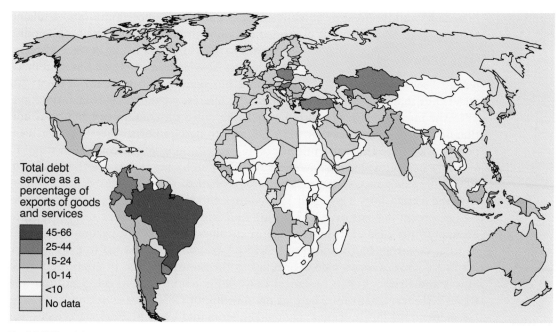

Fig 2.14: The debt problem: total debt service as a percentage of the value of exports of goods and services, 2003–2004

*Source:* Based on online data from World Bank's *World Development Indicators*

for every $100 earned through exports of goods and services in 2003–04, more than $30 was owed in long-term debt servicing. Worst off was Burundi, where two-thirds of all export earnings were cancelled out by debt servicing. The debt problem has been seriously aggravated, however, by patterns of international capital flows that have been stimulated by changing money market conditions rather than by the geography of trade. In order to avoid the punitive 'taxation' of profits and savings by the high inflation rates caused by the combination of trade imbalances and debt, the domestic creditors of LDC governments (i.e., anyone holding its currency or its interest-bearing debt) tend to move their money abroad. The result is capital flight. According to estimates by the International Monetary Fund (IMF) for 1995, for example, capital flight amounted to roughly half of the outstanding foreign debt of the most heavily indebted countries.

There is another problem. In the 1970s, world monetary reserves increased twelvefold with the availability of OPEC 'petrodollars' and as a by-product of the inflation that accompanied the break-up of the Bretton Woods system. The international banking system, awash with funds, began to 'recycle' the surpluses that oil companies had deposited with them. Bankers from developed countries suddenly found a willingness to lend to LDC governments. They found eager borrowers in LDCs desperate for capital. The result was that many LDC governments committed themselves to capital projects, wage bills and debt repayments that were more than they could finance through taxes.

By 1981 LDC debt amounted to US$739 billion. When 'Reaganomics' and monetarism drove interest rates up in the early 1980s, the debt burden became a debt crisis. In 1982 Mexico threatened to default on its debts, causing a widespread concern that such action could snowball to the point where international financial stability might be threatened. Recognizing this possibility (and realizing that their long-term interests depended not only on international financial stability but on reasonably healthy markets within LDCs), creditors in the developed countries allowed Mexico to reschedule its debts. This pattern of events has since been repeated several times. Brazil, for example, borrowed so much money in the 1970s and 1980s that it could no longer meet the interest payments. Between 1983 and 1989 the International Monetary Fund (IMF) bailed the country out, but on condition of austerity measures that were designed to curb imports. These included a 60 per cent increase in petroleum prices and a reduction of the minimum wage to US$50 a month, which gave workers half the purchasing power they had in 1940. The Philippine government, meanwhile, has had to reschedule its debt five times with the 'Paris Club', a group of 19 creditor countries. By 2002 the Philippines carried a foreign debt of over $33 billion and had reduced its debt-service ratio to around 20 per cent of its annual export earnings. By 2005 the accumulated debts of LDC countries had risen to over US$2.5 trillion. This has led to calls for rich lending countries to provide debt relief to the poorest LDCs. In 2000 the United States and Britain began to cancel LDC debts to the tune of $435 million and $1.43 billion respectively. Then, at the meeting of G8 countries (Canada, France, Germany, Italy, Japan, Russia, United Kingdom and USA) in 2005, agreement was reached to write off the entire $40 billion debt of 18 highly indebted LDCs to the World Bank, the International Monetary Fund and the African Development Fund. Addressing the magnitude of LDC debt, however, will require continued substantial and sustained efforts if the poorest countries are to break free of the crushing financial obligations of their accumulated debts.

## PATTERNS OF INTERNATIONAL AID

The debt issue leads us logically to the question of aid. Large-scale movements of aid began shortly after the Second World War with the Marshall Plan, financed by the United States to bolster wartorn European allies whose economic weakness, it was believed, made them susceptible to communism. During the 1950s and 1960s, as more LDCs gained independence, aid became a useful weapon in western and Sino-Soviet Cold War offensives to establish and preserve political influence throughout the world. By the late 1960s the list of donor countries had expanded beyond the superpowers to include smaller countries such as Austria, Denmark and Sweden, whose motivation in aid giving must be seen as more philanthropic than political. In addition, there was a greater geographic dispersal of aid, thanks largely to the activities of multilateral financial agencies such as the International Monetary Fund (IMF) and the World Bank.

Nevertheless, the geography of aid still has a strong political flavour. Bilateral aid from some countries reflects localized political aspirations and colonial ties. Thus much British and French aid is directed towards former African colonies, while Japanese aid is disbursed largely within Asia and aid from the OPEC countries has been directed mainly towards the 'frontline' Arab countries. More significantly for the LDCs, the end of the Cold War, together with the balance of payments difficulties of several developed countries, has ensured that levels of aid have diminished. Thus, whereas official development assistance from Organization for Economic Cooperation and Development (OECD) countries amounted to nearly 0.5 per cent of their total GNI in 1965, it had fallen to 0.3 per cent by 2006. The most striking decrease has been that of the United States, whose overseas development assistance as a percentage of GNI has fallen from 0.58 to 0.17. The Japanese, meanwhile, have never exceeded 0.3 per cent of their GNI in aid. It is true that some countries – Denmark, the Netherlands, Sweden and Norway, in particular – have steadily increased their aid giving to become the only DCs to have surpassed the UN target of 0.7 per cent of GNI. At these levels, aid cannot seriously be regarded as a catalyst for development or as an instrument for redressing core–periphery inequalities. By the same token, because most of this aid is 'tied' in some way to donor countries' exports or to specific military, educational or cultural projects, it is argued by many that, insignificant as it is in relative terms, it is sufficient to reinforce the initial advantage of the 'donors'.

## 2.4 INTERPRETATIONS OF INTERNATIONAL INEQUALITY

By as early as the 1960s it was clear that international spatial inequalities were becoming more rather than less pronounced. In this context, a virtual avalanche of critical writings appeared, claiming that the prosperity of the developed countries in the world economy (the USA, Europe and Japan, in particular) was based on *under*development and squalor in LDCs. The latter could not 'follow' the previous historical experience of developed countries because their underdevelopment was a structural requirement for development elsewhere. The development of Europe and North America, it was argued, *depended* on the systematic underdevelopment of LDCs. By means of unequal trade, exploitation of labour and profit extraction, the underdeveloped countries were becoming *increasingly* rather than decreasingly impoverished.

The writing of André Gunder Frank exemplifies the explanations of international economic change that arose from this critique. Frank rejected the idea that underdevelopment is an original condition, equivalent to 'traditionalism' or 'backwardness'. To the contrary, it is a condition *created* by integration into the worldwide system of exchange that originated in the 16th century: the 'world capitalist system'. The concentration of poverty and the lack of development are not, he argued, a consequence of geographical isolation or the failure of western technology, capital and values to spread. Rather, it stems directly from the nature of spatial relationships within the world capitalist system.

Frank (1967: 146–7) conceptualized a world metropolis (today the United States) and its national and international satellites and their leaders – national satellites like the southern states of the United States, and international satellites like São Paulo. Because São Paulo is a national metropolis in its own right, Frank additionally included São Paulo's satellites, the provincial metropolises, like Recife or Belo Horizonte, and their regional and local satellites in turn. Overall, Frank conceptualized a whole chain of metropolises and satellites, which ran from the world metropolis down to the hacienda or rural merchant, which are satellites of the local commercial metropolitan centre, which, in their turn, has peasants as their satellites. Globally, Frank saw a whole series of such constellations of metropolises and satellites.

An unequal structure to the world economy has been in place since Europeans first ventured out into the world in the 16th century. Although the form of the monopoly power of metropolis over satellites has changed (e.g., with the switch from merchant to industrial capitalism in the 19th century and following political independence for former colonies), the system of 'surplus expropriation' (the transfer of wealth from satellites to metropolis) has continued to fuel growth in some places at the expense of others.

Frank's approach is an example of what can be called 'dependency theory'. This has been a very influential approach to explaining global patterns of development and underdevelopment. It states, essentially, that development and underdevelopment are reverse sides of the same process. *Development somewhere requires underdevelopment somewhere else.* Independent development is impossible. Recent analyses have put more emphasis on the nature of the political and social structures created by external dependence and how these, in conjunction with the direct effects of external dependence, limit 'real' development (e.g., Slater, 1992). It is plain that concepts of underdevelopment and dependency are based (without stating it) on the notion of perpetual spatial disequilibrium between metropolis and satellites. However, as we suggested in Chapter 1 and will argue in more detail in the next chapter, the logic and demands of the world economy are in a continual state of reconstruction. The rise of the USA from satellite to metropolis, the challenge and the collapse of the Soviet Union, the appearance of the NICs and the increasing importance of transnational corporations are all contradictory to this notion of permanent spatial disequilibrium.

## SUMMARY

Brief reviews of the major aspects of international economic differentiation have illuminated both the dominance of core-periphery patterns and the extent of the gradient between core and periphery. Other important points to have emerged include the following:

- The existence of a distinctive group of semi-peripheral countries with intermediate levels of living. This group includes very different types: resource-exporting countries, both recently and newly industrializing countries, as well as countries such as China, India, poorer European countries like Greece and Portugal, the formerly socialist countries of eastern Europe and, of course, Russia.
- The speed and intensity of changes in patterns of economic activity and development associated with the globalization of economic activity under the influence of the strategies of transnational corporations.
- The degree of dependency of peripheral countries created by inequalities in resources, trading relationships, access to financial resources and control of economic activity.

## KEY SOURCES AND SUGGESTED READING

Beyon, J. and Dunkerley, D. (eds) 2000. *Globalization: The Reader*. New York: Routledge.

Dicken, P. 2007. *Global Shift: Mapping the Changing Contours of the World Economy* 5th edn. New York and London: Guilford Press.

Held, D. and McGrew, A. (eds) 2000. *The Global Transformations Reader*. Malden, MA: Blackwell.

Hutton, W. and Giddens, A. (eds) 2000. *Global Capitalism*. New York: New Press.

Lechner, F.J. and Boli, J. (eds) 2000. *The Globalization Reader*. Malden, MA: Blackwell.

Mittelman, J.H. 2000. *The Globalization Syndrome: Transformation and Resistance.* Princeton, NJ: Princeton University Press.

O'Meara, P., Mehlinger, H.D. and Krain, M. (eds) 2000. *Globalization and the Challenges of a New Century.* Bloomington, IN: Indiana University Press.

UNCTAD 2004. *Globalization and Development: Facts and Figures.* New York: UNCTAD.

UNDP (United Nations Development Programme) 2006. *Human Development Report 2006: Beyond Scarcity: Power, Poverty and the Global Water Crisis.* New York and Oxford: Oxford University Press.

Wallerstein, I. 1984. *The Politics of the World-Economy.* Cambridge: Cambridge University Press.

World Bank 2006. *World Development Report 2006: Equity and Development.* Oxford: Oxford University Press.

World Bank 2007. *World Development Report 2007: Development and the Next Generation.* Oxford: Oxford University Press.

## RELATED WEBSITES

International Monetary Fund: http://www.imf.org/
this UN agency offers financial and other information and data for the countries of the world and includes the latest edition of *The World Economic Outlook*

Population Reference Bureau: http://www.prb.org/
this website contains a wealth of information on population and population issues for individual countries and the world, and includes the latest *World Population Data Sheet*

United Nations Development Programme: http://www.undp.org/
this UNDP website offers excellent information on economic development issues for the LDCs. It contains the annual *Human Development Report* and the current human development index figures for the countries around the world

United Nations Environmental Program (UNEP): http://www.grida.no/
this UN website contains information and hyperlinks for environmental issues around the world

World Resources Institute: http://www.wri.org/
the website of this research body contains research and best practice on global environmental problems and includes *EarthTrends: The Environmental Information Portal*, which offers data and maps on environmental issues including water resources, forests, climate, etc.

# Chapter 3

# Geographical dynamics of the world economy

From one point of view the 1960s marked, as we saw in Chapter 2, the beginning of a new, more interdependent world economy. In particular, many firms operating in western Europe and the United States, and some elsewhere, began to reorganize their operations and thus improve their profitability by subcontracting some of their activities and internationalizing their production facilities. But from another viewpoint there was already a world economy in existence that was simply undergoing a process of 'globalization'. Beginning in the 16th century, but undergoing its greatest expansion and intensification in the 19th and 20th centuries, a world economy had evolved out of more localized economic systems. As it has become progressively more integrated, covering ever wider geographical areas and more and more economic activities (resource extraction, capital investment, trade in manufactures, services, etc.), it has undergone shifts in its mode of operation, as well as shifts in the relative importance of different world regions (Figure 3.1). Viewed in this larger historical context, the changes beginning in the late 1960s are the most recent manifestation of this evolutionary process.

The purpose of this chapter is, first, to sketch the historical development of the modern world economy; second, to pinpoint the geographical effects of state regulatory and macroeconomic actions; and, third, to identify the main causes and consequences of the current geographical reorganization of the world economy. The intention is to provide both a framework for understanding economic landscapes, to offer an outline of the historical context for the emerging trends in world economic geography examined in Part 4, and to give an overview of an important theoretical trend in the field of economic geography: geopolitical economy, the impact of states on the working of the world economy and the geography of economic activities.

**Shares of GDP**

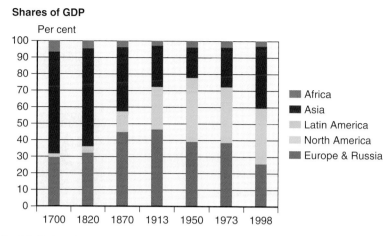

Fig 3.1: Shifting fortunes in the world economy (after Maddison)

*Source:* Based on Venables (2006: 63, Chart 1)

## 3.1  HISTORY OF THE WORLD ECONOMY

Six basic features of the world economy can serve to organize our account of it.

### 1. SINGLE WORLD MARKET

The modern world economy consists of a single world market. Within this market, producers exchange what they produce for the best price they can get. The price of products is not fixed but set as a result of competition for market share among producers. Price-setting markets, in this modern sense, took many years to become established, particularly since labour did not become a commodity to be bought and sold like any other (wage labour) until the late 18th century. Indeed, that point in time marks an important qualitative change in the nature of the world economy. European industrialization produced both a tremendous intensification of world trade and increasingly complex markets for raw materials and manufactured goods. Extra-European investment and trade also became much more important for the growth of Europe after the late 1700s. Major waves of international migration in the 19th and late 20th centuries testify to the periodic increase in geographical scope of the pools of labour on which firms and regions can draw to fuel their growth.

### 2. STATE SYSTEM

The modern world economy has always had a territorial division between political states. This division both pre-dates and grew along with the geographical expansion of the modern world economy. States can protect and stimulate infant industries and encourage the development of domestic production through tariffs, trade quotas (i.e., restricting access to 'domestic markets' of foreign-made goods) and financial incentives. The result is a competitive state system in which each state attempts to the best of its ability to insulate its economy from the rigours of the world market while trying to turn the world market to its advantage.

Obtaining competitive advantage does not always require conventional protectionist measures such as tariffs on competing products. Numerous historical examples attest to the importance of the mediating role of the state and other institutions, from the stimulus to US economic development that resulted from canal building in the early 19th century and the high spending on military goods since the Second World War, through Japan's disciplined conquest of market share in a wide range of industries after 1945 to Taiwan's highly organized entry into the global microelectronics industry in the 1980s. In some cases, for example in France, the connection between state policy and economic development has been especially close. A strongly coercive political atmosphere, along with government investment (especially in physical and social infrastructure such as roads, railways, schools, healthcare facilities) have been behind most successful attempts at overcoming France's disadvantages within the world market. Mobilization of national resources, in other words, does not usually arise naturally out of the free play of market forces but through the stimulus and direction given by government intervention.

## 3. THREE GEOGRAPHICAL TIERS

The modern world economy has developed a basic three-tiered geography as it has expanded to cover the globe (Figure 2.1). The early world economy consisted of Europe and those parts of South and Central America under Spanish–Portuguese control. The rest of the world was an external arena, essentially outside the workings of the world economy. Later, the rest of the world became incorporated – variously, by way of trade, colonization and imperialism. The world economy thus came to consist of a core (western Europe at first, joined later by the United States and Japan) and a periphery. The core is characterized by processes that involve some degree of control over the world economy and by the possession of advanced technology, diversified production and relatively high average incomes. The periphery is characterized by processes that lead to dependence and by primitive technology, undiversified production and relatively low average incomes. Uneven development at a global scale, therefore, is not a recent phenomenon or a mere by-product of the world economy; it is one of the world economy's basic features.

However, even as it expanded to incorporate ever greater parts of the world, the world economy was not without change. There has been movement between the two categories of core and periphery, as attested to by the 'rise' of the United States and Japan, and decline, as in the case of Spain and Portugal. A third geographical tier, the semi-periphery, applies to the processes operating in certain parts of the world to provide movement between periphery and core (and vice versa). This is a zone in which a mix of core and periphery processes is at work.

## 4. TEMPORAL PATTERNS AND HEGEMONY

The modern world economy has followed a number of cyclical patterns of growth and stagnation (see Box 3.1 for a review of two of the main cycles that have been identified in the world economy). States can differentially exploit or suffer from cyclical effects depending on their productive efficiency, commercial supremacy, ability to restrict competition from rivals and facility in responding to crises. Britain was able to dominate the world economy during the first two Kondratiev cycles through a mixed strategy of formal and informal imperialism (empire building and extensive investment outside its empire). The United States dominated during the next two by sponsoring a set of international economic institutions (such as the International Monetary Fund (IMF), the International Bank for Reconstruction and Development (the World Bank), and the General Agreement on Tariffs and Trade (GATT) and its successor, the World Trade Organization (WTO)) and international and regional security institutions (such as the United Nations and the North Atlantic Treaty Organization (NATO)) in order to represent and administer free market international capitalism after the Second World War. The term hegemony is often applied to instances of dominance such as those of Britain and the United States. This is a difficult and controversial concept but most definitions would accept the criterion that the leading state cannot be simply the strongest militarily but also must have the economic and cultural power to set and enforce the rules of international conduct that it prefers. American hegemony, therefore, does not only signify a shift in the identity of the hegemonic power from a previous one, but also a shift in the institutions and practices that the United States has brought to the world by virtue of its dominant position. These have included mass production/consumption (Fordism), limited state welfare policies, electoral democracy based on weak mass political parties and government economic policies directed towards stimulating private economic activities.

## Box 3.1 Long-wave economic fluctuations and spatial change

Within the dynamics of the capitalist mode of production there have been several kinds of cyclical fluctuation, each with different amplitudes, which have had profound effects on economic geography. Two of these – Kondratiev cycles and Kuznets cycles – are particularly important.

A series of cyclical movements in the overall rate of change of prices in the economy are known as Kondratiev cycles, after the Russian economist who first identified them. There is evidence from price and some growth data that since the late 18th century the world economy has gone through four complete Kondratiev cycles of (A) growth and (B) stagnation, and we are now in the fifth. Each one has been marked by a progressive acceleration in the rate of price increases for about 20 years, followed by a rapid inflationary spiral. After the peak, prices collapse, eventually reaching a trough some 50–55 years after the start of the cycle (see Figure 1.2). It is important to note that the evidence about trends in the world economy is generally better concerning the more recent cycles; the 19th-century ones are more difficult to discern and the data available are less reliable. When four cycles are identified they are usually presented in terms of the following approximate dates:

| | |
|---|---|
| I | (A) growth 1780–1815; (B) stagnation 1815–1848 |
| II | (A) growth 1848–1873; (B) stagnation 1873–1895 |
| III | (A) growth 1895–1918; (B) stagnation 1918–1940 |
| IV | (A) growth 1941–1973; (B) stagnation 1973–1992 |
| V | (A) growth 1992–? |

Superimposed on the Kondratiev fluctuations have been a variety of *business cycles* of different amplitudes. These can be regarded as the result of the fundamental dynamics of capitalist markets, in which expansion (production and supply increasing to meet increased consumer demand) is followed inevitably by overshoot (when overly optimistic producers and suppliers overestimate the rate of increase in demand) and then collapse (as overcapacity and excess inventory lead to falling profits, reduced asset values, pessimism and reduced levels of investment). The most significant of these cycles is the Kuznets cycle. This is a cycle of regular changes in the rate of economic growth, as measured by indicators such as per capita gross national income (GNI). As indicated on Figure 1.2, these are characterized by an expansion phase of 11–15 years, followed by a collapse phase of similar duration, which create the familiar business cycles of expansion/recession that attract so much public debate. They have affected many aspects of economic development, including the rhythm of investment in transport infrastructure, in city building and in migration.

In institutional terms some of the key features of the organizational evolution of capitalism correlate with the long-wave cycles. Competitive capitalism prevailed (before and) during the two Kondratiev cycles from the late 18th to the late 19th century. Small industrial firms operating in competitive national markets with foreign trade under rigid government control displaced more free-wheeling merchant capitalism. Organized capitalism developed through the next two cycles. In this period average firm size grew significantly and the new firms began to operate globally while maintaining strong regional bases within their home countries. Declining rates of profit under existing locational arrangements provided a powerful stimulus to global operations, particularly the establishment of factories that are free of the labour market constraints and environmental regulations increasingly prevalent in the USA and some European countries. The period since the early 1970s marks the emergence of an advanced (disorganized) capitalism: national markets are less regulated by national-based firms, and governments in general have less regulatory control over their national economies, average plant size has decreased, production has spread globally and service industries have grown faster than manufacturing ones (see Chapters 4–8 and 10–11 for more detailed descriptions).

## 5. INCORPORATION, SUBORDINATION AND RESISTANCE

One danger in focusing on the concept of 'world economy' is that local histories can be deprived of their integrity and specificity. In fact, the world's populations resist or adapt to incorporation into the world economy rather than simply accepting or succumbing to it, and different parts of the world have reacted distinctively to the expansion of the world economy. Hall (1986) provides a very useful typology of world economy impacts. Along a continuum of patterns of incorporation, he distinguishes a 'weak' pole of areas external to the world economy (external arenas) and a strong pole of fully fledged dependent peripheries. In between are areas where contact has been slight (contact peripheries) and an intermediate category of marginal peripheries (Table 3.1). The processes involved as an area shifts from the status of an external arena to a dependent periphery are also indicated in

Table 3.1. Market articulation refers to the nature of the capital and product flows between the expanding world economy and an area undergoing absorption. At the weak pole of the continuum are areas only slightly connected to the world economy, with the primary flow of influence from the core to the periphery. At the strong pole of the continuum, the exchange involved is important to core development. Although influence does flow in both directions, net product and capital flows generally favour the core.

**Table 3.1** Continuum of geographical incorporation into the world economy

| | Continuum of incorporation | | | |
| | None | Weak | Moderate | Strong |
| Type of periphery | External arena | Contact periphery | Marginal periphery | Dependent periphery |
|---|---|---|---|---|
| Market articulation | None | Weak | Moderate | Strong |
| Impact of core on periphery | None | Strong | Stronger | Strongest |
| Impact of periphery on core | None | Low | Moderate | Significant |

*Source:* Hall (1986: 392, Diagram 1)

Movement along the continuum is contingent rather than inevitable, both in terms of the pace and the eventual degree of dependence. The pace of transition towards strong incorporation depends on the strength of the state engaged in expansion and the nature of the world economy at the time. For example, in the 16th century Spanish expansion led less immediately to effective incorporation and the spread of market exchange than did British expansion in the 19th century. Plunder and religious zeal were more important to 16th-century Spain than 'bringing to market'. In the 19th century market exchange was effectively internationalized under British hegemony as production for the market everywhere replaced the mere exchange of commodities (Table 3.2). The British national economy had become the 'locomotive' of the world economy. But as its markets in Europe became more competitive, it was pushed into a widening of its markets elsewhere. The British Empire was an important part of this expansion. The internationalization of the British economy in the 19th century was a crucial element in the quickening pace and increased strength of incorporation worldwide (see Chapter 8).

## 6. ALTERNATIVE ADAPTATIONS

Finally, every part of the world has had its own particular relationship to the evolution of the world economy. In the case of the United States, for example, the existence from an early period of two contrasting and incompatible modes of socioeconomic organization within one territorial state – a plantation agriculture based on African slave labour in the south and a 'classic' capitalist or free enterprise economy in the north – was peculiarly American. Its heritage, in terms of the

**Table 3.2** Geographical development of the world economy in the nineteenth century

| Stage: | Developed | Developing | | Underdeveloped | |
|---|---|---|---|---|---|
| Factor intensity: | Capital | Labour | Land | Land | Labour |
| 1800 | Britain | Europe | | USA | India |
| 1840 | Britain | Europe | USA | Latin America<br>Australia<br>Canada | India<br>China |
| 1870 | Britain<br>Europe | | USA | Australia<br>Latin America<br>Canada<br>Africa | China |
| 1900 | Britain<br>Europe<br>USA | | Australia<br>Canada<br>Argentina<br>Mexico<br>South Africa | Latin America<br>Africa | India<br>China |

Source: Hansson (1952: 49–82)

relative regional underdevelopment of the south and racially polarized politics wherever there are concentrations of African–Americans, continues to this day. Likewise, the apartheid system of racial categorization and control in South Africa was a peculiarly South African response to the history of European settlement and economic exploitation in southern Africa. The nature of relations between the state and the economy also differs significantly among such nominally 'capitalist' states as Britain, Italy, France and Germany. This is the result of both the historical development of connections with the world economy and of different approaches to maintaining international competitive advantage. The whole process of development and underdevelopment is frequently mediated geographically through the actions of state-level regulation. Japan (see Chapter 5) and China (see Chapter 10) offer fascinating examples of this process. The most important experiment in providing a consciously designed *departure* from the guiding principles of the world economy was the 'model' of economic development established in the Soviet Union in the aftermath of the Russian Revolution of 1917 (see Chapter 10).

## 3.2 STATES AND THE WORLD ECONOMY

The emergence of the world economy in Europe coincided with, and was dependent on, the consolidation of territorial states within Europe and the emergence of the so-called Westphalian System. The Peace of Westphalia (1648), ending the Thirty Years' War in Europe, established several key principles which still have a lasting impact on the world: (1) the principle of the sovereignty of states and the fundamental right of political self-determination, (2) the principle of (legal) equality between states and (3) the principle of non-intervention of one state in the internal affairs of another state. These principles are still common to the way the international system operates today, which explains why the system of states is referred to as the 'Westphalian System'. From 500 political entities in Europe in 1500, there were not more than 25 territorial states in 1900. Modern territorial states have ever since been the political framework of the modern world economy. Thus, the expansion of the world economy has been accompanied by a parallel expansion of the interstate system as the sole form of political, military and administrative organization. As colonies achieved independence from the European empires they expanded the list of the world's states.

But the state is not a standardized entity in all countries. It includes very different institutions (different representative assemblies, bureaucracies, police forces, militaries, etc.), each a product of particular histories that adapted in phase to shifts in national development and position within the world economy. The relative power of states can be thought of in terms of three dimensions: (1) relative to one another (the hierarchy of states), (2) relative to their inhabitants and (3) relative to the 'globalizing' world economy (Harris, 1986: 145–69). The first – the hierarchy of states – has shown considerable variation historically, e.g., in the rise and decline of Britain and in the rise of the USA, Canada, Australia, New Zealand, Japan and the NICs. The second – the power of states relative to their inhabitants – seems to grow incessantly, particularly in the more developed economies, with respect to regulation, taxation and surveillance. However, the third – the power of states relative to other actors in the world economy – appears to be declining in general and to decline more as countries develop economically. It is this third dimension that attracts our attention before we proceed to the first and the second.

## STATES AND THE GLOBALIZING WORLD ECONOMY

The latest phase in the evolution of the world economy, labelled earlier (Figure 1.2) by the term globalized capitalism, has involved the erosion of national economies as the basic building blocks of the world economy. A transnational element has been in the ascendant in the form of the growth of a global market that is supplied by firms that organize their production and distribution without much reference to national boundaries. This 'global shift' in production has given rise to an explosion of foreign direct investment (FDI) and to the emergence of trade *within* large firms as the most rapidly expanding component of total world trade. Perhaps 30–40 per cent of US imports, for example, consists of parts and finished goods from the foreign subsidiaries of US-headquartered firms. Transnational corporations, therefore, are major engines in the growth of world trade. Chapters 7, 8 and 10 document the impact of this global shift on the geography of the world economy. However, one point that must be made here is that, rather than marking the eclipse of national boundaries, the globalization of production has occurred in large part *because* of them. *The spatial strategies of transnational corporations are designed to exploit national differences in labour forces, market conditions, regulatory environments and macroeconomic (fiscal and monetary) conditions.* Without this variation, the attraction to firms of shifting investments and moving production would be reduced. The challenge to states is to compete in this more integrated and volatile economic environment as effectively as possible.

There is, nevertheless, some danger of exaggerating the extent to which the globalization of production has involved the rise to power of global firms. Most so-called global companies are still strongly attached to their home countries. For example, non-national board membership on transnational corporations remains low. European and North American companies lead the trend towards global boards. In Japanese companies, in contrast, 'foreign directors are as rare as British sumo wrestlers' (*Economist*, 1993a: 69). This bias is manifested in the activities of even the most 'global' firms. When total sales decline, home markets tend to be protected at the expense of foreign ones. When firms expand abroad they continue to rely heavily on suppliers from their home countries. Antitrust laws and nationalism still make it hard for foreign firms to expand through takeovers. The difficulties encountered by British Airways and other European airlines in trying to join forces with various US airlines are a case in point.

The globalization of production has also been associated with many states and trading blocs (such as the European Union) devising industrial and trading policies that serve to protect and enhance their national economies by encouraging domestic and discouraging foreign investment (see Chapter 12 for more on economic, political and military integration among blocs of countries). An example is Airbus Industrie, which produces the European Airbus, and is a consortium of aerospace firms from different European countries collaborating to take on the big American producers such as Boeing. The United States and Britain are unique in the extent to which they have allowed their economic frontiers to expand beyond their national boundaries. Both had policies that protected infant industries and provided public investment in infrastructure (roads, railways, schools, hospitals, etc.) and research and development (R&D) (as in the federal support for the land-grant universities in the USA and government support of universities in general in both countries). Both are now faced with problems of deindustrialization that are more severe than those of many other countries, at least in part because of their neglect of the connection between government action and economic growth.

## INTERNATIONAL FINANCIAL SYSTEM

Of even greater alleged importance in reducing the power of states relative to the world economy is the international financial system, which provides the structural framework for trade and investment decisions and is much more integrated in the early 21st century than it was even a few decades ago. All forms of capital have become more mobile in time and space. Corporate and financial market decisions are now made within much tighter time schedules than was only recently the case. Currency exchange rates can now change several times a day compared to less than annually before 1970. Decisions about employing and shedding labour are now made weekly and monthly compared to quarterly before 1970 (Figure 3.2). Commodity, exchange and stock markets in world cities work around the clock shifting investments and setting prices that have different effects in different places because of their particular mixes of economic activities. Banking has become a global industry with the reduction of national and local barriers to operations and capital movements.

Flows of capital rather than trade now drive the world economy. The main recipients of FDI inflows remain developed countries, with almost 70 per cent of the total in 2005. When FDI is broken down by economic activity, services are the most important sector: Some 60 per cent of FDI stock is now in the services

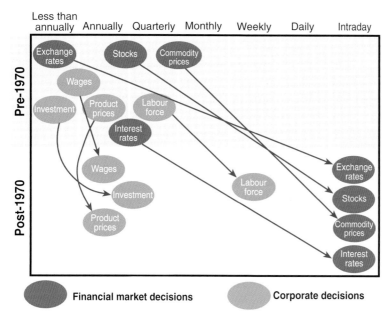

Fig 3.2: Increasing pace of the world economy

*Source:* Adapted from *Economist* (1983: 11, Figure 2)

industries, compared to less than 50 per cent a decade ago. The share of manufacturing in FDI inward stock has fallen from more than 40 per cent in 1990 to 35 per cent today, while the share of the primary sector has declined from 10 per cent to 6 per cent (UNCTAD, 2004).

Government policies towards FDI have been liberalized worldwide, partly as a result of the privatization of state-owned industries but also because of pressure from multilateral institutions such as the International Monetary Fund (IMF) and the World Bank, which insist on increased openness to FDI in return for favourable loan conditions. In some LDCs the IMF and the World Bank have cooperated to intervene in domestic politics by way of so-called structural adjustment programmes. Structural adjustment is a term used to describe the policy changes implemented by the IMF and the World Bank in developing countries. These policy changes are stipulations for getting new loans from the IMF or World Bank, or for obtaining lower interest rates on existing loans. These stipulations are implemented to ensure that the money lent will be spent in accordance with the overall goals of the loan. Structural adjustment programmes were created with the primary goal of reducing the borrowing country's macroeconomic imbalances. In general, loans from both the World Bank and the IMF are designed to promote economic growth, to generate income and to pay off the debt these countries have accumulated. Structural adjustment programmes are based on fiscal and monetary restraint, combined with deregulation and liberalization of national markets.

Even the most economically powerful countries are now less autonomous and more vulnerable to both foreign ownership of economic assets and shocks emanating from world financial markets. One commentator has gone so far as to proclaim in the subtitle of his book that global financial integration signifies the 'end of geography' (O'Brien, 1992). By this, he means the declining ability of states, even the most powerful ones, to regulate the financial sectors within their economies. This may well be true, but there are still very important institutional and cultural barriers to the free movement of capital. For example, knowledge about financial opportunities is still bound up with knowing the local investment 'scene', which largely depends on having access to local social networks that rely on relations of trust built up through social interaction and common social bonds.

Financial markets are undoubtedly more open than they were only 30 years ago, however. This opening up dates back to the collapse of the Bretton Woods system of pegged exchange rates that prevailed from 1945 until 1971 (see Chapter 2). Under that system, free trade and regulated finance ultimately proved incompatible; once the free trade became more significant in the 1960s the latter proved impossible to sustain. Confidence in a government's ability to maintain a fixed exchange rate (such as that of Britain in 1967) began to wane as capital controls proved incapable of neutralizing international capital movements. New, more flexible exchange rates after 1971 have proved relatively advantageous for large, relatively closed economies such as those of the United States and Japan. Some economists argue, however, that the costs of floating currencies have become increasingly high for smaller, open economies. According to this view, excessively volatile exchange rates disrupt domestic policymaking and reduce the ability of firms to make calculations about long-term rates of return on investment. In the long term, this may encourage the development of monetary blocs organized around the world's three major currencies: the US dollar, the euro and the Japanese yen.

## COLLABORATION AND INDEPENDENCE

Increased financial integration does not mean, however, that the world economy now runs rampant over national economies. Indeed, O'Brien, the prophet of the 'end of geography', suggests all kinds of barriers to the homogenization that his book's subtitle announces so dramatically. Individual governments (or state institutions such as central banks) can still influence international financial markets through industrial policies, budget deficits and by manipulating interest rates. But no single government can now control the system or completely control its own national economy. Even collaboration between governments, as in the G8 meetings of leaders from the main industrialized countries (Canada, France, Germany, Italy, Japan, Russia, United Kingdom and the USA), cannot always produce predictable effects on currencies, investment and trade flows. Nevertheless, collaboration, both formal and informal, and largely under American sponsorship, has become an important feature of the world economy. The willingness of governments from the strongest national economies (such as Japan and Germany) to pay a price for American leadership has persisted because increased international economic integration gives all countries a stake in maintaining stability. Participating in the global economy is now an important part of doing business anywhere.

## MANAGEMENT AND MEDIATION

The crux of the contemporary world economy, then, is the coexistence of national and global structures and attempts by states to manage the tensions between them. Transnational activities operate within states and under conditions imposed by them. Trade and tariff policies are still of vital importance in regulating trade and investment. For example, even as industrial countries' tariff levels have dropped steadily as a result of the GATT/WTO negotiations of the post-Second World War period, non-tariff barriers (quotas, voluntary trade restraints, etc.) have often increased, usually as a result of pressure on governments from domestic political coalitions. In a number of countries, especially the United States, there is a growing controversy among economists and politicians over the geographical distribution of the costs and benefits of open as opposed to more 'managed' trade. Some commentators argue that certain countries, particularly China and Japan, do not trade 'fairly', they impose too many restrictions on imports while they benefit from the relative openness of other countries to their exports.

Financial systems are important to the geography of the world economy because they mediate between political systems, on the one hand, and the global system of production, on the other. Largely as a result of national regulatory policy, national financial systems still differ profoundly in their connection with local industry and in their openness to foreign penetration. The German and Japanese financial systems, for example, are intimately connected with their conational industrial companies, whereas the US and the British systems are not only independent of but often appear to be at cross-purposes with the needs of the domestic manufacturing industry. This difference has important consequences, particularly in terms of the geography of investment. In Germany and Japan the fortunes of finance and industry are closely tied. Each has a stake in the other. In Britain, industry has had to compete with a wide range of alternative and often more attractive outlets for bank investment, inside and outside the country. At the same time, financial markets in Britain have been more readily accessible to investment from outside, creating in London a truly global financial centre.

In general, national financial systems differ along three dimensions (Zysman, 1983: 69). The first is the process whereby savings are transformed (by banks, etc.) into investments and allocated among competing uses: 'intermediation'. The second dimension is the degree to which prices are set in financial markets, by dominant financial institutions or by government: 'marketization', or price controls. The third is the amount of government intervention in the financial system: regulation. Combinations of the three dimensions differ significantly among countries and thus provide distinctive financial environments for internal economic development. The USA and Britain are capital market financial systems in which the intermediation of financial institutions is relatively weak, where prices are set in markets and there is limited state intervention in financial markets. There is little, if any, bias towards local industrial firms or long-run national economic development. Germany typifies a second model of a financial institution-dominated credit-based financial system in which bank intermediation dominates, prices are set in markets but the state and financial institutions are closely related. Large banks provide the bulk of the credit to domestic industrial firms and are usually represented on the governing boards of these firms. Finally, there are government-dominated credit-based financial systems, exemplified by France and Japan. In this case, state entanglement with industry (nationalized industry in France, private industry in Japan) has fundamental limiting effects on the autonomy of markets and financial institutions. Particularly in Japan the financial system has been structured traditionally to give a long-run orientation to industrial development. For example, the government-run Postal Savings system in Japan channels domestic savings through commercial banks into industrial investments.

For political–institutional reasons, therefore, national economies cannot always be confined solely to creating the optimal conditions for the operation of global industries within them, because national politics reflects conflicts of group and regional interests over tariffs and trade, and national economies have had distinctive trajectories in the development of the financial systems that underpin investment decisions by local firms (see Table 3.3). At the same time, the global economy is developing explicitly to optimize conditions for private business activities, at whatever cost to this or that national economy, including a firm's 'own'. An increasingly integrated world financial system is one mechanism for this. The 'global shift' in production is another. In some LDCs, international economic institutions such as the IMF and the World Bank have become so powerful in setting conditions under which loans will be granted that they have become the de facto governments of those countries. In a large number of African states the 'internationalization of the state' has gone so far that some commentators have referred to them as quasi-states, unable to direct their own economies without massive external assistance and not offering much in the way of citizenship or economic benefits to their populations. So: what, if anything, is the continuing significance of states in the contemporary context of expansive globalization?

**Table 3.3** Institutions and ideological basis of the world's dominant capitalisms

| Characteristic | American capitalism | Japanese capitalism | European social market | British capitalism |
|---|---|---|---|---|
| **Basic principle** | | | | |
| Dominant factor of production | Capital | Labour | Partnership | Capital |
| 'Public' tradition | Medium | High | High | Low |
| Centralization | Low | Medium | Medium | High |
| Reliance on price-mediated markets | High | Low | Medium | High |
| Supply relations | Arm's-length Price-driven | Close Enduring | Bureaucracy Planned | Arm's-length Price-driven |
| Industrial groups | Partial, defence, etc. | Very high | High | Low |
| Extent privatized | High | High | Medium | High |
| **Financial system** | | | | |
| Market structure | Anonymous, securitized | Personal, committed | Bureaucracy, committed | Uncommitted, marketized |
| Banking system | Advanced, marketized, regional | Traditional, regulated, concentrated | Traditional, regulated, regional | Advanced, marketized, centralized |
| Stock market | Very important | Unimportant | Unimportant | Very important |
| Required returns | High | Low | Medium | High |

**Table 3.3** *Continued*

| Characteristic | American capitalism | Japanese capitalism | European social market | British capitalism |
|---|---|---|---|---|
| **Labour market** | | | | |
| Job security | Low | High | High | Low |
| Labour mobility | High | Low | Medium | Medium |
| Labour/management | Adversarial | Cooperative | Cooperative | Adversarial |
| Pay differential | Large | Small | Medium | Large |
| Turnover | High | Low | Medium | Medium |
| Skills | Medium | High | High | Poor |
| Union structure | Sector-based | Firm-based | Industry-wide | Craft |
| Strength | Low | Low | High | Low |
| **The firm** | | | | |
| Main goal | Profits | Market share, stable jobs | Market share, fulfilment | Profits |
| Role of top manager | Boss-king, autocratic | Consensus | Consensus | Boss-king, hierarchy |
| Social overheads | Low | Low | High | Medium, down |
| **Welfare system** | | | | |
| Basic principle | Liberal | Corporatist | Corporatist, social democracy | Mixed |
| Universal transfers | Low | Medium | High | Medium, down |
| Means testing | High | Medium | Low | Medium, up |
| Degree education tiered by class | High | Medium | Medium | High |
| Private welfare | High | Medium | Low | Medium, up |
| **Government policies** | | | | |
| Role of government | Limited, adversarial | Extensive, cooperative | Encompassing | Strong, adversarial |
| Openness to trade | Quite open | Least open | Quite open | Open |
| Industrial policy | Little | High | High | Non-existent |
| Top income tax | Low | Low | High | Medium |

*Source:* Hutton (1995: 282)

## STATES AND THE GEOGRAPHY OF THE WORLD ECONOMY

The continuing importance of states in the world economy is manifested in a number of ways: first, in the organizing and mobilizing roles of states in the NICs; second, in the continuing geopolitical rivalry of the developed, industrialized countries; third, in the macroeconomic policies pursued by national governments and central banks to stabilize and reorganize their economies; fourth, in the continued importance of national governments as agents of social and political order within their territories; and, fifth, in the latitude and initiative of lower level governments in attracting and keeping economic activities within their jurisdictions.

## 1. The NICs

It is remarkable that if the larger NICs (i.e., excluding the Hong Kong SAR and Singapore because of their peculiarity as ethnic Chinese city states) are examined in detail, the fastest growing and otherwise best performing countries have all had national governments that have directly and actively intervened in their economies. In South Korea, for example, successive governments have played major roles in fostering economic growth. Adding government savings to deposits in nationalized banks, the South Korean government controlled two-thirds of South Korea's investment resources during the country's period of most rapid growth in the late 1970s. This power was used to guide investment in chosen directions through differential interest rates and easy credit terms. Korean export expansion, the main method of economic growth, was itself built on an economic base that was stringently protected from foreign imports. Activist governments orchestrated economic growth: 'In exchange for subsidies, the state ... imposed performance standards on private firms' (Amsden, 1989: 8). Elsewhere, subsidies have not always been tied so closely to performance and the result has been lower growth.

The recent experience of South Korea and some other NICs such as Taiwan should not therefore be interpreted as an entirely 'market' phenomenon. Economists on the political right and on the political left err when they ignore or systematically devalue the importance of state action in organizing and mobilizing resources for economic growth. Of course, not all states have either the institutional foundations or the resources to 'mobilize' for economic growth. South Korea and Taiwan had decisive advantages because of their ethnic homogeneity, their transport infrastructure inherited from Japanese colonialism, a history of land reform and American investment during the Cold War to help 'contain' China and the Soviet Union. In many other cases, ethnic divisions and organized corruption have turned states into barriers rather than facilitators of economic development. Their action or inaction continues to afflict their populations. One thinks of such examples as Zaire, Zimbabwe and Somalia in Africa (only three examples from a much longer list), Argentina and Venezuela in Latin America, and Sri Lanka and the Philippines in Asia (see Chapters 8 and 10).

## 2. States and geopolitical rivalry

Furthermore, states in the 'developed world' show few signs of disappearing (see Chapters 6 and 7). Indeed, under the conditions of economic restructuring that have affected most industrialized economies over the past 20 years, there has been a deepening of rivalry between many countries over trade, monetary and foreign policy. Successive US governments have used the devaluation and revaluation of the dollar to insulate the US territorial economy from the negative impacts of increased foreign competition and import penetration on the US economy. This has of necessity been at the expense of other currencies and other countries, especially Japan and the countries of western Europe.

This is an important example of how the most powerful states can use fiscal and monetary policies to stabilize and reorganize their economies at the expense of other national economies. Within their own boundaries they can also encourage or slow down the processes of restructuring that emanate from changes in the world economy. In the USA in the 1950s and 1960s defence spending and housing and transportation policies that stimulated suburban growth helped the development of

Fordist firms oriented to national markets (e.g., in automobile production). In Japan during the same period the government Ministry of International Trade and Industry (MITI) (reorganized as the Ministry of Economy, Trade and Industry (METI) in 2001) used an industrial life-cycle model to guide investment in new industries as 'old' ones achieved 'maturity'. Other countries had less direct industrial policies, often operating through government-owned industries (such as electricity or steel) to stimulate new industries and stabilize production. In the USA in the 1980s defence spending again and new financial services (stimulated through deregulation of banks and other financial institutions in the 1980s) became the focus of government attention. The large deficits in the federal government budget that began to accrue in the early part of the decade further stimulated the financial service industries through the need to attract and reward foreign investment. Regions and localities specializing in military production and finance were the beneficiaries. Increases in military spending were justified in terms of the security threat posed to the United States and its allies by another state with a different political–economic system: the (now) former Soviet Union. The demise of the Soviet Union promised both the reduction of military spending and the removal of the Cold War 'threat' on which the political commitment to the United States of such countries as Germany and Japan was based. The escalating threats of global terrorism and the spread of nuclear weapons to countries like Iran, Pakistan and North Korea, however, may provide US governments with a new approach to industrial policy and a new way of keeping allies (especially Germany and Japan) in line.

## 3. Macroeconomic policymaking

With the rise of international financial integration and highly speculative financial markets has come a concomitant rise in the political power of central banks (such as the Federal Reserve in the USA, the European Central Bank in Germany, the Bank of Japan or the Bank of England). This is because central banks in large financial markets have retained an ability to affect conditions in domestic and global markets by manipulating interest rates and the money supply. But these banks function differently in different countries and are subject to distinctive pressures emanating from the conjuncture of external influences and distinctive national institutional policy environments. For example, where a central bank is politically independent, and connections between industry and finance are weak, as in the USA, the central bank will be a 'rentier' bank, following restrictive monetary policies that benefit banks and other financial interests. However, where a central bank is independent but industry and finance are closely linked, as in many eurozone countries like Germany, France or Italy, the central bank will try to benefit business as a whole, choosing specific policies depending on the relative influence of labour. Prior to the advent of the euro and creation of the ECB, the Bundesbank in Germany gave a very high priority to maintaining price stability through fighting inflation. At least since the mid-1970s this seems to have produced higher aggregate economic growth than would otherwise have been the case. But it has required a general popular fear of inflation (perhaps based on the collective memory of the drastic price inflations of the 1920s and mid-1940s) for acceptance of the tight monetary policies that have been pursued. Finally, where the central bank is part of the government, industry and finance are linked and labour is cooperative, as in Sweden, central bank policy can be expected to be expansionary and, potentially, inflationary.

## 4. Governments and peoples

The corporate welfare state that developed under organized capitalism is under threat, however, in all these countries. The state is certainly still 'big' throughout the industrialized world and beyond (e.g., in India and China), but the Reagan administration in the USA and the Thatcher governments in Britain in the 1980s popularized the view that government spending on social services (Margaret Thatcher's 'nanny state') was a drag on national investment and growth because of the taxes that were required to pay for them. Overall, there has been a marked shift away from egalitarian liberalism toward a free market doctrine of neoliberalism (see Box 3.2). As the neoliberal paradigm establishes itself globally, this perspective is increasingly spreading beyond the bounds of the English-speaking world. Certainly, national governments in the core of the world economy now find themselves in the fiscal crisis that is a 'normal' condition in the rest of the world with demands on their resources increasing (e.g., ageing populations, increasing poverty) as their ability to meet them (e.g., loss of higher paying traditional manufacturing jobs and associated revenues) declines. However, governments in the industrialized world remain as the most important agents of social and political order within their territories. They differ only in the degree of 'bigness' as measured by laws passed, range and comprehensiveness of programmes, scope of government agencies and number and initiative of employees. The overall involvement of most governments in the lives of their citizens shows few signs of decline.

## Box 3.2 Neoliberalism

The failure of Keynesianism (the operational policy framework for egalitarian liberalism) to cope with the economic system shock of the sudden quadrupling of crude oil prices by OPEC in 1973, the consequent overaccumulation crisis, and the subsequent globalization of industrial production, all opened the way for radically different policy perspectives, setting in motion a shift away from the egalitarian liberalism that had dominated public policy in DCs like the United States and the United Kingdom since the 1930s. Just as the idea of market failures had been a powerful notion in the ideological shift from classical liberalism to egalitarian liberalism in the 1930s, so the idea of government failures became a powerful notion in undermining egalitarian liberalism (and especially the Keynesian welfare state) in the mid- to late-1970s. Governments, the argument ran, were inefficient, bloated with bureaucracy, prone to over-regulation that stifles economic development and committed to social and environmental policies that are an impediment to international competitiveness. As a result, egalitarian liberalism was eclipsed by neoliberalism, a selective return to the ideas of classical liberalism. Increased taxation (to fund spending on the casualties of deindustrialization), unemployment, and inner city decline led to resentment among more affluent sections of the taxpaying public who were caught up in an ever escalating material culture and wanted more disposable income for their own private consumption. With pressure on public spending, the quality of public services, public goods, and physical infrastructures inevitably deteriorated, which, in turn, added even more pressure for those with money to spend it privately.

The concept of the public good was tarred with the same brush as Keynesianism, as government itself (to paraphrase Ronald Reagan) came to be identified as the problem rather than the solution. Whereas market failures had been the rationale for the ascendance of egalitarian liberalism, government failures became the rationale for neoliberalism. Globalization also played a part: Keynesian economic policies and redistributive programmes came to be seen as an impediment to international competitiveness. Labour market 'flexibility' became the new conventional wisdom.

By the mid-1990s, neoliberalism had become the conventional economic wisdom. As Jamie Peck and Adam Tickell (2002) have pointed out, all this is part of a continuous process of political–economic change, not simply a set of policy outcomes. They have characterized the process in terms of a combination of 'rollback' neoliberalization and 'rollout' neoliberalization. Rollback neoliberalization has meant the deregulation of finance and industry, the demise of public housing programmes, the privatization of public space, cutbacks in redistributive welfare programmes, shedding many of the traditional roles of central and local governments as mediators and regulators, curbs on the power and influence of labour unions, and a reduction of investment in the physical infrastructure of roads, bridges and public utilities. Rollout neoliberalization has meant 'right-to-work' legislation, the establishment of public–private partnerships, the development of workfare requirements, the assertion of private property rights, the creation of free-trade zones, enterprise zones and other deregulated spaces, the assertion of the principle of 'highest and best use' for landuse planning decisions and the privatization of government services.

The net effect has been to 'hollow out' the capacity of the central governments while forcing local governments to become increasingly entrepreneurial in pursuit of jobs and revenues, and increasingly pro-business in terms of their expenditures. Indeed, the proponents of neoliberal policies have advocated free markets as the ideal condition not only for economic organization, but also for political and social life. Ideal for some, of course. Free markets have intensified uneven relationships among places and regions, the inevitable result being an intensification of economic inequality at every scale, from the neighbourhood to the nation-state.

## 5. Lower tier governments and economic development

In some countries, local levels of government are able to pursue policies of their own with respect to attracting and keeping economic activities. As some manufacturing and service industries have become more 'footloose' following the technological and organizational changes of the recent past (less tied through agglomeration economies to specific locations), a variety of factors once marginal to a firm's locational calculus have assumed greater prominence. Some of these can be subsumed under the rubric of local 'business climate'. In the United States, for example, the northern states of the manufacturing belt (the region stretching from Illinois to New York where most US manufacturing industry was concentrated from 1880 to the 1960s) tend to have higher personal income tax rates and greater provision of public goods and services (public education, social services, etc.) than states in the south and west. These conditions provide for less favourable business climates for certain industries than are found in the other regions.

Many states and localities throughout the country, however, have actively sought out businesses by offering tax breaks and subsidies. Many of the US states have offices in Europe and Asia designed to attract foreign investment, but much of the competition for businesses seems to involve attracting established firms and branch plants from other states. This has undoubtedly contributed to the decentralization of manufacturing industries within the country. The net contribution to national economic welfare is less substantial than might appear. In Europe, the European Union's Competition Policy attempts to restrict such wasteful zero-sum competition within its territory by placing restrictions on the provision of government incentives such as grants and subsidies to private companies. Increasingly, preparing local labour forces for higher skilled jobs through education and training, and thereby attracting 'higher value' industries, is seen as a much more important local economic development strategy (see Chapters 12 and 13).

## CONCLUSION

In a number of respects, therefore, territorial states and the political regulation of the economy that they provide are of fundamental importance in understanding the evolution of economic landscapes. But these states, far from being the same everywhere and staying the same over time, are intertwined in complex and contradictory ways with the world economy. States today must operate in a global economic environment in which they have become managers of internal–external transactions rather than, in coordination with national business, monopolists over discrete national territories.

Indeed, it has become a commonplace to observe that states are at one and the same time too large and too small for a wide range of social and economic purposes. They are often too large territorially to create full social identities and real national interests. This can be seen in the proliferation of ethnic and cultural movements around the world. It can also be seen in the difficulties involved in achieving national consensus in many states around national institutions and policies. For example, the postwar consensus on the 'welfare state' has been under attack in Europe and the United States. But existing states are for many economic purposes also too small geographically. They are increasingly 'market sectors' in an intensely competitive, integrated and interdependent world economy. Two propositions follow from this perspective, which inform the rest of this book:

1 First, economic power is no longer a simple attribute of states that have more or less of it. The growth of world trade, the activity of transnational corporations, the globalized world financial system, global production and regional trading blocs such as the European Union (EU) and the North American Free Trade Agreement (NAFTA) point towards an emerging new global world order, to which states must adjust.
2 Second, state and society/economy are no longer mutually defining. Uneven economic development within and between states has produced redefinitions of economic interests and political identities from national to regional and local levels. The economic restructuring associated with globalization has tied many local areas directly into global markets. Local areas are thus 'communities of

fate' in a world in which there is less possibility of shielding from competition within large territorial units than used to be the case. When such places have different orientations to the world economy, i.e., different commodities in trade, different trading partners and different exposures to foreign competition, the possibilities for national consensus on trade policy are much reduced. The growing redundancy of national governments as supranational entities (such as the EU) increase in importance, plus the challenge to national regulation from global markets, have conspired to stimulate new and revive old political identities, especially when ethnic and cultural divisions are defined geographically. In this context, therefore, the recent flowering of nationalist and separatist movements around the world is not so surprising. New spaces for political regulation at this level may have to coexist with older ones at a larger scale. Institutions at both levels will have to cope with real if also reversible pressures for global interdependence.

## 3.3 'MARKET ACCESS' AND THE REGIONAL MOTORS OF THE NEW WORLD ECONOMY

Wide acknowledgement that the world economy is currently undergoing a fundamental reorganization has not meant that there is agreement as to how and why this is happening. Agreement is confined only to the sense that the world economy has entered a phase of flexible production in which business operations around the world are increasingly taking the form of core firms (often transnational in scope) connected by formal and informal alliances to *networks* of other organizations – firms, governments and communities. The paradox of this trend, and the reason it has generated intense debate, is that while networking allows for an increased spanning of political boundaries by concentrated business organizations it also opens up the possibility of more decentralized production to sites with competitive advantages. At the same time, networks take on different forms with different sectors and in different places. Some networks have large corporations at their centres with geographically dispersed subcontractors and allied firms (for example, many car manufacturers) whereas others are clusters of firms in high-tech regions (such as California's Silicon Valley or Silicon Fen in Cambridge, to the north of London) or specialized industrial districts, such as those in Emilia-Romagna and Tuscany (parts of the so-called Third Italy – central and northeast Italy – where economic growth has been based on clusters of small firms specializing in the same industries, such as machine tools, shoes or woollen textiles). In all cases, however, sites are never isolated worlds unto themselves. They are linked through social connections and the benefits that come from either spatial divisions of labour (splitting different activities among different locations) or external economies of scale (the benefits that accrue from locating close to similar and complementary producers). The outcome is a world economy in which networks and flows bring together sites widely scattered around the world. Nevertheless, the vast majority of the tightest connections are found in and between Europe, North America and East Asia. The globalization of the world economy is not yet truly worldwide in its geographical scope.

One account of the source of this shift in the world economy from big, vertically integrated firms organized with reference to national economies to globe-spanning networks of production and finance emphasizes the declining rates of productivity and profits of major corporations in the years between 1965 and 1980. These declines seem tied more to falling rates of productivity (efficiency in the use of equipment and resources) than to rising labour costs. Although there have been recoveries in rates of profit at certain times in some economies (such as that of the USA) since the mid-1980s, these seem fuelled in part by suppressing wages and other labour benefits more than by returns to new technologies (such as computers) or new investment. This also reflects the results of the 'global turn' taken most aggressively by large (and other) American firms since the 1970s.

In any case, manufacturing industries in all of the major industrialized countries did experience a productivity and profitability crisis beginning in the 1970s. Out of this crisis came the urge to rationalize operations, 'downsize', divest relatively unprofitable activities and use relocation and diversification strategies to produce higher rates of return for investors. This massive shakeout had a number of consequences. These included the rapid spread of new technologies, the compression of the 'shelf life' of commodities to keep up demand (planned obsolescence) and increased competition to deliver goods and services quickly. Of particular importance, new transportation and communications technologies (such as containerization, fax machines and electronic mail) made it possible for businesses to move physical assets (such as machines), components, finished products and services and financial capital ever more rapidly from place to place or from one use to another.

In the background lay attempts by the governments of the most powerful states, particularly the United States, to open up the world economy to increased trade and investment across international boundaries. These reflected both the perceived interests of certain businesses coming from these countries in 'going global' to solve their problems and the ideological imperative (strongest in the United States) to build a 'free world' economy as an alternative to the closed-off and state-centred economies of the Soviet Union and its satellites. The exhaustion of Fordism also coincided with a number of general changes in the workings of the world economy, such as the collapse of the Bretton Woods system for fixing currency exchange rates in 1971, the oil price increases forced on world consumers by OPEC in 1973 and again in 1979 and the world debt crisis following the failure of borrowers (such as semi-peripheral countries including Mexico and Brazil) to pay back the loans made available to them from the 'petrodollars' recycled into the world economy by the oil producers.

The emerging character of the new world economy can be thought of both from the point of view of states and how they fit into the picture as firms reorganize and from the point of view of the firms and how they organize their networks geographically. The former is referred to by some commentators as an emerging 'market-access economy' in which states increasingly standardize the rules governing trade and investment in order to situate themselves more advantageously within the evolving international division of labour. The latter can be seen as territorially based production systems held together through networks and alliances of firms, governments and communities.

## 'MARKET-ACCESS' REGIME

Globalization is partly about firms attempting to cash in on the comparative advantage enjoyed in production by other countries and localities and to gain unimpeded access to their consumer markets. But it is also about governments wanting to attract capital and expertise from beyond their boundaries so as to increase employment, learn from foreign partners, and generally improve the global competitive position of 'their' firms. The combination of the two has given rise to a 'market-access' regime of world trade and investment. This is eroding the free trade regime that had increasingly predominated in trade between the main industrial capitalist countries in the post-Second World War period. In its place is a regime in which acceptable rules governing trade and investment have spread from the relatively narrow realm of trade to cover a wide range of areas of firm organization and performance.

Six 'pillars' of this 'market-access' system can be identified (Table 3.4). The first is a move away from the dominance of the US model of industrial organization in international negotiations towards a hybrid model in which there is less emphasis on keeping governments and industries 'at arm's length' and commitment to encouraging interfirm collaboration and alliances across as well as within national boundaries. In this new model, foreign firms are allowed to contest most segments of national markets, except in cases where clearly demarcated sectors are left for local firms.

A second pillar involves the increased cooperation and acceptance of global rules concerning trade, investment and money by national bureaucracies, with an increasingly powerful role also played by supranational and international organizations (such as the European Commission for the EU and the World Trade Organization, respectively; see Chapter 12). Two consequences are the blurring of lines of regulation between 'issue areas' (such as trade and foreign direct investment) and the penetration of 'global norms' into the practices of national bureaucracies (e.g., the international accounting standards (IAS) proposed by the International Accounting Standards Board Foundation or corporate governance principles drawn up by the OECD).

The third pillar is based on the increasing trade in services beyond national boundaries and the concomitant increased importance of services (banking,

**Table 3.4** Old and new pillars of world trade

| Old pillars of the free-trade regime | New pillars of the market-access regime |
| --- | --- |
| *Structure* | |
| **1** US model of industrial organization | Hybrid model of industrial organization |
| **2** Separate systems of governance | Internationalization of domestic policies |
| **3** Goods traded and services produced and consumed domestically | Globalization of services; eroding boundaries between goods and services |
| **4** Universal rules are the norm | Sector-specific codes are common |
| *Rules* | |
| **5** Free movement of goods; investment conditional | Investment as integrated co-equal with trade |
| **6** National comparative advantage | Regional and global advantage |

*Source:* Cowhey and Aronson (1993: 60, Table 4.1)

insurance, transportation, legal, advertising, etc.) in the world economy. One reason for this is that high-tech products (computers, commercial aircraft, etc.) contain high levels of service inputs. Servicing the 'software' that such products require has led to an explosion in business services. Another is that producers are demanding services that are of high quality and competitively priced. They can turn to foreign suppliers if appropriate ones are not available locally. Banking and telephone industries are two services that have experienced a dramatic increase in internationalization as producers have turned to non-traditional (frequently foreign – offshore) suppliers.

Fourth, international negotiations about trade and investment are now organized much more along sectoral and issue-specific lines than was the case in the past. One rule no longer fits all. But many of the new rules are essentially ad hoc, rather than formal.

The final two pillars concern the content of the rules of the market-access regime. One is an equivalence today between trade and investment, due largely to the activities of transnational corporations in expanding the level of foreign direct investment to astronomical highs. Local rules about how much of a finished product must be made locally (within a particular country) and worries about the competitive fairness of firm alliances, however, have also led to new efforts by governments in industrialized countries to regulate the flows of foreign investment. 'Levelling the playing field' has meant pressure and counter-pressure between governments to ensure at least a degree of similarity in regulation (in, e.g., cases of presumed monopoly or antitrust violations).

The final pillar involves the shift on the part of firms from a concern with national or home-base comparative advantage to a concern with establishing global or world–regional competitive advantages internal to firms and their networks. This reflects the overwhelming attractiveness of 'multinationality' to many businesses as a way of both diversifying assets, increasing market access, and enjoying the firm economies of scale that come from supplying larger markets.

Production facilities can be located to take advantage of other benefits that come from operating in multiple locations, particularly those offered by foreign sites. Foreign direct investment is often seen as the result of three sets of factors:

1 the advantages that accrue to firms abroad because of their technology and market power relative to competitors (ownership advantages)
2 the need to ensure returns on research and development (R&D) and other prior investments by controlling production and marketing rather than licensing to foreign firms (internalizing markets)
3 favourable foreign location conditions that encourage foreign operations rather than export (market size and needs, production costs, trade barriers) – (location advantages).

Business economists tend to emphasize the first two, whereas economic geographers tend to give more weight to the third. In particular, the geographers have tended to use the product life-cycle model to explain the trend towards increased relocation of certain production processes in foreign settings. In its original form this idea did not have any locational significance; it referred entirely to the tendency for products to move from being novelties to mass production to obsolescence. Vernon (1966) gave the product life-cycle a locational component by arguing that as production requirements change as a product 'ages' so do locational requirements. In particular, mass production is more labour intensive than the earlier phases of production. Hence, when a product reaches this phase in its life-cycle, it pays in terms of profitability to move production to where cheaper labour is available. Patterns of imports and exports adjust accordingly (Figure 3.3). This model faces a number of criticisms when applied without attention to the specific production requirements of different sectors, such as the overemphasis on labour intensity as a feature of mass production, the importance of automation in much mass production, the implicit assumption that industries and their products 'mature' rather than adjust or fail to adjust to changing conditions of production, the lack of attention to customized production in many product categories today and the neglect of the role of regulatory factors (such as tariffs and other import restrictions) in encouraging the movement of production facilities to countries other than the home one. (This last factor is one of the main reasons why Japanese car producers have moved some of their production to the USA and to Britain.)

The complexity of the global economy means that there is no single model of firm locational behaviour. New transportation and communication technologies have provided a 'permissive' environment in which firms can decentralize manufacturing and primary production activities yet maintain central control (e.g., networked computers, telecommunications, air travel). There is now the possibility of intensive interaction without geographical proximity. This by no means signals the end of regional specialization. The evolution of transnational strategies of production does not require the demise of older ones.

American firms such as Coca-Cola, McDonald's and Disney have been leaders in the shift to a 'borderless world'. Implicit in this approach is a sequence of organizational–geographical moves as firms shift from (1) exporting to (2) foreign sales outlets to (3) foreign production to (4) the world as an 'investment surface' with production spread around over a large number of locations in different countries. Firms have learned that they can improve their profitability if they use their economies of scope and coordination (returns to complexity and managerial capability in producing multiple products) to compete effectively for global markets

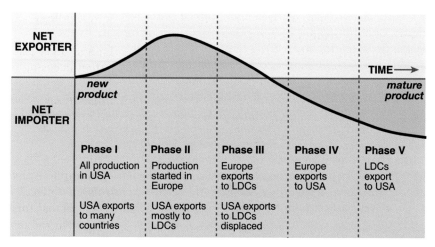

Fig 3.3: Product life-cycle model and possible effects on US production and trade (after Vernon, 1966)
*Source:* Adapted from Wells (1972: 15, Figure 1)

against local producers who may have advantages in economies of scale and local connections. Brand names, financial clout and managerial savvy can overcome these barriers. But this can happen only if foreign markets are opened up to competition, which is what the market-access regime is all about (see Box 3.3).

## Box 3.3 The semiconductor industry and the workings of the market-access regime

Semiconductors are the basic components in electronics technologies. Electronics technologies are at the heart of the informational revolution that has both allowed and encouraged the transformation of the world economy since the 1970s. Worldwide, the semiconductor business conducted nearly US$250 billion worth of transactions in 2006. From the early 1980s until the declines of the late 1990s (partly due to the Asian financial crisis and the lingering recession in Japan), the world market had been growing at around 15 per cent per year. More than 30 per cent of all semiconductors are exported, so it is a good candidate for showing the workings of the market-access regime. In the 1980s the Japanese makers broke through in world markets, weakening the grip of American producers, and further threatening the already fragile European industry. This challenge was particularly strong in the market for standard memory chips (the DRAM or dynamic random-access memory chips) as innovation was rapid and Japanese manufacturers cut prices steeply. It is the DRAM market that has the largest economies of scale and thus can in the long term underwrite other types of production. Not surprisingly, semiconductors became a key trade issue. In 2005, 23 of the top 50 semiconductor producers were US companies, but only two of them were in the top 10 – Intel (1) and Texas Instruments (3). Three European semiconductor companies made the top 10 – Infineon (4), ST (6) and Philips (10) – along with three Japanese companies – Renesas (5), Toshiba (7) and NEC (9). Samsung, from North Korea, stood at number 2, and TSMC, from Taiwan, stood at number 8.

The semiconductor industry began in the United States where it remains a key industry with over 65 per cent of global manufacturing capacity. By the end of 2006, the global market share of US firms amounted to 46 per cent and over three-quarters of these sales took place outside the US market. In the USA, the semiconductor industry is responsible for some 230,000 jobs with capital equipment worth $13 billion and R&D investments of $18 billion. Recently, sales growth has largely been driven by popular consumer products such as cell phones, MP3 players (like the iPod) and HDTV sets – all products that have proliferated as semiconductor technology has enabled dramatically lower costs coupled with improved functionality (SIA, 2007).

In Japan, the Ministry of International Trade and Industry (MITI) (now METI) accorded semiconductors the highest priority and worked to establish a major presence in global markets. In practice, Japanese success was the result of the marriage of the *keiretsu* system of big companies at the centre of affiliated networks to a national industrial policy. In particular, the Japanese firms enjoyed ready access to capital, and government policy reduced the risks of overextension and fostered domestic competition to achieve the best results in global markets. Out of this Japanese challenge came a whole new approach to global trade and investment in semiconductors. The first element was two US–Japan Semiconductor Agreements (1986 and 1991), which opened up Japan to foreign (US) firms and monitored charges of Japanese 'dumping' of semiconductors in the USA at below world prices. The second was the move of Japanese, European and US producers into a number of international corporate alliances. This is particularly critical. To anticipate future costs of R&D: 'Firms are turning to ICAs (international corporate alliances) to build common, global infrastructures for the next generation of technologies. Alliances also allow firms to reduce the cost and risk of fielding extensive product lines' (Cowhey and Aronson, 1993: 162).

The net effect is a perfect example of the market-access regime of trade and investment. The new structure of the semiconductor industry is a hybrid of Japanese, American and European models (pillar 1 in Table 3.4). International agreements are the main means by which the industry is regulated (pillar 2). The mix of hardware and software makes it hard to say where the product ends and servicing begins. What is clear is that both must be available on a worldwide basis for a product to be competitive (pillar 3). Since 1986 specialized industry codes have steadily displaced older industry-wide ones (pillar 4). Where chips were once traded relatively freely but there was not much foreign direct investment, there are now major networks across national boundaries based on international alliances. Semiconductor firms have gone global in their organization as well as in their search for markets (pillar 5). Finally, firms are building global and world–regional advantages in order to give them leverage over home and foreign markets (pillar 6). Product and technology flows are now so globalized that closing markets (national and regional) would doom affected producers to limited market share and to not participating in new rounds of innovation and product development.

## PRODUCTION NETWORKS AND REGIONAL MOTORS

From the business point of view, the response to the competitive pressures of the market-access regime has been to acquire greater flexibility through technological change, reorganizing labour relations and establishing links with other firms. One solution has predominated: the creation of networks among producers. This has several origins. One lies in attempts by large firms to reduce the size of their work-forces and to hive off activities to other firms. This process of vertical disintegration can be cost saving if a unionized labour force is replaced by a non-union one, for example, and it also taps into the specialized skills of suppliers and subcontractors. A second source lies in the attempt to penetrate foreign markets and build a global presence by collaborating with other firms (including erstwhile competitors). Thus, for example, Toyota entered into a joint venture with General Motors, while Nestlé has a joint venture with General Mills. The focus on production networks highlights the central role of geographical shifts in investment and production as a response to changes in the competitive environment experienced by firms in many economic sectors with the advent of the market-access regime.

## PRODUCTION NETWORKS

Four types of network among firms can be distinguished. The first type occurs with *craft-based industries*. These industries are themselves organized around *projects* more than firms per se. In construction, publishing, film and recording, architecture and software engineering, highly skilled workforces are employed by firms but share knowledge easily across firm boundaries. Consequently, such industries tend to cluster to take advantage of the external economies implicit in such sharing. External economies include such factors as a labour pool with relevant skills, a broad network of suppliers, excellent educational and training support and, perhaps most importantly, access to 'venture capital' knowledgeable about the nature of the business. But they also include intangibles such as a 'culture' accepting of innovation, tolerance of failure, local reinvestment, collaboration, promotion on merit and openness to new enterprises.

The second type of network involves *small firm industrial districts* such as those often associated with so-called 'Third Italy'. These are local integrated networks of producers with different firms specializing in different phases of the production process but competing for work with other local firms when new projects come along. Evidence suggests that they rely in equal measure on external economies of scale in production (collaborative production, local government financing, craft traditions, pools of skilled labour, etc.) and on what can be called non-traded interdependencies – a long history of social collaboration, institutionalized cooperation and agreement on social conventions governing everyday inter-firm relations.

The third type of network is that of *agglomerated big firm-based production systems*, such as that of Toyota and its ring of suppliers around Toyota City in Nagoya, Japan, Boeing and its suppliers around Tacoma-Seattle in the USA, and Fiat and its suppliers around Turin in northwest Italy. In some cases the suppliers pre-existed the emergence of the big firms, in others (as in Japan and South Korea), the dominant company financed the suppliers. Since the 1970s, however, the main process stimulating this kind of network has been the vertical disintegration of the big firms themselves. Whether territorially connected to them or not, large firms can now achieve improved flexibility by using subcontractors to carry out aspects of production that used to be performed within the boundaries of the firm. A high-tech industrial complex such as Silicon Valley is somewhere in between the first or 'classic' type of industrial district and the third or agglomerated big-firm production system, sharing features of both.

Fourth, there is the type of network represented by *strategic alliances between firms*. This is one of the most important innovations of the market-access regime, especially in terms of the extent to which strategic alliances take place between international competitors. 'Each partner brings to the marriage its own specialty – technology, financial power, access to government regulators or procurement officials – and its own constellation of small firm suppliers' (Harrison, 1994: 138). What each gains is the knowledge and connections intrinsic to the other to further their efforts at conquering global markets for their products. One logical consequence of alliances would be merger or acquisition of one partner by the other. But some national laws and customs set limits to this (e.g., American and Japanese laws restrict foreign acquisition of home-grown firms) and the goal of flexibility is best met by maintaining or recreating alliances rather than engaging in fully fledged mergers.

## NEW INTERNATIONAL DIVISION OF LABOUR

The first interpretations of the changing character of business organization and the associated changes in the economic geography of production focused on the emergence of a new international division of labour (NIDL). From this point of view, big transnational corporations were seen as creating a new global economic geography. One of the architects of this viewpoint, Stephen Hymer (1972: 114), imagined that the transnational corporations:

> [W]ould tend to produce a hierarchical division of labour between geographical regions corresponding to the vertical division of labour within the firm. It would tend to centralize high-level decision-making occupations to a few key cities in the advanced countries, surrounded by a number of regional sub-capitals, and confine the rest of the world to lower levels of activity and income.

As a result, the new international division of labour was seen as reflecting the hierarchical social division of labour within the big firms themselves. Hymer claimed that a tight space–process relationship was coming about, in which control and operational activities within firms would be completely separated. As suggested by Table 3.5 the close space–process relationship would take the form A to B to C. But the table reveals other possibilities: D, E and F. Logically, a major metropolis (or world city) could dominate all levels in the hierarchy of functions in absolute terms even with the *addition* of foreign operations. The advent of networks was largely responsible for confounding the simple story of the new international division of labour. Production networks allowed much more complex geographies of production than those predicted by Hymer's simple hierarchy. Big firms have changed their internal structures and external relations in ways that undermine their own internal hierarchies. So the analogy between internal (organizational) and external (geographical) hierarchies now seems overdrawn.

**Table 3.5** 'Hymer's stereotype', in which the space–process relationship takes the form A→B→C

| | Type of area | | |
| --- | --- | --- | --- |
| Level of corporate hierarchy | Major metropolis (e.g., London or New York) | Regional capital (e.g., Brussels or Denver) | Semi-periphery (e.g., Mexico, South Korea or China) |
| 1 Long-term strategic planning | A | | |
| 2 Management of divisions | D | B | |
| 3 Production, routine work | F | E | C |

*Source:* Sayer (1985: 13, Table 1)

More importantly, much of the explosion of foreign direct investment of the past 35 years has involved within core and not core to periphery/semi-periphery flows at a world scale. The DCs remain the principal destinations for FDI and attract almost three-quarters of global inflows. Cross-border mergers and acquisitions and strategic alliances continue to drive FDI and these remain concentrated in the DCs. This suggests how important market access has also become compared to the search for cheap labour in assembly processes. Increased competition for market shares by US and western European companies at home has forced a search for markets elsewhere that cannot be served by an export strategy. Supplier performance, alliances, and service to customers, as well as avoidance of tariffs and other trade barriers, have dictated that US firms move close to potential European markets and European firms move close to potential North American markets. Moving to the global periphery to minimize labour costs is a less important activity in terms of total investment.

## GEOGRAPHIES OF PRODUCTION NETWORKS

Lying at the heart of the geography of the world economy under market-access conditions are the tradeoffs between the benefits/costs to firms of clustering together and the benefits/costs to firms of conducting economic transactions over space. The former involves the cost-saving role of locating close to suppliers, subcontractors, competitors and specialized pools of labour. The latter come down to the costs of production involved in overcoming distance in the transactions implicit in production (bringing together inputs, serving markets, etc.).

Table 3.6 illustrates six possible scenarios in these trade-offs:

1  In one scenario, producers will seek out low-cost locations relative to basic inputs and/or markets. There is little or no incentive for firms to cluster together. This scenario is most pertinent for resource-based industries, resource-dependent industries, wholesaling and retailing (in which either transport costs and/or direct access to customers still figure prominently in firm locational decisions). The result is locational patterns that conform closely to the distribution of resources and population. Even in such cases, however, the situation facing firms is not the same as it once was. In particular, international transport and communications costs have declined steadily during the 20th century. Over the period 1930–2000, for example, transport costs fell by at least two-thirds in real terms (after taking inflation into account) (Figure 3.4).

   New types of ship design, containerization, improved logistics services and the almost universal availability of faxes and electronic mail have produced massive improvements in the efficiency of the shipping and land transport industries. So, even for industries in which there is major 'weight loss' during production (a major reduction in the amount of output relative to amounts of inputs) the 'friction' of distance is no longer the constraint on making decisions about where to locate plants that it undoubtedly once was.

**Table 3.6**  Spatial transaction costs versus externalities: six scenarios

|  | Spatial transaction costs | | |
|---|---|---|---|
|  | Low | Medium | High |
| *Externalities* | | | |
| Low | (4) | (5) | (1) |
| High | (3) | (6) | (2) |

*Source:* Based on Scott (1996)

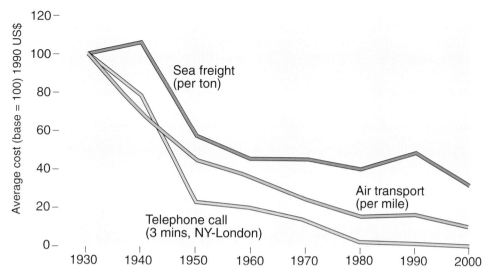

Fig 3.4: Cheaper transport and communications costs on the global highway

*Source:* Adapted from Busse (2002: 13, Figure 2)

2 A second scenario, in which external economies are significant but where transaction costs are high, defines the situation of industrial districts and
high-technology complexes (such as California's Silicon Valley). They have an
important focus on external economies while requiring heavy inputs of outside
resources and an orientation to external consumer markets. Intensive relations
between firms encourage agglomeration but there are limits to which this can go
before costs associated with serving outside markets and obtaining outside
resources start to go up.

3 A third scenario, essentially that of branch plant industrialization, sees the possibility of firms consuming external economies at a distance because of low
transaction costs. In this way, external economies can be internalized within a
firm (or inter-firm alliance) and then realized through dispersal of functions to
locations where they can achieve cost advantages (lower wage bills, etc.).

4 A fourth scenario is literally one where anything can be located anywhere. This is
the fantasy of some prophets of globalization who predict the 'end of geography'
as telecommuting and a radical decentralization of production characterizes all sectors. This is a state of spatial entropy in which there would be no spatial limits on
access to external economies. As yet, this appears to be more fantasy than reality.

5 More likely is a case in which, though external economies can be obtained at a
distance, transaction costs mandate attraction to markets or inputs.

6 Most important to the evolving world economy is the sixth scenario. Here, spatial transaction costs are assumed to be moderate (on average) but external
economies are high. There is thus a major incentive to cluster. Such clusters represent the major novelty in recent times. They are the concentrations of
innovative, knowledge-based and high-value producing industries (both manufacturing and services) that are increasingly driving the world economy. This is
why Scott (1996: 400) refers to them as the 'regional motors' of the world economy. The major reason for this claim is:

that contemporary forms of economic production and organization are rife with externality effects, having their roots in the augmenting levels of flexibility, uncertainty, product destandardization, and competitiveness that are some of the hallmarks of contemporary capitalist enterprise.

But in addition to the increasing returns to agglomeration in many leading sectors (such as high-technology industry, design-intensive consumer goods and financial and business services), many transactions are still intensely sensitive to the effects of distance:

> while spatial transaction costs have fallen dramatically across a wide front in recent decades, allowing many firms ready access to global markets, there still remain important kinds of transactions that are extremely sensitive to the effects of distance. External economies tend to be well developed in the interaction networks constituted by just such transactions as these and, in order to secure them, producers agglomerate together in geographic space.

The main geographical implication is that, with increasing world economic integration, the leading production activities will become more concentrated in metropolitan areas and their hinterlands. These are places with long-established competitive advantages, built up by trial and error over the years more than as the result of some single overriding locational advantage relative to other locations. This geographical path dependence seems set to continue, as in the old refrain 'the rich get richer and the poor get the blame'. Giant metropolitan areas such as Tokyo, São Paulo, New York, Mexico City, Shanghai, Los Angeles, Mumbai and Seoul, with populations in excess of 10 million in 2005, not to mention at least 40 other urban agglomerations in excess of 5 million apiece, constitute the dynamic centres of the world economy as national boundaries lose some of their grip on channelling the processes governing economic growth. Those who operate from these centres employed in occupations and sectors with a global market reach are able to cash in personally on the larger demand only they can satisfy because of *where they are*. London re-insurers, Hollywood actors, New York lawyers and Silicon Valley software engineers have the capacity to extract higher incomes because they embody major specialized activities of where they are from. They have global access in sectors for which there is high global demand.

What is also clear is that the flipside of this concentration of economic growth based on serving global markets is the increased marginalization of large parts of the world and their populations (see Chapter 7). These are not necessarily at great distance from the 'motors' themselves. Indeed, internal to the dominant metropolitan areas are rich and poor districts housing the increasingly polarized income groups that the new world economy seems to be bringing in its train. Many of the poor, when they find employment, find it in providing services for the more affluent, which is increasingly one of the driving forces behind local economic growth. Services for local consumption are responsible for much of the economic growth in large cities. Yet this growth depends on the incomes generated by the goods- and service-producing activities of industries oriented to national and global markets. Indeed, the growth of smaller cities and areas surrounding major cities is increasingly dependent on the growth of the networked economy. For example, much of the growth of employment and incomes in Britain in recent decades has been concentrated in an arc of 'growth areas' extending from Cambridge to Bournemouth, which can be seen as beneficiaries of the growth of the financial service industries in London. Computer hardware manufacturing and service, accounting, billing, paperwork and other 'back-office' functions have decentralized into London's hinterland. In the new 'services economy', in which both the most lucrative and the poorest paying jobs involve providing services to others (from banking and finance to fast food and house cleaning), globalization causes London to cast a new shadow over its hinterland.

One theoretical implication is unmistakable: the increased globalization of the world economy is leading not to a spreading out of economic growth or a homogenization of global space but to heightened differences between regions and localities. Some of the so-called world cities, such as London, Tokyo, New York, Hong Kong and Singapore have become centres of (among other things) financial and business services. Other regions, like the Third Italy, the American Midwest, Taiwan and Shanghai have a focus on manufacturing. Some regions remain primarily agricultural, whereas others are the sites of low-wage assembly or back-office functions. There is no single universal model of business organization that accounts for all of them. In an increasingly competitive world economy they are all the result of adaptive responses to pressures on states and firms to change their ways of doing business.

## SUMMARY

This chapter has laid out the historical–geographical perspective that lies behind the rest of this book. We have shown how the processes that produce the geography of economic activities evolve over time in conjunction with the evolution of the world economy. Particular attention has been paid to the specific features of the world economy and its evolution. These are:

1 the single world market
2 the state system
3 the three geographical tiers: core, periphery, semi-periphery
4 temporal patterns and hegemony
5 subordination and resistance
6 alternative adaptations.

Another section was devoted to examining the changing relationship between states and the contemporary world economy under conditions of globalized capitalism. The main conclusions are that states must now operate in a world in which (1) economic power is no longer best thought of as an attribute of states and (2) states and societies/national economies are no longer mutually defining entities. However, we stressed the continuing importance of states as regulators of economic activities. Historical experience suggests that a trend towards a globalized world economy can be reversed if there is an increase in economic nationalism or protectionism if a major economy such as that of the USA or of the European Union undermines the fairly open trading system that presently exists. A totally 'globalized' world economy will have political divisions with a geographical form.

The third part of the chapter introduced the idea of a 'market-access' economy, how it differs from the previously dominant free trade regime and the critical role of certain regional 'motors' to the emerging world economy. The importance of transnational corporations and strategic alliances between them was emphasized, along with the increasingly complex international division of labour in many economic sectors. The location of economic activities appears to involve a decreased reliance on the costs of assembling the factors of production (i.e., spatial transaction costs) – largely because of a dramatic decline in transportation costs – and an increased reliance on both traded and non-traded interdependencies (external economies), which encourages a clustering of specialized activities. Rather than encouraging a spreading out of manufacturing and service industries across the world, therefore, the market-access model of increased global economic interdependence produces a remarkable regional clustering of many activities. This reflects the competitive advantage achieved by certain locations (often for historic or geographical path dependence reasons) more than patterns of raw material availability or labour cost advantages. For certain sectors (e.g., pulp and paper or apparel, respectively) these factors maintain their relevance. But leading 'high-tech' sectors (such as information and biotechnologies) and many other sectors (such as stock trading, insurance and metal working) are wedded closely to particular locations.

Parts 2 and 3 of this book are taken up with exploring the specific economic–geographical consequences of the evolution of the world economy as described in the first and third parts of this chapter. Part 4 is concerned with some of the manifestations of the globalization/localization nexus at the centre of today's world economy that pose challenges to state management raised in the second part: the growth of regional trading blocs and decentralist reactions to the changing world economy.

## KEY SOURCES AND SUGGESTED READING

Cowhey, P.F. and Aronson, J.D. 1993. *Managing the World Economy: The Consequences of Corporate Alliances*. New York: Council on Foreign Relations Press.

Eichengreen, B. 1996. *Globalizing Capital: A History of the International Monetary System*. Princeton, NJ: Princeton University Press.

Gereffi, G. and Korzeniewicz, M. (eds) 1993. *Commodity Chains and Global Capitalism*. Westport, CT: Greenwood Press.

Hackworth, J. 2006. *The Neoliberal City. Governance, Ideology, and Development in American Urbanism*. Ithaca, NY: Cornell University Press.

Harrison, B. 1994. *Lean and Mean: The Changing Landscape of Corporate Power in the Age of Flexibility*. New York: Basic Books.

Maddison, A. 2001. *The World Economy: A Millennial Perspective*. Paris: OECD Development Centre Studies, 2001.

Malmberg, A. and Maskell, P. 1997. Towards an explanation of regional specialization and industry agglomeration, *European Planning Studies*, 5, 25–41.

Peck, J. and Tickell, A. 2002. 'Neoliberalizing space' in *Spaces of Neoliberalism. Urban Restructuring in North America and Western Europe*. N. Brenner and N. Theodore (eds). Oxford: Blackwell.

UNCTAD 2004. Development and globalization: facts and figures. New York: United Nations Conference on Trade and Development.

Venables, A.J. 2006. Shifts in economic geography and their causes, *Federal Reserve Bank of Kansas City Economic Review*, 31, 61–85.

Vernon, R. 1966. International investment and international trade in the product cycle, *Quarterly Journal of Economics*, 80, 190–207.

Wallerstein, I. 1979. *The Capitalist World-Economy*. Cambridge: Cambridge University Press.

## RELATED WEBSITES

World Trade Organization: http://www.wto.org/
the WTO includes research and documents on international agreements and conferences relating to world trade, including the GATT

United Nations Conference on Trade and Development (UNCTAD): http://www.unctad.org/
UNCTAD's website offers publications and data on trade, investment and economic development issues, including the latest edition of the *World Investment Report*, which contains information and data on TNCs and FDI.

*Fortune* magazine: http://www.fortune.com/
this website offers articles and information on private businesses, including the *Global 500* list of the world's largest companies

*Economist*: http://www.economist.com/index.html
this website offers articles and data on global issues of interest to economic geographers

Semiconductor Equipment and Materials International (SEMI): http://www.semi.org/
although aimed at business people, the website of this global industry association contains a wealth of information on the global semiconductor industry

# Part 2

# Rise of the Core Economies

In the next three chapters, we trace the emergence of the world's core economies, following their different paths towards increasing scale and complexity with case histories that illuminate many of the patterns, models and theories outlined in Part 1. We seek to show that the world's economic landscapes, however unique or exceptional they may seem, are now part of a single, overarching world economy. In Chapter 4, we describe the way in which this world economy came to be centred on Europe, how it came to be consolidated by the emergence of merchant capitalism and how the nature and organization of merchant capitalism came to be reflected in particular kinds of urban and regional change. In Chapter 5, we describe the very different trajectories that have marked the ascent of Europe, North America and Japan and within the world economy, emphasizing the spatial changes consequent on the emergence and evolution of industrial capitalism. In Chapter 6, the globalization of the core economies is described. But, although the emphasis throughout this part of the book is on the interactions of dominant forms of economic organization and major dimensions of spatial change, there is an important subtheme. This is the role of human agency in shaping and differentiating the mosaic of regional landscapes. What is done, where and how – under any form of economic organization – reflects human interpretations of how resources should be used. As Ron Johnston (1984: 446) noted, these interpretations:

> [A]re shaped through cultural lenses (which may be locally created, or may be imported); they reflect reactions to both the local physical environment and the international economic situation; they are mediated by local institutional structures; they are influenced by historical context; and they change that context, and hence the environment for future operations.

Picture credit: Paul Knox

# Chapter 4

# Pre-industrial foundations

In this chapter, we trace the emergence of an embryonic world economy centred on Europe, and describe the way in which Europeans became, as Robert Reynolds put it (1961: vii), the 'leaders, drivers, persuaders, shapers, crushers and builders' of the rest of the world's economies and societies. It was as a result of these changes that the core areas of Europe forged the template for the economic geography of the modern world. It must be recognized from the outset, however, that pre-industrial economic development was by no means exclusively a European phenomenon. The early trajectories of other parts of the world often eclipsed that of Europe and were sometimes important in influencing events in Europe itself. We begin, therefore, with a brief review that spans the origins and diffusion of the first, crucial 'revolution' in the development of agricultural systems, the rise of ancient empires, the establishment of urban systems and the spread of feudalism as the dominant mode of production. Our purpose here is not so much to attempt to provide a thumbnail sketch of early economic history as to point to the emergence and spatial implications of certain fundamental socioeconomic forces.

## 4.1 BEGINNINGS

We start from some basic distinctions provided by the world-systems theory of Immanuel Wallerstein. In his view, at one time all societies were minisystems: 'A minisystem is an entity that has within it a complete division of labour, and a single cultural framework' (1979a: 17). Such minisystems would include very simple hunting and gathering, and some agricultural societies. But they no longer exist. As soon as they became tied to empires or the world economy they ceased to be separate systems. Empires and the world economy are examples of what Wallerstein calls world-systems: units with a single spatial division of labour but multiple cultural systems. In the case of a unit with a common political system, there is a world empire; where there is no political integration, there is a world economy.

Relatively little is in fact known about the first transitions from primitive hunter-gathering minisystems to larger scale, agriculturally based world empires and world economies. Despite significant advances in the accuracy of archaeological research, we still have to rely on speculation as much as established facts. It is generally agreed, however, that the transition began in the Proto-Neolithic period (between 9000 and 7000 BC), when a series of innovations among certain hunter-gatherer peoples established the preconditions for agriculture. These innovations included (1) the use of fire to process food, (2) the use of grindstones and (3) the improvement of basic tools for catching, killing and preparing animals, fish, birds and reptiles. Given these preconditions, it was a relatively straightforward transition to a simple system of 'fallow' agriculture (or shifting cultivation) that involved sowing or planting familiar species of wild cereals or tubers on scorched land using a slash-and-burn system (cutting down the natural vegetation (e.g., forest) and burning it to release its nutrients into the soil). No special tools are required for such a system, neither is weeding or fertilization necessary, provided that cultivation is shifted in a couple of years to another burned plot after a few crops have been taken from the old one, which is then abandoned (left fallow) for a period of time.

Meanwhile, the domestication of cattle and sheep had begun. By the Neolithic period (7000 to 5500 BC), farming had developed to the point where stock breeding and seed agriculture were established techniques of food production. The switch from hunting and gathering to food production seems to have occurred very slowly, however – it was not a revolutionary change that suddenly transformed local practices. Archaeological evidence from a Neolithic village in western Asia, for example, shows that the wild legumes that were the major food item in 7500 BC were gradually replaced by cultivated grains over a span of almost 2000 years. Ester Boserup (1981) suggested that there was little incentive to switch to food production until population densities began to increase and/or wild food sources became scarce because hunting and gathering often provided adequate levels of subsistence with relatively low workloads. From this perspective, then, *demographic conditions as well as technological innovations were a critical precondition for economic change.*

## HEARTH AREAS

The weight of available archaeological evidence suggests that the transition to food production took place independently in several different agricultural 'hearth areas':

1 The earliest hard evidence comes from southwestern Asia, in the foothills of the Zagros Mountains of what are now Iran and Iraq, where radiocarbon analysis has dated the remains of domesticated sheep at around 8500 BC. In addition, evidence of early Neolithic activity has been found in other parts of southwestern Asia, particularly around the Dead Sea Valley in Palestine and on the Anatolian Plateau in Turkey.

2 A second early Neolithic hearth area was in South Asia, along the floodplains of the Ganges, Brahmaputra and Irawaddy rivers.

3 Later, from around 5000 BC, a third hearth area seems to have emerged in China, around the Yuan River valley in western Hunan.

4 Finally, there is evidence of independent agricultural organization in four regions of the Americas: the southern Tamaulipas area and the Tehaucán Valley in Central America, coastal Peru and the North American southwest. In these

regions, however, agricultural development not only came later but it was painfully slow, with widespread food production coming to dominate the exploitation of wild plants and game only after AD 1000.

Meanwhile, the agricultural 'revolution' had been diffused from southwestern Asia. By 5000 BC it had begun to spread eastwards, to southern Turkmenia and west-wards, via the Mediterranean and the Danube, into Europe; by 3000 BC it had reached the Sudan and Kenya (via the Nile), much of India (via Afghanistan and Baluchistan) and had penetrated Europe as far as Britain, Ireland and southern Scandinavia. By 1500 BC the last European stronghold of pure hunter-gatherer economies was the zone of tundra and coniferous forest stretching eastwards from the Norwegian coast.

Archaeological evidence is inevitably rather patchy, however, so that the patterns of diffusion from agricultural hearth areas remain a topic of considerable academic debate. More important to us here, however, are the eventual *outcomes* of the transition to food production:

- Most important of all for the long-term evolution of the world economy were the changes in social organization that resulted from the establishment of settled agriculture. The previous communal social order was steadily replaced by a kin-ordered system that laid the basis for a new, stratified social structure. Kin groups emerged as a 'natural' way of assigning rights over resources, and organizing the production and storage of food, but they also generated new social institutions to deal with the ownership of property and the formal exchange of goods.

- The increased volume and reliability of food supplies allowed much higher population densities and encouraged the proliferation of settled agricultural villages. Together with the new social institutions of kin-ordered societies, this, in turn, facilitated the development of non-agricultural crafts, such as pottery, weaving, jewellery and weaponry. Such specializations in their turn encouraged the beginnings of barter and trade between communities, sometimes over substantial distances.

## FRAMEWORK OF EARLY URBANIZATION

These outcomes of the agricultural revolution were effectively the preconditions for another 'revolutionary' change in the economic and spatial organization of the world: the emergence of cities and city systems. As with the evidence on the agricultural transition, our knowledge of the earliest cities is partly a function of where archaeologists have chosen to dig and partly a function of fortuitous factors such as the durability of building materials and artefacts. It now seems firmly established, however, that *urbanization developed independently in different regions, more or less in the wake of the local completion of the agricultural transition.* Thus the first region of independent or 'nuclear' urbanism, from around 3000 BC, was in southwestern Asia, in the Mesopotamian valleys of the Tigris and Euphrates and the Nile Valley (together making the so-called Fertile Crescent). By 2500 BC cities had appeared in the Indus Valley and by 1800 BC they were established in northern China. Other areas of nuclear urbanism include Central America (from around AD 1500). Meanwhile, of course, the original southwest Asian urban hearth had generated successive urban world empires, including those of Greece, Rome and Byzantium.

Explanations of these first transitions to city-based economies have emphasized several factors. Boserup (1981), for instance, stressed the role of local concentrations of population; Jacobs (1969) interpreted the emergence of cities mainly as a function of trade; while the classical archaeological interpretation rests on the availability of an agricultural surplus large enough to facilitate the emergence of specialized, non-agricultural workers.

Another important factor was the emergence of 'primitive accumulation' through the exaction of tributes, the control of fixed assets and/or the control of labour power – usually through some form of religious persuasion or despotic coercion. Once established, a parasitic elite provided the stimulus for urban development by investing its appropriated wealth in displays of power and status. This not only created the kernel of the monumental city but also required an increased degree of specialization in non-agricultural activities – construction, crafts, administration, the priesthood, soldiery and so on – which could only be organized effectively in an urban setting.

This kind of expansion, however, could only be sustained in the most fertile agricultural regions, where the peasant population could produce enough to support not only the parasitic elite but also the growing numbers of non-agricultural workers. In this context, the development of irrigation seems to have been a critical factor. It not only intensified cultivation and increased productivity; it also required the kind of large-scale cooperation that could only be organized effectively in a hierarchical, despotic society. Yet, even in the most fertile and intensively farmed regions, rank-redistributive economies could only expand beyond a certain point if overall levels of productivity could be increased: through harder work, improvements in technology or improvements in agricultural practices. All three solutions will have required more non-agricultural specialists and so will have reinforced the incipient process of urbanization:

> [A]dministrators and, perhaps, an army to oversee the harder work (their actions may have been accompanied by the élite taking to itself the ownership of land) in the first, craftsmen to create the tools in the second, and also, probably, miners and others to provide the raw materials; and 'researchers' to develop the new strains and the new technology (notably irrigation) in the third. Thus the demands for more production are reflected in the urban node as well as in the countryside, and continued growth of the society, to meet the never-satisfied demands of an expanding élite and its associates, leads to self-propelling urban growth.
>
> Johnston (1980: 52)

Such developments are ultimately limited by the size of the society's resource base, however. The obvious response – the enlargement of the resource base through territorial expansion – also tended to reinforce and extend the process of urbanization. All these changes would involve the creation of city-based jobs. Furthermore, whereas small-scale colonial expansion could be organized from one centre and controlled by a single elite group, expansion beyond easy reach of the main settlement (beyond, perhaps, a journey of a day or two) would require the establishment of secondary settlements, to act as the nodes for parts of the controlled territory, as intermediate centres in the flow of demands from elite to producers and of goods in return. *As long as growth was maintained, therefore, the empire would have to be continually enlarged, with an increasing number of urban control centres.* Hence the expansion of the Greek and Roman Empires, which laid the foundations of an urban system in western Europe (Figure 4.1).

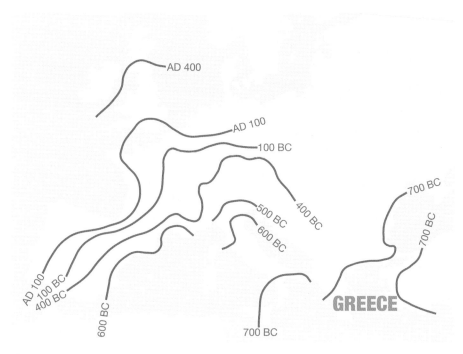

Fig 4.1: Urbanization of the classical world

Source: Based on Carter (1983: 21, Figure 2.2)

It would be wrong, however, to draw a picture of the steady growth, expansion and succession of ancient and classical empires. Urbanized economies were a precarious phenomenon, and many lapsed into ruralism before being revived or recolonized. In a number of cases, this was a result of demographic setbacks associated with wars and epidemics. Such setbacks left too few people to maintain the social and economic infrastructure necessary for urbanization. An early example of this kind of relapse occurred in the Indus Valley, where Aryan pastoralists displaced the urban economy in the middle of the second millennium BC. Elsewhere, it was changes in resource/population ratios that precipitated the breakdown and decay of urban economies. The demands of repair and upkeep of irrigation systems, for example, on top of the need for increasing productivity resulting from population growth, sometimes put overwhelming strains on the available peasant labour. After a while, investments were neglected, armies grew small, and the strength and cohesion of the empire was fatally undermined.

This kind of sequence seems to have been the root cause of the eventual collapse of the Mesopotamian empire and may also have contributed to the abandonment of much of the Mayan empire more than 500 years before the arrival of the Spanish. Similarly, the population of the Roman Empire began to decline in the 2nd century AD, allowing the infiltration of 'barbarian' settlers and traders from the German lands of east-central Europe (ultimately leading to the pillaging of Rome in the 5th century AD by the Vandals, an east Germanic tribe).

## RURAL CONSOLIDATION

Although the emergence of urbanization provided an important framework for future development, it was the reorganization and consolidation of rural areas that provided the immediate platform for the critical transition to merchant capitalism and the emergence of a European world economy. At the heart of this rural consolidation was the evolution of the elaborate feudal systems of medieval Europe, China, India and Japan.

In economic terms, feudal systems were characterized by being almost wholly agricultural, with 80 or 90 per cent of the workforce being engaged in mixed arable and pastoral farming and most of the rest occupied in basic craftwork. Moreover, most production was for immediate needs: very little of a community's output ever found its way to wider markets. The basis of the feudal system was the feudal estate, owned by lay or ecclesiastical lords, who delegated parcels of land to others in return for allegiance and economic obligations, the latter being fulfilled mainly in the form of money dues. The lords in their turn would normally owe allegiance and homage to higher lords from whom they held delegated grants of land. The labour power that ran each estate consisted of a peasant population, most of whom were serfs (descended from slaves and therefore not free in public law) or tenants whose freedom of movement, freedom to marry, freedom to leave property to their heirs and freedom to buy goods and sell their labour were closely circumscribed by public law. It was this sociopolitical institution – the peasantry – that was the key to feudal economic systems in that it formed the basis on which the feudal lords were able to accumulate wealth, through a combination of labour services, rents in kind, taxes, seigneurial dues, the issuance of money and payments for the use of essential services – milling, baking, olive pressing and so on – monopolized by the lords.

By AD 1000 the countryside of most of western Europe had been consolidated into a series of feudal agricultural subsystems that were largely autonomous. Every estate was more or less self-sufficient in the raw materials for simple industrial products. Some of the members of every rural household would be capable of specialized, non-agricultural, part-time activities such as cloth making or basketry; and nearly every community supported a range of specialist artisans and craft workers. In addition, most regions were able to sustain at least some small towns, whose existence hinged mainly on their role as ecclesiastical centres, defensive strongholds and administrative centres for the upper echelons of the feudal hierarchy. *Improbably, it was this economic landscape – inflexible, slow-motion and introverted – that nurtured the resurgence of trade and the revival of cities, thus setting the preconditions for the rise of merchant capitalism in western Europe.*

## 4.2 SUMMARY: EMERGING IMPERATIVES OF ECONOMIC ORGANIZATION

Before moving on to examine the transition to merchant capitalism and the emergence of the European world-system, it is useful to pause briefly in order to review some of the organizing principles that seem to have been important in delineating the formative stages of pre-industrial economic geography:

- Major changes in patterns of economic activity were gradual and incremental, even in 'hearth' areas or 'core' regions.
- Such changes were generally preceded by the development of critical innovations, particularly in technology and economic organization.
- Such innovations were a necessary but not sufficient condition to bring about radical change; institutional and sociopolitical changes were also necessary in order to exploit them.
- Demographic factors were also critical. Insufficient absolute numbers of potential workers sometimes hindered economic development, while changes in the balance between a population and its local resource base could be important in precipitating *either* progressive *or* regressive economic change.
- The law of diminishing returns provided an early impetus for territorial expansion. In addition to the obvious spatial consequences in terms of establishing dominant/subordinate territorial relationships, colonization was pivotal in the development of hierarchical urban systems and improved transportation. Colonization also stimulated the development of militarism, which itself induced important changes in spatial organization: through the importance of defensive sites for key settlements, for example. Finally, the environmental and social constraints laid bare by the law of diminishing returns was responsible for the emergence of a new geopolitical phenomenon – the state.

## 4.3 EMERGENCE OF THE EUROPEAN WORLD-SYSTEM

This section deals with the period from the first stirrings of the transition from feudalism to merchant capitalism in the 13th century, through the creation of the European world-system in the 16th and 17th centuries, to the proto-industrialization of the early 18th century, which laid the foundations for the Industrial Revolution. Our purpose here is to point to the emergence, interaction and spatial implications of the salient aspects of economic change. We must begin our examination of the emergence of the European world-system, however, with an obvious but often neglected question: 'Why Europe?'

### WHY EUROPE?

In the 12th century, almost half a millennium before Europe embarked on the path of capitalist development that was to shape, directly or indirectly, virtually the entire global economy, there were several well-developed 'economic worlds' in the eastern hemisphere. One was the Mediterranean region, whose principal elements included Byzantium, the Italian city states and Muslim North Africa. A second was the Chinese empire. The central Asian land mass from Russia to Mongolia was a third; the Indian Ocean/Red Sea complex was a fourth; and the Baltic area was on the verge of becoming a fifth.

Why did Europe become the locus of innovatory economic change? In particular, *why not China*? China had approximately the same total population as Europe and for a long time – well into the 15th century – was at least as far advanced in science and technology. Chinese ironmasters had developed blast furnaces that allowed the casting of iron as early as 200 BC. Iron ploughs were introduced in the 6th century, the compass in the 10th century and the water clock in the 11th. The Chinese were also significantly more advanced than the Europeans in medicine, papermaking and printing and the production of explosives. In addition, because China had retained an imperial system, it held a potentially telling advantage: its centralized decision making, extensive state bureaucracy, well-developed internal communications and unified financial system were well suited to economic development and territorial expansion.

China's failure to take off in the way Europe did must be attributed in part to its failure to pursue economic opportunities overseas. The Chinese had, in fact, matched early European exploratory successes by spanning the Indian Ocean from Java to Africa in a series of lucrative and informative voyages; but they simply lost interest in further exploration. One explanation for this lack of a colonizing mission is that they saw their own 'world' as the only one that mattered. Another is that they were distracted by the growing menace of Mongol nomad barbarians and/or Japanese pirates. A third explanation is that the centralized power structure of imperial China did not contain enough different interest groups for whom overseas exploration was an attractive proposition.

This last point is seen by some to be part of a broader set of structural constraints associated with the imperial form. The administration and defence of a huge population and land mass are held to have been a drain on attention, energy and wealth, which might otherwise have been invested in capital development. The imperial system also meant that cultural and social elites tended to be focused on the arts, humanities and self-promotion vis-à-vis the imperial bureaucracy. The centralization of decision making, meanwhile, is seen as having been insensitive to the economic potential of China's estimated 1700 city states and principalities. There is a link, too, between China's imperial framework and its failure to develop military technology (after having gained a flying start) in the way that enabled Europeans to turn exploration into domination: quite simply, the imperial court suppressed the spread of knowledge of gunnery because it feared internal bandits and domestic uprisings.

Another important difference in the trajectories followed by China and Europe was that European agriculture had become focused on the production of cattle and wheat, whereas Chinese agriculture was dominated by rice production. Because rice production requires relatively little land, China did not feel such a great need for territorial expansion. Conversely, Europe's reliance on wheat and cattle provided a strong impetus for territorial expansion and exploration, while the more extensive use of animal power in Europe meant that 'European man possessed in the 15th century a motor, more or less five times as powerful as that possessed by Chinese men' (Chaunu, 1969: 336). Finally, some writers have emphasized the lack of autonomy of oriental towns compared to their European counterparts. As we shall see, the legal and political autonomy of European towns was a crucial 'pull' factor in attracting rural migrants whose labour and initiative were central to the emergence of merchant capitalism. So much, then, for China; it remains for us to explain just how Europe became the hub of the embryonic world economy.

## CRISIS OF FEUDALISM IN EUROPE

The transition from feudalism to merchant capitalism in Europe remains an issue of considerable debate, largely because we do not know enough about the details or timing of the critical economic and social changes that took place between 1300 and 1450. As a result, a variety of theoretical interpretations have emerged, each emphasizing different elements in the transition. It is generally agreed, however, that the overall context for the transition was a phase of economic, demographic and political crisis brought about by the combination of steady population growth, modest technological improvements and limited amounts of usable land.

As a result of improvements in ploughing techniques, harnesses and basic equipment in the early feudal period, wheat yields rose significantly, leading to a steady rise in population over the 12th and 13th centuries. In response, the feudal economy kept up by reclaiming rough pastureland and woodland; and when this began to prove difficult (from around 1250) the response was to improve crop rotations and shorten the period of fallow. There were limits, however, to such adjustments (Figure 4.2 illustrates the land intensity of a medieval manor in England). The number of cattle that could be kept, for example, was fixed by climatic constraints, which limited the quantity of available winter forage and this, in turn, imposed a limit on the supply of fertilizer for arable farming. In the absence of further advances in agrarian technology, food shortages were an inevitable outcome and, in their wake, just as inevitably, came epidemics such as those of the Black Death (bubonic plague) in the 1340s, 1360s and 1370s. These problems were compounded by climatic fluctuations: the cold winters and late springs of the 14th century aggravated the food shortages, while some exceptionally hot summers helped to swell the population of the black rat, host to the rat flea, one of the two vectors of bubonic plague.

Another aggravating factor was the beginning of the Hundred Years War in 1335–45, which put many economies on a war footing. The result was a marked increase in taxation. This, in turn, initiated a downward economic spiral as levels of consumption fell, causing liquidity problems for noble treasuries and eventually leading to a rise in prices. This led to further rounds of tax increases, which provoked a political climate of endemic discontent. The combined result of these pressures was 'not only to exhaust the goose that laid the golden eggs for the castle, but to provoke, from sheer desperation, a movement of illegal emigration from the manor' (Dobb, 1963: 21).

The destination of all these fugitives from feudalism was the town, where different laws and tax systems prevailed. The late medieval European town (Cipolla, 1981: 146):

> [W]as the 'frontier', a new and dynamic world where people felt they could break their ties with an unpleasant past, where people hoped they would find opportunities for economic and social success, where sclerotic traditional institutions and discriminations no longer counted, and where there would be ample reward for initiative, daring and industriousness.

That the towns should appear so attractive was not simply the result of the legal status of their inhabitants, however. They had, ironically, begun to prosper at the height of feudal economic development. In order to meet the nobility's more sophisticated and ostentatious requirements, seigneurial incomes had been increasingly realized in the form of cash. *This obliged peasants to sell part of their produce on the market in order to pay rents and taxes and generally facilitated the trading of commodities.* There developed an embryonic pattern of regional trade in basic industrial and agricultural produce, and even some long-distance, international trade in luxury goods such as spices, furs, silks, fruit and wine. One consequence of this trade was an increase in the size and vitality of towns, as more and more merchants and craft workers emerged to cope with the demands of the system. This urban vitality was a major agent in the eventual crisis of feudalism. It helped to highlight the relative inefficiency of the self-sufficient feudal estate and transformed attitudes towards the pursuit of wealth.

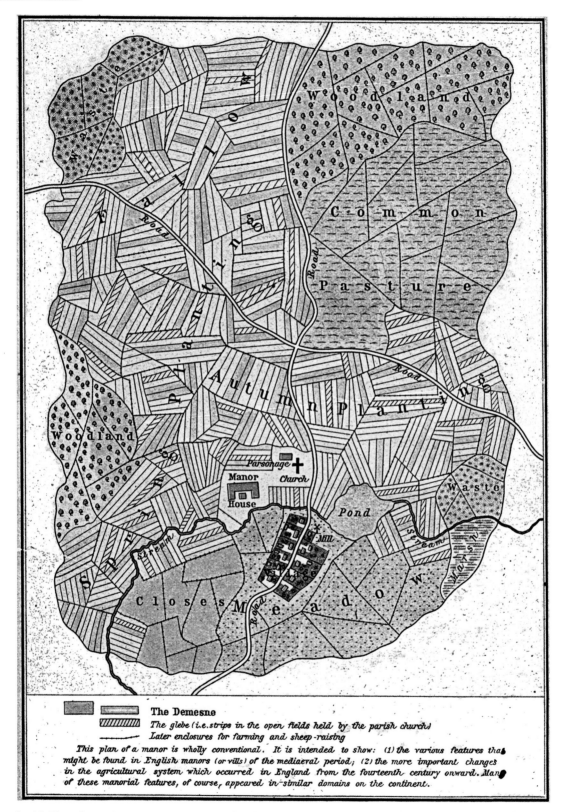

Fig 4.2: Plan of a medieval manor

*Source*: University of Texas Libraries map, available at http://www.lib.utexas.edu/maps/historical/shepherd/plan_mediaeval_manor.jpg

## RESURGENCE OF TRADE AND EXPANSION OF TOWNS UNDER MERCHANT CAPITALISM

Increased trade and urban growth were both a cause and an effect of the transition from feudalism; but they were also hallmarks of the new economic order. As the feudal system faltered and disintegrated, it was replaced by an economy that was dominated by market exchange, in which communities came to specialize in the production of the goods and commodities they could produce most efficiently in comparison with other communities (Figure 4.3). The key actors in this system were the merchants who supplied the capital required to initiate the flow of trade – hence the label 'merchant capitalism'.

In marked contrast to feudalism and earlier rank-redistributive and primitive subsistence economies, merchant capitalism was a self-propelling growth system in which the continued expansion of trade was vital: without it, neither merchants nor those dependent on their success – producers, consumers, financiers, etc. – could maintain their position, let alone advance it:

> Mercantile success required the merchants to buy as cheaply as possible, and to sell as expensively as possible; it also demanded that they trade in as large a volume of goods as possible . . . This created a contradiction, however, for the producers were also consumers (though not of the goods they produced), so that if the prices they received were low, they could not afford to buy large quantities of other goods and thus satisfy the demands of the merchant class as a whole. A consequence of this was a great pressure on producers to increase the volume of goods offered for sale, which meant increasing their productivity, while merchants put pressure on consumers to buy more, even if this meant them borrowing money in order to afford their purchases. Both processes . . . involved producers raising loans which they had to repay with interest; to achieve the latter, they had to produce more (or, if they were employees rather than independent workers, to work harder).
>
> Johnston (1980: 33–4)

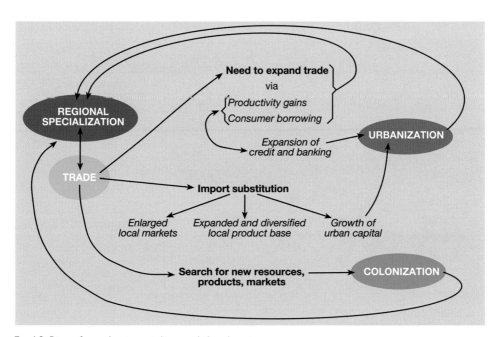

Fig 4.3: Rise of merchant capitalism and the changing space-economy

The regional specializations and trading patterns that provided the foundations for early merchant capitalism were predetermined to a considerable degree by the longstanding patterns that had been developed by the traders of Venice, Pisa, Genoa, Florence, Bruges, Antwerp and the Hanseatic League (which included Bremen, Hamburg, Lübeck, Rostock and Danzig; see Figure 4.4) from the 12th century. As the self-propelling growth of merchant capitalism took hold, centres of trade multiplied in northern France and the lower Rhineland, new routes across Switzerland and southern Germany linked the commerce of Flanders (in Belgium) more closely to that of the Mediterranean, and sea lanes – across the English Channel, North Sea and Baltic – began to integrate the economies of Britain, Scandinavia and the Hansa territories with those of the continental core. Very quickly, a trading system of immense complexity came to span Europe, from Portugal to Poland and from Sweden to Sicily. This trading system was based not on the luxury goods of earlier trade routes but on bulky staples such as grains, wine, salt, wool, cloth and metals.

The increased volume of trade fostered a great deal of urban development as merchants began to settle at locations that were of particular significance in relation to major trade routes and as local economies everywhere came to focus on market exchange. But once the dynamics of trade had been initiated, the key to urban growth was a process of import substitution, whereby externally produced goods and services are replaced with locally produced ones. In this way, local economies reinvest their income within their boundaries, which leads to a partial restoration of self-sufficiency and economic autarky. Although some things were hard to copy because of the constraints of climate or basic resource endowment,

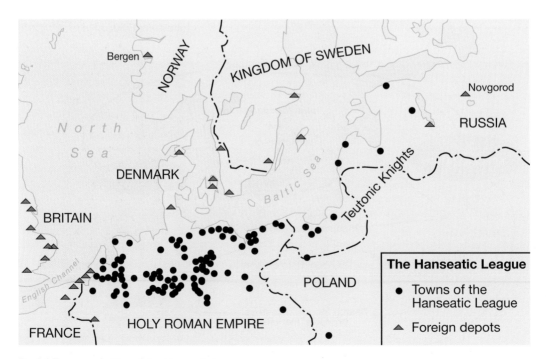

Fig 4.4: Towns and cities of the Hanseatic League

Source: Adapted from Hugill (1993: 50, Figure 2.5)

many imported manufactures could be copied by local producers, thus increasing local employment opportunities, intensifying the use of local resources and increasing the amount of local investment capital available. As Jane Jacobs argued, cities that replaced imports in this way could then afford new types of goods being produced in other cities. The newly imported innovations, in their turn, might then be replaced with local production, opening up the market for still more innovations from elsewhere. So the cities of Europe:

> [W]ere forever generating new exports for one another – bells, dyes, buckles, parchment, lace, carding combs, needles, painted cabinet work, ceramics, brushes, cutlery, paper, sieves, riddles, sweetmeats, elixirs, files, pitchforks, sextants – and then replacing them with local production, to become customers for still more innovations. They were developing on one another's shoulder.
>
> Jacobs (1984: 50)

As a result, patterns of trade and urban growth were very volatile; and long-term local success within the new economic order became increasingly dependent on:

- sustained improvisation and innovation
- repeated episodes of import substitution
- the discovery and control of additional resources and new kinds of resource.

## CONSOLIDATION AND EXPANSION

In the 15th and 16th centuries, a series of innovations in business and technology contributed to the consolidation of merchant capitalism. These included innovations in the organization of business and finance: banking, loan systems, credit transfers, company partnerships, shares in stock, speculation in commodity futures, commercial insurance, courier/news services and so on. The importance of these innovations lay not only in the way they oiled the wheels of industry, agriculture and commerce, but also in the way that they helped to encourage savings and to facilitate their use for investment. Furthermore, the routinization of complex commercial and financial activity brought with it the codification of civil and criminal legislation relating to property rights (e.g., patent laws); a development seen by some as being of critical importance because it provided an incentive for a sufficient number of innovators and entrepreneurs to channel their efforts into the embryonic capitalist economy.

Meanwhile, technological innovations succeeded each other at an accelerated rate. Some of these were adaptations and improvements of oriental discoveries – the windmill, spinning wheels, paper manufacture, gunpowder and the compass, for example. But in Europe, there was a real passion for the mechanization of the productive process as a means of increasing productivity. In addition to improvements based on others' ideas, there emerged a welter of independent engineering breakthroughs, including the more efficient use of energy in watermills and blast furnaces, the design of reliable clocks and firearms and the introduction of new methods of processing metals and manufacturing glass.

The advantages conferred by these breakthroughs were guarded jealously by the centres of innovation – northern Italy up to the 15th century; England and Holland in the 16th and 17th centuries – while competitors in other regions went to considerable lengths to acquire new technology at the first opportunity. Thus, for example, the Venetian government strictly prohibited the emigration of caulkers; and the Grand Duke of Florence gave a reward for the return, dead or alive, of emigrants from key positions in the brocade industry. The French actually kidnapped skilled ironworkers from Sweden; while many governments were happy to provide shelter and handsome rewards for migrant craftsmen who had knowledge of new techniques. These early examples of a 'brain drain' were complemented by the practice of temporary migration in the opposite direction in order to acquire new expertise, sometimes legitimately, sometimes covertly. But the most important vector for the diffusion of technological innovations came with the invention of the printing press using movable type. Within 20 years of its introduction by Johannes Gutenberg in Mainz around 1450, printing shops had spread throughout Europe, opening up vast new possibilities in the fields of knowledge and education.

It was the combination of innovations in *shipbuilding, navigation* and *naval ordnance*, however, that literally had the most far-reaching consequences for the evolution of the European space-economy. By the 14th century, European shipwrights were building ships skeleton first, as a vast saving of labour in comparison with previous methods. In the course of the 15th century, the full-rigged ship was developed, enabling faster voyages in larger and more manoeuvrable vessels that were less dependent on favourable winds. Meanwhile, the quadrant (1450) and the astrolabe (1480) were developed, and a systematic knowledge of Atlantic winds had been acquired. By the mid-16th century, England, Holland and Sweden had perfected the technique of casting iron guns, making it possible to replace bronze cannon with larger numbers of more effective guns at lower expense. Together, these advances made it possible for the merchants of Europe to establish the basis of a worldwide economy in the space of less than 100 years.

## MERCANTILISM AND TERRITORIAL EXPANSION

As we have already seen in relation to China, however, economic strength and technological ability do not necessarily lead to overseas expansion. What, then, translated Europe's economic power and technological superiority to a broader arena? Figure 4.5 summarizes the most important factors. The large number of impoverished aristocrats produced by western European inheritance laws and by expensive Crusades and local wars was one important factor. Discouraged from commercial careers by sheer snobbery and encouraged by a culture that romanticized the fighting man, these poverty-stricken gentlemen provided a plentiful supply of adventurers who were willing to die for glory and even more willing to exercise greed and cruelty in the name of god and country. This points to two other important factors: the evangelical zeal of the Church and the political competitiveness of the monarchies.

Above all, however, overseas expansion was impelled by the *logic of merchant capitalism* and the *law of diminishing returns*. Self-propelling growth could only be sustained as long as productivity could be improved and, after a point, this required food and energy resources that could only be obtained by the conquest – peaceful or otherwise – of new territories. Similarly, merchant capitalism required new supplies of gold and silver to make up for the leakage through trade with Byzantium, China and Arabia.

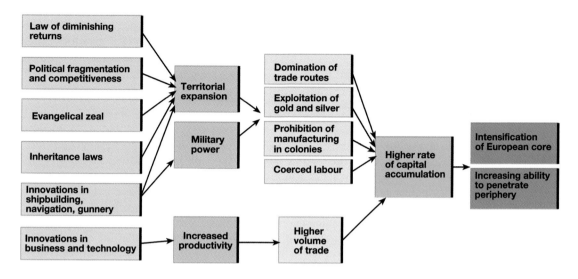

Figure 4.5 Emergence of a European-based world-system

Collectively, these motivations found expression in the dogma of mercantilism. Most European countries adhered to this dogma from the 16th century to the early 18th century. The basis of mercantilism was that national wealth was to be measured in terms of the amount of accumulated precious metal (gold or silver) and that the fundamental source of economic growth was a persistently favourable balance of trade. This was the economic 'logic' that justified not only overseas colonization but also the coercion of plantation labour and the prohibition of manufacturing in the colonies. It was also the logic that, on the domestic front, promoted thrift and saving as a means of accumulating capital for overseas investment. It required a high degree of economic regulation, sponsorship and protection by the government.

There is no need for us to reiterate here the pattern and sequence of European expansion and conquest (although it is worth noting that the overall thrust, overseas from Atlantic Europe rather than inland to the east, was essentially because the technological superiority of the Europeans was not as marked on land as it was on the seas: Asians could counterbalance technological inferiority with weight of numbers until after the mid-17th century, when European technology succeeded in developing more mobile and rapid firing guns). Europeans soon destroyed most of the Muslim shipping trade in the Indian Ocean and captured a large share of the intra-Asian trade. By bringing Japanese copper to China and India, Spice Island cloves to India and China, India cotton textiles to Asia and Persian carpets to India, European merchants made good profits and with them paid for some of their imports from Asia.

It was the gold and silver from the Americas, however, that provided the first major economic transformation, allowing Europe 'to live above its means, to invest beyond its savings' (Braudel, 1972: 268). In effect, the bullion was converted into effective demand for consumer goods and producer goods of all kinds – textiles, wine, food, furniture, weapons, ships – thus stimulating production throughout the economic system and creating the basis for a 'Golden Age' of prosperity for most of the 16th century. Meanwhile, overseas expansion made available a variety of new and unusual products – cocoa, beans, maize, potatoes, tomatoes, sugar cane, tobacco, and vanilla from the Americas, tea from the orient – which opened up large new markets to enterprising merchants.

As European traders came to monopolize intra-oriental trade routes, they were literally able to control the flow and patterns of trade between potential rivals. Because of this monopoly, European traders could identify foreign articles with a tested profitable market and ship them home to Europe, where skilled workmen could learn to imitate them. Once Europeans had begun manufacturing these products, it was their goods that were shipped to the rest of the world:

> For example, Europeans long prized the shawls which were made in the north of India in the Kashmir region; much later Scotchmen [sic] were making imitations of those shawls by the dozens per day; called 'Paisley' shawls, they swept the Kashmir shawls off the general market. Europeans admired the very hard vitrified china of the Chinese, and for a long while bought it to sell to other peoples, taking it from China and distributing it. But then the Europeans began to make it in France and elsewhere, and shortly true Chinese china had become a rare article on the world market while Europe was making and selling enormous amounts of its own 'china'. For a good while Europeans bought cottons of a very fine quality from India for markets in Africa, Europe, and America, but before too long they had imitated them in England and were shipping cheaper machine-made cottons back to India where they ruined the Indian cotton-weaving industry in its own home.
>
> Reynolds (1961: 45–6)

For Europe, the benefits of overseas expansion thus extended well beyond the basic acquisition of new lands and resources. In addition to the bullion and the opportunities for import substitution, overseas expansion also stimulated further improvements in technology and business techniques, thus adding a further dimension to the self-propelling growth of merchant capitalism. New developments were achieved in nautical mapmaking, naval artillery, shipbuilding and the use of sail; and the whole experience of overseas expansion provided a great practical school of entrepreneurship and investment. Most important of all, perhaps, was the way that the profits from overseas colonies and trading overflowed into domestic agriculture, mining and manufacturing. This contributed to an accumulation of capital that was undoubtedly one of the main preconditions for the emergence of industrial capitalism in the 18th century.

## THE WORLD OUTSIDE EUROPE: TRANSOCEANIC RIM SETTLEMENTS

Outside Europe, the most important features of the economic landscape to emerge as a result of merchant capitalism were the gateway towns and entrepôts that were established along the coastal rims of the Americas, Africa and south Asia. These *transoceanic rim settlements* (Figure 4.6) were of three main kinds:

1 *Trading stations*, such as Canton (now Guangzhou, China), Madras (now Chennai, India) and Goa (India), which grew up as the points of contact between Europe and the – as yet – relatively autonomous economic worlds of the orient. Few Europeans lived in these towns and cities and only in India was it possible to exercise any secure measure of political control over the large hinterland areas that served as ports.
2 *Entrepôts and colonial headquarters* for tropical plantations, such as Rio de Janeiro (Brazil), Georgetown (British Guiana), Port of Spain (Trinidad), Penang (Malaysia), Lagos (Nigeria), Lourenço Marques (now Maputo, Mozambique) and Zanzibar (Tanzania). Substantial numbers of European settlers were required

for administrative and military purposes, whereas the indigenous population provided field labour and manual labour in the towns. The colonial plantation system made intensive demands on labour, however, and when the indigenous supply was insufficient it was augmented by enforced movements of slave labour from other regions, thus creating distinctive ethnic cleavages among the populations of many colonies.

3 *Gateway ports* for the 13 farm family colonies on the northeastern seaboard of America (similar settlements were later established in South Africa, Australia and New Zealand). Although there were several distinctive groups – the Tidewater Colonies of Virginia (e.g., Jamestown, Baltimore), the New Towns of New England (e.g., Boston, Newport), the Middle Colony towns (e.g., New York, Philadelphia) and the colonial towns of the Carolinas (e.g., Charleston, Savannah) – they were essentially a direct extension of the west European urban system, peopled by west Europeans and oriented much more to their homelands than their hinterlands.

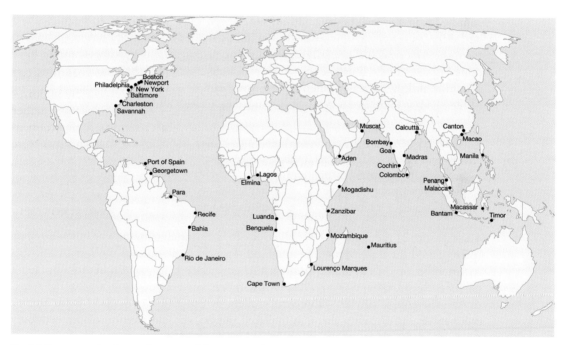

Fig 4.6: Transoceanic rim settlements of the mercantile era

## THE SHIFTING LOCUS OF ECONOMIC POWER

The dominant feature of the changing economic geography of Europe in the 16th and 17th centuries was a dramatic shift in the focus of economic activity from the Mediterranean to the North Sea. At the end of the 15th century, the Mediterranean was the most highly developed region in the world, with central and northern Italy as the hub of economic activity. During the 16th century, the relative prosperity of the Mediterranean was further enhanced as Spain and Portugal benefited immensely from the influx of treasure from the Americas. By the end of the 17th century, however, the Mediterranean had become a backward region in relation to the levels of prosperity generated by the Dutch economy; while England, hitherto a very marginal economy in European terms, stood poised to threaten the position of the Dutch as world leaders.

Between these two extremes of stagnation/regression and dynamic expansion was the experience of France, Scandinavia, Germany and much of the rest of continental Europe, where there was a general penetration of economic development and maturing of local economies: a consolidation of merchant capitalism, which helped to maintain the coherence of the European economy during a period of volatile change in its spatial organization. In detail, therefore, the changing centre of gravity of the European economy involved a complex of overlapping, interlocking and interacting regional struggles and transformations. The basic processes involved, however, were more general and they can be illustrated with reference to the decline of Spain and Italy and the rise of Holland and England.

## Spain

Spain provides a good example of the importance of import substitution. Quite simply, Spain declined because it had never been fully 'developed' to begin with; it had only been rich. The increased demand generated by its acquisition of bullion from the Americas did not stimulate domestic production as much as it might have done because of the bottlenecks in the productive system – the restrictive practices of guilds and the lack of skilled labour, for example – and the complacent attitude of the Spanish elite. In 1675 Alfonso Nuñez de Castro wrote:

> Let London manufacture those fabrics of hers to her heart's content; Holland her chambrays; Florence her cloth; the Indies their beaver and vicuña; Milan her brocades; Italy and Flanders their linens, so long as our capital can enjoy them; the only thing it proves is that all nations train journeymen for Madrid and that Madrid is the queen of Parliaments, for all the world serves her and she serves nobody.
>
> Cipolla (1981: 25)

The treasure of the Americas provided Spain with purchasing power but ultimately it stimulated the development of England, France, Holland and the rest of Europe. Meanwhile, Spain's artificial prosperity had induced the government to pursue a persistently warmongering policy, which represented a serious drain on the treasury. In the course of the 17th century, then, as the influx of bullion from Spain's colonies declined (partly through depleted mines), the momentum of the economy evaporated, leaving insufficient entrepreneurs and artisans to counterbalance an overabundance of bureaucrats, lawyers and priests, and a mounting national debt.

## Italy

Italy's decline was more complex, but its beginning can be dated more accurately: the end of the 15th century, when for almost 50 years northern Italy became the battlefield for an international conflict involving Spain, France and Germany. As a result there were not only famines and epidemics but also severe disruptions to trade at a time when trade was beginning to expand elsewhere. Buoyed up by the international boom in demand during the late 16th century, the economy made something of a recovery; but it was a recovery based on traditional methods of organization, which meant, among other things, that competition and innovation were suppressed by the renewed strength of craft guilds. Between 1610 and 1630 a series of external events led to the collapse of some of the Italians' major markets – the decline of the Spanish economy, disruptive wars in the German states and political instability within the Turkish empire. At the same time, many of Italy's competitors had been able to substitute domestic products for Italian imports. At this point, the self-propelling growth of merchant capitalism broke down. Unable, or unwilling, to respond through innovation and increased productivity, Italian entrepreneurs began to disinvest in manufacturing and shipping. By the end of the 17th century Italy was importing large quantities of manufactures from England, France and Holland, while exporting agricultural goods for which the terms of trade were poor: oil, wheat, wine and wool. Foreign trade had thus been transformed from an 'engine of growth' to an 'engine of decline'.

## The Netherlands

The Netherlands' 'economic miracle' of the 17th century was launched from a fairly solid platform of trading and manufacturing. Although overshadowed in the early phases of merchant capitalism by the prosperity of nearby Bruges and Antwerp, Holland (and Amsterdam in particular), had steadily developed an entrepôt function for northern Europe (importing flax, hemp, grain and timber; exporting salt, fish and wine), around which it had begun to establish a manufacturing base. From the stability of this base, the Dutch successfully rebelled against Spanish imperialism and emerged, in 1609, with political independence and religious freedom.

Thereafter, a combination of factors helped the Dutch to become leaders of the world economy for more than 150 years. One was the 'modernity' of Dutch institutions: relatively few restrictive guilds, a small nobility of landowners, and a relatively weak Church after the departure of the Spanish. Another was the vigorous pursuit of mercantilist policies, including not only a strong colonial drive and a massive commitment to merchant shipping but also an uncompromising stance towards competitors. For example, the Dutch blockaded Antwerp's access to the sea from 1585 to 1795, taking over its entrepôt trade and its textile industry. In relation to their drive to dominate trade, the Dutch were able to turn their geographical situation to great advantage, both developing ocean ports and exploiting the inland waterways that penetrated the heart of continental Europe. They were also able to benefit from a highly developed and very innovative shipbuilding industry whose output completely overshadowed that of the rest of Europe. Finally, the Dutch were the major beneficiaries of the flight of skilled craftsmen, merchants, sailors, financiers and professionals from the fanaticism and intolerance of the Spanish in Flanders and Wallonia (Belgium).

## England

England, at the end of the 15th century, was distinctly backward, with a small population (around 5 million, compared to more than 15 million in France, 11 million in Italy and 7 million in Spain) and a weakly developed economy. The only significant comparative advantage the English held was the manufacture of woollen cloth. The first real break for the English economy came in the first half of the 16th century, when Italian production and trade collapsed because of war and its ensuing disasters, leaving the English literally to capitalize on a sustained increase in woollen exports – a trend that was further enhanced by the progressive deterioration of English currency resulting from Henry VIII's extravagant military expenditures. The boom was halted in the mid-16th century, however, by the recovery of the Italian textile industry and by the war between the Dutch and the Spanish, which disrupted English exports.

By this time, however, English entrepreneurial and expansionist ambitions had become established and were articulated through a strong mercantilist philosophy. Like the Dutch, the English were able to take advantage of their geographical situation, at least in relation to transoceanic trade. They had also developed a strong navy and gave high priority to establishing a large merchant fleet and to acquiring colonial footholds. Like the Dutch, they also benefited from the skills of immigrants driven from France and the Low Countries by religious persecution. Innovation, improvisation and import substitution all played their part in ensuring a rapid escape from the mid-century economic crisis and, indeed, in building an economy to challenge that of the Dutch. The development of iron artillery in the 1540s, for example, enabled the English to arm their merchant ships, privateers and warships more extensively *and* at lower cost. Meanwhile, the exploitation of coal as a substitute for the relatively sparse and rapidly diminishing timber reserves not only helped the English to avoid an energy crisis but also helped to develop new processing techniques. 'Concentrating on iron and coal, England set herself on the road that led directly to the Industrial Revolution' (Cipolla, 1981: 290).

## SUMMARY

At this stage it is useful to review the major organizing principles that were important in delineating the evolving space-economy up to the eve of the Industrial Revolution. First, note that the observations we made in relation to early economic systems (pp. 98–99) appear as recurring elements in subsequent economic epochs. Thus we can confirm the gradual and incremental nature of major economic change.

We can also confirm the continuing importance of innovations in technology and business organization (although we should note that the innovative process to this point was carried out in small steps, by way of the gradual accumulation of improvements rather than by distinct bursts of invention which, as we shall see, have characterized economic change since the industrial era).

The importance of institutional and sociopolitical factors was also a recurring theme (as, for example, in the constraints of a centralized imperial system on the evolution of the Chinese economy, in the stimulus provided by European laws on property rights and the role of European governments in implementing mercantilist policies). Similarly, we must acknowledge the continuing interaction between demographic change and economic development and, finally, the continuing impetus for territorial expansion provided by the law of diminishing returns. In addition, however, we can identify several new dimensions of spatial-economic organization:

- The emergence of a true 'world economy', involving long-distance interaction based on a sophisticated spatial division of labour.
- The progressive elaboration of the world economy, with competitive ('price-setting') markets penetrating into more and more space, and more and more commodities, was *uneven*. Some sectors, countries and regions expanded more quickly than others and some spheres of opportunity and lines of communication were

penetrated more quickly than others, so that its early spread was in a selective, spatially discontinuous fashion.

- The pattern of specialization and the nature of economic interaction within the world economy resulted in the emergence of *core* areas, characterized by such mass market industries as had emerged (e.g., textiles, shipbuilding), international and local commerce in the hands of an indigenous bourgeoisie, and relatively advanced forms of agriculture; *peripheral* areas, characterized by the monoculture of cash crops by coerced labour on large estates or plantations; and *semi-peripheral* areas, characterized by a process of deindustrialization but retaining a significant share of specialized industrial production and financial control.
- The spatial organization of the European space-economy was based around a cluster of core areas in northwestern Europe: southeastern England and Holland, together with the Baltic states, the Rhine and Elbe regions of Germany, Flanders (Belgium) and northern France. Peripheral regions included northern Scandinavia, Britain's Celtic fringe (i.e., Scotland, Wales, Ireland), east-central Europe and all the transoceanic rim settlements and colonies. The semi-periphery consisted of the Christian Mediterranean region, which had been the advanced core area at the beginning of the merchant capitalist era.
- The articulation of the European world economy also produced a distinctive pattern of settlement and urbanization. Merchant capitalism was reflected in the urban landscape by a strengthening of the hierarchical system of settlements and the development of a central place system. The overseas territorial expansion associated with merchant capitalism was also reflected in a distinctive urban landscape, as illustrated in Figure 4.7. Johnston (1980: 74) once again provides a succinct description:

> In the initial stages of mercantile exploration no permanent settlement is established in order to obtain the required products (fish, timber and furs). Then the colony is settled by agriculturalists; the export of their products moves through local articulation points to the colonial port, and thence to the port in the homeland, which grows in size and status relative to its inland competitors. As settlement of the colony expands further inland, so both of the ports increase in size, railways replace rivers as the main traffic arteries within the colony, and internal gateways develop to articulate the trade of areas some distance from the port, while in the homeland places near to the original port benefit from the imports and a new outport is built to handle the larger volume of trade and the bigger vessels.

The emergence of the European world economy brought about a system of internal dynamics that involved three important mechanisms of spatial change:

1 The switching of investment from one area to another by merchants in response to the shifting comparative advantages enjoyed by local producers. These shifts in comparative advantage, in turn, were associated with technological innovations and improvements, institutional changes, currency fluctuations and so on.
2 Import substitution. Communities able to achieve repeated episodes of import substitution, as Jacobs (1984) pointed out, benefit from five aspects of economic development:
   - enlarged markets for new imports and innovations
   - an expanded and more varied employment base
   - new applications of technology to increase rural productivity

- a spillover of employment to rural areas as older, expanding enterprises are crowded out of cities
- growth of city capital.

3  Militarism and geopolitical change.

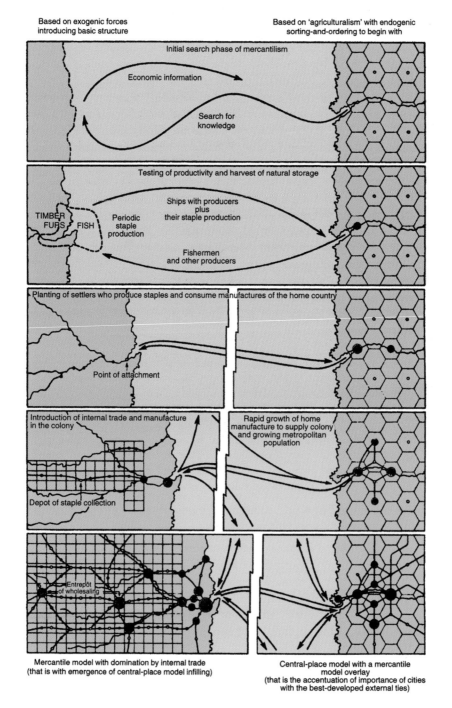

Fig 4.7: Colonialism and urban settlement patterns

Source: Based on Vance (1970: 151, Figure 18)

## KEY SOURCES AND SUGGESTED READING

Cipolla, C. 1981. *Before the Industrial Revolution. European Society and Economy, 1000–1700* 2nd edn. London: Methuen.

Clark, C. 1977. *World Prehistory in New Perspective*. Cambridge: Cambridge University Press.

De Vries, J. 1976. *Economy of Europe in an Age of Crisis, 1600–1750*. Cambridge: Cambridge University Press.

Diamond, J. 1997. *Guns, Germs, and Steel*. New York: W.W. Norton.

Diamond, J. 2005. *Collapse: How Societies Choose to Fail or Succeed*. New York: Viking.

Frank, A.G. 1998. *ReORIENT: Global Economy in the Asian Age*. Berkeley: University of California Press.

Jacobs, J. 1984. Cities and the wealth of nations, *Atlantic Monthly*, March, 41–66.

Johnston, R.J. 1984. The world is our oyster, *Transactions, Institute of British Geographers*, 9, 443–59.

Landes, D.S. 1999. *The Wealth and Poverty of Nations*. New York: W.W. Norton.

Reynolds, R. 1961. *Europe Emerges. Transition Toward an Industrial World-Wide Society*. Madison, WI: University of Wisconsin Press.

Tilly, C. 1992. *Coercion, Capital, and European States*. Cambridge, MA: Blackwell.

Wallerstein, I. 1980. *The Modern World-System II: Mercantilism and the Consolidation of the World-Economy 1600–1750*. London: Academic Press.

## RELATED WEBSITES

Ancient World History: http://members.aol.com/TeacherNet/Ancient.html
contains numerous hyperlinks to a variety of topics including *Ancient China to Modern Times*

Exploring Ancient World Cultures: an introduction to ancient world cultures on the world wide web: http://eawc.evansville.edu/
this University of Evansville website contains a wealth of resources on the classical world and includes *Search Argus*, a searchable online bibliography, available at http://argos.evansville.edu/

History Net: http://history.about.com/
offers articles and hyperlinks for 20th-century and earlier history

Internet Ancient History Sourcebook: http://www.fordham.edu/halsall/ancient/asbook.html
searchable online bibliography (maintained by Fordham University) offers a variety of resources on ancient history, including texts on Mesopotamia and China

Chapter 5

# Evolution of the industrial core regions

From the second half of the 18th century, industrialization brought a new pattern and tempo to the economic organization of the world economy and new dimensions to the world's economic landscapes. Today, economic geography within the tripolar core of the world economy is dominated by the physical, institutional and social legacies of industrial capitalism. The economic geography of the world's peripheral regions has, meanwhile, been shaped by their role in sustaining the industrial expansion of the core economies and more recently the NICs. In short, there are few of the world's economic landscapes that are not largely a product, directly or indirectly, of the industrial era. In this chapter, we outline the evolution of the economic geography of the industrial core regions, analyzing the major processes involved in the relative ascent and decline of countries and regions within the industrial core areas.

## 5.1 THE INDUSTRIAL REVOLUTION AND SPATIAL CHANGE

The transition during the late 18th and early 19th centuries from merchant capitalism to industrial capitalism as the dominant mode of production is conventionally ascribed to the Industrial Revolution. The Industrial Revolution, in turn, is conventionally depicted as a revolution in the techniques and organization of manufacturing, based on a series of innovations in the technology of production (e.g., Kay's flying shuttle (1733), Hargreaves' spinning Jenny (1765) and Cartwright's machine loom (1787)), and in transport technology and engineering (particularly the development of canal and railway systems). But technological advance was really part of a wider economic, social and political transition, whose origins and preconditions are to be found both in the Renaissance and Enlightenment. Indeed:

> [P]rior to 1800, living standards in the world economy were roughly constant over the very long run: per capita wage income, output and consumption did not grow. Modern industrial economies, on the other hand, enjoy unprecedented and seemingly endless growth in living standards.
>
> Hansen and Prescott (2002: 1202)

The most important context for technological advance was the existence within merchant capitalism of *industry* organized on capitalist lines by entrepreneurs employing wage labour and producing commodities for sale in regional and national markets. In addition, the *capital* that had been accumulated through trading provided the means for entrepreneurs to finance investment in the capital-intensive but highly productive technology of the Industrial Revolution.

From these roots, machine production and the organizational setting of the factory – machinofacture – emerged as the central characteristics of industrialization. While machinery provided the basis for higher levels of productivity, it was the factory setting that enabled this productivity to be exploited to the fullest possible extent. This was achieved through specialization – the assembly line division of labour – and internal economies of scale. At the same time, the concentration of workers in big industrial units generated urban environments that, themselves, represented a new dynamic force for economic, social and political change.

Like merchant capitalism before it, however, industrial capitalism had to confront the twin obstacles of market saturation and the law of diminishing returns. In response, industrialists have pursued a variety of strategies. In addition to the constant search for technological advances, these have included:

- pursuit of new ways of exploiting internal economies of scale and external economies of scale
- exploitation of new, cheaper sources of labour and/or raw materials and energy
- penetration of new (i.e., overseas) markets for existing products
- development of new products, either through new inventions (e.g., video recorders, microcomputers) or by the 'commodification' of activities previously performed within the household (e.g., food processing and preparation)
- acceptance of increasingly formalized relations with labour unions and governments, in order to establish a more stable context (economic, social and political) in which to operate.

As a result of all this dynamism, the changes imposed on economic landscapes by the first waves of the Industrial Revolution have been overwritten by a succession of episodes of industrial development, restructuring and reorganization. In addition, it is important to recognize the differences that were created between the major industrial regions as a result not only of variations in resource endowment and previous patterns of economic development but also because of variations in the relative timing and interaction of these episodes of industrial change.

## 5.2 MACHINOFACTURE AND THE SPREAD OF INDUSTRIALIZATION IN EUROPE

There was in fact not a single Industrial Revolution but several distinctive transitional phases, each having a different degree of impact, in different ways, on different regions and countries. *As new technologies shifted the margins of profitability in different kinds of enterprises, so the fortunes of specialized places shifted.*

These regional differentials, in turn, helped to influence the changing character of capitalism itself. A key aspect of this change was the evolving nature of economic, social, political and cultural relations under capitalism. These can be thought of as a series of successive regimes of accumulation – interrelated complexes of production, consumption and income distribution based on the ways in which capitalist firms are organized. Regimes of accumulation evolve in response to the opportunities and constraints created by new production, transportation and communications technologies. At the same time, this evolution is associated with a succession of technology systems that are imprinted, differentially, on to the world's economic landscapes. Associated with each regime of accumulation is a specific mode of regulation or set of local and historical economic and political arrangements and institutions that emerges to provide appropriate management for the operation of the successive regimes of accumulation (e.g., monetary and wage regulation, particular government–business relationships, trading regulation, etc.) and technology systems within the wider national and international context. Modes of regulation have four principal functions:

1  regulating the monetary system and financial mechanisms
2  regulating wages and collective bargaining
3  facilitating (or, in some circumstances, constraining) competition, and establishing the relations between the private sector and the public economy
4  establishing the roles of governments at various spatial scales.

It is possible to identify three major waves of industrialization in Europe, each consisting of several phases and each highly localized in its impact. The first wave saw the imprint of the first technology system of the Industrial Revolution, based on new iron and cotton textile technologies, using water power, trunk canals and turnpike roads. Even within the span of this first wave, however, the imprint was highly differentiated. 'Above all', Pollard emphasizes, 'the industrial revolution was a *regional* phenomenon' (1981: 14, emphasis added).

Figure 5.1 clearly highlights that, before the first wave of industrialization, the growth rate of GDP per capita in Europe was very close to zero for almost 1000 years. In England, the real wage was roughly the same in 1800 as it had been in 1300. Figure 5.1 also demonstrates that population growth was stagnant around zero prior to industrialization, largely reflecting the low pace of technological change.

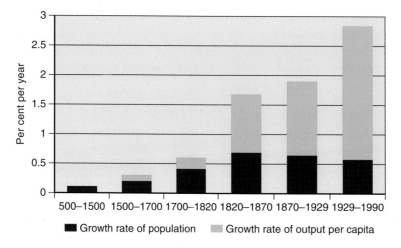

Fig 5.1: Output growth in western Europe, 500–1990
*Source:* Galor and Weil (2000: 808, Figure 1)

## FIRST-WAVE INDUSTRIALIZATION: BRITAIN

The springboard for the first wave of industrialization, which began in Britain around 1760, consisted of several local hearth areas of 'proto-industrialization'. These were areas with longstanding concentrations of industry based on a wage-labour force using the most advanced of the available industrial processes. This early industrial activity was highly localized because of industry's need to be near mineral resources and sources of water power and because of the importance of local canal systems. This localization was also a product of the principle of comparative advantage, whereby industry had been displaced into the areas that were least profitable for agriculture.

This pattern of proto-industrialization, with its external economies, infrastructural advantages and well-developed markets, helped to determine the nuclei of industrial development in Great Britain during the first phase of the first wave of industrialization, between 1760 and 1890. These included north Cornwall, eastern Shropshire, south Staffordshire, north Wales, upland Derbyshire, south Lancashire, the West Riding of Yorkshire, Tyneside, Wearside and parts of the central Lowlands of Scotland. Although these sub-regions shared the common impetus of certain key resources and innovations, each retained its own distinctive business transitions and industrial style. To use the terminology of regulationist theories, each had its own emergent mode of regulation and regime of accumulation. Much of the required capital was raised locally, labour requirements were drawn (in the first instance) from the immediate hinterland and industrialists formed themselves into regional organizations and operated regional cartels.

From the start, then, industrialization was articulated at the regional level; and this has been a feature of subsequent phases and waves. The second phase, between 1790 and 1820, reinforced the position of those embryo industrial regions with a coalfield base and saw the emergence of Ulster (Northern Ireland) and south Wales as industrialized regions. Meanwhile, the prosperity of the early starters – Cornwall, north Wales, eastern Shropshire and upland Derbyshire – declined markedly as their relative advantages were eclipsed by a combination of three different factors:

1  exhaustion of minerals, or the discovery of cheaper alternative supplies of them
2  inaccessibility to markets because of poor communications and/or relatively remote locations
3  lack of size to develop.

The third phase of the 'British' wave, between 1820 and 1850, was dominated by the expansion of the railway system. This did not foster any new industrial regions, but it did widen the market area of the existing industrial regions, drawing more of Britain into the sphere of industrial capitalism.

## SECOND-WAVE INDUSTRIALIZATION: A NEW TECHNOLOGY SYSTEM AND NEW REGIMES OF ACCUMULATION

It was at this point that industrialization began to spread to continental Europe. It should be emphasized, however, that this did not take the form of a straightforward spatial diffusion of industrialization or 'modernization'. By this time, a second technology system had begun to emerge, based on coal, steel, heavy engineering, steam power and railways. Exploiting these new technologies meant:

- drawing on new resources
- development of new labour practices (the spread of wage-labour norms)
- development of new corporate structures (large limited-liability firms that were national rather than local in scope)
- new relationships between governments and industry (increased government regulation of, and investment in, key industries).

Thus there evolved new regimes of accumulation and new modes of regulation.

Just as the British wave of industrialization was initially based on localized concentrations of proto-industrialization, so the second wave was launched from the proto-industrial regions of continental Europe. Initially, from around 1850, industrialization was concentrated in the Sambre-Meuse region of Belgium and in the valley of the Scheldt in Belgium and France. Subsequent phases saw the spread of industrialization: to the Aachen area, the right bank of the River Rhine around Solingen and Remscheid, and the Ruhr in Germany; to Alsace, Normandy and the upper Loire valley in France; and to the Swiss industrial district between Basel and Glarus.

Meanwhile, however, the initial advantage enjoyed by British industries over their would-be competitors on the continent meant that later industrializing regions had to confront a situation in which British industries, having secured comfortable advantages in technology, had come to dominate world markets. Britain also had a series of 'natural' geographical advantages: a compact territory with a large population, favourable conditions for intensive agricultural production and a rich variety of minerals, including coal. This competitive disadvantage for continental European industrial regions was compounded by the consequences of the Revolutionary and Napoleonic Wars of the early 19th century (as it was in the United States by the Civil War of 1861–65). Conscription, conflict and military occupation disrupted production and suppressed industrial expansion, allowing British industries to forge still further ahead on the basis of the new technology system (and, of course, a constantly evolving and adapting mode of regulation).

At the same time, continental entrepreneurs and governments did not have to industrialize by trial and error in the way that the British had: they could benefit from British experience and they could import British managers, workers, capital and technology. These regions of 'inner' Europe were differentiated one from another not only by their different mix of industries, but also by what economic historian Sidney Pollard calls the differential of contemporaneousness, whereby new technologies, ideas and market conditions reached different regions simultaneously but affected them in very different ways *because they were differently equipped to respond to them*. Thus, for example:

> Legislation permitting the easy formation of joint-stock companies spread quickly across Europe in the 1850s, and their contribution to overspeculation and widespread bankruptcies in the less sophisticated European economies has often been commented on. In banking, the backward economies, using the experience of the pioneers, could bypass some of the difficulties of the latter by enjoying the benefits of more efficient banks, ahead, as it were, of their own stage of economic growth.
>
> Pollard (1981: 188–9)

In general terms, however, the cumulative impact of innovations in first- and second-wave industrializers made for convergence: the French Nord (north) began to look and function increasingly like the central belt of the Scottish Lowlands, and the Ruhr began to look and function increasingly like the Sambre-Meuse region. At the same time, there was increasing divergence between those areas that had adopted an industrial base and those that had yet to follow suit. By 1875, the latter still covered a great deal of the map (Figure 5.2), but many of them were incorporated in the third wave of industrialization between 1870 and 1914.

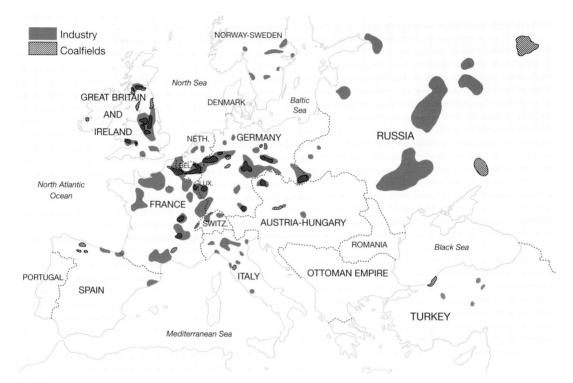

Fig 5.2: Europe in 1875

*Source:* Adapted from Pollard (1981: xv, Map 2)

## THIRD-WAVE INDUSTRIALIZATION: INTERMEDIATE EUROPE

The third wave of industrialization included 'intermediate Europe' – parts of Britain, France, Belgium and Germany that had not been directly affected by the first two waves, together with most of the Netherlands, southern Scandinavia, northern Italy, eastern Austria, and Catalonia in northeastern Spain. By this time, all European landscapes were beginning to be reorganized in response to the imperatives of a third technology system: one based on steamships, world shipping, the internal combustion engine, heavy chemicals and heavy engineering.

In the regions of 'intermediate' Europe, the imprint of this industrialization was distinctive in several important respects. There was little by way of antecedent development on which to base industrialization (apart from small enclaves in Barcelona, Milan-Turin and Vienna) and the relative amount of capital these regions were required to find in order to support industrialization was 10 times greater than during the first wave. This, together with the increasing sophistication of industrial technology and its related services, led central governments to take on ever increasing responsibilities. The economic role of the state among the later industrializers therefore tends to be more pronounced than in the countries of 'inner' Europe.

## PERIPHERAL EUROPE

The residual territories of western Europe – most of the Iberian peninsula, northern Scandinavia, Ireland, southern Italy, the Balkans and east-central Europe, which Pollard collectively terms the 'outer periphery' – remained, like the interstices of 'inner' and 'intermediate' Europe, mainly outside the fold of industrial capitalism, to be penetrated to different degrees over the next 50 years.

One of the reasons for the continued peripherality of these regions was that their entrepreneurs and governments often felt compelled to adopt the new technologies and forms of organization that had served the pioneer regions well, despite the reality of very different economic geographic settings in the periphery. Railway systems provide a simple illustration. Railway networks in pioneer regions had been able to integrate industrial development and operate profitably by carrying regular passenger traffic as well as heavy bulk freight like coal, ore and grain. The extension of railway systems to regions with neither an emerging industrial base nor sufficiently high density of population (as in Ireland, southern Italy, Spain and most of east-central Europe) invited heavy losses. The fact that most governments were willing to underwrite such losses reflects the potency of the railways as political virility symbols. What was not foreseen at the time, however, was that, rather than integrating national territories and fostering industrial development, the penetration of the railways to peripheral regions tended to result in their specialization in a subordinate, agricultural role: a special case of Pollard's 'differential of contemporaneousness'.

Another reason for continued peripherality is to be found in the very different nature of urban development within the later industrializing regions. In Britain, 'inner' Europe and 'intermediate' Europe there had been a symbiotic relationship between urban and industrial development (with cities providing capital, labour, markets, access to transport systems and a variety of agglomeration economies). In much of peripheral Europe, the 'demonstration effect' of these events led to a very different relationship, largely because of the attitudes of the elite:

> Railways were laid to royal palaces, gas or water mains supplied a narrow layer of privileged classes ... innovations intended for mass markets were misused for a narrow luxury market and either diverted resources, or led to burdensome capital imports ... Above all, the city became the gate of entry to new technology manufactures from abroad, spreading outward from Naples, Madrid, Budapest or St. Petersburg, to kill off native industry as unfashionable.
>
> Pollard (1981: 212)

In short, conspicuous consumption precluded import substitution, creating cities that inhibited rather than fostered industrial growth.

## DISLOCATION AND DEPRESSION

In the first half of the 20th century, the economic development of the whole of Europe was punctuated twice by major wars. The disruptions of the First World War were immense. The overall loss of life, including the victims of influenza epidemics and border conflicts that followed the war, amounted to between 50 and 60 million. About half as many again were permanently disabled. For some countries, this meant a loss of between 10 and 15 per cent of the male workforce. In addition, material losses caused a severe dislocation to economic growth: it has been calculated that the level of European output achieved in 1929 would have been reached by 1921 if it had not been for the war.

Economic dislocation in Europe was further intensified by several indirect consequences of the war. In terms of tracing the evolving economic geography of the core regions of the world, two of these were particularly important:

1  The *relative decline* of Europe as a producer compared with the rest of the world. Europe accounted for 43 per cent of the world's production and 59 per cent of its trade in 1913, compared with only 34 per cent of production and 50 per cent of trade in 1923. The main beneficiaries were the USA and Japan for manufactures and Latin America and the British dominions for primary production.

2  The redrawing of the political map of Europe. This created 38 independent economic units instead of 26; 27 currencies instead of 14; and 20,000 extra kilometres of national boundaries. The corollary of these changes was a severe dislocation of economic life, particularly in east-central Europe: frontiers separated workers from the factories, factories from their markets, towns from their traditional food supplies, and textile looms from their spinning sheds and finishing mills; while the transport system found itself only loosely matched to this new political geography.

Just as European economies had adjusted to these dislocations, the stagflation crisis of 1929–35 – the Great Depression – created a further phase of economic damage and reorganization throughout Europe. It should be emphasized, however, that the effects of the Depression varied a great deal from one sector of the economy to another and *from one region to another*. The image of the 1930s depends very much on whether attention is focused on Jarrow or Slough, on Bochum or Nice, on Glasgow or Geneva.

Meanwhile, the coherence of the European economic world began to disintegrate as individual countries attempted to protect their industries with import quotas and restrictions, currency manipulation and exclusionary trade agreements. The result was a substantial fall in trade, both in absolute terms and as a proportion of output, with the USA and Japan, once again, as the major beneficiaries.

## SECOND WORLD WAR AND RECOVERY

The Second World War resulted in a further round of destruction and dislocation. The total loss of life in Europe was 42 million, two-thirds of whom were civilian casualties. The German occupation of continental Europe involved ruthless exploitation. By the end of the war, France was depressed to below 50 per cent of its prewar level of living and had lost 8 per cent of its industrial assets. The United Kingdom lost 18 per cent of its industrial assets (including overseas holdings) and the USSR lost 25 per cent. Germany itself, however, lost 13 per cent of its assets and ended the war with a level of income per capita that was less than 25 per cent of the prewar figure.

After the war, the political cleavage between eastern and western Europe (which resulted from the imposition of what Winston Churchill called the 'Iron Curtain' along the western frontier of Soviet-dominated territory) resulted in a further erosion of the coherence of the European economy and, indeed, of its economic geography. Ironically, it was this cleavage that led to a surprisingly rapid economic recovery in western Europe: the USA, believing that poverty and economic chaos would foster communism, embarked on a massive programme of aid under the

Marshall Plan. This pump-priming action, together with the pent-up backlog of demand in almost every sphere of production, provided the basis for a remarkable recovery. By the early 1950s most of Europe had exceeded prewar levels of prosperity. By the early 1960s, European central banks were in a position to step in, when necessary, to support the US dollar. As Table 5.1 illustrates, growth rates throughout western Europe surged forward to impressive levels.

Table 5.1 Growth rates in Europe

| | Average annual per capita growth rate of real output | |
|---|---|---|
| | 1913–50 | 1950–70 |
| Austria | 0.2 | 4.9 |
| Belgium | 0.7 | 3.3 |
| Denmark | 1.1 | 3.3 |
| France | 1.0 | 4.2 |
| West Germany | 0.8 | 5.3 |
| Greece | 0.2 | 5.9 |
| Ireland | 0.7 | 2.8 |
| Italy | 0.8 | 5.0 |
| Netherlands | 0.9 | 3.6 |
| Norway | 1.8 | 3.2 |
| Portugal | 0.9 | 4.8 |
| Spain | −0.3 | 5.4 |
| Sweden | 2.5 | 3.3 |
| Switzerland | 1.6 | 3.0 |
| United Kingdom | 0.8 | 2.2 |
| **Western European average** | **1.0** | **4.0** |

*Source:* Adapted from Pollard (1981: 315, Table 9.2)

## Box 5.1 Core and periphery in Europe

The cumulative effects of the differential impact of successive waves of industrialization and reorganization have often been interpreted in terms of cores of capital accumulation and economic power, and peripheries of limited (or suppressed) potential for economic development. The relative affluence of western Europe's core regions is shown in stark fashion by Figure 5.3, which depicts a standard measure of regional success: GDP per capita, adjusted in terms of purchasing power to account for regional differences in the cost of living. Even though the cost of living is notoriously high around London, Paris and Milan, these regions enjoy a prosperity that is well above the overall level (indexed at 100 for the 27-member European Union). Europe's affluent core thus stretches between northern Italy and southeast England, including much of southern Germany, southeast France, the Ruhr area, Île de France, Belgium and the Netherlands. There are also affluent outliers in southern Ireland, Denmark, northeast Scotland, the Basque country of Spain, and the capital regions of Finland and Sweden. In contrast, Bulgaria, Romania, Latvia and much of Poland and the Czech Republic are decidedly peripheral, with index scores of under 65.

The European core has variously been interpreted as the triangular region defined by Lille-Bremen-Strasbourg (the 'heavy industrial triangle'), as an axial belt stretching between Boulogne and Amsterdam in the north and Besançon and Munich in the south, as a T-shaped region whose stem extends down the Rhine to Stuttgart; and so on. Such definitions can be confusing in their variability, but their main weakness is that they overlook the *interdependence* that exists between core and periphery. It is therefore more satisfactory to think in terms of a core consisting of a number of linkages or *flows* (capital, migrants, taxes, tourists, consumer fashions) *that bind core and periphery together, reinforcing their unequal but symbiotic relationship.*

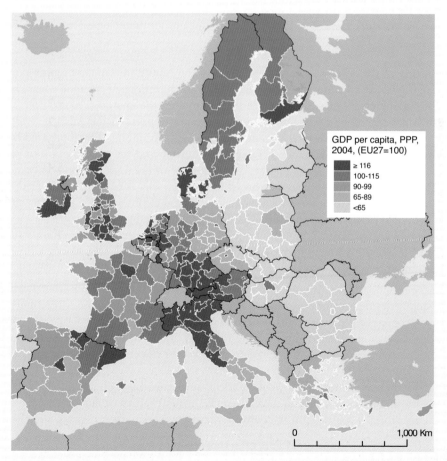

Fig 5.3: Core and periphery in Europe
*Source*: Based on data in Eurostat (2007)

## 5.3 FORDISM AND NORTH AMERICAN INDUSTRIALIZATION

The emergence of North America as the dominant component of the core of the world economy was essentially due to the fact that it had:

- vast natural resources of land and minerals
- a large and – thanks to immigration – rapidly growing market and labour force
- sufficient size to breed giant corporations with large research budgets, which helped to institutionalize the innovation process in a way that European industry had never done.

*Within* North America, the evolving pattern of spatial organization can be interpreted in terms of the interaction of (1) the geography of resources, (2) the introduction of major technological innovations (particularly in transport) and (3) movements of population. Thus:

> Major changes in technology have resulted in critically important changes in the evaluation or definition of particular resources on which the growth of certain urban regions had previously been based. Great migrations have sought to exploit resources – ranging from climate or coal to water or zinc – that were either newly appreciated or newly accessible within the national market. Usually, of course, the new appreciation or accessibility had come about, in turn, through some major technological innovation.
>
> Borchert (1967: 324)

The history of the development and evolution of the American economy found its clearest geographic expression in changing patterns of urbanization. At the time when Europe was experiencing the first waves of industrialization, the spatial organization of the North American economy was focused on the gateway ports of the Atlantic seaboard, each of which controlled a limited hinterland where the economy was dominated by the production of agricultural staples for export to Europe and the consumption of manufactured goods imported from Europe. From the end of the 18th century, however, the North American economy began to break loose from this dependent relationship and within 100 years it had become the dominant component of the world economy, articulated around a closely integrated but highly differentiated urban system.

A major factor in this metamorphosis was the *political independence* of the United States, which was formally achieved in 1783. This stimulated economic development in several ways:

1 Independence from Britain and national political integration under a federal system provided an important stimulus for economic links to be forged between the component parts of the old colonial system.
2 Independence meant that a much greater proportion of investment was financed by American capital, with the result that less of the profits were 'leaked' back to Europe.
3 Independence stimulated a proliferation of government employment, as every county seat and state capital developed the infrastructure of democracy.
4 The territorial expansion of the new country provided a large, rich resource base.

Both urban and economic development in this period, however, was constrained by the relatively primitive transportation system of the 'sail and wagon' epoch. It was not until the 1840s, when the second *technology system* of industrial capitalism (coal/steel/steam/railways) began to be exploited, that American industrialization took off.

# Box 5.2 Growth of the American manufacturing belt

The acceleration of industrialization in the United States in the 1840s was in part the result of the diffusion of industrial technology – particularly the wider industrial application of steam and the accompanying changes in the iron industry – and methods of industrial and commercial organization from the hearth area of the Industrial Revolution in Europe. In addition, the demand for foodstuffs and other agricultural staples, both in North America and abroad, stimulated the growth of industrial capitalism as farmers sought to increase productivity through mechanization and the use of improved agricultural implements. Increasing agricultural productivity, in turn, helped to sustain the growing numbers of immigrants from Europe, thus allowing them to be channelled into industrial employment in North America's mushrooming cities.

The development of the railway system was central to the evolution of this new economic order. Initially, the railways were complementary to the waterways as competitive long-haul carriers of general freight; but by the end of the 'iron horse' epoch the railway network had not only realigned the economic system but also extended it to a continental scale. In 1869, the railway network reached the Pacific when, at Promontory, Utah, the Union Pacific railway, building west from Omaha, met the Central Pacific railway, building east from Sacramento. By 1875 intense competition between railway companies had began to open up the western prairies as far as Minneapolis-St Paul and Kansas City. The significance of this was to be profound:

> Not only did this permit American enterprise to exploit fully the commercial advantages and scale economies of large, diversified natural resources and of the revolutionary technologies evolved in those decades, but it generated rapid, large-scale functional and spatial concentration of finance and management unimpeded by world events, creating a 'transcontinental' business mentality. Wide spatial separation of major resources, cities and markets, and adjacency to the easily penetrated Canadian economy all induced mental thresholds for thinking 'intercontinental' once imported resources and markets overseas became a necessary ingredient to sustain business activity at home, especially during and after the Second World War.
>
> Hamilton (1978: 26; emphasis added)

In short, the railways can be seen as the catalyst that allowed regional economies to develop into a continental economy that stood poised to become the leading component of the world economic system.

Meanwhile, the westward extension of the railways inevitably affected the fortunes of the inland gateway cities. Buffalo and Louisville, for instance, experienced slowed rates of growth and came increasingly to rely on more diversified regional functions. Further west, St Paul and Kansas City grew rapidly to become major wholesaling depots. The development of improved transportation networks also led to adjustments in spatial organization within the northeast, where fierce competition between the railways and water-borne transport, coupled with equally fierce rivalry between neighbouring cities, led to a marked increase in *intra*-regional trade. This helped to lay the foundations of what was to become the manufacturing belt.

In essence, the consolidation of the manufacturing belt as the continental economic heartland was the result of initial advantage. With its large markets, well-developed transport networks and access to nearby coal reserves, it was ideally placed to take advantage of the general upsurge in demand for consumer goods, the increased efficiency of the telegraph system and postal services, the advances in industrial technology and the increasing logic of economies of scale and external economies that characterized the late nineteenth century. The overall effect was twofold:

1    Individual cities began to specialize, as producers were able to gear themselves to national rather than regional markets:

Between 1870 and 1890, advances in milling technology and concentration of ownership supported the emergence of Minneapolis as a milling centre. Furniture for the mass market centralized in fewer, larger plants using wood-working machinery .. . The rise of national brewers between 1880 and 1910 is an example of national market firms encroaching on local-regional firms. The brewers in Milwaukee and St Louis achieved economies of scale in manufacture, used production innovations such as mechanical refrigeration, and capitalized on distribution innovations made possible by the refrigerated rail car and an integrated rail network.

Meyer (1983: 160)

Similarly, musical instrument manufacture and men's clothing emerged as specialties in Boston; meat packing, furniture manufacture, and printing and publishing in Chicago; coach-building and furniture manufacture in Cincinnati; textile manufacture in Philadelphia; and so on. In smaller cities, specialization was often much more pronounced, as in the production of iron and steel, and coach-building in Columbus, furniture in Grand Rapids, agricultural implements in Springfield, and boots and shoes in Worcester. Overall, there emerged a three-part segmentation of the manufacturing belt (Figure 5.4), with a heavy bias towards consumer goods production in the ports of Baltimore, Boston and New York, a producer goods axis between Philadelphia and Cleveland, and a western cluster of rather less specialized consumer-oriented manufacturing cities.

2    This specialization provided the basis for increasing commodity flows between individual cities, thus binding the manufacturing belt together. These linkages, in turn, generated important multiplier effects through wholesaling, finance, warehousing and transportation, adding to the cumulative process of regional industrial growth and increasing the region's comparative advantage. These advantages meant that the manufacturing belt was able to attract a large proportion of any new industrial activities with large or national markets, thus stifling the chances of comparable levels of industrialization in late developing regions.

This does not mean, of course, that other regions did not become industrialized. Rather, it was the scale and the intensity of industrialization that differed: later developed regions were able to support an array of locally oriented manufacturers, together with some nationally oriented activities based on particular local advantages or raw materials; but they were rarely able to attract manufacturers of producer goods for the national market.

Fig 5.4: American manufacturing belt in 1919 (after Conzen, 1981: 340, Figure 9.13)

*Source:* Based on Knox *et al.* (1988: 117, Figure 5.1)

## FORDISM, TAYLORISM AND REGIONAL ECONOMIC CHANGE

If the template of North American economic geography had been established by 1920, the full details of industrial capitalism were etched in between 1920 and 1940, when the arrival of truck and automobile transportation triggered a further series of shifts and adjustments. Road and air travel, along with improvements in electronic communications, increased the *capacity* and *efficiency* of the economy and facilitated the functional integration of both businesses and regions at an unprecedented pace. The 1920s were the 'new economic era', and the liberal reactions to industrialism, which had characterized the progressive era before the First World War, were quickly edged aside by consumerism and boosterism.

The larger companies based in the major metropolitan centres were best placed to take advantage of the increased capacity and efficiency of the economic system. As they did so, they also exploited new principles of economic organization based on a more intensive division of labour, assembly line production and 'scientific' management (also known as 'Taylorism'). The resulting increases in efficiency and productivity meant that many goods could be *mass produced* at low prices for mass markets. The consequent combination of mass production and mass consumption is generally referred to as a Fordist regime of accumulation, after Henry Ford, the automobile manufacturer who led the way in implementing these changes.

This new regime of accumulation required ever larger companies. A flurry of company mergers soon transformed the business structure of the economy, resulting in a relatively small number of very powerful corporations that now stood poised to dominate the economy. By 1920 over 30 per cent of all jobs and nearly 50 per cent of the country's production was accounted for by just 1 per cent of all firms:

> The Captains of Industry were clearly in charge. Across the country, territorial communities watched effective control over local production slip out of their grasp. Political power came to focus on the national level of territorial integration which, for the time being, effectively bounded the operation of most businesses.
>
> Friedmann and Weaver (1979: 22)

However, the new regime of accumulation associated with this 'new economic era' fostered some serious problems. Mechanized agriculture became so 'overproductive' that commodity prices plummeted; while the industrial market became unstable as a result of the labyrinth of holding companies that had been created. In October 1929 the stock market collapsed, triggering the Great Depression in which millions of workers lost their jobs. Because of the regional division of labour that had emerged over the previous 50 years, some areas suffered particularly acute social and economic problems. The political response took the form of a 'New Deal' in which the central government took on much more responsibility, both for overall economic growth and for regional economic well-being. Before long, this evolved into a system of public macroeconomic management that came to be known as Keynesianism (after the doctrine of British economist John Maynard Keynes). In these changes, we can see that a significant shift occurred in the mode of regulation associated with the Fordist regime of accumulation, the focus of economic policies changing from regulating the supply side to a finely tuned management of the demand side.

With the outbreak of war in Europe in 1939, the entire North American economy entered a phase of accelerated growth; and in the aftermath of the war, the United States and Canada emerged not only with stronger and more efficient industries but also with new technologies and with control over new international markets. The United States, in its new, more outward-looking role as leader of the capitalist world, was able to dictate the pattern of world affairs through the terms of the Marshall Plan, its control of the Organization for European Economic Cooperation (OEEC) (forerunner of the OECD and established to administer US and Canadian postwar reconstruction aid in Europe under the Marshall Plan) and the Bretton Woods agreement (which established a new framework for international economic relations). By 1960 GNI per capita stood at US$2513 in the USA, compared with US$1909 in Canada, US$1678 in Sweden, US$1259 in the UK, US$1200 in West Germany, US$1193 in France and US$421 in Japan. By this time, however, the economic geography of North America had begun to respond to the imperatives of the new technology systems and regimes of accumulation of globalized capitalism, themes that we explore in detail in Chapter 7.

## 5.4 JAPANESE INDUSTRIALIZATION: TWO ECONOMIC MIRACLES

The rise of the Japanese economy to join western Europe and North America at the core of the modern world economy represents a major achievement and it poses some important questions in relation both to the theory and reality of economic organization and spatial change. In particular, how was it that a relatively resource-poor country like Japan was successful in industrialization, while resource-rich regions elsewhere in Asia and in Latin America were not? In other words, in what way was Japan an exception to the rest of the periphery?

Broadly speaking, the answer lies in the fact that the Japanese economy, although organized along feudal lines until well into the 19th century, was autonomous; it had never been penetrated by the capitalism of the other core regions. Moreover, the transition from feudalism to capitalism took place as a deliberate attempt to preserve national political and economic autonomy. But, even though Japan was 'lucky' in not having been politically and economically subordinated, the path to progress via industrialization was still obstructed by the other core regions' pre-emption of the technology, the infrastructure and the capital for industrial development. This raises a second important question: 'How were these obstacles overcome?' The answer, again in general terms, lies in the combination of a proto-industrial base and a strategy of military aggression, flooding overseas markets with cheap products and copying and adapting western technology – a strategy that was achieved at the expense of authoritarian government, widespread exploitation and acute regional disparities.

## THE FIRST MIRACLE: FROM FEUDALISM TO INDUSTRIAL CAPITALISM

Japan's transition from feudalism to industrial capitalism can be pinpointed to a specific year – 1868 – when the feudal political economy of the Tokugawa regime was toppled by the restoration of imperial power. For over 200 years, just as an industrial system was developing in the western hemisphere, the Tokugawa regime had attempted to sustain traditional Japanese society. To this end, the patriarchal government of the Tokugawa family excluded missionaries, banned Christianity, prohibited the construction of ships above 50 tons, closed Japanese ports to foreign vessels (Nagasaki was the single exception) and deliberately suppressed commercial enterprise. At the top of the feudal hierarchy were the nobility (the *shogunate*), the barons (*daimyos*) and warriors (*samurai*). Farmers and artisans represented the productive base exploited by these ruling classes; and only outcastes and prostitutes ranked lower than merchants.

In terms of spatial organization, the economy was built on a closed hierarchy of castle towns, each representing the administrative base of a local *shogun*. The position of a town within this hierarchy was dependent on the status of the *shogun*, which, in turn, was related to the productivity of the agricultural hinterland. As a result, the largest cities – which were to become the foundations for subsequent economic growth – emerged among the alluvial plains and the reclaimed lakes and bayheads of southern Honshu. At the top of the hierarchy was Edo (now Tokyo), which the Tokugawa regime had selected as its capital in preference to the traditional imperial capital of Kyoto. Bloated by soldiery, administrators and the entourages of the nobility in attendance at the Tokugawa court, Tokyo reached a population of around a million by the early 19th century. Kyoto and Osaka were next largest, with populations of between 300,000 and 500,000; and they were followed by Nagoya and Kanazawa, both of which stood at around 100,000.

With cities of this size, it was very difficult to suppress commerce and prevent the breakdown of the traditional political economy. As in feudal Europe, the peasantry fled the countryside in increasing numbers in response to a combination of taxation, technological improvements in agriculture, and the lure of the relative freedom and prosperity of cities. At the same time, the cities evolved into important centres of domestic manufacture: nodes of proto-industrial development that were to become the platform for Japan's subsequent development. Meanwhile, prolonged peace had reduced both the influence and the affluence of the *samurai*, drawing increasing numbers of them towards commercial and manufacturing activities. Thus:

> former peasants mingled with former warriors in secular occupations coordinated as much by market forces as by feudalistic regulations. A class-based commercial society thus developed despite the efforts of the Tokugawa leaders to maintain the pre-industrial, status-oriented society of old Japan.
>
> Light (1983: 158)

By the early 19th century, Japan had moved into a period of crises: famines and peasant uprisings, presided over by an introverted and self-serving leadership. In 1853 US Admiral Perry arrived in Edo Bay to 'persuade' the *shogunate* to open Japanese ports to trade with the USA and other foreign powers. This neocolonialist threat galvanized feelings of nationalism and xenophobia and precipitated a period of civil war among the *shogunate*. The outcome was the restoration of the Meiji imperial dynasty in 1868 by a clique of *samurai* and *daimyo* who were convinced that Japan needed to industrialize in order to maintain national independence.

Under the slogan 'national wealth and military strength', the new elite of ex-warriors set out to modernize Japan as quickly as possible. A distinctive feature of the entire process was the very high degree of state involvement. Successive governments intervened to promote industrial development by fostering capitalist monopolies (*zaibatsu*). In many instances, whole industries were created from public funds and, once established, were sold off to private enterprise at less than cost. Because early manufacturing was motivated strongly by considerations of national security, it was iron and steel, shipbuilding and armaments that were prominent in the early phase of Japanese modernization. The latest industrial technology and equipment were bought in from overseas and advisers (chiefly British) were brought in to supervise the initial stages of development. Meanwhile, the state indulged in high levels of expenditure on highways, port facilities, the banking system and public education in its attempt to 'buy' modernization. Similarly, the railway system was financed by the state under British direction before being sold to private enterprise.

The Japanese financed this modernization by harsh taxes on the agricultural sector. As a result, there began a sharp polarization between the urban and the rural economies, characterized by the impoverishment of large numbers of peasant farmers. Yet the more productive components of the agrarian sector were able to contribute significantly to Japanese economic growth. Improved technology, better seedstock and the use of fertilizers provided an increase of 2 per cent per annum in rice production during the last quarter of the 19th century and the first part of the 20th century, thereby helping to feed the growing non-farm sector without great dependence on food imports. It is important to note that these increases in agricultural productivity were not absorbed by population growth, as has been the case for most latecomers to industrialization. The Japanese demographic transition arrived later – after increases in agricultural productivity had helped to finance an emergent industrial sector but in time to provide an expanding labour force and market for industrial products.

Several other factors helped to foster rapid industrialization in Japan in the late 19th and early 20th centuries. One was the cultural order that allowed the Japanese to follow government leadership and accept new ways of life: a recurring theme in modern Japanese economic history. Another was the success of educational reforms: 95 per cent of all children of school age were receiving an elementary education by 1905. Third, Japanese sericulture (silk production) provided the basis for a lucrative export trade with which to help finance expenditure on overseas technology, materials and expertise. It has been estimated that, between 1870 and 1930, the raw silk trade alone was able to finance as much as 40 per cent of Japan's entire imports of raw materials and machinery. Finally, and most important, were the benefits deriving from military aggression. Naval victories over China (1894–95) and Russia (1904–05) and the annexation of Korea (1910) not only provided expanded markets for Japanese goods in Asia but also provided indemnities for the losers (which paid for the costs of conquest) and stimulated the armaments industry, shipbuilding, and industrial technology and financial organization in general.

By the early 1900s, a broad spectrum of industries had been successfully established. Most were geared towards the domestic market in a kind of pre-emptive import substitution strategy. The textile industry, however, had already begun to establish an export base. Unable to compete with western countries in the production of high-quality textiles, the Japanese concentrated on the production of inexpensive goods, competing initially with western producers for markets in Asia. Their success derived largely from labour-intensive processes in which high productivity and low wages were maintained through a combination of (1) exhortations to personal sacrifice in the cause of national independence and (2) strict government suppression of labour unrest.

## JAPAN ADVANCES

During the First World War, Japan was able to become a major supplier of textiles, armaments and industrial equipment on world markets, to almost double its merchant marine tonnage, and to establish a balance of payments surplus. Between 1919 and 1929 this position was consolidated, again under government sponsorship. Steel manufacturing, engineering and textiles were further developed and aircraft and automobile industries were established. Meanwhile, Japanese innovations began to emerge, weakening the dependence on western technology and providing an important competitive advantage. This pattern of progress was halted, however, by the stagnation of international trade that followed the stock market collapse of 1929 and the subsequent depression. Once again, state intervention provided a critical boost. A massive devaluation of the yen in 1931 allowed Japanese producers to undersell on the world market, while a Bureau of Industrial Rationalization was set up to increase efficiency, lower costs and weed out smaller, less profitable concerns.

Although these interventions helped to sustain Japanese industrialization and improve Japan's overall economic independence, they led directly towards crisis. Western governments – particularly that of the United States – began seriously to resist the purchase of Japanese goods. In Japan, the austerity resulting from devaluation and rationalization precipitated social and political unrest. The government response was to indulge in further military expenditure and to adopt a more aggressive territorial policy. In 1931 the Japanese army advanced into Manchuria to create a puppet state. In 1936 a military faction gained full political power and, declaring a Greater East Asian Co-Prosperity Sphere, set about full-scale war with China the following year. In 1939 Japan attacked British colonies in East Asia and by 1940 the Japanese 'had become heavily committed to an industrial empire based on war. In that year, 17 per cent of the entire national output was for war purposes' (Kornhauser, 1989: 119). By this time, as the rest of the world quickly realized, Japan had attained the status of an advanced industrial economy. The military leaders overplayed their hand, however, by attacking the United States. With defeat in 1945, Japanese industry lay in ruins. In 1946 output was only 30 per cent of the prewar level; and the United States, having begun to weaken the power of the *zaibatsu* and to impose widespread social and political reforms, was set to impose punitive reparations.

## THE SECOND MIRACLE: POSTWAR RECONSTRUCTION AND GROWTH

Within five years, the Japanese economy had recovered to its prewar levels of output. Throughout the 1950s and 1960s the annual rate of growth of the economy held at around 10 per cent, compared with growth rates of around 2 per cent per annum in North America and western Europe. After beginning the postwar period at the bottom of the international manufacturing league table, Japan had risen to join the other developed countries by the 1980s (Figure 5.5). By 1980, for example, Japan had outstripped, even in *absolute* terms, all of the major industrial core countries in the production of ships, automobiles and television sets and only the Soviet Union was producing more steel.

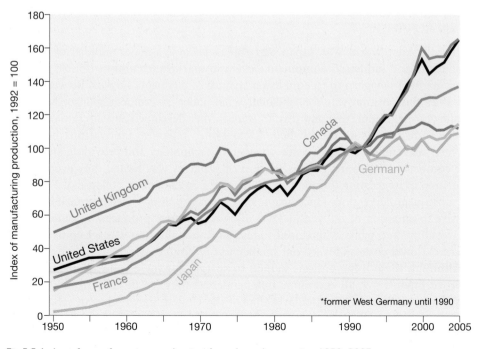

Fig 5.5: Index of manufacturing production for selected countries, 1950–2005

Source: Based on online data from US Department of Labor, Bureau of Labor Statistics, *International Comparisons of Manufacturing Productivity and Unit Labor Cost Trends*

Explanations of this 'miracle' have identified a variety of contributory factors. One of the most important, in the first instance, was the reversal of United States' policy. Cold War strategy, in response to China's pursuit (in 1949) of a communist path to development, dictated that the initial punitive stance should be replaced by massive economic aid in order to create a bastion against the spread of communism in East Asia. In return for providing an offshore bastion in the containment of the Soviet Union during the early Cold War, Japan was allowed to re-enter the world economy on terms that were favourable to its economic growth. For example, high Japanese tariffs were tolerated at the same time that the USA was sponsoring a world economic order based on tariff reduction or removal. The Korean conflict (1950–53) helped to reinforce this logic and at the same time stimulated the Japanese economy through US expenditure on Japanese supplies and military bases. Once under way, the reconstruction of the Japanese economy was able to draw on some of its previously established advantages: a well-educated, flexible, loyal and relatively cheap labour force, a large national market with good internal communications, a good geographical situation for trade within Asia, a high degree of cooperation between industry and government and a model of industrial organization – derived from the *zaibatsu* – big enough to compete with the transnational corporations of western Europe and North America.

In addition, several *new* factors helped to metamorphose reconstruction into spectacular growth. These included the following:

1 Exceptionally high levels of personal savings (e.g., 19.5 per cent of personal disposable income in 1980, compared with 4.7 per cent in the United States), which helped to fund high levels of capital investment.

2 The acquisition of new technology: between 1950 and 1969 Japan was able to acquire, for around US$1.5 billion in royalties and licences, a body of thoroughly tested US technology that had cost the United States US$20 billion *a year* in research and development (R&D). More recently, Japanese investment in domestic R&D has overtaken (in relative terms) that of both western Europe and North America, providing important advantages in production technology and product design. Overall, Japanese investment in technology in 1980 amounted to 6 per cent of its industrial turnover, compared with 1 per cent in the United States. Despite sluggish economic growth in the 1990s, Japanese expenditure on R&D as a percentage of GDP (3.13 per cent) remained higher than that of both western Europe and North America (e.g., the United Kingdom (1.88 per cent), Germany (2.49 per cent), USA (2.69 per cent) and Canada (1.99 per cent)) in 2004. This is also well above both the averages for the EU (1.81 per cent) and the OECD countries (2.2 per cent) (OECD, 2006).

3 New means of government support. On the one hand, the construction of a rigid and sophisticated system of import protection – both tariff and non-tariff barriers – shielded domestic markets from overseas competition. On the other hand, the growth of domestic industry was fostered by a multitude of tax concessions and by the provision of investment finance through the Japan Development Bank. Most important of all, however, was the orchestration of industrial growth by the Ministry of International Trade and Industry (MITI) (reorganized as the Ministry of Economy, Trade and Industry (METI) in 2001). In particular, MITI identified key recovery sectors (e.g., steel, shipbuilding) and potential growth sectors (e.g., automobiles, electronics, computers) and facilitated their

development by providing finance, ensuring protection from foreign competition, subsidizing technological development and arranging corporate mergers. MITI also organized Japanese corporations into business networks (known as *keiretsu*), setting up favourable trade policies, technology policies and fiscal policies to help Japanese industry compete successfully in the world economy.

This second economic miracle was remarkable not only for its overall success in terms of economic performance but also because it represented a unique path to development, one that was able to combine economic growth with income distribution. Real wages (that is, the effective purchasing power of wages) rose substantially, while income inequality was reduced to one of the lowest levels in the world. Equally remarkable was the interdependence of government and industry, characterized by some as 'Japan, Inc.'. Also important was the exceptional degree of social stability and management–labour cooperation during this phase of tremendous change. This stability and cooperation was, like the interdependence of government and industry, a reflection of Japanese nationalism and people's commitment to rebuilding the nation. The same sense of national identity and purpose helped foster people's adherence to traditional values and lifestyles, their willingness to work many more hours than their European and American counterparts and their willingness to defer consumption, thus providing a pool of savings that could be invested in Japanese industry.

## Box 5.3 Regional dimensions of Japanese industrialization

The pace and weight of postwar industrialization have dramatically rearranged the economic landscape that existed at the close of the Tokugawa period. In many ways, the changes wrought on the Japanese landscape parallel those that occurred in response to the industrialization of western Europe and North America. Existing urban centres (the castle towns) grew differentially according to their adaptability as regional industrial, commercial or administrative centres; while new kinds of specialist settlements – ports, mining towns, heavy manufacturing towns and transport centres – emerged and grew rapidly to become major nodes of urbanization. Similarly, the expansion and diversification of the industrial economy imposed a progressive spatial division of labour. The logic of agglomeration economies and economies of scale made for regional specialization, something that was strongly encouraged by government policies through MITI. Within this overall transformation, one distinctive feature to emerge was the large company town. This, of course, was a reflection of the unique role of the *zaibatsu* in Japanese industrialization. The early leaders among the *zaibatsu* – Mitsui, Mitsubishi and Sumitomo – inevitably came to dominate their host cities (which included Omuta, Niihama, Nobeoka and Nagasaki); while later established *zaibatsu*, as well as some of the corporate giants spawned by postwar growth, sponsored new company towns in newly industrializing regions (the city of Hitachi, northeast of Mito, for example).

What was most distinctive about the geography of industrialization in Japan, however, was the sheer intensity of development that was crammed into the relatively limited amount of suitable land. The economic miracle of the 1960s was founded on the import of raw materials and the manufacturing and export of finished products. Japan's resurgent industries thus flourished best in coastal locations, close to deepwater ports. The megapolitan Pacific Corridor between Tokyo and Kobe is the embodiment of these developments. It developed into the core region of modern Japanese industrialization because it not only had several deepwater ports but also large pools of skilled labour and relatively large amounts of flat land. The entire region, known as the Tokaido megalopolis, is comparable in size and scope to the megapolitan area in the United States that stretches from Boston through New York and Philadelphia to Washington. The Tokaido megalopolis contains more than 50 million people and accounts for more than 80 per cent of Japan's total GDP. In 2000 Osaka alone accounted for a GDP that was greater than those of all but eight countries in the world. Transportation has been a key factor in the successful development of the Pacific Corridor. Although port facilities were a precondition for the region's success, internal connections within the region were poor, making it difficult for manufacturers and suppliers to exploit agglomeration economies and restricting the movement of workers and consumers. In response, the Japanese government undertook a massive programme of infrastructure investment. The showpiece of this programme is the Shinkansen railway system. First opened in 1964 to coincide with the Tokyo Olympic Games, the 'bullet trains' of the Shinkansen have turned the entire Pacific Corridor into a daily commuter belt.

The Pacific Corridor's prewar industrial base was dominated by cotton, silk, other textiles, toys, glass and porcelain. These industries are still present in the region but have been dwarfed by the growth of iron and steel, heavy metal products and machinery, shipping and shipbuilding, petrochemicals, paper products, ceramics, automobile and truck manufacturing, cameras, scientific instruments and electrical and electronics goods of all kinds. Tokyo itself has grown into a world city of the first rank, with a banking and financial sector that compares to those of London and New York. The population of the Tokyo metropolitan area in 2005 was 26.4 million.

The growth of the Pacific Corridor has inevitably brought serious problems: overcrowding, congestion, environmental pollution and ground subsidence. Meanwhile, the concentration of economic activity in the Pacific Corridor has resulted in a relative lack of development elsewhere. Japan is thus characterized, like Europe and North America, by a centre–periphery pattern. In the Japanese case, the periphery consists of northern Hokkaido, Honshu, Kyushu and Shikoku. Like peripheral regions within older core nations, they have experienced the backwash effects of metropolitan development: selective outmigration, restricted investment (both public and private), and limited employment opportunities. In addition, much of the periphery has a climate that most Japanese find severe, thus compounding feelings of deprivation and remoteness.

More recently, the high costs of operating in Japan have begun to weigh on Japanese corporations, straining their allegiance to the nationalist project of economic development. Many larger Japanese corporations have moved production facilities elsewhere in East and Southeast Asia in search of lower production costs and expanding markets. METI attempted to counter the consequent loss of Japanese capital and technology by developing a technopolis programme that sought to establish the infrastructure necessary to lure Japanese capital to domestic high-tech industries. However, METI no longer has direct influence over Japanese corporations, neither do these corporations decide their strategies primarily within the framework of Japan's economic interests.

This decoupling of the systematic interdependence between Japanese government and industry means that places and regions in Japan are becoming much more interdependent with places and regions elsewhere. It also means that it is increasingly difficult to sustain the system of lifelong tenure for workers in large corporations, which has distinguished Japanese employment practices for decades. Not surprisingly, people's willingness to work long hours and defer consumption in the cause of national economic development has also declined. This unravelling of Japan's successful system of economic development has been reflected in a series of recent economic and political crises. It is also beginning to be reflected in shifting values and lifestyles. Traditional patriarchal values and nationalistic bureaucratic indoctrination have little meaning for the generation that has grown up in affluence.

## 5.5 EMERGENCE OF 'ORGANIZED' CAPITALISM

The development of the industrial economies of the trinodal core brought with it a number of important changes in the nature of economic, social, political and cultural relations (or, put another way, changes in technology systems, regimes of accumulation and modes of regulation), each of which became woven into the urban and regional landscapes of the industrial core regions. Collectively, these changes characterize what has been called 'organized' capitalism. Its principal features include (Lash and Urry, 1987: 3–4):

1  Concentration and centralization of industrial, banking and commercial capital as markets became increasingly regulated; the increased interconnectedness of finance and industry; the proliferation of cartels.
2  Emergence of extractive and manufacturing industry as the dominant economic sector.
3  Concentration of industrial capitalist relations within relatively few industrial sectors and within a small number of countries.
4  Expansion of empires and the control by the core economies of markets and production in overseas settings.
5  Increasing separation of ownership from control and the elaboration of complex managerial hierarchies within companies.
6  Growth of a new managerial/scientific/technological intelligentsia and of a bureaucratically employed middle class.
7  Emergence of 'modernism' – a cultural–ideological configuration involving the glorification of science and technical rationality, a machine- and future-oriented aesthetic and a nationalistic frame of reference.
8  Growth of collective organizations in the labour market: trade unions, employers' associations, nationally organized professions, etc.
9  Regional economic specialization.
10  Dominance of particular regions by large metropolitan areas.
11  An increasing inter-articulation between countries and large monopolies and between collective organizations and countries as states increasingly intervene in social conflicts and become involved in welfare state legislation.

Clearly, organized capitalism and its attendant regime of accumulation and mode of regulation did not emerge in the same way everywhere. There are three main factors that determined the timing of these changes and the extent to which a particular national economy developed the characteristics of 'organized' capitalism:

- First is the *point in history at which it begins to industrialize*: the earlier this was, the less 'organized' capitalism became, because later industrializers needed to begin at higher levels of concentration and centralization of capital in order to compete with established industrial economies.
- Second is the *extent to which pre-industrial institutions survived* into the capitalist period:

  Britain and Germany became more highly organized capitalist societies than France and the United States: this is because the former two countries did not experience a 'bourgeois revolution' and as a result, guilds, corporate local government, and merchant, professional, aristocratic, university and church bodies remained relatively intact.

  Lash and Urry (1987: 5)

- Third is the *size of the country*: for the industry of small countries to compete internationally, resources had to be channelled into relatively few sectors and firms. This, in turn, meant that coordination between state and industry was facilitated.

German capitalism became 'organized' during the last quarter of the 19th century, while American capitalism was organized fairly early on at the top (e.g., through the concentration of industry, increasing inter-articulation of banks, industry and the state and the formation of cartels) but very late and only partially at the bottom (e.g., the development of national trades union organizations, working-class political parties and the welfare state). British capitalism, in contrast, was organized rather early at the bottom but late at the top; while French capitalism only came to be organized, at both top and bottom, after the Second World War.

The characteristics of organized capitalism thus came to be woven into the urban and regional landscapes of the core regions rather unevenly. Meanwhile, they came to represent not just a distinctive set of economic, social, political and cultural relations, but also the context – the preconditions – for further transformations of capitalism and the new economic landscapes to emerge with the onset of globalized capitalism.

## CHANGING ROLE OF THE STATE

It is no accident that the rise of competitive capitalism and the evolution of industrial economies took place side by side with the emergence of the modern nation-state. Within Europe, it was the system of nation-states, once established in place of the earlier dynastic kingdoms and empires, that fostered the economic, social and political organization required by the Industrial Revolution. At the same time, strong competitiveness between nation-states provided a strong incentive for technological innovation. It is important to bear in mind, however, that few nation-states were 'natural' entities developed from distinctive cultural or philosophical bases. Rather, they were *constructed* in order to clothe, and enclose, the developing political economy of industrial capitalism. It follows that the process of building nation-states involved the resolution of successive crises that arose from the interaction of territory, economy, culture and government.

One series of crises arose from the long struggle to make state boundaries fit populations with feelings of (or at least the potential for) common identity. This struggle involved (1) states attempting to build nations from a diversity of peoples, and (2) peoples with a common identity, nations, attempting to create an autonomous state. The former has often involved the penetration by powerful regions or groups of neighbouring territories with different cultures, languages and economic institutions. As a result, many nation-states came into being with inbuilt core–periphery contrasts, with sociopolitical tensions compounding economic differentials. We examine the reaction to these developments in Chapter 13.

Another series of crises arose from the increasing degree of organization required by capitalism. The evolution of the industrial core regions posed a succession of problems, which resulted in *more* state intervention in a *greater variety* of fields. The initial advantage gained by British manufacturers with the advent of the Industrial Revolution soon prompted businessmen elsewhere to realize that the old doctrine of *laissez-faire* and free trade only served the interests of the dominant economy. As a result, governments everywhere were looked to as protectors – through tariffs and quotas – against low-priced British imports.

Meanwhile, the coming of the railway involved the state in another sphere – investment in infrastructure – because of the railways' economic and strategic importance. Problems of public health, working conditions, housing and civil disorder induced further kinds of state involvement, as did the need to provide a stable price system for the successful operation of private industry, the need to manage the cyclical fluctuations of the industrial economy and the need to improve the quality of the workforce and its managers through formal education. Of course, the *capacity* of governments to intervene in all these matters was dependent on economic growth. Nevertheless, it was by no means the wealthiest economies that led the way in terms of state activity, since public expenditure is mediated through the complex arena of politics.

In detail, then, the development of state functions has been complex. It is possible, however, to identify two major trends in the nature of the changes that have taken place:

1   The *centralization* of the functions of states, whereby local and regional activities have been rationalized into centralized national bureaucracies as the organization of government has attempted to keep up with the changing scale of economic organization. With increasingly powerful central bureaucracies, the power of politicians at both local and national levels has been constrained and this, in turn, has led to crises in the legitimacy of political institutions. One response has been the intensification of demands for the regional devolution of power by the representatives of communities in peripheral areas. Another has been the growth of forms of direct action in the shape of grassroots pressure groups. These are both examined in more detail in Chapter 13.

2   The dramatic expansion of the *public economy* as governments became increasingly drawn into the creation of welfare states. In most core countries, the public economy channels a vast amount of resources into everything from defence, health, education and income security to transport, infrastructural development and industrial investment; and conditions the whole of the private economy through everything from price guarantees and labour laws to tax structures and import tariffs. Italy, Sweden and the United Kingdom had by the 1970s reached

the stage where more than 50 per cent of their GDP was committed to public expenditure and most of the other industrial core countries are now approaching this figure, having almost doubled their share of their respective national economies since the 1950s. This is despite government downsizing through privatization (the sale of government assets and contracting out services to the private sector) in the 1980s and 1990s, as occurred most visibly in the United Kingdom, where public expenditure nevertheless remains high, but is now at just under 40 per cent of GDP. Public expenditure is still high in countries that have not pursued an aggressive privatization programme, such as in the Scandinavian countries of Sweden (55 per cent) and Denmark (52 per cent).

Indeed, the sheer magnitude of the public economy has come to blur the boundary between the public and the private sectors. Many governments have even been impelled to intervene – for a variety of reasons – to prevent the collapse of private business corporations (examples have included the US government's efforts to rescue Lockheed and Chrysler in the 1970s, the UK government's efforts in the 1980s to sustain British Leyland, as well as the US government airline bailouts after the terrorist attacks on New York and Washington on 11 September 2001). Most important of all, governments everywhere have become the largest single consumers of the goods produced by private-sector enterprise. In short, the public economy is pervasive in its effects on economic well-being.

## GEOGRAPHY OF THE PUBLIC ECONOMY

Nearly all this public sector activity has a geographical expression. One of the most obvious examples is the deliberate bias of regional policy and planning, which we examine in Chapter 13. In this section, we emphasize the spatial bias – often unintentional – that results from other aspects of the public economy.

The geography of public finance is a complex subject and it is hazardous to attempt detailed comparisons between countries. It is possible, however, to identify major categories of activity and to illustrate their spatial implications with specific examples. In this context, it is convenient to recognize four major categories of government *expenditure*:

1 The salaries of central government employees, including clerks, bureaucrats and other workers in the armed forces, education, public health, the nationalized industries, the police and the courts. Expenditure on these salaries is of course localized in capital cities. In Washington, DC, for example, almost one-third of all earnings come from federal employment. In addition, government salaries can have an important impact in small or medium-sized cities that have been selected for specific functions – defence installations, for example, or decentralized branches of the bureaucracy (as in the UK government's relocation of social security offices from London to Newcastle upon Tyne).

2 Transfer payments to particular population groups (e.g., the elderly, the unemployed, families with dependent children) and particular industries (e.g., agricultural subsidies and guaranteed prices). These expenditures involve complex flows of monies and are geographically localized only in as much as the 'target' populations and industries are localized.

3  Purchasing and subcontracting from businesses in the private sector. This includes a wide range of items – buildings, roads, dams, power stations, military equipment, office equipment and publishing, for example – which can make for highly localized impacts. Defence expenditure has been researched in some detail and it provides good examples of the kind of bias that can result from government purchasing. It seems that the employment generated by defence expenditure generally tends to be sufficiently localized (because it is concentrated in the hands of just a few giant corporations – e.g., General Dynamics, McDonnell-Douglas, United Technologies, Boeing, General Electric, Lockheed and Hughes Aircraft in the USA) as to create significant multiplier effects. But the resultant spatial bias seems to bear no consistent relationship to core–periphery patterns or to dimensions of economic geography. In the UK, defence expenditures after the Second World War came to sustain around 1.25 million jobs – about 5 per cent of all employment – and pay for around 25 per cent of all the R&D activity undertaken in the country. Both the direct spin-off from the employment and the indirect 'seedbed' effects of R&D tended to reinforce the core–periphery structure of the UK economy, with the southeast, the southwest and the East Midlands benefiting most while the likes of Yorkshire and Northern Ireland were under-represented both in terms of job creation and R&D activity. In the USA, by way of contrast, defence procurements tended to be biased away from the industrial core. Taking R&D activity as well as prime defence contracts into account, and allowing for the effects of subcontracting, it was California that benefited most from Department of Defense spending, together with Washington (state), Massachusetts, Maryland, Arizona and Connecticut.

4  Local government expenditure. In many core countries, this soon came to approach the levels of expenditure by central governments (although a large portion of local expenditure is always dependent on revenues provided by central governments in the form of grants and revenue-sharing funds). What is most striking about local government expenditure is that, after fulfilling their statutory obligations, local governments vary a great deal both in the amount they spend and the categories of their expenditure. This reflects a complex interaction between local resources, local needs and the local political climate.

In order to gauge the net impact of these expenditures, we have to set them against the geography of *taxation*. Such an exercise is very difficult to achieve at any level of detail, but we can illustrate the kind of biases that can emerge by reference to federal taxes in the USA. Around 40 per cent of all federal revenues are derived from personal income taxes, with another 25 per cent coming from taxes on pension trusts and a further 15 per cent from taxes on corporate profits. *To a large extent*, therefore, the geography of federal revenues reflects the geography of income and economic health.

Yet the *structure* of the tax system can have less straightforward geographical implications. The federal tax breaks that are geared to encourage business investment in new equipment and machinery, for example, tend to benefit growth industries in growth areas; as do the more generous rates of depreciation allowed for new industrial and commercial plants. Contrariwise, it should be acknowledged that studies of industrial location have established fairly clearly that tax differences between states are not a significant factor in inducing industrial *relocation*.

Although it is not possible to quantify the local effect of these structural characteristics of the tax system, it is possible to specify the magnitude of the *net* flows of monies between the federal government and individual states. Interstate differentials in such flows have tended to diminish during the postwar period as the federal tax system has become more uniformly progressive and as state variations in per capita incomes have narrowed. Differences between states remain substantial, however, with a marked disadvantage of states in the manufacturing belt and the northeast. This has been interpreted by some as a product of the manipulation of the political 'pork barrel'. Certainly the traditional dominance of the democrats in the Deep South ensured the seniority of its federal senators and thus the chairmanship of committees of Congress controlling the allocation and distribution of federal funds. Moreover, members of Congress do seek positions on the committees of Congress that control the allocation and distribution of federal funds, they do seek membership on the committees and subcommittees most relevant to the needs of their constituents, and many decisions are blatantly taken for electoral reasons. But political and electoral variables are weak predictors of the overall geography of federal outlays.

What is important about patterns of federal expenditure in the present context is that the *marginal impact* of the flow of federal funds seems to have been much greater in the south and west. By improving the infrastructure of communications, transportation, sewage facilities and energy, the federal government helped to establish the *preconditions* for the development of new industries in the Sunbelt. By direct and indirect investment in electronics research, semiconductors, computers, aeronautics and scientific instruments in the south and west, the federal government enabled the Sunbelt to capture some of the most dynamic activities of the advanced capitalist economy.

## INCREASING GLOBAL INTERDEPENDENCE

Although the industrial core regions have been the focus of this chapter, the historical process of industrialization must be seen in a global perspective. Quite simply, the ascent of the industrial core regions could not have taken place without the foodstuffs, raw materials and markets provided by the rest of the world. In order to ensure the availability of the produce, materials and markets on which they were increasingly dependent, the industrial core countries vigorously pursued a second phase of colonialism and imperialism, creating a series of 'trading empires'.

As soon as the Industrial Revolution had gathered momentum, European colonial powers embarked on the inland penetration of mid-continental grassland zones in order to exploit them for grain or stock production – although the detailed pattern and timing of this exploitation was heavily conditioned by innovations such as the railways, barbed wire and refrigeration – hence the settlement of the prairies and the pampas in the Americas, the *veldt* in Africa and the Murray-Darling and Canterbury Plains in Australasia. The emigration that fuelled this colonization was itself a major factor in the economic development of the core regions, siphoning off the 'surplus' population that was generated by demographic transition and swollen by the rationalization of rural economies. Meanwhile, as the demand for tropical plantation products increased, most of the tropical world came under the political control – direct or indirect – of one or another of the industrial core countries.

The outcome of this expansionism was that the colonies and client states of the industrial core began to specialize in the production of those foodstuffs and raw materials (1) for which there was an established demand in the industrial core and (2) for which they held a comparative advantage. *This specialization, in turn, established a complex pattern of interdependent development that was articulated, above all, in patterns of international trade.* From the start, however, this expanded and more closely integrated international system was unevenly balanced. On the one hand, the influence of the core countries on the cultural and institutional organization of the peripheral countries has moulded their economic organization to fit core-oriented needs and core-inspired philosophies of 'development' (see Chapters 9 to 11). On the other, a variety of barriers and imperfections have blunted the effectiveness of international trade as an 'engine of growth'. While *some* of the semi-peripheral and peripheral national economies were able to achieve considerable momentum as a result of the stimulus provided by rapidly increasing levels of demand transmitted from the industrial core regions, many were not. In very general terms, the type and profitability of activity in semi-peripheral and peripheral regions was determined by effective distance from the industrial core that represented their major market. Within the resultant zones of specialization, the beneficial effects of trade were conditioned by a variety of factors, including variations in climate, topography, pre-existing systems of agriculture, and population densities. In practice:

> The trade impetus to growth was … immensely important for Argentina and Uruguay in Latin America, South Africa and Zimbabwe (formerly Southern Rhodesia) in Africa, Australia and New Zealand, and, to a lesser extent, in Sri Lanka (formerly Ceylon). Elsewhere, there was a significant impact, *but this was inadequate to get sustained development going*, for example on the west coast of Africa. For countries such as India, Pakistan, Bangladesh, Iraq and Iran, *the export trades were too small relative to the total population* to provide much impetus for development, except in very restricted areas.
>
> Chisholm (1982: 88, emphasis added)

In short, the once-and-for-all benefits of specialization and international trade enabled some regions and countries to ascend within the world-system while enhancing the position of those at the top. For the rest, the subsequent prospects of economic growth through trade have been further diminished by the inbuilt differential between themselves and the better off in terms of access to capital, since this translates into a differential in the use of technology; and this, in turn, keeps productivity at relatively low levels. As a result, the amount of labour power required to produce a given quantity of exports from the industrial core will generally be much less than that needed to produce an equivalent value of exports from peripheral countries. From this point of view, the international trade system is characterized by unequal exchange.

Attempts to shortcircuit this inbuilt handicap by borrowing capital with which to purchase new (but not always appropriate) technology have almost always resulted in a debt trap as compounded interest on loans has outpaced increases in the rate of productivity.

In addition, many peripheral countries have been affected by another inbuilt handicap: the differential elasticities of demand for their products vis-à-vis those of their trading partners in the industrial core. In general, elasticities of demand for the primary commodities that have become the staples of the periphery are low, so that even fairly large price reductions in overseas markets elicit only a modest rise in demand. Similarly, demand for these products will only increase very slightly in response to increases in the purchasing power of consumers in the core countries. Conversely, elasticities of demand for manufactured goods are generally very high. The net result is that the terms of trade have tended to work to the cumulative advantage of the industrial core.

In other words, although the world economy has come to be characterized by interdependent relationships as a result of the spatial division of labour, it is the *periphery* that has carried the burden of dependency and this is one of the themes that we explore in detail in Part 3.

## 5.6 PRINCIPLES OF ECONOMIC GEOGRAPHY: LESSONS FROM THE INDUSTRIAL ERA

It will be clear from the case histories in this chapter that the increasing complexity of economic organization and spatial change makes it difficult to generalize about organizing principles or characteristic features. What we can do, however, is to emphasize once more the recurring importance of certain elements and the emergence of others in interacting to produce the economic landscapes of the industrial core regions during the industrial era. Among those that carried over from previous eras are:

- distribution of natural resources – with iron ore and coal exercising a central role in the industrial era
- demographic change – particularly (1) the timing of the demographic transition in relation to industrialization and (2) the role of large-scale migrations in relation to changing labour markets
- technological change – including improvements and innovations in transport and communications
- colonialism and territorial expansion as responses to the law of diminishing returns
- changes in institutional and sociopolitical settings
- changes in the spatial distribution of investment in response to the shifting comparative advantages enjoyed by producers in different areas
- import substitution as a mechanism of ascent within the world economy
- militarism and geopolitical change as a mechanism of ascent within the world economy.

In addition, the industrial era saw the emergence of several new dimensions of spatial-economic organization and the increased prominence of others:

- extension of the world economy to a global scale with a corresponding extension of the spatial division of labour and the consequent intensification of the interdependencies between core, semi-periphery and periphery
- replacement of 'liberal' merchant capitalism with a competitive and, later, an increasingly organized form of industrial capitalism characterized by distinct, specialized regional economies organized around growing urban centres
- eclipse of the European core of the world economy by the ascent of the United States and Japan
- emergence of distinctive core–periphery contrasts within the industrial core territories of the world economy

- agglomeration of industrial activity as a result of the logic of economies of scale and the multiplier effect
- modification of urban systems by the addition of new kinds of towns and cities – mining towns, heavy manufacturing centres, power centres and transport nodes – and the rapid growth of larger pre-industrial cities as they benefited disproportionately (because of their established markets, entrepreneurship, trading links and commercial infrastructure) from the various growth impulses that characterize industrialization
- imprint of cyclical fluctuations in the pace and nature of economic activity
- 'differential of contemporaneousness' in regional economic development – a phenomenon linked to the uneven impacts of the process of technological diffusion and changing technology systems
- adaptation of private firms to the changing opportunities and constraints of different technology systems, resulting in evolving 'regimes of accumulation', from simple manufacturing, through machinofacture, to Fordism
- adaptation of wider society to these changing regimes of accumulation, resulting in another evolutionary process – that of changing modes of regulation – in which the increasing intervention of governments in economic development was the single most important development
- emergence of an 'organized' form of capitalism, founded on the power and authority of independent countries, characterized by a sophisticated interdependence of firms, industries, regions and governments, and forming the basis for core-periphery relationships at various geographic scales.

## KEY SOURCES AND SUGGESTED READING

Borchert, J. 1967. American metropolitan evolution, *Geographical Review*, 57, 301–32.
Castells, M. 2000. *The Information Age: Economy, Society and Culture: Volume 1, The Rise of the Network Society* 2nd edn. Oxford: Blackwell.
Dunford, M. 1990. Theories of regulation, *Society and Space*, 8, 297–321.
Galor, O. and Weil, D. 2000. Population, technology and growth: from Malthusian stagnation to the demographic transition and beyond, *American Economic Review*, 90(4), 806–28.
Hansen, G. and Prescott, E. 2002. Malthus to Solow, *American Economic Review*, 94(2), 1205–17.
Haywood, J. 1998. *Historical Atlas of the 19th Century World 1783–1914*. New York: Barnes & Noble.
Hugill, P. 1994. *World Trade since 1431: Geography, Technology, and Capitalism*. Baltimore, MD: Johns Hopkins University Press.
Hugill, P. 1999. *Global Communications since 1844: Geography, Technology, and Capitalism*. Baltimore, MD: Johns Hopkins University Press.
Pollard, S. 1981. *Peaceful Conquest: The Industrialization of Europe, 1760–1970*. Oxford: Oxford University Press.

## RELATED WEBSITES

George C. Marshall Foundation: http://www.marshallfoundation.org/
the Marshall Foundation's website contains a summary of the Marshall Plan, examples of its uses, with maps and photographs and consideration of the plan's origins

History Learning Site: http://www.historylearningsite.co.uk/
this Association of Teachers website contains hyperlinks to a wealth of information on British history including the Industrial Revolution and the Second World War

Internet Modern History Sourcebook: http://www.fordham.edu/halsall/mod/modsbook14.html
this searchable online bibliography (maintained by Fordham University) offers a variety of
resources on modern history, including texts on the Industrial Revolution and the Second
World War

Ministry of Economy, Trade and Industry: http://www.meti.go.jp/english/index.html
METI (formerly the Ministry of International Trade and Industry (MITI)) provides statistics and
reports on Japan's economy, trade and industry

Organization for Economic Cooperation and Development: http://www.oecd.org/
OECD's website contains economic and trade information and reports for the 30 industrialized
countries comprising the OECD (e.g., Australia, Canada, France, Germany, Japan, New Zealand,
United Kingdom, United States)

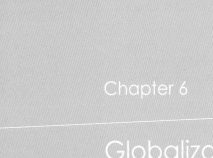

Chapter 6

Globalization of
production
systems

Picture credit: Paul Knox

After the Second World War the economies of the industrial core regions began to enter a substantially different phase in terms of *what* they produced, *how* they produced it and *where* they produced it. This phase is sometimes referred to as advanced or disorganized capitalism. It typically involves a combination of ingredients:

> Most especially: the accelerated internationalization of economic processes; a frenetic international financial system; the use of new information technologies; new kinds of production; different modes of state intervention; and the increasing involvement of culture as a factor in and of production.

> Thrift (2002: 19)

It evolved in response to the increasing inflexibility of the old system of Fordist industrial capitalism. Faced with the saturation of domestic consumer markets, increasing overseas competition, increasing costs of unionized labour and of governmental welfare provision, the industrial corporations of the core economies began to pursue new and more flexible strategies. They reorganized themselves, redeployed their operations and revised their relationships with labour unions and governments. The result has been the deindustrialization of the core economies, the industrialization of certain semi-peripheral countries and the expansion of financial and business services on a global scale.

## 6.1 TRANSITION TO ADVANCED CAPITALISM

The shift to advanced capitalism has been a result of the cumulative interaction of several processes. As in all of the previous major economic transitions we have described, the importance of these processes has been revealed only after a period of *crisis* for the old order. In this case, the crisis was thrown into focus by a phase of stagflation and intensified by a sudden increase in the price of oil.

## PRELUDE: CRISIS OF FORDISM

The crisis for the Fordist regime of industrial capitalism emerged abruptly in the early 1970s, throwing into reverse the postwar industrial boom. This reversal is clearly illustrated by the performance of the US economy. In overall terms, the US economy performed exceptionally well from the late 1940s right through to the early 1970s. Real disposable income per capita rose from just over US$2200 (in constant 1972 dollars) in 1947 to over US$3800 in 1972. The 1960s were particularly prosperous, with economic growth averaging over 4 per cent per year, thus expanding GNI by 50 per cent over the decade. Meanwhile, the average family obtained a real increase of over 30 per cent in its disposable income; these were the years of J.K. Galbraith's 'affluent society'.

After the early 1970s, however, US economic growth averaged only 2.2 per cent, while productivity in the private business sector, having increased at around 3.3 per cent per year in the 1960s, fell away to 1.3 per cent per year in the 1970s: 'By 1979, the typical family with a $20,000 income had only 7 per cent more real purchasing power than it had a full decade earlier. The years had brought a mere $25 more per week in purchasing power for the average family' (Bluestone and Harrison, 1982: 4). Unemployment, having remained steady at round 4.5 per cent until the early 1970s, almost doubled over the next five years, levelling off at around 10 per cent by the mid-1980s. The rate of inflation doubled from around 2.5 per cent per year in the 1960s to over 5 per cent per year in the mid-1980s. Meanwhile, in 1971, the US economy had moved, for the first time during the 20th century, into a negative trade balance with the rest of the world: a performance repeated in 19 of the next 21 years.

The 'system shock' precipitated by the rise in oil prices in 1973 as a result of the OPEC cartel has been widely cited as a major cause of this downturn (in 1973–4, petroleum prices quadrupled as a result of the cartel's actions). The evidence is inconclusive, however. Similarly, it has been difficult to establish the 'guilt' of other popular scapegoats, such as the role of labour unions in obtaining wage increases in excess of productivity. Rather, the crisis of the 1970s must be seen as the product of a conjunction of trends whose origins can be traced to the 1960s or before. Hamilton (1984) identified several such trends:

1 The stagflation phase of economic long waves. With the downswing of the Kuznets cycle (see Box 3.1) there was a slowing down of economic growth and a steady fall in profits, particularly in the industrial core countries of the OECD. This was associated with falling levels of demand for capital goods, particularly transport, building, mining and factory equipment (e.g., ships, vehicles, machinery, machine tools) and, hence, steel. Overall, rates of growth in the OECD countries fell from an annual average of 5 to 6 per cent between 1963 and 1973 to around 2.5 per cent between 1973 and 1978 and less than 1 per cent between 1979 and 1982.

At the same time, rising levels of inflation, associated with the upswing of the Kondratiev cycle (see p. 59), generally served to reduce profits and hampered capital accumulation. This resulted in greater dependency on financing investment via the banking sector. This, in turn, meant high interest rates that retarded technological investment and so hindered competitiveness. Inflation also raised labour costs, thus increasing the urgency of technological investment (particularly automation) at a time when capital was expensive. The result was the widespread depression of both capital-intensive industries (e.g., steel, shipbuilding, vehicles, appliances) *and* labour-intensive industries (e.g., textiles, clothing, footwear).

2 Increased international monetary instability, which took two major forms:

- Overvaluation of exchange rates as a result of the transition (in the early 1970s) from fixed exchange rates to floating exchange rates. Where currencies were overvalued (e.g., the currencies of oil and/or gas producers such as the Netherlands, Norway and the United Kingdom, and, more recently, the USA), the loss of international competitiveness resulted in import penetration and a consequent decline in industrial capacity (Figure 6.1). In the USA, import

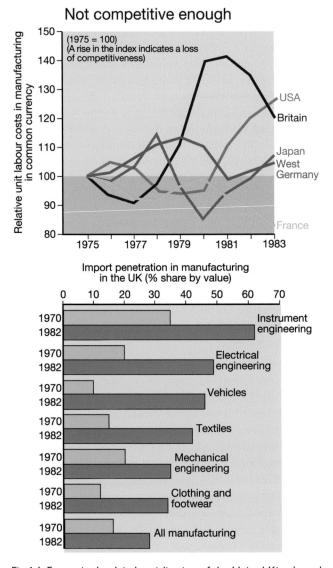

Fig 6.1: Forces in the deindustrialization of the United Kingdom: dramatic loss of competitiveness (1978–83) and consequent import penetration, converting the country from a net exporter to a net importer of manufactures

*Source:* Based on Hamilton (1984: 352, Figure 2)

penetration in clothing and textiles increased from 34 per cent in 1980 to 55 per cent in 1986; import penetration in shoes increased from 50 to 81 per cent, in computers from 7 to 25 per cent; and in automobiles from 35 to 40 per cent.

- Problems of indebtedness among NICs and some LDCs following massive borrowing from the 'petrodollar' surpluses created in the OPEC countries (see p. 51). In addition to the international financial instability associated with uncertainty caused by debt rescheduling and fears over national bankruptcies, this created a strong incentive for NICs and LDCs to increase their exports – of cheap manufactured goods as well as traditional staples – to the core regions in order to obtain the necessary foreign exchange. This, in turn, increased the competitive pressure on the labour-intensive sectors of the core economies.

3 The strengthening, throughout the 1960s, of social values associated with social welfare provision (e.g., retirement pensions, healthcare, anti-poverty programmes) and environmental protection. Although this created new markets for some products and services, it also raised some industrial costs and contributed to a higher tax burden on both consumers and producers.

4 The introduction of innovations and technological changes in response to escalating energy and labour costs created feedback effects that depressed demand in 'traditional' industrial activities. Energy-saving designs in transport and heating, for example, reduced the demand for steel; while innovations in microelectronics reduced the demand for electromechanical products.

5 A resurgence of political volatility, which reduced the extent of stable business settings and so inhibited several dimensions of world trade, including east–west trade (until 1989 and the fall of communism) and trade involving much of Central America, southwestern Asia and Southeast Asia.

## TOWARDS FLEXIBILITY: PRECONDITIONS

Meanwhile, just as in previous major economic transitions, the processes themselves that resulted in the shift to advanced capitalism have drawn on a number of *preconditions* developed during the preceding era (i.e., during organized, Fordist industrial capitalism). Three main factors are involved:

1 new, enabling technologies in transport and telecommunications
2 changing patterns of demand and consumption
3 corporate restructuring.

### 1. Enabling technologies and economies of scope

The resolution of the crisis of Fordism and the emergence of advanced capitalism have been made possible, in part, by the availability of 'permissive' technology of two kinds:

- *Circulation*: improvements in transport and communications technologies (widebodied cargo jets, containerization, email networks, computerized business systems, communications satellites, optical-fibre networks, etc.), which have reduced the time and costs of circulation, bringing a wider geographic market within the scope of an increasing range of business activities. This 'global reach' has also been advanced through the economic development of peripheral areas and the standardization of products across cultures (the latter itself being a function of the development of communications media).

- *Production*: improvements in production technologies (electronically controlled assembly lines, automated machine tools, computerized sewing systems, robotics, etc.) have allowed for a finer degree of specialization in many production processes, and facilitated a routinization of many operations. This, in turn, has led to the deskilling of many production systems, while at the same time increasing the *separability* (and therefore the spatial fragmentation) of their constituent parts. This has made it easier for managers to take advantage of new sources of cheaper and less militant labour. Advances in the manufacture and use of synthetic materials have also extended the locational capability of many industries, since raw materials have traditionally been the most restrictive of all factors of production.

The impact of these enabling technologies is difficult to overstate. During the past three decades the global network of computers, telephones and televisions has increased its information-carrying capacity a million times over. Telecommunications satellites allow for hundreds of thousands of simultaneous telephone conversations. Figure 6.2 shows the tremendous explosion that has occurred in the number of internet users (from 4.4 million in 1991, to 40 million in 1995, to almost 400 million in 2000 and over 1 billion by 2005) who now access somewhere between an estimated 15–30 billion web pages, to which an estimated 10 million new pages are added every day. International air cargo has increased from about 9 million tons of freight and nearly 22 billion ton kilometres in 1976 to over 40 million tons of freight and more than 100 billion ton kilometres by 2007. The emergence of a tripolar world economy has encouraged the development of round-the-world shipping services that could link the three main cargo-generating zones of Europe, North America and East Asia. Thus there emerged, by the mid-1980s, the flexible, intermodal and global

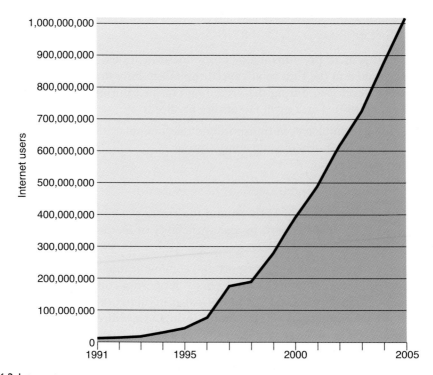

Fig 6.2: Internet users

*Source:* Online data from World Research Institute, available at http://earthtrends.wri.org/; and CIA *World Factbook*, 2007, available at http://www.odci.gov/cia/publications/factbook/

transportation services offered by several container lines: Evergreen (Taiwan), United States Lines (USA), Senator (Germany) and Maersk (Denmark). In addition, some shipping lines, such as American President Line and P&O Line, acquired inland trucking operations, and railway companies became involved in ocean-borne transport (e.g., the merger of CSX and Sea-Land in the United States).

## Box 6.1 Technological breakthroughs of the 1970s

All key information technologies that underpin the emerging informational economy of the twenty-first century are part of a massive diffusion of commercial and civilian applications since the 1970s. The giant leap forward in the diffusion of microelectronics in all machines came in 1971 with the invention by an Intel engineer, Ted Hoff, of the microprocessor (the computer on a chip). The advent of the microprocessor turned the electronics world, and indeed the world itself, upside down when it began to diffuse in the mid-1970s. The microcomputer was invented in 1975 and the first successful commercial product, Apple II, was introduced in April 1977, around the same time that Microsoft started to produce operating systems for microcomputers. The Xerox Alto, the matrix of many software technologies for personal computers, was developed at PARC labs in Palo Alto in 1973. The first industrial electronic switch appeared in 1969 and digital switching was developed in the mid-1970s and commercially diffused in 1977. Corning Glass first industrially produced optic fibre in the early 1970s. Also by the mid-1970s, Sony started to produce VCR machines commercially, on the basis of 1960s' discoveries in America and England that never reached mass production. And last, but not least, it was in 1969 that the US Defense Department's Advanced Research Projects Agency (ARPA) set up a new, revolutionary electronic communication network that would grow during the 1970s to become the internet. It was greatly helped by the invention by Cerf and Kahn in 1974 of TCP/IP, the interconnection network protocol that ushered in 'gateway' technology, allowing different types of network to be connected. Two Chicago students, Ward Christensen and Randy Suess, invented the modem in 1978 when they were trying to find a system to transfer microcomputer programs to each other through the telephone to avoid travelling in the Chicago winter between their distant locations.

Adapted from Castells (2000: 42, 44, 47, 53, 54)

We should also note that the introduction of new circulation and production technologies has in many cases created a powerful second-order effect: economies of scope, the capacity to provide entirely new products and/or services through the flexible use of the same production or service network. Thus, for example, the computerized records developed by airlines have lent themselves to an increased scope of business that includes hotel reservations and rental cars. Similarly, the credit records of major retailing firms have provided a base for them to exploit economies of scope. In the United States, Sears, exploiting its access to its retail credit customers (currently about 60 million), has offered at different times insurance services (through Allstate), investment services (through Morgan Stanley Dean Witter) and real estate services (through Coldwell Banker).

Another important aspect of enabling technologies concerns their capacity for flexibility during periods of intense competition or changing market conditions. The following example is from the insurance industry in the United States:

> In the mid-1960s, when the insurance industry was stable and heavily regulated, insurance companies automated their back-room activities to obtain dramatic gains in productivity in handling premium billings and collections. As wildly fluctuating interest rates hit the industry in the mid-1970s, companies had to change their product rapidly to attract premiums and to offset the effects of customers borrowing against their policies at low interest rates. *Only those companies that had flexibly designed computer and control systems could deploy their products rapidly enough to obtain a competitive edge* ... Smaller companies could not afford the huge initial costs of needed technologies and sold out or merged with larger companies who could benefit from their distribution networks. A flexibly automated back room became a key element in survival and competitive success.
>
> Quinn (1987: 137, emphasis added)

Finally, we must recognize the differential of contemporaneousness (see also p. 120) in the uneven spatial impact of these enabling technologies. Following Sachar and Öberg (1990), we can see that new technologies have different implications for different regions within the world economy:

- In the core countries, high technology creates new jobs, particularly in financial and business services. It creates new products, facilitates new production and distribution processes and new forms of corporate organization, but reduces the need for employment in manufacturing.
- In semi-peripheral countries, high technology brings an increase in manufacturing employment, increases in productivity and an overall improvement in their competitiveness in the international economy.
- In peripheral countries, new technologies are often too expensive to acquire or deploy. As a result there is a relative decline in both productivity and international competitiveness. To the extent that new technologies are deployed, their main effect is to displace jobs in labour-intensive sectors, thus adding to a sprawling informal sector in urban economies and putting pressure on the public sector to absorb labour in government-sponsored jobs.

## 2. Changing patterns of demand and consumption

Shifting patterns of consumer demand have also been an important precondition for the evolution of advanced capitalism. Within core countries, the Fordist mode of industrial capitalism, based as it was on mass production coupled with mass consumption, began to be the victim of its own success as mass markets for many of its staple products – such as cars and refrigerators – came close to being saturated. As the affluent societies of the core countries satisfied more and more of their wants, market saturation could only be avoided by skilful marketing campaigns and continuous modifications in products and packaging. Even so, mass produced goods were less and less effective in satisfying one of their main roles in affluent societies: that of positional goods, possessions that serve as measures of socioeconomic status. As more and more people were able to acquire mass produced *positional goods* – a nice home, new cars, televisions, etc. – so more people sought the distinction of custom-made, stylish, high-design and fashionable products. Social distinctions, previously marked by the ownership of a basic set of consumer goods on a sliding scale of size/quality, now had to be established via the symbolism of ensembles of positional goods. The problem for producers following the Fordist mode of accumulation was not just that their mass produced products were rapidly losing their appeal to the most affluent consumers but also that their strategies and processes of production were too inflexible to cater to the many different (and rapidly changing) market niches for positional goods. The result was that many firms began to adopt more flexible forms of production, using new production and circulation technologies in order to exploit a variety of niches within the overall market. One of the classic success stories in this respect is the Benetton company (see Box 6.2).

## Box 6.2 How Benetton satisfies changing consumer demand

In 1965 the Benetton company began with a single factory near Venice. In 1968, it acquired a single retail store in the Alpine town of Belluno, marking the beginning of a remarkable sequence of corporate expansion. Benetton is now a global organization with about 5000 retail outlets in 120 countries and its own investment bank and financial services organizations. It achieved this growth by exploiting computers, new communications and transportation systems, flexible outsourcing strategies and new production process technologies – such as robotics and CAD/CAM (computer-aided design/computer-aided manufacturing) systems – to the fullest possible extent.

Benetton employs well over 8000 people worldwide, 400 of whom are located in the company's home base of Ponzano, near Treviso, in Italy. From here, Benetton managers coordinate the activities of its nearby high-tech production pole at Castrette, its other Italian, eastern European and Asian factories, and its more than 300 outside suppliers in order to stock its worldwide network of retail outlet franchises and directly owned and managed megastores. In Ponzano, the firm's designers create new shirts and sweaters on CAD terminals; but their designs are produced only for orders in hand, allowing for the coordination of production with the purchase of raw materials – the Japanese *kanban* or just-in-time (JIT) production system. In factories, rollers linked to a central computer spread and cut layers of cloth in small batches according to the numbers and colours ordered by Benetton stores around the world. Sweaters, gloves and scarves, knitted in volume in white yarn, are dyed in small batches by machines similarly programmed to respond to sales orders. Completed garments are warehoused briefly (by robots) and shipped out directly (via private package delivery firms) to individual stores, to arrive on their shelves within an average of seven days in Italy and 15 throughout the rest of the world; more than 10 million garments are shipped each month.

Sensitivity to demand, however, is the foundation of Benetton's success. Niche marketing and product differentiation have been central to this sensitivity, which requires a high degree of flexibility in exploiting new product lines. Key stores patronized by trend-setting consumers (such as the megastores on the Champs-Elysées in Paris and on Omotesando Street in Tokyo) are monitored closely, and

> Benetton stores' cash registers operate as point-of-sale terminals, so that immediate marketing data are available to company headquarters daily. Another notable feature of the company's operations is the way in which different market niches are exploited with the same basic products. In Italy, Benetton products are sold through 11 different retail chains, each with an image and décor calculated to bring in a different sort of customer.

Although the postwar era of steadily increasing affluence in the core economies came to an abrupt end with the stagflation crisis and OPEC oil price increases of the mid-1970s, the shift away from mass markets to niche markets did not slow. Rather, it intensified as a new materialism took root. The chief actors in this change were the 'babyboomers' whose formative years had been spent in the post-war economic boom. Their reaction to mass consumption was a countercultural movement with a collectivist approach to the exploration of freedom and self-realization. The failure of this countercultural movement (in particular, the failure of the sit-ins, protest marches, general strikes, student–worker alliances and civil disorder of 1968) meant that self-realization slid into self-centred and narcissistic lifestyles: the basis for new market niches. But the real cause of the materialism of the babyboomers was the shock of emerging onto housing and labour markets just as the economies of the core countries were experiencing a phase of stagflation compounded by the recessionary effects of the OPEC oil price rise. Wages stood still while consumer prices ballooned.

Millions of babyboomers, raised to take for granted steady improvements in levels of living, found themselves unable to fulfil the American Dream (or the European or East Asian version of it). Their response was to pursue materialism for its own sake. They saved less, borrowed more, deferred parenthood, comforted themselves with affordable luxuries that were marketed as symbols of style and distinctiveness and generally surrendered to the hedonism of lives infused with extravagant details: gourmet foods, designer clothes, jewellery, winter vacations and extravagant electronic and other gadgets. The point here is that all of this represented consumer demand not for mass produced products but for a rapidly changing array of high-quality products whose value as positional goods had a relatively short life. This meant that producers had to be flexible enough to be able, like Benetton, to identify and exploit finely differentiated market niches.

Between core countries, meanwhile, there has been a homogenization of markets. Similar trends in income distribution and consumer tastes have been reinforced by television (especially CNN, MTV and syndicated light entertainment series) and international travel. Together with decreasing relative costs of transport and communications, this has meant that *market niches have merged across national boundaries, thus making it possible for producers to exploit economies of scale in the production of upmarket products*. To a lesser degree, the same processes have extended from core countries to the more affluent consumers of *semi-peripheral* and *peripheral* countries, thus allowing the marketing of 'world products' (e.g., German luxury automobiles, British raincoats, Italian sweaters, Swiss watches, French wines, American soft drinks, Japanese consumer electronics) to global market segments. Barnet and Cavanagh (1994: 15–16, 166) describe the emergence of what they call the 'global shopping mall':

The Global Shopping Mall is a planetary supermarket with a dazzling spread of things to eat, drink, wear, and enjoy ... [Through] the rise of global advertising, distribution, and marketing ... dreams of affluent living are communicated to the farthest reaches of the globe ... Even in the rural areas of the Philippines any city of over 20,000 will have at least one 'supermarket', usually a one-room affair about the size of an old New Hampshire general store. In the fishing and rice-farming town of Balanga, Bataan, the San José Supermarket offers Philip Morris's Tang and Cheez Whiz, Procter & Gamble's Pringle's potato chips, Hormel's Spam, Hershey's Kisses, RJR Nabisco's Chips Ahoy, Del Monte's tomato juice, Planter's Cheez Curls, and Colgate-Palmolive's toothpaste.

## 3. Logic of corporate restructuring

One of the most important preconditions for the emergence of advanced capitalism and the globalization of business activity has been the restructuring of the corporate world. In response to changing circumstances, private business has had to develop new strategies in order to survive; strategies that have significantly altered the fortunes of different kinds of cities, regions and countries.

Two of the most important outcomes overall have been corporate concentration and centralization. Concentration involves the elimination of small, weak firms in particular spheres of economic activity, partly through competition and partly through mergers and acquisitions. Centralization involves the merging of the resultant large enterprises from different spheres of economic activity to form giant 'conglomerate' companies with a diversified range of activities. Such corporations are often *transnational* in their operations, having established overseas subsidiaries, taken over foreign competitors, or bought into profitable foreign businesses.

In every industry, there are limits both to the extent to which productivity can be increased and to which consumers can be induced to purchase more. As competition to maintain profit levels becomes more intense, some firms will be driven out of business while others will be taken over by stronger competitors in a process of horizontal integration. A successful automobile manufacturer, for example, might buy out other automobile manufacturers.

Meanwhile, the chances of new firms being successful tend to be diminished, since the larger existing corporations are able to draw on economies of scale in order to edge out smaller competitors by price cutting. But even giant corporations cannot prevent market saturation indefinitely; and they are in any case always vulnerable to unforeseen shifts in demand. A common corporate strategy has therefore been to engage in vertical integration (taking over the firms that provide their inputs and/or those that purchase their output) in an attempt to capture a greater proportion of the final selling price. The automobile manufacturer, for example, might take over companies that make specialized components like engines or car navigation systems; and/or companies that distribute or sell automobiles. The net result is the *concentration of production*, within most industries, in the hands of a diminishing number of increasingly large companies.

Alternatively – or in addition – diagonal integration (taking over firms whose activities are completely unrelated to their own) offers the chance of gaining access to more profitable markets and/or less expensive factors of production. Staying with the same example, the automobile manufacturer may buy into energy, advertising or entertainment companies. The net result in this case is the *centralization* of assets, jobs, production and decisions about economic life in the hands of an even smaller number of even larger companies.

The extent of these trends can be illustrated in relation to the US economy during the postwar period. Spearheaded by the large corporations that had established themselves through early flurries of horizontal integration in the 1900s (e.g., US Steel, International Harvester, American Tobacco, General Electric) and vertical integration in the 1920s (e.g., General Foods, B.F. Goodrich and the major petroleum companies), 'big business' began to exert an increasing influence on economic life. Although the incidence of horizontal mergers was greatly reduced by antitrust (antimonopoly) legislation (e.g., the Celler Kefauver Act 1950), vertical and diagonal integration proceeded at unprecedented rates, generating around 3000 mergers per year in the peak years of the late 1960s. Since the early 1970s, concentration ratios (the percentage of total sales attributable to the four largest firms) had increased across a broad spectrum of industries. Several major industries, including motor vehicles, telephone equipment, turbines and cookies and crackers, are each almost completely dominated by four (or fewer) firms (Table 6.1). For example, despite diversification into the growing assortment of competing breakfast options for on-the-go consumers (e.g., ready-to-eat breakfast bars, bagels and muffins or quick-serve food outlets such as McDonald's), Kellogg's (29.2 per cent), General Mills (27.4 per cent), PepsiCo's Quaker Oats (13.8 per cent) and Kraft's Post division (12.8 per cent) still shared together over 83 per cent of the declining cold cereal market in 2003.

Meanwhile, giant conglomerates had begun to emerge as a result of diagonal integration. The first of these was Textron Incorporated, established only in 1943 when it sold blankets and other textile products to the US Army. By 1980 it had been involved in buying or selling over 100 different companies in industries as

**Table 6.1** Percentage of value of shipments accounted for by the four largest companies in selected manufacturing industries in the USA, 1992–2002

| Industry | Percentage of value of shipments | | |
| --- | --- | --- | --- |
| | 1992 | 1997 | 2002 |
| Cigarettes | 93 | 99 | 95 |
| Cookies and crackers | 56 | 60 | 67 |
| Guided missiles and space vehicles | 71 | 89 | 96 |
| Household laundry equipment | 84 | 90 | 93 |
| Household refrigerators and freezers | 82 | 82 | 85 |
| Household vacuum cleaners | 59 | 69 | 78 |
| Motor vehicles | 84 | 82 | 81 |
| Petrochemicals | – | 60 | 85 |
| Semiconductor machinery | 41 | 44 | 60 |
| Telephone apparatus | 51 | 54 | 56 |
| Turbine and turbine generator set units | 79 | 78 | 88 |

*Source:* US Census Bureau, *Economic Census* (five-yearly; various years)

diverse as textiles, aerospace, machinery, watch bracelets and pens. Textron was by no means an isolated example, however. As early as 1955 the majority of mergers taking place in the USA were diagonal, conglomerate mergers. By the early 1990s nine out of every 10 mergers involved conglomerate companies.

As a result of all this merger activity, giant conglomerates increasingly influence the world's core economies. For example, between 1950 and 1980 the 50 largest US corporations increased their share of the total value added in *all* manufacturing from less than 20 per cent to nearly 30 per cent; and the largest 200 increased their share from 30 per cent to 50 per cent. Similar trends have occurred in the service sector (where the control of variety stores, department stores, car rental firms, motion picture distribution and data processing had become particularly central-ized) and in the agricultural sector (where less than 10 per cent of all farms, in terms of sales, account for 75 per cent of the total market value of all agricultural products sold). In the USA, for example, the 10 largest cable operators serve about 85 per cent of all cable subscribers, with the largest three, Comcast, AOL TimeWarner and Charter together serving about 56 per cent of all cable sub-scribers: Comcast (provides cable, internet and phone services to more than 20 million subscribers), AOL TimeWarner (over 10 million subscribers), Charter (over 6 million), Cox (over 6 million), Adelphia (over 5 million) and Cablevision (serves over 3 million subscribers). Three giant conglomerates, AT&T (38.0 per cent), MCI (19.8 per cent) and Sprint (10.1 per cent), shared nearly 70 per cent of the long-distance telephone market in 2004. Five companies dominated the mobile phone market in 2005 with the following shares of subscribers: Cingular Wireless (26.8 per cent), Verizon Wireless (25.4 per cent), Sprint Nextel (22.2 per cent), T-Mobile (10.7 per cent) and Alltel (5.3 per cent). Five companies dominated the global PC market with shipments amounting to almost 50 per cent of the nearly 55 million units shipped in 2006: Dell (17.7 per cent), Hewlett-Packard (14.8 per cent), Lenovo (7.3 per cent), Acer (5.2 per cent) and Toshiba (3.5 per cent).

Surfers are now even visiting fewer sites on the internet than in the 1990s. Online music has also seen a shift to fewer providers. EMusic, MP3.com, MyPlay and Napster were expected to push the five big record labels out of business. Instead, they were each bought out. Vivendi Universal purchased EMusic and MP3.com, while Bertlesmann bought Napster and MyPlay. Although Vivendi later sold off EMusic and MP3.com to two different companies, the online distribution of music is still dominated by a small number of large companies, including iTunes and Vivendi which purchased BMG (the musical arm of Bertlesmann).

Because of their size, the larger elements of US conglomerates have also come to exert an increasing influence in the *international* economy. This is not surprising given that the annual sales of the very largest business enterprises like Wal-Mart and General Motors are greater than the GDP of countries such as Norway and Portugal. Perhaps more significant is the fact that *the combined overseas output of US-based transnational corporations (TNCs) is now larger than the GDP of every country in the world except the USA itself.* As we shall see (Chapter 12), this new dimension of the international economy has come to represent a serious economic threat to small countries and it has prompted the creation of a variety of interna-tional and supranational economic and political organizations.

It should be stressed that the USA has by no means been the only core country to generate giant conglomerates. Major TNCs have been bred in Europe, Japan,

Canada and Australasia in response to the same logic that has applied to the USA; and some NICs and peripheral countries now have large home-based transnational corporations. Indeed, these companies have been increasing their share of world markets at the expense of US-based companies; and some of them have extended their operations to the USA itself. The South Korean electronics giant Samsung, for example (the 46th largest corporation in the world in 2006, with a global work-force of 229,000 and sales of US$141 billion in 2005) has multiple subsidiaries and affiliates that produce, market and sell a wide range of electronic parts and components including next generation memory chips, computer and telecommunications equipment, colour TV picture tubes and glass bulbs. The company's 600 designers work in design centres in Seoul, London, Milan, Los Angeles, San Francisco, Tokyo and Shanghai. Overall, the number of transnational corporations increased from just over 7000 in the early 1970s to more than 77,000 in 2005. Together, these corporations have about 770,000 foreign affiliates and account for more than US$19 trillion in worldwide annual sales.

## EVOLUTION OF TRANSNATIONAL CORPORATE ACTIVITY

The current importance of transnational corporations in the world economy is the result of an evolutionary process that can be characterized in terms of three distinctive phases. With reference to the experience of US-based TNCs, these phases were as follows:

- *Phase I*: Beginning in the 19th century and extending to 1940, this phase was dominated by investment directed at obtaining raw materials – mainly oil and minerals – for domestic manufacturing operations.
- *Phase II*: After the Second World War, some of the leading corporations began to use foreign direct investment (FDI) in overseas production operations as a means of penetrating foreign consumer markets. Initially, the focus of this investment was western Europe, where the Marshall Plan programme, NATO rearmament and the US military presence in West Germany provided useful information feedback and points of entry to an expanding consumer market. Meanwhile, the establishment of the US dollar as the world's principal reserve currency at the 1944 Bretton Woods conference (see Chapter 2), had made it much easier for US companies to buy into foreign industries. It was not long before many US firms began to penetrate the expanding markets of parts of the rest of the world, particularly in Latin America. The resulting mergers and acquisitions often led to the restructuring of corporate production processes.

  Bulova Watch is a good example. Bulova originally manufactured watch movements in Switzerland and shipped them to Pago Pago in American Samoa where they were assembled and shipped for sale in the United States. Bluestone and Harrison (1982: 114) reported that Corporation President Harry B. Henshel said about this arrangement: 'We are able to beat the foreign competition because we are the foreign competition.' Since then Bulova has extended its operations to Mexico.

  Between 1957 and 1967, 20 per cent of all new US machinery plants, 25 per cent of new chemical plants and over 30 per cent of new transport equipment plants were located abroad. By 1970, almost 75 per cent of US imports were transactions between the domestic and foreign subsidiaries of transnational corporations. By the end of the 1970s overseas profits accounted for one-third or more of the overall profits of the hundred largest transnational producers and banks.

• *Phase III*: During the 1970s the crisis and destabilization associated with the episode of stagflation brought growing competition from goods produced in the NICs with cheap labour. In addition, the collapse of the Bretton Woods agreement in 1971 increased the value of the US dollar, thus making imported goods cheaper and so making it easier for European and Japanese TNCs to penetrate US markets. In response, US transnational corporations began to restructure their production processes once again, eliminating the duplication of activities between domestic and foreign-based facilities and reorganizing the division of tasks between them.

Effectively, this third phase has meant:

1  retaining existing facilities that require high inputs of technology and/or skilled labour (e.g., headquarter offices in North America and western Europe)
2  the further redeployment of capital, bringing peripheral countries into the production space of US companies in order to benefit from lower labour costs (in 2005 the costs of hourly compensation for production workers in manufacturing industries in Hong Kong, Singapore, South Korea and Taiwan were between about 24 and 57 per cent of those for US workers; in Mexico and Brazil, they were between 10 and 17 per cent; and in China, they were about 3 per cent)
3  withdrawing from locations where unskilled and semi-skilled labour is more expensive (i.e., North America and western Europe – in 2005, e.g., the costs of hourly compensation for production workers in manufacturing industries in Germany, Switzerland and the Scandinavian countries were between about 121 and 166 per cent of those for US workers), either by opening foreign factories or using foreign subcontractors.

Thus, for example, General Electric added 30,000 foreign jobs to its payroll during the 1970s while reducing its US employment by 25,000. Similarly, the RCA Corporation increased its foreign workforce by 19,000 while reducing its US payroll by 14,000. Nike is a good example of the consequences of this third phase. This company sold its manufacturing plants in the United States and United Kingdom and now subcontracts out all of its production. The geography of Nike's production network has changed over time to reflect changing labour costs across the LDCs. Nike shoe production was initially carried out in Japan, but was later relocated to Taiwan and South Korea. Today, Nike products are manufactured in more than 700 factories by subcontractors employing over 500,000 workers across 50 countries with low labour costs, including Albania, Argentina, Bangladesh, Belarus, Brazil, Bulgaria, Chile, China and South Africa.

## 6.2 PATTERNS AND PROCESSES OF GLOBALIZATION

Most of the world's population now lives in countries that are either integrated into world markets for goods and finance or rapidly becoming so. As recently as the late 1970s only a few peripheral countries had opened their borders to flows of trade and investment capital. About one-third of the world's labour force lived in countries like the former Soviet Union and China with centrally planned economies and at least another third lived in countries insulated from international markets by prohibitive trade barriers and currency controls. With nearly half the world's labour force among them, three giant population blocs – China, Russia and India – have rapidly integrated into the global market. Many other countries, from Mexico to South Korea, have deep linkages.

Globalization, although incorporating more of the world, more completely, into the capitalist world-system, has intensified the differences between the core and the periphery. Between 1960 and 2006 the average per capita income in the wealthiest 20 countries grew from 18 to 36 times that in the poorest 20 countries. Some parts of the periphery have almost slid off the economic map. In Sub-Saharan Africa, economic output fell by one-third during the 1980s. Unlike many other LDCs that managed to restore growth in the early 1990s, Sub-Saharan Africa experienced growth during the 1990s that merely matched the population growth rate (with average annual GDP growth of only 2.5 per cent for 1990–2000) due to 'a combination of adverse external developments, structural and institutional bottlenecks and policy errors' (UNCTAD, 2001). Although GDP growth had risen to over 5 per cent by 2005, average incomes in Sub-Saharan Africa are lower today than in 1990 and even lower than in the 1960s. Indeed, the persistent economic peripherality of Sub-Saharan Africa in the contemporary global economy, exacerbated by the impacts of the HIV/AIDS epidemic, is probably a much more threatening condition than the dependency of the colonial period.

Meanwhile, globalization has resulted in the consolidation of the core of the world-system. The core is now a close-knit triad of the geographic centres of the United States, the European Union (EU) and Japan. Most of the world's flows of goods, capital and information are within and between these three centres. In 2003–05, for example, the United States, the EU and Japan accounted for 54 per cent of world inflows of foreign direct investment and 75 per cent of FDI outflows. The share of the EU's FDI inflows into the triad was 75 per cent in 2003-05, compared to 62 per cent in 1978–80. The enlarged EU now accounts for almost half of global inward and outward FDI flows and stocks. The importance of both the United States and Japan's inward and outward FDI flows and stocks has not kept pace. Although the LDCs have seen a significant increase in both inward and outward FDI flows and stocks (with inflows and outflows rising from 20.3 to 35.9 and from 3.0 to 12.3 between 1978–80 and 2003–05 respectively), the United States, the EU and Japan continue to dominate the world's periphery, with each centre having particular influence in its own regional expansion zone: its nearest peripheral region.

Allen Scott (1996) conceptualized this situation as a patchwork of global metropolitan regions, 'regional economic motors', each one being the site of dense networks of specialized but complementary forms of economic activity, together with large and multifaceted labour markets and specialized infrastructures offering powerful agglomeration economies. The central metropolitan area of each regional motor is surrounded by a hinterland occupied by ancillary communities, prosperous agricultural zones, local service centres and the like. The hinterlands of some of these regional motors may coalesce with one another (as in the actual cases of Boston/New York/Philadelphia, Los Angeles/San Diego/Tijuana, Milan/Turin/Genoa and Tokyo/Nagoya/Osaka).

These regional economic motors are linked by intense flows of capital, information, goods and people. Beyond them, there are large residual expanses of the contemporary world that lie at the extensive economic frontiers of advanced capitalism (former colonies, physically isolated regions and so on). These are underdeveloped areas that have been unable to build the economic organizations that might provide the basis for sustained growth in a global economy. Nevertheless, these areas are interspersed at times by 'islands' of relative prosperity and economic opportunity that are on a path toward higher levels of agglomerated development. In the 1960s and 1970s examples included Hong Kong, Singapore, Taiwan, Seoul and Mexico City. Since then others have followed, including Bangkok, Kuala Lumpur and São Paulo-Rio de Janeiro, and more recently, the growing number of global metropolitan regions in China and India.

## INTERNATIONAL REDEPLOYMENT AND LOCATIONAL HIERARCHIES

The cumulative result of the globalization of economic activity has been the creation of *locational hierarchies* of activities. The aggregate outcome involves:

1  localized concentrations of high-level management in world cities (see Chapter 7)
2  smaller concentrations of mid-level management and administration in large metropolitan areas in core countries and in the capital cities of NICs and some peripheral countries
3  clusters of research and development (R&D) activity in high-tech, innovative milieux – technopoles – (see Chapter 7) within the core countries
4  regions specializing in advanced, high-tech industrial production, mostly within the core countries
5  decentralized pockets of routinized industrial production – branch plants – in (a) the peripheral regions of core countries and (b) the metropolitan areas of NICs and some peripheral countries.

These tendencies, and the fact that they have been influenced so much by the locational strategies of transnational corporations equipped to undertake a 'global scan' in pursuit of the most profitable redeployment of activities, have contributed to the idea of the emergence of a new international division of labour (NIDL) (see Chapter 1).

It should be acknowledged that not all firms or industries are equal in their need or their capability to engage in international redeployment of this kind. It is the largest companies – the transnational corporations – that are in the best position to take advantage of the advances in circulation and production technology. Probably the best developed example – and the most researched – is provided by the automobile industry, where the clearly defined national markets of the early postwar period have been almost entirely replaced by production and marketing on a global scale. In 1976 Ford introduced the Fiesta, a vehicle designed to sell in Europe, South America, the Asian market and for a time in North America. The Fiesta was assembled in several different locations from components manufactured in an even greater number of locations. The Fiesta became the first of a series of Ford 'world cars', which still includes the Mondeo. Ford's international subsidiaries, which used to operate independently of the parent company, are now functionally integrated, through computers and video teleconferences.

The other automobile companies have organized their own global assembly systems (Figure 6.3). They employ modular manufacturing for their world cars based on a common underbody platform yet with the flexibility to adapt the interior, trim, body and ride characteristics to local conditions in different countries: Volkswagen's best selling European Golf (US Rabbit), for example, GM's Corsa and Fiat's Palio and Siena models deriving from its 'Project 178' world car

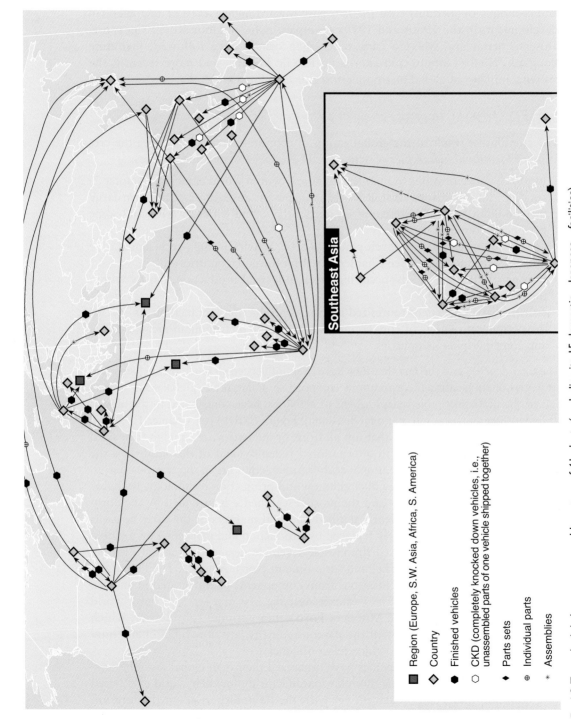

Fig 6.3: Toyota's global overseas assembly system of 41 plants (excluding its 15 domestic – Japanese – facilities)

Region (Europe, S.W. Asia, Africa, S. America)

Country

Finished vehicles

CKD (completely knocked down vehicles, i.e.,
unassembled parts of one vehicle shipped together)

Parts sets

Individual parts

Assemblies

Southeast Asia

*Source:* Based on Toyota (2001: 11–12, Table 1.5)

platform. Ford's Focus in North America, for example, has larger front and rear bumpers. Honda produces two distinct versions of the same car from its Accord world car platform: the more powerful, bigger and more comfortable Accord for American drivers and the smaller sportier Accord aimed at European and Japanese drivers. According to Plunkett Research, nearly two-thirds of the 50 million cars and light trucks that roll off the production lines each year are made by just five supergroups of global corporations – in order of size: General Motors (which includes Saturn, Saab, Daewoo, Suzuki and Isuzu), Toyota (with Lexus and Daihatsu), Ford (incorporating Volvo, Jaguar, Land Rover and Mazda), DaimlerChrysler (with Mercedes-Benz, Smart and Maybach) and Honda.

## FLEXIBLE PRODUCTION SYSTEMS

Concurrent with the changing competitive strategies of firms, there have been some significant changes in the organization of production systems in many industries. These are often expressed in terms of a transition from Fordism to flexible production systems, or Neo-Fordism. In Neo-Fordism, the logic of mass production coupled with mass consumption has been modified by the addition of more flexible production, distribution and marketing systems.

This flexibility is rooted in forms of production that enable manufacturers to shift quickly and efficiently from one level of output to another and, more importantly, from one process and/or product configuration to another. It must be understood as a change that involves flexibility both *within* firms and *between* them. Within firms, a great deal of the flexibility of Neo-Fordism is attributable to the exploitation of new technologies. Computerized machine tools are capable of producing a variety of new products simply by being reprogrammed, often with very little downtime between production runs for different products. Different stages of the production process (sometimes located in different places) can be integrated and coordinated through computer-aided design (CAD) and computer-aided manufacturing (CAM) systems. Computer-based information systems can be used to monitor retail sales and track wholesale orders, thus allowing producers to reduce the costs of raw materials stockpiles, parts inventories and warehousing through sophisticated small-batch, just-in-time production and distribution systems. The combination of computer-based information systems, CAD/CAM systems and computerized machine tools has also helped firms to be flexible enough to exploit specialized niches of consumer demand, rendering geographically scattered upscale markets accessible to economies of scale in production. This kind of flexibility depends on new labour practices as well as new technologies, however (Table 6.2). There are two main aspects to this. One is the increasingly flexible use of labour within firms, which requires individual workers to perform a wider variety of tasks. Taken to its extreme, this trend has in some instances substituted 'craftwork' for production line work. The other is the increasingly flexible size and quality of the labour force required at any one plant. This trend has substituted overtime, part-time and temporary employment for permanent, full-time jobs.

Between firms, the flexibility inherent to Neo-Fordism has been achieved through the *externalization* of certain functions. One way of doing this has been to restructure permanent and hierarchically structured administrative, managerial and technical units within large corporations into flatter, leaner and more flexible forms

**Table 6.2** Contrasts in the production process and the labour process: Fordism and flexible accumulation (Neo-Fordism)

| Fordism | Flexible accumulation (Neo-Fordism) |
| --- | --- |
| **Production process** | |
| Mass production of homogeneous products | Small batch production |
| Uniformity | Flexible production of a variety of product types |
| Large buffer stocks and inventory | No stocks (just-in-time inventories) |
| Testing quality ex-post (rejects and errors detected late) | Quality control as part of the process (immediate detection of errors) |
| Rejects are concealed in buffer stocks | Immediate rejection of defective parts |
| Loss of production time because of long set-up times, defective parts, inventory bottlenecks, etc. | Reduction of lost time as a result of shorter set-up times, fewer defective parts, just-in-time deliveries meeting changing demand, etc. |
| Resource driven | Demand driven |
| Vertical and (in some cases) horizontal integration | Vertical disintegration |
| Cost reductions through wage control | Cost reductions through subcontracting |
| **Labour** | |
| Single task performance by worker | Multiple tasks |
| Payment per rate (based on job design criteria) | Personal payment (detailed bonus system) |
| High degree of job specialization | Elimination of job demarcation |
| Vertical labour organization | More horizontal labour organization for key workers |
| No or little on-the-job training | Ongoing on-the-job training |
| No learning experience | On-the-job learning; learning-by-doing integrated into long-term planning |
| Emphasis on diminishing worker's responsibility (disciplining of labour force) | Emphasis on worker's co-responsibility |
| Greater job security for unionized workers | High job security for key workers. No job security and poor labour conditions for temporary workers/increasing informal activities. No job security for workers employed by subcontractors |

*Source:* Albrechts and Swyngedouw (1989: 75, Figure 1)

of organization that can make increased use of outside consultants, specialists and subcontractors. This has led to a degree of vertical disintegration among firms (see Chapter 3). Another route to externalization has been to participate in joint ventures, in the licensing or contracting of technology, and in strategic alliances involving design partnerships, collaborative R&D projects and the like. Strategic alliances are an important contributor to the intensification of economic globalization. Having grown to well over 20,000 per year in 2004 (up from 5200 in 1996), the number of strategic alliances in the USA now far exceeds the number of more traditional (and more expensive) mergers and acquisitions. A survey of America's fastest growing companies identified that more than half the CEOs are involved in an average of three strategic alliances. Strategic alliances drove 30 per cent of all revenues in 2004 (Chernesky, 2006).

The numerous strategic alliances between the world's largest automakers include parts-sharing agreements and joint ventures in research, as well as in manufacturing. Toyota of Japan, for instance, has dozens of agreements with car and other companies, including an agreement with Nissan to collaborate on hybrid vehicle technology. GM and Daimler Group have also agreed to collaborate in developing hybrid vehicle technology. GM and ChevronTexaco agreed to collaborate on fuel cells (seen as the more environmentally friendly successor to the internal combustion engine). Other products of strategic alliances include the Pontiac Vibe hatchback, a Toyota Matrix that is made in California and marketed in the United States by General Motors; the Suzuki Swift that is marketed in Canada by GM as the Daewoo Kalos/Chevrolet Aveo; and the Jaguar, made in England by a wholly owned Ford subsidiary.

The Nestlé food company's strategic alliances, for example, include a joint venture with General Mills, called Cereal Partners Worldwide (CPW), and one with New Zealand's leading dairy company, Fronterra to supply dairy products throughout the Americas, called Dairy Partners Americas. Nestlé also has a joint venture with the Coca-Cola Company, called Beverage Partners Worldwide (BPW), in which the Swiss company cooperates with Coca-Cola in exchanging technologies and in marketing. Nestlé has, for example, licensed its Nestea and Enviga brands of ready-to-drink teas to Coca-Cola in the United States and to BPW for the rest of the world.

Such alliances have become an important aspect of global economic geography, as transnational corporations seek to reduce their costs and to minimize the risks involved in their multimillion-dollar projects. Strategic alliances serve several functions, they:

- allow transnational corporations to link up with local 'insiders' elsewhere in order to tap into new markets
- provide a quick and inexpensive means of swapping information about technologies that help to improve their products and their productivity
- reduce the costs of product development
- spread the costs of market research.

## Box 6.3 Changing geography of the clothing industry

The clothing industry provides a good example of the way in which local economic geographies are affected by an industry's response to globalization. In the nineteenth century, the clothing industry developed in the metropolitan areas of core countries, with many small firms using cheap migrant or immigrant labour. In the first half of the twentieth century, the industry, like many others, began to modernize. Larger firms emerged, their success based on taking advantage of mass production techniques for mass markets and on exploiting principles of spatial organization within national markets. In the United States, for example, the clothing industry went through a major locational shift as a great deal of production moved out of the workshops of New York to big, new factories in smaller towns in the south, where labour was not only much cheaper but less unionized.

Then, as the world economy began to globalize, semi-peripheral and peripheral countries became the least cost locations for mass produced clothing for global markets. In 1960, less than 7 per cent of all apparel purchased in the United States was imported; in 2007, the American Apparel & Footwear Association reported that 90 per cent was imported. Leisure wear – jeans, shorts, T-shirts, polo shirts and so on – was an important component of the homogenization of consumer tastes around the world and it could be produced most profitably by the cheap labour of young women in the peripheral metropolitan areas of the world. The hourly compensation (including benefits) of clothing workers in the United States is about $10 for a 37-hour week and in western Europe it is about US$17 an hour; for a 60-hour week, their counterparts in Asia (excluding Japan) average about US$3 an hour, with the labour costs in China and India under US$1 an hour. There are also inequalities in the wages of male and female workers (even in Europe, men in the textile, clothing and footwear industries make 20 to 30 per cent more than women). While the retail margin on domestically made garments sold in Europe and the United States is 70 per cent or so, the retail margin on clothing made in workshops in countries such as Indonesia and Thailand is 100 to 250 per cent. A typical example of how the sale price of a $100 garment is divided up would be: $50 to the retailer, $35 to the manufacturer (who spends $22.50 on textiles) and $15 to the contractor, who pays the garment workers $6. The apparel and textile industries together represent the largest industrial employer in the world. Apparel, over half of that industry, employs more than 20 million workers in the garment industry, of whom 75 per cent are women. Studies of the industry have shown that some of the female workers are as young as 12 – girls from rural villages who have been sent to work as sewing machinists in city workshops, sleeping eight to a room, sewing seven days a week from 8 am to 11 pm. Child labour is also widespread in subcontracting arrangements that make use of homeworkers.

This globalization of production has resulted in a complex set of commodity chains. Many of the largest clothing companies, such as Liz Claiborne, have most of their products manufactured through arrangements with independent suppliers (over 340 factories in the case of Claiborne), with no one supplier producing more than 4 or 5 per cent of the company's total output. These manufacturers are scattered throughout the world, making the clothing industry one of the most globalized of all manufacturing activities (see Figure 6.4). Claiborne has its goods produced simultaneously in 40 countries, mainly in Asia, the Caribbean and Central America, including China/Hong Kong, Cambodia and Mexico. The actual geography of commodity chains in the clothing industry is somewhat volatile, with frequent shifts in production and assembly sites as companies and their suppliers continuously seek out new locations with lower costs.

Although cheap leisure wear can be produced most effectively through arrangements with multiple suppliers in peripheral, low-wage regions, higher end apparel for the global marketplace requires a different geography of production. These products – women's fashion, outerwear and lingerie, infants' wear and men's suits – are based on frequent style changes and high-quality finish. This requires short production runs and greater contact between producers and buyers. The most profitable settings for these products are in the metropolitan areas of the core countries – London, Los Angeles, Milan, New York, Paris and Stuttgart – where, once again, migrant and immigrant labour provides a workforce for 'designer' clothing that can be shipped in small batches to upscale stores and shopping malls around the world.

The result is that commodity chains in the clothing industry are quite distinctive in terms of the origins of products destined for different segments of the market. Fashion-oriented retailers in the United States who sell designer products to upmarket customers obtain most of their goods from manufacturers in a small group of high-value-added countries including France, Italy, Japan, the United Kingdom and the United States. Department stores that emphasize 'private label' products (i.e., store brands, such as Nordstrom) and premium national brands will obtain most of their goods from established manufacturers in semi-peripheral East Asian countries. Mass merchandisers who sell lower priced brands buy primarily from a third tier of lower cost, mid-quality manufacturers, while large-volume discount stores like Wal-Mart import most of their goods from low-cost suppliers in peripheral countries like Bangladesh, China and the Dominican Republic. Finally, some importers operate on the outer fringes of the international production frontier, seeking out very cheap but low-quality products from new sources in peripheral countries with no significant experience in clothing manufacture.

## INTERPRETATIONS OF CORPORATE FLEXIBILITY

The increased flexibility in economic organization can be interpreted in two rather different ways. One interpretation, that of *flexible specialization*, sees the trend toward flexible production systems in a permanent and positive light. In short, new technologies have opened up the possibility for the decline of the large integrated firm and for the growth of a production system organized around clusters of small firms. Much is made of cases such as the 'Third Italy' (central and northeast Italy) where such clusters have emerged over the past 30 years. Alfred Marshall's (1920) model of the industrial district is sometimes used to provide a theoretical argument for the clustering of specialized industries in specific localities: this emphasized

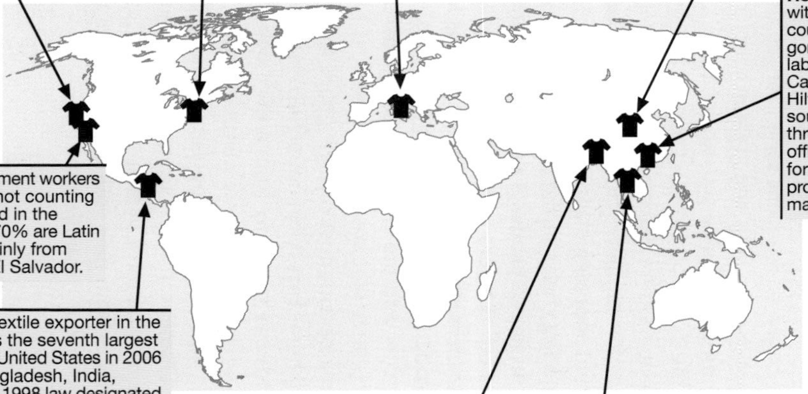

Liz Claiborne routinely ships 5 million items each week in the United States alone and sources its clothing from 340 factories in 40 countries, especially in Asia. Chinese suppliers in supply-chain cities containing factories, dormitories for workers, textile mills, and button and other supplies are attractive to US companies like Liz Claiborne. Luen Thai Holdings's supply-chain city in China's Guangdong Province allows Liz Claiborne to locate all but its core designers and trend spotters close to the factory floor. This cuts production time and gets garments to customers more quickly by eliminating the need to ship prototypes back and forth between the factory and Liz Claiborne's offices in **New York**.

Levi Strauss & Co has regional headquarters in **San Francisco**, Brussels and Singapore. Product designers are located primarily in the United States, Belgium, Japan and Korea, with over 700 different suppliers in about 50 countries. Since 1992, the company has kept databases to track contractors' work practices and labour relations based on its supplier code of conduct. The company withdrew sourcing from Myanmar (Burma) because of concerns over human rights violations.

**Italy** is the world's second-largest exporter of apparel, after China. Most of its products are higher quality garments that are consumed in other European countries (especially Germany and France), the United States and Japan.

Despite the imposition of US and EU safeguard quotas between 2005 and 2008 following the termination of the Multi-Fibre Agreement (MFA) quotas at the end of 2004, **China** remains the world's largest exporter of textiles and apparel, followed by its special administrative region of Hong Kong. China's textile and garment exports have increased steadily to well over US$55 billion annually. As the standard of living has increased in sync with China's rising exports, its domestic apparel market has grown. Two-thirds of China's textile products are now for a domestic market that is expected to increase in tandem with the country's growing middle-income group.

**Hong Kong** can no longer compete with the lowest-cost manufacturing countries, so its manufactures have gone up-market. Premium designer labels—including Donna Karen, Calvin Klein, Ralph Lauren, Tommy Hilfiger and Yves Saint Laurent—source their apparel in Hong Kong through their own or other buying offices. Many of Hong Kong's former lower-end garments products are now subcontracted to manufacturers in China.

**Thailand** is one of a handful of peripheral countries that has been able to break into the ranks of the world's major clothing exporters. Textiles and clothing together are the largest manufacturing industry, and, after computer parts, the country's second largest export industry. Thailand's 2,500 garment companies, 450 dyeing, printing and finishing companies, 1,300 weaving and knitting companies, and 150 spinning businesses and 18 synthetic fibre manufacturers employ more than 1 million workers who generate over US$6 billion in export earnings annually.

Of the well over 60,000 garment workers in **Los Angeles County**, not counting the many workers involved in the informal economy, about 70% are Latin American immigrants, mainly from Mexico, Guatemala and El Salvador.

**Honduras** is the largest textile exporter in the Caribbean Basin and was the seventh largest exporter of apparel to the United States in 2006 (after China, Mexico, Bangladesh, India, Indonesia and Vietnam). A 1998 law designated the entire country as a free trade zone. More than 250 companies employ well over 100,000 workers (mostly young women), who assemble in excess of 120 million garments for companies such as The Gap, Hanes and Wrangler, with a value of about US$2 billion.

Clothing is the leading industry in **Bangladesh**, with export earnings of US$8 billion (of which over 90% goes to the United States and the European Union) representing about 75% of the country's annual exports. Buyers of Bangladeshi clothing include Levi Strauss, H&M, Marks & Spencer, Wal-Mart, The Gap and Nike. Garment exports have risen spectacularly since the early 1980s despite the termination of the Multi-Fibre Agreement (MFA) quotas and preferential access to the major Western markets at the end of 2004. The clothing sector employs about 1.5 million workers (mostly poor young women).

Fig 6.4: The changing global distribution of clothing manufacturing

specialized labour pools, external economies from proximity accruing to firms in the same industry, and the availability of specialized inputs and services. This is, of course, nothing more than a restatement of the main arguments for any kind of agglomeration or localization economies (Krugman, 1991: 35–67). It has, however, become popular to restate them in terms of the 'new institutional economics' (Williamson, 1985) as 'internalizing transaction costs' within regions rather than inside firms. A more radical point of view is that trust, loyalty and partnership between firms are vital to the establishment of the 'new' industrial districts, if not to the old ones of Alfred Marshall's model. Thus, the social conditions for small-scale production, in combination with (1) a history of artisanal activity, (2) nearby centres of innovation, (3) assistance from local governments and (4) consensus between labour and management, are all basic requirements for the functioning of industrial districts engaged in flexible production (Harrison, 1992). From this point of view, there is a sociology to the new industrial district that sets limits to its diffusion elsewhere.

On the basis of a series of national case studies (Silicon Valley in the USA, the Île de France technopole in France and the Third Italy), Scott (1988b: 106) has used the phrase 'regime of flexible accumulation' to describe this new wave of economic–geographical organization. The basic proposition is that irrespective of the particular industries involved (e.g., shoes, clothing, machine tools, computers) there is a major drive toward geographical concentration of industries even for manufacturing so-called 'mature products' (those towards the end of a product life-cycle). Rather than specialization at a regional scale of agglomeration, however, a more localized pattern of specialization is now under way. This is because small firms are its major agents and they prosper best as the providers of goods to rapidly changing markets when they are able to share information, labour traditions and inter-industry links.

Responding to criticisms of the industrial district model (such as that it ignores the continuing importance of large firms and exaggerates endogenous (local) conditions relative to world markets and the international division of labour) several authors have provided more synthetic accounts. For example, Scott (1992) now argues that large producers can play an important part in inducing and maintaining the growth of (high-technology) industrial districts. He suggests that the usual division of production units between flexible and mass producers is insufficient. He identifies a third type, the *systems house*, flexible producers that benefit from economies of scope flowing from R&D or design synergies, with a variegated internal structure of job specialization and batch production (as opposed to mass production) of complex products. These systems houses do not stand alone or operate with branch plants. They are usually connected with nearby flexible producers. They are the 'hubs' for high-technology industrial districts such as those in southern California, Cambridge, UK, Baden-Württemberg, Germany, and Tokyo and Kyoto in Japan.

Scott, for one, does not see this model of industrial districts as incompatible with an internationalized world economy. Indeed, he sees this phenomenon as itself 'the interlinkage of industrial districts across the globe … as a mosaic of regions consisting of localized networks of transactions (i.e. industrial districts) embedded in global networks of transactions' (Scott, 1992: 274). One study (Henderson, 1989) has attempted to show for one industry – semiconductor (computer chip) production – how its technical and social divisions of labour (broadly, R&D/unskilled and white male/female immigrant (USA) or female rural-to-urban migrants (east Asia) divisions) and the need for access to some protected markets (Europe) have produced a specific set of locational patterns of production activities. The 'American' semiconductor industry now links *production complexes* (Henderson does not use the language of industrial districts or flexible production) in the United States with others in, for example, Scotland and Hong Kong. Contrary to NIDL models, however, cheap labour is not the sole attraction of any of these locations. For example, there is now an indigenous electronics industry in some countries of East Asia oriented to local rather than American, European or other external demand.

A second interpretation of the Fordist/neo-Fordist divide, that of flexible accumulation, sees the methods of flexible production more as a response to a crisis of capital accumulation in some sectors of industrial production rather than a fully fledged new mode of production. From this point of view it is the growth and transformation of financial markets in the 1980s and the introduction of flexible production as a means of disciplining the power of labour that attract attention. In the first case, it is argued that through the 'explosion in new financial instruments and markets (e.g., junk bonds), coupled with the rise of highly sophisticated systems of financial coordination on a global scale', the financial system has forced the increase in 'the geographical and temporal flexibility of capital accumulation' (Harvey, 1990: 194). In the second case, the declining rate of profit in the 1970s led firms to a strategy of decentralized production to undermine the power of labour (and reduce wage bills), which had increased under Fordism, yet still maintain centralized control. Many of the often 'idealized' small firms of the Third Italy are indeed subcontractors for larger firms searching for alternatives to their large unionized labour forces.

It is important to note, however, that several criticisms have been directed at these interpretations, most especially the first one of flexible specialization:

- Not all the apparently 'flexible' methods of production are in fact that flexible. Simple oppositions such as 'rigid' and 'flexible', and 'Fordist' and 'neo-Fordist' impose a structure on an industrial history that is not all that simple. In particular, the labour processes in different industries, the market and macroeconomic features of different sectors, and the 'organizational cultures' of the firms and areas involved combine to produce a range of industrial geographies along the spectrum between locational fixity and global mobility (Amin and Thrift, 1992: 574).
- Large firms are now adopting many of the methods that were seen as the exclusive province of small firms clustered in industrial districts (as acknowledged by Scott). Some enter into strategic alliances to produce certain items even with firms that are their direct competitors (e.g., Toyota with GM or Toyota with Volkswagen and Daimler Group). They can do this even with dispersed production facilities.
- The geographical boundaries of industrial districts are not usually carefully defined; partly, this is a result of a lack of consensus about the transactions and flows that must be internalized geographically for a district to 'exist'. Some new industrial districts sprawl over large areas and overlap with other districts, whereas others are small and exclusive. Does the same logic of production govern both of these types of industrial space?
- Missing from most discussions of both models is attention to the specificity (in terms of industries, technologies and limited areas) of the 'new spaces' associated

with flexible production, prior spatial divisions of labour in the affected areas (and elsewhere where a shift to flexible production is not taking place) and the influence of government policies, especially with respect to technical education, innovation policy, tax incentives and trade barriers.

- Little is known of how local conditions interact with global competitive conditions to affect the fortunes of industrial districts. What is known suggests that such districts are not immune to the problems of international competition that afflict Fordist firms (see Box 6.4 and Chapter 13). Decreases in US defence spending since the end of the Cold War, for example, have seriously affected the fortunes of some industrial districts, such as California's Silicon Valley (which, however, survived earlier defence-spending cutbacks in the 1970s when its semi-conductor companies switched to selling their chips to the civilian market).

- Scholars who live in places experiencing the new forms of economic development emphasize the 'shift' to flexible production. The so-called Los Angeles 'school' (Scott is a leading member) uses examples of new production complexes from southern California, Massachusetts (Route 128) or the Third Italy as if they were drawn from a universal sample or provide a window on the future everywhere. The view of traditional manufacturing workers from the 'rustbelt' of the USA, for example, would be considerably less sanguine about the break with mass production and the possible universality of flexible production. Many large firms in the northeast of the USA continue to move production abroad or invest in automation. In many manufacturing industries, Fordist principles of production still prevail. (For an excellent review of the various problems with flexible production models, see Gertler, 1992.)

## Box 6.4 'New' industrial districts of the Third Italy

The Third Italy (central and northeast Italy) is an often cited example of one of the flexible production systems organized around clusters of small firms that have emerged during the past 30 years. Small firms are seen as the best providers of goods to rapidly changing markets in a localized pattern of specialization where they are able to share information, labour traditions and inter-industry links. Yet, in many cases, the tradition and style of the Italian artisanal approach have had to be adapted to modern production methods. Many of the often 'idealized' small firms of the Third Italy are in fact subcontractors for larger firms searching for alternatives to their large and more expensive unionized labour forces. Some of the largest Italian shoe manufacturers have even relocated production to lower cost east European countries such as Hungary, Romania and Slovenia, and to Asia. Even the small upmarket Italian shoe firms and their workers are not immune to the problems of international competition that afflict Fordist firms. Italian exports have been impacted by increased production in Brazil, China and Vietnam. Job losses have occurred as some smaller businesses have folded and others have been forced into mergers or acquisitions. International competition has stimulated businesses to strengthen their position at the top end of the market by investing in R&D and new technology, design techniques to improve quality and comfort and to create innovative models and colours. Italy remains the foremost shoe manufacturer in the European Union, the fifth largest footwear manufacturer worldwide and the third largest footwear exporter in the world. Despite the higher cost of producing shoes in the Third Italy, the small upmarket shoe manufacturers there are betting that they and their quality shoes will survive international competition (Galbraith, 2001).

## THE GLOBAL OFFICE AND THE INFORMATIONAL ECONOMY

The globalization of production systems and the growth of transnational corporations have brought about another important change in patterns of local economic development: producer services like financial and business services are now no longer locally oriented ancillary activities but important global industries in their own right. The new importance of financial and business services was initially a result of the globalization of manufacturing, an increase in the volume of world trade and the emergence of transnational corporate empires. It was helped along by advances in telecommunications and data processing. Satellite communications systems and fibre-optic networks made it possible for firms to operate key financial and business services 24 hours a day, around the globe, handling an enormous volume of transactions. Linked to these communications systems, computers permit the recording and coordination of the data.

As banking, finance and business services grew into important global activities, however, they were themselves transformed into something quite different from the old, locally oriented ancillary services. The global banking and financial network now handles trillions of dollars every day (with an estimated US$3 trillion or more in straight currency transactions, and tens of billions of dollars in transactions in fixed-income bonds and notes every trading day) – no more than 10 per cent of which has anything to do with the traditional world economy of trade in goods and services. International movements of money, bonds, securities and other financial instruments have now become an end in themselves because they are a potential source of high profits from speculation and manipulation. Several factors have supported this development:

- The institutionalization of savings (through pension funds and so on) has established a large pool of capital managed by professional investors with few local or regional allegiances or ties.
- Deregulation of banking and financial services, as governments in many countries have lifted restrictions and regulations in the hope of capturing more of their growth.
- The quadrupling of crude oil prices in 1973 generated so much capital for oil-rich countries that their banks opened overseas branches in order to find enough borrowers. In many cases, the borrowers were companies and governments in peripheral countries that had previously been considered poor investment prospects. The internationalization of financial services soon paid off for the big banks. By the mid-1970s, about 70 per cent of Citibank's overall earnings came from its international operations, with Brazil alone accounting for 13 per cent of the bank's earnings in 1976.
- A persistent trade deficit of the United States vis-à-vis the rest of the world (a result of the postwar recovery of Europe and Japan) created a growing pool of dollars outside the United States, known as eurodollars. This supply in turn created a pool of capital that was beyond the direct control of the US authorities.

- 'Hot' money (undeclared business income, proceeds of securities fraud, trade in illegal drugs and syndicated crime), easily laundered through international electronic transactions, also found its way into the growing pool of eurodollars. It is estimated that between 1 and 3 trillion US dollars are laundered each year through the global financial system. Even though the margin between these two estimates is enormous, the lower figure of US$1 trillion is still incredibly high.
- The initial response of many governments (including the US government) to balance-of-payments problems was to print more money – a short-term solution that eventually contributed to a significant surge in inflation in the world economy. This inflation, because it promoted rapid change and international differentials in financial markets, provided a further boost to speculative international financial transactions of all kinds.

Together, these factors have amounted to a change so important that a deep-seated restructuring of the world economy has resulted. Banks and financial corporations with the size and international reach of Citigroup (which now includes Smith Barney), Mizuho Financial Group, Deutsche Bank, Sumitomo Mitsui Banking Corporation or Nomura Holdings are able to influence local patterns and processes of economic development throughout the world, just like the major transnational corporations involved in the global assembly system. In addition, key producer services (such as market research, accountancy, advertising, banking, corporate insurance and corporate legal services) have proliferated, adding an important new dimension to the world's economic landscapes. Nearly four out of every five jobs in the USA and UK are in the service sectors. Having lost another 100,000 manufacturing jobs the previous year, the total number of workers in manufacturing employment in Britain had by 2000 fallen to fewer than 4 million – representing only 15 per cent of all full-time workers. By 2006 the number of manufacturing workers had fallen to less than 3 million – representing only 11 per cent of all full-time workers.

Perhaps most important of all, the combined effect of all this has been to create an emergent informational economy. The informational economy represents a new mode of economic production and management in which productivity and competitiveness rely heavily on the generation of new knowledge and on the access to, and processing of, appropriate information. As we saw in Chapter 1, the most important economic sectors in this informational economy are high-technology manufacturing, design-intensive consumer goods and business and financial services. In the industrial mode of development, the main source of productivity lies in the introduction of new energy sources and in the ability to decentralize the use of energy throughout the production and circulation processes. 'In the new, informational mode of development the source of productivity lies in the technology of knowledge generation, information processing, and symbol communication' (Castells, 2000: 17). Between 30 and 50 per cent of total gross value added (GVA) in most core economies is now knowledge based, including industries such as computers, software, pharmaceuticals, education and television. Over the past few decades, high-tech manufacturing has been the fastest growing area of world trade. High-tech industries have almost doubled their share of manufacturing output, to around 25 per cent and knowledge-intensive services are growing even faster, accounting for eight out of every 10 new jobs in the core economics.

## BUSINESS SERVICES AND METROPOLITAN GROWTH

The fastest growing service sector in Europe, North America, Japan and in scattered locations elsewhere in East Asia (e.g., Hong Kong, Singapore) has been that of business services. Most of these activities employ personnel either in managerial or information-processing positions. Demand for these services comes from other firms rather than the general public. Consequently, these services are located close to their main customers, overwhelmingly in and around large cities. Several factors have acted to reinforce this trend. The first is their *internationalization*. Agglomeration economies (access to clients and competitors, proximity to technical services, availability of qualified personnel) are so powerful across most of these services that they are disproportionately located in major cities. But ease of communication has made it possible for firms to operate across different cities rather than restrict themselves to one. The spread of manufacturing and conglomerate TNCs has encouraged successful business service firms to follow suit, establishing multi-city offices to service their transnational accounts. Second, the *deregulation* of national markets (especially in banking and finance) has also strengthened the relationship between certain large cities with well-established institutions (exchanges and commodity markets) and business services. A relatively small number of centres (London, Tokyo, Chicago, New York) has benefited disproportionately from this trend. These world cities have become vital control points within a world economy breaking the bounds previously imposed by national restrictions.

## BUSINESS SERVICES AND FLEXIBLE ECONOMIES

It can be argued that the processes of subcontracting and small firm growth associated with flexible production give rise to 'new' service activities and increase the dependence of manufacturers on the purchase of services from independent vendors. Typically, 'intermediary' functions in economic activity, such as wholesaling, have been regarded as internal to large *vertically integrated firms* (all functions carried out within one firm) or ignored because of an assumption that producers trade directly with one another. However, wholesaling has persisted and, recently, expanded. Glasmeier (1990) makes a plausible case for the view that the emergence of 'high-tech' industrial districts, such as Silicon Valley and Baden-Württemberg, Germany, depended from the start on the coexistence of manufacturers and merchant wholesalers. In the case of Austin, Texas, which Glasmeier examines in detail, the wholesalers serve as agents of interregional trade, bringing parts and products from outside the local complex into the local economy. Over time, national and regional wholesalers have displaced local ones in importance to the local manufacturers. This suggests both the importance of merchant wholesalers to the development of industrial districts and the role of exogenous (extra- or non-local) agents in local development. The growth of industrial districts cannot be explained just in terms of local social conditions or the nature of manufacturing processes.

Christopherson (1989) argues that the attention given to flexible production in manufacturing has obscured the increasing importance of flexibility in the labour markets of service industries. She points out that by the 1980s in the United States 80 per cent of the new jobs were in retail, health and business services, and that perhaps 25 per cent of all service jobs were 'flexible' jobs involving part-time work or independent subcontracting. Large firms increasingly dominate the growing service industries but to cut costs they make expanded use of subcontracting and part-time (usually female and minority group) employees. Indeed, a major feature of the restructuring of labour markets in the USA and Britain in the period since 1970 has been the 'feminization' of employment in the expanding service sectors at the same time that more highly paid and predominantly male manufacturing jobs have been disappearing. In the retail and health sectors 'worksites' are decentralized and administrative functions separated spatially from the delivery of the services themselves even as large firms become dominant. The services are increasingly standardized from place to place; much like the physical settings such as regional shopping centres, shopping malls and suburban medical buildings in which they are located.

*Spatial homogenization* rather than local specialization, therefore, characterizes the emerging spatial pattern of major service industries and the flexible employment on which they are coming to rely. This flexibility is more difficult to romanticize than that associated with manufacturing. It involves serious reductions in incomes compared to those paid in the 'old' Fordist manufacturing industries. It also reduces the overall 'power' of the workforce through exploiting gender and ethnic divisions (e.g., it is 'natural' to pay women less) and spatially dispersed worksites to restrict employment security and limit labour organizing.

## SUMMARY

In this chapter, we have seen how the crisis of Fordism, coupled with trends associated with corporate restructuring, technological advances and shifting consumer demand have begun to result in the globalization of economic activities that were previously localized within the core economies. Among the salient features of these changes are the following:

- The emergence of production hierarchies within the large companies that have come to dominate most industries. These hierarchies have tended to result in separate locational settings for (1) high-level corporate control, (2) production requiring high inputs of skilled labour and new technology; intermediate administration and R&D activities and (3) routine production.
- The organization of the world economy into three broad international regions:
  1 the highly integrated and very diversified industrial and control centres of the core of North America, Europe, Japan and Australasia
  2 the semi-periphery of resource-exporting countries, recently industrialized or 'old' NICs, and newly industrializing or 'new' NICs, mostly in the world's 'middle regions' (eastwards from Mexico, through the Mediterranean to East and Southeast Asia) as well as China, Russia and parts of the southern hemisphere including India
  3 the relatively thinly industrialized periphery that makes up most of the southern hemisphere (such as Sub-Saharan Africa), which is highly dependent on the core.
- Persistence within each of these broad regions of nested hierarchies of countries and regions at different levels of economic development. Thus the periphery contains core regions and semi-peripheral regions (as, e.g., the Lagos/Ibadan region and Abidjan region respectively in West Africa), the semi-periphery contains core regions and peripheral regions (e.g., the Calcutta-Hooghly-Howra conurbation and Uttar Pradesh respectively in India), and the core contains regions that are, relatively, semi-peripheral and peripheral (e.g., Portugal or Greece and east-central Europe respectively in Europe).

## KEY SOURCES AND SUGGESTED READING

Bingham, R.D. and Hill, E.W. (eds) 1997. *Global Perspectives on Economic Development*. New Brunswick, NJ: Center for Urban Policy Research.

Cooke, P. 2005. Regional asymmetric knowledge capabilities and open innovation exploring 'Globalization 2' – a new model of industry organisation, *Research Policy*, 34, 1128–49.

Harrison, B. 2007. Industrial districts: old wine in new bottles?, *Regional Studies*, 41, S107–S121.

Leinbach, T.R. and Brunn, S.D. (eds) 2001. *Worlds of E-Commerce: Economic, Geographical and Social Dimensions*. Chichester: John Wiley & Sons.

Markusen, A. 2003. Fuzzy concepts, scanty evidence, policy distance: the case of rigour and policy relevance in critical regional studies, *Regional Studies*, 37, 701–17.

Scott, A.J. 2006. *Geography and Economy*. Oxford: Clarendon Press.

Scott, A.J. and Storper, M. 2003. Regions, globalization, development, *Regional Studies*, 37, 579–93.

Thrift, N.J. 2002. A hyperactive world, in R.J. Johnston, P.J. Taylor and M. Watts (eds) *Geographies of Global Change. Remapping the World in the Late Twentieth Century* 2nd edn. Oxford: Blackwell.

UNCTAD 2001. *World Investment Report 2001*. New York and Geneva: United Nations.

UNCTAD 2006. *World Investment Report 2006: FDI from Developing and Transition Economies: Implications for Development*. New York and Geneva: United Nations.

## RELATED WEBSITES

Center for Globalization and Policy Research: http://www.sppsr.ucla.edu/cgpr/
this UCLA centre provides information and downloadable working papers on the globalization of production

International Labour Organization: http://www.ilo.org/
this UN agency offers research and data on labour issues around the world, including information about work standards, child workers, etc.

United Nations Conference on Trade and Development (UNCTAD): http://www.unctad.org/
UNCTAD's website offers publications and data on global production and trade

United Nations Industrial Development Organization: http://www.unido.org/
this UN agency website provides research and data on industry and manufacturing around the world and includes a searchable database with statistics on manufacturing (value added, employment, etc.) for each country, available at http://www.unido.org/Regions.cfm?area=GLO

World Trade Organization: http://www.wto.org/
the WTO's website includes research and documents on a variety of issues related to global production and trade

# Part 3

# Spatial transformation of core and periphery

In the next five chapters, we examine the spatial transformations of the core and periphery, paying special attention to the changing relationships between core and periphery outlined in Chapters 2 and 3. In Chapter 7, the spatial implications of the latest form of economic organization on the capitalist countries of the world's core regions are examined. In Chapter 8, we examine the spatial transformations in the periphery and semi-periphery that have occurred as a consequence of both an older colonialism and a more recent interdependent global capitalism. Attention is also paid, however, to how the consequences have varied depending on local relations and institutional responses. In Chapters 9, 10 and 11, three major economic activities, agriculture, manufacturing and services are examined both with respect to their roles in economic development and their changing geographical patterns, particularly from the perspective of the periphery and semi-periphery. The emphasis throughout this section is on the impacts of and responses to the evolving modern world economy in both the developed and the less developed countries and to the changing relationships between them.

# Chapter 7

# Spatial reorganization of the core economies

Picture credit: Anthony Bayford

The evolution of advanced (disorganized) capitalism and the emergence of an informational economy have led to a significant reorganization of the economic geography of places and regions throughout most of the world. We shall examine the nature and implications of these changes for the economic landscapes of the NICs and LDCs in Chapter 8. In this chapter, we focus our attention on urban and regional change in the core countries, emphasizing the overall impact of corporate reorganization in creating new industrial spaces and affecting regional economic well-being.

It is important to note at the outset that the globalization of the economy described in the previous chapter has resulted in a relative *increase* in the importance of cities and regions as agents of economic development:

> In a world economy whose productive infrastructure is made up of information flows, cities and regions are increasingly becoming critical agents of economic development ... Precisely because the economy is global, national governments suffer from failing powers to act upon the functional processes that shape their economies and societies. But regions and cities are more flexible in adapting to the changing conditions of markets, technology and culture. True, they have less power than national governments, but they have a greater response capacity to generate targeted development projects, negotiate with multinational firms, foster the growth of small and medium endogenous firms, and create conditions that will attract the new sources of wealth, power, and prestige.

> Castells and Hall (1994: 7)

As at the international level, the major components of urban and regional change have hinged on the redeployment of routine production capacity from high-cost to low-cost locations, and the retention/localization of facilities requiring high inputs of technology and/or skilled labour in key locations with appropriate resources and amenities. As a result, two countervailing trends characterize the 'new' economic geographies of Europe, North America, Australasia and Japan: *decentralization* and *consolidation*. Decentralization has led to an attenuation of regional and interurban gradients in economic well-being; consolidation has contributed to an increased spatial differentiation in terms of the conditions of production and exchange, and the hierarchical structure of control.

At the same time, we have to consider the effects on core countries of wider changes in the world economy and in the regime of capitalist accumulation. We begin, therefore, with a brief outline of the main outcomes of these secular changes. In the broadest of terms, three key changes can be identified: a transformation of the relationship between capital and labour; the creation of new regional divisions of labour; and the development of new roles for the state. Together, they amount to the beginning of a distinctive new context for economic development in core countries.

## 7.1 A NEW CONTEXT FOR URBAN AND REGIONAL CHANGE

Neo-Fordism has emerged as a new regime of accumulation as companies throughout the developed world have exploited new technologies and new strategies in order to remain competitive in a globalizing economy. In the process, the relationship between capital and labour has been transformed, with capital recapturing the initiative over wage rates and conditions that had been established under 'organized' industrial capitalism. New technologies have played a major role in this transformation. The introduction of robotics in factories and information-processing technologies in offices, for example, has made for dramatic increases in productivity but has also created a long-term threat: that of substituting machines for workers, thus placing labour in a weak bargaining position.

Neo-Fordism has also created a new interregional and international division of labour, as large corporations have pursued flexible strategies in order to deal with, and exploit, the 'time–space compression' introduced by new transport and telecommunications technologies such as long-distance fibre-optic systems, regional telecommunications systems, satellite teleports, 'smart' buildings and microwave communications. Paradoxically, this 'annihilation of space' and 'electronic colonialism' has *heightened the importance of geography*. The reduction of spatial barriers has had the effect of magnifying greatly the significance of what local spaces contain because the new flexibility of the business world enables relatively small differences between places to be quickly, if temporarily, exploited to good effect. As a result, there has been an acceleration of shifts in the patterning of uneven development on the basis of particular local mixes of skills and resources: *a continuously variable geometry of labour, capital, production, markets and management.*

Last, but not least, Neo-Fordism has required the development of new roles for the state and the public sector: reduced direct government intervention in the economy and a decreased emphasis on providing for collective consumption (school, hospitals, community services, etc.). The dilemma facing most governments was that the deindustrialization recession accentuated the vulnerability of more and more people while making it increasingly difficult – politically as well as economically – to finance existing programmes. As a result, a 'new conservativism' in the orientation of central and local governments emerged. This new conservatism was associated with an ideological stance based on the assertion that the welfare state had not only generated unreasonably high levels of taxation, budget deficits, disincentives to work and save, and a bloated class of unproductive workers, but also that it may have fostered 'soft' attitudes towards 'problem' groups in society. The consequent restructuring of the welfare state was most pronounced in the United Kingdom and the United States, where the Thatcher and Reagan administrations respectively embarked on programmes of privatization in health, housing and education, accompanied by cuts (some absolute, some relative) in higher education, in programmes for the unemployed, those with disabilities and the elderly and in regional policy budgets. In the United Kingdom, closer controls on local government expenditure by the central government led to corresponding cuts at the local level, particularly in depressed towns and cities where the incidence of need for welfare services is high but local fiscal resources are low.

This last point is central to the emergence of a new *mode of regulation* that, in turn, is tied in to the emergence of the new neo-Fordist or flexible regime of accumulation. Following Jessop (1992), we can characterize this emerging mode of regulation in general terms as involving a commitment to supply-side innovation in flexibility, with specific manifestations in several areas:

- a change in the regulation and conduct of labour markets, involving (1) a shift away from centralized collective bargaining towards company- or plant-level negotiations, and (2) an increasing tolerance of insecurity and marginality in the wage relations and employment conditions of unskilled workers
- flatter, leaner and more flexible forms of corporate organization that are suited not only to externalization but also to joint ventures and to public–private partnerships
- more flexible forms of credit: the result of deregulation of financial markets and the internationalization of finance and financial services, which has effectively reduced the degree of control that can be exerted by individual national governments
- displacement of Keynesian welfare states by 'workfare states':

> The emerging state form will no longer be concerned mainly with securing full employment within a national economy but with guiding and promoting the structural competitiveness of the national economy by intervening on the supply-side to encourage innovation; and it will no longer be concerned to generalise norms of mass consumption but to articulate policies to the need to promote greater flexibility.
>
> Jessop (1992: 32)

Table 7.1 illustrates some of the main contrasts between the characteristics of states under the two systems:

- The 'hollowing out' of national government as a result of (1) the displacement of national power upwards through pan-regional agreements and transnational organizations (see Chapter 12) and downwards to regional and local governments (see Chapter 13) and (2) increasing cooperation among local and regional governments in key fields such as R&D and technology transfer in ways that bypass their respective national states.

It has been suggested that this emerging mode of regulation, together with the imprint of Neo-Fordism and the globalization of economic activity from the core (as described in this chapter) marks the beginning of a new phase of capitalism. Lash and Urry (1987) describe this phase as one of disorganized (advanced) capitalism, to

Table 7.1 Contrasts in the characteristics of states: Fordism and flexible accumulation (Neo-Fordism)

| Fordism | Flexible accumulation (Neo-Fordism) |
| --- | --- |
| Regulation | Deregulation/regulation |
| Rigidity | Flexibility |
| Collective bargaining | Division/individualization |
| Socialization of welfare (welfare state) | Privation of collective needs and social security <br> Soup kitchen state for the underprivileged |
| International stability through multilateral agreements | International destabilization |
| Centralization | Decentralization and sharpened inter-regional/inter-city conflicts |
| The 'subsidy' state/city | The 'entrepreneurial' state/city marketing |
| Indirect intervention in markets through income and price policies | Direct state intervention in markets through procurement |
| Company-financed R&D | State-financed R&D |
| Industry-led innovation | State-led innovation |

*Source:* Albrechts and Swyngedouw (1989: 75, Figure 1)

distinguish it from the previous phase that was dominated by a closely regulated and highly organized relationship between labour, capital and government at the level of a country. Disorganized capitalism, in contrast, is characterized by:

1 deconcentration of capital within national markets, a growing separation of finance from industry and the decline of cartels (as a result of the growth of a world market, the increasing scale of industrial, commercial and banking enterprises and the general decline of tariffs)
2 decline in the absolute and relative size of the core working class and the expansion of a service class of professional, white-collar workers in core economies as they deindustrialize
3 decline in the importance and effectiveness of national-level collective bargaining and a growth in company and plant-level bargaining (as companies exert their new leverage in order to impose more flexible forms of organization)
4 increasing independence of large monopolies from direct control and regulation by individual national states
5 decline in average plant size because of shifts in industrial structure, substantial labour-saving capital investment, the hiving off of various subcontracted activities and the export of labour-intensive activities to underdeveloped countries and to peripheral regions within core economies

6  decline of metropolitan dominance within core countries – the loss of jobs and population from inner city areas and an increase in jobs and population in smaller towns and some rural areas

7  weakening of the degree to which industries are concentrated in specific countries and regions as a result of the new, variable geometry of the international division of labour – 'each nation or locality develops its own kind of industrialization process even as it may depend on, and partake of, global investment flows and multinational industrial production systems' (Storper, 1987: 591)

8  decline in the salience and class character of political parties, an increase in cultural fragmentation and pluralism, the emergence of a 'global' culture and an international consciousness and the ascendance of a 'postmodern' cultural–ideological configuration (Table 7.2).

**Table 7.2** Contrasts in ideology: Fordism and flexible accumulation (Neo-Fordism)

| Fordism | Flexible accumulation (Neo-Fordism) |
| --- | --- |
| Mass consumption of consumer durables: the consumption society | Individualized consumption: 'Yuppie' culture |
| Modernism | 'Post'-modernism |
| Totality/structural reform | Specificity/adaptation |
| Rationalism | Deconstructionism |
| Socialization | Individualization The 'spectacle' society |

*Source*: Albrechts and Swyngedouw (1989: 75, Figure 1)

## 7.2 SPATIAL REORGANIZATION OF THE CORE ECONOMIES

In this section, we examine two important trends in the economic geography of the core economies, both of which have occurred within the context of the globalization of economic activity and the secular shifts within core countries from manufacturing to informational economies. The first of these trends is the regional, inter-metropolitan and metropolitan *decentralization* of certain categories of both manufacturing and service employment. The second is the regional and inter-metropolitan *consolidation* of other kinds of activities.

### 1. SPATIAL DECENTRALIZATION AND EXTERNAL CONTROL

Decentralization has operated at regional, metropolitan and inter-metropolitan scales in response to a variety of complex and often cross-cutting processes of reorganization and adjustment.

### Regional decentralization

Regional decentralization is a product of the migration of some firms and the 'births' and 'deaths' of others, together with the transfer of productive capacity by plant shutdowns in core, metropolitan regions and the opening of new branch plants (or the expansion of existing ones) in declining or peripheral cities and regions of core countries. The result has been the creation of what have been called 'branch-plant economies' and 'module production places' in the peripheral regions of most core countries.

A useful distinction can be made between diffuse industrialization and branch-plant industrialization (Hudson, 1983). The former has been directed towards the reserves of unskilled labour in rural regions, while the latter has been directed towards the skilled manual labour reserves of declining industrial regions. The areas of central and northeastern Italy provide classic examples of *diffuse* industrialization, much of it resulting from the decentralization of companies from the Milan-Turin area in response to the increasing shortage, cost and militancy of labour there. On the one hand, diffuse industrialization typically involves activities in which labour costs are an important part of overall production costs *and* in which there has been little scope for reducing labour costs through technological change; it can thus be seen as an expression of the product life-cycle model of industrial location. Empirical studies have shown that the main attractions of rural locations for such activities have been:

- availability of relatively low-cost labour
- inexpensive supplies of easily developed land
- lower levels of taxation
- low levels of unionization.

*Branch-plant industrialization* proper, on the other hand, typically involves activities that require significant inputs of technology and of skilled (or at least experienced) labour and that also require a certain degree of centrality in order to assemble and distribute raw materials and finished products. Good examples are provided by many former textile cities – Dundee in the United Kingdom, for example, and Amiens in France – where branch plants in a variety of 'light' industries (including tyres, light engineering and, more recently, computer software and biotechnology) have moved in to take advantage of 'surplus' labour, cheap factory space and an established infrastructure. It is not only manufacturing activities that are being decentralized, however. While many places have developed branch-plant economies on the basis of assembly line activities, some have attracted white-collar information-processing or wholesaling functions. Omaha, Nebraska, for example, has become the '800' telephone exchange centre of the United States, based partly on its reliable telecommunications and electric power infrastructure; Roanoke, Virginia, with its easy access to major trucking routes, has become the centre for a number of mail-order (catalogue and internet) and teleshopping operations.

The twin processes of diffuse and branch-plant industrialization, combined with the process of mergers and acquisitions, have meant that regional decentralization has come to be characterized by increasing levels of external control. By as early as 1973 in the northern region of England, for example, 78 per cent of manufacturing employment was controlled by companies with headquarters outside the region, compared with 57 per cent in 1963. In the southern states of the USA, fewer than one-third of the new jobs created in manufacturing plants between 1969 and 1976 belonged to southern-based corporations.

As at the international level, it has been the large transnational corporations that have been particularly important in influencing the extent and spatial pattern of external control. In the United States, the total number of jobs in foreign-owned firms jumped from 2.0 million in 1980 to over 5.0 million by 2006. Many of these jobs have been in manufacturing and most have been controlled by British, German, Japanese, Canadian, French, Dutch or Swiss companies. In several states, Japanese-owned companies alone account for between 4 and 8 per cent of all manufacturing employees. Many Japanese automobile companies are clustered in the USA's 'automobile alley' of states that include Ohio, Kentucky and Tennessee (Figure 7.1). In high-tech, high-growth industries, about 20 per cent of all employment in the United States is in foreign firms. While the extent of employment in foreign-owned firms in states with the largest concentrations of US high-tech employment (e.g., California and Massachusetts) is relatively low, as much as 50 per cent of all high-tech employment in several states (including Wisconsin, Indiana and North Carolina) is controlled by foreign firms.

Because of the degree of external control involved in regional economic decentralization, it has become a moot point as to how much long-term benefit will accrue to the regions involved. On the *positive* side, it can be argued that branch-plant economies and module production places benefit by having access to the

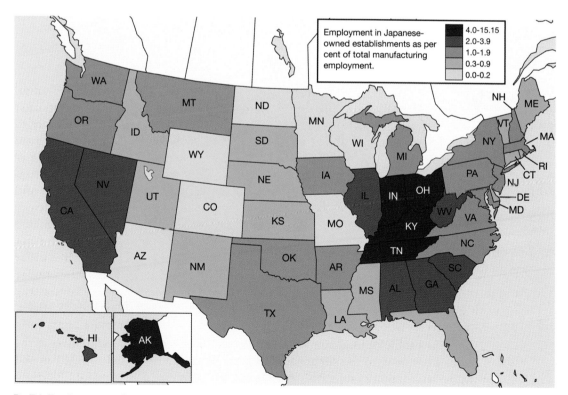

Fig 7.1: Employment in Japanese-owned manufacturing establishments in the United States, 2002

*Source*: Based on online data from US Bureau of the Census, 2002 Economic Census

financial resources and technological and administrative innovations of the parent firm. Moreover, some locations have attracted 'higher order' corporate functions, such as research and development (R&D) (Figure 7.2). The location of foreign-owned industrial R&D facilities in the USA, for example, is concentrated in those areas that also offer specialized expertise in certain university departments: Silicon Valley, around Stanford and Berkeley universities (for computers, semiconductors, computer software and biotechnology), the Los Angeles metropolitan area (for a variety of R&D, including automotive design), New Jersey, especially around Princeton University (for drugs and chemicals), the Research Triangle Park in North Carolina (for biotechnology and telecommunications), and the Boston, Massachusetts, region, particularly around the Massachusetts Institute of Technology (MIT) (for computers). R&D in some regions is highly specialized in certain industries, such as Detroit, Michigan, for automotive facilities and Richardson, Texas, for telecommunications.

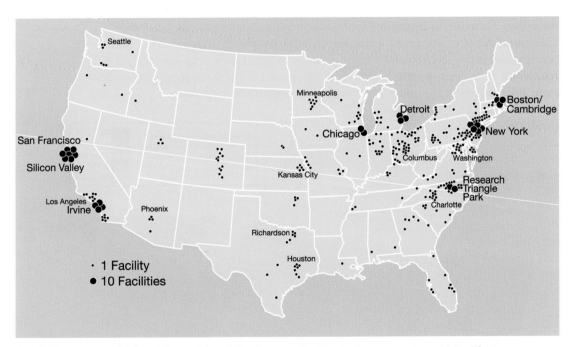

Fig 7.2: Foreign-owned industrial research and development facilities in the conterminous United States
*Source:* Dalton and Serapio (1999: 26, Figure 3)

On the *negative* side, it has been suggested that the absence of 'higher order' corporate functions in other locations can:

1  limit the profile of local employment opportunities, leading to a *deskilling* of the local workforce, to the suppression of entrepreneurial drive and enthusiasm and to the retardation of technological innovation
2  result in a very open regional economy, so that international economic fluctuations are transmitted into the region relatively quickly. The corollary of this is that because externally controlled plants are poorly integrated with the local economy, their own potential multiplier effects are limited

3   increase the vulnerability of branch-plant economies to the further redeployment
of capital – branch-plant economies in the core countries are placed in direct competition with those of the NICs, which typically have much lower factor costs.

## Metropolitan decentralization

Metropolitan decentralization (the exodus of industry and employment from inner-
city areas to suburbs) can in fact be traced to the 1930s; but since the early 1970s
the process has begun to dominate patterns of urban development in a number of
countries. Historically, the major impetus for metropolitan decentralization has
been employers' desire to sidestep the increasing militancy of labour in inner-city
neighbourhoods. Suburban locations have also been attractive to many industries
because of the availability of larger tracts of relatively cheap land. Given this basic
attractiveness, successive improvements in transport and communications have
greatly accelerated the process of decentralization.

   Residential suburbanization, meanwhile, has provided labour supplies – including
cheap, non-unionized, female labour – that have encouraged the suburbanization of
more firms. A mutually reinforcing process was thus set in motion. At the same time,
the intensification of some of the locational disadvantages of inner-city areas – higher
taxes, congestion, restricted sites and so on – began to push some firms out. The
stagflation episode of the 1970s threw the cumulative effect of all these factors into
focus for many firms, as profits were sharply squeezed. What was most pronounced
was the 'shakeout' of routine and labour-intensive inner-city areas – some of it destined for relocation in the suburbs, but much more destined for relocation in rural
areas, peripheral regions of core economies, peripheral countries or the bankruptcy
courts. *The overall result was a sharp acceleration in the relative rate of growth of
employment in the suburbs and a sudden intensification of the 'inner city problem'.*

## Inter-metropolitan decentralization

At the inter-metropolitan level, the most striking aspect of decentralization has
involved service industries, particularly business services. Corporate reorganization,
facilitated by advances in telecommunications, has resulted in a general decentralization of routine business services down the urban hierarchies of core countries.
The process has been geographically selective, with a relatively small number of
metropolitan areas (in the northeast and 'Sunbelt' including Dallas, Houston,
Huntsville, Los Angeles, Newark, San Francisco, San José, Tampa and Washington,
DC) enjoying a disproportionately high proportion of employment in business services. This phenomenon is surprising to some observers, who had expected that new
communications technologies would allow for the dispersion of 'electronic offices'
and, with it, the decentralization of an important catalyst for local economic development. A good deal of geographic decentralization of offices has occurred, in fact,
but it has mainly involved 'back-office' functions that have been relocated from
metropolitan and business district locations to small-town and suburban locations.

   Back-office functions are record keeping and analytical functions that do not
require frequent personal contact with clients or business associates. The account-
ants and financial technicians of high-street banks, for example, are back-office
workers. Developments in computing technologies, database access, electronic data
interchanges and telephone call-routing technologies are enabling a larger share of
back-office work to be relocated to specialized office space in cheaper settings,

freeing space in the high-rent locations occupied by the bank's front office. For example, the US Postal Service uses multiple optical character readers (MLOCRs) to read addresses on mail, which is then barcoded and automatically sorted for delivery. Digitally scanned images of addresses that the MLOCRs cannot read are transmitted electronically to the remote barcoding system, which has a high-tech neural net processor that effectively reads almost all addresses, no matter how poorly written. Mail with addresses that still cannot be read using this automated system is sent to one of three mail recovery centres (formerly dead letter offices) for workers to examine. The three mail recovery centres are distributed throughout the country, in such places as Atlanta, where wage rates are relatively low.

Among the more prominent examples of back-office decentralization from US metropolitan areas have been the relocation of back-office jobs in American Express from New York to Salt Lake City (Utah), Fort Lauderdale (Florida), Phoenix (Arizona) and Greensboro (North Carolina); the relocation of Hertz's reservations and data-entry operations to Oklahoma City and Saraland, Alabama; and the relocation of Citibank's MasterCard and Visa divisions to Tampa and Sioux Falls.

Internationally, this trend has taken the form of offshore back offices. By decentralizing back-office functions to offshore locations, companies save even more in labour costs. While Zurich-based Swissair, for example, now does its accounting in Mumbai, India, several New York-based life insurance companies have established back-office facilities in Ireland. Situated conveniently near Ireland's main international airport, Shannon, they ship insurance claim documents from New York via Federal Express, process them and beam the results back to New York via satellite or transatlantic fibre-optic line (Figure 7.3). Similarly, US companies have offshore back offices in the Caribbean, and particularly in Anglophone countries such as Barbados and Jamaica. American Airlines moved its data-processing centre from Tulsa to Barbados in 1981 (Figure 7.3) and, through its subsidiary Caribbean Data Services (CDS), later expanded operations to Jamaica and the Dominican Republic. Chapter 11 provides an in-depth examination of service outsourcing and the implications for both the LDCs and the DCs.

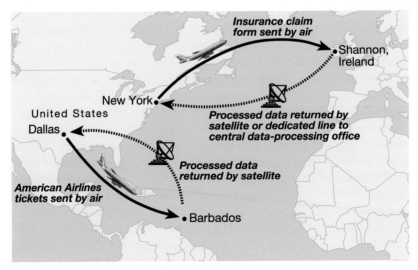

Fig 7.3: International back offices

*Source:* Adapted from Stutz and Warf (2007: 279, Figure 8.27)

## Box 7.1 The Sunbelt

Regional, metropolitan and inter-metropolitan decentralization are individual components in what is ultimately a multidimensional dynamic of spatial change. The growth of the US Sunbelt provides a good example. The Sunbelt phenomenon can be interpreted as the *combined* product of diffuse industrialization, inter-metropolitan decentralization and metropolitan decentralization. Such an interpretation is supported by the types of employment growth that characterize the rise of the Sunbelt: (1) production jobs in branch plants in industries such as textiles, clothing and electronics; (2) production jobs in branch plants and in locally based firms in high-growth industries – mainly in computer hardware, scientific instruments, aerospace and chemicals and plastics; and (3) service jobs catering both to these industries and to the increased population attracted to the retirement and leisure communities.

In very general terms, it appears that Sunbelt states such as Arizona, California, the Carolinas and Texas have been able to benefit from relative advantages in terms of labour costs, labour unionization, land costs, energy costs, local taxation, local government boosterism and federal expenditure patterns. In addition, Sunbelt cities have proved attractive to industries because they did not have a legacy of inefficient layout and infrastructure. As Gordon put it (1979: 78): 'They could be constructed from scratch to fit the needs of a new period of accumulation in which factory plant and equipment were themselves increasingly predicated upon a decentralized model ... There was consequently no identifiable downtown factory district ... Automobiles and trucks provided the connecting links, threading together the separate pieces. The corporate city became ... The Fragmented Metropolis.'

## 2. CONSOLIDATION AND AGGLOMERATION

The structural and functional consolidation of certain activities under advanced capitalism has made for countertrends that have strengthened the economic well-being of many of the largest and most central components of the space-economies of the core countries.

The fundamental reason for the consolidation of certain economic activities in such settings is that:

> Large towns offer larger local markets, with the associated internal economies of scale, plus greater external economies than are available in smaller places, and together these allow production costs which are often significantly lower than those in smaller towns: once transport costs began to fall substantially, so that they were less than the production cost differential between the large-town and the small-town firm, the former could begin the invasion of the latter's market.
>
> Johnston (1980: 110–11)

The sectoral shifts and manufacturing specializations of advanced capitalism have also worked in favour of many large cities and metropolitan regions. Manufacturers of many sophisticated new high-value-added products have been drawn to such locations. The reasons for this are several:

- complex links that these new products have with established industries
- their dependence on risk capital in the early stages of development
- their need for access to a large, affluent and sophisticated market during the early stages of marketing.

Similarly, large parts of the rapidly expanding service sector have been drawn towards metropolitan locations because of the kind of environment and workforce required by information-processing, coordinating, controlling and marketing activities.

Corporate restructuring and new competitive strategies have added to the agglomerative and recentralizing trends of certain economic activities in metropolitan settings. The flexibility of Neo-Fordism requires a new social division of labour with access to a large and fluid labour pool (containing part-time and temporary workers as well as highly skilled workers – attributes that are most readily found in metropolitan settings). Equally important, metropolitan settings are essential to the *externalization* of certain functions and the more extensive use of outside consultants, subcontracting, joint ventures, strategic alliances and collaborative R&D that characterize flexible production systems.

Finally, the national and international redeployment of activities by large conglomerate companies has also contributed to the consolidation of certain activities in the central regions and metropolitan areas of the developed countries. In particular, there has been *a marked localization of two key functions: headquarters offices* and *R&D establishments*. Indeed, the distribution of these two functions has come to represent an important dimension of the 'new' economic geography of advanced capitalism.

## Box 7.2 Agglomeration and the 'relational turn' in economic geography: Motor Sport Valley

[I]t is precisely the social, institutional, cultural and political embeddedness of local and regional economies that can play a key role in determining the possibilities for or constraints on development; and thus why spatial agglomeration of economic activity occurs in particular places and not others ... it is not merely a case of recognizing that the mechanisms of economic development, growth and welfare operate unevenly across space, but that those mechanisms are themselves spatially differentiated and in part geographically constituted; that is, determined by locally varying, scale-dependent social, cultural and institutional conditions.

Martin (1999: 75, 83)

Since the mid-1990s, many economic geographers have become increasingly concerned with the ways in which the socio-spatial relations among agents and structures shape the spatial organization of economic activities. In 2003, the *Journal of Economic Geography* devoted a special issue to the 'relational turn' in economic geography (see, for example, Boggs and Rantisi, 2003).

Henry and Pinch (2000) offer a case study of the agglomeration of the British motor sport industry in 'Motor Sport Valley' to show how this relational economic geography allows economic geographers to conceptualize geographical specialization as the construction of a socially embedded and 'relational' economic system. By global standards, the British motor sport industry is a classic example of a leading regional agglomeration. This agglomeration – the 'Silicon Valley of Motor Sport' or 'Motor Sport Valley' – is located in the vicinity of Oxford (northwest of London) and dominates the world's racing car industry.

Motor Sport Valley began as a network of small companies but now includes investment from some of the world's largest automobile manufacturers, including Ford, Nissan, Subaru, Mercedes-Benz, Volvo and General Motors, in addition to international sponsors from other sectors of the economy, including primarily tobacco. About three-quarters of the world's single-seater racing cars are designed and assembled in this region, including the vast majority of the most competitive Formula One, Championship Auto Racing Teams and Indy Racing League cars. The region is also the base for a large number of rallying teams.

Henry and Pinch argue that Motor Sport Valley can best be conceptualized as a 'knowledge community' that comprises a socially and spatially embedded economic system facilitating the generation and rapid dissemination of knowledge about the best ways to design and manufacture racing cars. Their case study analysis found that a key characteristic of the industrial organization and labour market of motor sport is a set of processes involving a continual 'churning' of people and ideas, in this case, centred on, and within, Motor Sport Valley. This 'churning' is a process of producing and circulating knowledge within the knowledge community and regional production centre of Motor Sport Valley. As workers move among companies, for example, they carry with them knowledge and ideas about how things are done in other companies, which helps to raise the level of knowledge throughout the industry and within the region.

Henry and Pinch report on concerns about the geographical mobility of motor sport production within the context of the growth of industry in the NICs (see Chapter 10). Because the success of Motor Sport Valley depends largely on knowledge, it may be easy to shift this expertise to another region, for example, to California by the capital-rich US automobile manufacturers. These authors argue, however, that this concern underestimates the (knowledge-laden) production process of the fast moving motor sport industry. 'The knowledge of the British motor sport industry is encapsulated in particular people, objects and ways of doing things which are themselves constructed *in a particular place*' (Henry and Pinch, 2000: 140), in this case, Motor Sport Valley.

## CORPORATE CONTROL CENTRES AND WORLD CITIES

The United States provides a good example of the changing geography of corporate headquarters. Historically, the most striking feature of the geography of corporate headquarters in the USA has been the dominance of the 'manufacturing belt' in general and of New York and Chicago in particular. Elsewhere, the pattern of headquarters offices has tended to reflect the geography of urbanization, so that the more important 'control centres', in terms of business corporations, have been the major entrepôts and central places that developed under earlier phases of economic development, as points of optimal accessibility to regional economies.

With the arrival of advanced capitalism the relative importance of the control centres of the manufacturing belt has decreased somewhat, with cities in the Midwest,
and in the south and the west increasing their share of major company headquarters
offices. Atlanta, Denver, Houston, Minneapolis and Seattle have been the major beneficiaries of this shift, although no new control centres have emerged to counter the
dominance of New York, Chicago and the other major cities of the northeast. One
interpretation of this shift is that it is simply a reflection of changes in the central
place system: high-order urban areas tend to be higher order business control centres
because of their reserves of entrepreneurial talent, the array of support services they
can offer and their accessibility in both a regional and a national context.

In overall terms, 'there has been a process of *cumulative and mutual reinforcement*
between relatively accessible locations and relatively effective entrepreneurship'
(Borchert, 1978: 230, emphasis added). This has made for a high degree of inertia in
the geography of economic control centres and this, in turn, has consolidated the economic position of the metropolitan areas of the northeast through the multiplier effects
of concentrations of corporate headquarters, whereby the vitality of the corporate
administrative sector contributes to the growth and circulation of specialized information concerning business activity, thus generating further employment in a relatively
well-paid sector and sustaining the area's attractiveness for headquarters offices.

The concentration of corporate headquarters offices has contributed to the emergence of a few places within the international urban system as world cities, dominant
centres and sub-centres of transnational business, international finance and international business services – what Friedmann (1986) called the 'basing points' for global
capital. These 'world cities', it should be stressed, are not necessarily the biggest
within the international system of cities in terms of population, employment or
output. Rather, they are the 'control centres' of the world economy: places that are
critical to the articulation of production and marketing under the contemporary
phase of world economic development. Because these properties are difficult to
quantify, it is not possible to establish a definitive list or hierarchy of world cities. It
is possible to identify world cities on the basis of their role in articulating the functions of the global economy associated with financial markets, major corporate
headquarters, international institutions, communications nodes and concentrations
of business services (Figure 7.4). On this basis, all but two of the dominant and
major world cities – Hong Kong and Singapore – are located in core countries. The
relative importance of secondary and minor world cities is very much a function of
the strength and vitality of the national economies that they articulate (Figure 7.4).

Despite the limitations of attempting to portray the system of world-systems on a
map and the impossibility of capturing the major economic and other interconnec-
tions among them, following Friedmann, it is possible to discern a linear character to
the world city system that connects, along an east–west axis, three distinct but interrelated subsystems: an Asian subsystem centred on the Tokyo-Hong Kong-Singapore
axis, with Seoul an important secondary world city, and quite a few minor world
cities such as Shanghai already growing in global importance; an American subsystem based on the three primary world cities of New York, Chicago and Los Angeles,
linked to secondary world cities such as San Francisco in the west, Toronto in the
north and Mexico City and São Paulo in the south, thus bringing Canada, Central
and South America into the American orbit; and a west European subsystem focused
on London, Paris, Frankfurt and Milan, with linkages across a large number of sec-

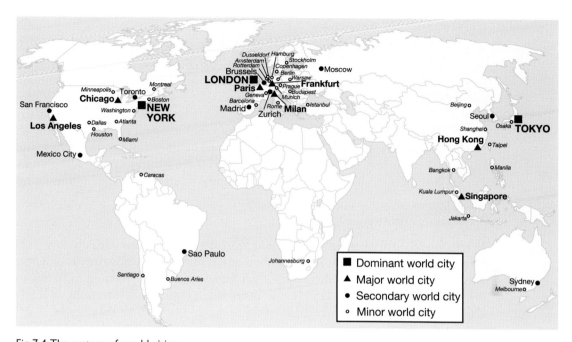

Fig 7.4: The system of world cities

*Source:* Adapted from Globalization and World Cities (GaWC), available at  http://www.lboro.ac.uk/gawc/; Friedmann, 1986, 1995; Knox 1995

ondary and minor world cities from Madrid to Moscow and from Brussels to Istanbul, linked to Johannesburg, the only (minor) world city in Africa.

Friedmann and later Sassen (2001) contributed to a better understanding of the global context for how, for example, business services tend to agglomerate in particular corporate control centres and particularly in world cities. This work, however, tended to result in a focus on the agglomeration within individual world cities like New York, London and Tokyo. Following Castells' (2000) notion of a 'space of flows', Taylor's (2004) world city network concept additionally stresses the importance of the interrelationships between world cities. For Taylor, the agglomeration of business activities in particular world cities is less important than the global connectivity of these cities. In fact, Taylor's most recent conceptualization of world cities in the global economy fits nicely with Immanuel Wallerstein's world-system theory that forms an important underlying explanatory framework for this book (see Chapter 2):

> Wallerstein's (1979a) description of core processes can be interpreted as city-making processes (both produce spatially clustered 'high-tech' outcomes), and peripheral processes – the development of underdevelopment ... In the contemporary world-economy, therefore, the core is defined by the processes of new work that are constituting the world city network, and the periphery is the rest of the world beyond the world city network. The semi-periphery is defined in Wallersteinian terms as locales where core and periphery processes are approximately balanced; these are cities in the erstwhile 'third world' that are now part of the world city network but are also 'mega-cities' (pernicious population 'town' growth that is a periphery process). This is what makes cities such as São Paulo, Mexico City, Mumbai, Johannesburg and Bangkok among the most interesting settlements in the first decades of the twenty-first century.
>
> Taylor (2007: 296)

## CENTRES OF INNOVATION

As Castells notes (2000: 65), the development of the information technology revolution has contributed to the formation of milieux of innovation where important commercial discoveries interact and are tested in a recurrent process of trial and error. These milieux require 'spatial concentration of research centres, higher-education institutions, advanced-technology companies, a network of ancillary suppliers of goods and services, and business networks of venture capital to finance start-ups'.

The geography of these milieux has important implications for urban and regional development. Malecki, who has examined the geography of R&D activity in the USA in detail, suggests that the overall pattern can be interpreted in terms of:

1 availability of highly qualified personnel
2 corporate organization.

In relation to the former, he suggests that amenity-rich locations (cities with a wide range of cultural facilities, well-established universities and pleasant environments), which are attractive to highly qualified personnel tend to be favoured as locations for R&D activity. Malecki (1991) also notes that existing concentrations of R&D activity tend to be attractive because of the potential for 'raiding' other firms.

In relation to corporate organization, it seems that corporate-level or long-range R&D is best performed in or near headquarters complexes in a central laboratory where intra-organizational interaction can be fostered. In firms with independent divisions producing quite different product lines, however, R&D activity tends to be located in separate divisional laboratories. Such a pattern is particularly common for conglomerates that have acquired firms with active R&D programmes in existing laboratories. Finally, some industries, whatever the organizational structure of the firms involved, require R&D laboratories to have close links with production facilities, resulting in a relatively dispersed locational pattern corresponding to the pattern of plant location.

The net result of these locational forces is in fact *a marked agglomeration of R&D laboratories in major control centres and manufacturing regions*. It is the metropolitan areas of the manufacturing belt that dominate the geography of corporate R&D activity. As Malecki points out, most of these are either major control centres with a significant element of headquarters office activity. Elsewhere, R&D tends to be concentrated in 'innovation centres' – university cities with diversified economies, some high-technology activity and a strong federal scientific presence (e.g., Austin, Texas; Huntsville, Alabama; Lincoln, Nebraska).

In terms of locational *trends*, Malecki has shown that:

> Although industrial R&D appears to be evolving away from a dependence on some large city regions, especially New York, it remains, at the same time, a *very markedly large-city activity* ... The comparative advantage of city size, particularly in centres of corporate headquarters location, manufacturing activity and university and government research, shows little sign of reversing.
>
> Malecki (1979: 321, emphasis added)

In short, R&D laboratories, like headquarters offices, exhibit a strong tendency for consolidation, accompanied by a certain amount of decentralization. This pattern has important implications for regional economic development, for the urban areas in which concentrations of R&D activity exist will in future be able to consolidate their comparative advantage over other areas in the generation of new products and new businesses. They will also benefit from the short-term multiplier effects of employment generation in a particularly well-paid sector. Conversely, cities and regions with little research and development activity will be at a disadvantage in keeping up with the new economic content of advanced capitalism.

## 7.3  OLD INDUSTRIAL SPACES

One of the most striking overall changes within core economies has been the decline in the traditional industrial manufacturing employment base. Initially, this took the form of a relative decline: growth in the postwar boom period was much greater in the service sector of most economies than it was in the manufacturing sector. With the globalization of economic activity, however, there has been an *absolute* decline in core manufacturing employment (see, for example, Figures 7.5 and 7.6). Whereas in 1960 manufacturing in the most industrialized OECD countries generated between 25 and 42 per cent of the GDP and accounted for similar proportions of their employment, the comparable figures for 2006 were in the range of 10 to 30 per cent.

The decline has been most pronounced in the early industrializers of northwestern Europe. In the United Kingdom, for example, more than 1 million manufacturing jobs disappeared, *in net terms*, between 1966 and 1976 – a fall of 13 per cent. This decline affected almost every sector of manufacturing, not just the traditional pillars of manufacturing – shipbuilding (–9.7 per cent), metal manufacture (–21.3 per cent), mechanical engineering (–14.5 per cent) and textiles (–26.6 per

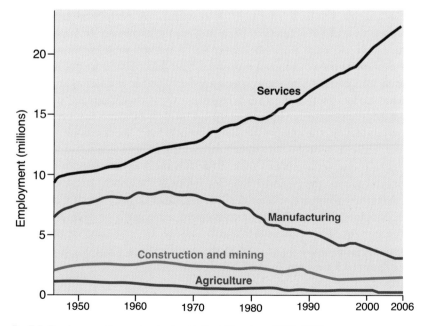

Fig 7.5: Employment by sector in the United Kingdom, 1946–2006

*Source*: Based on online data from UK Office for National Statistics, *Workforce Jobs by Industry*, available at http://www.statistics.gov.uk/statbase/

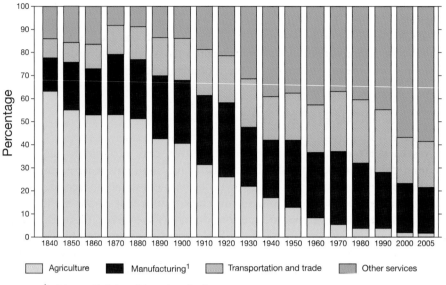

Fig 7.6: Employment shares, by economic sector, USA, 1840–2005

*Source:* Based on online data from US Bureau of Labor Statistics, *Employment and Earnings, 2006*, available at http://www.bls.gov/bls/cps/

cent) – but also its former growth sectors and the bases of the fourth Kondratiev cycle – motor vehicles (–10.1 per cent) and electrical engineering (–10.5 per cent). In the West Midlands – traditionally regarded as a 'leading' region within Britain – a net loss of 151,117 manufacturing jobs between 1978 and 1981 helped to redefine the region as part of Britain's 'rust belt'. It is within the peripheral regions of the United Kingdom that the problem has been most acute, however. In Lancashire, for example, the textile industry alone shed over half a million jobs.

In short, the decline of the traditional industrial base has been most pronounced in the regions that had come to be most specialized in Fordist industrial manufacturing. For some communities in these regions, the consequences of plant shutdowns have been disastrous. In Youngstown, which became the symbol of American industrial decline, the closure of the Campbell Steel Works in 1977 eliminated over 10,000 jobs at a stroke. In overall terms, it has been estimated that the mid-Atlantic region (New Jersey, New York, Pennsylvania) experienced a net loss of over 175,000 jobs during the period 1969–76, whereas the south Atlantic region (Delaware, District of Columbia, Florida, Georgia, Maryland, North Carolina, South Carolina, Virginia, West Virginia) experienced a net gain of over 2 million jobs in the same period. This represents a job loss of 1.5 per cent in the mid-Atlantic region and a gain of 24.4 per cent in the south Atlantic region, compared with a net gain of some 15 per cent in the USA as a whole.

Deindustrialization on this scale brought with it a number of *downward-spiralling* multiplier effects, including the substantial contraction of major segments of intra-regional, vertically integrated production chains (e.g., ore mining, coalmining, steel production, marine engineering and shipbuilding) and the disappearance of inefficient, more labour-intensive firms and sections of production chains (e.g., in textiles), leaving the old industrial regions only finishing, specialized and high-quality product lines (e.g., in clothing), which now become dependent on supply linkages that are often 'stretched' overseas.

It would be misleading, however, to place too much emphasis on the demise of old industrial regions. Many cities within such regions have attempted to make the transition to an advanced economy. Within the Ruhrgebiet of Germany, for example, an economic renaissance is in evidence at the site of an old steel plant, which was bulldozed to make way for one of Europe's largest shopping centres: a US$1.5-billion megamall with over 200 stores, a 12,000-seat arena, a 1200-seat food court with a giant 48-screen video wall offering continuous closed-circuit programming, a 30-restaurant 'gastronomy' annex anchored by Planet Hollywood, hotels, cinemas, an artificial canal, an amusement park and 10,500 parking spaces. The only structure to survive from the steel plant is a huge gas tank, which contains exhibits and offers a view from the top when using the elevator. CentrO, as the huge shopping complex that opened in 1996 near Oberhausen is called, draws more than 60,000 visitors every day, with 22 million people visiting in its first year. Such developments show that local efforts can help to counter the regional economic decline associated with deindustrialization. Nevertheless, it is important to note that, in comparison with the jobs lost in traditional industries, employment in retailing, food and leisure provides a much less desirable base: typically, jobs are less well paid, with less security and fewer benefits. Major new shopping complexes such as this one, can also draw shoppers away from existing retail and entertainment establishments in a region.

We should also note that the process of deindustrialization (i.e., the *relative* decline of manufacturing jobs), while localized within old industrial regions has affected every region within core countries. In the United States, for example, even California, the archetypal Sunbelt state, was seriously affected by company shutdowns. In Los Angeles alone, almost 18,000 manufacturing jobs were lost between 1978 and 1982, many of them the result of plant closures by large corporations such as Ford, Pabst Brewing, Max Factor, Uniroyal and US Steel. In the state as a whole in the single year of 1980, more than 150 large plants closed down, displacing more than 37,000 workers. In short, the overall losses of the manufacturing belt conceal a complex and uneven pattern of ebbs and flows.

## 7.4 NEW INDUSTRIAL SPACES

Advanced capitalism has not only seen the evolution and alignment of the 'old' economy, it has also seen the emergence of *new* industries based on entirely new technologies: semiconductors and computer software, for example and, more recently, biotechnology, photovoltaics and robotics. These were the precursors of the fifth Kondratiev upswing (see Box 3.1). The possibility thus emerges of an entirely new dimension to the economic landscapes of the developed countries, with concentrations of high-tech ('sunrise') industries initiating new patterns of urban and regional growth through new 'production ensembles' with new multipliers of cumulative causation.

Studies of high-tech industries in the United States confirm that job creation has been significant and is likely to continue to expand. By 2006, 5.8 million people (about 4 per cent of total US employment) were employed in high-tech industries, including over 2 million in service industries such as data processing and commercial testing laboratories.

The growth of some of these industries has certainly been explosive. Employment in computer software companies in the United States, for example, doubled during the 1970s to 250,000, and grew to about 1,900,000 by 2006. Employment in robotics rose from around 10,000 in 1980 to about 100,000 in 1990. By 2000 nearly 600,000 people were employed by companies in the factory automation industry (manufacturing robotic equipment, e.g., equipment to assemble, test, inspect, measure, move and package manufactured goods). Of course, a much greater number of jobs in other industries have been *displaced* by the application of robotics. Whether the growth in high-tech industries will be sufficient to cancel out the effects of continued deindustrialization and international redeployment is by no means certain, however. By the mid-1990s, many US high-tech companies had begun to experience acute problems as a result of the combination of the sluggishness of the overall economy, overproduction and the persistence of Japanese non-tariff barriers to trade. Some companies – including Intel, Texas Instruments, Micron Technology and National Semiconductor – laid off workers; others went out of business altogether. Nevertheless, it should be recalled that, in the context of economic long waves, the effects of high-tech innovations are not likely to be fully developed until at least a decade or more after the beginning, around 1990, of the fifth Kondratiev upswing.

It should also be noted that in terms of occupational structure the expansion of high-tech employment is a microcosm of the trends that have dominated advanced capitalism (in this connection, see also Box 7.3). Studies in California, for example, 'suggest that the occupational, ethnic and gender composition of new jobs in high-tech sectors will tend to worsen the current trend toward the "disappearing middle", that is, toward a labour force bifurcated between high-paid professionals and low-paid service workers' (Markusen, 1983: 19). In relation to corporate structure, high-tech industry is distinctive for its tendency towards the proliferation of small breakaway companies set up by key employees; but at the same time the larger and more established firms have soon been drawn into the process of mergers and acquisitions, either as the dominant element (in horizontal and vertical integration) or as a subsidiary element (in diagonal integration).

## Box 7.3 The digital divide

The so-called 'digital divide' refers to the gap in opportunities between individuals, households, businesses and areas at different socioeconomic levels to access advanced information and communication technologies (ICTs) for a variety of activities. The digital divide exists both within countries (for example, between urban and rural areas or between richer and poorer neighbourhoods) and between countries or groups of countries (for example, between the LDCs and the DCs). Despite the initial promises that advanced ICTs could benefit everyone everywhere, as Warf (2001: 3, 16) argues:

> geography still matters ... electronic systems simultaneously reflect and transform existing topographies of class, gender, and ethnicity, creating and recreating hierarchies of places mirrored in the spatial architecture of computer networks.

> Far from eliminating differences among places, systems such as the Internet allow their differences to be exploited ... often reinforcing existing relations of wealth and power.

Within DCs such as the USA and the United Kingdom, for example, while there is increasing use of the internet by people regardless of race, ethnicity, income, education or gender, internet users are still predominantly white, middle income and male. Even more striking is the fact that an estimated one-third of the world's people, mostly in the LDCs, have never made a telephone call, much less sent an email or surfed the World Wide Web (especially in rural areas in the LDCs (see Chapter 9)). As indicated by a variety of measures, the digital divide between the LDCs and DCs is growing. For example, between 1997 and 2006 alone, the digital divide in internet host penetration between Africa and North America grew from a multiple of 272 to 732 (see Table 7.3). In addition, the changing nature of the modes of accessing the internet is reinforcing the digital divide. The number of individuals and companies who have become broadband subscribers in the DCs has risen dramatically compared to those in the LDCs. Aside from the benefits for individuals, broadband would increase the capacity of businesses in the LDCs to engage in more sophisticated e-business processes and delivery via the internet, thereby maximizing the economic benefits of ICTs.

The primary concern is that lack of access to and development of information, communication and e-commerce technology will prevent many people from benefiting from the new knowledge-based economy. In this regard, governments and other organizations operating within the LDCs in particular face enormous challenges as they attempt to promote growth in and access to ICTs. Meanwhile, although the digital divide between the LDCs and DCs has been an international topic of debate for a number of years, limited action or funds have been forthcoming from the DCs to help address the issue.

Table 7.3 Internet hosts per 1000 inhabitants

|  | 1997 | 2000 | 2006 |
|---|---|---|---|
| North America (USA and Canada) | 46.28 | 168.68 | 600.44 |
| Oceania | 26.81 | 59.16 | 270.04 |
| Europe | 6.13 | 20.22 | 86.12 |
| Central and South America | 0.48 | 2.53 | 23.97 |
| Asia | 0.53 | 1.96 | 11.63 |
| Africa | 0.17 | 0.31 | 0.82 |

Source: OECD (2001b: 13); CIA Factbook 2007

## TECHNOPOLES

The locational impact of expanding high-tech activities has received a great deal of attention. A phenomenon that has received significant attention has been the emergence of technology-oriented complexes or 'technopoles' (Castells and Hall, 1994), and the archetype has been in Santa Clara county – 'Silicon Valley' – in California. In the 1950s Santa Clara was a quiet agricultural county with a population of about 300,000. By 1980, it had been transformed into the world's most intensive complex of high-tech activity, with a population of 1.25 million. During the 1970s, the high-tech industries of Santa Clara county generated over 40,000 jobs a year, each new job creating at least two or three additional jobs in other sectors – an extremely high multiplier effect in comparison with the figure of about one new job created for every new manufacturing job in buoyant (by national standards) metropolitan economies such as San Francisco's.

The development of Silicon Valley in the first instance is generally attributed to the work of Frederick Terman, a professor (and, later, vice-president) of Stanford University at Palo Alto, in the northwestern corner of Santa Clara county. As early as the 1930s Terman began to encourage his graduates in electrical engineering to stay in the area and establish their own companies (one of the first was founded by William Hewlett and David Packard in a garage near the campus; it is now one of the world's largest electronics firms). By the end of the 1950s Terman had persuaded Stanford University to develop a special industrial park for such fledgling high-tech firms, creating a hothouse of innovation and generating significant external economies – including a specialized workforce and a specialized array of business services – which have not only sustained the continued agglomeration of high-tech electronics enterprises but also attracted other high-tech industries. Nearly one-third of all biotechnology companies in the United States, for example, are located in California, and the San Francisco Bay area has the largest concentration of these companies in the country. California's 53,000 biotechnology workers represent more than half the national total. Stanford University, meanwhile, found itself in receipt of an increasing flood of donations from grateful companies. In 1955 alone, these amounted to around US$500,000 annually; by 1965 they exceeded around US$2 million and in 1976 they had reached US$6.9 million.

This kind of linkage between university research and high-tech activity is seen by many to be the key to the emerging geography of the fifth Kondratiev cycle. Not only do the new industries thrive on a symbiotic relationship with one another and university research departments, but key workers also tend to favour technology complexes associated with top-flight universities since they provide abundant social and cultural activities and a job market that allows individuals (and spouses) to switch jobs without relocating. Such areas soon acquire a reputation as the 'right place to be', and this often counts for more than cost-of-living or quality-of-life factors. Where, as in Silicon Valley, the 'right place to be' happens to offer the additional bonus of an attractive environment and climate, the result is explosive growth. An important point in this context, as Hall (1981: 536) observed, is that 'university systems, even in a country as dynamic as the United States, have a great deal of built-in inertia'. Large, top-drawer universities like Harvard, MIT, Berkeley and Stanford are secure in their status, but few other institutions seem destined to join them. The result is that, outside these potential areas, there are few places in the USA where a high-tech industrial base is likely to be developed – apart, perhaps from the research triangle (Raleigh-Durham-Chapel Hill) that has already been established in North Carolina around Duke University and the University of North Carolina.

Similarly, there are few environments in other developed countries that are likely to attract a critical mass of high-tech activity, despite the proliferation of 'technology parks' – or, to be more accurate, *designated* technology parks. One exception is France, where an ambitious programme of national technological research centres (CNRT) has involved designating 18 CNRTs (Figure 7.7), with special tax breaks and subsidies designed to attract not only high-tech industries such as electronics, nanotechnology and biotechnology but also to develop a supportive infrastructure of universities and R&D labs.

At the same time, technopoles come in a variety of formats:

> Most notably, it is clear that in most countries, with the important exceptions of the United States and, to some extent, Germany, the leading technopoles are in fact contained in the leading metropolitan areas: Tokyo, Paris-Sud, London-M4 Corridor, Milan, Seoul-Inchon, Moscow-Zelenograd, and at a considerable distance Nice-Sophia Antipolis, Taipei-Hsinchu, Singapore, Shanghai, São Paulo, Barcelona, and so on.
>
> Castells (2000: 421)

Fig 7.7: French National Centres for Technological Research (*Centres Nationaux de Recherche Technologique* (CNRT))

## DECENTRALIZATION OF HIGH-TECH EMPLOYMENT

Almost all existing high-technology complexes are very much a suburban phenomenon. As Markusen (1983: 26) noted in relation to the early development of the Silicon Valley and Route 128 (Boston) complexes, they are 'newly developed, auto-based, suburban areas whose jobs and tax base do not overlay the inner-city poor nor the central city jurisdiction'. But, because high-tech firms have tended to be very self-conscious about their 'address', these suburban complexes have become crowded and expensive. The outcome has been the familiar combination of corporate functional and spatial reorganization. More routine production tasks and downstream marketing and service functions are beginning to be dispersed, while managerial and developmental activities are retained in order to maximize the external economies of the 'right address'.

Research has suggested that American computer firms have kept their R&D and administrative activities in places like California and Massachusetts while moving their production facilities to southeastern states to take advantage of lower labour costs. Furthermore, some of the larger corporations in the computer and semiconductor fields have already begun to redeploy at the international scale, partly to acquire foreign technology and expertise and partly in search of cheaper labour, both highly qualified and semi-skilled. There is now an international division of labour in the US integrated circuit industry, for example, with skilled production functions decentralized to settings such as central Scotland, assembly and testing in the likes of Hong Kong and Singapore and assembly operations in metropolitan areas of peripheral countries like the Philippines, Malaysia and Indonesia – leaving only R&D functions to the innovation centres of the USA itself. Because of this sort of international redeployment, the central belt of Scotland – 'Silicon Glen' – in the mid-1990s made one-third of the personal computers and half of the laptops sold in Europe, much of which came from factories owned by companies such as Motorola, National Semiconductor, Nippon Electric (NEC) and General Instrument. As with the local branch-plant economies generated by the decentralization of traditional manufacturing industries, these regional concentrations of decentralized high-tech industry did not seem to generate many local linkages or multiplier effects. More importantly, Silicon Glen is now suffering from the lingering effects of the global electronics downturn since 2001 and the steady relocation of electronics manufacturing to eastern Europe and China. The export output of the Silicon Glen electronics sector peaked by 2000 at about US$22 billion and has fallen to less than half that figure since then.

## FLEXIBLE PRODUCTION REGIONS

While the imprint of the new, high-tech industries of advanced capitalism cannot be said to amount to an entirely new dimension of the economic landscapes of the core countries, their new industrial spaces have clearly contributed an additional component to existing landscapes. Meanwhile, however, other industries have been changing, leaving their imprint on the economic geography of the core. The crisis of Fordism, combined with the opportunities afforded by new production process and circulation technologies, by changing patterns of consumer demand, and by corporate restructuring and new competitive strategies, has led to the emergence of a phenomenon that *can* be described as a new dimension of the economic landscapes of the core countries. 'Flexible production regions' have emerged in many

## Box 7.4 The Celtic Tiger

Comparing Ireland's incredible economic boom to that of the 'Asian Tigers' (Hong Kong, Singapore, South Korea, Taiwan), economist Kevin Gardiner, when working for the US investment bank, Morgan Stanley, coined the term 'Celtic Tiger'.

As recently as the mid-1980s, Ireland had an unemployment rate of nearly 20 per cent, the highest debt per capita in the world and a GDP per capita of only 63 per cent of its nearest neighbour, the United Kingdom. Beginning in the early 1990s, Ireland began to enjoy astonishing growth rates of between 5 and 10 per cent of GDP. By the end of the decade, unemployment was down to 4.5 per cent, the national debt was down and the country's GDP per capita had outstripped those of the United Kingdom and even Germany.

The underlying causes of Ireland's economic growth and massive foreign investment, especially from US TNCs, include its openness to international trade and investment, low corporate taxes, low wages, a skilled workforce from decades of government investment in education, a stable national economy, appropriate budget policies, EU membership and adoption of the euro and regional aid for investment in infrastructure and training from the European Union.

The Celtic Tiger roared until the global economic downturn of 2001 when the economy was impacted by the significant decline in investment in the global IT industry. By the end of 2003, however, the so-called 'Celtic Tiger Mark 2' was showing signs of strong recovery with an annual average of about 5 per cent in GDP growth. Despite being a small country – with a population of just over 4 million – Ireland nonetheless produces one-quarter of all personal computers sold in Europe. TNCs including Dell, IBM, Apple and Hewlett-Packard have large facilities in Ireland.

Concerns about the future growth of the 'Celtic Tiger Mark 2' relate to the country's rising wages, inflation, infrastructure that has failed to keep pace with the rapid growth, excessive public spending and the implications for Ireland's continued competitiveness of the accession to the European Union of eight eastern European countries in 2004 and two more in 2007. Additional concerns relate to the slowdown in national productivity growth rates, which had been among the highest of the OECD countries. Of greatest concern is the fact that recent economic growth in Ireland has shifted away from exports and toward domestic construction activity and consumer demand financed by high levels of personal borrowing.

core economies as a result of the interplay of flexible production systems, existing labour markets and the fixed capital of older industrial spaces.

Flexible production regions, which may contain elements of branch-plant industrialization (see p. 186) along with a mixture of other new functions and activities, are seen as the product of Neo-Fordism, in which the emphasis on flexibility results in the externalization of certain functions and the vertical disintegration of organizational structures, which in turn lead to locational convergence and spatial agglomeration. Allen Scott, who has contributed most to this interpretation, sums up the central tendency as follows: 'vertical disintegration encourages agglomeration, and agglomeration encourages vertical disintegration' (1986: 224). The result is a series of regions or production complexes whose dynamics 'revolve for the most part around the social division of labour, the formation of external economies, the dissolution of labour rigidities, and the reagglomeration of production' (1988a: 181).

The archetypal flexible production region is the so-called Third Italy (Emilia-Romagna, Tuscany, the Marches, the Abruzzi and Venetia), where branch-plant industrialization has combined with highly skilled local labour markets, well-developed infrastructure and economies of scale and scope arising from the spatial division of labour between specialized firms to create a regional network of innovative, flexible and high-quality manufacturers whose products include textiles, knitwear, jewellery, shoes, ceramics, machinery, machine tools and furniture (see Box 6.4). Other examples of flexible production regions based on a similar mixture of design- and labour-intensive industries include Jutland (Denmark), the Swiss Jura and southern Germany (Table 7.4).

**Table 7.4** Propulsive industries and new industrial spaces

| Propulsive sector | Typical features | Cited examples |
|---|---|---|
| **Craft industries** | | |
| Labour-intensive craft industries, e.g., clothing, furniture | Exploitation of 'sweatshop' labour; often high level of immigrants; subcontracting and outworking | New York, USA<br>Los Angeles, USA<br>Paris, France |
| Design-intensive craft industries, e.g., jewellery | High-quality products. Extreme social division of labour (but class polarization subdued in some examples) | Jura, Switzerland<br>Southern Germany<br>Emilia-Romagna (Third Italy), Italy<br>Central Portugal<br>Jutland, Denmark |
| **High-technology industries** | Segmented local labour markets with skilled managerial cadres and disorganized and malleable (non-union; temporary) fractions of the labour force | Route 128, Boston, USA<br>Orange County, CA, USA<br>Silicon Valley, CA, USA<br>M4 corridor, UK<br>Scientific City, France<br>Austin, TX, USA<br>Boulder, CO, USA<br>Cambridge, UK<br>Grenoble, France<br>Montpellier, France<br>Sophia Antipolis, France |
| **Office and business services** | Preferentially based on white-collar labour – including low-wage female labour. Very diversified and prone to agglomeration | London, UK<br>New York, USA<br>Tokyo, Japan |

*Source:* Tickell and Peck (1992: 199, Table 2)

Networks of manufacturers in high-technology industries form the basis of a second group of flexible production regions. Here, the agglomerating tendencies of new industries have resulted in localized growth in relatively new metropolitan settings: for example Orange County and Silicon Valley in California; Scientific City, Grenoble, and Montpelier in France; and the M4 corridor in Britain (Table 7.4).

These examples support Scott's observation that flexible production regions 'are almost always some distance – socially or geographically – from the major foci of Fordist industrialization' (1988b: 14). The argument, as we have seen, is that the interests of flexibility are best served by avoiding the rigidities (from outdated infrastructure to outdated institutions and labour relations) of Fordist settings. Yet we must recognize that it is quite possible for flexible, neo-Fordist manufacturers to establish successful enclaves *within* older industrial regions and metropolitan areas. Examples include the design- and labour-intensive clothing industry in New York, clothing, high-tech electronics and furniture in Milan and clothing and motion pictures in Los Angeles. Equally, it is legitimate to interpret the localized networks of producer services within world cities as a specialized form of flexible production region. We are forced to conclude, therefore, that although flexible production regions represent a new dimension within the economic landscapes of the core, they do not represent an absolute or fundamental break from the old. As with previous transitions, the old order of things does not, and cannot, simply disappear. Thus:

> As far as the geography of change is concerned, it is necessary to grasp the coexistence and combination of localizing and globalizing, centripetal and centrifugal, forces. The current restructuring process is a matter of a whole repertoire of spatial strategies, dependent on situated contexts and upon balances of power.
>
> Amin and Robins (1990: 28)

## Box 7.5 Hollywood and the cultural economy of cities

Allen Scott (2005: 1) begins his book, *On Hollywood*, with the following:

> One of the defining features of contemporary society, at least in the high-income countries of the world, is the conspicuous convergence that is occurring between the domain of the economic on the one hand and the domain of the cultural on the other. Vast segments of the modern economy are inscribed with significant cultural content, while culture itself is increasingly being supplied in the form of goods and services produced by private firms for a profit under conditions of market exchange. These trends can be described variously in terms of the aestheticization of the economy and the commodification of culture.

The cultural economy can be defined as a group of sectors (cultural products industries) that produce goods and services – including jewellery, live theatre, music recording, film production – whose symbolic value to consumers is high relative to their practical purpose. Scott's work on Hollywood is of interest to economic geographers because it argues for the vital role of agglomeration economies and localized increasing returns to scale in allowing this 'industrial district' to become the largest and most influential cultural products agglomeration in the world.

Scott (2005: 8) offers five thematic arguments that address how the history, geography, economic structure and cultural energies of the Hollywood motion picture industry combine to hold Hollywood together as a spatial unit, while endowing those producing within this agglomeration with potential long-term competitive advantages.

First, Hollywood emerged as the main centre of the US motion picture industry (in competition with New York) because its pioneering model of film production generated an expanding system of agglomeration economies. By the 1920s, the 'old' classical studio system of production was securely in place and Hollywood had risen to unparalleled dominance nationally and internationally.

Second, following the Second World War, a 'new' Hollywood developed as the 'old' studio system was transformed into a more diffuse organizational pattern of production. This greatly enhanced the role of Hollywood as a concentrated industrial district, intensifying its place-specific competitive advantages. Important in this process were the significant extension of flexible production systems in Hollywood and the fundamental shift in the role of the major film production companies as they began to act more as sources of financial and coordination services for independent producers in combination with overall marketing and distribution services.

Third, the film production companies in Hollywood, as part of an industrial district, include not only the units of production from which they derive their principal identity, but also the countless other companies in ancillary sectors – including soundstages, set design and construction, prop houses, digital visual effects, agents and talent managers – which directly and indirectly provide the critical physical inputs and services necessary to keep the entire system operational through complex webs of spatial and functional relationships.

Fourth, the Hollywood production system depends on a large number of workers with a diverse range of skills.

Fifth, Hollywood, like other industrial districts, depends for its economic success on an efficient productive base in conjunction with the effective marketing and distribution of its final products. Companies in Hollywood have been remarkably aggressive in marketing and have established an extensive international distribution system so that their outputs can be exported efficiently. Part of globalization, this diffusion of American culture from Hollywood has had not only important economic but also profound cultural implications globally.

## 7.5 REGIONAL INEQUALITY IN CORE ECONOMIES

We have seen that the evolution of advanced capitalism and the emergence of an informational economy have led to a significant reorganization of the economic geography of places and regions throughout the developed world. This reorganization has modified many of the core–periphery patterns of regional development associated with industrial capitalism. Yet core–periphery patterns and regional economic disparities have by no means disappeared. Rather, they have been reconfigured and intensified. Core regions within developed countries have typically been centred on urban–industrial heartlands, but have recently been modified by the geography of service activities, particularly producer services and by the imprint of the new spatial divisions of labour associated with globalization, decentralization and agglomeration.

Europe provides a good example of the kind of regional differentiation that is characteristic of contemporary core economies. The overall core–periphery contrasts that were the legacy of industrial capitalism (Figure 5.3) have carried over into substantial disparities. Figure 7.8 shows the range and variability of regional economic well-being across the European Union, as measured by GDP per capita based on purchasing power parity (PPP; see Chapter 2). While the most affluent regions of the continental core of the European Union (e.g., in Germany, Italy, the Netherlands) have per capita incomes that are well over 100 per cent of the EU average, some of the least developed EU regions, especially Bulgaria and Romania, have incomes that are well under 50 per cent of the EU average.

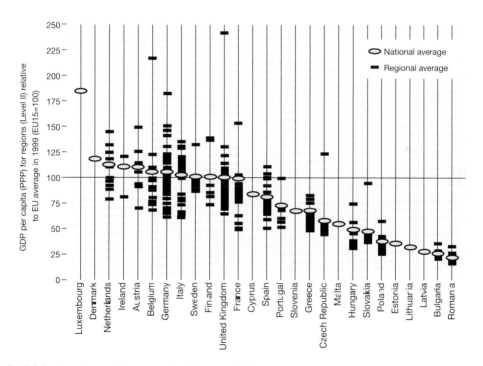

Fig 7.8: Regional inequality across the European Union

*Source:* Adapted from Dunford (2002)

Within this broad pattern of regional inequality there exist sharp local variations. Figure 7.9 shows the geography of 'economic performance' of local districts in England, as measured by an index based on income and employment deprivation. In general terms, the whole of England to the southeast of a line drawn between the Severn Estuary and Lincolnshire can be considered to be Britain's economic core. At the heart of this region is a prosperous hub centred on Greater London and extending outward for a radius of about 100 kilometres, encompassing the

M4 motorway corridor to the west of London, the M3 belt to the southwest and the M11 corridor to the north. In general, high economic performance in Britain is associated with a southeastern location (with the obvious exception of the deprived inner-city neighbourhoods of London), with planned expansion and proximity to the motorway system and with relatively high levels of employment in finance, banking, insurance and related producer services.

Britain's traditional industrial heartland (districts in the northwest, Yorkshire and Humberside, and the northern Midlands) now fares no better than the long-recognized periphery of northern England, Wales and Scotland. Within this broad periphery, the worst performing districts are widely scattered around the coalmining

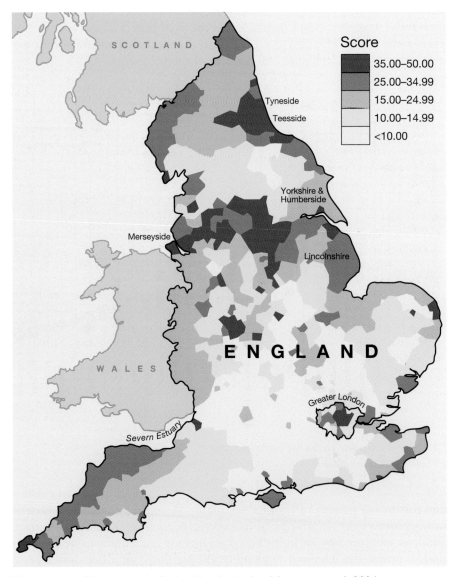

Fig 7.9: An index of deprivation in England, by district level (average score), 2004

*Source*: Based on UK Office of the Deputy Prime Minister (2004: 157, Annex L), available at
http://www.viral.info/iod/iodpdf/odpm_urbpol_029534.pdf

and heavy industrial districts of Tyneside (Newcastle), Teesside (Middlesbrough), South Yorkshire (Sheffield), Merseyside (Liverpool), central Scotland and south Wales. The fundamental cleavage reflected in this core–periphery pattern is echoed by a broad spectrum of social and economic data, to the point where it became common to refer to Britain's political economy in terms of the 'two nations' of north and south.

## Box 7.6 National economic development and regional inequality

The relationship between overall levels of development and the intensity of regional disparities is central to theory in economic geography. Much of the conventional wisdom on the subject is derived from a major study by Williamson (1965), who examined inter-regional income disparities in a sample of 24 countries. The results of this analysis suggested that the greatest regional inequalities were associated with countries at a semi-peripheral level of development, with much smaller differences within both the most- and the least-developed countries (Figure 7.10).

Williamson interpreted these cross-national results as a consequence of the dynamics of economic development, suggesting that the onset of industrial development precipitates sharp increases in regional inequality, which are subsequently reduced as the economy matures.

Both the results and the interpretation of Williamson's work have been questioned on several grounds, however. The reliability of data and the appropriateness of measurement techniques are crucial: depending on the researcher's selections, anything can be proved.

Reviewing the large number of empirical studies that have followed Williamson's work, Krebs (1982) showed that, even allowing for different measurement techniques, the idea of divergence followed by convergence in regional disparities does not meet with strong support. In terms of the spatial concentration of both per capita incomes (see, e.g., Figure 7.11) and of economic activity (see, e.g., Figure 7.9), the evidence often points to spatial polarization or, at best, no change.

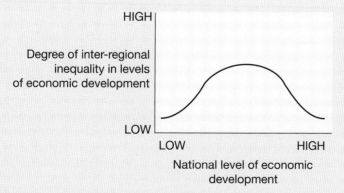

Fig 7.10: Relationship between inter-regional inequality and levels of economic development, as posited by Williamson (1965)

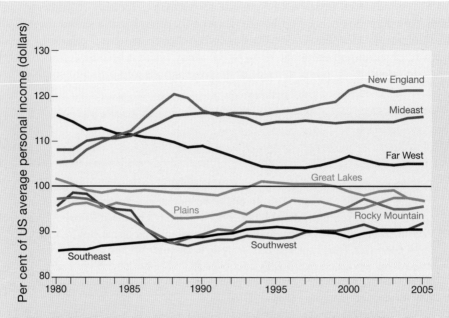

Fig 7.11: Regional trends in per capita incomes in the United States, 1980–2005

*Source*: Based on US Department of Commerce, Bureau of Economic Analysis, online *Regional Economic Accounts*, available at http://www.bea.gov/bea/regional/

Finally, we must remember to set these trends within the context of the long-wave rhythms of the world economy. Although the relationships between economic long waves and regional inequality are an under-researched topic, it is clear from our discussion in Chapters 1 and 3 that a fundamental consequence of the succession of Kondratiev cycles is that each new phase of economic development, based on new technology systems, and requiring new resources and new markets, initiates a round of 'creative destruction' that leaves an indelible imprint on economic landscapes and, therefore, on the pattern and intensity of regional inequality. Furthermore, there are dynamics to the political economy that stem from the rhythm of economic long waves and that feed back to influence the whole question of inequality within countries. Thus, for example, periods of economic growth and low inflation tend to generate widespread satisfaction and a lack of enthusiasm for altering the status quo. During such periods, conservative political parties tend to be in the ascendant, while labour unions tend to become moderate and weak. At the same time, these are the periods during which voters are most likely to feel able to afford to pay for redistributive policies. While we have no adequate single theory or explanation to account for these relationships, it is clear that we must consider regional inequality within the broader context of economic change. Viewed in this way, regional inequality never disappears: it is a perennial consequence of uneven development, of the see-sawing of capital from one set of opportunities to another. We may see regional inequality diminish, over the long-term, in one part of the world; but elsewhere, and at different spatial scales, inequality will persist or intensify.

## INTERPRETATIONS OF REGIONAL ECONOMIC INEQUALITY

The most widely known explanation of regional economic inequality is that of Myrdal (1957). This is based on the contention that changes in the location of economic activities in a market economy produce cumulative advantages for one region rather than a straightforward equalization of growth across all regions. Cumulative causation refers to the spiral build-up of advantages that occurs in specific geographic settings as a result of the development of agglomeration economies, external economies and localization economies. Agglomeration economies are the cost advantages that accrue to individual firms because of their location within such a cluster. These advantages are sometimes known as external economies. External economies are cost savings that result from advantages that are derived from circumstances beyond a firm's own organization and methods of production. Where external economies and local economic linkages are limited to firms involved in one particular industry, they are known as localization economies. These economies are cost savings that accrue to particular industries as a result of clustering together at a specific location.

Myrdal pointed out that the spiral of local growth involved in cumulative causation would tend to attract people – enterprising young people, usually – and investment funds from other peripheral areas. In some cases, this loss of entrepreneurial talent, labour and investment capital is sufficient to trigger a cumulative *negative* spiral of economic disadvantage in these other areas. With less capital, less innovative energy and depleted pools of labour, industrial growth in peripheral regions tends to be significantly slower and less innovative than in regions with an initial advantage and an established process of cumulative causation. This then tends to limit the size of the local tax base, so that local governments find it hard to furnish a competitive infrastructure of roads, schools and recreational amenities. Myrdal called these disadvantages *backwash effects*: negative impacts on a region (or regions) of the economic growth of some other region that take the form, for example, of outmigration, outflows of investment capital and the shrinkage of local tax bases. They are important because they help us to explain why regional economic development is so uneven and why core–periphery contrasts in economic development are so common.

Myrdal recognized that peripheral regions do sometimes emerge as new growth regions and he provided a partial explanation of them in what he called spread effects. Spread effects are the positive impacts on a region of the economic growth of some other region. This growth creates levels of demand for food, consumer goods and other manufactures that are so high that local producers cannot satisfy them. This demand provides the opportunity for investors in peripheral regions to establish a local capacity to meet the demand. Entrepreneurs who attempt this are also able to exploit the advantages of cheaper land and labour in peripheral regions. If these effects are strong enough, they can enable peripheral regions to develop their own spiral of cumulative causation, thus changing the interregional geography of economic patterns and flows (Figure 7.12).

Myrdal's influential model was followed by others based on similar logic. Hirschman's (1958) model assumes 'polarization' and 'trickling-down effects' but sees early polarization producing a countervailing trend (and, thus, interregional equilibrium) rather than the cumulative intensification of initial advantage. Hicks' (1959) model was more like Myrdal's in its emphasis on cumulative causation but it gives greater attention to flows of labour and capital from *growing* to *lagging* regions.

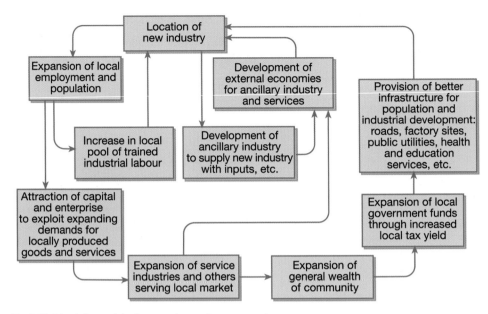

Fig 7.12: Myrdal's model of regional cumulative causation

Not all industries are equal in the extent to which they stimulate growth. Perroux (1955; 1961) argued that the locations of 'propulsive industries' (those that attract other industries and stimulate new ones in the vicinity) serve as the distinguishing characteristic of regions that achieve high rates of economic growth. As a propulsive industry grows, it attracts other linked industries and creates a set of agglomeration economies. A growth pole is formed and a growth centre develops. In the 1920s shipbuilding was a propulsive industry. In the 1950s and 1960s automobile manufacturing was a propulsive industry and in today's informational economy high-tech manufacturing, design-intensive consumer goods and business and financial services are propulsive industries.

Krugman (1991) suggests a more complex and more formal model to account for a core–periphery pattern of economic development and for the possibility of its transformation. He argues that the relationship between demand and production established during an early phase of industrialization locks into place an interregional imbalance through the conjoint operation of increasing returns to scale in plant operations, transportation costs and demand. As he puts it:

> Given sufficiently strong economies of scale, each manufacturer wants to serve the national market from a single location. To minimize transportation costs, she chooses a location with large local demand. But local demand will be large precisely where the majority of manufacturers choose to locate. Thus there is a circularity that tends to keep a manufacturing belt in existence once it is established.
>
> Krugman (1991: 15)

However, once the population of a peripheral region reaches critical mass it may serve to stimulate production facilities. A dramatic shift in regional fortunes may follow. Local 'boosterism', faith in a locality's future possibilities and policies that reflect this can also prove decisive in reversing regional imbalance: 'Nothing', therefore, 'is forever' (Krugman, 1991: 26). This is an argument for a rapid reversal in regional fortunes, rather than for slow regional balancing, cores becoming peripheries and vice versa. Krugman argues that increasing returns to scale, imperfect competition and historical accident conspire to produce geographical concentration. But the identity of the favoured region is not set for all time – a new pattern of concentration can break the historic mould.

## SUMMARY

In this chapter, we have seen how the crisis of Fordism and the sectoral shifts and changing business structures of the emerging era of advanced capitalism have begun to reshape the economic landscapes of the industrial core regions. Several aspects of this transition are of special importance:

- The spatial reorganization of core economies is the product of several interdependent processes, including the globalization of some core area economic activity, a shift from manufacturing towards service industries, development of neo-Fordist production processes and competitive strategies and the beginnings of a new mode of regulation.
- The imprint of the shift towards service employment has had two main dimensions: deindustrialization and economic decline in regions of traditional heavy industries and rapid growth (a new bout of cumulative causation) in metropolitan settings that have attracted higher order producer services.
- This shift overlapped with a phase of stagflation and with the globalization of some core area economic activity, with the result that certain aspects of change have been intensified and others have been introduced. The globalization of economic activity, for example, has intensified the effects of deindustrialization; while the pressures of stagflation have contributed to radical changes in the role of the public economy.
- Corporate reorganization has resulted in an increase in the external control of regional economies, with the consequence that the industrial systems of old industrial regions have become fragmented while those of newly industrializing regions have become segmented or truncated.
- Net effects of change have resulted in simultaneous spatial trends involving both decentralization and agglomeration, each highly selective in terms of the regions and economic activities involved.
- The diverse mixes of industry, workers and infrastructure inherited from the industrial era have mediated the broader processes of structural change and reorganization, so that different kinds of regions have evolved in different ways. *There have been four broad trajectories of change.* In the first, restructuring in response to a legacy of declining industry has been the dominant process. Examples include the old manufacturing heartlands of northern England, south Wales, central Scotland and the US manufacturing belt. In some rural areas and peripheral regions, in contrast, the dominant process has been one of decentralization of footloose, labour-intensive industries from the metropolitan areas and core regions. Examples include parts of the southern USA such as the Carolinas. A third trajectory is characterized by regions whose industry has developed at or just above the national average, sustained by a consistent supply of new investment. Examples include most of southeast England and, in the USA, the Boston-New York-Washington, DC-Richmond corridor. Finally, there are some regions whose attributes have made them attractive to new industries and/or to

new investments aimed at exploiting new competitive strategies and new production processes. These encompass 'new industrial spaces' such as the high-tech concentrations of Orange County and Silicon Valley and 'flexible production regions' such as north-central Italy.

- Overlying these categories there has been a general accentuation of the importance and prosperity of large metropolitan areas, while many smaller towns and, in particular, many of the specialized new towns spawned by industrial capitalism (mining towns, heavy manufacturing towns and so on) have declined.

## KEY SOURCES AND SUGGESTED READING

Bryson, J.R., Daniels, P.W., Henry, N. and Pollard, J. (eds) 2000. *Knowledge, Space, Economy*. London: Routledge.

Castells, M. 2000. *The Information Age: Economy, Society and Culture: Volume I, The Rise of the Network Society* 2nd edn. Oxford: Blackwell.

Cox, K.R. (ed.) 1997. *Spaces of Globalization: Reasserting the Power of the Local*. New York: Guilford Press.

Masscy, D. 2005. *For Space*. London: Sage.

OECD 2001. *Understanding the Digital Divide*. Paris: OECD.

Scott, A.J. 2000. *The Cultural Economy of Cities: Essays on the Geography of Image-Producing Industries*. London: Sage.

Scott, A.J. 2001. *Global City-Regions: Trends, Theory, Policy*. New York: Oxford University Press.

Taylor, P.J. 2004. *World City Network: A Global Urban Analysis*. London: Routledge.

Taylor, P.J., Derudder, B., Saey, P. and Witlox, F. (eds) 2007. *Cities in Globalization: Practices, Policies and Theories*. London: Routledge.

Warf, B. 2001. Segueways into cyberspace: multiple geographies of the digital divide, *Environment and Planning B: Planning and Design*, 28, 3–19.

## RELATED WEBSITES

Center for Globalization and Policy Research: http://www.sppsr.ucla.edu/cgpr/
this UCLA website provides information and downloadable working papers on the globalization of production

CIO.com: http://www.cio.com/research/global/
while aimed at businesspeople, this website provides up-to-date information and articles on information technology and the world economy

Community Research and Development Information Service of the European Union (CORDIS): http://cordis.europa.eu/en/home.html
the EU's CORDIS website is a resource for research and development in the European Union, offering information on national and regional development activities in the member states, including the national technological research centres (CNRT) programme in France

Digital Divide Network: http://www.digitaldividenetwork.org/
this Benton Foundation website (in partnership with funding agencies such as the Ford Foundation and Annie E. Casey Foundation) provides research and data on the digital divide from a variety of perspectives

Globalization and World Cities (GaWC) Study Group and Network: http://www.lboro.ac.uk/gawc/
provides an excellent source of information on world cities

# Chapter 8

# Dynamics of interdependence: transformation of the periphery

Picture credit: Paul Knox

If local isolation was rarely complete and development was rarely totally independent, the coming of the modern world economy led to greater and greater interaction between different parts of the world. In this chapter, we focus on the cumulative consequences of this increased interdependence for those regions incorporated into the world economy on terms initially and decisively disadvantageous to them. This is not to say that the terms of interdependence have always remained absolutely disadvantageous, although this is true, for example, in the case of Central America and large parts of Sub-Saharan Africa. Particularly since the late 1960s, the major oil-producing countries (e.g., Saudi Arabia, Iran, Venezuela, Nigeria and Indonesia) and the newly industrializing countries (NICs) (such as Taiwan and South Korea and, most recently, China) have challenged the static picture of a 'fixed' industrial core and a 'fixed' non-industrial periphery. The world economy now has a vibrant semi-periphery of NICs and resource-based economies. This chapter begins with a discussion of how existing economies were transformed into colonial ones. A second section identifies the major ways in which these colonial economics were enmeshed and maintained within the world economy. A third section identifies the importance of frameworks of administration introduced by Europeans. A fourth section discusses the cultural mechanisms that facilitated integration into the world economy. The final two sections explore the contexts of change in the nature of interdependence since the 1960s, respectively the global context (the new international division of labour, decolonization and the Cold War) and several national political–economic strategies or 'models' of development that challenge or, more typically, have adapted to the dominant 'liberal' one.

## 8.1 COLONIAL ECONOMIES AND THE TRANSFORMATION OF GLOBAL SPACE

The modern world economy began with the global expansion of trade and conquest by European merchants, adventurers and statesmen (Figure 8.1). But a distinction should be drawn between pre-capitalist colonial rule, notably that of Spain and Portugal in Latin America, and the new colonialism that was associated with the growth and global expansion of west European capitalism, beginning in the 16th century and itself undergoing successive shifts in development. The major purpose of pre-capitalist colonialism was the extraction of tribute from subject peoples and its major mechanisms involved political–territorial control. In contrast, the 'new colonialism' was associated primarily with economic objectives and mechanisms. Direct political–territorial control, although often advantageous, was not essential. The emphasis initially was on the exploitation of raw materials. After the Industrial Revolution in Britain, however, markets for manufactured goods became an equally important objective. Realizing both of these objectives required a restructuring of the economic landscapes of the colonized societies.

Territorial conquest, with or without the elimination of indigenous peoples, and the planting of either settler enclaves or slave plantations and mining enterprises were the major features of European expansion through the 18th century. For much of the 19th century, however, many societies that remained or became formally independent were under the economic domination of European and, increasingly, American capitalists. With the 'German challenge' to British hegemony in the 1870s, there was a new 'scramble' for territorial conquest as rival

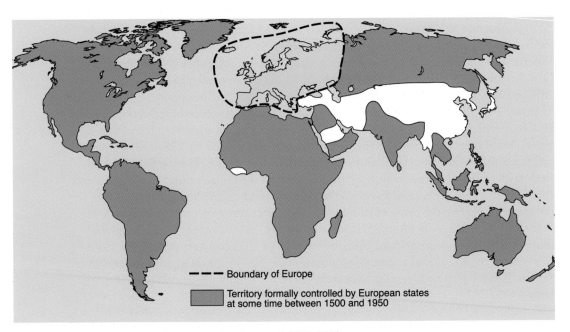

Fig 8.1: Geographical extent of European political control, 1500–1950

Source: Based on Taylor (2000: 106, Figure 3.1)

colonial powers attempted to pre-empt one another, especially in Africa. This coincided with the emergence of capital export as a major stimulus to intervention and domination, as profit rates in the periphery exceeded those in the core.

In both territorial (colonial) and interactional (commercial) forms, capitalist expansion entailed a forcible transformation of pre-capitalist societies whereby their economies were internally disarticulated and integrated externally with the world economy. They were no longer locally oriented but had now to focus on the production of raw materials and foodstuffs for the 'core' economies. Often they became extremely dependent on monoculture in order to confer the blessings of comparative advantage (the purported benefits of specializing in goods that a country can produce at a lower relative cost while importing goods for which its own production costs are relatively higher) on the developed world. At the same time they also provided markets for the manufactured goods exchanged in return. For many parts of the world this relationship still holds true today.

The dramatic transformation of the existing geography of production that the reorientation towards the core entailed is not sufficiently noted. Before the Industrial Revolution and European capitalist expansion, Asian and other countries that are now conventionally characterized as LDCs contained a far larger share of world manufacturing output than did Europe. Bairoch's (1982) calculations of industrial output by world region during the course of the 19th century, for example, reveal a picture not simply of a higher rate of industrialization in core countries but also of deindustrialization in the periphery as the cheaper European products forced traditional producers elsewhere out of business (see Chapter 3).

The division between 'developed' and 'underdeveloped' economies, therefore, which had been moderate before now grew enormously. This was the main geographical consequence of the coming of the world economy. The conditions for the development of 'national economies' did not exist neither were they permitted to exist in the 'dependent world' that came into existence during the course of the expansion of the European world economy (see Chapter 3). The unequal core–periphery structure of the world economy has been in place since the Europeans first ventured out into the world in the 16th century. From this point of view, underdevelopment is not an original condition, equivalent to 'traditionalism' or 'backwardness'. On the contrary, it is a condition created by integration into the world economy. At the same time, however, the die is not permanently cast in confining some places and peoples to an underdeveloped condition. Examples such as the United States, Japan, Australia and the NICs suggest that upward mobility is possible for some states/regions initially in an underdeveloped state. What is equally clear is that for large parts of the world such mobility is either difficult or next to impossible. To understand the geography of the world economy we need to understand such cases as well as the 'successful' ones.

During the early years of incorporation into the world economy the periphery tended to become specialized in the extraction of raw materials (from gold bullion to furs and spices) and production of plantation crops (such as tobacco, cotton and sugar). As time wore on, plantations and extractive industries were sometimes supplemented by labour-intensive manufacturing that took advantage of cheap colonial labour. By the mid-20th century, Latin America, Asia and Africa were organically linked to and financially dependent on western Europe and the United States. The emergence of the United States as a dominant force and the growth of the Soviet bloc, however, undermined the monopoly of political control exercised by the European powers over large parts of the world. A process of decolonization began with the independence of the south Asian countries in 1947. This brought the possibility, however constrained (as the experience of Latin America, politically 'independent' since 1820, shows), of more autonomous development.

## IMPOSITION OF REGIONAL SPECIALIZATIONS

The 19th century was an especially critical period in the creation of colonial economies (Figure 8.2). Whole regions were made to specialize in the production of a specific raw material (such as gold, spices or cotton), food crop (such as bananas) or 'stimulant' (such as tea or tobacco). Many of these had a prior history, such as the sugar-producing areas of the Caribbean or the cotton-growing regions of the United States, India and Egypt. But the Long Depression (1883–96), a major down-turn in the world economy (the II(B) phase of Kondratiev's long-wave cycle (see Box 3.1)) – due, among other things, to decreased profitability in manufacturing – ush-ered in a major spurt in the global expansion of capitalism and intensified regional specialization. During this time period more and more resources and labour were drawn into an increasingly differentiated world economy.

Adam Smith and David Ricardo, writing well before this period, had envisaged a global division of labour in which each country would freely choose the com-modities it was most suited to produce and freely exchange its optimal commodity for the optimal commodities of others. Unfortunately, this economic vision of com-parative advantage, basic to most modern theories of international trade, ignores both the historical-political conditions under which commodities were selected and the costs faced by a specialized commodity economy in terms of vulnerability to the vagaries of 'world' demand. Competitive advantage, established through

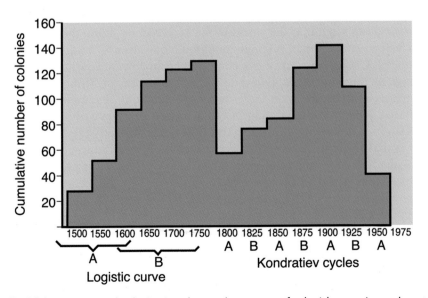

Fig 8.2: Long waves and colonization: the two long waves of colonial expansion and contraction
*Source*: Based on Taylor (2000: 115, Figure 3.4)

market dominance and political power, makes more sense as the significant determinant of the global map of production.

In the late 19th century, 'choice' of commodity was often imposed by force or through market domination. Moreover, once embroiled in the global system of regional specialization, an economy had to organize its factors of production in order to foster capital growth, or fall by the wayside. At the same time, other regions, without some initial advantage in raw material, climate, social organization or accessibility, became providers of labour power to the new outposts of global capitalism. Three examples, out of a host of possibilities, illustrate how externally oriented colonial economies were created on the basis of regional specialization: bananas in Central America, rubber in Malaya and tea in Sri Lanka.

Bananas are hardly a major food staple, but the creation of banana plantations in the late 19th century affected many areas, especially in Central America. Introduced into the Americas by the Spaniards, the banana became a staple crop among the lowland populations of Central America. In the 1870s it became a plantation crop as an American entrepreneur engaged in railroad construction in Costa Rica experimented with commercial banana production to increase the profitability of his railroad. As a result of this initiative was developed the United Fruit Company, incorporated in 1889 as a corporation engaged in the marketing of bananas from Central America in the United States. Over the years, the company produced bananas on plantation-estates in Costa Rica, Panama, Honduras, Colombia and Ecuador. Geographic dispersal had a number of advantages:

> [It] enabled the Company to offset political pressures in any one host country. Dispersal also allowed it to take advantage of suitable environments in different locations, thus reducing the chance that floods, hurricanes, soil depletion and plant diseases could bring production to a halt in any one of them. To further reduce these risks, the Company acquired a great deal more land than it could use at any one time, to hold as a reserve against the future. In some areas it formed relationships with local cultivators who grew bananas and then sold them to the Company.
>
> Wolf (1982: 324)

Much of the labour on the plantations was recruited locally, especially in Colombia and Ecuador, but in parts of Central America workers were brought from the English-speaking islands of the Caribbean. This resulted because of the difficulty the company faced in obtaining labourers from the populated highlands to work in the lowlands, and the firm's preference for a workforce that could be socially isolated and made wholly dependent on the company. The role of these foreign workers gradually decreased as host governments' limited immigration and encouraged their native populations to engage in wage labour on the plantations. Bananas are still an important export crop, especially for Panama and Costa Rica.

Wild rubber from Brazil dominated the world market for most of the 19th century. In 1876, however, Amazonian rubber seeds were smuggled from Brazil to England where they were prepared for planting in Malaya. Malayan rubber plantations grew from 5000 acres in 1900 to 1,250,000 acres in 1913. During this expansion, a class of managers for companies operating from London supplanted an original planter class. Labourers were initially imported from southern India but over time many plantations came to employ local Malays. Although plantation production remained dominant, many Malay cultivators tapped their own rubber trees as a source of cash income. Rubber increasingly replaced irrigated rice, a food staple, as the major commodity produced by small-scale proprietors. It remains so to this day.

Finally, among the range of commodities destined for consumption in the industrial world, some were neither foodstuffs (such as bananas) nor industrial crops (such as rubber). Such commodities as sugar, tea, coffee, cocoa, tobacco and opium were of fundamental importance in the global expansion of the world economy. Explaining the popularity of these 'stimulants' is not easy. Some accounts suggest that the work behaviour required under industrialization favoured the sale of these stimulants (except opium, a special case, as its main initial market was China) because they provided 'quick energy' and prolonged work activity. Others suggest that some (e.g., sugar and cocoa) provided low-cost substitutes for the traditional and increasingly costly diet of pre-industrial Europe. Whatever the basis to demand; by the late 19th century the stimulants were of great and increasing importance in world trade (see Mintz, 1985, for a splendid discussion of sugar and its role in world trade). Tea had become 'the drink' of English court circles in the late 17th century. It came entirely from China. Demand was so great that in the early 18th century tea replaced silk as the main item carried by British ships in the Chinese coastal trade. At the time of the American War of Independence, as the 'Boston Tea Party' reminds us, tea was the third largest import, after textiles and iron goods, of the American colonies. Some tea plantations were established in Assam (northeast India) in the 1840s, but until the opening of the Suez Canal Indian tea could not compete with the Chinese tea carried by the famous clipper ships around the Cape of Good Hope. With the opening of the canal and decreasing cost of steamship transportation, Indian 'black' teas became commercially competitive with the green teas of China. In the 1870s tea plantations spread with great speed throughout the uplands of what was then Ceylon (now Sri Lanka). This was done by confiscating peasant land through the device of 'royal condemnation' and then selling it to planters. By 1903 over 400,000 acres were planted in tea shrubs.

Tea cultivation is extremely labour intensive. To obtain the necessary labour, the Ceylon tea planters imported Tamil labourers from southern India. These Tamils, not to be confused with the long-resident Sri Lankan Tamils of northern and eastern Sri Lanka, now number over 1 million people, in a region in which the upland or Kandyan Sinhalese are about 2 million. As a consequence, an ethnic conflict has been imposed on top of an economic conflict between Sinhalese cultivators and Tamil plantation workers. Tea remains an important export crop in the contemporary Sri Lankan economy.

Many other examples could be added to these three to demonstrate the degree to which regional specialization was the classic motif of the colonial economies as they developed at an accelerating rate in the late 19th century. The long depression of that time in Europe and the United States stimulated an unprecedented expansion of the world economy into all parts of the globe as European and American capitalists sought to maintain capital accumulation in the face of declines in industrial production. Commodity production for a world market was not new but in its late 19th-century 'explosion' it 'incorporated pre-existing networks of exchange and created new itineraries between continents; it fostered regional specialization and initiated worldwide movements of commodities' (Wolf, 1982: 352).

## 8.2 ECONOMIC MECHANISMS OF ENMESHMENI AND MAINTENANCE IN THE COLONIAL WORLD ECONOMY

How was it that the regional specialization that began in the late 19th century was possible? And how did it evolve over time? Answering these questions requires us to focus on the means by which an integrated world economy was created: flows of capital investment, networks of communication and marketing, movements of commodities and people, and transportation – urban networks as channels of diffusion and concentration.

### TRADE AND INVESTMENT

The period 1860–70 inherited from the earlier centuries of colonial expansion two major systems of economic interaction, an Atlantic system built on the 'triangular trade' between Europe, Africa and the Americas (Figure 8.3) and a Eurasian system built on trade with India, East Asia and Southeast Asia. In the mid-19th century the Atlantic system in its classic form collapsed. It was replaced by a system based on a mix of competitive colonialism, regional specialization and investment in infrastructure (especially railways).

Between 1830 and 1876 there was a vast increase in the number of colonies and the number of people under colonial rule (Figure 8.2). There was also a tremendous

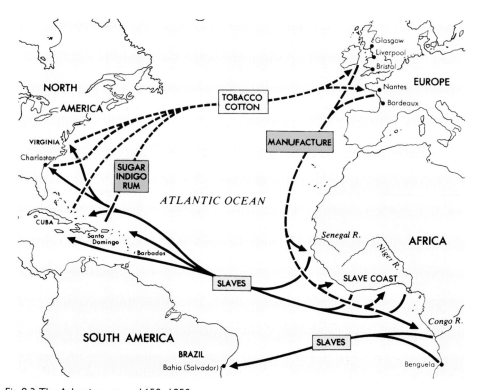

Fig 8.3: The Atlantic system, 1650–1850

*Source:* Based on Duignan and Gann (1985: 12, Map 1)

expansion of foreign investment by European states and capitalists in the late 19th and early 20th centuries (Table 8.1). Moreover, there was an important shift in the geographical distribution of both investment and exports. British trade and investment, to use the most important example, shifted away from India, Europe and the United States, especially with respect to investment in the first two and with respect to exports to the third, from the 1870s on. South America and the British dominions (Australia, Canada, New Zealand and South Africa) became more important, especially with respect to investment. However, the pattern was to fluctuate considerably over the years as some regions/states increased and others decreased in attractiveness to investors (Figure 8.4).

Table 8.1  Stock of foreign capital investment held by Europe, 1825–1915 (US$ billion)

|         | 1825 | 1855 | 1885 | 1915 |
|---------|------|------|------|------|
| UK      | 0.5  | 2.3  | 7.8  | 19.5 |
| France  | 0.1  | 1.0  | 3.3  | 8.6  |
| Germany | 0.1  | 1.0  | 1.9  | 6.7  |
| Others  | –    | –    | –    | 11.4 |
| **Total** | **0.7** | **4.3** | **13.0** | **46.2** |

Source: Warren (1980: 62, Table 1)

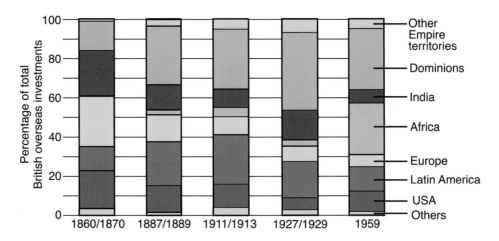

Fig 8.4: Geographical distribution of British foreign investment, 1860–1959
Source: Based on Hobsbawm (1968: 303, Figure 33)

The geographical switching of investment, however, was not always obviously economic in motivation. In particular, European incorporation of Africa into the world economy was based largely on competitive colonialism. Local settlers, as in South Africa, sometimes developed their own local 'imperialisms' and when challenged by other settlers or hostile natives called in the 'Motherland'. The relative weakness of many African polities also invited direct intervention. Once one European state was involved, others were tempted to engage in pre-emptive strikes to limit the damage to their 'interests'. Between 1850 and 1914 Africa was divided into a patchwork of European colonies and protectorates (Figure 8.5).

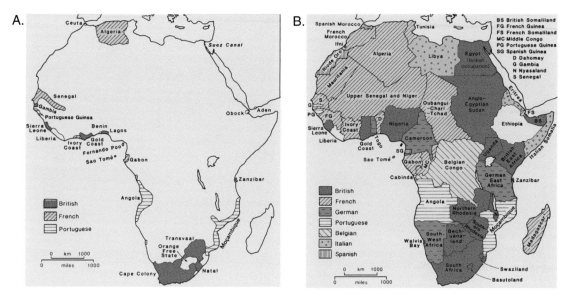

Fig 8.5: Colonization of Africa: (A) 1850; (B) 1914
*Source:* Based on Christopher (1984: 28–9, Figures 2.1 and 2.2)

## TRANSPORT ROUTES

At the global level the colonial system was bound together by a network of steamship and communication (postal, telegraph and, later, telephone) routes. These became progressively more dense and interconnected from the 1860s onwards. The Suez and Panama Canals were important in providing shorter and less hazardous routes between 'home ports' in Europe and North America and colonial destinations. By 1913 the world economy was effectively integrated by a system of regularly scheduled steamship routes (Figure 8.6). A world telegraph system enabled orders to be placed and shipments to be embarked for a large number of ports around the world (Figure 8.7).

Within colonies, railway building was the major mechanism of spatial transformation. In most of Africa and Asia, with the important exceptions of India, South Africa and north China, railways were not mechanisms for creating integrated colonial economies but, rather, means for moving a basic export commodity for shipment to Europe or North America. However, railways were often an important investment in their own right rather than a burdensome state responsibility. This was especially the case in South America and China, if much less so in India and Africa. In Argentina, for example, although the road and railway networks were oriented towards the River Plate Estuary and the capital city of Buenos Aires, they

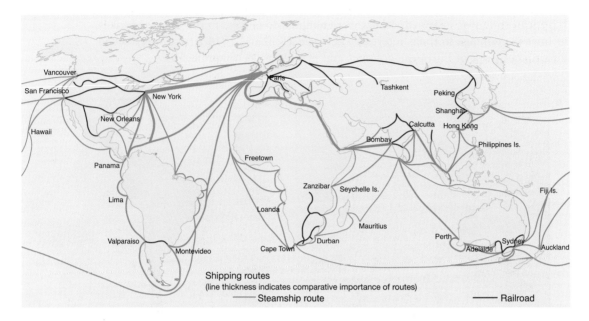

Fig 8.6: World steamship routes, by volume of trade, 1913

*Source*: Based on Latham (1978: 33, Map 2)

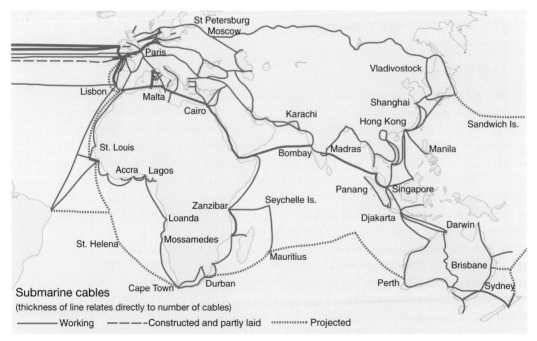

Fig 8.7: Telegraph system in Asia and Africa, 1897

*Source*: Based on Latham (1978: 36, Map 3)

provided a relatively dense grid for the rich commercial agriculture of the Argentinean pampas (Figure 8.8). This produced a transport system considerably more interconnected and integrated than the simple linear systems prevalent in Central America, Southeast Asia and most of Africa. In short, spatial integration into the colonial world economy did not take the same form everywhere.

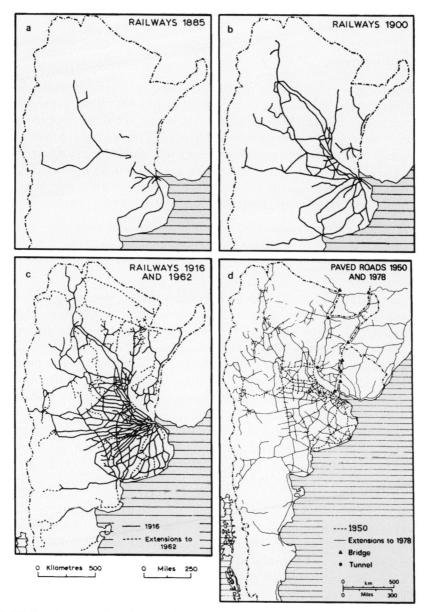

Fig 8.8: Development of roads and railways in the River Plate region of South America, 1885–1978
Source: Based on Crossley (1983: 401, Figure 9.3)

Whatever the precise nature of the railway networks, there was a tendency for all networks to focus on one or, at most, several coastal ports. These became 'privileged' locations, often assuming the role of administrative as well as economic centre for the entire colony. Specialization in the export of raw materials and concentration of administrative functions thus had the effect of stimulating the disproportionate growth of these 'links' to the world economy. This was especially marked in India (with Bombay, Calcutta and Madras) and Africa (for example, Cape Town, Dakar, Lagos).

## SETTLEMENT SYSTEMS

But the character of the colonial system also put limits on the growth of the dominant or primate cities. There was only a limited stimulus to the growth of a distinctive urban economy. The orientation of urban networks was towards exploitation of hinterlands rather than an industry- and service-based urban economy. It was only with political independence that a new dynamic for urban growth occurred as the primate cities shifted from being mechanisms for colonial control to their contemporary role 'as the corporate representative of the people of the former colony' (Fiala and Kamens, 1986: 28). As Rondinelli (1983: 49) points out:

> [C]olonial activities often stimulated the growth of secondary cities. In some cases they were encouraged to grow as colonial administrative posts or as transfer and processing centres for the exploitation of mineral and agricultural resources in the interior of a country.

Regions without a history of urbanization before colonialism were not surprisingly the most easily and strongly reoriented to the colonial world economy. In Malaysia, for example, cities grew up in the interior where crops were grown for export or where other exportable commodities (tin, especially) were exploited. These cities were connected by railway and road to port cities that grew as processing and transfer points. In regions with a long pre-colonial history of urbanization, such as western Nigeria, roads and railways were often built to bypass traditional centres of trade, such as Benin City, Ife and Sokoto. New, more effectively colonial cities grew up at nodes in the transportation network. As one study notes: 'Fortune rode the trains. [Towns] that received terminals grew, but those that did not stagnated or declined, as did many river ports' (Gugler and Flanagan, 1978: 27–8).

## REALIGNMENT OF TRADE AND PRODUCTION

The outcome of the new extension of the world economy and the intensification of trade within regions that were already incorporated was a substantial increase in world trade. The nature of the system of trade has led to its naming as a crossover system of trade. How important was the contribution of Asia, Africa and Latin America? The answer is: of great importance. By 1913 Asia and Africa provided more exports to the world economy than either the USA and Canada or the UK and Ireland (Table 8.2). In 1913 Asia also had a share of world imports almost as large as the USA and Canada combined (Table 8.3). What happened was that the industrializing countries of Europe and North America bought increasing amounts of raw materials and foodstuffs from the undeveloped economies and ran up large trade deficits with these regions. Britain, however, as a result of its free trade policy, ran up substantial deficits as a result of importing manufactured goods and investing heavily in the industrializing countries (especially the United States and Germany). In turn, Britain financed its deficits through the export of manufactured goods to the undeveloped world. Thus the circle of international trade and dependence was closed.

Table 8.2  World exports by region, 1876–1937, per cent of total

| Exports | 1876–80 | 1896–1900 | 1913 | 1928 | 1937 |
|---|---|---|---|---|---|
| USA and Canada | 11.7 | 14.5 | 14.8 | 19.8 | 17.1 |
| UK and Ireland | 16.3 | 14.2 | 13.1 | 11.5 | 10.6 |
| Northwest Europe | 31.9 | 34.4 | 33.4 | 25.1 | 25.8 |
| Other Europe | 16.0 | 15.2 | 12.4 | 11.4 | 10.6 |
| Oceania | | | 2.5 | | 2.9 | 3.5 |
| Latin America | 24.1 | 21.7 | 8.3 | 26.3 | 9.8 | 10.2 |
| Africa | | | 3.7 | | 4.0 | 5.3 |
| Asia | | | 11.8 | | 15.5 | 16.9 |

*Source:* Yates (1959: 32, Table 6)

Table 8.3  World imports by region, 1876–1937, per cent of total

| Imports | 1876–80 | 1896–1900 | 1913 | 1928 | 1937 |
|---|---|---|---|---|---|
| USA and Canada | 7.4 | 8.9 | 11.5 | 15.2 | 13.9 |
| UK and Ireland | 22.5 | 20.5 | 15.2 | 15.8 | 17.8 |
| Northwest Europe | 31.9 | 36.5 | 36.5 | 27.9 | 27.8 |
| Other Europe | 11.9 | 11.0 | 13.4 | 12.5 | 10.2 |
| Oceania | | | 2.4 | | 2.6 | 2.8 |
| Latin America | 26.3 | 23.0 | 7.0 | 23.4 | 7.6 | 7.2 |
| Africa | | | 3.6 | | 4.6 | 6.2 |
| Asia | | | 10.4 | | 13.8 | 14.1 |

*Source:* Yates (1959: 33, Table 7)

India and China were particularly important to this world pattern of trade and payments. It was Britain's trade with India and China that compensated for a negative balance of payments with the United States, industrial Europe, Canada, South Africa and New Zealand. Without the 'Asian surplus' Britain would not have been able to subsidize the growth of these other economies. So, far from being 'peripheral' to the growth of the world economy, the undeveloped world, especially India and China, was vital.

Between 1918 and 1939 this system of multilateral trade suffered a number of setbacks. One was the overall decline in trade as the world experienced a major depression. But the worst was the decline in Britain's relative position as the linchpin of the colonial world economy. This reflected both successful industrialization in India and China displacing British products (especially cotton textiles) and increased competition from Japan in Britain's 'traditional' colonial markets. But another problem was the overproduction of the main export crops and raw materials. As a consequence, commodity prices fell and so did demand for manufactured goods. The successful expansion of plantations and mines, therefore, ultimately undermined the system of capital circulation and accumulation that their introduction had brought into existence in the 19th century.

The onset of the Great Depression of the 1930s effectively ended the expansionist regime of international trade established in the late 19th century. The major industrial states reacted to the Depression by raising tariffs and devaluing their currencies. These shifts in economic policy were premised on the assumption that Britain would remain 'open' as the linchpin of the colonial world economy. But, as Stein (1984: 375) puts it: 'Depression left Britain unable and unwilling to accept an increasingly asymmetric bargain.' Not until the 1970s would world trade return to the relative levels that it had achieved in the early 1900s.

Military spending and massive increases in domestic consumption of domestic manufactures provided the keys to economic recovery in western Europe and the United States in the 1940s and 1950s. Although this did lead to increased demand for many of the industrial raw materials and foodstuffs produced in the 'periphery', there was no longer the crossover system of trading linkages. If anything, the European colonial states and, above all, the United States now came to have direct links to specific sites of exploitation in the periphery without the necessity of the infrastructure and administrative investments that had limited short-run payoffs. This approach favoured direct investment and the creation of subsidiaries by transnational corporations rather than portfolio investment and conventional trade. Advantages hitherto specific to the United States – the cost effectiveness of large plants, economies of process, product and market integration – had become the proprietary rights of large firms. The world was now their oyster, rather than that of the colonial states: 'American governments could preach against colonialism while large American [and other] firms colonized the world' (Agnew, 1987: 62).

In the early part of the 20th century the major share of accumulated foreign direct investment (FDI) was in the less developed countries (LDCs) (62.8 per cent in 1914). Total FDI came overwhelmingly from Britain (45.5 per cent) and the USA (18.5 per cent). Since the Second World War, however, most foreign direct investment has been between the industrialized economies. By the early 1970s only about 30 per cent of FDI was directed to the LDCs (which has since fallen to about 20 per cent); although after western Europe, Latin America was the major recipient region. By the early 1970s also, the USA, with nearly 50 per cent, was the major source of total FDI (Dunning, 1983). This has decreased since to about 30 per cent with the growth of Japanese, European and some NIC FDI. The dramatic post-Second World War expansion in FDI, therefore, has not involved all parts of the world on equal terms. In terms of flows of FDI, the LDCs have, on the whole, become less central to the world economy than they were previously. From this point of view at least, the end of colonialism was something of a mixed blessing.

## 8.3 INFLUENCE OF COLONIAL ADMINISTRATION ON INTERDEPENDENCE

Many of those who colonized the world from Europe, in both the 16th and the 19th centuries, saw their activities as part of a historic 'mission' of western civilization: to bring progress to backward and barbarian peoples. Lord Lugard, the famous British colonial administrator, maintained that Britain stood in a kind of apostolic succession of empire:

> [A]s Roman imperialism ... led the wild barbarians of these islands [the British Isles] along the path of progress, so in Africa today we are re-paying the debt, and bringing to the dark places of the earth ... the torch of culture and progress.

> Ranger (1976: 115–16)

At best the political ideas of the European imperialists were that:

> [P]olitical power tended constantly to deposit itself in the hands of a natural aristocracy, that power so deposited was morally valid, and that it was not to be tamely surrendered before the claims of abstract democratic ideals, but was to be asserted and exercised with justice and mercy.

> Stokes (1959: 69)

The chief problem was to understand and pacify the indigenous colonized. The Nigerian novelist Chinua Achebe (1975: 5) puts this as follows:

> To the colonialist mind it was always of the utmost importance to be able to say: I know my natives, a claim which implied two things at once: (a) that the native was really quite simple and (b) that understanding him and controlling him went hand in hand – understanding being a precondition for control and control constituting adequate proof of understanding.

This approach provided the ideology for what Hopkins (1973: 189) referring to the British in Africa, has called the 'art of light administration', administration without too much long-run investment or explicit (and expensive) violence.

The colonial regimes themselves never amounted to more than a thin veneer of European officials and soldiers on top of complex networks of local collaborators. In India in the 1930s, for example, 4000 British civil servants, 60,000 soldiers and 90,000 civilians ruled a country of 300 million people. The British were able to do this:

> by constructing a delicately balanced network through which they gained the support of certain favoured economic groups (the Zamindars acting as landed tax collectors in areas such as Bengal, for example), different traditional power holders (especially after the Great Mutiny of 1857, the native princes), warrior tribes (such as the Sikhs of the [sic] Punjab), and aroused minority groups such as the Muslims.

> Smith (1981: 52)

This kind of brokerage system was to be found in every colonial territory without a large European settler population. Sometimes a foreign economic presence was crucial (the Chinese in Southeast Asia; the Lebanese in West Africa; European settlers in Algeria and Kenya). Often there were alliances with new or traditional ruling groups (the Princely States in Malaya; the Ottoman bureaucracies in Tunisia and Morocco; the Hashemite family in Mesopotamia and Syria). Above all, local rivalries were exploited to advantage, as in Madagascar, India and China. Even in the face of nominal local political independence, as in China or Latin America, colonial imperatives and administrative models had considerable influence through imported school curricula and business practices (e.g., British influence was strong in Argentina and Venezuela; German influence was strong in Chile and Brazil).

Alliances and administrative structures were far from static and differed from colony to colony and between colonial powers. But one change *was* permanent. The new colonies, often vastly bigger than the territorial units they superseded, created markets of unprecedented size. Internal tolls and other restraints on trade disappeared. Sumptuary laws that prevented people of low status from acquiring luxury goods were abolished. All forms of servitude that interfered with the wage economy were outlawed. The great tribal migrations of eastern and southern Africa were brought to a close. New judicial methods were introduced and old ones eliminated. Schools and hierarchical systems of local administration were established.

The colonial powers operated in different ways. In Africa, for example, the British administration was more civilian and decentralized than the French and Belgian administrations. Its officials:

> [P]rided themselves on being gentlemen and amateurs, rather than on being military, legal or administrative specialists. The British pioneers set up an administrative hybrid based partly on British metropolitan models and partly on models derived from colonial India and Ireland.
>
> Gann and Duignan (1978: 355)

In particular, there was a dispersal of administrative power.

Any description of the particularities of administration in the various territories would require much more space than is available here (see Gann and Duignan, 1978; Gifford and Louis, 1971, for some of the details). One example must suffice. In Nigeria, Britain's most populous colony in Africa, the coastal (Lagos) and northern (Kaduna) regions were administered in completely different ways. The coastal region had a longstanding commercial base and export trade, tied to Liverpool and England's northern (e.g., Lancashire) industries. Consequently:

> Lagos governors ... tried to please north country British businessmen by emphasizing the needs of trade, communications and public health, by avoiding wars and punitive expeditions, by their reluctance to impose direct taxation, and by their determination to maintain a policy aimed at 'peaceful penetration' and commercial development.
>
> Gann and Duignan (1978: 209)

The northern region was a borderland and its international trade was limited:

> In this region the tone of administration was military; the British ruling group was linked to London and the Home Counties [the southeast of England] rather than to Lancashire ... Government emphasized prestige instead of profit, hierarchy in place of diversity.
>
> Gann and Duignan (1978: 209)

In all colonies, however, priority was given to communication, transport and medical care. Railways were built both to promote agricultural and mineral exports and to facilitate the movement of police and army detachments. Post offices, telegraphs and telephones gradually tied together the local administrative units. Indicative of the centrality of transportation networks to colonial administration was the fact that public works departments were often the first government units established in a territory. As Gann and Duignan (1978: 271) emphasize: 'By 1914 all the British African dependencies possessed a basic infrastructure of specialized services, the most important of which was the creation of a modern transportation network.'

An important cultural import into the colonies, therefore, was the assumption that the state should both encourage development and provide social services – education, agricultural instruction, etc.:

> The very notion of the state as a territorial entity independent of ethnic or kinship ties, operating through impersonal rules, was one of the most revolutionary concepts bequeathed by colonialism to post-colonial precedent ... All of them have taken over, in some form or other, both the boundaries and the administrative institutions of their erstwhile Western overlords.
>
> Gann and Duignan (1978: 347)

## 8.4 MECHANISMS OF CULTURAL INTEGRATION

The imposition of colonial rule and, more generally, western penetration of societies outside Europe, involved a great deal of violence and war. But, once established, 'law and order' involved the imposition of western values as much as terminating local conflicts and suppressing practices (witchcraft, infanticide, bride burning) that Europeans regarded as 'barbaric'.

The social effects of European values were paradoxical. On the one hand, old values were destroyed, as missionaries and schoolteachers attacked animistic creeds, polygamy and other customs. Families often broke up as some members 'converted' to Christianity and others did not. On the other hand, some people used the new ways to establish new bases of authority. In particular, western-educated natives became indispensable to European rule and influence. Interpreters, clerks, foremen and police sergeants were cultural pioneers; they represented the new order and profited from it.

The economic effects were also double-edged. As restraints on trade disappeared, commercial agriculture and trade spread in extent and intensity. Yields increased as agricultural techniques improved, and trade proved more profitable as new communications linked previously isolated interiors with coastal entrepôts. Yet, as a consequence, the certainties and rhythms of local life broke down and traditional skills were devalued. Above all, new types of consumption, while adding to the comforts of life of those with sufficient disposable income, led to the destruction of many local industries and the growth of dependence on manufactured imports from the colonial 'Motherland'. In this context, obligations to community and chief began to weaken. Money became the major metric for assessing social status. This was in part because money could help purchase an education:

> Education, in turn, brought power and influence. These new opportunities profoundly affected life in the village, and the village ceased to be an almost self-contained unit, absorbing all the interests of its people. Instead, cash-cropping and wage labour for limited periods gradually came to occupy a much more central position in the cultivator's life.
>
> Gann and Duignan (1978: 367)

The growth of 'free' labour was a process that was 'always uneven and idiosyncratic' (Marks and Rathbone, 1982: 13). It depended on spatial variation in the extent of competition for labour; conflicts of interest between firms and the colonial states; and the availability of alternatives to wage labour. But once colony-wide labour and other markets were effectively created, the prospering of commercial enterprises (both foreign and indigenous), such as mines and plantations, depended on an increasingly efficient and productive labour force to operate new equipment and machinery. This required measures to both increase labour force stability (housing, minimum wages) and attempts to upgrade the health, literacy and skills of employees. Of course, employee organizations also played a role in pressuring for these changes. Consumption demands, and hence demands for higher incomes, tended to increase in concert with the increase in permanent wage employment.

It is evident that in many colonies there were dramatic improvements in education and health. In Africa in the period 1910–60 the number of children attending school grew much faster than had school enrolments in Europe in the boom years of 1840–80. There were also significant increases in life expectancy (e.g., in Ghana in 1921 it was 28 years; in 1980 it was 45; and by 2000 it was 57) and reductions in infant mortality rates. To the British colonial authorities education was an important means of inculcating both 'modern' work habits and a commitment to the class structure of colonialism. At the centre of colonial education, was:

> the idea of work – taught to those who lacked property – emphasizing regularity, the organization of time and human energy around the work routine, and the necessity of discipline. It was a moral and cultural concept … Prohibitions against drinking and dancing … were as much a part of changing concepts of labour as forced recruitment, vagrancy laws, and the insistence that workers put in regular hours.
>
> Cooper (1980: 69–70)

But, above all, it was necessary 'to get workers to internalise cultural values and behaviour patterns that would define their role in the economy and society' (Cooper, 1980: 70).

This conception of education was particularly characteristic of the British colonies. Other colonies either failed to develop the capitalist labour markets to which it was a reaction (e.g., sections of the French colonies on the southern margins of the Sahara Desert) or were severely underfunded for public activities (e.g., the Belgian Congo and Portuguese colonies). But British policy brought a price. It was precisely the educated elite that 'formed the vanguard of the nationalist movements, and the more "disciplined" African workers became, the more effective were their trade union organizations in pursuing not only economic, but political anti-colonial objectives' (Sender and Smith, 1986: 66). As taught in colonial schools, western concepts of 'democracy' and 'justice' served to undermine the legitimacy of the western empires that had introduced them.

The growth of wage labour incorporated women as well as men into the colonial world economy, although at significantly lower levels of participation. More importantly, however, the spread of wage employment disrupted existing sexual divisions of labour, often to the detriment of women. Women remained powerfully constrained by family, marriage, religion and so-called 'domestic duties', even while engaged in wage employment. But norms, power and traditional patterns of authority based on gender, as well as age, caste and lineage, were subject to radical challenge because of wage labour, education, migration and urbanization. Lonsdale (1985: 730) quotes from one Zulu chief in southern Africa who in 1905 expressed his opposition to the cultural changes of the time as follows:

> Our sons elbow us away from the boiled mealies in the pot when we reach for a handful to eat, saying, 'we bought these, father', and when remonstrated with, our wives dare to raise their eyes and glare at us. It used not to be thus. If we chide or beat our wives and children for misconduct, they run off to the police and the magistrate fines us.

Cultural change was not always one way, however. Some pre-capitalist and pre-colonial social and religious institutions were strengthened. More accurately, perhaps, 'new' syncretic traditions were invented out of elements of past traditions. Mission-educated elites often invented mythic histories of ancient empires and new nationalist traditions both to legitimize their quests for political power and to protect themselves in the new labour markets. Adaptation was at least as common as straightforward assimilation in many colonial settings.

Ultimately, however, cultural incorporation, whether by adaptation or assimilation, undermined the sociopolitical relation of dominance/subordination that colonialism existed to reproduce. Even when the idiom of dominance was *improvement* rather than *order*, native groups were not always persuaded of the natural superiority of colonial ways. Langley's (1983: 223) conclusion concerning American colonial adventures in the Caribbean is a fitting epitaph to the cultural contradictions of the entire colonial enterprise:

> Striving to teach by example, they found it necessary to denigrate the cultural values of those whom they had come to save ... Their presence, even when it meant a peaceful society and material advancement, stripped Caribbean peoples of their dignity and constituted an unspoken American judgement of Caribbean inferiority. Little wonder, then, that the occupied were so 'ungrateful' for what Americans considered years of benign tutelage. But, then, Americans do not have in their epigrammatic repertory that old Spanish proverb that Mexicans long ago adopted: 'The wine is bitter, but it's our wine.'

## 8.5 CHANGING GLOBAL CONTEXT OF INTERDEPENDENCE

The colonial world economy began to disintegrate after the Second World War. The crossover trading system effectively ended in the 1930s. The Second World War's build-up of industrial capacity for military purposes in the United States and the Soviet Union produced two superpowers without overseas colonial empires and European decolonization further undermined the colonial world order. In the 1950s and 1960s the so-called 'Third World' (of politically independent but often politically non-aligned and always less prosperous countries) was born. Large parts of Asia and Africa now joined Latin America as a largely non-industrial and ex-colonial but still 'dependent world' (Figure 8.9). The initial tendency was to attempt to achieve economic self-reliance through national strategies of industrialization and diversification of trading partners. This was the first change in relation to the global context of interdependence.

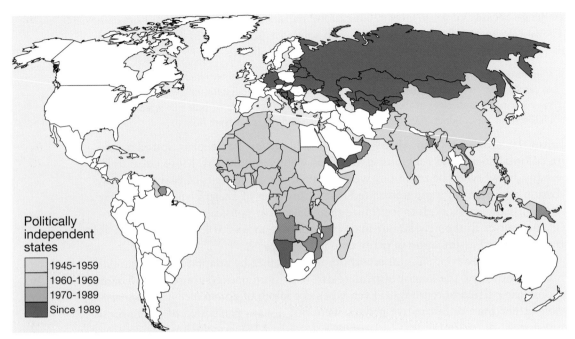

Fig 8.9: New states of the world since the Second World War

*Source*: Updated from Edwards (1985: 209, Figure 8.1)

## END OF COLONIALISM AND NATIONAL STRATEGIES OF DEVELOPMENT

As new states came into existence, so did attempts to stimulate industrial development and economic growth. From the Depression of the 1930s on and especially during the Second World War, stagnation and shipping blockades had encouraged some import substitution in the colonies. Increasingly traders and merchants in the richer peripheral countries looked to manufacturing industry as a source of capital accumulation. Leading politicians also saw in industrial development both national and personal advantage (see Chapter 10 for more details on the preference for industrialization).

Most importantly, however, the barter terms of trade (the ratio between the prices of exports and the prices of imports) for many of the basic commodities exported to the 'core' have deteriorated (Table 8.4). Basic commodity prices (largely those for raw materials) have declined relative to those for manufactures (Table 8.4). One consequence has been a widening gap between what peripheral countries received for their exports and what they had to pay for their imports. The resulting deterioration in the general barter terms of trade between richer and poorer countries was widely viewed as inevitable – given the low elasticity of demand for LDCs' primary commodities (as incomes rose in developed countries there was not a parallel increase in the consumption of goods from LDCs), the persisting low wages in the primary production sector in the LDCs (lowering local consumption power) and the high protective barriers for competing primary production (mainly temperate agricultural products, such as sugar beet and cereals, and largely erected in the 1930s) in the developed countries.

In fact, while real prices for almost all primary commodities have declined since the early 20th century, the rate and volatility of decline has varied considerably across primary commodities and relative to manufactures. This volatility of real

**Table 8.4** Barter terms of trade and world prices for primary product commodity groups, 1961–2002

|  | 1961–62 | 1970–72 | 1980–82 | 1990–92 | 2000–02 | 2002 |
|---|---|---|---|---|---|---|
| *Index of barter terms of trade: primaries against manufactures (1990–92 = 100)* | | | | | | |
| Least developed countries (e.g., Haiti, Mali, Afghanistan) | | | | | | |
|     Agricultural products | 120 | 121 | 120 | 100 | 86 | 84 |
|     Manufactured products | 190 | 175 | 165 | 100 | 76 | 70 |
| Other developing countries (e.g., Argentina, Egypt, Pakistan) | | | | | | |
|     Agricultural products | 115 | 125 | 125 | 100 | 97 | 98 |
|     Manufactured products | 175 | 169 | 164 | 100 | 90 | 89 |
| *Price indices (2000 = 100)* | | | | | | |
|     Tropical beverages | 48 | 62 | 182 | 98 | 89 | 89 |
|     Vegetable oilseeds | 63 | 74 | 150 | 114 | 103 | 117 |
|     Agricultural raw materials | 44 | 40 | 111 | 125 | 97 | 94 |
|     Food | 46 | 58 | 152 | 121 | 102 | 102 |
|     Minerals | 33 | 49 | 100 | 116 | 92 | 87 |

*Source:* Based on FAO (2004: 48, Table 5); UNCTAD (2005: Table 2.2)

prices received by primary commodity exporters, combined with a *perception* of a deteriorating barter terms of trade, inspired the first post-independence leaders to embark on policies that led away from specialization in primary commodity production. Recent years have not offered much encouragement as prices for the principal non-fuel primary commodities in world trade have continued to decline, especially for the least developed countries (Table 8.4).

Pessimism about the future prospects for primary commodities was reinforced by the view that the primary sector was inherently backward compared to the manufacturing sector: because of the latter's multiplier effects and, allegedly, greater economies of scale. Consequently, the pursuit of industrialization could be justified 'theoretically' as well as materially (see Chapter 10).

The promotion of industry came from either protection – from reserving domestic markets for domestic industry – or, later, establishing export enclaves and attracting foreign and local capital to finance branch plants. Once established, and/or protected through their early, vulnerable years, new industries would be able to compete globally. A predilection for protection, in many cases, reflected both a positive interpretation of the past practices of such countries as the United States, Japan and Germany, which had in their day protected 'infant industries' and the conception of an 'activist' state common to many ex-colonial territories.

During the 1960s exports of manufactures from LDCs grew quickly, from around US$3 billion in 1960 to over US$9 billion in 1970. As a percentage of total world trade in manufactures this was an increase of from under 4 per cent to 5 per cent. In the 1970s growth was even more rapid. By 1980 LDC-manufactured exports were more than US$80 billion or over 9 per cent of the world total. This growth is part of the new international division of labour (NIDL; see also pp. 39–47). One of the most notable features of the period 1960–80, however, and perhaps even more notable since then, has been the polarization of performance and prospects between different regional groupings of LDCs. Almost 75 per cent of the total of LDC-manufactured exports comes from 11 NICs (Brazil, China, Hong Kong, India, Indonesia, Malaysia, Mexico, Singapore, South Korea, Taiwan and Thailand). In most of these cases – especially Hong Kong, Malaysia, Mexico, Singapore, South Korea and Taiwan – industrial growth has been export led (export enclave) rather than import substitution (protection). Since 1980 this pattern has become institutionalized, with the bulk of the foreign direct investment, bank lending and trade relating to manufacturing production outside of the DCs concentrated in East Asia, parts of Latin America and eastern Europe.

Just over 66 per cent of all LDC merchandise exports (manufactures, food, agricultural raw materials, fuels, ores and metals) are now sold to DCs. Both high levels of protection in the DCs and the risk of increased protection in the future limit this market. Since the early 1970s the level and uncertainty of protective trade barriers to LDC manufactured exports have increased tremendously, particularly so-called hard-core non-tariff barriers such as quotas, voluntary export restraints and the Multifibre Agreement (MFA) (involving quotas by the DCs on textile and clothing imports from the LDCs between 1974 and 2005). This is especially the case for relatively more finished products. Between 1966 and 1986, the share of imports affected by all non-tariff measures increased by more than 20 per cent for the USA, around 40 per cent for Japan and 160 per cent for the EC. By 1986 21 per cent of LDC exports to the industrialized world were covered by these barriers even as average tariff rates and coverage declined. The Uruguay round of the General Agreement on Tariffs and Trade (GATT), however, incorporated some significant steps towards trade liberalization. Beginning in 1994, voluntary export restraints were abolished and the highly protectionist quota regime for textiles and clothing began to be phased out.

Manufactured goods can be classified into two main product groups: producer goods – capital goods (e.g., machinery and equipment, including transport equipment) and intermediate goods (e.g., raw materials and semi-finished items) – and consumer goods, of which textiles and clothing are the largest single category in international trade. Capital goods account for about half of all manufactured goods traded in the world economy (up from 46 per cent in 1990). But different world regions account for different shares of the two product categories. For example, DCs supply 72 per cent of world exports of machinery and transport equipment and 42 per cent of textiles and clothing. LDCs are important only as suppliers of textiles and clothing and certain light industrial products, mainly consumer goods (with the important exception of electronics components and automobile components, in the case of countries such as Brazil, Mexico and South Korea). The specialization of trade flows between LDCs and DCs, therefore, extends today beyond the distinction between primary commodities and other goods to apply *within* the category of manufactured goods.

## ROLE OF TRANSNATIONAL CORPORATIONS

The growth of trade in manufactures in the 1970s, after a 40-year period in which manufacturing production was intensively concentrated in the DCs and there was more limited DC–DC as well as DC–LDC trade in manufactures, was influenced by the growing significance of transnational corporations and of contractual coopera-tion between firms in different countries. Transnational corporations (TNCs) have long been active in manufacturing in LDCs. As we saw in Chapter 6 and discuss fur-ther in Chapter 10, they tended at first to duplicate plants around the world in order to gain access to protected markets or to make use of local raw materials. The production by TNCs of cars (e.g., in Brazil), agricultural engineering products (e.g., in South Africa and Mexico) and pharmaceuticals (e.g., in India) across a range of LDCs are examples. This kind of manufacturing production still exists, especially in countries with large internal markets. In Brazil, for example, in the mid-1970s to take an extreme case, almost 50 per cent of industrial output was produced by TNCs and more than 90 per cent of TNC production was sold locally.

Since the 1960s, however, much TNC involvement in LDCs has also involved what is known as global sourcing. As a result of technical change, especially reduc-tions in transportation costs, and the appeal of cheap (often female) labour in certain countries, production activities that once were adjacent spatially can now be dispersed widely. Many so-called light industrial processes are especially suited to the separation of various stages of production. In particular, labour-intensive stages (as in the product life-cycle model) can be located to take advantage of both the enormous international spread in wage levels and the exchange rate fluctua-tions between currencies that have been a feature of the world economy since the early 1970s. With respect to wage levels, the footwear industry faces wage costs of about US$10 per hour in the United States but under US$1 in Bangladesh, the Philippines and Trinidad and Tobago; Chinese textile workers earn less than US$0.50 per hour compared to a US rate of about US$13 (the higher skills and productivity of workers in the textile industry translate into higher wages com-pared to the clothing and footwear industries).

One industry that has engaged in global sourcing on a massive scale (and, perhaps, for this reason, is somewhat exceptional) is the consumer electronics com-ponents and products industry. This industry has two characteristics that have encouraged the shift to global sourcing: discrete production segments, of which some are extremely labour intensive and require a 'flexible response' because of short product cycles that make automation uneconomic; and compact products (parts and components) that can be shipped relatively cheaply. East Asian locations with cheap, reliable, literate and tractable (largely female) labour forces have been especially attractive to this industry (and some others such as textiles and clothing). Governments have often facilitated the process of establishing component and assembly plants through the provision of export processing zones (EPZs), subsidies and tax advantages, and the enforcement of the 'political stability' highly valued by TNCs and their local subcontractors.

## CHANGES IN MARKETS FOR PRIMARY COMMODITIES

For many LDCs, however, there is still a heavy dependence on trade in primary commodities (see Chapter 9). But the primary commodity sector has become extremely heterogeneous with respect to trading conditions since the Second World War. Four major categories stand out in this regard: fuels (mainly petroleum), non-fuel minerals, grains and other agricultural products. These product groups have experienced very different price movements and, to some extent, quantity fluctua-tions over the past 50 years. The non-food commodity prices have been especially volatile. Generally, manufactures have increased in price to the disadvantage of primary commodity exporters. But there have been two periods, 1949–52 and 1973–80, when demand for primary non-food commodities was extremely strong and commodity prices surged. In particular, in the years 1973–80, inflation and uncertain economic conditions in the DCs boosted the prices of agricultural raw materials. Since 1980, however, the relative price strength in the fuels and agricultural products groups has largely disappeared and the value of commodity export earnings in these sectors has sunk precipitously in relation to the prices of manufactures and minerals. Perhaps the most negative price movement from the perspective of most LDCs has been in the price of grains. There has been a long-term decline in world grain prices. This reflects tremendous increases in production the world over, but especially in the United States and other DCs. Normal yields per hectare are now more than twice what they were in 1950. The real price of wheat, however, is now about half what it was 100 years ago.

Across all primary commodities, commodity agreements between producing and consuming countries (cocoa, tin, sugar and natural rubber) and producer cartels (most famously, OPEC for petroleum) have failed to reduce volatility and raise the prices of primary commodities relative to those of manufactures because of fundamental differences of interest between producers and consumers and among producers. Even OPEC, after successfully raising the price of oil between 1973 and 1979, has been riven by conflict and the failure to attract some major oil producers (such as Britain, Mexico and Norway) to its ranks. This failure has encouraged further attempts at industrialization as the major strategy of economic development. However, price volatility acts to reduce the industrial potential of 'mineral economies' (Auty, 1991). This is one of the 'Catch-22s' of the contemporary world economy. Dependence on oil is said to sometimes lead to what is called the 'resource curse'. This suggests that rather than a blessing, reliance on a primary commodity for which there is tremendous world demand can give rise to a range of negative effects such as encouragement of corruption (particularly when state-owned companies have a monopoly), a rise in the exchange rate between the country's currency and others that can then raise inflation and squeeze out investment in agriculture and manufacturing, and pressure to share revenues by investing in prestige projects and providing subsidies that do not stimulate long-term economic growth.

Some countries, however, especially those in Sub-Saharan Africa, could probably benefit from increased attention to primary commodities. The macroeconomic policies of many African governments have worked to undermine their region's shares of world export markets across a range of primary commodities (Figure 8.10). Since the early 1970s real export earnings have remained stagnant or declined significantly in 25 out of 33 countries in Sub-Saharan Africa for which data are available. The whole of this region, with over 640 million people, has export revenues that are less than those of Singapore, a city state of 4 million people.

Inelasticity of demand in the DCs (expressed in deteriorating barter terms of trade) cannot explain the magnitude of these declines; neither can the absence of commodity diversification, since those countries with a relatively diversified structure of agricultural exports – such as Tanzania – have not experienced more favourable trends in export earnings than more specialized ones. Sender and Smith (1986: 127) explain the absolute decline of Sub-Saharan Africa's contributions to world commodity markets in terms of 'the continued dominance of anti-trade ideologies and export pessimism' that are:

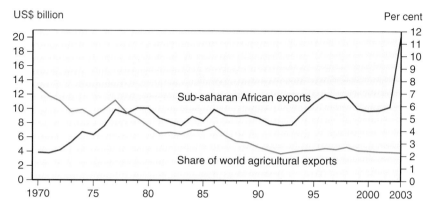

Fig 8.10: Sub-Saharan African exports

*Source:* Based on USDA (2002: 19)

probably explained by the political hegemony of nationalism. It remains expedient for the national bourgeoisie, or for those determining the form and nature of state intervention, to deflect criticism by resort to anti-imperialist rhetoric and to blame foreign scapegoats for economic failure.

However, this is probably too narrow a perspective. Political agendas and social problems of a more general nature have also played important roles. In the immediate post-independence period, considerable political energy was expended in diversifying import and export markets rather than building larger ones. This was a direct result of trying to slay the 'colonial dragon' as the newly independent countries tried to become less dependent on their former colonial powers. Governments have also been faced with major ethnic divisions and rivalries, fragile political institutions, and 'superpower' infiltration and manipulation. The Nigerian Civil War in the early 1970s, frequent military coups d'état and American or Soviet covert operations in most African countries are symptomatic examples of the diversions from economic policymaking that have faced political elites in Sub-Saharan Africa (and to a lesser extent also in Latin America and Asia) since the 1940s.

## DISPARITIES WITHIN THE PERIPHERY

Disparities among LDCs have increased substantially since the 1970s. Several groups have emerged and can be distinguished. First, there are those NICs that have grown rapidly and are important exporters of manufactured goods. These include the 'old' NICs such as South Korea, Taiwan and Hong Kong, and newer NICs, predominantly in Asia (e.g., Malaysia, Thailand), but including Brazil and Mexico. In 1960 the East Asian NICs only accounted for 5 per cent of total LDC exports and in 1980 for 10 per cent but, by 2005, this had risen closer to 50 per cent.

Then there is a group of countries that experienced reasonable growth until the late 1970s but because of high debt loads struggled during the 1980s in particular. Examples would include Argentina, Brazil and the Philippines. A couple of countries in this group with less serious debt problems, Costa Rica and Colombia, managed to continue their economic diversification away from primary commodities. A third group remains very dependent on raw material exports but export demand has held up to some extent. Examples would include oil exporters such as Nigeria, Ecuador and Cameroon.

Finally, there are two groups of low-income countries mainly in Sub-Saharan Africa and Asia. The Asian group – Afghanistan, Bangladesh, China, India, Nepal, Pakistan and Sri Lanka – is populous and, until recently, its countries isolated themselves from the world economy through protectionist policies. China has been the most aggressive in 'opening up' to trade and foreign investment and the impact of this is now most apparent in China's coastal areas, especially around Hong Kong and in the vicinity of Shanghai. Sub-Saharan Africa has had the poorest record of economic growth over the past 20 years. Most countries in the region have experienced declining or stagnant export earnings in the 1980s and 1990s. They are heavily dependent on foreign aid and investment by multilateral institutions such as the World Bank (but on the dangers of overaggregating the African case, see Grant and Agnew, 1996).

## EFFECTS OF THE COLD WAR

The end of colonialism did not usher in an era of equivalently 'sustainable' national development everywhere in the former colonial world; that much should be clear from the preceding discussion. The factor initially most responsible for this was the Cold War between the United States and the former Soviet Union, which, while encouraging 'aid' programmes of one kind or other, also encouraged militarization and political instability. After the Second World War the world was effectively divided into two spheres of influence with large parts of the new 'Third World' of former colonies as a zone of superpower competition (Figure 8.11). In certain cases, such as, for example, South Korea and Taiwan, superpower aid (US in these cases) contributed to economic growth. In many African countries aid has helped achieve major improvements in physical and social infrastructure, although much of the most productive aid has not come from the superpowers, which have specialized in military aid and technical assistance (intelligence gathering) rather than direct economic assistance. International agencies (the UN, World Bank, etc.), and some European countries (particularly the Scandinavian countries and the Netherlands) have provided much of the more economically 'useful' aid (on aid, see Chapter 2).

In other cases, 'models' of development were imported from either the United States ('free enterprise') or the Soviet Union (central planning) and then supported/ undermined from outside by each of the superpowers. This often led to increased militarization both of governments and national budgets as internal opponents were repressed and external patrons satisfied. Between 1960 and the collapse of the Soviet Union by 1991, more than 11,700,000 people were killed in 143 major wars and episodes of political violence (those with more than 1000 deaths attributable to them). Most of these were in the LDCs.

## GLOBALIZATION OF CAPITAL

A second change in the global context of interdependence since the demise of colonialism and the rise of national development strategies, and increasingly important since the 1970s, has been the increased pace and internationalization of the world economy as noted in Chapters 3 and 6. Capital has become much more mobile, both in time and space. For example, before 1972, currency exchange rates

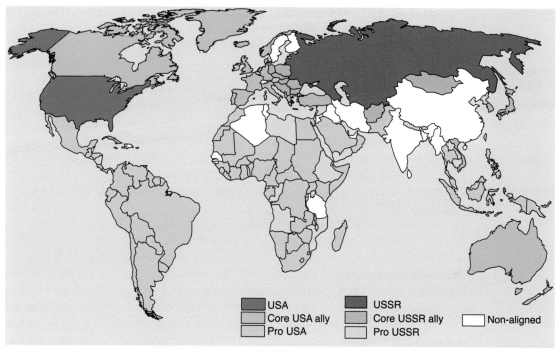

Fig 8.11: Soviet and US spheres of influence, 1982
*Source*: Based on O'Loughlin (1989: 302, Figure 11.1)

changed once every four years on average, interest rates moved twice a year and companies made price and investment decisions no more than once or twice a year (see Figure 3.2). All this has changed. There is now an almost constant review of prices and investment decisions, a constant instability and disorder. This places an even greater premium on the ability of firms and governments in LDCs to react within some coherent national framework to changes in the global political–economic environment.

Nowhere is this clearer than with respect to the world financial system. As we have seen, the growing integration of the world economy and the loosening of government control over exchange rates (when the major industrial governments, led by the United States, abandoned the Bretton Woods system of semi-fixed currency exchange rates in 1971) stimulated the growth of a massive *private* international monetary system. This system was organized around eurodollars, a term that originally meant US dollar deposits in banks in Europe but now refers to dollars that circulate outside the United States, which are used for world trade and are not regulated by the US government. This global currency mushroomed between the mid-1970s and the early 1980s as a result of the enormous dollar surpluses earned by the OPEC countries from oil sales. The large banks that received these funds sought borrowers who:

> could be charged enough interest to enable the banks to earn a profit. The banks first moved Eurodollars into Third World countries, saddling them with a US$1 trillion debt burden by the end of 1986, compared to less than US$100 million in 1973.

Instead of supporting new productive investment, however, a large portion of this debt went into luxury consumption. Over US$200 billion disappeared through capital flight from the Third World back to the industrial countries.

Wachtel (1987: 786)

This phenomenon was particularly deleterious for poor oil importers (who had to finance their oil imports) and countries with ambitious development plans (into which outside capital could be pumped). Many of them are still locked into debt repayment schedules that require them to devote the lion's share of their export earnings to servicing their debts. In Latin America, for example, since the early 1980s there has been a persistent net outflow of capital 'reflecting a "scissors movement" of declining grant aid and mounting debt repayments' (Cook and Kirkpatrick, 1997: 63).

After 1982, when Mexico and certain other major Latin American borrowers effectively defaulted on loan repayments, the eurodollars have shifted into funding the US budget deficit, into firm mergers and acquisitions in the United States and Europe and into the world's stock markets. But the burden of debt, in both the form of repayment and the inability to borrow fresh capital with outstanding debt, has emerged as a major new barrier to economic development (see Figure 2.14). In the 1980s net financial flows to LDCs initially decreased as commercial bank lending dried up. Since 1986 government and multilateral agency (World Bank, etc.) aid and foreign direct investment by TNCs have increased substantially. But only in 1989 did total flows equal the 1982 figure and, within this, aid increased from 38 to 55 per cent of the total. Since then private investment has increased somewhat, including both portfolio and foreign direct investment, but debt service still soaks up significant proportions of all capital inflows. This is borrowing to pay back what was previously borrowed rather than productive investment in economic activities that improve the lot of the LDCs and their populations. In the years between 1990 and the Asian financial crisis in 1997 in particular, most new bank lending from the DCs went to Asia, whereas the other regions had to rely more on foreign direct investment (as in Latin America) or on aid and multilateral loans from international organizations (e.g., the International Monetary Fund in Sub-Saharan Africa).

## DEBT AND INSTABILITY

If the 1970s are remembered for two major oil price shocks (in 1973 and 1979) and a persisting downturn in the world economy, the 1980s were marked by three global phenomena. One was the international debt problem, which effectively undermined growth in many LDCs for most of the decade. Although a variety of international agreements renegotiating interest payments reduced the overall severity of the international debt crisis in the 1980s, debt burdens remain at historic highs and effectively undermine the possibility of future credit-led economic development (Corbridge, 1993, offers a thorough overview of this phenomenon). The absolute debt load of LDCs peaked during the mid- to late 1990s at around 39 per cent of their combined GDP after declining in a cyclical fashion to 33 per cent in 1990 from a previous high of around 37 per cent in 1986. So debt is a problem that still haunts many LDCs' economies. Its impact varies widely, however, and is not a direct function of the absolute size of the debt. For example, as of 1999 Mexico had a huge debt of US$166.9 billion but its debt–service ratio (interest and principal payments as a share of all exports) was 'only' 25.1 per cent, whereas, at the other extreme, Colombia with a debt of US$34.5 billion had a debt–service ratio of 43.5 per cent. A second was the volatility of exchange rates, illustrated most vividly by the steep appreciation of the US dollar until 1985, followed by a dramatic descent until the late 1990s, at which point it began to appreciate again so that by the early 2000s it had reached levels not seen since the mid-1980s. These shifts have had important effects on the imports and exports of countries whose currencies are 'pegged' in value to global currencies such as the US dollar. Commodities become more or less expensive depending on the shifts in the value of the global currency. The net impact has been negative for all LDCs. Finally, the US federal government and national trade deficits, emerging spectacularly after 1983, produced growth in the USA at the expense of stagnation elsewhere. Investment that could have gone to the LDCs under other circumstances was diverted to the USA to finance the deficits. This also raised interest rates on outstanding loans such as those held by heavily indebted LDCs. Consequently, high interest rates and low commodity prices rather than the debt loads incurred in the 1970s were probably the major barriers to growth in the LDCs in the 1980s. On balance, the 1980s was not a good decade for the LDCs as a whole. Likewise, the period since 1990 has hardly been stellar given the declining terms of trade for primary commodities, the debt loads incurred but not yet paid off and the economic woes of a number of the NICs precipitated by the Asian financial crisis of 1997.

## Box 8.1 The Asian financial crisis

The early 1990s in East Asia was a time of rapid economic growth. Doubts about the 'East Asian Miracle' surfaced in 1996, however, as observers pointed to a slowdown in exports, excess capacity in many industries and declining earnings. In 1997 the currency and financial crisis that erupted in Thailand in July spread to South Korea, Malaysia and Indonesia; Hong Kong, the Philippines and Singapore were less hard hit; China and Taiwan were least affected although they still experienced a slowdown in growth.

The crisis in East Asia deepened in late 1997 and had spread to the rest of the world by 1998. Speculative attacks in other semi-peripheral countries – notably Brazil and the Russian Federation – caused economic difficulties and capital flight. On Wall Street, the Dow Jones Industrial Average recorded its second and third biggest losses in August. Efforts by the individual East Asian countries themselves, combined with assistance from the IMF and World Bank among others, helped bring the crisis under control to the extent that, by March 1999, the Dow closed above 10,000 for the first time in its history. The East Asian economies rebounded and enjoyed a growth rate of 4.1 per cent in 1999 and close to 6 per cent by 2000.

Some of the factors that precipitated this crisis in East Asia, which have been targeted with macroeconomic and structural policies, include national financial weakness (overvaluation of currencies pegged to the US dollar, large volumes of short-term capital inflows and exposure to short-term debt), inadequate regulatory oversight of financial and other businesses, high corporate indebtedness, failed management and overcapacity in key manufacturing sectors.

## CONTINUED CORE–PERIPHERY POLARIZATION?

From one point of view, the net effect of the changes in the global context for inter-dependence has been an increased division between the LDCs, on the one hand, and the DCs, on the other. National income and purchasing power statistics support this interpretation. But, from another point of view, the periphery has, in fact, developed rapidly. This interpretation is supported by data on output, health and education. One way of reconciling these discordant interpretations is to argue that the post-colonial world economy has come to rest on increasingly diffused global production but has lacked a similar attainment of a global spread of consumption. The relatively low incomes available in LDC factories and plantations have put a cap on local purchasing power even as local labour forces were made more efficient (through improved health and education) and increased their output.

The problem with this reconciliation and the interpretations on which it is based is that they are geographically overaggregated. The experience of different groups of LDCs has been different, as suggested previously by the 'grouping' of countries. On the one hand, some of the Latin American countries, for example, are relatively large and have relatively high levels of per capita income (e.g., Brazil, Argentina). Some of them did achieve considerable income growth in the 1960s and 1970s on the basis of industrialization to satisfy local markets (import substitution). Most of them, however, were heavy importers of oil (Mexico and Venezuela were exceptional) and their industrial sectors were generally uncompetitive in world markets. They were hit in the 1970s by the combination of oil price rises and their failure to switch to export-oriented manufacturing in the boom years of the late 1960s. They had to borrow to ease the oil shock adjustment instead of paying for it with export earnings. They are now caught in a 'debt trap' of accumulated loans compounded by the high interest rates of the early 1980s, and the growth of trade barriers to the manufactures they export to the United States and western Europe.

The Sub-Saharan African countries, on the other hand, are much poorer on the average than Latin American or East Asian countries and their low level of output in all sectors is undermined by their even faster rates of population increase. They are economies with small industrial sectors and a heavy dependence on primary commodities. As commodity prices dropped in the 1980s (see Table 8.4), the Sub-Saharan African countries were forced to borrow to maintain minimal levels of consumption. Their debt burden is similar to that of the most indebted Latin American countries. The consequence, as in Latin America, is a general reduction in the standard of living but in contexts where it is already desperately low.

Finally, Asian countries have, on average, managed the best over the past 20 years. They have been more successful in maintaining economic growth as a secular trend and adjusting to short-run cyclical downturns such as the world recessions of 1974–75, 1979–82, 1989–93 and 2000–02. The East Asian NICs, the most dynamic economies in the region, have been able to expand their export of manufactures. They now account for almost 50 per cent of LDC total exports of manufactures. Although, like the Latin American countries, they borrowed heavily in 1974–75 to adjust to the oil price increases, their export performance has allowed them to keep relatively good borrowing terms and adjust more easily to the massive interest rate increases of 1980–81. Yet, they are not without their own difficulties. Even before the Asian financial crisis, growth rates were slowing throughout East Asia in the mid-1990s indicating that there may be limits to an export-based strategy of economic development when established markets stagnate or decline and growth is more reliant on cheap labour and high savings than on technological and organizational innovation. The rise of the East Asian NICs, however, has altered the global development picture in fundamental ways. For one thing, their high rates of economic growth have translated into declining national poverty rates. Because of the numbers of people involved this can be made to seem as if this is a trend across the entire periphery. In fact, poverty reduction has been much less evident elsewhere. This means that there are increasingly significant differences *within* the periphery and between semi-peripheral and truly peripheral economies with respect to poverty and overall quality of life.

## 8.6  ALTERNATIVE MODELS OF DEVELOPMENT?

In the face of the failure of many LDCs to maintain, let alone increase, their production output and the consumption levels of their populations, the models of development on which national development efforts have been based have been called into question. This coincides with the growing questioning of the American model of competitive capitalism (especially the lack of effective national trade and industrial policies) in the USA and the collapse of the Soviet command economy model in the (former) Soviet Union and eastern Europe. Neither of these models can any longer be said to offer a simple way out of the 'development impasse'. The spread of more liberal and open trading policies in the 1980s and 1990s did produce benefits for some countries, particularly the NICs, but these have been strictly limited geographically. This is undoubtedly the dominant model at the moment; sponsored by the main international economic institutions (such as the IMF, WTO and World Bank) as well as by the TNCs and major global banks.

It is in this context that new 'models' have appeared to replace previous ones. Perhaps the three most important ones today are based on (1) a synthesis of liberal reforms and social democracy as practised in parts of western Europe, particularly in Sweden, (2) the Chinese experiment in globalization since 1978 and, to a much more limited extent, (3) Islamic economic practices. Each of these alternative models is noted briefly.

The European experience is seen as relevant because it combines both a focus on economic growth with an emphasis on reducing income inequalities and social exclusion. The problem is that historical experience suggests that both rarely take place at the same time. It has been only with considerable struggle that subordinated groups have been able to wrest various programmes and social rights from their national governments often in the face of resistance from dominant groups such as local and foreign capitalists. The great Chinese experiment since 1978 is also sui generis in that it combines a government regulated macroeconomy with considerable decentralization of power over industrial and financial affairs to a range of other actors including domestic capitalists, local governments and TNCs. Finally, practices and beliefs drawn from the Islamic religion have become important in southwest Asia, North Africa and other parts of Asia (e.g., Indonesia). The prohibition of usury or 'excessive' interest charged on monetary loans is one of the more concrete and obviously appealing features of Islamic economics. But, as yet, no system of political economy based on Islamic principles has been established in any country (including Iran). The conclusion of Katouzian (1983: 164), one of the leading authorities on Islamic economics, seems appropriate:

> While one may empathize with the desire to construct an indigenous ideology that can be identified with the Islamic beliefs and practices of its advocates particularly in view of the havoc caused by selective application of Western ideas under the late Shah [of Iran], it is no more to be expected that Islam can provide a comprehensive economic system than that the latter could be based on Christianity, Judaism, or any other traditional religio-political system.

In practice what is happening is more by way of different adaptations to a dominant liberal capitalism than the adoption of full-bloodied alternatives to it. If some places have seen a full-scale adoption of a market-access capitalism in which barriers to the flow of goods and capital have been radically reduced, others have seen the continued or renewed imposition of state regulation. Some places with heavy state regulation have been able to successfully incorporate themselves into global trade and capital circuits primarily through the export of manufactured goods and services (Table 8.5). These are usually populous states such as India and China with distinctive competitive advantages in different sectors. Smaller countries emphasizing exports typically must make themselves much more open to the potential turbulence of the world economy. Resource-oriented economies likewise divide into two main groups according to the degree of state regulation and direction. Here, scale of production also seems to matter but the patterns are more unstable in that the role of different strong political leaders, such as Putin in Russia and Chavez in Venezuela, and their ability to exploit upswings in global demand for their countries' oil and natural gas, seem to be more determining of policy choices than the structural characteristics of their economies per se.

Table 8.5 Adaptations to global capitalism

|  | State-regulated | Market-access |
|---|---|---|
| Export of manufactures/services | China, India | Taiwan, South Korea |
| Export of oil and gas | Russia, Venezuela | Nigeria, Saudi Arabia |

## SUMMARY

In this chapter, we have surveyed the dynamics of interdependence between the core and the periphery of the world economy from the colonial period to the present day. We have identified the following points as being of critical importance:

1 Existing economies were transformed into colonial ones through regional specialization in primary commodity production.
2 In the late 19th and early 20th centuries, a 'crossover' multilateral system of trade, with Britain as its linchpin, integrated the world economy.
3 The 'crossover' system was progressively displaced by foreign direct investment (FDI) from transnational corporations (TNCs). American firms were especially important.
4 Colonialism created the conditions for wage labour and gave priority to improving communications, transportation and medical care. The European-

style territorial state became accepted as the basic political unit for regulating economic activity.

5  Western values had paradoxical effects. On the one hand, values of work discipline and private property were disseminated. On the other, new syncretic traditions were invented.

6  With decolonization, new states came into existence that attempted to encourage industrialization.

7  For many years much manufacturing in the LDCs was import substitution. Since the 1960s, however, TNCs have engaged in global sourcing: dispersing some production functions to appropriate sites in LDCs and exporting components/products back to the USA, western Europe or Japan. Some NICs have developed their own export-oriented industries.

8  Many LDCs are still heavily dependent on the export of primary commodities, the prices of which are highly volatile and have tended to decline against those of manufactured goods over time.

9  Cartels and production agreements have largely failed to stabilize the production or prices of most primary commodities. The success of OPEC in relation to petroleum beginning in the 1970s is the one exception.

10  The Cold War between the United States and the former Soviet Union and the increased pace and internationalization of the world economy placed serious constraints on development efforts. The global 'debt crisis' of the early 1980s has been another especially important constraint.

11  The integration of production within the world economy has not been matched by an integration of consumption. However, different world regions of the periphery have had different experiences in this regard: the Asian countries (especially the East Asian NICs) have been most successful, the countries of Sub-Saharan Africa least so.

12  Alternative models of development, from Europe, China and Islamic traditions, have arisen to challenge the dominant US/Soviet ones because of the failure of the dominant ones to manage social inequalities or generate sustainable economic development. But more typical in practice have been adaptations to the dominant liberal capitalism of the globalizing world economy involving greater or lesser degrees of state intervention versus more whole-hearted acceptance of market-access policies.

The next three chapters take off from this general perspective on the transformation of the periphery and semi-periphery to examine contemporary patterns of agriculture, industry and services, paying special attention to the changing relationships between core and periphery outlined in Chapters 2 and 3.

## KEY SOURCES AND SUGGESTED READING

Amsden, A. 2007. *Escape from Empire: The Developing World's Journey through Heaven and Hell.* Cambridge, MA: MIT Press.

Banerjee, A.V., Bénabou, R. and Mookherjee, D. (eds) 2007. *Understanding Poverty.* Oxford: Oxford University Press.

Cook, P. and Kirkpatrick, C. 1997. Globalization, regionalization and third world development, *Regional Studies*, 31, 55–66.

Corbridge, S. 1993. *Debt and Development.* Oxford: Blackwell.

Diakosavvas, D. and Scandizzo, P. 1991. Trends in the terms of trade of primary commodities, 1900–1982: the controversy and its origins, *Economic Development and Cultural Change*, 39, 231–64.

Fiala, R. and Kamens, D. 1986. Urban growth and world polity in the nineteenth and twentieth centuries: a research agenda, *Studies in Comparative International Development*, 21, 23–35.

Grant, R.J. and Agnew, J.A. 1996. Representing Africa: the geography of Africa in world trade, 1960–1992, *Annals of the Association of American Geographers*, 86, 729–44.

Powell, A. 1991. Commodity and developing country terms of trade: what does the long run show?, *Economic Journal*, 101, 1485–96.

Sender, J. and Smith, S. 1986. *The Development of Capitalism in Africa*. London: Methuen.

Wachtel, H.M. 1987. Currency without a country: the global funny money game, *The Nation*, 245, 26 December, 784–90.

Weinthal, E. and Luong, P.J. 2006. Combating the resource curse: an alternative solution to managing mineral wealth, *Perspectives on Politics*, 4(1), 35–53.

Wolf, E.R. 1982. *Europe and the People without History*. Berkeley, CA: University of California Press.

## RELATED WEBSITES

American Memory, Library of Congress: http://memory.loc.gov/ammem/aapchtml/
contains *From Slavery to Freedom: The African-American Pamphlet Collection, 1824–1909* comprising nearly 400 pamphlets from the Rare Book and Special Collections Division, published from 1824–1909, by African–American authors and others who wrote about slavery, African colonization, emancipation, reconstruction and related topics

Asian Development Bank: http://www.adb.org
the ADB is a multilateral development finance agency (owned by countries in the Asia–Pacific region) whose goal is to reduce poverty in Asia and the Pacific. In addition to information about ADB and its activities, this website contains data and research covering, for example, the Asian financial crisis

Facts on File News Service: http://www.facts.com/
provides news information from internet sources, with weekly updates from the *Facts on File World News Digest*, in addition to regular updates from Reuters. Its country profiles provide a detailed history, which includes the colonial past of former colonies

United Nations and Decolonization: http://www.un.org/Depts/dpi/decolonization/main.htm
provides information on decolonization for the countries that have gained their independence and joined the United Nations since the Second World War

United Nations Conference on Trade and Development (UNCTAD): http://www.unctad.org/
offers publications and data on trade, investment and economic development issues as they relate to the LDCs, including the latest edition of the annual *Least Developed Countries Report* and the annual *Trade and Development Report: Developing Countries in World Trade*, as well as the annual *World Investment Report*, which contains information and data on DC and NIC TNCs, and FDI in the LDCs

World Bank: http://www.worldbank.org/
offers research and statistics on economic development and world trade as it relates to the LDCs, including its 2002 publication, *Globalization, Growth and Poverty: Building an Inclusive Economy*, and its annual edition of *Global Economic Prospects*

# Chapter 9

# Agriculture: the primary concern?

Picture credit: Xiaojing Chen

'Development' is often equated with the structural transformation of an economy whereby agriculture's share of the national product and of the labour force declines in relative importance. Agriculture has often been viewed as a 'black box from which people, and food to feed them, and perhaps capital could be released' (Little, 1982: 105). This perspective, long dominant among planners and politicians and common to both the American and the former Soviet models of development, reflected the low elasticity of demand for food (demand increases very little with higher incomes), the secular global trend towards higher labour productivity in agriculture (the same output can be produced by fewer workers because of technology, fertilizers, etc.), the limited multiplier effect of agriculture and the secular tendency for the barter terms of trade to turn against countries that export primary commodities and import manufactured goods.

However, it is almost certain that the world's population will rise to over 9 billion by the middle of this century. It is equally certain that most of the growth in population between now and then will take place in the LDCs. Consequently, these countries in particular will need to increase their food production to supply the additional people and to increase their standard of living. At the same time they face two major constraints: much land is unsuitable for agricultural purposes (Figure 2.5) and their involvement with the world economy often reduces their food self-reliance without sufficient compensation in other sectors.

The purpose of this chapter is to describe the contemporary state of agriculture in the 'periphery' of the world economy. To this end, the chapter is organized as follows: a first section establishes the importance of agriculture as an economic sector and stresses the dual trends of increased agricultural production for the world market and decreased food self-reliance; a second section discusses the general relationships between land, labour and capital in the periphery with special attention to efforts at rural land reform; third, the capitalization of agriculture in the periphery by transnational corporations is described; fourth, and last, the role of science and technology in agriculture in the periphery, especially in the form of the so-called Green Revolution, is assessed.

## 9.1 AGRICULTURE IN THE PERIPHERY

The countries of the periphery have all been significantly involved with modern commercial farming since the beginning of western colonization in the 16th century. But subsistence and production for local markets have remained of great, if decreasing, importance. Malassis (1975) identifies four types of agricultural system in the periphery: (1) the 'customary' farm involving common ownership of land for both cultivation and grazing; (2) the 'feudal or semi-feudal' estate, hacienda and latifundia; (3) 'peasant agriculture', including minifundia (small, subsistence farms), commercial farms and share cropping; and (4) capitalist plantation or mechanized agriculture based on wage labour. These four types of farm organization produce three types of commodity: (a) commercial foods, primarily cereals for the domestic market; (b) subsistence foods, primarily for personal use; and (c) export crops, where the major market is overseas. The historical trend in agriculture in most countries of the periphery has been from (1) and (2) to (3) and, especially, (4) in farm organization and from (a) and (b) to (c) in types of agricultural commodity.

However, the three continents of the periphery – Africa, Asia and Latin America – differ in terms of agricultural organization and performance. Above all, Sub-Saharan Africa is, or has been until recently, abundant in land and sparse in population; Asia is largely short of land relative to population; and Latin America contains both areas with large populations and areas with few inhabitants. Agriculture is also of much greater relative importance in Sub-Saharan Africa and Asia than in Latin America, both in terms of employment and contribution to national product.

### WOMEN'S WORK

It is also important to recognize that in agriculture in the LDCs it is the women rather than the men who are overwhelmingly more important as the source of workers. Indeed, the 'gender dimension' is not a secondary consequence of variations in agricultural organization but 'a fundamental organizing principle of labour use' (Joekes, 1987: 63). Regional differences are apparent, however, indicating the contingencies of resource endowment and carrying capacity. More women are involved in agriculture in Africa, relatively speaking, than elsewhere. In 2000 the UN FAO estimated that at least 75 per cent of all women in the labour force in Sub-Saharan Africa were involved in agriculture, compared to 68 per cent in India, 70 per cent in China, 62 per cent in other low-income Asian countries (such as Bangladesh and Cambodia) and 35 per cent in middle-income Asian countries (such as Malaysia and South Korea). In Latin America the comparable figure is a very low 10 per cent. This reflects the greater degree of mechanization (and export crop orientation) in Latin American agriculture and higher levels of female rural to urban migration compared to other regions. Official figures may capture the female day labourers on larger commercial farms but certainly miss many of the subsistence farming activities carried out predominantly by women. Labour force participation data usually involve very narrow definitions of agricultural activity focused on land cultivation and large-scale livestock keeping. While many of the men migrate to find work, they leave behind the women, whose largely unrecorded role in agriculture includes tending to the fields and the animals. Women also do most of the domestic work: processing food crops, preparing meals, fetching water, collecting fuel wood, and caring for the children, elderly and sick (an increasing burden in the face of the HIV/AIDS pandemic).

However, although women have the primary responsibili they usually do not have control. National law or local < the right to secure title or inherit land, which means they credit and improve their conditions.

In a few communities, government agencies and non-pr recognized this untapped economic potential have beg information, education and access to credit.

## FORMS OF AGRICULTURAL ORGANIZATION

Forms of agricultural employment and organization also tend to differ among the regions of the world. 'Mechanized agriculture' and export crops have become of greatest importance in Latin America. Green Revolution agriculture has become most widespread in producing wage and peasant foods in lowland Asia with pockets in Latin America and North Africa. 'Resource-poor' agriculture, producing a range of crops, predominates in Sub-Saharan Africa and areas of poor soils and drainage elsewhere. Production differences reflect these organizational and endowment differences.

While per capita food production in the periphery has not matched that of the core, and in many cases has not kept up with population increases, spectacular growth in the production of specific crops for export to the core was characteristic of the 1970s and 1980s in particular. In Latin America by the late 1970s, commercial agriculture, centred primarily in the large farm sector, was estimated to account for half of all agricultural production, nearly one-third of the cultivated area and one-fifth of the entire workforce. For example, sugar production increased by over 200 per cent in El Salvador, Guatemala and Honduras between 1965 and 1977. The production of sugar in these three countries has continued to increase since then, by over 100 per cent. Beef production in the Dominican Republic grew at 7.6 per cent per annum between 1970 and 1979. It continued to grow at 4.6 per cent annually throughout the 1990s. Sorghum production, unimportant in Brazil before 1970, rose to over 1.5 million metric tons by 2005. The expansion of export production and regional specialization has been most characteristic of agriculture in Latin America. In Sub-Saharan Africa, however, export crops have failed to maintain global market shares even as total agricultural production increased (see Table 8.4). This reflects both declining productivity in the export sector and government attempts to direct investment into industrialization rather than agricultural commodities. Food production has been dismal, particularly in the context of rapid population increase. In Asia, both productivity and production have increased enormously because of fertilizers and the application of new technologies, but most growth has been in cereals (especially rice and wheat) production rather than 'special' export crops such as those of growing importance in Latin America (e.g., fruits and beef). The problems for the Asian countries are their high land–population ratios and the competition they face from agriculture in the United States and western Europe in the crops (such as wheat and rice) in which their growth has been concentrated. US, EU and Japanese subsidies and market protection for agricultural production deprive Asian (and other LDC producers such as Argentina) of both higher prices and international markets. Lower production of cereal crops in the core of the world economy would produce higher world prices (through a decrease in the amount produced) and greater access of LDC producers to DC markets.

## 9.1 The coffee commodity chain

Coffee is the world's second most valuable traded commodity, behind oil. There are about 25 million farmers and coffee workers in over 50 countries producing coffee. Coffee was historically developed as a cash crop in colonial economies, planted by peasants or wage labourers on large plantations for sale in the core countries. It is currently the largest food import of the United States. The coffee 'commodity chain' today involves a string of producers, middlemen, exporters, importers, roasters and retailers before reaching the consumer (see Chapter 1). Global consumption has increased tremendously over the past 20 years, owing much to the 'Starbucks'® phenomenon: the spread of coffee shop franchises of this or other similar brands all over the world. Around 70 per cent of world production is of Arabica beans, used for higher grade and specialty coffees, with 80 per cent coming from Latin America. The rest is Robusta coffee, grown mainly in Africa and Asia. Typically, coffee farmers and workers receive extremely low wages relative to the final retail price of coffee. This has encouraged the development of the Fair Trade in Coffee Movement to try to improve working conditions and wages for producers (see Box 2.4). Most small farmers sell to middlemen, while large estate owners usually process and sell their crop directly overseas at prices fixed by the New York or other international coffee exchanges. Most importers purchase green coffee from established exporters and estate owners in producing countries such as Brazil and Colombia. They then hold the stocks selling gradually to roasters to both maintain the price and to control supply. Importers are thus the key agents in the coffee commodity chain. Roasters, of whom there are around 1200 in the United States today, usually have a set of recipes and sell to large retailers under such brands as Maxwell House (Kraft) and Sanka (Philip Morris), Folgers and Millstone (Procter & Gamble), and Nestlé. Although these large roasters account for 60 per cent of green coffee volume in the USA, some roasters produce as few as 500 bags a year for the specialty coffee market of high-end coffee shops. With the highest profit margins in the value chain, roasters are thus a key link on the road from producers to consumers. Retailers sometimes now roast their own beans but, by and large, they sell either beans or coffee to the general public. Supermarkets and other shops account for about 60 per cent of retail sales with coffee shops making up the rest. Other foodstuffs and industrial raw materials follow similar commodity chains geographically linking together producers and consumers living and working in different places.

## PROBLEMS

Each of the three major regions of the periphery/semi-periphery faces distinctive problems with respect to its agriculture. For Latin America, it is the expansion of export crops at the expense of local food crops. As a consequence, food imports are often necessary. For Sub-Saharan Africa, it is the total deterioration of agriculture in the face of population pressure on marginal land, low productivity, government bias against investment in agriculture and fluctuations in export earnings. Food imports are now an absolute necessity. For Asia, production of cereals has increased greatly but prices have been low because of global 'gluts'. Hence, increased agricultural production has not generated the capital necessary for investment in other sectors such as industry. When prices increase, local populations must pay the increase or substitute other cereals that are imported, more often than not, from western Europe or the United States. Between 1975 and 2005 food production per capita increased substantially and consistently only in China, Malaysia and Indonesia among all LDCs (Table 9.1).

Table 9.1 Food production per capita for selected countries (1999–2001 = 100)

|  | 1975 | 1980 | 1985 | 1990 | 1995 | 2000 | 2005 |
|---|---|---|---|---|---|---|---|
| China | 41.5 | 44.7 | 54.9 | 63.8 | 81.6 | 100.2 | 117.8 |
| Malaysia | 52.2 | 60.7 | 69.3 | 87.4 | 94.8 | 98.4 | 114.4 |
| Indonesia | 63.0 | 71.1 | 82.4 | 93.6 | 107.2 | 100.5 | 115.2 |
| Philippines | 99.3 | 105.9 | 93.4 | 98.2 | 95.0 | 99.8 | 104.6 |
| Sri Lanka | 95.3 | 125.4 | 114.3 | 101.1 | 108.4 | 101.7 | 102.8 |
| Mexico | 84.4 | 91.8 | 95.8 | 89.4 | 97.9 | 98.8 | 101.5 |
| Ghana | 94.7 | 69.5 | 68.6 | 59.7 | 89.5 | 99.2 | 108.6 |
| India | 74.3 | 73.2 | 83.4 | 89.4 | 93.6 | 99.1 | 97.6 |
| Nigeria | 78.1 | 65.1 | 66.0 | 82.3 | 97.9 | 100.4 | 93.4 |
| Bangladesh | 98.9 | 94.0 | 90.8 | 91.4 | 84.1 | 102.9 | 98.8 |
| Côte d'Ivoire | 104.5 | 94.9 | 91.8 | 90.7 | 94.9 | 102.0 | 93.8 |
| Haiti | 156.4 | 151.5 | 146.8 | 117.5 | 97.2 | 103.0 | 94.2 |
| Zimbabwe | 149.9 | 119.8 | 133.2 | 110.4 | 72.2 | 105.3 | 84.9 |
| United States | 88.8 | 91.0 | 97.5 | 92.4 | 94.1 | 101.6 | 100.5 |

Source: Based on FAO (FAOSTAT), available at http://faostat.fao.org

Although the world as a whole produces sufficient food for everybody, 777 million people in the LDCs, one in five of the population is chronically undernourished. As many as 2 billion people fill themselves daily with adequate food calories but lack a diet balanced in needed nutrients. Hunger and inadequate diets are especially serious in Africa, where 34 per cent of the population is chronically undernourished. Comparable figures are 11 per cent in Latin America and 19 per cent in Asia. In these world regions conditions have improved since 1970 when 19 per cent and 40 per cent, respectively, were chronically underfed. In Africa there has been little or no improvement (35 per cent in 1970). The remarkable improvement in Asia owes much to improved rural healthcare, which protects people from falling sick and losing income or work and subsequently disrupting family food supply, and increased crop yields. Another way of putting the food problem would be to compare food production per capita in the three regions. In this perspective, Asia has seen an impressive 78.3 per cent increase from 1961 to 2005 and Latin

America has experienced a 44.8 per cent increase. In Africa, food production per capita has *dropped* by 8.2 per cent over the same period.

In large parts of the periphery today agriculture is a vulnerable sector: either orientated externally or subject to the vagaries of world market prices without the protection and subsidies enjoyed by agriculture in the core. Yet it is absolutely vital. Vast numbers of people are still employed in or are immediately dependent on agriculture. And, whatever the model of economic development adopted, any hope of improving living standards in general depends on increasing agricultural production.

## 9.2 LAND, LABOUR AND CAPITAL

Agriculture in the contemporary periphery rests on a foundation of agrarian history and recent changes can only be understood in this context. Central to agrarian history the world over has been the impact of market forces on landholding patterns and the structure of rural social relationships. Although rural areas are often characterized as static and traditional, the historical record shows frequent changes in agricultural practices and labour relationships in response to global and domestic political–economic conditions. But some features of landholding systems and rural life have persisted from the period of incorporation into the world economy. In this section the mix of 'old' and 'new' in the agricultural organization of different parts of the contemporary periphery (Latin America, Sub-Saharan Africa, Asia) will be examined.

### LATIN AMERICA

In Latin America, conquest and colonial domination created patterns of subsistence and commercial agriculture based on large landholdings. After independence, this characteristic and its corollary, an exploited and powerless peasantry, became firmly entrenched as the region was firmly tied into the world market as a producer of primary commodities. Between the 1850s and 1930s the various countries of Latin America came to depend on the export of one or two primary export commodities to the industrial countries – first Britain and later the United States. The older hacienda system, albeit complex and varied in its particulars from place to place, went into decline to be replaced by a plantation system that already had a considerable history in the sugar plantations of northeast Brazil and the Caribbean (Table 9.2).

The growth of export-oriented agrarian capitalism was associated with the emergence of a politically powerful landed elite linked to foreign investors and commercial agents dealing in primary commodities. Agriculture for domestic consumption was largely ignored and through control over governments the agricultural elite was able to increase its hold over land, labour and capital.

The concentration of landholding and the marginalization of peasant agriculture did not occur without resistance. Agrarian uprisings and social banditry were widespread. In Mexico, the 1910 uprising was a major impetus to the revolution; strikes were extremely common in the corporate plantations of coastal Peru in the period 1912–28; in Colombia, rural violence by agrarian tenant syndicates directed against commercial coffee producers lasted well into the 1930s. The 1930s also was a period of rural unrest in the Brazilian northeast and in El Salvador among dispossessed peasants and unemployed plantation workers.

Table 9.2 Land, labour, capital and markets: haciendas and plantations

| | Haciendas | Plantation |
|---|---|---|
| Markets | Relatively small and unreliable, regional, with inelasticity of demand; attempt to limit production to keep prices high | Relatively large and reliable; European, with elasticity of demand; attempt to increase production to maximize profits |
| Profits | Relatively low; highly concentrated in small group | Relatively high; highly concentrated in small group |
| Capital and technology | Little access to capital, especially foreign; operating capital often from Church; technology simple, often same as that of peasant cultivators | Availability of foreign capital for equipment and labour; foreign direct investment late in nineteenth century; relatively advanced technology, with expensive machinery for processing |
| Land | Size determined by passive acceptance of indigenous groups; attempt to monopolize land to limit alternative sources of income to labour force; unclear boundaries | Size determined by availability of labour; relatively valuable with carefully fixed boundaries; much unused land; relatively cheap |
| Labour | Large labour force required seasonally; generally indigenous; informally bound by debt, provision of subsistence plot, social ties, payment in provisions | Large labour force required seasonally; generally imported; slavery common; also wage labour |
| Organization | Limited need for supervision; generally hired administrators/ managers, absentee landlord | Need for continual supervision and managerial skills; generally resident owner/manager |

*Source:* Grindle (1986: 30, Table 3.1)

When the world economy collapsed in the 1930s so too did export-oriented agriculture. This spurred the emergence of active nationalists, often in the military, who wanted to increase industrialization and diminish reliance on the export of primary commodities. Between 1930 and 1934 there were 12 forcible takeovers of power – from Argentina to Peru to El Salvador. Argentina, Brazil, Chile, Colombia, Mexico and Uruguay all instituted import substitution industrial strategies. These led to a massive movement of people off the land. For the region as a whole, in 1920, only 14 per cent of the population lived in urban areas, but by 1940 the proportion had risen to 20 per cent. In Argentina, Chile and Uruguay, urban percentages reached 35–45 per cent of the population. One major consequence of this was a decline in the grip of the landholding elite over national politics in some countries as urban professional and working classes grew in size and influence.

This change, however, can be exaggerated. Many countries continued to rely on the export of one or few primary commodities – the Central American and Caribbean countries, but also Argentina, Colombia and Chile – and rural land remained concentrated in the hands of the landed elite. What was different was the emergence of nationalist and populist movements committed to industrialization rather than export agriculture.

Pursuing policies of import substitution had important effects on agriculture. For one, manufacturing surpassed agriculture in its contribution to gross domestic product in a number of countries (Argentina, Brazil, Chile, Mexico, Uruguay and Venezuela) in the 1940s. Much of the new capacity was concentrated in or near the capital cities of the states that were its major sponsors (Buenos Aires, Rio de Janeiro, Santiago, etc.).

Industrialization required a 'draining' of agriculture for resources (cheap food, raw materials) and capital (foreign exchange, taxation). As a consequence, a premium was placed on efficiency in agricultural production. This was thought to require large holdings, the spread of technological innovation and capitalization (heavy capital investment). Between 1940 and 1960 there was a massive migration of people from the countryside to the cities as a consequence of mechanization and the expansion of large landholdings at the expense of small tenants and proprietors.

In the 1960s import substitution became increasingly expensive as the 'easy phase' emphasizing light consumer goods was played out and the prodigious expense of moving into heavier capital goods became apparent. In a process that accelerated during the 1970s, a new development model based on export promotion slowly displaced import substitution. According to this model, agriculture had been neglected and, although no substitute for industrialization, more efficient production of domestic food crops and increased agricultural exports were important in both maintaining political stability and obtaining foreign exchange. After 1965 public investment in rural areas and agriculture increased in a large number of Latin American countries.

Government policies have discriminated heavily in favour of the larger landowners. The geographical distribution of official credit, research and extension, infrastructure, mechanization and Green Revolution inputs reflects the geography of landholding. In Peru, for example, about half the credit supplied by the Agricultural Development Bank between 1940 and 1965 went to cotton growers, who were among the wealthiest coastal agricultural exporters. Food crop producers – largely peasants – were mainly ignored by the bank. In Mexico in 1970, mechanization was used on 25.7 per cent of the crop area of farms of more than 5 hectares but was used on only 4.3 per cent of the crop area of farms less than 5 hectares in size. In Brazil all government policies have tended to reinforce the emphasis on commercial agriculture in the south and east regions at the expense of the northeast and small-scale producers everywhere.

This is not to say that large-scale capitalist agriculture has completely displaced peasant production. Far from it. A large section of the agricultural labour force is still 'part-peasant' in that it supplements its wage earnings with the produce of its often less-than-subsistence plots. This serves to sustain capitalist agriculture through reducing the costs of reproducing a labour force. In many parts of Latin America, therefore, large-scale capitalist agriculture and small-scale peasant production still coexist uneasily. The past is still present.

## SUB-SAHARAN AFRICA

In Sub-Saharan Africa, unlike Latin America (or Europe), access to labour not land was always the basis of economic and political power. From 1830 to 1930 agriculture in Sub-Saharan Africa underwent an incredible expansion in the form of small-scale commercial farming. Some commercial farming had existed prior to this period, for example in the Hausa-Fulani and Mandinka states of northwest Africa, but the introduction of new crops and the expansion of existing ones into previously uncultivated areas increased the scale and geographical distribution of commercial agriculture. Of special importance were such crops as cocoa, cotton, coffee, groundnuts and oil palm, which were grown mainly for export markets. They spread along with European traders, the introduction of foreign capital, the shifting objectives of native farmers and traders and, finally, colonial rule. This was the 'cash crop revolution' (Tosh, 1980) that brought Africa into the world economy and capitalism into Africa.

Colonial rule involved massive intervention in existing agriculture through forced labour and taxation. Taxation, in particular, provided a fresh stimulus to cash cropping. In some parts of Africa, especially the east and south, taxation also encouraged labour migration to mines, plantations and industries established by European settlers. In West Africa, however, labour migration pre-dated colonial rule. It was of a seasonal nature and involved the integration of farming in the interior with migration to more fertile but labour-deficient coastal areas. In West Africa cash cropping by small-scale farmers and long-distance labour migration at harvest time were indigenous phenomena that increased in intensity after the onset of colonial rule. Elsewhere, cash cropping and labour migration were relatively novel and related much more to either European settlement (as in South Africa, Zimbabwe or Kenya) or European initiatives in mining and plantation agriculture (as in Zambia and Zaire).

Another distinctive feature of West Africa as compared, for example, to Kenya was that the production of food and cash crops was complementary rather than competitive. Even today food crops such as plantains, cocoyams and peppers are grown to provide shade for young cocoa trees. Moreover, the period of peak labour demand for cocoa harvesting (November–February) complements the peak labour demand periods for the cereal-growing areas to the north (May–July and February–March). Cocoa farms, therefore, have rarely faced a maximum price for labour and the commercial cocoa industry can coexist with the market for labour in food crop production.

In Kenya, however, the European settlers specialized in the production of food crops and their production cycle matched that of subsistence producers. They consequently had to compete for labour with the subsistence sector. In addition, the establishment of estates or plantations in Kenya involved the confiscation of land from subsistence producers and the subsidy of commercial production at the expense of the subsistence sector.

The rate of agricultural production slowed markedly during the 1930s and the Second World War. It was only in the 1950s, when world prices for many export crops increased as the industrial countries entered into their long boom of the 1950s and early 1960s, that there was a rapid expansion in export crop production. But the increase in demand for Africa's export crops was short lived, peaking as early as 1956. Since then cash cropping and commercialized livestock farming have been concentrated in the districts where they were dominant 50 years ago. With the exception of sugar, most new planting (of cocoa, coffee or tea) has taken place within the areas that were already the major producers in the early 1950s.

In those districts in which agricultural production has intensified or expanded, it has involved different types of farming. For example, in Côte d'Ivoire, plantations have been the major agent of growth, whereas in Ghana, Kenya and Sudan it has been small-scale peasant cash crop production that has been responsible for most growth. Indeed, in Kenya the small-scale farming sector has largely replaced the plantation sector as the most dynamic in terms of commercial production.

Total agricultural production (cash crops and food staples) increased substantially in Sub-Saharan Africa over the period 1980–2005 (Table 9.3). However, the rate of population increase over the region as a whole has meant that there has been no increase overall in per capita terms, with many countries experiencing a decrease in per capita agricultural production (Table 9.3). Most African governments have adopted policies that seek to depress food prices to feed their burgeoning populations. This often leads them to set higher prices for large-scale producers because of presumed efficiencies (and political influence?). Penalizing the food production sector is meant both to stimulate export crop production and feed increasingly large urban populations. In fact it has discouraged farmers, especially the mass of small-scale farmers, from increasing their production through investment in increased productivity.

Table 9.3 Index of total (and per capita) agricultural production: selected African countries (1999–2001 = 100)

|  | 1980 | | 1990 | | 2000 | | 2005 | |
|---|---|---|---|---|---|---|---|---|
| Côte d'Ivoire | 51.3 | (96.2) | 72.9 | (92.3) | 103.6 | (103.5) | 98.5 | (90.8) |
| Ghana | 39.2 | (69.6) | 46.5 | (59.7) | 99.2 | (99.3) | 120.6 | (108.2) |
| Kenya | 53.4 | (99.6) | 82.1 | (106.3) | 97.4 | (97.4) | 105.3 | (97.9) |
| Malawi | 49.7 | (91.4) | 60.3 | (72.5) | 103.6 | (103.6) | 100.4 | (90.8) |
| Mozambique | 78.6 | (116.1) | 78.6 | (104.2) | 94.5 | (94.5) | 107.5 | (98.4) |
| Nigeria | 36.4 | (65.0) | 62.0 | (82.6) | 100.5 | (100.4) | 106.1 | (93.4) |
| Senegal | 45.0 | (76.2) | 73.2 | (93.5) | 101.2 | (101.2) | 100.8 | (89.4) |
| Sierra Leone | 102.6 | (140.2) | 125.3 | (136.8) | 93.7 | (94.0) | 114.3 | (94.7) |
| Tanzania | 68.6 | (126.9) | 89.1 | (119.1) | 99.8 | (99.8) | 109.9 | (99.8) |
| Zambia | 63.8 | (110.0) | 82.4 | (104.6) | 97.8 | (97.6) | 104.5 | (98.5) |
| Zimbabwe | 63.8 | (111.5) | 81.2 | (98.1) | 106.7 | (106.6) | 74.4 | (72.5) |
| Sub-Saharan Africa | 55.2 | (96.4) | 73.0 | (95.1) | 99.2 | (99.2) | 108.1 | (95.9) |

Source: Based on FAO (FAOSTAT), available at http://faostat.fao.org/

The trade policies of DCs and the advice their experts offer have also contributed to the problems of African agriculture. North America, western Europe and Japan may practise fairly free trade in the manufactured goods and services in which they may have comparative advantages but they are relentlessly protectionist about food-stuffs; precisely the sector in which African countries can offer competitive products. For example, US government subsidies to its sugar, tobacco and groundnut farmers lead to lower prices for US-produced crops than would be the case without the subsidies. This deprives African producers of potential markets. With respect to advice, Africa has been on the receiving end of some of the worst advice ever offered by people from one part of the world to another. The litany of disasters resulting from advice offered by foreign experts is much too long to provide here. Two examples must suffice. In Burkina Faso and elsewhere in the dry Sahel region of north-central Africa the UN Food and Agricultural Organization (FAO) encouraged local farmers to grow potatoes. A bumper crop resulted, which then rotted unsold in local markets where potatoes were seen as an exotic crop without any history in local diets. By Lake Turkana in East Africa, Norwegian experts persuaded Turkana cattle herdsmen to give up their cattle and take up fishing only to find out that the cost of chilling the fish exceeded what they could bring in city markets. Not only was the fishing equipment a wasted investment but the Turkana were now also without their cattle. They ended up on food aid provided by the surpluses bought up by the US and other governments as a result of overproduction brought about by their subsidy programmes to cereal producers and dairy producers.

But countries differ in the relative extent to which farmers must bear the brunt of tax and price-setting policies. It all depends on the political base of governing elites and the origins of marketing organizations. In Ghana and Zambia in the 1980s, for example, urban-based politicians put the burden on small-scale farmers to a much greater extent than the rural-based politicians of Kenya. In Ghana, the Cocoa Board is a patronage organization, whereas in Kenya, producers control the marketing organizations. Interestingly, the increase in total agricultural production in the 1980s was higher in Kenya than in Ghana and Zambia (see Table 9.3). In Kenya, this benefited both food production for domestic consumption and increases in sales of export crops. Subsequent liberalization and privatization in Ghana, however, have contributed to significantly increased production in the 1990s (Table 9.3).

Three trends have nevertheless been fairly general over the past 30 years. One has been the increased importance of wage labour, especially with respect to export crops. This has further 'monetized' the rural economy and reduced the degree of reliance on domestic groups (families) as sources of farm labour. This in turn has reinforced the role of long-distance migration in agricultural labour and given some districts the specialized role of 'migrant labour reserve' for other districts in which export agriculture is important. For example, even with restrictions on international migration, Togo and Benin in West Africa have been a major source of temporary and permanent migrants to Côte d'Ivoire and Ghana (Figure 9.1).

A second trend has been the changing role of women in African agriculture. Women have become central to the production of food crops on small-scale farms such as those that dominate throughout Sub-Saharan Africa. As Swindell (1985: 179) puts it:

> As men have become more involved in commercial cropping and non-farm occupations, so women have become increasingly responsible for the cultivation of food staples. This is especially true in those areas where the out-migration of men is persistent, and it could be argued that the expansion of commercial cropping and the industrial labour force has been built on the backs of women farmers.

The third trend has been growth in agricultural production through extending areas under cropping or grazing rather than through raising yields. Green Revolution technologies (high-yield varieties, fertilizers, etc.), mainly addressed to cereal production,

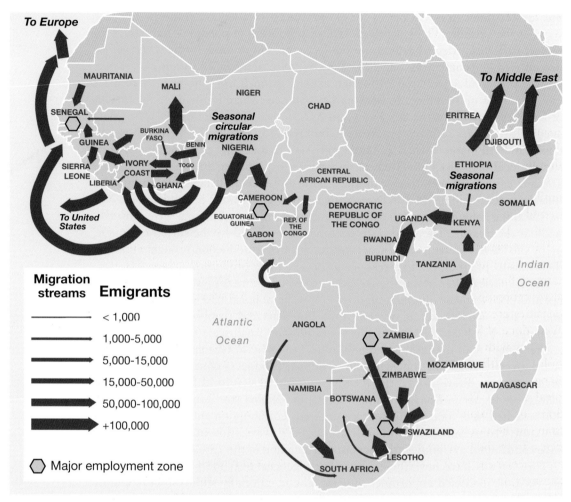

Fig 9.1: External migration flows in Sub-Saharan Africa

*Source:* Based on Aryeetey-Attoh (1997: 136, Figure 5.4); Marston *et al.* (2008: 248, Figure 5.32)

have been either inappropriate or not widely adopted in Sub-Saharan Africa. Whatever the cause, however, commercial agriculture has become extensive rather than intensive. This has led to farming on poor soils in areas with unreliable rainfall and the displacement of subsistence agriculture onto ever more marginal terrain. Sen (1981a) implicates this trend as a major factor in the famines that have afflicted many parts of Africa over the past 20 years. Civil wars, poor food distribution networks and the degradation of soils through lack of crop rotation have also played some part.

Although much of African agriculture has become increasingly commercialized, it remains largely small scale and still involves domestic groups or families. The level of agricultural production, however, has not kept up with the world's highest rates of population increase. In many countries there are now major national food deficits. At the same time government policies in many countries have had the effect of discouraging agricultural production both for food staples and export crops. But in most countries farming must remain the dominant activity for the

foreseeable future if only because an incre
requisite for industrial development. At p.
import substitution is limited by the small si,
can only grow if the incomes of farmers rise.

## ASIA

Asian agriculture presents a more complex pi,
America or Sub-Saharan Africa. On the one hand, t
tion densities are here but, on the other, population.
systems with quite different and distinctive features.
until recently, was between China, where there was nc
of and the rural economy has been organized around '
1954 to 1979), and those countries such as Malaysia a
export agriculture (rubber and sugar, respectively) is impc           _ping
tenancy (renting with payment in kind to landlords) predor.        _ue the plantations. But in general there is a high incidence of tenancy       _sian countries and
share cropping is its major form, especially in those areas where rural population
densities are very high (Bangladesh, Java, Central Luzon (in the Philippines), the
West Zone of Sri Lanka and eastern and southern India).

Along with the preponderance of tenants goes an extreme concentration of landholding, although less on average than in Latin America (Table 9.4). In
Bangladesh, 87 per cent of the farms account for 43 per cent of the total agricultural area; in Thailand, one-fifth of the farms cover 3 per cent of the total area.
Some of the figures in Table 9.4 suggest that the proportion of small farms (less
than one hectare) is increasing in some Asian countries, including India. Other evidence from India suggests two types of change in historical patterns of rural social
structure: the growth in some areas of the class of self-employed cultivators or rich
peasants, favoured by 1950s land reform (e.g., Gujarat) and the transformation of
large landowners into capitalist farmers employing migrant labourers (e.g.,
Punjab). Both changes are signs of increasing commercialization of agriculture even
as share-cropping tenancy persists in 'marginal' areas to provide labour reserves for
seasonal and cyclical purposes at little or no cost to the commercial sector.

In the colonial period, governments concerned themselves either with plantation
agriculture or with raising taxes from other forms of agriculture. In India, the
British created a class of landed aristocrats called *zamindars* as revenue collectors
for the government. The *zamindars*, however, did not have any real interest in
improving agriculture. Over time they and other intermediaries became an
immense burden on actual cultivators whose rents included not only revenue for
the government but also income for the various intermediaries. After independence,
India, Pakistan and other countries in South and Southeast Asia where this system
prevailed, abolished intermediary tenures. However, many of the old intermediaries
continued to cultivate their holdings through tenants and share croppers on the
same exploitative terms as before. Only in China, South Korea and Taiwan did
land redistribution lead to an effective abolition of the power of large landlords.

Since independence, however, total agricultural production has increased at rates
at least commensurate with population growth in most Asian countries.
Unfortunately, much of the growth has been concentrated in export crops or
cereals (wheat, rice) rather than across the board. Moreover, the unequal social struc-

...on in Asia and Latin America

| | Year | % of farms <1 hectare | % of total agricultural area covered by farms <1 hectare |
|---|---|---|---|
| **Asia** | **1970** | **48.9** | **8.36** |
| | **1980** | **49.5** | **8.54** |
| | **1990** | **53.3** | **10.11** |
| Bangladesh | 1960 | 51.6 | 15.20 |
| | 1974 | 66.0 | 24.00 |
| | 1996 | 86.7 | 42.70 |
| India | 1961 | 39.8 | 6.80 |
| | 1971 | 50.6 | 8.97 |
| | 1977 | 54.6 | 10.72 |
| | 1986 | 57.8 | 13.39 |
| | 1997 | 61.6 | 17.20 |
| Philippines | 1960 | 11.5 | 1.60 |
| | 1971 | 13.6 | 1.91 |
| | 1981 | 22.7 | 3.78 |
| | 1991 | 36.6 | 7.30 |
| Thailand | 1963 | 18.5 | 2.50 |
| | 1978 | 15.9 | 2.28 |
| | 1993 | 19.7 | 3.01 |
| | 2003 | 22.7 | – |
| **Latin America** | **1970** | **14.0** | **0.13** |
| | **1980** | **9.1** | **0.07** |
| | **1990** | **8.6** | **0.09** |
| Brazil | 1970 | 8.1 | 0.08 |
| | 1980 | 9.1 | 0.08 |
| | 1985 | 11.1 | 0.10 |
| | 1996 | 10.5 | 0.08 |
| Panama | 1971 | 26.1 | 0.25 |
| | 1981 | 41.0 | 0.50 |
| | 1990 | 46.7 | 0.55 |
| | 2001 | 52.7 | 0.62 |
| Paraguay | 1981 | 8.6 | 0.03 |
| | 1991 | 9.8 | 0.04 |

*Source:* Based on FAO, *National Agricultural Censuses*, various years, available at http://www.fao.org/

*Note:* 1 hectare = 2.477 acres

ture of most rural areas has ensured an upward drift of the benefits of increased production. Rural poverty has increased as agricultural production has increased.

A major source of increased production of cereals (especially wheat) since the 1960s has been the Green Revolution. This had its most significant impact in both Punjabs (since Partition, there is one in India and one in Pakistan) and the Indian state of Haryana where irrigation facilities could be utilized. Benefits have accrued disproportionately to large farmers and the technologies involved (new seed varieties, heavy applications of chemical fertilizers) cannot be applied in areas without irrigation facilities: 80 per cent of the cultivated area in India, 90 per cent in Bangladesh.

In general, over the past 40 years most Asian governments have not favoured agriculture. Many have pursued pricing and credit policies similar to those noted earlier for Sub-Saharan Africa. This seems also to be true at least for considerable periods in the case of China. Indian development plans until the late 1970s were systematically biased against the agricultural sector. Yet there is a direct relationship between agricultural yields and a price structure that favours the agricultural sector. The countries with the highest ratios of product prices (e.g., rice) to input costs (e.g., fertilizer cost) are also where yields are highest. The three countries with the highest rice yields per hectare in Asia, Japan, South Korea and Taiwan also have perhaps some of the poorest soils in Asia. Government policies (especially subsidies for inputs such as fertilizers) and egalitarian rural social structures (all farmers are rewarded) are the most plausible causes of the differences in crop yields. One negative effect of this, however, is a high level of water pollution produced by the heavy use of subsidized fertilizers.

According to the United Nations, three-quarters of the world's 'absolute poor' (those unable to maintain a minimum nutritional standard) live in Asia and more than four-fifths of them live in rural areas. The most common feature of the rural poor in the region is landlessness or limited access to land. Poor rural households tend to have larger families, lower educational attainment and higher underemployment. While the Green Revolution helped to achieve the most rapid and widespread decline in poverty, hunger and premature death in history during the 1970s and 1980s, progress has since stalled. Appropriate technologies remain to be developed for the agriculturally marginal areas that are home today to about 40 per cent of the rural poor. In China, for example, nearly 65 million officially recognized poor people live in remote, mountainous areas: 'In the 1990s, poverty reduction fell to less than one third of the rate needed to meet the United Nations' commitment to halve extreme poverty by 2015' (IFAD, 2001: 2).

## 9.3 RURAL LAND REFORM

In Latin America and Asia, the landholding and tenurial systems have been periodically 'reformed' as a result of pressure from peasant movements, government attempts to make agriculture more efficient and productive, and external pressures from TNCs and international development agencies. Certain models have sometimes been followed depending on whether efficiency or equity has been the overriding goal. In the former case, the Taiwanese and South Korean experiences are emphasized; in the latter, the Chinese experience is often the model. However, in practice, agricultural reform, especially land reform, is overwhelmingly a sociopolitical process rather than a technical one of choosing a model and then following it.

At one time or another, but especially between 1960 and the early 1970s, virtually every country in Latin America and Asia passed land reform laws. A wide range of arguments have been proposed to justify a role for land reform in agricultural development. There are perhaps four justifications that have been most common and they have appealed differentially to different social groups. The first of these is a 'conservative' argument: land reform is a minimal concession for political stabilization. The second is a 'liberal' argument: land reform is needed to create a class of capitalist farmers and expand the domestic market. Third, there is the 'populist' argument: small farms are more efficient (and equitable) than large ones. Fourth, the 'radical' argument: peasants are rapidly being dispossessed of their status as independent producers and are prisoners of cheap food policies and agro-export policies, consequently land reform towards collective production (collective farms, state farms) is necessary, if insufficient, for economic development.

Most actual land reform policies have been of the 'liberal' type, concerned with creating a reform sector. A total of 35 land reforms are classified in Table 9.5, including those in the same country when a land reform programme was later redefined (e.g., Chile). All the diagonal reforms on this table are redistributive ones in the sense that they either increase the size of the reform sector without changing the non-reform sector (1, 7 and 13 in Table 9.5) or involve expansion of the reform sector (25). Reforms 2, 3 and 4 are oriented towards eliminating 'feudal' (or other pre-capitalist) remnants from agriculture rather than redistributing land. In each case the transition to capitalism is dominated by (2) a landed elite, (3) farmers or (4) peasants.

The only possible reforms, as opposed to drastic changes, once a capitalist agriculture has been established are either shifts in the type of agrarian structure (8, 9, 14) or distributive reforms within a given type (7, 13, 19, 25). All reforms can give way to counter-reforms: Chile essentially switched to (12) from (3) after the 1973 military coup, Guatemala returned to (11) from (3) after the military coup of 1954. The Chinese, Cuban and Algerian cases are ones of land reform involving the collectivization of agriculture that were part of more 'radical' programmes of sociopolitical change. But since the early 1980s China has shifted to a mixed system of collective ownership but private use. The recent redistribution of land from large capitalist farms to small peasant holdings in Zimbabwe and some other African countries has destroyed the existing agricultural system without effecting either improvements in production or in the incomes and status of the new farmers.

The most widespread and successful (in the sense of lasting) land reforms have been those facilitating the creation of a capitalist agriculture (1–5 in Table 9.5). In Latin America the combination of anti-feudal land reforms with more spontaneous development of capitalism has both removed most feudal remnants and put an end to reform efforts. A similar conclusion can be drawn for Asia. Reform efforts generally ended in the early 1970s. By and large they cannot be said to have lived up to their promise for the needs of the bulk of the rural population irrespective of the nature of the reform undertaken. However, in some cases, such as Taiwan and South Korea after the Second World War, and China's land privatization since 1978, rural land reform appears to have served as a prerequisite for later industrialization by increasing crop yields and through increased rural earnings providing capital for industrial investment.

## 9.4 CAPITALIZATION OF AGRICULTURE

Spontaneous change, therefore, has now become much more important than reform in agricultural development. Over the past 20 years there has been a substantial increase in direct and indirect investment by transnational corporations (TNCs) in the agriculture of a number of peripheral countries. In many countries, TNCs, attracted

Table 9.5 A typology of land reforms

| | Post-land reform | | | | |
|---|---|---|---|---|---|
| **Mode of production in whole society** | Semi-feudal | Capitalist | | Socialist | |
| **Mode of production in agriculture** | Semi-feudal | Capitalist | | | Socialist |
| **Land tenure** | Semi-feudal estates and reform sector | Capitalist estates and reform sector | Capitalist farms and reform sector | Peasant farms | Socialist farms |
| Semi-feudal estates | (1) Mexico 1917–34 Taiwan 1949–51 Colombia 1961–67 Chile 1962–67 | (2) Bolivia 1952– Venezuela 1959– Philippines 1963–72 Ecuador 1964– Peru 1964–69 Colombia 1968– | (3) Mexico 1934–40 India 1950– Guatemala 1952–54 Egypt 1952–66 Iran 1962–67 Chile 1967–73 | (4) South Korea 1950– Taiwan 1951–63 Iraq 1958– | (5) China 1949–52 |
| Capitalist estates | (6) | (7) Costa Rica 1962–76 | (8) Peru 1969–75 Philippines 1972–79 | (9) | (10) Cuba 1959–63 Algeria 1961–71 |
| Capitalist farms | (11) Guatemala 1954– | (12) Chile 1973– | (13) Mexico 1940– Dominican Rep. 1963– Egypt 1961– South Africa 1994– | (14) Zimbabwe 1980– | (15) |
| Peasant farms | (16) | (17) | (18) | (19) | (20) |
| Socialist farms | (21) | (22) | (23) Russia 1991– | (24) | (25) Cuba 1963– China 1952–78 China 1979– Algeria 1971–77 |

Pre-land reform — Mode of production in whole society:
Semi-feudal (Semi-feudal estates) | Capitalist (Capitalist estates, Capitalist farms) | Socialist (Peasant farms, Socialist farms)

by cheap land and labour, appropriate physical conditions, improved infrastructure and a decline in the relative profitability of other sorts of investment, have increased their involvement in export-oriented agriculture and the production and distribution of seeds, pesticides and fertilizers. Thailand, for example, which exported no pineapples in the early 1970s, had, by 1979, become the major world exporter after Hawaii because the US company Castle and Cooke had moved a major part of its pineapple operations out of Hawaii. Similarly, the Philippines, which exported no bananas in 1960s, had become one of the world's major exporters by the mid-1970s. This was again due almost entirely to new TNC investment. So, just as TNCs that specialize in manufacturing use global sourcing, agricultural TNCs have turned to multiple sites of production to lower labour costs, gain year-round supplies for seasonal crops (e.g., strawberries in January in western Europe from Chile) and to avoid labour and environmental regulations. Over the past 30 years the global food industry has been one of the world's fastest growing industries.

Of great importance, however, was the prior emergence in western Europe, Japan and North America of a highly capital-intensive agriculture serving a food system in which consumers increasingly demanded high-value products (such as lean beef, chicken products and fresh fruit and vegetables) at the same time as marketing and distribution were concentrating in the hands of large-scale wholesalers and supermarket chains. Economies of scale could be realized within large vertically integrated firms that supplied the new wholesalers and direct retailers. Global sourcing is an extension into the periphery of a shift towards industrialized agriculture that was well under way by the 1950s in the United States and western Europe, with beef cattle lodged in 'lots' for fattening and chickens stacked on top of one another in battery houses. The recent demand for 'organic produce', very fresh fruit and vegetables and worries about contamination of the beef food chain – prompted by the outbreak of 'mad cow disease' (bovine spongiform encephalopathy (BSE)) in Britain – however, may signal the limits of the globalization of food production when consumer tastes and demands in urban and export markets resist the imposition of mass produced items. Different food products now have different food systems associated with them. Only some are amenable to global sourcing.

It is in Latin America that the capitalization of agriculture by TNCs has been both most extensive and intensive. Of the six countries usually identified as the 'new agricultural countries' in which agricultural investment has been concentrated, four are in Latin America: Argentina, Brazil, Chile and Mexico. The other two are Hungary and Thailand, where the governments have promoted agricultural investment for urban and export markets, focusing on such high-value food products as meats, fruits and vegetables. Sometimes control is exercised directly by purchase of land and involvement in production. For example, between 1964 and 1970 US-based TNCs purchased 35 million hectares of agricultural land in Brazil alone. Increasingly, however, TNCs and international development agencies (the World Bank, the US Agency for International Development (AID), etc.) are encouraging traditional rural elites to become commercial elites, practising mechanized farming of export crops that are processed and marketed by the TNCs or by contracting out to peasant producers. These strategies reflect both fear of the revolutionary potential of peasant movements in traditional agrarian social structures and the need for TNCs to keep a low profile lest they become the targets of nationalization drives.

## AGRIBUSINESS

The impact of agribusiness investment in the agriculture of the periphery, therefore, is not restricted to the development of export enclaves or plantation enclaves as was characteristic of an earlier phase in the development of the world economy. Rather, its most important effect is probably the way in which it channels capital to a class of rural capitalists and thus consolidates TNC control over entire national agricultural systems. The penetration of peripheral agriculture by international agribusiness is, in effect, just another aspect of the new international division of labour.

Between 1966 and 1978, for example, US investment in Latin American agriculture expanded from US$365 million to US$1.04 billion, growing from 15 per cent to 21 per cent of total US foreign direct investment (FDI) in Latin America. This investment was heavily concentrated in Argentina, Brazil, Mexico and Venezuela, where the growing urban middle and upper classes provided a domestic supplement to US demand for so called 'luxury foodstuffs' (meat, fruits and vegetables). As demand grew for the fertilizers, pesticides, herbicides, improved seeds and agricultural machinery needed by the 'new' agriculture, TNCs such as Du Pont, W.R. Grace, Monsanto, Exxon and Allied Chemical were increasingly involved in local production.

TNCs and foreign portfolio investment capital were involved in a variety of ways. In the state of Sinaloa in northern Mexico, for example, 20–40 per cent of the credit for agricultural production in the 1970s came from north of the border. In Argentina, the amount of foreign capital in beef production decreased, while it increased in the packing and processing industries. In Mexico and Central America, contract production linked national producers with TNCs. Foreign banks have become major agricultural lenders. For example, the San Francisco-based Bank of America became heavily involved in Guatemala in the 1970s, lending for major development projects such as converting forest to pasture for beef production, and providing speculative export loans.

### Local impacts of agribusiness

The consequences have been manifold. At a global level there has been a marked reorientation of Latin American export agriculture from Europe to the United States. Before the Second World War exports were strongly oriented to Europe. At a national level there has been an extraordinary expansion of some crops at the expense of others, especially traditional food staples. Some crops that were not widely produced in the 1960s have grown at enormous rates: sorghum in Brazil, Venezuela and Colombia; soybeans in Paraguay, Argentina and Brazil; and palm oil in Ecuador (Table 9.6).

More profitable products destined for affluent urban and foreign markets have replaced the food staples. In Chile fruits and livestock replaced wheat and sugar beet; sorghum replaced corn in Mexico and Brazil; livestock replaced the basic crops throughout the region as indicated by statistics showing the vast expansion of permanent pasture lands at the same time croplands either decreased in area (as in Mexico and Venezuela) or increased only moderately (as in Costa Rica, Colombia, Panama and Honduras). In some places increased livestock production also stimulated the expansion of feed grain production, often on land that formerly produced the food staples of middle- and low-income groups.

Shortfalls in food staple production have necessitated the increased import of basic food items. Until 1973 agricultural exports grew steadily even if they did not keep pace with imports. Since then, however, weaker economic conditions in the

**Table 9.6** Growth of some export crops in selected Latin American countries (metric tons)

|  | 1961 | 1970 | 1980 | 1990 | 2000 | 2005 |
|---|---|---|---|---|---|---|
| *Sorghum* | | | | | | |
| Brazil | 5 | 2000 | 180,292 | 236,250 | 779,608 | 1,520,540 |
| Venezuela | 0 | 6532 | 352,611 | 376,384 | 581,526 | 385,440 |
| Colombia | 4300 | 118,000 | 430,520 | 777,400 | 217,565 | 252,940 |
| *Soybeans* | | | | | | |
| Paraguay | 2100 | 41,293 | 537,300 | 1,794,618 | 2,980,060 | 3,988,000 |
| Argentina | 957 | 26,800 | 3,500,000 | 10,700,000 | 20,200,000 | 38,300,000 |
| Brazil | 271,488 | 1,508,540 | 15,155,804 | 19,897,804 | 32,734,958 | 51,182,050 |
| *Palm oil* | | | | | | |
| Ecuador | 167,000 | 150,000 | 244,930 | 835,697 | 1,339,400 | 1,929,919 |

*Source:* Based on FAO (*FAOSTAT*), available at http://faostat.fao.org

United States and western Europe have reduced demand for Latin America's agricultural exports (such as 'January' strawberries) at the same time as the cost of imported food (and other products such as fertilizers and machinery) increased appreciably. The increased preference of affluent consumers in North America and western Europe for 'local' produce has also eaten into the potential demand for foodstuffs imported over long distances. Thus, the new agricultural production tends to recapitulate both the volatility of demand and the declining terms of trade associated with the historic production of agricultural commodities in peripheral economies.

Nevertheless, the penetration of foreign agribusiness has had important effects on rural populations. One effect has been the increased concentration of land holdings in the hands of capitalist farmers and TNCs such that:

> Throughout the region, tenants and sharecroppers were replaced by agricultural workers, and permanent workers were displaced by part-time labourers. Given these changes, landowners could minimize the costs of maintaining a labour force through periods when it was not needed and expand cropping or live stocking areas by taking over lands that had been assigned to resident labourers, tenants, and sharecroppers. Labour costs were thus reduced for the entrepreneur, and the available pool of labourers, forced to provide for their own maintenance during inactive periods, was enlarged.
>
> Grindle (1986: 98)

Another effect has been to increase the need to borrow, and hence the indebtedness, of surviving peasant farmers and part-time labourers. Debt is nothing new for peasant farmers. As the meaning of subsistence changed in a monetized economy to include 'urban goods' and processed foods, so too did the importance of money. In the past, money was obtained through the sale of labour for cash wages or sale of market crops. Debt arose because of the need to store and transport crops and pay for inputs before cash was available. Often yields and cash wages were so low that more debt was incurred merely to survive. Today debt is also incurred by the necessity of competing against the capitalist export sector for land, inputs and water resources.

## THE CYCLE OF INDEBTEDNESS

In order to manage the higher debt load, peasants must farm their land more intensively. This only exacerbates the problem. Traditional farming methods such as crop rotation and fallow agriculture are replaced by monoculture to grow the most remunerative crop. This process leaches and depletes the soil, leading to poor harvests and soil erosion. As a consequence, more fertilizers and new seeds are required, thus deepening the cycle of indebtedness. Warman (1980: 238) described the cycle of indebtedness that has followed the increased capitalization of agriculture in central Mexico:

> The peasant has to combine several sources of credit, on occasion all of them, in order to bring off the miracle of continuing to produce without dying of starvation. He does it through a set of elaborate and sometimes convoluted strategies. Some people plant peanuts only in order to finance the fertilizers for the corn crop. Others use official credit to finance planting a cornfield or for buying corn for consumption in the months of scarcity, while they resort to the local bourgeoisie or the big monopolists in order to finance a field of tomatoes or onions. Many turn to usurers [money lenders] to cover the costs of an illness or a fiesta … Given what they produce in a year, what is left after paying the debts does not go far enough even for food during the dry season, much less for starting a crop on their own. For them, obtaining a new loan is a precondition for continuing cultivation, one that must be combined with the sale of labour if they are to hold out to the next harvest. Each year the effort necessary to maintain the precarious equilibrium increases.

Peasants, then, are survivors as much as victims. Increasingly, wage labour has come to provide a major portion of family income even for peasants who own land. Often this has involved temporary long-distance migration. In Guatemala, for example, the coffee, cotton and sugar harvests in December and January involve the seasonal migration of an estimated 1 million highland Indians. Temporary wage labour on nearby plantations and capitalist farms, however, is perhaps the major form of adaptation.

## DRUG CROPS

In some areas peasants have also supplemented their incomes by switching to the cultivation of drug crops. The market for these crops in the United States and Europe has grown exponentially since 1970 and the crops can be grown in remote areas on low-grade soils. Given the illegality of drug crops in world trade, remoteness becomes a virtue rather than the liability it is in more legitimate trade. Afghanistan (even after Taliban rule) and Myanmar (Burma) are important sources of heroin destined for American and European markets. In three Latin American countries, Peru, Colombia and Bolivia, the value of cocaine exports is estimated to be US$690 million per annum. Of course, much of the proceeds goes to 'drug barons', public officials and intermediaries. But for many peasants, the drug traffic is one of the only ways they have of paying their debts and, thus, responding to the disruptions consequent on the capitalization of agriculture by TNCs and foreign investment. Profits from drugs also fuel the insurgencies of ethnic and political opponents of existing governments. The main routes of surreptitious export change frequently in response to both new alliances between producers and intermediaries and successful efforts by police forces at intercepting the drugs before they hit the streets of American and European cities. Some commentators see the 'laundering' of profits from the international drug business as a major activity in some offshore financial centres. The drugs business is not new. It has ancient roots. In the 19th century opening up China to the export of opium from India was one of the main causes of the war between Britain and China that was, as a result, called the Opium War. Illicit though it may now be, the global trade in drugs fits into the long history of the trade in stimulants as an important part of the growth of the modern world economy (see Chapter 8).

## THE CASE OF THE BEEF BOOM IN CENTRAL AMERICA

An interesting case study in the capitalization of Latin American agriculture is the so-called 'beef boom' in Central America in the 1970s and early 1980s. This led to the emergence of Central America as a major supplier of beef to the United States when it had been previously relatively insignificant. It resulted from the tremendous increase in demand for beef in the United States as a result of the emergence of fast-food franchises such as McDonald's and BurgerKing, catering to a population increasingly given to 'eating out'. The new franchises were not particularly demanding of high-quality beef; what they wanted was quantity that could be formed into patties of equal size and weight by sufficient grinding and tenderizing. But the quantity needed was so huge that the fast-food chains (and 'TV dinner' makers) needed to look beyond the USA for their supply. Sources such as Australia, New Zealand and Canada were subject to severe quota limitations that were part of intensive 'tit-for-tat' trade negotiations on the part of the US government in the GATT. South America was 'out' because of the prevalence of foot and mouth disease. Central America was favoured by US government policy to help 'friendly' governments diversify their exports in the face of the perceived 'geostrategic threat' from Cuba and the Soviet Union in the region. By 1979 Central America had acquired 93 per cent of the share of the US beef quota available to LDCs.

A number of TNCs and individuals found it profitable to respond to the demand for beef from Central America. Some very large US companies became involved through subsidiaries and joint ventures. For example, R.J. Reynolds owned huge grazing ranches in Guatemala and Costa Rica at that time through its then subsidiary, Del Monte, and directly processed and marketed its beef through a variety of outlets: 'Ortega' beef tacos, 'Chun King' beef chow mein and 'Delmonte' Mexican foods. It also sold beef through 'Zantigo' Mexican restaurants (Kentucky Fried Chicken). One of the largest firms in the Central American beef business was Agrodinamica Holding Company, formed in 1971 with 60 per cent of the stock owned by wealthy Latin Americans and 40 per cent of the stock owned by the American ADELA Investment Company. This operation controlled thousands of acres of pasture in Central America, owned numerous packing plants and ran a Miami (Florida) beef import house and wholesale distributor.

Other TNCs became involved in supplying the beef business with inputs (grass seed, barbed wire, fertilizers, feed grains and veterinary supplies). Pulp and paper companies, such as Crown Zellerbach and Weyerhauser, invested in cardboard box factories to supply packing houses with containers for shipping the beef. Finally, fruit companies with access to large blocks of land turned them into money-making properties.

TNCs, however, were not the only beneficiaries. Wealthy families with access to large amounts of 'marginal' and forest land turned them into pasture. Some urban-based professionals (lawyers, bankers, etc.) also became involved as 'weekend ranchers' of peripheral areas previously untouched by commercial agriculture.

The massive displacement of peasants by ranchers and cattle, however, met with tremendous resistance. As Williams (1986: 151) put it: 'The receding edge of the tropical forest became the setting of a conflict between two incompatible systems of land use, one driven by the logic of the world market, the other driven by the logic of survival.' The violence and civil war throughout much of Central America in the 1970s and 1980s bore no small relationship to the expansion of the beef export business.

The Central American 'beef boom' ended in the 1980s, however, due to declining international beef prices and reduced US demand as real incomes stagnated and consumers became more health conscious. The US Congress also passed a more restrictive meat import act in 1979, which significantly reduced Central America's access to the US market. Beef exports from Costa Rica, Guatemala and Honduras were prohibited on several occasions as the USA enforced laws prohibiting the import of substandard beef and beef with pesticide residues. During the 1980s and early 1990s the US government also prohibited meat imports from Nicaragua and Panama for political reasons. To make matters worse, cattle ranchers' costs (inputs and taxes) were rising. A major blow was the decision in 1987 by BurgerKing, which at one time bought 70 per cent of Costa Rica's beef exports, to stop buying Latin American beef because of criticism of the 'hamburger connection' (Kaimowitz, 1995).

This criticism relates to other important consequences associated with the capitalization of agriculture: deforestation and environmental degradation. Much of the loss of forest in Central America, the Amazon Basin of Brazil and in Southeast Asia has been due to the extension of ranching as well as timber extraction and the burning of timber as fuelwood. While the rate of deforestation in Central America is estimated to have declined from 4,000,000 hectares per year in the 1970s to 300,000 hectares in the 1990s, at this current rate, Central America will lose its remaining forest in under 60 years. A related stimulus to the incredible pace at which tropical forests have been disappearing since the 1970s has been the need to pay off the debts incurred in expensive industrialization campaigns. The opening of forest land to capital-intensive agriculture has been one strategy for swapping natural resources for income to repay debts. Five of the world's 'mega-debtors' – Brazil, India, Indonesia, Mexico and Nigeria – all rank among the top 10 deforesters. The conversion from forest to pasture or cultivation can also increase soil compaction, soil erosion and nutrient depletion – particular problems in marginal locations with less fertile soils. During the rainy season, erosion in places with steeper slopes can contribute to devastating flooding and mudslides in the flatland areas. The capitalization of agriculture in the periphery, therefore, has had correlates other than increased productivity, the establishment of comparative advantage in export crops and the increased import of food crops.

## 9.5 SCIENCE AND TECHNOLOGY IN AGRICULTURE

The beef export boom in Central America would not have been possible without the importation of techniques of 'scientific agriculture'. In this context, this involved creating 'new' breeds of cattle by combining 'beefier' attributes with high resistance to pests and tropical heat, transforming pasture management by sowing higher yield grasses and fertilizers, enhancing water supplies by digging new wells and ponds and providing better veterinary care to cattle herds.

The past 40 years have witnessed an intensive drive on the part of international development agencies (such as the Food and Agriculture Organization (FAO) of the UN and the World Bank), some national governments and agribusiness to intro-duce scientific farming into agriculture in LDCs. The results have been controversial. From one point of view, yields have been increased and, especially in parts of Asia but to a degree also elsewhere, agricultural productivity and produc-tion have been significantly increased. Of particular importance have been the new wheat, maize and rice varieties associated with the so-called Green Revolution. It is generally acknowledged that the gains from these new varieties (and the fertilizers and irrigation they require) have been concentrated in certain districts of India, Pakistan and Sri Lanka, the central Philippines, Java in Indonesia, peninsular Malaysia, northern Turkey and northern Colombia. In addition to increased yields, the new techniques can involve an increase in demand for labour in land prepara-tion, fertilizer application and harvesting, and increases in the wages of agricultural labourers (as in Indian Punjab). Doubts are sometimes expressed, however, about the sustainability of these trends in yields and labour use.

From another point of view, scientific agriculture is largely an instrument of commercialization and capitalization rather than a mechanism for improving agri-cultural productivity and production per se. This is not to say that new seed varieties, fertilizers, etc., are always inappropriate; rather, that it all depends on the sociopolitical context in which they are applied. In particular, research efforts in scientific agriculture have been heavily biased towards certain commodities that are either most important in the industrialized countries or significant in world trade. The very small amount of research on important food staples such as cassava, coconuts, sweet potatoes, groundnuts and chickpeas is especially noteworthy. The 'research system' gives high priority to export crops such as cattle, cotton and sorghum and to those such as rice and wheat that have 'wide adaptability': the ability to transfer a new variety from one region to others. Wide adaptability can be criticized, however, for its potential in reducing genetic variety and making crops more vulnerable to disease.

A more frequent criticism of scientific agriculture, particularly in its manifesta-tion as the Green Revolution, is that it primarily benefits larger, more prosperous farmers who have readier access to the necessary inputs and credit sources. At the same time it encourages the 'debt cycle' among poorer peasants and part-time labourers discussed earlier. Moreover, the new varieties require increased depend-ence on the acquisition of energy-intensive inputs (such as fertilizers and agricultural machinery), largely controlled by TNCs.

The substitution of feed crops – crops for feeding animals rather than direct human use – and export food crops for local food crops has been one important recent impact of scientific agriculture. Some observers refer to this as the 'second green revolution', meaning that it has produced a new wave of crops, whereas the earlier trend produced greater yields of staple crops. This is not only biased in favour of farmers with capital, it also can lead to the neglect of food crops funda-mental to local diets. As a result, while exporting increasing quantities of meat and fruits, some countries find themselves having to import beans, wheat and maize to feed their rural populations.

Evidence from such diverse settings as Mexico, India and Bangladesh suggests that where capital-intensive agriculture is introduced into areas with an uneven distribution of resources it exacerbates the condition of the rural poor by marginalizing subsistence systems, such as share cropping, and encourages the polarization of land control between a class of capitalist farmers, on the one hand, and the mass of the rural population, on the other. The impact of scientific agriculture, therefore, cannot be separated from issues of social structure.

## Box 9.2  Science and rice

For half of the world's population, overwhelmingly in Asia, the life-cycle revolves around rice. In Vietnam, a child's first solid food is rice gruel. In Taiwan, chopsticks stuck in a mound of cooked rice symbolize death. Getting a good job in Singapore is an 'iron rice bowl' and unemployment is a 'broken rice bowl'. The characters for Toyota and Honda, the great car companies, mean in Japanese, 'bountiful rice field' and 'main rice field', respectively. For people in places where rice has long been the main staple of everyday diet, rice means just about everything that is important: birth, death, power, wealth, virility, fertility, vitality and so on. The oldest recorded cultivation of rice occurred in what is today Thailand in 4000 BC, although the crop is thought to have originated in Africa. Its cultivation spread widely but rice became the staple crop in Southeast and East Asia. Elsewhere, wheat and other cereal grains tended to be more important. The great advantage of rice lies in its yields which, on average, are twice as large as those of wheat. Today, rice feeds more people than any other crop. Although more wheat is harvested annually than rice, over 20 per cent of that harvest goes to feed animals. Virtually the entire annual rice harvest (598.2 million metric tons in 2000) goes to feed people, mostly in Asia, where more than 60 per cent of the world's population lives. In Bangladesh, Cambodia, Indonesia, Laos, Myanmar, Thailand and Vietnam, 56 to 80 per cent of daily calories come from rice. Rice has what botanists call 'developmental plasticity': it can grow in a wide variety of circumstances. It flourishes best, however, in the humid tropics. The three largest producers, China, India and Indonesia, produce and consume about 60 per cent of the world's rice. With only 4 per cent of the world's rice in world trade, a stable local supply is crucial to the food supply of most Asian countries. All the world's exports, about 24 million tons, would not meet demand from India for more than two months. From the 1930s to the 1950s rice yields in Asia stagnated, while improved healthcare led to a doubling of the population. The application of chemical fertilizers did little to improve the situation. The established types of rice grew, but they grew too tall, fell under their own weight and rotted in the flooded fields in which they were cultivated. A new strategy came in the early 1960s as a result of research on new hybrid varieties of rice carried out at the International Rice Research Institute (IRRI) in Los Banos, Philippines. IR8, one of the first new varieties, was spectacularly successful in raising yields. It grew faster – maturing in 130 rather than the usual 180 days – and allowed farmers to harvest two or even three crops a year from the same land. It also produced twice as much rice as either of the parent varieties. This variety and subsequent ones were so successful in doubling the world's rice crop that they were called 'miracle varieties'. They and new wheat varieties led to the declaration of a 'green revolution' in which the war on hunger and famine was said to have been won. This was premature. By the 1980s the IRRI had engineered 250 new varieties of rice that are planted in 106 countries; but at the same time world rice production has flattened out and the population has kept on growing. A simple answer might be just to plant more land in rice. In Asia, however, little or no land is left for expansion. So the pressure is on to increase yields even further through more varieties better fitted to specific ecological conditions and, due to genetic modification, pest resistant. Insects and diseases destroy nearly 25 per cent of rice crops. The question of the moment is whether or not yields can be increased indefinitely even with genetically modified varieties. The levelling-out of production in recent years might suggest that the limits to scientific agriculture in rice production have now been reached.

## SUMMARY

Since the early 1960s GDP growth rates have been faster in the less developed countries than in the developed countries (4.2 per cent per annum compared to 3.2 per cent). In addition, despite large rates of population growth, the per capita incomes of the periphery taken as a whole have grown at about 2.2 per cent per annum. Agricultural production has also increased, in contrast to the stagnation of the colonial period in many Asian and some African countries. Food production per capita in Latin America and Asia grew by 5 to 10 per cent from 1960 to 1970 and from 1970 to 1980. In Asia, these rates accelerated to over 20 per cent from 1980 to 1990 and from 1990 to 2000. In Latin America, although the rates slipped somewhat from 1980 to 1990, the growth of food production rebounded to a more than 15 per cent increase from 1990 to 2000. Only in countries with birth rates of 3 per cent or more, as in parts of Sub-Saharan Africa, or where there were major social upheavals, such as Central America, Bangladesh, Cambodia and Vietnam, is this picture particularly misleading. Throughout the periphery the incidence of chronic hunger and malnourishment has declined since 1970, however, despite civil strife, wars and natural disasters such as droughts, floods and earthquakes.

At the same time, however, the incidence of rural indebtedness and poverty and the loss of land for food production to meet local demand have increased enormously. This is because increased agricultural production in the context of the modern world economy is no guarantee that the people involved in achieving it will see its fruits. This chapter has attempted to show how this can be the case by detailing the effects of progressive commercialization and capitalization. When export crops displace subsistence uses and food staple production, increased agricultural production does not necessarily benefit rural populations. Far from it. They often find themselves ensnared in webs of poverty and indebtedness that are the direct product of modern scientific agriculture in contexts where there are few alternatives to agricultural employment. In reaching this conclusion the argument of this chapter has involved making the following major points:

1 Agriculture is often given a subsidiary role in models of development followed by governments even when it is a vital source of sustenance and employment. For a variety of reasons, national government pricing and credit policies have tended to drain agriculture in favour of the industrial–urban sector.

2 The three continents of the periphery – Africa, Asia and Latin America – differ significantly in terms of agricultural organization and performance.

3 It is also important to recognize that in agriculture in the LDCs, it is the women rather than the men who are overwhelmingly more important as the source of workers, especially in Sub-Saharan Africa.

4 There is a long history of commercial agriculture in the periphery. Until recently, however, it was a plantation or export enclave sector surrounded by a largely subsistence sector.

5 Rural land reform has tended to encourage the development of capitalist agriculture rather than benefit the interests of peasant farmers.

6 Rural land reform, and the recent activities of governments and transnational corporations have produced a much more widespread commercialization and capitalization (increasingly capital-intensive type) of agriculture. This has been most marked in Latin America but can also be seen elsewhere.

7 'Scientific' agriculture has tended to reflect and reinforce the capitalization of agriculture even as it has increased yields for a limited number of agricultural products, mainly a few staples such as rice and wheat and those in export trade.

## KEY SOURCES AND SUGGESTED READING

De Janvry, A. 1984. The role of land reform in economic development: policies and politics, in C.K. Eicher and J.M. Staatz (eds) *Agricultural Development in the Third World*. Baltimore, MD: Johns Hopkins University Press.

Fine, B. 1994. Towards a political economy of food, *Review of International Political Economy*, 3, 519–45.

Goodman, D. 2003. The quality 'turn' and alternative food practices: reflections and agenda, *Journal of Rural Studies*, 19, 1–7.

Grindle, M.S. 1986. *State and Countryside: Development Policy and Agrarian Politics in Latin America*. Baltimore, MD: Johns Hopkins University Press.

Hayami, Y. 1984. Assessment of the Green Revolution, in C.K. Eicher and J.M. Staatz (eds) *Agricultural Development in the Third World*. Baltimore, MD: Johns Hopkins University Press.

IFAD 2001. *Regional Strategy Paper: IFAD Strategy for Rural Poverty Reduction in Asia and the Pacific*. Rome: IFAD.

Joekes, S.P. 1987. *Women in the World Economy*. New York: Oxford University Press.

Rosset, P., Patel, R. and Courville, M. (eds) 2007. *Promised Land: Competing Visions of Agrarian Reform*. San Francisco: Food First.

Swindell, K. 1985. *Farm Labour*. Cambridge: Cambridge University Press.

UNFPA 2001. *The State of World Population 2001*. New York: UNFPA.

Warman, A. 1980. *'We Come to Protest': The Peasants of Morelos and the National State*. Baltimore, MD: Johns Hopkins University Press.

Williams, R.G. 1986. *Export Agriculture and the Crisis in Central America*. Chapel Hill, NC: University of North Carolina Press.

## RELATED WEBSITES

Agriculture page of the Food and Agriculture Organization (FAO) of the United Nations: http://www.fao.org/ag/

the FAO's agriculture page provides information and hyperlinks related to agriculture in the LDCs, including material on the Green Revolution and agribusiness. It also offers the national agricultural censuses that contain land and tenure statistics for a variety of countries. *FAOSTAT* is a searchable database with agriculture and food statistics for the countries around the world. The FAO's website also has a section on gender and food security, available at http://www.fao.org/Gender/gender.htm

International Fund for Agricultural Development: http://www.ifad.org/
this UN agency is concerned with addressing the structural problems relating to poverty and hunger that impact adversely on food production in the LDCs. The IFAD website contains publications, data and photographs of agriculture in Africa, Latin America and Asia

International Labour Organization: http://www.ilo.org/
this UN agency offers research and data on labour migration for agricultural workers

United Nations Office for Drug Control and Crime Prevention: http://www.odccp.org
this UN website provides reports and statistics on the global drug trade, and the associated problems and issues it generates

United Nations Population Fund: http://www.unfpa.org/
the UNPF website contains information on population issues and the LDCs. It offers the latest edition of *The State of World Population Report*, which in 2001 focused on population and environmental change, and contained a section on women and the environment

# Chapter 10

# Industrialization: the path to progress?

In the 1950s and 1960s the development strategies of many less developed countries placed considerable emphasis on manufacturing industry, which was considered to be the leading sector of economic development. More recently, as the industrialized countries have 'lost' some branches of manufacturing to locations in the global periphery and some LDCs have embarked on aggressive export-oriented development strategies, it seems that efforts at industrialization can pay off. But what exactly has been the result of several decades of industrialization in the LDCs?

In the LDCs over the past 40 years value added in manufacturing (MVA) has risen at a rapid pace. The increase is relative, however. The LDCs supplied 8.2 per cent of world MVA in 1960, 14.4 per cent in 1980 and still only 29.8 per cent by 2005. Moreover, industrialization has been highly concentrated. From 1966 to 1975, four countries, representing 11 per cent of the population of the LDCs, accounted for over half the increase of the LDCs' MVA. Eight countries (Argentina, Brazil, India, Indonesia, Iran, Mexico, South Korea and Turkey) with 17 per cent of the total population produced about two-thirds of the increase. From 1975 to 2005, however, Argentina dropped out and China, Malaysia, Singapore, Taiwan and Thailand were added to the list. The presence of China and India on this list raises the proportion of the population of the LDCs in the high-growth category to 60 per cent.

At the same time, growth rates of MVA have been lowest in the poorest countries. In Sun-Saharan Africa the growth of manufacturing has been particularly slow. In 1975 manufactured production represented 5 per cent of the GDP of the Sun-Saharan African LDCs as opposed to 16 per cent for the Asian ones and 25 per cent of those in Latin America and the Caribbean. By 2000 the comparable figures were approximately 13 per cent for the Sun-Saharan African LDCs, 26 per cent for Asia (29 per cent in East Asia, 14 per cent in South Asia), and 19 per cent for Latin America and the Caribbean.

In all LDCs, irrespective of their growth rates, industrial production has been characterized by a particular expansion of heavy industries: iron and steel, machinery and chemicals. Over the entire period 1950–2000 this expansion was more rapid than the growth of food processing or textile, clothing and shoe industries.

This point needs emphasizing because of the tendency to assume, because of increasing exports of goods such as clothing and shoes to Europe and the United States, that light and consumer goods industries have grown the most. However, since the 1960s, the industrial mix of many LDCs has undergone significant change. After the Second World War, industrialization, even if involving foreign investment by TNCs, was largely concerned with import substitution. Since the early 1960s the possibilities of substitution have dwindled in the face of the mounting costs of establishing heavy industries and as new subcontracting and global sourcing strategies of TNCs have replaced the older strategy of direct establishment of subsidiaries. In this new global context, a fundamental reorientation has taken place in the most industrialized LDCs in East Asia and Latin America. In these countries an increasing proportion of industry is oriented towards exporting manufactured goods, mostly to the developed countries.

The shift towards an export orientation was facilitated by rapid economic growth (and increasing consumer incomes) in the developed countries (especially in western Europe and Japan) and the liberalization of world trade beginning in the 1960s. Above all, however, it reflects a change in national industrialization strategy. The role of the state remains central. Like import substitution, export-oriented development strategies involve a strong managerial role for the state in adjusting to new global pressures. The states that have been most successful in doing so, such as South Korea and Taiwan, are now among the leading industrializers. But the ideological and institutional context has changed fundamentally. The focus has moved from self-sufficiency in a world of national economies to gaining competitive advantage in a global economy organized around principles of market access.

In this chapter, the progress of industrialization in the LDCs is examined in four complementary ways. First, the national and global stimuli to industrialization are described. Particular attention is directed towards the role of industrialization in national ideologies of modernization, the practical basis to the demand for industrialization and the global context for the shift from import substitution to export-oriented export strategies. Second, the problems facing industrialization in the LDCs are reviewed, focusing on the limits to industrialization posed by certain national-level and global constraints. Third, the geographical pattern of industrialization is surveyed at global, regional and urban scales. Finally, industrialization in Russia and China is profiled. China, in particular, is profiled for its experience of industrialization over the recent past because it calls into question the sustainability of the core–periphery structure of the world economy as it is presently organized. Along with such potential industrial powers as Brazil, Russia and India, China's rapid rise within the global manufacturing system could signal the beginning of a shift towards a very different world economy than the one we see today. The so-called BRIC (Brazil, Russia, India and China) economies are seen by some commentators as the emerging beneficiaries of the export-oriented globalization of the past 40 years.

## 10.1 NATIONAL AND GLOBAL STIMULI TO INDUSTRIALIZATION

The central attention given by many LDCs to industry is partly a result of the prestige of this sector, which is widely considered the hallmark of development. Although the notion of 'industrialization-in-general' can be criticized on grounds of vagueness and lack of attention to the specific mix of industries and their relation to the needs of the mass of the population, industrialization figures prominently in most national ideologies of modernization. Perhaps China for part of the 1960s was something of an exception, at least in theory; but even there the lure of industrialization as a development strategy proved stronger than ideological commitment to rural–agricultural development.

Interestingly, in the core of the world economy, particularly in western Europe, industrialization has always given rise to various 'discontents'. Contempt for the production of worldly goods shows up even in the writings of the classical economist, Adam Smith. Later concerns have been more with the nature of industrialization, in particular the 'balance' between heavy and consumer goods industries. These ideas have had their most vocal expression among those east Europeans who decried the 'overemphasis' of the now defunct communist governments on heavy industry and Latin American complaints about the 'lack' of heavy industry. However, the association between industrialization and progress is now strongly established. Only environmental activists, a rare breed in most LDCs, question the unrelenting priority given to industrial development.

## THREE MYTHS

Three ideas of mythic proportions are at the centre of the claim that national industrialization is the path to progress, even though they are of questionable empirical validity. Interestingly, they all involve negative views of agriculture as much as positive endorsements of industry and they all imply a simple sectoral logic of development as movement from agriculture to industry. The word 'myth' does not imply falsehood so much as an unexamined idea that comes to guide thought and action.

First, agriculture is viewed as having more limited stimulus effects on other economic activities than industry. In other words, industry is seen as providing multiplier effects that agriculture cannot provide. The best refutation of this particular idea is the key role that agriculture played in the early industrialization of Europe and the continued importance of agriculture in the economies of the developed world. Of course, in each case investment was required to develop forward linkages to consumer industry (food processing, etc.) and backward linkages to input providers (fertilizers, etc.). In each case farmers were also important as consumers of industrial products, when not penalized by low prices for their products, and as significant financiers of industrial investment, through savings and taxation. Adelman (1984) has proposed that precisely these stimulative features of agriculture can be used to substitute 'agriculture-demand-led-industrialization' (ADLI) for import substitution and export-oriented development models.

Second, farmers have a reputation for conservatism whereas industrialists (and workers) are viewed as agents of modernization. Imprisoned in ancient and traditional cultures, farmers, especially peasant farmers, are without dynamism and rationality. Yet, again, this idea is easily refuted by evidence from all over the world. For example, as shown in Chapter 9, there is a strong link between producer prices and yields of rice in different Asian countries. Corn (maize) production in Thailand, bean production in the Sudan and wheat production in India and Pakistan have all increased as prices have increased and decreased when prices have declined. These are hardly indications of conservatism and lack of responsiveness to commercial incentives.

Third, for many governments industry is seen as the only productive sector. Only in industry, the argument goes, are there increasing marginal returns through economies of scale in production. Moreover, the average productivity of workers in industry is higher than that of those in agriculture. However, the productivity of other factors, capital in particular, is probably higher in agriculture. In most of the countries for which data exist, the gross marginal capital–output ratio is lower and hence productivity is higher in agriculture than in other sectors. In the United States, the only country with a sufficiently long statistical series, the total productivity of all factors has increased faster in agriculture than in other sectors.

## PRACTICAL RATIONALES FOR INDUSTRIALIZATION

Whatever the empirical merit of the three ideas, they have become firmly entrenched and associated with modernization through industrialization. Manufacturing industry is widely viewed as the path to progress and it figures prominently in most national development ideologies and plans. These ideologies, whatever precise roles they reserve for 'private' business and state direction, have been reinforced by certain practical problems facing most governments. There are perhaps three that appear most important. One of them concerns the terms of trade in exchanging primary commodities for manufactured goods. As suggested in Chapter 9, there are good grounds for pessimism about the growth potential in general of primary production (raw materials and agricultural exports) because of the deteriorating barter terms of trade with manufactured goods. However, for specific primary commodities and specific countries, investment in primary production can be preferable. Nevertheless, by and large, governments have not been persuaded of this. They can even point to the case of the OPEC cartel – the most successful attempt in the history of the world economy to bolster the price of a primary commodity – to illustrate the limitations of primary production. From its dominant position in 1973–74, OPEC has become less and less able to govern the world price of oil. This reflects both adjustment strategies in consumer countries (energy conservation, shifts to non-OPEC suppliers), and the emergence of political conflicts and different production strategies among member countries (the Iran/Iraq war of the 1980s; long-term market share and conservation of oil reserves versus rapid production, e.g., Saudi Arabia versus Nigeria). It is easy to infer from the experience of OPEC the long-run limitations of a development strategy based on primary production for world markets.

Second, many LDCs have massive unemployed and underemployed populations concentrated increasingly in urban areas. Deteriorating living conditions in the countryside (see Chapter 9) and the availability of better public services in urban areas have encouraged large-scale rural-to-urban migration, often in the absence of industrialization. To survive in the cities, people engage in a wide range of 'informal sector' economic activities as street vendors, shoeshine boys, stall keepers, public letter writers, auto mechanics, taxi drivers, subcontractors, tailors, drug dealers and prostitutes. Sometimes these activities can be linked to industrialization of a formal variety through subcontracting, but often they cannot. International migration, both temporary and permanent, is sometimes an alternative for those with better education and greatest initiative. But, among other things, this produces a 'brain drain' that poor countries can ill afford. It is in this context that expansion of employment in manufacturing industry can often become an important national imperative.

A third incentive for industrialization comes from the state-building activities of national elites. National industrialization can be a 'prestige' goal around which national populations can be mobilized. All governments are also under pressure to industrialize in order to compete with other countries. Pressure comes from both domestic elites, especially the military, and from foreign allies and patrons. Some of the emphasis on heavy industries undoubtedly derives from this pressure. The significant growth of military industries in the LDCs is directly related to it. Industry is also an important instrument of political favouritism and patronage. Governments can reward 'loyal' social and ethnic groups and punish 'disloyal' ones, by directing industrial activities towards some places and away from others. Industrialization, therefore, often involves political stimulation, of both 'noble' and 'ignoble' varieties.

The national industrialization drives that took place in the aftermath of decolonization had limited effects until the late 1960s, except in those countries with large domestic markets and long-sustained import substitution policies (e.g., Brazil and Mexico). The spread and intensification of industrialization since the late 1960s coincides to a certain extent with the declining rate of profit in the industrialized countries (see Chapter 3) and the consequent shift in strategy by TNCs from high-wage/high-consumption forms of production in the industrialized countries (Fordism) towards spatially decentralized forms of production in which low-wage labour forces are important in certain phases (see Table 10.1). This suggests that the changing global context has been fundamentally important in stimulating the recent expansion of manufacturing industry in some LDCs. In other words, the new international division of labour in manufacturing and its associated spatial decentralization of many production activities (largely related to the international product life-cycle model) are closely related to the 'crisis' of capital accumulation in the industrialized countries. A new geography of manufacturing employment has been the result (Table 10.2).

The extent to which cost advantages for TNCs (particularly low-cost labour) have entirely spurred the growth of the NICs can be exaggerated. In the first place, TNCs do not dominate production in the NICs. Even in Brazil, a country that for many years had had a high proportion of TNC investment relative to local sources, foreign direct investment (FDI) declined from the mid-1970s, until this trend was reversed during the late 1990s as a result of currency and trade reforms. Second, governments in the NICs have controlled foreign investment, preferring investment by banks and other financial interests to FDI: 'Productive capital has largely remained under the control of local corporations; most foreign capital has entered countries either as bilateral or multilateral aid or as financial capital' (Webber and Rigby, 1996: 453). Nevertheless, export-based industrialization, as opposed to import substitution, does allow firms to pay lower wages than they would have to if the local economy had to absorb all of the supply. This has broken the local geographical bonds between production and consumption on which organized capitalism was based. The expansion of industry in the LDCs, therefore, has some basis in cost advantages, even if these are not ones that accrue largely to TNCs and it has had the consequence of increasing the competitiveness of world markets across a wide range of manufacturing industries.

But perhaps the best and most simple evidence that costs alone cannot explain the spread of industrialization to the LDCs is that export-oriented industrialization did not concentrate where wage rates were lowest. It has been concentrated mainly in certain countries with other characteristics. The most successful ones, the East

**Table 10.1** Labour conditions in global manufacturing

|  | Average hourly earnings in manufacturing in 2005 (US$) | Strike and lockouts in manufacturing 1990–2005 (average annual) |
|---|---|---|
| United States | 23.65 | 9 |
| Canada | 23.82 | 107 |
| United Kingdom | 25.66 | 41 |
| Germany | 33.00 | Not available |
| Portugal | 7.33 | 135 |
| Australia | 21.76 | 164 |
| Japan | 24.91 | 50 |
| Mexico | 2.63 | 32 |
| Hong Kong | 5.65 | 0 |
| South Korea | 13.56 | 83 |
| Singapore | 7.66 | 0 |
| Taiwan | 6.38 | Not available |
| Sri Lanka | 0.54 | 65 |

*Source:* Based on United States Department of Labor, *International Comparisons of Hourly Compensation Costs for Production Workers in Manufacturing* (Table 2), available at http://www.bls.gov/; International Labour Office (ILO) *LABORSTA Internet,* available at http://laborsta.ilo.org/

**Table 10.2** Changing geography of manufacturing employment: paid employment in manufacturing (millions of people)

| Region/country | 1980 | 1995 | 2005 | Overall change |
|---|---|---|---|---|
| United States and Canada | 21.4 | 20.3 | 18.5 | −2.9 |
| Japan | 12.1 | 11.9 | 11.4 | −0.7 |
| Western Europe[1] | 28.2 | 25.9 | 23.7 | −4.5 |
| *Core countries* | *61.7* | *58.1* | *53.6* | *−8.1* |
| South Asia[2] | 6.9 | 8.9 | 10.5 | +3.6 |
| Southeast and East Asia[3] | 68.6 | 115.3 | 96.7 | +28.1 |
| Latin America[4] | 8.7 | 9.1 | 16.2 | +7.5 |
| *Semi-peripheral and peripheral countries* | *84.2* | *133.3* | *123.4* | *+39.2* |

*Source:* Based on Peet (1987), p. 781; UNIDO *(Reference Information:* http://www.unido.org/); United Nations *(Monthly Bulletin of Statistics On-Line:* http://esa.un.org/unsd/mbsdemo/mbssearch.asp); International Labor Organization (online *Labor Statistics Database:* www.ilo.org/)

*Note:* [1]Austria, Belgium, France, Germany, Italy, Netherlands, Portugal, Spain, Sweden, United Kingdom; [2]Bangladesh, India, Sri Lanka; [3]China, Hong Kong, Malaysia, Philippines, Singapore, South Korea, Taiwan, Thailand; [4]Brazil, Mexico, Venezuela

Asian NICs of China, South Korea, Taiwan, Singapore and Hong Kong, were ones in which the state and local industrial capital were closely interlocked and receptive to massive foreign investment. Moreover, they are the ones in which much of the foreign investment was in the form of private bank credit or strategic alliances between TNCs and local partners rather than direct investment by TNCs. They thus maintained more local control over investment decisions. In addition, the privileged geopolitical arrangements of South Korea and Taiwan with the United States were important in opening American markets and making available American aid and investment in return for the East Asian countries' forward role in 'containment' of mainland China and the Soviet Union. Since the late 1980s there has been an increased level of FDI in East Asia, much of it flowing between East Asian countries rather than emanating from outside the region. The East Asian financial crisis of 1997 reinforced this trend as some FDI that would otherwise have gone into Southeast Asian countries (e.g., Thailand, the Philippines and especially Indonesia), was diverted to East Asian countries (e.g., South Korea, Taiwan, as well as China and Hong Kong). Indeed, between 1991 and 2000 private financial flows to the LDCs grew rapidly after stagnating in the 1980s but 'official' (governments, World Bank, etc.) investment tailed off having been more important than private flows throughout the 1980s. This has led some commentators to see a foundation being laid for a future boom in peripheral industrialization. However, though the global context may well trigger the *possibility* for industrialization, especially of the export-oriented type, it never guarantees its realization. Various contingencies – political, economic, social – intervene to determine *where* it takes place.

## 10.2 LIMITS TO INDUSTRIALIZATION IN THE PERIPHERY

There are a number of constraints that will probably limit the spread and intensification of the export-oriented industrialization that has lain behind the impressive growth of the NICs since the 1970s.

### PROFIT CYCLES

The declining rates of profit in the industrialized countries – between the 1960s and the mid-1980s – may have been cyclical rather than secular. There is evidence that corporate profitability in the USA, for example, began to rebound in the late 1980s after a 15-year downturn. The more critical analyses of this trend argue that the return to profitability has been fuelled by stagnant wage rates. This may mean that locating production facilities or engaging in subcontracting in the LDCs can be less attractive to US TNCs. However, the figures (as reported by the US Department of Commerce, e.g., 4.57 per cent average after-tax return on capital in manufacturing in the USA in 1988 compared to 2.87 per cent in 1985, 3.99 per cent in 1975 and 4.80 per cent in 1965) may reflect the falling dollar after 1985 helping American-based manufacturers in foreign markets and the increased return on foreign investments rather than improving domestic profitability (e.g., the European operations of General Motors lifted what would otherwise have been an even more dismal rate of profitability in the late 1980s). Certainly the picture is a complex one, with not only countries but also industrial sectors (electronics, automobiles, etc.) having different trajectories in profit rates over time.

In addition, some of the giant American TNCs, such as IBM and GE, that pioneered the shift in production to the new international division of labour (NIDL) through the creation of foreign assembly operations in the LDCs have become lacklustre performers, challenged in the most profitable production lines by more innovative smaller firms with currently more localized patterns of production in industrial districts because of their reliance on immediate response from independent subcontractors.

## PROTECTIONISM

There are inherent limits to the generalization to other LDCs of the export successes of the NICs. To begin with, the period 1950–73 was one of unusually high growth in world trade. Whereas global trade expanded only at 1 per cent per annum during 1910–40, the period 1953–73 saw an increase in total trade of 8 per cent per annum, and of 11 per cent per annum for manufactures. The consequence was an increased interdependence in the world economy as trade barriers were lowered. Since the late 1970s, however, protectionism has remained a response in the industrialized countries in times of declining rates of economic growth and increased unemployment, domestic inflation and balance of payments deficits. It is the LDCs that have become the major advocates of global trade liberalization. Cline (1982) estimated that if all the LDCs had the same export intensity as Hong Kong, Singapore, South Korea and Taiwan, there would be a shift from 16.4 to 60.4 per cent of aggregate DC manufactured imports originating in the LDCs. Given the reliance of the NICs on DC markets, the likelihood of this expansion without protectionist responses seems extremely unlikely. As Cline (1982: 89) concludes:

> It is seriously misleading to hold up the East Asian G4 [Gang of Four, i.e., Hong Kong, Singapore, South Korea and Taiwan] as a model of development because that model almost certainly cannot be generalized without provoking [a] protectionist response ruling out its implementation.

Of course, Cline's generalization from the current NICs to all LDCs represents an extreme scenario. There is still considerable scope for building up export markets in both DCs and other LDCs. In particular, there is evidence that the established NICs are now transferring some of their more labour-intensive industries to countries that have a short-run comparative advantage. For example, Taiwanese firms have subsidiaries in China and Malaysia, and Hong Kong firms have subsidiaries in China and the Philippines. Among the LDCs, consequently, adjacent countries are not necessarily condemned to see their neighbours who enjoy an initial advantage permanently monopolize the positions they have won in world markets, even though they must of necessity start out as subservient to them.

## ACCESS TO TECHNOLOGY

The TNCs that have been involved in setting up subsidiaries or engaging subcontractors in the NICs must now respond to protectionist pressures in the DCs where their final markets are concentrated. This will involve substituting radical new automation technologies for low-wage labour. Even if the technology diffuses evenly at a global scale, production costs will decline more steeply in the DCs than in the NICs. In addition, new economies of scale associated with batch production for customized as opposed to mass markets and new external economies associated with a close geo-graphical integration of component suppliers and final assembly in 'last minute', just-in-time (JIT) and 'zero inventory' production systems can reduce the attractiveness of global sourcing. There is already evidence that some assembly of electronic circuits is being brought back to DCs from LDCs, and the introduction of new technologies and new production systems may further reduce the need for cheap, unskilled labour.

It is important to note again, however, that the growth of the NICs is not uniquely due to the activities of foreign TNCs. Domestic firms, including an increasing number of TNCs from the NICs themselves play important roles, partic-ularly in such export sectors as electronics, automobiles, textiles, clothing and shoes. By 2000, for example, foreign sales accounted for more than 25 per cent of total sales for the 10 largest East Asian TNCs (as ranked by foreign assets, e.g., Hutchinson Whampoa from Hong Kong, Samsung Corp. from South Korea). Only in Latin America and, to a certain degree, in China have the expansion of foreign TNCs and the growth of exports been closely related; but the control of foreign TNCs over most of the new automation and information technologies can limit their transfer when these TNCs are not locally dominant.

## DEBT AND CREDITWORTHINESS

The success of export-oriented industrialization has been tied to the growth of enormous debt loads underwritten by FDI, official aid agencies and international banks. Among the most problematic features of the world economy by the late 1990s was the absence of any new actors willing to finance industrialization in the LDCs and the appearance of a global 'credit shortage' because of the emergence of eastern Europe (especially the former East Germany) and the former Soviet Union (particularly Russia) as competitors in world financial markets. The institutions that did play a central role in the past are largely unwilling to do so now. Perhaps the only institution that has substantially increased its lending and encouraged others to do likewise is the International Monetary Fund (IMF). But the IMF still lends relatively little compared to the size of LDCs' current account deficits and attaches conditions to loans that many countries with strong state direction find undesirable and damaging to long-run development.

Even in the 1970s lending, especially private bank lending, was concentrated in the LDCs with relatively high per capita incomes and those with already impressive growth records. The four largest borrowers (Mexico, Brazil, South Korea and the Philippines) accounted for over 60 per cent of total accumulated non-OPEC LDCs' debt to international banks in December 1982. Much of the money lent came from recycled 'petrodollars' in the context of declines in credit demand from traditional clients in the DCs in the wake of the 1974–75 recession. This situation is not likely to repeat itself even though in the 1990s private lending from banks and stock markets to East Asia and Latin America did increase after declining precipitously in the 1980s.

## RESEARCH AND DEVELOPMENT (R&D) CAPACITY

The new leading sectors of industrial growth in the world economy are the so-called 'information technologies'. The USA, Europe and Japan lead the way in world demand for these technologies and their products. Consequently, success in the global information processing and electronics industries requires a research and development (R&D), production, marketing and political lobbying base inside all three regions of demand. Given the importance of politics – especially in the form of lobbying against protectionist threats – established TNCs and countries with large public sector investments in information technologies are at a distinct advantage. Those companies and countries struggling to gain entry beyond the labour-intensive, assembly level will be faced with formidable barriers, not least the absence of local protection in the face of US-led attempts in such international institutions as the GATT over the past 10 years at 'deregulation' of LDC domestic markets.

## POLARIZATION AND INSTABILITY

The non-city state NICs (the experience of Singapore and Hong Kong is not immediately relevant to most LDCs) with the highest growth rates – particularly South Korea and Taiwan – have enjoyed a unique set of circumstances that are not generalizable to other peripheral settings. In particular, they inherited the transport and education infrastructure imposed by Japanese colonialism. Later, massive US aid in the 1950s – for geopolitical purposes – stabilized their economies and tight controls on imports plus government allocation of foreign exchange and capital promoted export-led growth. In addition to land reform (see Chapter 9) in both South Korea and Taiwan, state enterprises were a key part of national growth strategies in the 1970s, accounting for 25 per cent to 35 per cent of total fixed investment. In South Korea – following the practice of Japan – interest subsidies and other incentives that rewarded performance were employed to induce private companies to develop major industries and focus on exports.

Crucially, relatively equal income distribution in South Korea – where the richest 20 per cent receive 5.3 times the income of the poorest 20 per cent – has allowed the government to adopt policies pursuing efficiency and growth with limited social and political unrest. By contrast, Latin American countries such as Brazil (until its fiscal reforms, beginning in 1994), where the comparable income differential exceeds a factor of 26, have run larger government budget deficits through financing redistributive programmes to the poor that help prevent political unrest while yielding to the demands of the rich to limit taxation. In such circumstances the extreme inequality of incomes limits government fiscal flexibility (Table 10.3).

## WEIGHT OF POPULATION GROWTH

Finally, it seems that export-oriented industries can make, and have already made, an important contribution to the creation of new employment in certain small countries. However, it would probably be a mistake to believe that these industries can make anything other than a marginal contribution to employment in the periphery as a whole. As of 1980 the World Bank estimated the total number of direct jobs created by export industries in the poorest LDCs as between 2 and 3 million, about 10 per cent of total industrial employment in these countries, or, in other terms, less than 0.5 per cent of the total labour force of some 850 million people. Even considering multiplier effects, the total number of direct and indirect jobs created came to 5–10 million, around 1 per cent of the total labour force. As this labour force of over 1 billion today is growing at an annual rate of 2.0 per cent (down from 2.3 per cent in the 1980s and 1990s), the number of workers added every year to the total labour force is about twice as large as the entire labour force employed in jobs cre-

Table 10.3 International variations in the concentration of incomes (higher figures indicate greater inequality)

| | Year | Ratio of income of lowest 5th/income of highest 5th |
|---|---|---|
| *Low Human Development Index* | | |
| Zambia | 1998 | 17.2 |
| Burkina Faso | 1998 | 13.6 |
| Côte d'Ivoire | 2002 | 9.7 |
| Ethiopia | 1999 | 4.3 |
| *Medium Human Development Index* | | |
| Brazil | 2001 | 26.4 |
| Colombia | 1999 | 22.9 |
| South Africa | 2000 | 17.9 |
| China | 2001 | 10.7 |
| Philippines | 2000 | 9.7 |
| Thailand | 2000 | 8.3 |
| Tunisia | 2000 | 7.9 |
| Indonesia | 2002 | 5.2 |
| Sri Lanka | 1999 | 5.1 |
| India | 1999 | 4.9 |
| Russian Federation | 2002 | 4.8 |
| *High Human Development Index* | | |
| United States | 2000 | 8.4 |
| United Kingdom | 1999 | 7.2 |
| New Zealand | 1997 | 6.8 |
| Canada | 1998 | 5.8 |
| Germany | 2000 | 4.3 |
| Norway | 2000 | 3.9 |

*Source:* Based on UNDP (2005: 270–73, Table 15)

ated by export-oriented manufacturing. Across all LDCs, therefore, export industries cannot possibly absorb the additional labour force arriving each year or even reabsorb those unemployed due to cyclical shifts in demand for export products. Even restricting attention to seven NICs or potential NICs (Brazil, Egypt, India, Mexico, the Philippines, South Korea and Taiwan), total jobs created during the 1960s by the export of manufactured goods represented only 3 per cent of total employment. However, for small countries with high levels of industrial exports the picture is somewhat different. Thus in Taiwan in 1969 one job in six was created by manufactured exports and in South Korea in 1970 one job in 10 was created by exports of all kinds. These numbers doubled in the 1980s. Moreover, for the city states such as Hong Kong and Singapore, with their dynamic producer service (finance, organization, research) sectors as well as large concentrations of export-oriented manufacturing industries, the figures are even higher. By 2000 in Taiwan, one of the most consistently successful NICs over the past 20 years, the 22 million population had a GDP per capita (US$17,400) about one-third larger than that of Portugal (US$11,060) or Greece (US$11,960), universal schooling and healthcare and the world's fourth largest gross international reserves (holdings of monetary gold, special drawing rights, reserves of IMF members held by the IMF and holdings of foreign exchange under the control of monetary authorities) after Japan, China and the USA. Taiwanese business is a major investor throughout Asia, contributing to the industrialization of coastal China even though 'officially' still on a war footing against the mainland (see later section on China).

It is not, however, only the absence of large dependent peasant and urban populations that gives the smaller states of East Asia distinct advantages in relative job creation from export-oriented manufacturing. These countries have concentrated until recently on labour-intensive export industries, such as textiles, clothing, and electrical and mechanical assemblage. These industries use a great deal of labour per unit of production and this labour is unskilled. They also employ disproportionately large numbers of women whose social position can be exploited to suppress wages and limit union organization. As Joekes (1987: 90) puts it: 'Women's lesser education and their expectation (born of past experience) of receiving little training make them apparently suited to unskilled occupations and, most importantly, prepared to stay at such unskilled jobs, however monotonous they may be.'

Moreover, these countries initially managed to limit capital-intensive production in order to maximize the return on their higher labour–capital ratios in export-oriented manufacturing. This sets them apart from other NICs that have much lower capital/labour ratios in export industries and higher levels of capital-intensive production for domestic markets (e.g., Brazil). It also leads to an improvement in income distribution as well as employment creation, since the heavy reliance on unskilled labour implies that relatively more of the incomes generated by export industries will go to the poorest segments of the population and less to those classes rich in capital or technical skills. The peculiar historical development of the East Asian NICs in job creation by export industries, therefore, is not readily duplicated by larger countries – or some smaller ones, for example, Puerto Rico – in which incomes and wealth are divided unequally and in which powerful sociopolitical classes have a vested interest in maintaining the status quo.

## 10.3  GEOGRAPHY OF INDUSTRIALIZATION IN THE PERIPHERY

As stated earlier, beginning in the late 1960s and 1970s a number of LDCs underwent a rapid process of industrialization, financed in part by the export of investment capital from the developed world. These countries, the NICs, were the ones where growth was fastest. But growth was not limited to them. What is most important is to grasp the dynamics of industrialization underway since the 1970s. If the 1980s, the 1990s and the period since 2000 generally have not seen the same overall dynamism, with very important exceptions such as China and India, it is the process of industrialization that demands our attention.

## TRAJECTORIES OF INDUSTRIALIZATION

Figure 10.1 illustrates one way of doing this. This shows the groupings of countries resulting from applying Sutcliffe's (1971) three 'tests' of industrialization:

- Test One, at least 25 per cent of GDP in industry.
- Test Two, at least 60 per cent of industrial output in manufacturing.
- Test Three, at least 10 per cent of the total population employed in industry.

This last test measures the impact of the industrial sector on the population as a whole. Seven groupings and two paths to industrialization result from applying the three tests. The groupings are as follows:

A    Fully industrialized countries that pass all three tests.

B    Countries that pass the first two tests but with limited 'penetration' into the population or the economy as a whole. These are semi-industrialized countries.

A/B  Borderline cases (e.g., Greece).

C    Countries that pass the first and third tests. A large industrial sector (in mining or oil) affects the population widely, but manufacturing is weak.

D    Countries that pass the second test only. A small industrial sector dominated by manufacturing.

E    Countries that pass the first test only. A substantial industrial, but non-manufacturing, sector has limited impacts on the population.

O    Other countries, i.e., non-industrialized countries, failing all three tests.

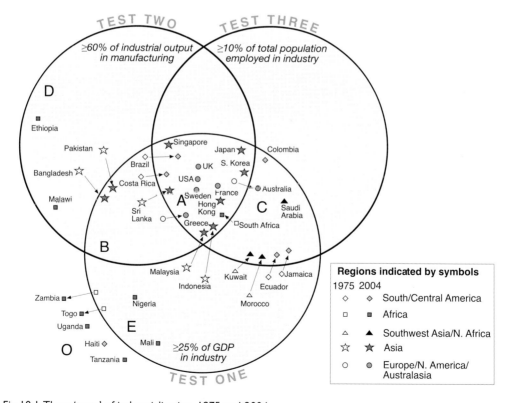

Fig 10.1: Three 'tests' of industrialization, 1975 and 2004

Source: Based on online data from World Bank, Tables 2.1, 2.2, 2.3, 4.2, World Development Indicators, 2006, available at http://devdata.worldbank.org/wdi2006/

There are two possible paths to industrialization given this categorization. They are E → C → A, where, for example, a mining enclave expands to involve the total population and manufacturing develops later; or D → B → A, where manufacturing leads to increases in industrial output and later towards a more industrial labour force.

If data for 2004 are used as well as data for 1975, a number of shifts are discernible. A number of D → B → A moves are clearly visible; most of the NICs (see later) fit this model (Figure 10.1). The E → C → A path, characteristic in the past of the USA, Australia and South Africa, and the expected route, perhaps, of the members of OPEC and other mineral-rich economies, is also of importance, but as yet at an early stage. It is clear, however, that, although there are some important examples of industrialization in the periphery, most LDCs are not industrializing, are industrializing quite slowly or are deindustrializing (losing manufacturing industry), a new phenomenon since 1975.

One problem with this type of analysis is that it provides minimum thresholds for defining industrialization but misses the point that after achieving these levels economies typically begin to lose jobs in manufacturing and experience an expansion of their producer and financial service industries. Manufacturing in itself is then no longer the driving force behind economic growth. This is what has happened in all of the so-called industrialized countries or DCs, where services are now a much more important component of their economies than is manufacturing. For example, in the USA by 2000, services accounted for 72 per cent of GDP, manufacturing had fallen to 18 per cent, and only 15 per cent of jobs were in manufacturing.

The conclusion about the general lack of industrialization at the periphery is reinforced by focusing more directly on rates of growth in manufacturing output. Figure 10.2 shows that the high rates of growth in the period 1995–2005 were relatively concentrated geographically. There is no 'exclusive' list of NICs, as different

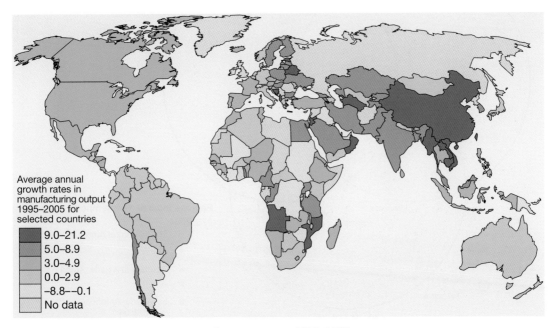

Average annual growth rates in manufacturing output 1995–2005 for selected countries

9.0–21.2
5.0–8.9
3.0–4.9
0.0–2.9
–8.8--0.1
No data

Fig 10.2: The geography of growth in manufacturing output, 1995–2005

*Source*: Based on World Bank, *Country at a Glance Tables*, available at http://www.worldbank.org/

indicators lead to the inclusion of different countries. Also, there has been some volatility over time. The 1980s and 1990s were not particularly good decades for the NICs as a whole. Latin American NICs such as Brazil and Mexico fared worse in the 1980s than in the 1990s. The Asian financial crisis impaired the economic performance of many Asian NICs in the late 1990s. Back in 1979 the OECD recognized 10 countries as NICs (Brazil, Hong Kong, Greece, Mexico, Portugal, Singapore, South Korea, Spain, Taiwan and the then Yugoslavia) on the grounds of 'fast growth of the level and share of industrial employment, an enlargement of export market shares in manufactures, and a rapid relative reduction in the per capita income gap separating them from the advanced industrial countries' (OECD, 1979). In Figure 10.2, only two of these NICs had manufacturing output growth rates between 1995 and 2005 exceeding 5 per cent per year (South Korea (7.6) and Singapore (5.3)), two had 3.6 per cent (Spain and Portugal), one had 3.1 per cent (Mexico), one had 2.5 per cent (Greece), one had 1.3 per cent (Brazil), the former Yugoslavia no longer exists and growth rates are not available for the other two. Of the other countries with high growth rates (5 per cent or more), some are major oil exporters (e.g., Oman (10.6)) or starting from tiny industrial sectors (e.g., Vietnam (11.0)). Some are 'new' NICs (e.g., China (10.1), India (5.5).

## EXPORT PROCESSING ZONES

The NICs such as South Korea, Singapore, Mexico, Taiwan and, predominantly, China, have been especially active in export-oriented industrialization (Figure 10.3). Some of this industry has been attracted to and is concentrated geographically in export processing zones (EPZs) or 'free trade zones' (also see Chapter 2). These are limited areas in which special advantages accrue to investors. These include duty-free entry of goods for assembly, limited restrictions on profit repatriation, lower

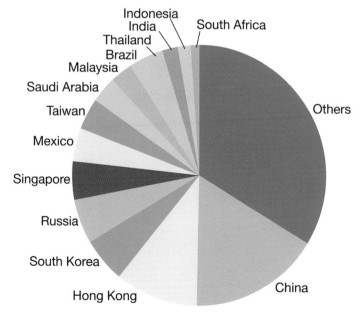

Fig 10.3: Share of certain NICs in total LDC exports, 2005–06 by value

*Source:* Based on online data from *CIA World Factbook 2007*, available at http://www.odci.gov/cia/publications/factbook/

taxation, reduced pollution controls and constraints on labour organization (strikes banned, etc.). The intention of EPZs is to attract local and international companies with the capital to set up factories oriented to export production; and much of the industry in EPZs is owned by TNCs. According to the World Bank (2002), the number of these EPZs mushroomed from only a handful in the 1970s to more than 500 in 73 countries by the late 1990s. Most of the EPZs cluster around major markets: North America, western Europe and Japan. The share of employment in the EPZs is substantial in some LDCs, especially when taking into account that the agricultural and informal sectors still employ a significant percentage of the population. While Mauritius is particularly high at 17 per cent, EPZ employment shares are about 5 per cent in the Dominican Republic and 2 to 4 per cent in Honduras and Costa Rica. EPZ production is concentrated in textiles and clothing, microelectronic assembly, and the assembly of cars and bicycles. More specifically, it is the labour-intensive stages of production that are characteristic of the EPZs (Figure 10.4).

In Mexico by 1978, 60 per cent of the *maquiladoras* – the assembly plants located in EPZs along the US border since the programme of tax breaks for American business began in 1965 – were engaged in electrical and electronic assembly and 30 per cent were involved in textiles and clothing. In the Asian EPZs, over 50 per cent of the employment is in electronics, with the clothing and footwear industries second. The build-up in electronics has been especially marked since the early 1970s. The total amount of employment in EPZs, however, is relatively small. In Mexico, *maquiladora* employment in 1980 was only around 110,000, although, by 1992, the

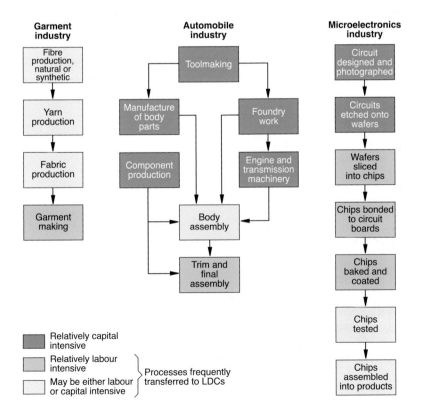

Fig 10.4: Labour processes in three manufacturing industries
*Source:* Based on Crow and Thomas (1985: 49)

year before Mexico joined NAFTA, it had grown to 500,000, and by 2001 it exceeded 1 million. An estimated 2.5 million workers are directly employed in EPZs in Asia. Most of the workers are unmarried women between the ages of 17 and 23.

Such young women, earning around US$1.90 per hour, accounted for between 70 and 90 per cent of employment in Mexican EPZs in 2000. Within Asia, young women account for 94 per cent of EPZ employment in Vietnam, 90 per cent in Sri Lanka and Thailand, 87 per cent in Malaysia, 77 per cent in Taiwan and 74 per cent in the Philippines. Young women are preferred as workers because their wages tend to be lower than men's and because they are considered 'nimble fingered' and 'more able to cope with repetitive work' (Armstrong and McGee, 1986). Certainly, very little training is required and wages are very low. Often an exploitative trainee system is used in which 'trainees' are paid only 60 per cent of the local minimum wage and are repeatedly fired and rehired so as to obtain a permanent 40 per cent reduction in the wage bill.

Many of the EPZs also do not appear to have generated major multiplier effects. Links to local economies are generally limited especially in Latin America. In the Mexican case the North American Free Trade Agreement (NAFTA) with the United States and Canada has removed the need for the special border EPZs now that the whole of Mexico has become a giant EPZ. However, Scott (1987) has shown that in some Asian cases, the activities of TNCs led to the growth of both 'diffusion facilities' owned by local firms engaged in higher level (not solely assembly) operations and locally owned subcontract assembly houses. The former are concentrated in South Korea, Taiwan and Hong Kong, the latter are found in Thailand, Malaysia, Singapore, the Philippines, Hong Kong, Taiwan and South Korea. In Malaysia, for example, the presence of foreign TNCs in the electronics industry since the 1970s has contributed to the development of local suppliers (Figure 10.5). Many of these local companies have been established by former employees who, after acquiring technical and marketing expertise from the TNC, left to set up their own spin-off companies.

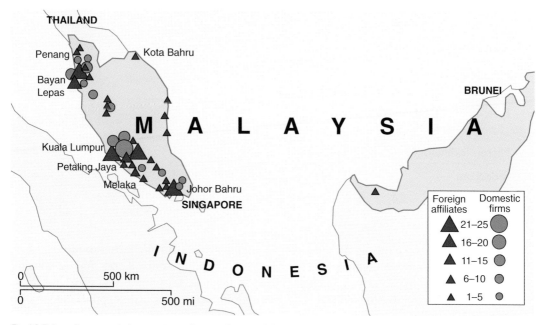

Fig 10.5: Locally owned electronics industry plants in Malaysia, 1999

Source: Adapted from UNCTAD (2001: 74, Box Figure II.4.1)

## TRANSNATIONAL INVESTMENT PATTERNS

Foreign direct investment by US TNCs has shifted dramatically over time. In 1969 most investment in electronic assembly was in Hong Kong, South Korea, Taiwan and Singapore. By 1983 the Philippines and Malaysia had become relatively more important. By 2002, China had become the prime location for US chip plant construction. This kind of foreign direct investment, therefore, is relatively footloose and sensitive, not only to marginal shifts in wage rates, local fiscal conditions and political 'instability', but also, in the case of China, to potential markets in populous LDCs, especially after they become members of the World Trade Organization (WTO). To spread their risks, however, many of the top US TNCs engaged in electronic assembly operations in Asia have plants in a number of different locations in different countries (Table 10.4). Intel, for example, has five different manufacturing facilities in three Asian countries (including China).

Table 10.4 Electronic plants in East and Southeast Asia in 2006 owned or leased by top US electronics corporations

| US rank | Company | China | Hong Kong | Japan | Malaysia | Indonesia | Philippines | Singapore | S. Korea | Taiwan | Thailand | Total |
|---|---|---|---|---|---|---|---|---|---|---|---|---|
| 1 | Intel | 2 | | | 2 | | 1 | | | | | 5 |
| 2 | Texas Instruments | 2 | | | 1 | | | | | 1 | | 4 |
| 3 | Sanmina-SCI | 4 | | | 2 | 1 | | 1 | | | 1 | 9 |
| 4 | Solectron | 5 | | 3 | 1 | 1 | | 3 | | 1 | | 14 |
| 5 | Jabil Circuit | 5 | | 1 | 1 | | | 1 | | | | 8 |
| 6 | Applied Materials | 2 | | | | | | | | 1 | | 3 |
| 7 | Advanced Micro Devices | 1 | | 1 | 2 | | | 1 | | | 1 | 6 |
| 8 | Freescale Semiconductor | 1 | | 1 | 1 | | | | | | | 3 |
| 9 | Micron Technology | 1 | | 1 | | | | 1 | | | | 3 |
| 10 | Broadcom | 1 | | 1 | 1 | | | 1 | | 2 | | 6 |
| | **Total** | 24 | 0 | 8 | 11 | 2 | 1 | 8 | 1 | 4 | 2 | 61 |

Source: company websites

In textiles and clothing there has also been a tendency for the most labour-intensive activities to move away from Hong Kong, Singapore, South Korea and Taiwan to other parts of Asia. Bangladesh, China, Indonesia, Sri Lanka and Thailand have become especially important: 'The clothing industry uses little capital and is very mobile. All you need is a shed, some sewing machines, and lots of cheap nimble fingers' (*Economist*, 1987: 67). Partly this has been a product life-cycle effect, as wage rates for unskilled labour have increased in the older NICs. Perhaps of great-est importance in this geographical shift, however, has been the imposition since 1974 of strict quotas (quantity restrictions) on textiles and clothing by the USA and European countries on imports from established producers in many LDCs. These multifibre arrangement (MFA) quotas set businesspeople from Hong Kong and South Korea, the major figures in this industry, searching for countries with higher quotas and low production. Hong Kong has also redirected its production to non-quota high-quality specialized fashion items and used China to fill its own quotas on basic clothing products. China has been allowed a large expansion simply because the DCs are keen to expand their exports of capital goods (e.g., steel, weapons) to such a large market and do not want to invite retaliatory action on their exports in the face of a clothing quota decrease.

The Agreement on Textiles and Clothing (ATC) is bringing trade in textiles and clothing in line with the rules of the WTO. In 2005, the MFA – intended as a tem-porary measure to give the DCs time to adjust to competition from the LDCs – began to be phased out. In the meantime, some DCs have shown a willingness to remove quotas for individual countries that open their markets in return. In 2001, for example, the EU lifted all quotas for textile and clothing imports from Sri Lanka in exchange for tariff reductions and commitments on non-tariff barriers to trade. During the 1980s Japanese sources displaced American and European ones as the major investors in the countries of Asia. Even as Japanese foreign direct investment in the USA and Europe followed an incredible growth rate during the late 1980s, Japan's stock of investment in Asia, already higher than that of the USA or Europe by 1985, grew faster than either of the other two. Despite its economic woes during the 1990s, Japan's investment in Asia remained higher than that of the EU or the USA (in 1998, for example, Japan's FDI in East Asia was US$72 billion, compared to US$65 billion from the EU and US$45 billion from the USA). This has led to talk of an East Asian economic bloc forming under Japanese dominance. Certainly, Japan's investment in manufacturing in neighbouring Asian countries has involved Japanese companies moving production abroad in a sector in which Japan has been losing comparative advantage. Moreover, increasing Japanese FDI in Asia has not been restricted to investment in manufacturing:

> More recently, increases in FDI have been associated with the rapid growth of spend-ing on research and development by Japanese firms. Some Japanese FDI has also been triggered by policy actions that make it advisable to move production of certain goods to other countries. Trade frictions ... may have encouraged Japanese firms to invest in Asia so as to build 'export platforms' for the US market.
>
> Bayoumi and Lipworth (1997: 12)

In fact, the evidence suggests that the region is moving, but only slowly, towards an intra-regional bias in trade and direct investment flows such as is evident in western Europe. East Asian trade and investment barriers are being reduced or eliminated as part of voluntary efforts by Asia Pacific Economic Cooperation group (APEC) mem-bers (see Chapter 12) and in conjunction with WTO agreements. As yet, however, East Asia in general and Southeast Asia in particular, including such countries as Malaysia, Indonesia, Thailand and the Philippines (despite their membership in ASEAN; see Chapter 12), do not form an incipient trading bloc diverting trade through some deliberate strategy of economic regionalism.

However, there is undoubtedly a degree to which regional proximity to a historically dominant trading and investment partner underpins the success of the old NICs and the emerging NICs close by. Most of the successful new export-oriented economies are adjacent to other ones and at least one important already industrialized economy. But although this is necessary, it is not a *sufficient* condition. Other factors such as underlying productivity conditions, political regime strength and stability, adaptability (rather than factor endowments or resources) and a mix of import substitution and export-oriented industrialization are among the most vital ingredients. The economies of East Asia, including the emerging NICs of Southeast Asia, have major advantages with respect to all of these factors. It is interesting to see how the formerly centrally planned economies of eastern Europe are gaining competitive advantage in like manner from their proximity to western Europe and reasonably well-developed infrastructures and well-trained labour forces.

## REGIONAL LINKAGES AND INDUSTRIAL EVOLUTION

It should be emphasized, however, that although the EPZs and the spatial division of labour within East Asia are symptomatic of the importance of 'offshore production' for final markets in the developed countries, it would be mistaken to see peripheral industrialization solely in these terms. For one thing, local markets for electronic components and semiconductor devices have grown rapidly in East Asia over the past few decades. US factories now ship about 27 per cent of their production to consumers in East Asia. This has encouraged the establishment of marketing, sales and after-sales service facilities in the region, especially in Hong Kong and Singapore. These two centres now function as nodes in a global system of producer services located in major world cities. They have also become important global banking and financial centres as a result of their coordinating roles in East Asian manufacturing industry. One factor facilitating this has been the international networks between 'ethnic Chinese' groups (often family or kinship based) in East Asia and North America.

Also of great importance, however, local firms have developed a wide range of industries oriented towards producing final products for export. Beginning in the early 1960s, for example, South Korea pursued an aggressive export-oriented industrial policy. In the early 1960s, familiarity with manufacturing acquired during the earlier import substitution period was used to develop a number of export 'infant industries' by obtaining manufacturing licences, loan capital and imported business 'know-how' (Table 10.5). These were mainly labour-intensive activities. But even with low wages it was not until the late 1960s that productivity and quality were high enough to make these industries, textiles, clothing and footwear, internationally competitive. The South Korean government subsidized this process by using currency depreciations to boost exports, making tax concessions and providing cheap loans.

During a second stage, 1967–71, other 'infant' industries were encouraged as the initial group achieved international competitiveness. These were more technologically advanced industries such as electronic assembly and shipbuilding. In shipbuilding, production went from 25,000 gross tons in 1970 to 996,000 gross tons in 1975; the ships built were also increasingly large and simple (such as supertankers and bulk carriers) with greater potential for automated production. By 1976 the Korean shipbuilding industry was globally competitive.

**Table 10.5** Stages in South Korea's export-oriented industrial development

| | 1962–71 Industrial takeoff | | 1972–81 Heavy/chemical industry drive | | 1982–present Technology-intensive industry drive | |
|---|---|---|---|---|---|---|
| | 1962–66 | 1967–71 | 1972–76 | 1977–81 | 1982–91 | 1992–present |
| *Infant industries* | Textiles<br>Clothing<br>Footwear | Electronic assemblies<br>Shipbuilding<br>Steel<br>Chemicals (fertilizers) | Motor vehicle assembly<br>Consumer electronics<br>Special steels<br>Precision goods (watches, cameras)<br>Turnkey plant building<br>Metal products | Automotive components<br>Machine tools<br>Machinery assembly<br>Simple instruments<br>Heavy electrical machinery assembly | Semiconductors<br>Precision machinery | Microelectronics<br>Bioengineering<br>Aerospace<br>Optics<br>Chemicals (fine)<br>New materials<br>Robotics |
| *Industries becoming competitive* | | Textiles<br>Clothing<br>Footwear | Electronic assemblies<br>Shipbuilding<br>Steel<br>Chemical (fertilizers) | Motor vehicle assembly<br>Consumer electronics<br>Special steels<br>Precision goods<br>Turnkey plant building<br>Metal products | Automotive components<br>Machine tools<br>Machinery assembly<br>Simple instruments<br>Heavy electrical machinery assembly | Semiconductors<br>Precision machinery |
| *Self-sustaining industries* | | | Textiles<br>Clothing<br>Footwear | Electronic assemblies<br>Shipbuilding<br>Steel<br>Chemicals (fertilizers)<br><br>Textiles<br>Clothing<br>Footwear | Motor vehicle assembly<br>Consumer electronics<br>Special steels<br>Precision goods<br>Turnkey plant building<br>Metal products<br><br>Electronic assemblies<br>Shipbuilding<br>Steel<br>Chemicals (fertilizers)<br><br>Textiles<br>Clothing<br>Footwear | Automotive components<br>Machine tools<br>Machinery assembly<br>Simple instruments<br>Heavy electrical machinery assembly<br>Motor vehicle assembly<br>Consumer electronics<br>Special steels<br>Precision goods<br>Turnkey plant building<br>Metal products<br>Electronic assemblies<br>Shipbuilding<br>Steel<br>Chemicals (fertilizers)<br><br>Textiles<br>Clothing<br>Footwear |

*Source:* Linge and Hamilton (1981: 33, Table 1.9; Kai-Sun et al. (2001, Chapter 3)

In the early 1970s a third 'wave' of industries was in the process of creation including motor vehicle assembly and consumer electronics. For instance, the automobile industry, which began in South Korea in 1967, produced 83,000 units by 1977 (and 3.5 million units by 1985). By the early 1980s, therefore, South Korea had acquired a wide range of internationally competitive and self-sustaining industries. And, despite the increasing technological sophistication of each wave of innovation, considerable emphasis was still placed on the original labour-intensive industries; although some of these were increasingly decentralized to other Asian locations. The South Korean policy of widening its manufacturing base is the most successful model of the kind of development policy being pursued by all the NICs. The country's 'technology-intensive' industry drive since the early 1980s has been toward more high value industries, including semiconductors, bioengineering, aerospace and even robotics (Table 10.5). Peripheral industrialization, therefore, is not just the offshore processing or assembly work for TNCs that a single-minded focus on EPZs would imply.

## AGGLOMERATION AND NEW INDUSTRIAL COMPLEXES

Peripheral industrialization is organized at the intra-national and urban levels as well. Coastal and metropolitan areas have been favoured locations, because of infrastructural advantages and ease of external access. Even in countries with little export-oriented industry this pattern is evident. In Nigeria, for example, and despite the transfer of the federal capital in 1991 to the more centrally located Abuja, well over 50 per cent of the country's industrial employment remains concentrated in Lagos and five other coastal states. In East Asia and Latin America much of the new manufacturing industry of the past 30 years is found in the major metropolitan areas. Both foreign and indigenous investment tends to be attracted by the amenities, basic infrastructure and political access characteristic of the larger urban areas (see the section headed 'Production networks and regional motors' in Chapter 3 for why this is the case). When urban growth is already concentrated in a primate city, such as Bangkok in Thailand, recent growth has tended to reinforce its primacy. This seems to be especially true of foreign direct investment.

The case of Japanese direct investment in East Asia is illustrative. It has been highly concentrated in the national capitals and their immediate vicinity. This is the case whether investment is measured by number of firms, employment or capital, although capital concentration is most pronounced. The Japanese electronics industry has had three major manufacturing agglomerations in East Asia (Figure 10.6): (1) Singapore and vicinity, including nearby Johor Bahru in Malaysia and Batam Island in Indonesia; there is also significant Japanese investment along the Singapore–Malaysia corridor, which links agglomerations in Malaysia from Kuala Lumpur as far north as Penang; (2) Taipei and vicinity, including Hsinchu Industrial Park and western corridor cities running from Taichung to Kaohsiung; and (3) Hong Kong and vicinity, including major concentrations in Guangdong Province such as Shenzhen, stretching northwards along the east coast of China to South Korea (Aoyama, 2000). More recently, locations in China have been the overwhelming beneficiaries of Japanese companies moving production facilities from relative higher cost to lower cost sites, presumably still within the hinterlands of major metropolitan areas (Table 10.6).

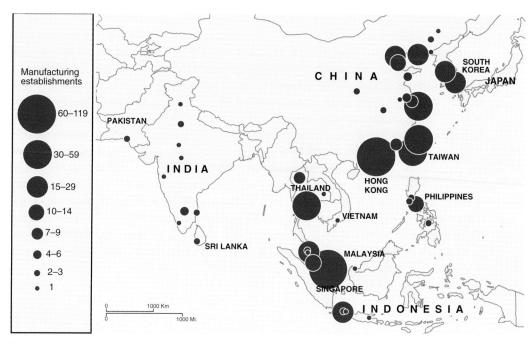

Fig 10.6: Manufacturing establishments of the Japanese electronics industry in Asia, 1995
*Source:* Aoyama (2000: 228, Figure 2)

Table 10.6 Relocation of electronics production by Japanese companies in East Asia, 1999–2003

| Country of divestment | Country of relocation | | | | | | Total |
|---|---|---|---|---|---|---|---|
| | China | Thailand | Malaysia | Indonesia | Vietnam | Japan | |
| Malaysia | 4 | 1 | | | | | 5 |
| Taiwan | 3 | 1 | | | 1 | | 5 |
| Singapore | 3 | | | 2 | | | 5 |
| Thailand | 3 | | | | | | 3 |
| Philippines | 2 | | | | | | 2 |
| South Korea | 1 | 1 | | | | | 2 |
| Indonesia | | | 2 | | | | 2 |
| China | | | | | | 1 | 1 |
| Total | 16 | 3 | 2 | 2 | 1 | 1 | 25 |

*Source:* Based on Belderbos and Zou (2006: 19, Table 10)

In a number of urban areas there are also incipient industrial complexes redolent of Silicon Valley in California and other high-technology complexes in developed countries (also see Chapters 2, 3 and 7). They are made up of both foreign-owned (US, European and Japanese) and locally owned assembly plants, and a surrounding constellation of linked activities. Hong Kong, Manila, Seoul, Singapore, Penang (see Figure 10.5) and Taipei all have such complexes. Scott (1987) used the Manila case to illustrate how a complex can arise in an initial context of low general economic development. The Manila complex originally consisted of a core of nine major US-owned semiconductor branch plants. These were served by 14 locally owned subcontract assembly houses and three specialized capital-intensive 'test and burn' facilities; there were also a number of specialized tool and die, and metal shops. Some of these were 'captive' to or totally dependent on the US-owned assembly plants but most were independent, local operations. Today, an increasing number of US firms are locating engineering and manufacturing design, call centres, back-office operations, outsourcing centres and software development in the three information technology (IT) zones in Manila (Eastwood City, Fort Bonifacio and Filinvest). The US and Philippine companies cluster together to minimize transactional costs and gain joint access to Manila International Airport. They are also at the centre of a metropolitan labour market, which provides production workers who have considerable experience with the norms and rhythms of assembly work, and a pool of technicians and engineers with the necessary skills.

Attempts have been made in many LDCs to decentralize manufacturing activities to regional growth poles (see Chapter 7 for a discussion of the models of regional change on which these ideas are based). For example, beginning in 1967 the government of Indonesia established a set of tax incentives for 'priority sectors' that were to be located in 11 industrial zones. The idea was to decentralize suitable industries away from the island of Java in general and the political capital of Jakarta in particular. The policy has failed. At a time when Indonesia's MVA growth rate was the highest in the world (1973–81) – 14.6 per cent per annum – more than half of both domestic and foreign investment was in Java (56.8 per cent of foreign and 64.6 per cent of domestic investment). Only resource-based industries have pulled some investment away from the centre even in the presence of significant tax incentives. Similar failures have been reported from Latin America, Africa and other parts of Asia.

The possibility of industrialization throughout the periphery under present global conditions is limited. The process of industrial growth is not a linear diffusion process spreading throughout the globe. Indeed, there are a number of cases not only of a lack of any growth at all (largely, but not entirely, in Sun-Saharan Africa) but also of stagnation and even (as in Argentina) of deindustrialization. The causes of stagnation are numerous: for example, the migration of labour from Yemen to the oil-rich states of the Persian Gulf; the civil war during the late 1970s in Nicaragua; the pursuit of extreme 'free market' monetarist policies by governments in Argentina. Consistent industrialization in the face of global downturns and increasingly competitive world markets seems to require at a minimum, in Petras's (1984: 199) words: 'a cohesive industrializing class linked to a coherent policy, promoting an internal market and selective insertion in the international market'.

## 10.4 RISE AND FALL OF THE SOVIET MODEL OF INDUSTRIALIZATION

The experience of the former Soviet Union and its eastern European satellites provides a very different model of industrial development (although in terms of spatial organization, the differences between them and capitalist industrial countries were fewer than might be expected) that was influential throughout the world, particularly in poorer countries, from the 1940s until the 1980s. It should be emphasized at the outset that the economies of the former Soviet Union and its satellites were *not* based on a true socialist or communist mode of production in which the working class had democratic control over the processes of production, distribution and development. Rather, they seem to have evolved as something of a hybrid, in which a bureaucratic class used state power to exploit workers and to compete for power and economic advantage in the world economy. Social objectives aside, their experience can be interpreted as the pragmatic response of latecomers whose leadership felt they could only industrialize by disengaging from their semi-peripheral role in the world economy in order to pursue modernization and economic development through highly centralized and rigidly enforced government direction.

Eventually, the constraints imposed by excessive state control, the inherent disadvantages that resulted from (1) the absence of entrepreneurship and competition and (2) the dissent that resulted from the lack of democracy, combined to bring the experiment to a sudden halt (in 1990). By then, parts of the Soviet world empire had been able to achieve a relatively advanced stage of industrial development; but none of the survivors of the experiment, including Russia, has achieved better than semi-peripheral status in the world economy.

## REVOLUTIONARY ECONOMIC REORGANIZATION

Since the time of Peter the Great (around 1700), Tsarist Russia had been attempting to modernize. By 1861, when Alexander II decreed the abolition of serfdom, Russia had built up an internal core with a large bureaucracy, a substantial intelligentsia and a sizeable group of skilled workers. The abolition of feudal serfdom was designed to accelerate the industrialization of the economy by compelling the peasantry to raise crops on a commercial basis, the idea being that the profits from exporting grain would be used to import foreign technology and machinery. In many ways, the strategy seems to have been successful: grain exports increased fivefold between 1860 and 1900, while manufacturing activity expanded rapidly. Further reforms, in 1906, helped to establish large, consolidated farms in place of some of the many small-scale peasant holdings. But the consequent flood of dispossessed peasants to the cities created acute problems as housing conditions deteriorated and labour markets became flooded.

These problems, to which the tsar remained indifferent despite the petitions of desperate municipal governments, nourished deep discontent, which eventually, aggravated by military defeats and the sufferings of the First World War, spawned the revolutionary changes of 1917. It was not the peasantry or the oppressed provincial industrial proletariat, however, which emerged from the chaos to take control. It was the Bolsheviks, a radical element drawn largely from the professional and middle classes, whose orientation from the beginning favoured a strategy of economic development in which the intelligentsia and skilled industrial workers would play the key roles.

In the first instance, however, the ravages of war and the upheavals of revolution precluded the possibility of planned economic reorganization of any kind. Thus the centralization of control over production and the nationalization of industry resulted as much from the need for national and political survival as from ideological beliefs. Similarly, it was rampant inflation that led to the virtual abolition of money, not revolutionary purism. By 1920 industrial production was still only 20 per cent of the prewar level, crop yields were only 44 per cent of the prewar level and national income per capita stood at less than 40 per cent of the prewar level.

In 1921 the New Economic Policy was introduced in an attempt to catch up. Central control of key industries, foreign trade and banking was codified under *Gosplan*, the central economic planning commission. But in other spheres – and in agriculture in particular – a substantial degree of freedom was restored, with heavy reliance on market mechanisms operated by 'bourgeois specialists' from the old intelligentsia. Improvement in national economic performance was immediate and sustained, with the result that recovery to prewar levels of production was reached in 1926 for agriculture and the following year in the case of industry.

Soon afterwards, however, there occurred a major shift in power within the Soviet Union. This power shift swept aside both the New Economic Policy and its 'bourgeois specialists'. They were replaced by a much more centralized allocation of resources: a command economy operated by a new breed of engineers/managers/ *apparatchiks* drawn from the new intelligentsia that had developed among the membership of the Communist Party. With this shift there also came a more explicit strategy for industrial development. Like Japan, the Soviet Union chose to withdraw from the capitalist world-system as far as possible, relying instead on the capacity of its vast territories to produce the raw materials needed for rapid industrialization. As in Meiji Japan, the capital for creating manufacturing capacity and the required infrastructure and educational improvements was extracted from the agricultural sector. The foundation of Stalin's industrialization drive was the collectivization of agriculture. This involved the compulsory relocation of peasants into state or collective farms, where their labour was expected to produce bigger yields. The state would then purchase the harvest at relatively low prices so that, in effect, the collectivized peasant was to pay for industrialization by 'gifts' of labour.

In the event, the Soviet peasantry was somewhat reluctant to make these gifts, not least because the wages they could earn on collective farms could not be spent on consumer goods or services: Soviet industrialization was overwhelmingly geared towards manufacturing producer goods such as machinery and heavy equipment. It proved very difficult to regiment the peasants. Requisitioning parties and tax inspectors were met with violence, passive resistance and the slaughter of animals. At this juncture Stalin employed police terror to compel the peasantry to comply with the requirements of the Five-Year Plans that provided the framework for his industrialization drive. Severe exploitation required severe repression. Dissidents, along with enemies of the state uncovered by purges of the army, the bureaucracy and the Communist Party, provided convict (*zek*) labour for infrastructural projects. Together, some 10 million people were sentenced to serve in the *zek* workforce, to be imprisoned or to be shot. The barbarization of Soviet society was the price paid for the modernization of the Soviet economy.

## ECONOMIC AND TERRITORIAL EXPANSION UNDER STATE SOCIALISM

The Soviet economy did modernize, however. Between 1928 and 1940 the rate of industrial growth increased steadily, reaching levels of over 10 per cent per annum in the late 1930s: rates that had never before been achieved and that have been equalled since only by Japan and China. The annual production of steel had increased from

4.3 million tons to 18.3 million tons; coal production had increased nearly five times; and the annual production of metal-cutting machine tools had increased from 2000 to 58,400. In short: 'An Industrial Revolution in the Western sense had been passed through in one decade' (Pollard, 1981: 299). When the Germans attacked the Soviet Union in 1941 they took on an economy that, in absolute terms (although not per capita), had output figures comparable with their own.

The Second World War cost the Soviet Union 25 million lives, the devastation of 1700 towns and cities and 84,000 villages and the loss of more than 60 per cent of all industrial installations. In the aftermath, the Soviet Union gave first priority to national security. The *cordon sanitaire* of independent east European countries that had been set up by the western allies after the First World War was appropriated as a buffer zone by the Soviet Union. Because this buffer zone happened to be relatively well developed and populous it also provided the basis of a Soviet world empire as an alternative to the capitalist world economy, thus providing economic as well as military security.

However, the Soviet Union felt vulnerable to the growing influence and participation of the United States in world economic and political affairs, and Stalin felt compelled, in 1947, to intervene in eastern Europe. In addition to the installation of the 'Iron Curtain', which severed most economic linkages with the west, this intervention resulted in the complete nationalization of the means of production, the collectivization of agriculture, and the imposition of rigid social and economic controls. The Communist Council for Mutual Economic Assistance (CMEA or COMECON) was also established to reorganize the eastern European economies in the Stalinist mould – even to the point of striving for autarky for individual members, each pursuing independent, centralized plans. This proved unsuccessful, however, and in 1958 COMECON was reorganized by Stalin's successor, Khrushchev. The goal of autarky was abandoned, mutual trade among the Soviet bloc was fostered and some trade with western Europe was permitted.

Meanwhile, the whole Soviet bloc gave high priority to industrialization. Between 1950 and 1955 output in the Soviet Union grew at nearly 10 per cent per annum, although it subsequently fell away to more modest levels until the fall of communism. The experience of the east European countries varied considerably, but, in general, rates of industrial growth were high during the Soviet era. Equally important was the structural transformation of industry, for although producer goods remained dominant, the economic base of all Soviet bloc countries expanded to the point where per capita consumption of food, clothing and other consumer goods came to be much closer to that of the capitalist core countries than to that of the peripheral and semi-peripheral countries of the capitalist world economy.

## ECONOMIC GEOGRAPHY OF STATE SOCIALISM

As in western Europe, North America and Japan, industrialization brought about radical changes in the economic landscapes of the Soviet Union and eastern Europe. But did the state socialism, or statism, that guided Soviet bloc industrialization result in qualitatively different economic landscapes? At face value, there were sound reasons for anticipating substantial differences. Central planning and control of economic development meant that ideological objectives could be translated into administrative fiat, while the absence of a competitive market eliminated risk and uncertainty, precluded the influence of powerful monopolies and facilitated the rapid dissemination of technological innovations.

In practice, however, spatial organization within the Soviet bloc did not exhibit any real distinctive dimension. As in the industrial core regions of the west and Japan, the industrial landscape came to be dominated by the localization of manufacturing activity, by regional specialization, by core–periphery contrasts in levels of economic development and by agglomeration and functional differentiation within the urban system. The reasons for this were several:

1 At the most fundamental level was the unevenness of natural resources and the consequent unevenness of population and economic development inherited from the pre-socialist era.
2 The principles of rationality and the primacy of *national* economic growth took precedence over ideological principles of spatial equality. As a result, Soviet planners applied the logic of agglomeration economies, developing *territorial production complexes*: planned groupings of industries designed to exploit local energy resources and environmental conditions. As developed by the Tenth Five-Year Plan (1976–80), these territorial production complexes were broadly defined, designed to foster broad-scale agglomeration economies among specialized sub-regional territorial production complexes.
3 The extensive bureaucracy required by command economies meant that a pronounced 'control hierarchy' developed:

> Central places in the spatial control hierarchy will have disproportionate numbers of high-level business and party posts. This, along with the tendency for the world of culture, the arts and education to concentrate spatially, will create local élites, as in Moscow, enjoying living standards substantially better than those of the mass of people.
>
> D. Smith (1979: 341–2)

Conversely, places at the lower end of the control hierarchy offered limited occupational opportunities and limited access to upper level jobs.

4 Centralized economic planning was unable to redress unwanted spatial disparities because large parts of the system came to be characterized by inertia, insensitivity, conservatism and compartmentalization. As a result, resource allocation was strongly conditioned by *incrementalism*, whereby those places already well endowed by past allocations got proportionally large shares of each successive round of budgeting.
5 Places and regions that were able to establish an initial advantage (by proximity to market or raw materials, for instance) were generally able to maintain a significant competitive advantage over other regions. Turnock, reviewing the outcomes of 'socialist' location principles, observed that: 'Despite oft-repeated assertions forecasting the impending elimination of backward regions, through appropriate allocations of investment under the system of central planning, growth rates continue to show wide spatial disparities' (1984: 316).

We can briefly illustrate both the extent of the resultant unevenness in economic development and the degree to which the economic landscapes of industrial socialism, like those of industrial capitalism, were dominated by core–periphery contrasts.

Within the former Soviet Union, the major contrast was always between, on the one hand, the richly endowed, relatively densely peopled, highly urbanized core of the manufacturing belt that stretches across Russia from St Petersburg (formerly Leningrad) in the north and eastern Ukraine in the south, through the Moscow and Volga regions to the Urals and, on the other hand, the rest of the country. Within the latter there are vast reaches where physical isolation and harsh environmental considerations have prevented all but a veneer of modern economic development and where tribal folk still pursue local subsistence economies. Much of the rest of what was Soviet Central Asia and the southern portion of Kazakhstan also lagged well behind in terms of economic development, largely because of the fundamental problem of physical isolation. In addition, however, there were parts of the European portion of the former Soviet Union that remained some way behind the levels of development achieved in the centre. These included Belorussia, eastern Latvia, Lithuania and western Ukraine – regions with large rural populations that were systematically excluded from Stalin's industrialization drive.

Such inequalities eventually contributed to the vulnerability of the Soviet system as an alternative model of economic development. The critical economic failure, however, was state socialism's inflexibility and its consequent inability to take advantage of the new technology system that was developing among capitalist core countries: 'Soviet statism failed in its attempt … to a large extent because of the incapacity of statism to assimilate and use the principles of informationalism embodied in new information technologies' (Castells, 2000: 13).

The dramatic failure of state socialism led to a period of radical change in the geography of the former Soviet Union with many of the constituent republics breaking away to form separate states. The former states of Yugoslavia and Czechoslovakia have been broken up into smaller entities; East Germany has been absorbed into Germany; and many eastern European countries (including Hungary, Poland, the Czech Republic and the Baltic States) have been drawn rapidly into the European Union's sphere of influence.

Russia, meanwhile, has had to reconstitute its economic geography through a chaotic transition towards a market economy. In the process, all local and regional economies have been disrupted, leaving many Russian people to survive through a semi-formal 'kiosk economy'. Many accounts suggest that criminal business has flourished amid the chaos of Russia's transition, with one estimate putting the share of the country's GDP generated by organized crime at nearly 15 per cent.

After well over a decade of transition and preoccupation with such pressing economic issues, Russia and the rest of the former Soviet Union have yet to address adequately the legacy of environmental degradation and health problems created by Soviet bloc industrialization (although the countries of eastern Europe, in particular, have benefited from European Union (EU) funding for environmental planning and remediation). In Russia, government funds for social and environmental programmes have been limited as overall GDP fell dramatically: by 29 per cent in 1992 and a further 13 and 13.5 per cent each in 1993 and 1994, 4.2 per cent in 1995 and 3.5 per cent in 1996. After a slight recovery (0.9 per cent) in 1997 GDP fell again (by 5 per cent) in 1998 (at a time when Russia devalued the rouble and defaulted on its IMF loan), before recovering to 5.4 per cent in 1999 and 8.3 per cent in 2000, due partly to the rise in the price of oil and gas, Russia's two main exports. Material production fell, as industrial production declined 9.6 per cent throughout the 1990s.

Foreign capital has flowed into Russia, but it has been targeted mainly at the fuel and energy sector, natural resources and raw materials (which in 2000 accounted for more than two-thirds of Russia's total exports) rather than manufacturing industry. By January 2001 companies from the USA, the leading foreign direct investor into Russia, had invested $5.49 billion in the fuel, transportation, engineering and communications sectors. As a result, Russia became increasingly dependent on oil and gas reserves in Siberia and further east (including off the coast of Sakhalin Island in the Pacific and along the Arctic Ocean coast), which together accounted for more than two-thirds of Russian exports by 2005. Industry is now almost entirely concentrated in European Russia and low levels of investment in manufacturing because of more attractive outlets in resources and foreign markets mean that the costly forced industrialization of the Soviet Union is now leading to a slow deindustrialization and increased interregional income inequalities with state employment as the only growth factor in many parts of contemporary Russia.

## 10.5 CHINA'S RISE IN THE WORLD ECONOMY

China is the economic development success story of the last few decades. With the largest population of any country in the world, 1.3 billion, China had a growth in GDP that averaged about 10 per cent each year during the 1980s and 1990s respectively (against a 3.5 per cent average for all LDCs during each of these decades). In the 1980s and 1990s China's rates of growth in GDP, agriculture, industry, manufacturing and services were among the highest in the world. The average annual rate of growth in manufacturing was particularly impressive. Only South Korea, Indonesia and Thailand had growth rates similar to China's 10.4 per cent between 1980 and 1990. But these countries did not come close to matching China's 13.9 per cent growth in manufacturing between 1990 and 1999. As a result, by 1994, China was already a little more advanced than South Korea had been in 1970 in terms of output per capita of some basic industrial products such as electricity, steel, cement, cotton fabrics and cotton yarn. China, with one-fifth of the world's population, is now only a generation behind the older NICs of East Asia in conventional indicators of economic development. As measured by GDP, China already has the world's fourth largest national economy, after the USA, Japan and Germany; almost 20 per cent that of the USA.

Much of the growth of manufacturing has been concentrated in coastal China, especially in the zones around Shanghai and Hong Kong that have been opened to foreign investment (Figure 10.7). Originally 'experimental', as the communist leadership in Beijing worked out a new model for maintaining political control over China while trying to absorb foreign capital, technology and management practices, the special economic zones (SEZs), such as Shenzhen in Guangdong Province on the border with Hong Kong, have become the nodal points for reforming the Chinese economy as a whole. Under the leadership of Den Xiaoping from 1978, China embarked on a thoroughgoing reorientation of its economy away from the autarchic China of the 1960s when agriculture and national economic self-sufficiency were the priorities. The new model involved privatizing collective farms, closing or privatizing parts of state industry, dismantling central planning in favour of private entrepreneurship and market mechanisms, and fully integrating China into the world economy. Economic growth has been elevated above the class struggle.

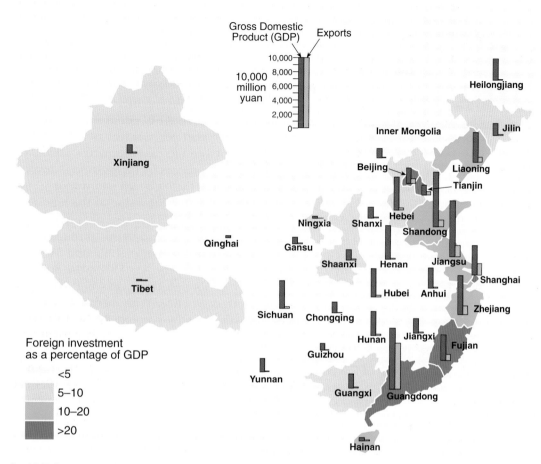

Fig 10.7: Geography of GDP growth, foreign investment and exports in China
*Source:* China Data Center, University of Michigan, China Map Library (Figure a 140 (2000))

Some 68 per cent of Chinese, 857 million people in 2001, still live on the land. The first economic reforms concentrated on privatizing peasant agriculture, taking a leaf out of the book of their East Asian neighbours in privileging rural land reform. This increased farm production and rural incomes tremendously, providing capital for industrialization and improvements in infrastructure in some restricted areas. 'World standards' were brought to bear on the economy through the establishment of SEZs to attract foreign technology and management. The dramatic success of Guangdong Province in southern China transfixed managers and bureaucrats elsewhere. In 1979, three of the original four SEZs in China were established in Guangdong (with the fourth in Fujian Province across the strait from Taiwan). These SEZs have attracted capital and expertise from outside, particularly from Hong Kong and Taiwan. Much of the investment is in joint ventures or inter-corporate alliances (such as those referred to in Chapter 3) between foreign firms and local enterprises operated by local governments and cooperatives. But throughout China the industrial structure increasingly resembles that of its East Asian neighbours rather than its former 'ideological friends' in eastern Europe and the former Soviet Union; Chinese manufacturing output is now dominated by a large number of small firms with mixed state and private (often foreign) participation rather than giant state companies as in the past.

Guangdong represents the most obvious example of industrial transformation. The province's industrial output during the 1980s, largely of goods such as clothes, shoes, electrical appliances and toys, rose 15 per cent per year (for an example, see Box 1.3 on Barbie). Industrial output continued to increase during the 1990s, by 16 per cent annually. The promotion of high-tech sectors by the provincial government translated into an increase in output value of the high-tech industry of 50 per cent each year during the 1990s. In 1999 the production value of the high-tech sector reached around US$25.6 billion, representing 13.9 per cent of Guangdong's industrial output. Total exports from the province, funnelled mostly through Hong Kong, accounted for 77.8 per cent of Guangdong's output in 1999 and 36.9 per cent of China's exports by 2000. During each year of the late 1990s, the province chalked up over US$100 billion annually in foreign trade, making it the top province in China as measured by foreign trade volume. With more than 86 million people, Guangdong experienced a growth in GDP of around 12.5 per cent per year in the 1980s and more than 9 per cent in the 1990s. For comparison, Thailand (population 61 million), a frequently cited example of an 'emerging' NIC, had a GDP growth of 7.6 per cent during the 1980s and 4.7 per cent in the 1990s.

From one point of view, this and similar development in coastal China represent the reintegration of Hong Kong and Taiwan with their continental hinterlands after a long period of separation. Low labour and land costs allied to high labour productivity have been major attractions. China's high export quotas to the EU and the USA have also been important. But more than 'pure' economics has been at work. The surge of investment has been led by ethnic Chinese within networks that stretch from south and east China all over Southeast Asia and around the 'Pacific Rim'. Common languages – Cantonese for Hong Kong and Guangdong, the Fujianese dialect for Taiwan and the closest provinces on the mainland – and a common culture eased the flow of money, managers and trade. Taiwan and China are officially still on a war footing, Taiwan being the refuge for the nationalist government after the communist revolution in 1949 and all economic relations are carried on through Hong Kong. But in 1992 China displaced Malaysia to become the biggest single destination for Taiwanese foreign direct investment. With the 'spillover' of investment and trade to the mainland, China is following economically where Taiwan led. And in 2001, under mounting pressure, the Taiwan government rescinded its 52-year-old ban on direct trade and investment with the mainland.

The euphoria engendered by the recent economic transformation of coastal China should be tempered somewhat by recognizing a number of serious barriers to the continuation of present trends. One is the poor condition of the transport infrastructure, particularly the railways in the interior: China has one of the world's smallest railway networks relative to population and arable land. The development along the south and east coasts, while supported by central government as a growth pole policy, has created significant and still growing disparities in growth and incomes between coastal and interior regions as the advantaged regions build up their external links. This spatial polarization has already generated internal political conflict. The millions of rural workers who migrated to coastal cities to find a job and a better standard of living have added to the growth pressures in these localities. Regional 'resource wars' have erupted when some regions implemented questionable administrative and other measures in an effort to restrict interregional resource flows. Central and local government bargaining over development policies and resource allocations have become particularly heated when some disadvantaged areas felt they were receiving less favourable treatment by central government. As a result, reducing regional inequality, which is seen as a threat to China's future prosperity, stability and unity, has been propelled to the top of the central government's policy priorities. Be that as it may, poverty in China remains a major problem, with at least 10 per cent of the population living below the national poverty line. This is estimated to be around 127 million people. Their condition contrasts markedly with that of those who have cashed in on the opening up of the Chinese economy (Figure 10.7).

A second problem is the continuing drain on central government revenues of state-owned firms. In particular, coal and oil companies are important loss makers because of government insistence on subsidized energy prices. Third, local governments have acquired considerable autonomy in pushing credit expansion and investment. This has led to an overheating of the national economy as expanding credit chases a shrinking money supply controlled from the centre. Fourth, for all of the success in creating a private economy there is still a level of government regulation without a guaranteed rule of law, which makes for an arbitrary application of rules and encourages corruption among civil servants.

At the root of many of these problems is the lack of political change paralleling the economic change. Unlike the countries of eastern Europe and the former Soviet Union, which have undergone political change prior to economic reform, China has created an increasingly capitalist economy within a still formally socialist state. The consensus view among professional 'China watchers' is that the Chinese Communist Party is now largely irrelevant to economic life and, as the revolt of the movement for greater political democracy that was violently suppressed in Tiananmen Square in Beijing in 1989 showed, its monopoly of state power is unacceptable to many. As one commentator expressed it: 'Communism in China will probably end not with a bang but a whimper' (MacFarquhar, 1992: 28). The capitalist genie unleashed in 1978 is probably too well established now to put back in the lamp of communist autarky.

Internal political conflicts aside, China's rapid economic growth has produced a degree of political hysteria in some other countries, not least in the United States. Yet, access to China's presumably gargantuan market has long been the prize most celebrated in the US idea of a 'Pacific Century'. Now, however, the emergence of China as a major supplier of consumer goods to the USA, the huge build-up of US dollar reserves by the Chinese Central Bank and the presumed base its high rate of economic growth will give China in the political–military competition of Great Power politics have conspired to produce an increasing sense of threat in some quarters. The bilateral trade deficit between the USA and China attracts particular hostility when, in fact, much of this reflects calculations that ignore the complexity of contemporary production chains and the imbalance between currencies, which, in turn, reflects high Chinese savings and considerable American profligacy or consumer spending beyond available incomes. At the same time, China is seriously overrated as both an economic and a political challenge. At least during the Cold

War, China was a 'beacon for many in the developing world. China now is a beacon for no one, and, indeed, an ally to no one. No other supposedly great power is as bereft of friends' (Segal, 1999: 25). China's reliance on US export markets, the close linkage of the Chinese currency, the yuan, to the US dollar, and the heavy dependence of Chinese economic growth on foreign investment now all limit its external leverage. US critics of China's rise should rest more easily.

## Box 10.1  Dreaming the BRIC future

In 2003 economists at the US investment bank, Goldman Sachs, predicted that over the next 50 years, Brazil, Russia, India and China – what they termed the BRIC economies – could become a major force in the world economy, primarily as manufacturing centres (particularly in the case of China and India) but also as major resource economies (particularly in the case of Russia and Brazil). Using a variety of economic indicators, the Goldman Sachs economists projected GDP growth and incomes per capita for the BRICs to 2050. Although incomes are likely to be lower than the average for individuals in the G6 industrialized countries (the USA, Japan, Germany, France, UK and Italy), GDP growth rates would be much higher so that by 2050 the BRIC economies together would be larger than the G6 (see Table 10.7). The shift from the G6 to the BRICs is most dramatic in the first 30 years with only India expected to grow much above 3 per cent per year in the last decade. Relative growth in the size and skills of labour forces as well as the overall competitive advantage of the BRIC economies in crucial sectors are the motors driving this vision of the future. The major overall assumption is that the BRICs must at least maintain their present levels of openness to the world economy and follow development policies that privilege their respective competitive advantages, such as Russia in natural gas, Brazil in agribusiness and certain manufacturing sectors, India in manufacturing and producer services and China in manufacturing. Of course, declining populations (particularly as dramatic as that in Russia), slower growth in the economies to which exports would be directed (such as the USA and Japan), and persistent problems such as massive underinvestment in road and other public infrastructure in India, rapidly increasing income inequalities between regions as in China and Brazil, massive corruption (in all countries) and the lack of symmetry between the shifts in the location of basic economic activities and the persistent dominance of the G6 countries (particularly the USA) in financial and monetary matters will limit the possibilities for a smooth transition to a truly new world economic order in which the core expands spectacularly to include the BRICs.

Table 10.7 The BRIC road to economic growth

| | BRICs | | | | G6 | | | | | | BRICs | G6 |
|---|---|---|---|---|---|---|---|---|---|---|---|---|
| | Brazil | China | India | Russia | France | Germany | Italy | Japan | UK | US | BRICs | G6 |
| **Projected US$ GDP** | | | | | | | | | | | | |
| 2000 | 762 | 1078 | 469 | 391 | 1,311 | 1,875 | 1,078 | 4,176 | 1,437 | 9,825 | 2,700 | 19,702 |
| 2010 | 668 | 2,998 | 929 | 847 | 1,622 | 2,212 | 1,337 | 4,601 | 1,876 | 13,271 | 5,441 | 24,919 |
| 2020 | 1,333 | 7,070 | 2,104 | 1,741 | 1,930 | 2,524 | 1,553 | 5,221 | 2,285 | 16,415 | 12,248 | 29,928 |
| 2030 | 2,189 | 14,321 | 4,935 | 2,980 | 2,267 | 2,697 | 1,671 | 5,810 | 2,649 | 20,833 | 24,415 | 35,927 |
| 2040 | 3,740 | 26,439 | 12,367 | 4,467 | 2,668 | 3,147 | 1,788 | 6,039 | 3,201 | 27,229 | 47,013 | 44,072 |
| 2050 | 6,074 | 44,453 | 27,803 | 5,870 | 3,148 | 3,603 | 2,061 | 6,673 | 3,782 | 35,165 | 84,201 | 54,433 |
| **Projected US$ per capita** | | | | | | | | | | | | |
| 2000 | 4,338 | 854 | 468 | 2,675 | 22,078 | 22,814 | 1,8677 | 32,960 | 24,142 | 34,797 | | |
| 2010 | 3,417 | 2,233 | 804 | 5,948 | 26,314 | 26,877 | 23,018 | 36,172 | 30,611 | 42,926 | | |
| 2020 | 6,302 | 4,965 | 1,622 | 12,527 | 30,723 | 31,000 | 27,239 | 42,359 | 36,234 | 48,849 | | |
| 2030 | 9,823 | 9,809 | 3,473 | 22,427 | 35,876 | 33,898 | 30,177 | 49,944 | 41,194 | 57,263 | | |
| 2040 | 16,370 | 18,209 | 8,124 | 35,314 | 42,601 | 40,966 | 33,583 | 55,721 | 49,658 | 69,431 | | |
| 2050 | 26,592 | 31,357 | 17,366 | 49,646 | 51,594 | 48,952 | 40,901 | 66,805 | 59,122 | 83,710 | | |

Source: Goldman Sachs (2003: 19–20, Appendix II)

## SUMMARY

According to the World Bank (1983), the aggregate rate of growth of both industrial (mineral resources plus manufacturing) and manufacturing output were over 3 per cent per annum for 34 low-income countries (e.g., Bangladesh, Cambodia and Sierra Leone) and over 6 per cent per annum for 59 middle-income countries (e.g., Mexico, Oman and South Korea) over the period 1960–81. These rates were higher than those for the industrialized countries and, consequently, the share of the LDCs in the world's manufacturing output rose somewhat: from 17.6 per cent in 1960 to 18.9 per cent in 1981. Their combined share of world exports of manufactures rose from 3.9 per cent to 8.2 per cent in the same period. Or, from a slightly different perspective, the LDCs' share of the manufactured imports of all industrial countries rose from 5.3 per cent in 1962 to 13.1 per cent in 1978. At the same time, the share of the GDP of the low-income countries coming from the industrial sector rose from 25 per cent in 1960 to 34 per cent in 1981. For manufacturing the rise was only from 11 to 16 per cent. In the middle-income group the changes were from 30 to 38 per cent for industry, and from 20 to 22 per cent for manufacturing alone. Much of this growth was concentrated in a relatively small group of NICs such as South Korea and Taiwan.

With some notable exceptions to the general trends, including China, the East Asian NICs and some Southeast Asian countries, the growth of manufacturing industry in the periphery and its penetration of DC markets did not deepen much in the 1980s and 1990s, even though it spread somewhat beyond the older NICs. Annual rates of growth in manufacturing averaged 4.9 per cent in the 1980s and 5.8 per cent in the 1990s for all LDCs (7.7 per cent average in the 1980s and 2.7 per cent in the 1990s for the low-income countries, and 4.6 per cent in the 1980s and 6.3 per cent in the 1990s for the middle-income ones). The OECD (major industrialized) countries averaged 3.3 per cent per annum through the decade of the 1980s and 3.6 per cent annually between 1993 and 2002. At the same time the LDCs' share of the manufactured imports into all industrial countries sank to 12.4 per cent in 1999, having fallen from 12.9 per cent in 1990 and 13.1 per cent in 1978.

These figures call into question the generally optimistic conclusion of Warren (1980) and others (see Chapter 8) that a massive industrialization of the periphery is under way. Indeed, this chapter has suggested that there are significant constraints on the industrialization of the periphery and the 1970s provided a time period uniquely favourable to the type of development that did take place. Indeed, even in that time period a number of economies stagnated or deindustrialized (e.g., Argentina). The economic problems of the industrial core have not created inevitable advantages for industrialization in the global periphery. Any advantages have been created there rather than simply given from the outside.

Some of the major conclusions are as follows:

- Industrialization plays a major role in national ideologies of modernization and is seen as a solution to various major practical economic and social problems.
- The spread and intensification of industrialization since the late 1960s coincided with the declining rate of profit in the industrial core.
- Much of the new industrialization is export oriented rather than directed (as in import substitution) to domestic markets.
- There are limits to the development of this industrialization: such as improving profit rates in the industrial core, protectionist measures in export markets,

technological changes that reduce the attractiveness of low-wage locations, incredible debt loads and relatively limited employment effects. Most LDCs are either not industrializing or are industrializing only very slowly.

- Export processing zones (EPZs) represent one geographical form taken by the new international division of labour (NIDL), but 'offshore production' of components or assembly is not the only feature of peripheral industrialization. There are now important industries engaged in the production of locally created final products.

- The new industrialization has favoured existing metropolitan areas and coastal regions. Attempts at decentralization to growth poles have not met with much success.

- The profile of China's industrialization reflects a conscious decision by the Chinese government to re-engage with the world economy after a long period on its margins. As a geographical extension of the existing NICs of East Asia, China represents the main wave of new industrialization in the world economy during the last few decades. This was anything but a global trend. But some commentators suggest that China's rapid growth will soon be followed by that of some other very large peripheral and semi-peripheral economies (the three other BRIC economies) that benefiting from economies of scale also have resources and capacities that could lead to a major shift in the balance of power within the world economy.

## KEY SOURCES AND SUGGESTED READING

Agnew, J.A. 2005. A new 'Pacific Century'? North America and the Pacific Rim, in *The USA and Canada 2005* 7th edn. London: Europa.

Castells, M. 2000. *The Information Age. Economy, Society, Culture, Volume I. The Rise of the Network Society* 2nd edn. Oxford: Blackwell.

Chen, X. 2005. *As Borders Bend: Transnational Spaces on the Pacific Rim*. Lanham, MD: Rowman & Littlefield.

*Economist* 2006. The physical internet: a survey of logistics, 17 June.

Goldman Sachs 2003. Dreaming with the BRICs: the path to 2050, *Global Economics Paper No. 99*. https://www.gs.com

Naughton, B. 2007. *The Chinese Economy: Transitions and Growth*. Cambridge, MA: MIT Press.

UNCTAD 2001. *World Investment Report 2001*. New York: United Nations.

UNIDO 2005. *Industrial Development: Global Report*. New York: United Nations.

Wolf, M. 2006 The answer to Asia's rise is not to retreat from the world, *Financial Times*, 15 March, 15.

Wood, T. 2007. Contours of the Putin era, *New Left Review*, 44, 53–68.

World Bank 2001. *World Development Indicators, 2001*. Washington, DC: World Bank.

World Bank 2006. *World Development Report 2005*. New York: Oxford University Press.

## RELATED WEBSITES

Brazilian Embassy: http://www.brasilemb.org/
the Brazilian embassy's Washington Office website provides a wealth of information on the country, with topics that include the economy, trade, the environment and social issues

Business Information Service for the Newly Independent States (BISNIS): http://www.bisnis.doc.gov/
although sponsored by the US Department of Commerce with the goal of providing US companies with information on the business opportunities in the former Soviet Union, this

website provides a wealth of information for economic geographers who are interested in this region

China Today: http://www.chinatoday.com/
this website provides a variety of information on China related to topics such as culture, history, government, finance, health and education

International Labour Organization: http://www.ilo.org/
this UN agency's website offers research and data on labour issues around the world, such as in the textile, clothing and footwear industries. The ILO also has a separate site devoted to EPZs, available at http://www.ilo.org/public/english/dialogue/govlab/legrel/tc/epz/

United Nations Conference on Trade and Development (UNCTAD): http://www.unctad.org/
offers publications and data on trade, investment and economic development issues as they relate to the LDCs, including the latest edition of the annual *World Investment Report*, which contains information and data on FDI in the LDCs

World Trade Organization: http://www.wto.org/
the WTO's website includes research and documents on international agreements and conferences relating to world trade, including the multifibre arrangement (MFA) and the Agreement on Textiles and Clothing

Chapter 11

# Services: going global?

Picture credit: Wikipedia

oncerns about recent outsourcing have received enormous attention in the media and in political circles in developed countries such as the United States and the United Kingdom. Outsourcing in general, and the outsourcing of services in particular, has provoked a vocal reaction on the part of some politicians, unions, workers and others. While the earlier trend associated with deindustrialization and the outsourcing of traditional manufacturing activities from the developed countries was treated initially with the same negative response, the first reports of service outsourcing were greeted not only with similar concern but also with profound shock. Unfounded as it was, the conventional wisdom had been that the developed countries would exploit their competitive advantage in service activities – impervious as they were to outsourcing – to more than fill any employment void left by outsourced industrial activity.

This misconception can partly be traced back to the 1940s and the Fisher-Clark thesis which suggested a 'three-sector' division of economic activities into agriculture, industry and services (Figure 11.1). This thesis maintained that increasing wealth over time in an economy will be associated with a shift from agriculture to manufacturing and then to service employment because wealthier societies consume more services such as entertainment, education and healthcare. Figure 11.2 shows this positive relationship between levels of per capita income and percentages of workers employed in services. Rich core countries such as Australia, Japan, Norway, the United Kingdom and the United States tend to be concentrated at the 'high' end of the graph while poor peripheral countries like Bangladesh, Vietnam, Cambodia, Uganda and Tanzania are at the 'low' end.

Viewed as non-tradable – needing to be both produced and consumed in the same location – services were seen, therefore, as immune to outsourcing. Certainly, a look back at Figures 7.5 or 7.6 shows the strong and steady growth in service employment in absolute and percentage terms in developed countries such as the United States and the United Kingdom; the percentage of the workforce in service jobs has risen to more than 75 per cent in these countries, with most new jobs

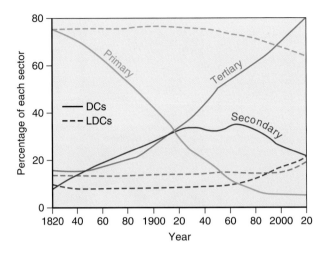

Fig 11.1: Changing share of employment in primary, secondary and tertiary sectors of the economy
*Source:* Adapted from Rubenstein (2005: 301, Figure 9-3)

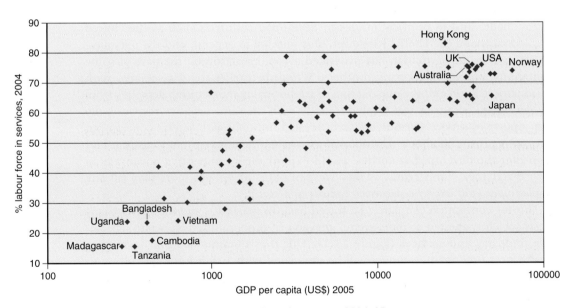

Fig 11.2: Service employment and GDP per capita, selected countries, 2004–05
*Source:* World Bank, online *World Development Indicators 2006*; IMF, World Economic Outlook Online Database 2006

being added in the service sector. Developed countries such as France, Germany, Japan, the United Kingdom and the United States also rank highest in terms of the percentage of the world's total services produced (Figure 11.3).

During the last decade or so, however, advances in information and communications technologies, in association with the profit-seeking strategies of both large and small corporations, have resulted in an increasing amount of services becoming tradable – capable of being outsourced and produced in one location for consump-

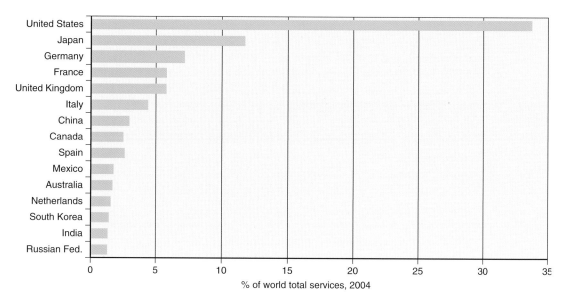

Fig 11.3: The world's largest service providers, 2004

*Source:* World Bank, *World Development Indicators* online 2006

tion in another. In addition, the rather simplistic notion of a straightforward sequential shift from manufacturing to services is no longer valid given such insights as the interdependence of manufacturing and service activities and the experience of LDCs like China where manufacturing and service employment growth has been concurrent rather than sequential.

In this chapter, the shift to services and the contemporary geography of services in both the LDCs *and* DCs, and the interactions between them, are examined in six complementary ways. First, we begin with an attempt to define and theorize services, including the issue of whether the distinction between services and manufacturing is in fact redundant. Second, the national and global stimuli to service growth are described. Third, the benefits and drawbacks of service outsourcing for both the DCs and the LDCs are discussed. Fourth, important national and global constraints on the growth of services faced by certain LDCs are highlighted. Fifth, the geographical pattern of services is surveyed at global, regional and urban scales. Sixth, a variety of services are profiled, including international retailing, tourism, financial services and business services.

## 11.1 DEFINING AND THEORIZING SERVICES

The Fisher-Clark thesis encouraged a tendency to focus on the differences between manufacturing and services. Consequently, services have conventionally been defined negatively, comprising what remains after agriculture, mining and manufacturing are excluded (CRIC, 2006).

Certainly, some differences between manufacturing and services have important implications for the LDCs and the DCs. The manufacturing and service labour markets, for example, differ in a number of ways. Many services – including customer services, entertainment and education – tend to be relatively more labour intensive and less easy to mechanize than manufacturing. Labour-intensive non-tradable services like hotels and restaurants will be more secure from outsourcing than tradable services like call centres or data entry. This has implications also because of the difference in the gender composition of services compared to manufacturing. In the DCs, women, as well as minorities, have historically dominated lower paid 'pink-collar' jobs in the clerical, secretarial, retail, restaurant, teaching and childcare fields. This is also an issue in terms of concerns about the bifurcated nature of the income distribution in services when contrasted with that for manufacturing. Despite the limited evidence for any difference in the wage distribution between services and manufacturing (Stutz and Warf, 2007), the loss of factory jobs in manufacturing, which had allowed a middle-income lifestyle, and the bifurcation between high-skilled high-paying service jobs in producer services like finance or research and development (R&D) versus low-skilled low-paying service jobs in restaurants and hotels have been seen as promoting a polarization of income groups in the DCs.

The distinction between services and manufacturing also has implications for measuring and studying services. For example, should services be measured as a set of industries or a series of occupations? A secretary who works in a factory and one who works in a bank may have similar duties. Categorized by industry, the secretary in the bank would be in services and the one in the factory would be in manufacturing; categorized by occupation, however, both secretaries would be in the service sector.

Although there is no generally agreed on definition, there is general agreement on the major components of the service sector (Bryson *et al.*, 2004: 7). The following seven components of the service sector can also be further categorized into private (marketed) and public (non-marketed) sectors. As a result of the private sector's concern for the profit motive of business operations, the internationalization of services has mostly entailed marketed services (Bagchi-Sen and Sen, 1997):

1 Finance, insurance and real estate (FIRE) including commercial and investment banking, insurance of all kinds (property, medical, casualty), and the residential and commercial real estate business.
2 Business services including legal services, advertising and marketing, public relations, accounting, research and development, personnel training, recruitment, architecture and engineering and consulting.
3 Transportation and communications, including the electronic media, trucking, shipping, railroads, airlines and local transportation (buses, taxis, etc.).
4 Wholesale and retail trade, including major wholesalers who supply major retailers. Eating and drinking establishments, personal services and repair and maintenance businesses are closely affiliated.
5 Entertainment, hotels and motels – part of tourism.
6 Public services at all government levels – only recently viewed as part of the service economy – including public servants, the armed forces, public school teachers, public healthcare professionals and police and fire departments.
7 Nonprofit services, including churches, charities, museums and non-profit healthcare agencies.

The absence of a generally agreed on definition – given that many consumers in the DCs especially use a variety of services in their everyday lives – does not prevent most people from having some idea of what is meant by services. Conventionally, again following the Fisher-Clark thesis, services have been defined – in contrast to tangible manufactured goods – as involving the production and consumption of intangible inputs and outputs. What, for example, is more intangible than the voice of a teacher sharing knowledge or the touch of a doctor carrying out a medical examination on a patient? But the distinction between tangible manufactured goods and intangible services is not clear cut. Many services come with tangible elements – what about the textbook written by the teacher or the injection given by the doctor?

Many manufactured goods provide a service; washing machines wash clothes, microwaves cook food, an automobile provides transportation. There are few manufactured goods which do not involve services in their production; indeed, an increasingly integral part of the manufacturing process depends on services such as research, design and marketing. Similarly, most services depend on manufactured goods; for example, an airline flight requires a reservation and security check at the airport certainly, but making a reservation requires a computer and, since 9/11 especially, the security check requires an increasing amount of machinery to scan travellers and their luggage. The distinction between services and manufacturing has come to be seen increasingly as redundant:

> Neither manufacturing nor services is inherently better than the other; they are inter-dependent. Computers are worthless without software writers; a television has no value without programmes … Before long no one will care whether firms are classified under manufacturing or services. Future prosperity will depend not on how economic activity is labelled, but on economies' ability to innovate and their capacity to adjust.
>
> *Economist* (2005: 82)

Howells' (2003) notion of service encapsulation of goods and materials is useful for understanding how services are increasingly incorporated into manufactured products. Over time, many manufactured products have come to be offered not in their own right to consumers, but in terms of their wider service attributes. This has occurred in two ways. First, the manufactured product can be offered along with closely aligned service products in a single package. Figure 11.4 shows a variety of services that may be sold with a manufactured product over its lifetime, including those involved in purchasing and arranging delivery of the product, maintenance and repair, related support activities and repurchase, disposal or recycling.

Fig 11.4: Service encapsulation

*Source:* Adapted from Howells (2003: 10, Figure 1)

Second, instead of buying a manufactured product in a single one-time purchase, a consumer can buy the service which the manufactured product provides as part of a continuing process involving long-term customer contact through service delivery. In the case of an automobile, for example, a customer can lease a car and use the vehicle without buying it. Another example, from the computer industry, is where, instead of purchasing computers to carry out certain tasks, a company purchases computer services.

Encapsulation is a particularly helpful concept because it illustrates the interdependence between manufacturing and services; each can produce innovations not only in its own sector but also in the other. A manufactured product can generate service innovations. The cranes made by Liebherr, for example, now come with special software programming to better control and run these machines. Similarly, services can promote innovations in manufacturing, for example, through product improvements based on feedback from market research surveys.

Consequently, rather than defining services in terms of what they are not, or even in terms of what they are, a potentially better way to define services would be to ask what is changed by the service and how. Whereas manufacturers change raw materials and energy into products, services physically, spatially or temporally change a person, manufactured product or information. Some services transform people, as when a customer receives a haircut from a hairstylist or an operation in a hospital to remove an appendix. Other services can change manufactured products by repairing them or by transporting them from one location to another. Still other services, such as financial services, transform information, such as the balance in a person's bank account (CRIC, 2006).

## 11.2 NATIONAL AND GLOBAL STIMULI TO THE GROWTH OF SERVICES

Bryson *et al.* (2004: 11–14) suggest six main forces that are driving the growth of services. These forces operate at a number of spatial scales, including national and global, involve a range of contemporary and historical factors and play out differently depending on national and local contexts.

### RISING PER CAPITA INCOMES

Rising incomes in most core and many semi-peripheral countries have contributed to an increase in service employment. Services have a high elasticity of demand – increases in personal income generate a significant increase in domestic demand for services. As per capita income rises, people tend to try to minimize the time they devote to everyday tasks. In core countries, for example, many people who can afford to will pay for services like lawncare or homecleaning; they may also eat in restaurants more frequently instead of cooking at home. The growth of tourism has been fuelled by the consumption of services with a particularly high elasticity of demand, such as transportation, hotels and entertainment.

## GROWING DEMAND FOR HEALTHCARE AND EDUCATIONAL SERVICES

The growth in domestic demand for healthcare and educational services, particularly in core economies, has also contributed to the growth in services. Demographically, the aging of the population in many core economies has meant that demand for healthcare has risen on the part of middle-aged and elderly people who require relatively high levels of medical care. At the same time, factors such as the changing labour market, the need for advanced skills in the workplace and the ability to offer classes via the internet, to name a few, have resulted in greater demand for educational services.

## INCREASINGLY COMPLEX DIVISION OF LABOUR

An increasingly complex division of labour has helped fuel the growth in services in general and producer services in particular. An ever more complicated commercial environment has forced companies to depend on a variety of services, including accountancy, research and development, marketing and advertising, and public relations. High-tech equipment in modern office buildings requires skilled maintenance, repair and security services.

## GROWING SIZE AND ROLE OF THE PUBLIC SECTOR

The growing size and role of the public sector has been a factor in the growth of the service sector. First, despite efforts to curtail government employment through strategies such as privatization, public sector employment has continued to increase; in many countries, public sector employees, from national to local levels, comprise the largest employee group. Second, government laws and regulations have created the need for legal, financial and other experts to assist companies to negotiate the increasingly complex legal environment.

## INCREASING INTERNATIONAL TRADE IN SERVICES

The increase of trade in services among countries has also contributed to the growth in services. Globally, trade in services, including tourism and business services, has grown to about 20 per cent of all international trade (UNCTAD, 2006). The opportunity for further major growth is considerable as more services become tradable (no longer needing to be produced and consumed in the same location).

## RAPID GROWTH IN OUTSOURCING SERVICE FUNCTIONS

The rapid growth in outsourcing service functions from core to semi-peripheral countries by both large and small companies which have exploited advances in information and communications technologies has also led to the growth in services.

## Box 11.1 Bucking the Fisher-Clark thesis in China? Concurrent growth of manufacturing and services

Instead of a straightforward sequential shift from agriculture to manufacturing to services as suggested by the Fisher-Clark thesis, LDCs such as China have seen concurrent rather than sequential manufacturing and service growth. Between 1995 and 2005 industry in China saw an average annual rate of growth of 9.9 per cent; services grew by 9.7 per cent. By 2006, industry as a percentage of GDP had risen to 46.2 per cent (up from 43.1 per cent in 1985); the percentage of GDP in services was 40.7 (up from only 28.5 in 1985). The percentage of the labour force in industry rose to 24 per cent (up from 17 per cent in 1985), while that for services rose from 12 to 31 per cent.

A number of factors are responsible for the dramatic expansion of the service sector in China (Lu et al., 2002; Yang, 2004). First, like the DCs, as per capita incomes have risen in China, domestic demand for services has increased faster than the demand for food and daily necessities. Second, although most research has focused on foreign direct investment (FDI) in manufacturing, a significant amount of foreign capital is being invested in the service sector. Third, Chinese state policies associated with the economic reforms since 1978 have been an important factor in the growth of services. In particular, the large-scale privatization of state-owned enterprises has been a major reason underlying the strong growth in the service sector. Privatization is more straightforward for trade and service companies than for manufacturing ones because there are fewer government restrictions and lower startup costs. Fourth, urban planning in the central parts of larger Chinese cities, which was designed to improve social and environmental conditions, has restricted or removed industry while encouraging services.

The strong growth of China's service sector has led some to speculate that its software-outsourcing industry may soon rival India's. A recent study of China's software industry by the McKinsey Global Institute, however, indicates that it will be many years before China poses a threat to India's dominance. The highly fragmented software industry in China needs to be consolidated in order to achieve the size and expertise needed to win large international projects. The top 10 companies for IT services in China have only about a 20 per cent share of the market; India's top 10 companies have a 45 per cent share. The Chinese companies are too numerous and too small: almost 75 per cent of China's 8000 software service providers have 50 employees or fewer. In contrast, India has fewer than 3000 software service companies, with at least 15 of these having more than 2000 employees. Some of these Indian companies have a global clientele, including Infosys Technologies Inc., Tata Consultancy Services and Wipro Technologies. China also needs to make regulatory and organizational changes to protect the intellectual property of clients.

# 11.3 SERVICE OUTSOURCING: BENEFITS AND DRAWBACKS FOR ALL?

Before discussing the outsourcing of tradable services, it is necessary to decipher the often confusing terminology that is used in the academic and other literature. While it is helpful to differentiate between the terms in order to understand the outsourcing process itself, a look at Table 11.1 reveals the flashpoint for those concerned about the loss of employment in services (or manufacturing) in the DCs. This table captures how the different kinds of outsourcing can all involve work undertaken *abroad* by foreign workers.

**Table 11.1** Deciphering outsourcing terminology

|  | Outsourcing/offshoring | | | |
|  | Where | | How | |
|  | Domestically | Abroad | Affiliated company (internal) | Unaffiliated company (external) |
|---|---|---|---|---|
| Outsourcing | ✓ | ✓ | | ✓ |
| Offshoring | | ✓ | ✓ | ✓ |
| Captive outsourcing | | ✓ | ✓ | |
| Offshore outsourcing | | ✓ | | ✓ |

*Outsourcing* can be done domestically or abroad and always involves work done externally, by an unaffiliated company (Table 11.1). In contrast, *offshoring* is always done abroad, but the work can be done either internally, by an affiliated company, or externally, by an unaffiliated company. *External* outsourcing – where the work is done by unaffiliated companies (including independent foreign subcontractors, as in *offshore outsourcing*) – is common for tradable services which can be standardized easily, such as back-office work. *Internal* outsourcing – where the work is done by foreign affiliates as in *captive outsourcing* – is reserved for situations where strong control of a 'core competency' activity is vital (for example, in research and development), sensitive information is involved, internal interaction is crucial, or a company is attempting to capture savings and other advantages.

While the outsourcing of services is still at a relatively early stage, it is seen as representing the leading edge of changes in global production. UNCTAD (2004) predicts that a 'tipping point' is rapidly approaching that will reflect a shift to a new international division of labour in the production of services. OECD estimates place the total number of jobs that could potentially be affected by domestic or international outsourcing at close to 20 per cent of total employment in DCs such as the United States, Canada, the United Kingdom, Germany and Australia. Despite certain similarities in the outsourcing of both services and manufacturing activities, important differences are expected to fuel an acceleration in service outsourcing.

First, although the service sector is much larger than the manufacturing sector, only about 10 per cent of service output currently enters international trade (compared with more than 50 per cent for manufacturing). This means that there is significant room for growth. Second, the rate of increase in the amount of services that has become tradable, and so capable of being outsourced, has been more rapid for services than for manufacturing. Third, while manufacturing companies have been the ones which have primarily carried out the outsourcing of goods production, companies in all sectors of the economy are outsourcing service functions. Fourth, skill levels are typically higher for outsourced services than for outsourced manufacturing, and as educational and skill levels continue to improve in many LDCs, there will be more opportunities for outsourcing white-collar jobs from the DCs. Fifth, services which are outsourced may be more mobile than outsourced manufacturing activities (because service activities may require lower capital investment, for example in buildings and machinery, compared to manufacturing).

As already mentioned, the outsourcing of services has received enormous – mostly negative – attention in the media and in political circles in many DCs. It is important to consider, however, not only the potential drawbacks but also the potential benefits of service outsourcing for both the DCs and the LDCs. The likely drawbacks for the DCs, including the loss of service sector jobs in particular, have received much more attention than the possible benefits. Yet a number of scholars have pointed out that service outsourcing may allow companies in the DCs to enhance their competitiveness by reducing expenditures and improving quality and delivery – with positive benefits for the companies and their national economies.

In a 2004 article about service outsourcing from DCs like the United States, Uday Karmarker asked whether companies in the service sector in the DCs can survive the outsourcing of service jobs. Karmarker acknowledged that there would be painful job losses for service workers in the DCs, but that the focus should not be on the loss of outsourced service jobs but on the benefits to the global competitiveness of companies in the service sector in the DCs. A 2004 study by the Information Technology Association of America (ITAA) has argued that outsourcing service jobs may ultimately create jobs, boost productivity and lower inflation in the United States. The labour cost savings from outsourcing can allow companies to sell goods more cheaply or at a greater profit, allowing more capital for purchasing equipment, building facilities, and undertaking research and development. In addition, service outsourcing can allow the DCs to restructure toward more productive and higher value activities that generate higher wage jobs. The underlying argument is that the outsourcing of certain service activities and jobs should not be met with cries for protectionist policies in the DCs, but embraced, because outsourcing may contribute to the competitiveness of service sector companies in the DCs by creating a new international division of labour in service production.

Although anxiety about the outsourcing from the DCs is high, the majority of service outsourcing is still currently taking place domestically (UNCTAD, 2004). Only 1–2 per cent of all business process outsourcing (BPO) – such as insurance claims processing, billing services, credit card services, telemarketing and research and development – is done internationally. Most outsourcing is done domestically, with much of the remainder going from the DCs to other DCs. More than half of all export-oriented FDI projects related to call centres, for example, went to other DCs during 2002–03. Ireland and Canada are among the top offshore locations for services. Of the estimated nearly US$40 billion offshore service exports in 2003, India ($12.2 billion), Ireland ($8.6 billion), Canada ($3.8 billion) and Israel ($3.6

billion) accounted for more than 70 per cent of the total market for outsourced services (mostly in software development and other IT-enabled services). The remaining nearly 30 per cent was shared among 'other Asia' ($7.5 billion, of which China accounted for $3.4 billion and the Philippines for $1.7 billion), Latin America ($2.3 billion, of which Mexico accounted for $0.5 billion), eastern Europe ($0.6 billion), Australia ($0.4 billion), Russia ($0.3 billion) and South Africa ($0.1 billion) (Farrell, 2005).

The benefits of service outsourcing for LDCs like India include the creation of higher skill jobs involving better pay, training and transferable skills and associated infrastructure investment that can contribute to further local job growth. The potential drawbacks for some LDCs include the possible relocation of outsourced service activities to other more competitive LDC locations unless worker skills and local infrastructure are continuously upgraded. There are also the perceived negative impacts on culture and tradition of such a rapid increase in employment opportunities for more educated young people, deepening any already entrenched social divisions. Generous salaries by LDC standards are creating a class of western-style consumers. In countries such as India, young, urban women with well-paid back-office jobs are now considering the possibility of a career, rather than the traditional route to financial security of early marriage.

## 11.4 LIMITS TO SERVICE EXPORT GROWTH IN THE SEMI-PERIPHERY AND PERIPHERY?

Not all services *can* be outsourced. Services with a low potential for being outsourced typically include the following features: a strong face-to-face servicing requirement; low information content; a work process not depending on telecommunications and the internet; low wage differentials relative to similar occupations in the DCs; high setup barriers; and significant social networking requirements, including proximity to customers in order to gain a thorough knowledge of markets or a local presence in order to gain an understanding of technical requirements such as legal codes or healthcare regulations.

Consequently, despite the strong forces driving the growth of services, there are significant constraints – related to technology and infrastructure; education and training; government regulations and policies; and corporate strategies – that can limit the growth of services and prevent certain LDCs from capturing some of the service outsourcing market, especially for IT-enabled services.

### TECHNOLOGY AND INFRASTRUCTURE

Technological limitations to the growth of service export growth in some LDCs include the fact that not all data can be converted to digital form for use by computer and made amenable to outsourcing. In addition, as we saw in Chapter 7 when discussing the so-called digital divide, Africa has less than 1 internet host per 1000 inhabitants (compared to a high of 600 internet hosts per 1000 inhabitants in the United States and Canada) (see Table 7.3). In fact, limited infrastructure, such as telecommunications, reliable power sources, and financial services and distribution logistics can limit the growth of export services. While the type of infrastructure needed varies, most IT-enabled services require dependable telecommunications and internet access.

The city of Mumbai and the southern states in India – which have enjoyed the greatest success in attracting outsourced services – have benefited from their proximity to the landing points of two submarine fibre-optic cables (Figure 11.5). This has provided a competitive advantage because fibre optics are usually cheaper and more efficient than satellite links.

While the DCs are well-connected by submarine cables, many LDCs are still not linked into this telecommunications network, with the result that they are limited in their ability to develop competitive bases for service exports. Figure 11.5 shows how the United States, Europe, and East and Southeast Asia have good cable capacity, but that only one major cable connects parts of Africa to the rest of the world – the SAT-3 cable. In fact, in Sub-Saharan Africa, only Angola, Benin, Cameroon, Côte d'Ivoire, Gabon, Ghana, Mauritius, Nigeria, Senegal and South Africa are linked directly to this cable.

## EDUCATION AND TRAINING

Lack of education and training is a limiting factor in knowledge-intense services. While the kinds of skill needed differ depending on the kinds of services, most outsourced IT-enabled services involve information processing of various kinds. The strong software export performance of India partly reflects government education and training policies that have produced a large pool of technically trained English-speaking workers. Most software companies are in Mumbai and Bangalore, where the software industry initially developed. With other growing urban centres, specifically New Delhi and its surroundings, Andhra Pradesh and Tamil Nadu, these five areas contain nearly 50 per cent of India's diploma-granting technical institutions.

Fig 11.5: Submarine fibre-optic cable network, 2006

*Source*: Based on UNCTAD (2004: 206, Figure V.3); TeleGeography research, PriMetrica, Inc. submarine cable map, available at http://www.primetrica.com

Special skills are also needed for more routine services. Call centres need workers not only with good language abilities but also solid customer support skills, telesales abilities, data-entry and processing skills.

But sustained strong growth in service outsourcing to India, Israel, the Philippines and South Africa depends on the continued availability and low cost of the necessary worker skills. Despite success so far, there is concern that LDCs like India may not be able to keep pace with the demand for qualified workers; shortages of trained workers can force wages up and make a country less attractive as an outsourcing destination.

## Box 11.2 A day in the life of a call centre worker in India

Parag Arora, 23, works at the call centre of a British multinational in Mumbai. He has a BA in economics from Delhi University and earns around 3000 rupees (£38 or US$74) a week.

*4 pm* Parag works nights to coincide with office hours in Britain and the United States, and so wakes up in the afternoon. He shares an apartment with three other call centre workers

*5 pm* Breakfast/lunch: *paratha* (a type of bread stuffed with vegetables), *dal* (lentils), *subzi* (a cooked vegetable dish) and *idli* (a fluffy rice cracker dipped in savoury sauce)

*5.30 pm* Parag relaxes with friends, plays computer games, does some shopping or goes to the cinema

*11 pm* The journey to work on the bus should take only 20 minutes, but the streets are often choked with traffic

*12 midnight* The 10-hour shift begins with a short team meeting on targets before the workers don their headsets. Parag deals with credit card queries such as payment problems. Workers must aim for an average call-handling time of two and a half minutes – the system also monitors how often customers are put on hold (which implies you need to ask for help). More than 2000 people are employed in the call centre and about 700 work on any given night

*5 am* A half-hour break and a meal in the crowded canteen: similar dishes to lunch (Chinese food is also popular). Workers are permitted another two 15-minute breaks during their shift

*10 am* Parag leaves work. The shifts are hard to adjust to, as they change every few weeks; invariably they involve working late into the morning. He works a five-day week but his days off vary

*11 am* Bed

*Source: New Statesman, 30 January 2006*

## GOVERNMENT REGULATION AND POLICIES

The regulatory and legal framework in some less developed countries can place limits on the growth of export services. There is a need for a competitive regulatory environment that encourages competition among service providers, which includes a deregulated telecommunications environment facilitating dependable and competitively priced service. Governments in LDCs such as China also need to address the concerns of many in the United States and the European Union in particular about poor data security and intellectual property protection. Developed countries such as Ireland and Canada, as well as higher cost LDCs like Singapore, emphasize their strong regulatory frameworks compared to those in China and even India when competing for service outsourcing work.

The WTO's General Agreement on Trade in Services (GATS) covers all internationally traded services. The goals of service liberalization in the GATS context are greater competition and non-discrimination against foreign services and service providers. The liberalization of services involves the reduction or elimination of barriers which affect services certainly, but also the removal of legally established monopolies or oligopolistic market structures, discriminatory taxation and limits on foreign investment in services. The GATS negotiations on the liberalization of services, however, have proceeded extremely slowly (WTO, 2004).

## CORPORATE STRATEGIES

Corporate decision making can result in limited opportunities for service export growth in some LDCs. Companies differ on their perception of risk and assessment of the benefits of internationally outsourcing services. In the United Kingdom, for example, the Royal Bank of Scotland – in contrast to competitors such as Barclays and HSBC – decided not to outsource certain financial services abroad. In some situations, for example, the information that is to be processed can be confidential; this can increase transaction costs and limit the desirability of outsourcing. Consequently, any assessment of the potential for service outsourcing needs to include an analysis of corporate strategies and organizational limitations.

# 11.5 GEOGRAPHY OF SERVICES

The major forces driving the growth in services and service outsourcing, combined with the constraints on service growth discussed earlier, mediated by local political, economic and other contexts, have produced an uneven geographical pattern at global, regional and urban spatial scales.

## PATTERNS AND TRAJECTORIES

A milestone for services was reached in 2006. For the first time, worldwide employment in services as a percentage of total employment increased to 40 per cent, surpassing the percentage in agriculture (which decreased to 38.7 per cent). Despite this overall increase in service employment, the percentage of workers employed in services is uneven among different parts of the world, with implications for both the DCs and the LDCs (Table 11.2).

The developed countries now have almost three-quarters of their workforce in service employment, followed by Latin America and the Caribbean with nearly two-thirds and the central and eastern European countries, Russia, and the Middle East and North Africa with about half their workers in services. The remaining regions – East Asia, Sub-Saharan Africa, South Asia, Southeast Asia and the Pacific – all have only between one-quarter and one-third of their workers in services (Table 11.2).

Table 11.2 Changing employment in services as a percentage of total employment

| | Service employment as % of total employment | |
|---|---|---|
| | 1996 | 2006 |
| World | 35.5 | 40.0 |
| Developed countries (DCs) and European Union | 66.4 | 72.7 |
| Central and eastern Europe (non-EU) and Russia, Central Asia, the Transcaucasus | 45.8 | 50.3 |
| East Asia | 20.7 | 25.8 |
| Southeast Asia and the Pacific | 32.7 | 35.2 |
| South Asia | 25.3 | 29.5 |
| Latin America and the Caribbean | 56.5 | 61.4 |
| Middle East and North Africa | 48.6 | 47.4 |
| Sub-Saharan Africa | 22.9 | 28.2 |

*Source:* Based on ILO (2007: 12, Table 5)

Looking at a more detailed level, there is significant variation in the percentage of workers employed in services among the LDCs (Figure 11.6). Countries in Latin America, such as Peru, Argentina and Uruguay, as well as many in the Middle East, including Jordan, Oman, Saudi Arabia and Israel, have more than 75 per cent of their workers in services. While Hong Kong and Singapore also have more than 75 per cent, India and China are only at about 30 per cent. Most countries in Sub-Saharan Africa have less than 30 per cent of their workers employed in services.

While more and more services are becoming tradable, a significant amount remains non-tradable, especially in the LDCs. In this connection, although the official statistics from the World Bank and International Labour Organization (ILO) indicate that there is relatively low employment in services in the LDCs compared to that in the DCs, it is important to keep in mind that these data do not include jobs in services in the informal economy. In some of the poorest LDCs, the informal economy represents a large proportion of GNI and is associated with incredibly low per capita incomes. Low-income countries in Sub-Saharan Africa such as Tanzania, Nigeria and Zimbabwe, which have perhaps 50 per cent or more of their GNI generated within the informal economy, contrast sharply with the richest DCs including the United States, United Kingdom and Australia (Figure 11.7).

In many cities in the LDCs more than one-third of the population works in the informal sector; in some cities this figure is more than two-thirds. Across Africa, the ILO has estimated that informal sector work is growing 10 times faster than formal sector employment. Although service jobs in the informal sector – including driving pedicabs, dress or shoe repair and prostitution – may seem marginal from the point of view of the world economy, they support more than a billion people around the world. In many LDCs, the informal sector includes the world's most vulnerable workers – women and children.

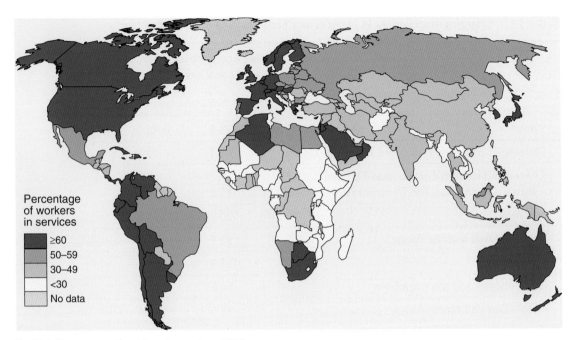

Fig 11.6: Percentage of workers in services, 2004
*Source:* World Bank, online *World Development Indicators 2006*; ILO online data; *CIA Factbook 2007* online

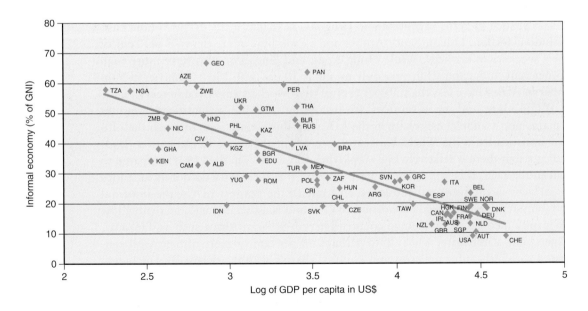

Fig 11.7: Informal economy and level of development
*Source:* Adapted from ILO (2004: 229, Figure 5.3)

Economic geographers recognize that the formal and informal sectors are interconnected – the informal sector represents an important resource for the formal sector. The informal sector provides a huge range of cheap services and goods that reduce the cost of living for employees in the formal sector, allowing employers to keep wages low. Although this arrangement does not contribute to economic growth or help alleviate poverty, it does keep many companies competitive within the global economic system. For export-oriented businesses, in particular, the informal sector provides a considerable indirect subsidy. And while this subsidy is often passed on to consumers in the DCs in the form of lower prices, the poorest households in the LDCs are forced to resort to increasingly drastic strategies for coping with worsening poverty.

The average annual percentage growth in services between 2000 and 2004 captures the relatively high rates of growth in services in LDCs such as China (9.8 per cent) and India (8.2 per cent) which started out with relatively low levels of services (Figure 11.8). The relatively slower growth rates of the DCs reflect the fact that these countries already have large service economies to begin with.

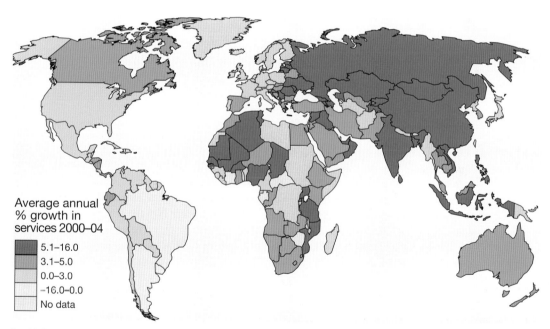

Average annual % growth in services 2000–04

- 5.1–16.0
- 3.1–5.0
- 0.0–3.0
- −16.0–0.0
- No data

Fig 11.8: Average annual percentage growth in services, 2000–04

*Source:* World Bank, online *World Development Indicators* 2006

Figure 11.9 shows the value of service production in 2004. The United States dominated with US$9 trillion, followed by Japan ($3 trillion) and Germany, France, the United Kingdom and Italy (with between $1 and $2 trillion each). China was next ($792 billion), ahead of Spain, Canada, Mexico, Australia, the Netherlands, South Korea, India and the Russian Federation.

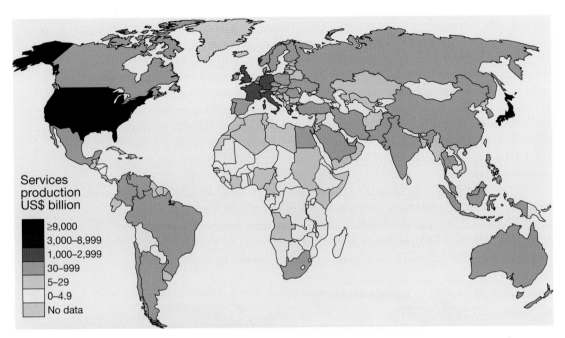

Fig 11.9: Service production (US$ billion), 2004

*Source:* World Bank, online *World Development Indicators* 2006

## INTERNATIONAL TRADE IN SERVICES

World service exports rose to about 20 per cent of total merchandise and service exports by 2005 (up from 15 per cent in 1980). Growing at an annual rate of 10 per cent, the value of service exports had risen to US$2,415 billion by 2005. In terms of world exports and imports of commercial services and concerns about the outsourcing of services by some in the DCs, however, North America and Europe export more services than they import; Central and South America with the Middle East import about the same amount of services as they export; Russia and other countries in Asia and Africa import more than they export (Figure 11.10).

While countries differ in their service trade performance, fewer than two dozen countries – comprising a small number of DCs with an even smaller number of LDCs (China (with Hong Kong), South Korea, India and Singapore) – account for three-quarters of total world exports, with the top five countries (United States (15 per cent), United Kingdom (8.1 per cent), Germany (6.3 per cent), France (5.1 per cent) and Japan (4.5 per cent)) accounting for almost 40 per cent of world service exports alone.

The fastest growing part of the world service sector comprises knowledge- and information-related services. OECD statistics on trade in services indicate that between 1998 and 2003, world service exports grew at an annual rate of 5.6 per cent. The fastest growing service exports were computer and information services (20 per cent), insurance (17 per cent) and financial services (9.7 per cent).

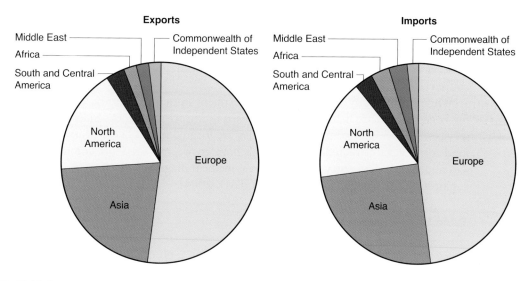

Fig 11.10: Exports and imports of services, 2005

*Source:* Based on WTO (2006: 10, Appendix Chart 1)

## TRANSNATIONAL INVESTMENT PATTERNS

The structure of foreign direct investment has shifted toward services. During the 1990s services became the largest sector in FDI worldwide. By 2002, services had risen to almost two-thirds of world FDI stock (up from less than one-half in 1990 and only one-quarter in 1970).

The increase in FDI by global service corporations is due to a number of factors:

- delivery of many non-tradable services requires a physical presence in foreign markets
- companies are adopting internationalization strategies on the strength of their home market success in building and strengthening their competitive advantage for investment overseas
- many countries have relaxed their regulation of service industries and foreign service providers with the result that these countries are more open to FDI
- information and communications technologies have allowed more service companies to locate their facilities in lower cost locations worldwide (Bryson *et al.*, 2004).

Capturing some of the escalating global FDI is a priority for many less developed countries. Nevertheless, the growth of FDI in services initially occurred among the developed countries, as the historically dominant home countries for FDI in services. The LDCs joined the process during the second half of the 1980s after they began to open their service sector to FDI (particularly through privatization). Since the early 1990s, countries in central and eastern Europe as well as Russia have also joined the process.

Services, valued at about US$500 billion, accounted for two-thirds of all FDI inflows in 2002; the developed countries accounted for the largest share (72 per cent). Likewise, outward FDI in services continues to be dominated by the developed countries, particularly the United States, the European Union and Japan. Reflecting the growth in services in less developed countries such as India and China, outward FDI in services by the less developed countries began to increase significantly from the 1990s – from only 1 per cent in 1990 to 10 per cent by 2002.

## EXPORT PROCESSING ZONES (EPZS)

Many LDCs offer financial and other incentives to attract foreign investment, not only in manufacturing, but also in services. Subsidies are used to attract a variety of service industries, but are most common in tourism, transportation and financial services.

While traditionally used to attract investment in manufacturing, export processing zones (EPZs) are increasingly being used to attract investment in export-oriented services. Most EPZs for service industries are located in the LDCs (Table 11.3). The kinds of services attracted to these EPZs have grown rapidly, from commercial services and simple data entry to call centres, medical diagnoses, architectural, business, engineering and financial services (UNCTAD, 2004).

**Table 11.3** EPZs targeting services, 2004

|  | Number of countries with EPZs for services |
| --- | --- |
| World | 91 |
| Asia and the Pacific | 26 |
| Latin America and the Caribbean | 26 |
| Africa | 20 |
| Central and Eastern Europe | 13 |
| European Union and other developed countries | 6 |

*Source:* Based on ILO data, available at http://www.ilo.org/epz

These EPZs offer a strong technology support infrastructure including modern communication technologies, reliable power supplies and a highly skilled workforce. Incentives include 100 per cent exemption from import duties and general sales taxes, full repatriation of earnings and preferential customs clearance. The emphasis on the skills and language abilities of the workers for IT-enabled service jobs contrasts with the low- or semi-skilled workers advertised by the traditional manufacturing EPZs.

In India, many of the outsourced services have been attracted to dedicated technology parks for IT services that were established by individual states. India's first software technology parks were set up in 1990 in Bangalore, Bhubaneshwar and Pune. There are now 39 of these parks, accounting for about 80 per cent of India's software exports.

## AGGLOMERATION AND NEW BUSINESS SERVICE CONCENTRATIONS

As we saw in Chapter 7, business services tend to agglomerate in particular corporate control centres, particularly in world cities. Barney Warf (2007) argues for the use of actor-network theory to better understand why some forms of service production are concentrated in a small number of urban centres like world cities, while other services are more dispersed globally. He makes a distinction between two kinds of knowledge: standardized knowledge, which includes forms of information that are easily transmitted from one person to another, such as quantitative data, publicly known rules and standards and orderly records; and tacit knowledge, which includes information that is not standardized, changes rapidly and is often not put in writing. Actor-network theory focuses on questions of power, politics and social relations and highlights the fact that the global service economy is the contingent outcome of actors situated in networks. In conjunction with the 'cultural turn' in economic geography (see Chapter 7), the use of actor-network theory is a way to help make sense of the emerging geographies of centrality and peripherality unleashed by the globalization not only of manufacturing but also of services.

> High value-added services, using skilled labor and tacit forms of knowledge, are highly agglomerated in the world's global cities. Such functions tend to be deeply embedded territorially and thus the competitive advantages of established centres are difficult to reproduce. In contrast, relatively low value-added service functions, such as back offices, call centres, and offshore banks, are increasingly dispersed to the world's low wage periphery. These operations, relying upon disembedded, standardized knowledge, are footloose and change locations frequently. These two sets of services represent opposite poles of one continuous process that geographically segregates functions on the basis of their value-added and types of skills and knowledges utilized. Both types of services are embodied in people and embedded in local and international contexts, forming complex mixtures of the local and global.
>
> Warf (2007: 1)

Research on changing occupational structure and the use of computers in the workplace by Levy and Murnane (2004) supports this assessment. They found that since the 1960s in the United States, the percentage of employees has risen in occupations that emphasize 'expert thinking' involving solving problems for which there are no rule-based solutions. Examples include diagnosing an illness of a patient whose symptoms seem strange or repairing an automobile that does not run well but which the computer diagnostics indicate has no problems. Similarly, the percentage of employees has risen in occupations that emphasize 'complex communication' involving interacting with other workers in order to acquire information, to explain it or to persuade others of its implications for action. Examples include managers motivating people whose work they supervise or an engineer describing why a new design for a DVD player is an improvement over previous designs. While computers can help, these are not tasks that computers can be programmed to solve and so are not easily amenable to outsourcing to the LDCs.

In contrast, the percentage of employees in the United States has fallen in occupations that emphasize routine cognitive tasks requiring mental skills that are well described by logical rules. Examples include recording new information provided by insurance customers and evaluating mortgage applications. Because these tasks can be accomplished by following a set of rules, they are prime candidates for computerization and to outsourcing to the LDCs.

## 11.6 VARIETY IN THE INTERNATIONALIZATION OF SERVICES

As we have seen, there is a wide variety of marketed services ranging from producer services (FIRE and business services) to transportation and communications, wholesale and retail trade, to entertainment, hotels and motels (part of tourism). In concluding this chapter, we briefly examine the internationalization of some leading services, namely, retailing, tourism and financial and business services.

### INTERNATIONALIZATION OF RETAILING

On the supply side, since the 1970s, the sales of the world's largest international retailers have grown considerably. In 1976 the total sales of the then largest retail company in the world – Sears Roebuck – were less than US$15 billion (equivalent to $55 billion in 2007 dollars). By 2007, Wal-Mart – the world's largest retailer today – had sales of $345 billion.

The largest retail companies have been more conservative than many other tradable services when entering foreign markets (Bryson *et al.*, 2004). The stores and receipts of many of the largest retailers are largely domestic (including, in the United States, Home Depot, Lowe's, Kroger, Walgreen and Target). Based on the location of their stores, only a few of the world's largest retailers – Wal-Mart (USA), Ahold (Netherlands), Carrefour, Pinault and Auchun (France), Metro, Aldi, Tengelmann, Rewe, Lidl and Schwarz (Germany), Delhaize (Belgium), IKEA (Sweden) and Tesco (UK) – can be considered truly global operators. Of these, only IKEA, Arhold, Delhaize, Tengelmann and Pinault have more than 50 per cent of their sales from foreign markets (Currah and Wrigley, 2004).

With the exception of Wal-Mart, most of the largest international retailers (with annual international sales of more than US$1 billion and operations in 10 or more countries) are from western Europe. In fact, Wal-Mart remained a domestic US company until as late as 1991 when it opened a Sam's Club near Mexico City (see Box 11.3). It currently derives just over one-fifth of its sales from foreign countries.

### Box 11.3 Wal-Mart®

The US giant, Wal-Mart, the largest retailer in the world and the second largest company after Exxonmobil, had net sales of US$345 billion in 2007. Based on the value of its annual sales, if it were a country, Wal-Mart would rank 26th in the world, ahead of Indonesia, Denmark and South Africa and just behind Austria, Poland and Saudi Arabia. The company employs 1.8 million workers worldwide, about the same number as the entire population of Botswana and more than the combined populations of Cyprus, Luxembourg and Malta.

Wal-Mart became an international operator only in 1991 when it opened a Sam's Club near Mexico City. Today, in addition to Wal-Mart's more than 4000 stores in the United States, the company operates over 2700 more in Argentina, Brazil, Canada, China, Costa Rica, El Salvador, Guatemala, Honduras, Japan, Mexico, Nicaragua, Puerto Rico and the United Kingdom (see Table 11.4). The company usually enters new markets by acquiring foreign operators, such as ASDA in the United Kingdom and Seiyu in Japan.

Table 11.4 Wal-Mart stores

| Country | 1997 | 2007 | Change 1997–2007 | |
|---|---|---|---|---|
| | | | # | % |
| United States | 2740 | 4022 | 1282 | 46.8 |
| Argentina | 6 | 13 | 7 | 116.7 |
| Brazil | 5 | 299 | 294 | 5880.0 |
| Canada | 136 | 289 | 153 | 112.5 |
| Central America | 0 | 413 | 413 | |
| China | 2 | 73 | 71 | 3550.0 |
| Indonesia | 2 | 0 | −2 | −100.0 |
| Japan | 0 | 392 | 392 | |
| Mexico | 152 | 889 | 737 | 484.9 |
| Puerto Rico | 11 | 54 | 43 | 390.9 |
| United Kingdom | 0 | 335 | 335 | |
| **Total** | **3054** | **6779** | **3725** | **122.0** |

*Source:* Wal-Mart 1997 and 2007 annual reports

The company is expected to concentrate increasingly on joint ventures since it was forced to pull out of Germany in 2006 where it faced stiff competition from much larger local rivals such as Aldi and Lidl & Schwarz. Wal-Mart sold its 85 German stores to Metro after it failed to repeat the extraordinary success it had achieved in the USA in Europe's largest economy. Analysts concluded that Wal-Mart's US approach to business did not translate well into German. In addition to having to conform to strict German labour laws, Wal-Mart's efforts to superimpose its own culture did not go smoothly. For example, Wal-Mart's initial requirement that its sales associates smile at customers was interpreted by male German shoppers as flirting; or requiring employees to bag groceries for customers was not appreciated by German customers who traditionally prefer to handle their own food and bag their own groceries. The consensus is that Wal-Mart learned important lessons in Germany; the company is currently in a joint venture to explore retail opportunities in India.

Wal-Mart's sales strategy – based on offering products at 'everyday low prices' – allows the company to minimize extensive advertising and promotional campaigns. The company can maintain low prices because it simplifies its purchasing activities and keeps costs down with suppliers by offering a relatively narrow choice of the most popular products combined with some particularly high-volume items.

In 2002 Wal-Mart established Wal-Mart Global Procurement Services to manage the company's direct import business and factory direct purchasing. This unit of the company is responsible for identifying new suppliers, sourcing new products, building partnerships with existing suppliers and managing the global supply chain of Wal-Mart's direct imports. Wal-Mart sources its products from more than 70 countries worldwide, working from offices in about two dozen countries including low-wage countries such as Bangladesh, Brazil, China, Guatemala, Honduras, India, Indonesia, Mexico, Nicaragua, Pakistan, the Philippines, Sri Lanka, Thailand and Turkey. Tight inventory management is maintained using computerization.

Wal-Mart has been criticized for a variety of practices including its extensive product sourcing in low-wage LDCs, and its low wages and poor worker benefits in its stores in the DCs, combined with its resistance to union representation for its workers. A low degree of unionization, however, is not unique to Wal-Mart; it is something that distinguishes today's service employers from the traditional manufacturing enterprises in the developed countries in the past.

Williams (1992) identified five major reasons why retailers typically decide to internationalize their operations. First, growth-oriented goals in a highly competitive domestic market can lead companies to consider new foreign markets in order to maintain sales and profits. Second, there may be limited domestic market growth opportunities because of market maturity, saturation, exhausted or unsuitable diversification possibilities and excessive government regulations. Third, there may be opportunities to implement internationally appealing and innovative retail concepts in some LDC markets. Fourth, more passive, reactive or subjective opportunities for enhanced sales and profits may arise from offers of joint ventures from foreign partners or through acquisition of foreign retail competitors. Fifth, senior management may be driven to apply their retail 'know-how' and techniques to foreign markets. In addition, technological breakthroughs, trade liberalization and the opening up of markets to FDI are vitally important policy changes that allow companies to expand internationally.

The international expansion of the largest retailers has been uneven. With the important exception of Africa, where smaller southern African retailers such as Shoprite and Pick'n Pay dominate, the largest global retailers are extending their presence primarily into Latin America, East Asia and central and eastern Europe. Within these regions, these large retailers target the most attractive markets with the largest consumer bases. In Latin America, for example, much of this foreign investment has gone to Argentina, Brazil and Chile; in East and Southeast Asia, the investment has gone to Malaysia, South Korea, Taiwan, Thailand and, increasingly, China; and in central and eastern Europe, the investment has gone to the Czech Republic, Hungary, Poland and, to a lesser extent, Slovakia (UNCTAD, 2004).

At the same time that these large retailers have been expanding into foreign markets, they have been internationalizing their supply networks. Gereffi's (2001) notion of a buyer-driven commodity chain is useful in conceptualizing this arrangement (see Figure 1.4). A commodity chain refers to the entire range of activities involved in the design, production and marketing of a product. *Buyer-driven* commodity chains cover those industries in which large retailers, marketers and branded manufacturers play pivotal roles in establishing decentralized production networks in a number of usually LDC exporters. This pattern of trade-led industrialization has become common in labour-intensive, consumer goods industries such as garments, footwear, toys, housewares, consumer electronics and a variety of handicrafts. Production is usually undertaken by tiered networks of contractors in the LDCs who make finished goods for foreign buyers. The product specifications are supplied by the large retailers or marketers who order the goods:

> One of the main characteristics of the firms that fit the buyer-driven model, including retailers like Wal-Mart, Sears Roebuck, and J.C. Penney, athletic footwear companies like Nike and Reebok, and fashion-oriented apparel companies like Liz Claiborne and The Limited, is that these companies design and/or market – but do not make – the branded products they order. They are part of a new breed of 'manufacturers without factories' that separate the physical production of goods from the design and marketing stages of the production process. Profits in buyer-driven chains derive not from the scale, volume, and technological advances as in producer-driven chains, but rather from unique combinations of high-value research, design, sales, marketing, and financial services that allow the retailers, designers, and marketers to act as strategic brokers in linking overseas factories and traders with evolving product niches in their main consumer markets.
>
> Gereffi (1999: 1)

In general, buyer-driven commodity chains are designed to keep costs down and involve forcing consolidation at all stages of the commodity chain in the less developed countries. Some of the negative outcomes for suppliers and workers in the LDCs are captured by this Oxfam (2004, p. 6) quote:

> [I]nternational mergers and acquisitions and aggressive pricing strategies have concentrated market power in the hands of a few major retailers, now building international empires. These companies have tremendous power in their negotiations with producers and they use that power to push the costs and risks of business down the supply chain. Their business model, focused on maximizing returns for shareholders, demands increasing flexibility through 'just-in-time' delivery, but tighter control over inputs and standards, and ever-lower prices.

Reardon *et al.* (2003) offer a typology for considering the supply network practices for supermarkets that can usefully be applied to the buyer-driven commodity chains of the largest international retailers:

1 Centralized procurement using a distribution centre serving multiple stores has replaced individual store procurement. This reduces administrative costs and increases the efficiency of the procurement network for retailers. It favours suppliers in the LDCs who can meet the retailers' delivery, volume and quality requirements.
2 Logistics improvements have accompanied procurement consolidation. Retailers are applying modern technologies to the supply chain in order to track inventory and delivery. Suppliers in the LDCs receive this technology transfer and training from the retailers themselves or from local consultants.
3 Retailers are increasingly using local specialized wholesalers – sidestepping or transforming the traditional wholesale system. Dealing directly with specialized wholesalers who are dedicated to and capable of meeting the specific needs of the retailers reduces the retailers' costs and ensures greater control over quality and delivery.
4 The increasing use of quasi-formal and formal contracts with price controls has formalized procedures for local suppliers. The large retailers typically draw up short-term contracts which give them the flexibility to adjust their supplier network and force LDC suppliers to bid for each new contract.

5 With little or no enforced public standards, the large retailers have imposed private certification and standards on their entire supplier network in order to harmonize product quality across LDC suppliers. Not surprisingly, many small LDC suppliers have found it impossible to meet these requirements and have been dropped from the procurement lists of the major retailers.

On the demand side, the national and global stimuli to the growth in services, including rising per capita incomes, have given rise to new shopping habits not only in the DCs but also in LDCs like China and India. In addition, breakthroughs in information technology have allowed consumers to access services using computers and the internet. E-shopping has added an additional dimension to retailing which does not involve traditional shopping venues, such as shopping malls and individual stores.

## INTERNATIONAL TOURISM

The globalization of the world economy has been paralleled by a globalization of the tourist industry. Even in those parts of the world that do not have much of a base in primary commodities, are not an important part of manufacturing commodity chains and are not closely tied into the global financial network, international tourism can offer the otherwise unlikely prospect of economic development. The growth of international tourism has been fuelled by rising incomes and the consumption of services with a particularly high elasticity of demand – including transportation, hotels and entertainment.

International tourism reached an all time high of more than 789 million international trips in 2005 (up from just 147 million in 1970) (Figure 11.11). Visitors from the more affluent countries of the world – particularly the United States, United Kingdom, Japan, France, Italy, Canada and the Netherlands – made these

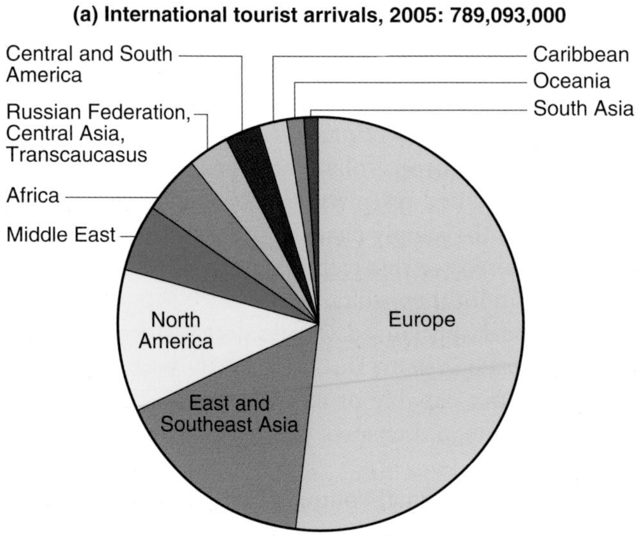

**(a) International tourist arrivals, 2005: 789,093,000**

Fig 11.11: International tourist arrivals and receipts, 2006

*Source*: Based on WTO (2006: 10, Appendix Chart 1)

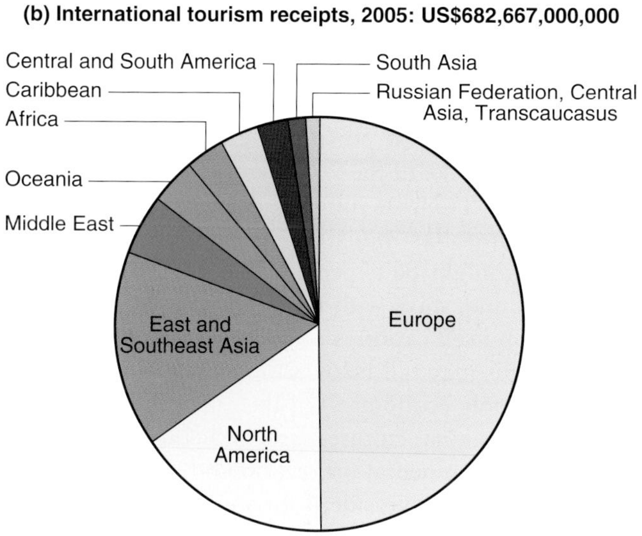

**(b) International tourism receipts, 2005: US$682,667,000,000**

Fig 11.11: *Continued*

trips. Since 1990 international tourist arrivals have increased steadily at a rate of 4 per cent each year. About half of these trips are for leisure, recreation and vacations; one-sixth for business; and the remainder for other purposes.

In 2005 international tourism earnings reached nearly US$683 billion (Figure 11.11). It is one of the world's largest industries, with as many as one in every 10 workers worldwide involved in transporting, feeding, housing, guiding or amusing tourists and with the global stock of lodging, restaurant and transportation facilities estimated to be worth more than $3 trillion.

What is most striking, however, is not so much the growth in the number of international tourists as the increased range of international tourism. Thanks largely to cheap long-distance flights, a significant proportion of tourism is now transcontinental and transoceanic. Europe (52 per cent) and the Americas (16 per cent) remain the most popular tourist destinations (Figure 11.11). The top destinations in Europe are countries bordering the Mediterranean – France, Spain and Italy. The United States alone offers tourist magnets such as Florida, Hawaii, Las Vegas and New York. But countries in Asia, Africa and the Pacific had grown to nearly one-third of the industry by 2005 (Figure 11.11). This, of course, has made tourism a central component of economic development in countries with sufficiently exotic wildlife (for example, Kenya), scenery (Nepal), beaches (the Seychelles), shopping (China and Hong Kong), culture (China, India and Indonesia) or sex (Thailand).

But, although tourism can provide a basis for economic development in the less developed countries, it is often a mixed blessing. Tourism certainly creates jobs, but they are often seasonal. Dependence on tourism also makes for a high degree of economic vulnerability. Tourism, like other high-end aspects of consumption, depends very much on matters of style and fashion. As a result, once thriving tourist destinations can suddenly find themselves struggling for customers. Some places are sought out by tourists because of their remoteness and their 'natural', undeveloped qualities and it is these that are most vulnerable to shifts of style and fashion. Nepal is a recent example of this phenomenon: it is now too 'obvious' as a destination and consequently the tourist industry in Nepal is having to work hard to continue to attract sufficient numbers of tourists. Bhutan, Bolivia, Estonia and Vietnam have been 'discovered' and are coping with their first real growth in tourism. Tourism in these more exotic destinations is also vulnerable in other ways: to political disturbances, natural disasters, outbreaks of disease or food poisoning and atypical weather. International tourism certainly fell in the wake of the 9/11 terrorist attacks, with destinations that depended significantly on US tourists suffering disproportionately.

Although tourism is a multibillion-dollar industry, the financial returns for tourist areas are often not as high as might be expected. The greater part of the price of a package vacation, for example, stays with the organizing company and the airline. Typically, the tourist region itself captures only 40 per cent. If the package involves a foreign-owned hotel, this may fall below 25 per cent. The costs and benefits of tourism, however, are not only economic. On the positive side, tourism can help sustain indigenous lifestyles, regional cultures, arts and crafts and provide incentives for wildlife preservation, environmental protection and the conservation of historic buildings and sites. On the negative side, tourism can adulterate and debase indigenous cultures and bring unsightly development, pollution and environmental degradation. Tourism can also involve exploitative relations that degrade traditional lifestyles and regional cultural heritages as they become packaged for outsider consumption. Traditional ceremonies, which formerly had cultural significance for the performers, are now enacted solely to be watched and photographed. In the process, indigenous cultures are edited, beautified and altered to suit outsiders' tastes and expectations.

Such problems, coupled with the economic vulnerability of tourism, have led to the idea of 'ecotourism' as a more sustainable strategy for economic development in peripheral regions. Ecotourism emphasizes self-determination, authenticity, social harmony, preserving the existing environment, small-scale development and greater use of local techniques, materials and architectural styles. Despite being a poor country, Costa Rica, for example, has won high praise from environmentalists for protecting more than one-quarter of its territory in biosphere and wildlife preserves. The payoff for Costa Rica is the escalating number of tourists who come to visit its active volcanoes, palm-lined beaches, cloud forests and tropical parks. In 2005 Costa Rica received about 1.5 million tourists. Tourism is the country's largest source of foreign exchange, followed closely by bananas, coffee, sugar, the textile industry and, more recently, the production of microchips.

## Box 11.4  Abu Dhabi, a tourist Mecca?

Many semi-peripheral countries have made a significant transition toward becoming service economies. Of these, some oil-rich states in the Persian Gulf are deliberately attempting to diversify their oil-dominated economies toward services such as banking and hosting conventions. They are also attempting to become tourist Meccas by investing in expensive tourist amenities, including luxury hotels, shopping malls and golf courses. Saudi Arabia, for example, with more than 9 million visitors in 2005, now ranks among the top 25 international tourist destinations in the world.

The United Arab Emirates (UAE) is quickly catching up, following an aggressive policy to position itself as a major Persian Gulf tourist destination. In 2007 the head of Abu Dhabi's tourism agency and the French Culture Minister signed a 30-year agreement to open a Louvre Museum outlet in this Persian Gulf boomtown. France will receive US$525 million alone for the use of the Louvre brand name. The deal also involves a gift of $33 million to renovate a wing of the Paris Louvre, which will house Islamic art and be named for the longtime UAE ruler, Sheik Zayed bin Sultan Al Nahyan. In addition to the hundreds of millions of dollars in construction costs, a further $750 million will be spent to bring French staff and 300 loaned pieces of art to the Louvre Abu Dhabi for its opening some time after 2012. The waterfront museum is designed to be the centrepiece of a cultural district with the goal of attracting millions of well-heeled tourists each year.

Not everyone is happy about what some see negatively as the globalization of French culture. In France, opponents argue that the French government is exploiting art for trade. The Louvre Abu Dhabi will also have to overcome significant cultural barriers in the Islamic art world where representations of the human body, even fully clothed, can be a religious taboo.

## INTERNATIONALIZATION OF FINANCE

Having addressed the patterns of international finance in earlier chapters (see, for example, Chapters 2 and 3) we focus here on the internationalization of finance from the perspective of the LDCs in terms of transnational banks and FDI in financial services, foreign exchange transactions and offshore banking centres. Several factors – with implications for the LDCs – have reinforced the globalization of financial services. A particularly important factor has been the advances in information and telecommunications technologies, allowing the digital flow of capital, which has significantly reduced the transaction and transmission costs associated with moving money. Another has been the institutionalization of savings in the developed countries (through pension funds and the like), which has established a large pool of capital managed by professional investors with few geographical allegiances or ties. Another has been the trend toward 'disintermediation' – which involves borrowers (especially large corporations) raising capital and making investments without going through the traditional, intermediary channels of financial institutions. Yet another, and probably more important, factor has been the deregulation of financial markets that occurred in many developed countries in the 1980s.

Financial services have traditionally accounted for the largest share of FDI in services in every part of the world. In the LDCs, the share in FDI stock in services is relatively high, at more than 20 per cent. The stock of FDI in financial services grew by 1.5 times between 1990 and 2002, to US$250 billion. In banking alone, cross-border mergers and acquisitions (M&As), the primary means of foreign entry into LDC markets during the 1990s, rose to nearly $80 billion during 1995–2003 (compared to an inflation adjusted $2.5 billion during 1987–94). As we saw in Chapter 2, Europe and North America dominate the list of the 20 largest financial conglomerates. The European Union (specifically France, Germany, Italy, the Netherlands, Spain and the United Kingdom) has 65 per cent of the top 20 financial conglomerates, followed by the United States with 20 per cent, and Switzerland with 15 per cent (Table 2.4).

There has been a large increase in the presence of banks from the developed countries in the less developed countries, especially in East Asia, Latin America and eastern Europe. In East Asia, countries such as China, South Korea and Taiwan have recorded increases in the number of banks from the developed countries of 50 per cent or more. The increases have been much greater in other parts of the world, especially in Argentina, Brazil, Colombia and Venezuela in Latin America, and in Hungary and Poland in eastern Europe (Cornford, 2004).

UNCTAD has reported that an estimated one-third of the world's financial TNCs are from the less developed countries. These banks, however, tend to be relatively small by international standards and less internationally active (with a physical presence in relatively few foreign banking markets). A significant percentage of the foreign subsidiaries of these financial TNCs are concentrated within the region of the home LDC. In fact, 48 per cent of the banks from Africa, Latin America and the Caribbean, and South, East and Southeast Asia have their foreign subsidiaries in the region of their home country (compared, for example, to 37 per cent for the banks from the EU). These figures indicate the relatively strong intra-regional nature of the financial TNCs in terms of physical presence, particularly in the LDCs.

In addition, the number of banking entities (branches, subsidiaries, etc.) from the less developed countries that operate in London and New York, for example, actually decreased between 1996 and 2002 (from 153 to 122 in London and from 118 to 90 in New York). This retrenchment has been due to a number of factors including banking consolidation associated with domestic and cross border M&As and banking problems in parent countries (for example, recent banking-cum-external-payments crises in several less developed countries) (Cornford, 2004).

Nevertheless, just as some NICs developed their own transnational corporations to compete with those of developed countries, so some have begun to develop relatively large and aggressive banks with an increasing interest in international opportunities. Singapore's four largest banks, for example, have more than 50 overseas branches, 20 overseas subsidiaries and affiliates and more than 30 representative offices in overseas locations including Beijing, Hong Kong, Jakarta, London, Los Angeles, Manila, New York, Seoul, Sydney, Taipei, Tokyo and Vancouver.

In addition, the effects of the rapid spread of e-finance in recent years are not limited to the DCs. E-finance involves electronic financial services that are delivered online, through mobile phones or other remote mechanisms or through smart cards (embedded with a microprocessor and/or a memory chip allowing information on the card to be added, deleted or otherwise manipulated). The World Bank reports that some LDCs with underdeveloped financial systems are using e-finance to leapfrog ahead in some areas of finance, including banking. In some African countries, for example, electronic cash and smart cards are being offered as savings and payment services for low-income customers who do not have access to traditional banks and conventional bank accounts. Evidence from Brazil and South Korea indicates that e-finance can be introduced quickly even when basic financial infrastructure is weak or non-existent (Table 11.5).

At the same time, however, there is enormous variation in the extent of electronic banking and brokerage services across both the DCs and the LDCs. This variation is not closely related to level of development however. In some countries, DC as well as LDC, electronic delivery of financial services remains in its infancy. Meanwhile, other countries have experienced the rapid penetration of e-finance. In Sweden, e-finance accounts for more than one-third of financial

Table 11.5 Spread of e-finance: selected countries

| | Online banking (customers as % of bank customers) | Online brokerage (transactions as % of brokerage transactions) | E-money (no. of merchant terminals per 100,000 people) | Business environment ranking, 2000–04* |
|---|---|---|---|---|
| **Core** | 8 | 27 | 427 | 8.2 |
| Australia | 4 | 22 | 10 | 8.1 |
| France | 2 | 18 | 1 | 8.2 |
| Germany | 12 | 32 | 73 | 8.3 |
| Italy | 1 | 16 | 7 | 7.7 |
| Japan | | 32 | | 7.4 |
| Netherlands | 15 | 40 | 1898 | 8.8 |
| Norway | 8 | 25 | 1059 | 8.0 |
| Sweden | 31 | 55 | 418 | 8.3 |
| United Kingdom | 6 | 26 | 3 | 8.8 |
| United States | 6 | 56 | 35 | 8.7 |
| **Semi-periphery** | 5 | 30 | 71 | 7.0 |
| Brazil | 5 | 6 | 1 | 6.4 |
| China | | 3 | | 5.9 |
| Czech Republic | 1 | 90 | | 7.0 |
| Hong Kong | 5 | 1 | 351 | 8.5 |
| Hungary | 6 | | 1 | 7.1 |
| India | 11 | 2 | | 6.0 |
| Mexico | 3 | 41 | 2 | 6.8 |
| Singapore | 5 | 10 | 332 | 8.6 |
| South Korea | 13 | 65 | | 7.3 |
| Thailand | 1 | | 1 | 7.3 |

Note: * Business environment rankings range from a score of 10 as best to 5 as poor. The rankings combine more than 70 indicators to measure the attractiveness of business environment (including the strength of the economy, outlook for political stability, regulatory climate, taxation policy and openness to trade and investment)

Source: Based on Claessens et al. (2002: 6: Table 1)

transactions. In some LDCs, such as the Czech Republic and Mexico, e-finance penetration is also high for some financial services (Table 11.5). At the same time, however, significant challenges to the spread of e-finance in some LDCs relate not only to the availability of technology and infrastructure (including access to mobile phones, computers, the internet) but also to the enabling regulatory environment, involving security and related infrastructure for e-transactions, information and privacy, and contract enforcement.

In addition, the increasing use of electronic money has changed the nature of international financial investments in ways that may not benefit the LDCs. For example, foreign investments are already beginning to shift away from more tangible FDI to intangible portfolio investments such as stocks and bonds. The issue here is that whereas FDI can generate tangible levels of employment and facilitate technology transfer, portfolio investments typically create few jobs (Bryson *et al.*, 2004).

Moreover, despite the dominance of electronic money flows, the majority of the foreign exchange transactions – nearly 75 per cent – are still made in only three currencies: the euro, the US dollar and the Japanese yen. Certainly the market opens each day in East Asia while it is still evening in the United States; financial transactions then look west, travelling along fibre-optic cables, typically from Tokyo to Hong Kong to Singapore to Bahrain to Frankfurt or Paris to London and then on to the United States (Figure 11.12). But London has maintained its preeminence as the premier world centre, exchanging US$500 billion in currencies each year, followed by New York with $300 billion and Tokyo with $200 billion.

Not all the needs of the global financial system, however, can be met by conventional financial services. The need for secrecy and the desire for shelter from taxation and regulation have resulted in the emergence of offshore banking centres. The incredible increase in the digital flow of global capital has allowed many of these offshore banking centres to be located in the LDCs – in microstates and on islands (Figure 11.13). There are five major specialized offshore banking centre nodes in the geography of worldwide financial flows: the Caribbean (including the Cayman Islands, Bahamas, British Virgin Islands, Panama, Costa Rica), Europe (including the Isle of Man, Jersey, Luxembourg, Liechtenstein, Andorra, San Marino), the Middle East (including the Lebanon, Bahrain, Cyprus), East and Southeast Asia (including Hong Kong, Singapore, Labuan) and the South Pacific (including Nauru, Vanuatu, the Cook Islands).

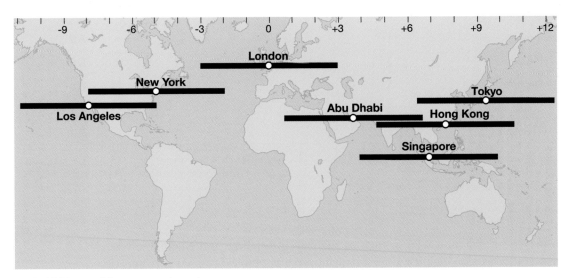

Fig 11.12: The world's major stock markets

*Source*: Based on Stutz and Warf (2007: 276, Figure 8.25)

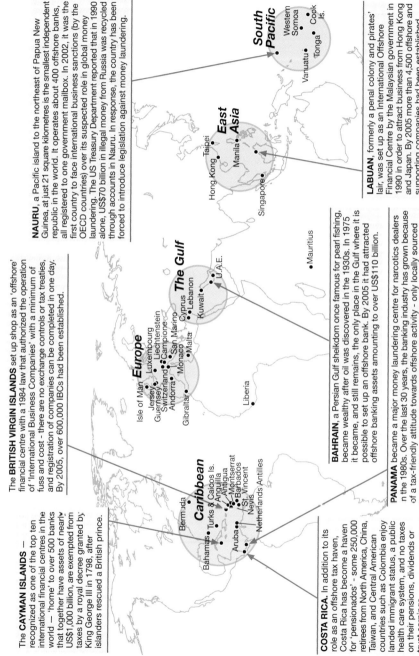

The **CAYMAN ISLANDS** — recognized as one of the top ten international financial centres in the world — 'home' to over 500 banks that together have assets of nearly US$1,000 billion, are exempted from taxes by a royal decree granted by King George III in 1798, after islanders rescued a British prince.

The **BRITISH VIRGIN ISLANDS** set up shop as an 'offshore' financial centre with a 1984 law that authorized the operation of 'International Business Companies' with a minimum of fuss and cost - there are no exchange controls or tax treaties, and registration of companies can be completed in one day. By 2005, over 600,000 IBCs had been established.

**NAURU**, a Pacific island to the northeast of Papua New Guinea, at just 21 square kilometres is the smallest independent republic in the world. It operates about 400 offshore banks, all registered to one government mailbox. In 2002, it was the first country to face international business sanctions (by the OECD countries) over its suspected role in global money laundering. The US Treasury Department reported that in 1990 alone, US$70 billion in illegal money from Russia was recycled through accounts in Nauru. In response, the country has been forced to introduce legislation against money laundering.

**LABUAN**, formerly a penal colony and pirates' lair, was set up as an International Offshore Financial Centre by the Malaysian government in 1990 in order to attract business from Hong Kong and Japan. By 2005 more than 4,500 offshore and supporting companies had been established. About 65 offshore banks, over 100 insurance and insurance related companies and 30 trust companies, as well as numerous legal and accounting firms have decided to take advantage of Labuan's zero tax on dividends, interest and royalties and its 3 per cent tax on net profits. The asset base of Labuan's offshore banking sector is estimated to be more than US$50 billion.

**COSTA RICA**. In addition to its role as an offshore tax haven, Costa Rica has become a haven for 'pensionados' - some 250,000 retirees from North America, China, Taiwan, and Central American countries such as Colombia enjoy landed immigrant status, a public health care system, and no taxes on their pensions, dividends or trust earnings.

**BAHRAIN**, a Persian Gulf sheikdom once famous for pearl fishing, became wealthy after oil was discovered in the 1930s. In 1975 it became, and still remains, the only place in the Gulf where it is possible to set up an offshore bank. By 2005 it had attracted offshore banking assets amounting to over US$110 billion.

**PANAMA** became a major money laundering centre for narcotics dealers in the 1980s. Over the last 30 years, the banking industry has grown because of a tax-friendly attitude towards offshore activity - only locally sourced income is taxed - and the absence of exchange controls and tax treaties. More than 120,000 companies, including over 140 banks, trade or hold assets externally. In 2000, the country's lax banking legislation landed it on an international blacklist, from which it was removed in 2001 following substantial reforms to its banking laws to conform to 40 recommendations in a code of good practice governing money laundering. Panama's participation in the worldwide search for terrorist funds in offshore bank accounts since the September 11, 2001 attacks in the US has helped the country establish that it is no longer the freewheeling tax haven it was during the government of General Noriega.

Offshore banking centre nodes

Fig 11.13: Major world areas of offshore banking

*Source:* Based on Stutz and Warf (2007: 278, Figure 8.26)

The main attraction of these offshore financial centres is simply that they are less regulated than financial centres elsewhere. They provide low- or no tax settings for savings, and havens for undeclared income and for hot money. They also provide discreet markets in which to transact currencies, bonds, loans and other financial instruments without coming to the attention of regulating authorities or competitors. The US Internal Revenue Service estimates that about US$300 billion ends up in offshore financial centres each year as a result of tax evasion schemes. Overall, about one-half of the world's business transactions are done in offshore banks and one-third of all the world's money resides offshore.

## INTERNATIONALIZATION OF BUSINESS SERVICES

We conclude this chapter by briefly examining the internationalization of business in terms of business process outsourcing (BPO) to the LDCs in general, and to India in particular. Instead of building in-house expertise, while still maintaining the secure and reliable provision of non-core IT services, large corporations in the United States initially outsourced to other large companies domestically. The largest IT and BPO service providers and their intermediaries include companies in the DCs, particularly the United States, such as Accenture, Computer Sciences Corporation (CSC), Electronic Data Systems Corporation (EDS) and IBM. The largest IT and BPO service providers also include companies in the LDCs, particularly India, such as Infosys Technologies, Tata Consultancy Services and Wipro (see Table 11.6).

The internationalization of IT-enabled services, including BPO, to LDCs such as India, has been driven by the corporate strategies, beginning in the early 1990s, of companies in the United States, Europe and Japan particularly. US companies began outsourcing to India the conversion of custom-made software programs from one operating system to another. This time-consuming and tedious operation could be outsourced easily to an LDC such as India. The Indian programmers were much less costly than their US counterparts and had the necessary skills, speed and attention to detail to perform the work (UNCTAD, 2003).

As the birthplace of BPO, the United States still dominates. UNCTAD (2004) reported that more than two-thirds of India's exports of software services go to the United States. European companies have shown less inclination, with less than 40 per cent of the largest European TNCs outsourcing business services to the LDCs so far. Some companies have decided not to outsource (yet) and, as in the United States, a few companies have moved operations back in response to customer complaints. Of course, service outsourcing varies across Europe, with the United Kingdom accounting for the largest share of business process outsourcing, most closely mirroring the United States.

The kinds of service activity involved now include, not only call centres, computer network support, legal services, accounting and procurement, but also software development, research and development and engineering services:

> BPO is a varied and flexible process. Service providers may provide rudimentary data entry services, or they may take over management functions or operations and become responsible for the entire process. Clients may outsource to several outsourcing providers. They may outsource data center management functions to one provider, network management functions to another, and business processes and help desk functions to still others. The BPO vendor may be a small local business or a large company, perhaps larger than the client.

UNCTAD (2003: 137)

Table 11.6 Major international business process outsourcing (BPO) corporations

| Company and headquarters | Specialty | Low-cost locations | Offshore revenue range |
|---|---|---|---|
| Accenture (USA) | Software development, network support, finance and accounting (F&A), human resources (HR) procurement, insurance operations, general banking | India, Philippines, Spain, China, Czech Republic, Slovakia, Brazil, Australia | Over US$5 billion |
| Affiliated Computer Services (ACS) (USA) | F&A, HR, payroll, procurement, telecom, transportation, healthcare operations, general banking, mortgage processing | India, China, Dominican Republic, Ghana, Guatemala, Jamaica, Malaysia, Mexico, Spain | $1 billion– $5 billion |
| Capgemini (France) | Software development | Canada, Mexico, Spain, Poland, India, Australia | $1 billion– $5 billion |
| Computer Sciences Corp. (CSC) (USA) | Software development, insurance operations, demand management | Canada, Bulgaria, Ireland, India, Mexico, Malaysia, South Africa, Spain | Over $5 billion |
| Electronic Data Systems Corp. (EDS) (USA) | Software development, network support; F&A, HR, payroll, demand management, procurement, insurance, general banking, telecom, transportation, healthcare operations | Canada, Mexico, Brazil, Argentina, India, Australia, South Africa, Spain, Hungary | Over $5 billion |
| Hewitt Associates (USA) | HR, payroll, procurement | India, China, Philippines, Thailand, Malaysia, Czech Republic, Poland, Hungary, Brazil, Mexico, Argentina, Chile | Over $5 billion |
| Hewlett-Packard (USA) | F&A, payroll, procurement | India | Over $5 billion |
| IBM (USA) | Software development, network support, F&A, HR, payroll, procurement, insurance operations | India, Brazil, China, Mexico, Belarus, Philippines, South Africa, Romania, Argentina | Over $5 billion |
| Infosys Technologies (India) | Software development, network support, banking, mortgage processing | India, Czech Republic, China, Australia | $1 billion– $5 billion |
| Tata Consultancy Services (India) | Software development, R&D/engineering, F&A, telecom, transportation, hospitality operations | India, Hungary, Brazil, Uruguay, Chile, China | $1 billion– $5 billion |
| Wipro (India) | Software development, R&D/engineering, demand management, mortgage processing, transportation operations, healthcare operations, banking, mortgage processing | India, Canada | $1 billion– $5 billion |

*Source:* Based on information from the information technology research and advisory company, Gartner, Inc., available at http://www.gartner.com

BPO so far has tended to be concentrated in a relatively small number of LDCs. The necessary technology and infrastructure requirements, including fibre-optic submarine cables (see Figure 11.5), are less potentially ubiquitous than even a skilled workforce (which a national government's education and training policies can promote). The main outsourcing destinations for BPO in the LDCs are India, Israel, the Philippines and South Africa, but Merrill Lynch's list of up and coming destinations include Argentina, the Czech Republic and China in particular, but also Poland, Brazil, Mexico, Pakistan, Russia and Ukraine.

## Box 11.5  India's competitive advantage in BPO

The main LDC outsourcing destination by far for BPO is India. This country accounts for about two-thirds of the global market in outsourced IT-enabled services and almost half of outsourced BPO. Large cities in India, particularly Bangalore, Delhi and Mumbai, are attractive to BPO because of their large pool of skilled English-speaking workers, good information and communication technologies, convenient time zone difference for companies in the DCs and relative political stability. In addition, low labour costs are a factor: in the United States, the average salary for a computer programmer is about US$70,000, versus $8000 in India. India's established track record in the field of IT-enabled services, including software development, has allowed this country to continue to benefit from its initial advantage in this area.

In addition, large Indian corporations – including Infosys Technologies, Tata Consultancy Services and Wipro – now engage in BPO themselves (so-called 'double-sourcing'), especially when the BPO does not depend on good language abilities or when the Indian companies need a presence in a foreign market close to its customers (see Table 11.6):

> Infosys Technologies was created in 1981 in Bangalore. With over 52,000 employees worldwide, it now provides consulting and IT services to clients globally. The company has pursued an international strategy to strengthen its competitive position and become a global player. Infosys has over 30 foreign affiliates worldwide, covering all countries and territories where its major customers are located. Infosys Technologies' global initiative began with the opening of its first subsidiary in the United States in 1987. Its first European subsidiary was created in the United Kingdom in 1996, followed by affiliates in Belgium, Germany and Sweden (1997), France (2000), the Netherlands (2001) and Switzerland (2002). In 2005, Infosys set up its first overseas operations center in the Czech Republic and bought RASInfo (France).

> UNCTAD (2006: 131)

By 2006 in India, whereas the percentage had remained largely the same for industry (27.3 per cent), services as a percentage of GDP had risen to 54.4 per cent (up from 39.9 per cent in 1985). Average annual growth in services between 1995 and 2005 was high by international standards – 8.2 per cent. While still having a large percentage of its workers in agriculture (60 per cent), India now has about 30 per cent of its workers in services. Services outsourcing plays an important role in creating jobs, particularly for women, who are employed primarily, however, at the low end of BPO. Women tend to work in call centres or perform data entry and other business operations that require lower level skills than their male counterparts.

India has recorded high growth rates in the export of services, with an increase of 42 per cent in 2005–06 alone at which point its service exports had risen to US$61.4 billion. Growth has been particularly rapid in software, business, financial and communication services. In 2005 India's share and ranking in world commercial services' exports was 2.3 per cent and 11th respectively (compared to only 1 per cent and 29th respectively for world merchandise exports). Concerns about India's continued service outsourcing dominance relate to whether the country can grow quickly enough to accommodate the 40 foreign companies that, on average, set up in business in India each month. The main concerns are whether India can keep up with the growing demand for skilled workers, and address serious congestion, power outages, rising costs and competition from other established and up and coming LDC competitors such as Argentina, China, the Czech Republic, the Philippines and South Africa, to name a few.

Currently, India's position appears to be strengthening. This is because companies in the DCs are increasing their outsourcing to LDCs such as India of more complex 'core competency' service functions like R&D and software design that are associated with greater innovation and higher value (see Figure 11.14). Especially in situations where companies have their own India-based development teams, the decision has increasingly been made to allow these teams to take sole responsibility for the development of certain service products, including conceptualizing and building new features and modules. In addition, whereas in the past, a constraint on greater innovation and value in BPO in India was distance from customers in the DCs, the internet has changed everything. Now that the internet provides the customers for companies such as Amazon, Google and Yahoo!, access to the information and needs of customers has been equalized for the development teams in India. As a result, Amazon and Google designed their development centres in Bangalore to generate completely new service products, rather than to act merely as back offices for their US operations.

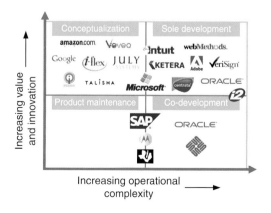

Fig 11.14: Computer product companies operating in India, 2005

*Source*: based on Zinnov (2005: 2, Figure 3)

## SUMMARY

In this chapter, we have examined the shift to services and the contemporary geography of services in both the less developed countries and the developed countries, as well as the interactions between them. We have identified the following points as being of critical importance:

- Services can be categorized into a number of major components, including finance, insurance and real estate; business services; transportation and communications; wholesale and retail trade; entertainment, hotels and motels; public services; and non-profit services.
- The distinction between services and manufacturing has come to be seen increasingly as redundant. The notion of service encapsulation of goods and materials is useful for understanding how services are increasingly incorporated into manufactured products.
- Major forces that are driving the growth of services include rising per capita incomes; growing demand for healthcare and educational services; an increasingly complex division of labour; the growing size and role of the public sector; increasing international trade in services; and the rapid growth in outsourcing service functions.
- Service outsourcing involves not only potential drawbacks but also potential benefits for the developed countries and the less developed countries.
- There are significant constraints – related to technology and infrastructure; education and training; government regulations and policies; and corporate strategies – that can limit the growth of services and prevent certain LDCs from capturing some of the service outsourcing market, especially for IT-enabled services.
- In 2006, for the first time, worldwide employment in services as a percentage of total employment increased to 40 per cent, surpassing the percentage in agriculture.
- The percentage of workers employed in services is uneven among different parts of the world. The developed countries have almost three-quarters of their workforce in services; followed by Latin America and the Caribbean with nearly two-thirds; and the central and eastern European countries, Russia and the Middle East and North Africa with about half their workers in services. The remaining regions of the world have only between one-quarter and one-third of their workers in services.
- There is significant variation in the percentage of workers employed in services among the LDCs. LDCs including Peru, Argentina, Saudi Arabia and Israel all have 75 per cent or more of their workers in services. For China and India, the figure is about 30 per cent. In Sub-Saharan Africa, most countries are below 30 per cent.
- LDCs including China and India have seen relatively high rates of growth in services. Nevertheless, the United States has the highest production of services; followed by Japan, Germany, France, the United Kingdom and Italy. China is next, ahead of Spain, Canada, Mexico, Australia, the Netherlands, South Korea, India and the Russian Federation.
- World service exports rose to US$2,415 billion or 20 per cent of total merchandise and service exports by 2005. The United States, United Kingdom, Germany, France and Japan together account for almost 40 per cent of world service exports.

- The structure of foreign direct investment has shifted toward services. The developed countries account for the largest shares of FDI in services.
- Export processing zones (EPZs) are increasingly being used to attract investment in export-oriented services by the LDCs.
- High value-added services, using skilled labour and tacit forms of knowledge, are highly agglomerated in world cities. In contrast, relatively low value-added service functions, such as back offices, call centres and offshore banks are increasingly dispersed to low wage peripheral countries.
- As the world's largest retailers like Wal-Mart have been expanding into foreign markets, they have been internationalizing their supply networks. Their buyer-driven commodity chains create opportunities and drawbacks for suppliers in the LDCs. E-shopping has added an additional dimension to retailing that does not involve traditional shopping venues.
- International tourism reached an all time high of more than 789 million international trips in 2005. Although tourism can provide a basis for economic development in many LDCs, it is often a mixed blessing. In contrast, 'eco-tourism' can offer a more sustainable strategy for economic development in some peripheral regions.
- The internationalization of finance has created opportunities and challenges for the LDCs in terms of the operation of transnational banks and FDI in financial services, the continued dominance of London, New York and Tokyo over foreign exchange transactions despite the increasing use of electronic money, and the concentration of offshore banking centres in the LDCs.
- The internationalization of business in terms of BPO was begun by US TNCs. The kinds of service activity involved now include not only call centres, computer network support, legal services, accounting and procurement, but also software development, research and development and engineering services. The main outsourcing destinations for BPO in the LDCs are India, Israel, the Philippines and South Africa.

## KEY SOURCES AND SUGGESTED READING

Amiti, M. and Wei, S.-J. 2005. Fear of service outsourcing: is it justified?, *Economic Policy*, 42, 307–47, available at http://www.oecd.org/dataoecd/44/24/35333668.pdf.

Brunn, S. (ed.) 2006. *Wal-Mart World: The World's Biggest Corporation in the Global Economy*. New York and London: Routledge.

Bryson, J.R., Daniels, P.W. and Warf, B. 2004. *Service Worlds: People, Organisations, Technologies*. London and New York: Routledge.

CRIC 2006. *Innovation in Services*. CRIC Briefing No. 2. Manchester: Centre for Research on Innovation and Competition, University of Manchester.

Coffey, W.J. 2000. The geographies of producer services [progress report], *Urban Geography*, 21(2), 170–83.

Cuadrado-Roura, J.R., Rubalcaba-Bermejo, L. and Bryson, J.R. (eds) 2002. *Trading Services in the Global Economy*. Cheltenham: Edward Elgar.

Daniels, P.W. and Bryson, J.R. 2002. Manufacturing services and servicing manufacturing: knowledge-based cities and changing forms of production, *Urban Studies*, 39, 977–91.

Karmarkar, U. 2004. Will you survive the services revolution?, *Harvard Business Review*, June, 82(6), 101–7.

Stutz, F.P. and Warf, B. 2007. *The World Economy: Resources, Location, Trade and Development* 5th edn. Upper Saddle River, NJ: Pearson Education, Inc.

Tickell, A. 1999; 2001; 2002. *Progress in Human Geography* [progress reports on the geography of services]. Vol. 23, 633–9; Vol. 25, 283–92; Vol. 26, 791–801.

UNCTAD 2004. *World Investment Report 2004: The Shift towards Services*. New York and Geneva: United Nations.

## RELATED WEBSITES

China Today.com: http://www.chinatoday.com/
this commercial website offers a variety of material and hyperlinks to even more information about trade and investment in services in China

Department of Information Technology, Ministry of Communications and Information Technology, Government of India: http://www.mit.gov.in/
India's Department of Information Technology (DIT) is part of the country's Ministry of Communications and Information Technology. Its main objective is to help make India a major global information technology player. The DIT website offers information and data on India's IT sector

International Labour Organization: http://www.ilo.org/
this UN agency offers research and data on labour issues around the world, including information related to the services sector

United Nations Conference on Trade and Development (UNCTAD): http://www.unctad.org/en/enhome.htm
UNCTAD's website offers publications and data on trade, investment and economic development issues, including the latest edition of the *World Investment Report*, which contains information and data on TNCs and FDI as they relate to the services sector

World Tourism Organization (WTO): http://www.world-tourism.org/
this UN agency and leading international organization in the field of tourism serves as a global forum for tourism policy issues and a practical source of information and data on tourism

# Part 4

# Adjusting to a new global economy

I n this concluding part of the book, we examine some of the reactions to the emergence of ever larger and more powerful economic forces and the time–space compression that have come to characterize the world economy. In Chapter 12, we explore the changing role of national states within the world economy, emphasizing the relationships between economic change and the new geopolitics and, in particular, the spatial consequences of international and supranational political and economic integration that have occurred in response to the increased scale, sophistication and interdependence of the modern world economy. In Chapter 13, we examine the other side of the coin: decentralist reactions to the changing world economy. Here, the focus is on regionalism and regional policy, nationalism and separatism and grassroots movements towards economic democracy. Finally, in Chapter 14, we review the key arguments that have shaped the book, emphasizing the dynamic interdependence of global and local change.

Picture credit: Paul Knox

# Chapter 12

# International and supranational institutionalized integration

Picture credit: © European Community, 2007

In this chapter, we return to the theme of the relationship between economic development and the role of the state. As Parts 2 and 3 have shown, nation-states have been crucial, both in the struggle for domination over the world economy within the core and as peripheral and semi-peripheral economies have struggled to reduce their dependency on core economies. As the world economy has become more and more globalized, however, nation-states throughout the world economy have had to explore cooperative strategies involving international and supranational ('trading bloc') political and economic integration of various kinds. This chapter outlines the rationale for these strategies, describes the scope of the major international and supranational organizations and illustrates some of the more important spatial implications of international and supranational institutionalized integration. Arguably the most successful of the attempts at supranational integration, the European Union, receives the most detailed examination in this chapter simply because its impacts on the world economy have been the greatest. Although it should be borne in mind that international institutions regulating trade, such as the World Trade Organization (WTO), have also become increasingly important if less visible arbiters of the global economic integration process. This is why we also examine the WTO in some detail.

## 12.1 ECONOMIC CHANGE AND THE NEW GEOPOLITICS

In order to understand the emergence of international and supranational organizations, we must first remind ourselves of the shifting economic and geopolitical foundations of the world economy since the Second World War. In the aftermath of the war, the capitalist world economy was reordered as a more open system. It was a system without the economic barriers of the trading empires that had been set up in the years previously. Instead, it was based on free market capitalism with stable monetary relations and rapidly diminishing barriers to trade. This required, first of all, an *orderly* world, internally peaceful and secure from outside threats. Second, it required leadership in providing and furthering mechanisms for establishing a stable reserve standard for international currency exchange rates and for ensuring access to world trade markets. The one state that could provide military order – the United States – was also the only state economically strong enough to impose order on the economic system. The Soviet world empire had turned inward in its attempt to restructure its economy and society along different ideological lines, but its existence was extremely important because (until its dissolution in 1991) it served to mobilize an ideological reaction – anti-communism – that provided both an economic stimulus and political solidarity within the core economies.

In short, the world economy was characterized by the hegemony of the United States. Under US hegemony, as we saw in Chapter 5, the world economy came to be characterized by Fordism, the socioeconomic system that links mass production with mass consumption. A tense but durable relationship among big business, big labour and big government enabled Fordism to provide the basis for the long postwar boom and unprecedented rise in living standards throughout much of the capitalist world. This boom was also crucially dependent on the massive expansion of world trade and international investment flows made possible under the umbrella of US financial and military power. Following the Bretton Woods Agreement of 1944 that made the US dollar the world's reserve currency (see p. 48), Fordism was implanted in Europe and Japan, either directly, during the occupation phase, or indirectly, through the Marshall Plan and foreign direct investment (FDI) by US companies. The consequent opening up of foreign trade, observes Harvey (1988: 4):

> permitted surplus productive capacity (and potentially surplus labour reserves) to be absorbed in the United States, while the progress of Fordism internationally meant the formation of global mass markets and the absorption of the mass of the world's population, outside the communist world, into the global dynamics of a new kind of capitalism ... At the input end, the opening up of foreign trade meant the globalisation of supply and often ever cheaper raw material. This new internationalism also brought a host of other activities in its wake – banking, insurance, hotels, airports, and, ultimately, tourism. It also meant a new international culture and a new global system of gathering and evaluating information.

The immediate postwar period (1947–60) saw, therefore, the rise of a series of industries – automobiles, steel, petrochemicals, rubber, etc. – that acted as the propulsive engines of economic growth, coordinated through the collective powers of big labour, big business and big government. And out of this there arose a series of grand production regions in the world economy – the Midwest of the United States, the West Midlands of Britain, the Ruhr in West Germany and the Tokyo-Yokohama production region in Japan – managed from worldwide financial and governmental centres such as New York and London and reaching out to dominate an increasingly homogeneous world market.

The logic of Fordist production also fostered, as we have seen (Chapter 6), the emergence of transnational corporations (TNCs) with the capacity to move capital and technology rapidly from place to place, drawing opportunistically on resources, labour markets and consumer markets in different parts of the world. TNCs have now gone far beyond the point where they can be seen simply as extensions of a specific national economy; and even some small firms have now acquired both the capability and the propensity to operate globally. The significance of this is that, *although private companies are by no means absolute masters of their own fate, they do have the ability (as compared with governmental units) to redefine their commitments and objectives in response to the changing opportunities presented by the globalization of the world economy.*

Within this new context of political and economic interdependence, regional and international shifts in economic and political power began to occur, as we saw in Chapters 5 and 6: shifts that the policies of particular governments seemed powerless to prevent by normal means. The ascent of the NICs has brought a new dimension to the world economy in the form of second-order economic powers that have effectively created a new hierarchical geopolitical system. Meanwhile, as the regional influence of NICs has grown, so they have come to exert an independent effect on the landscapes of the world's core economies:

> None has had a greater political/psychological effect on the major powers than the omnipresence of persons, symbols and signs in Europe's great cities, and in such American cities as New York, Miami, New Orleans and Los Angeles. In Europe, billboards advertising Asian, African and Latin American Airlines, store signs in Arabic script, national airline offices and ethnic food restaurants from three continents, a plethora of Arabic-language newspapers displayed prominently in kiosks and, above all, the businessman, tourist, shopper, student and adolescent youth from these newly-powerful countries demonstrate that the world has changed. They have joined the overseas symbols of American power – the Hilton, the Holiday Inn, Hertz, Avis, ESSO, Mobil, IBM, the English-language newspaper, the American bar and restaurant, and the tourist, student and businessman – to share the landscape of sight, sound and taste with Americans.
>
> Cohen (1982: 227)

In the core economies, meanwhile, the prosperity associated with the Fordist regime had been replaced by uncertainty, destabilization and crisis resulting from the conjunction of an extended episode of stagflation associated with the declining performance of many businesses at the same time that labour was increasingly militant (1965–79) and the 1973 OPEC oil embargo. This created national economic management problems that could not be solved without accelerating the inflation that had undermined the role of the US dollar as the international reserve currency.

As a consequence, the role and relative power of nation-states began to change significantly. Economic circumstances reduced the ability of governments to deliver full employment as well as a full range of welfare services; and the growth of the global financial system blunted the power of individual countries to pursue independent fiscal and monetary policies with any degree of success. In particular, the United States had to struggle hard to maintain its hegemony, running a mounting trade deficit and an enormous public debt and having persistently to devalue the dollar in order to maintain competitiveness with Japan and Germany.

In the decentralized, restructured and consolidated world economy that emerged in the 1980s, new communications technologies, new forms of corporate organization and new business services were intensifying time–space compression, decreasing the time horizons of both public and private decision making and making it easier to spread those decisions over an ever wider space. As we saw in Chapter 7, one result has been the acceleration of shifts in the patterning of uneven development as more flexible corporate organization and flexible production systems have been able to quickly exploit particular local mixes of skills and resources. Another outcome is that local governments are being forced to be much more competitive with one another as they attempt not only to protect their economic base during a time of upheaval and transition, but also to identify and exploit some competitive edge with which to lure the newly flexible flows of finance and production. This intergovernmental competition has bred so-called 'entrepreneurial' cities, whose governments have been drawn beyond questions of tax policies, infrastructure provision and service delivery to explore public/private partnerships, foster favourable 'business climates' and initiate controls on labour through contract negotiations with municipal workers.

## 12.2 INTERNATIONAL AND SUPRANATIONAL INSTITUTIONALIZED INTEGRATION

It is within this changing economic and geopolitical context that we have to see the various attempts to adjust to the modern world economy through strategies of international and supranational economic and political integration. We should nevertheless remember that, as Parts 2 and 3 of this book have shown, the dominant processes in both intra-core rivalry and in the struggle by the semi-periphery and periphery to escape from dependency have been dominated by conflict and competition. Economic nationalism, whether drawing on practical examples (e.g., 18th-century Britain and 19th- and 20th-century Japan; see Chapters 5 and 10 respectively), political ideology (e.g., Juan Péron in Argentina and Getúlio Vargas in Brazil in the 1940s and 1950s) or development theory (e.g., the import substitution industrialization espoused by Raoul Prebisch), continues to dominate global economics and geopolitics.

Having acknowledged this, however, we must also recognize the long-term trend among the world's national economies towards the progressive integration and interdependence of local, regional and national economic systems. *What has happened is that the logic of the world economy has in many ways transcended the scale of nation-states.* The logic and apparatus of statehood are not conducive to international and supranational integration, economic or political; but the outcomes of Neo-Fordism have forced many states to explore cooperative strategies of various kinds. As a result, the world's economic landscapes now bear the imprint, in a variety of ways, of international and supranational economic and political integration.

### THE LOGIC OF INTEGRATION

The increased scale, sophistication and interdependence of the modern world economy would not have been feasible were it not for the fact that new technologies and new forms of corporate organization gradually made it possible to conquer several of the frictions that tend to operate against hierarchical flows of production and consumption. In addition to the obvious – for geographers – friction of distance itself, these include the frictions associated with spatial variations in social organization and culture. As railroads, the telegraph, automobiles, aircraft, computer networks, satellite communications systems and fibre optics have successively 'shrunk' the globe, Fordist principles of mass production have brought about a convergence of patterns of social organization and radio and television have undermined local and regional cultures and replaced them with an international culture characterized by the language and artefacts of consumerism: American Express, Benetton, BurgerKing, Coca-Cola, Gucci, Laura Ashley, Marlboro, Mercedes-Benz, MTV, Rolex, Sony, Visa and so on.

The framework of nation-states, however, is a source of friction that has persisted. The main reason for this, of course, is that the functional logic of statehood hinges on reinforcing *differences between* nations while reinforcing *similarities within* nations. In order to establish the required feelings of common identity, even the oldest states have had to engage in the process of creating and diffusing a distinctive identity. Much of the ideology and symbolism of nation-states in Europe, for example, has centred on the systematic mythologizing of history, reinforced by the stereotyping of outsiders. One very important outcome of this was the jingoism and xenophobia that set the context for the First World War, nurtured the ambitions of the Third Reich, and hampered postwar attempts to establish common economic and legal frameworks.

Among the more explicit functions of nation-states that have contributed to the frictions affecting the world economy are those relating to national security and the promotion of homogeneous internal standards and conditions. The latter include controlling fiscal and monetary policy, upholding labour contracts, establishing standards for everything from education to ball bearings, and overseeing key industries such as telecommunications.

Once a significant amount of economic activity had spilled beyond national boundaries, however, countries had to confront the need to rethink these activities in order not to become isolated or to become even more vulnerable to underdevelopment. In short, *it was the international trade system that provided the major impetus for countries to be drawn into various forms of institutionalized integration.* For core countries, the objective was primarily to protect and consolidate existing advantages through increased international security, access to wider markets, investment opportunities and labour markets. For peripheral and semi-peripheral countries, the objective was primarily to minimize or reduce dependency through harnessing more resources and more investment potential. In addition, most countries were able to subscribe, in public at least, to the more lofty ideals of good international relations and a more equitable international economic order.

The particular *advantages* of formalized international and supranational integration include:

1  potential for economies of scale, particularly for the smallest countries and the weakest national economies
2  potential for creating multiplier effects from the existence of enlarged markets
3  potential for strengthening regional interaction by easing the movement of labour, goods and capital.

The particular *disadvantages* of formalized international and supranational integration include:

1  potential loss of national sovereignty over a broad spectrum of issues
2  potential for the intensification of internal inequalities as a wider geographical context makes for more pronounced processes of uneven development.

## TYPES AND LEVELS OF INTEGRATION

Figure 12.1 summarizes the 'where' of international and supranational economic integration since 1945. In practice, integration can be pursued in a variety of ways and at different levels. It can be *formal*, involving an institutionalized set of rules and procedures (e.g., United Nations Organization, European Union (EU, formerly the European Community or EC), General Agreement on Tariffs and Trade (GATT)); or *informal*, involving coalitions of interests (UN voting blocs). It can be *inter*national, involving attempts to foster integration between countries (North Atlantic Treaty Organization (NATO); the **African Union (AU)**, formerly the Organization of African Unity (OAU); the World Trade Organization (WTO)); or *supra*national, involving a commitment to an institutionalized body with certain powers over member states (EU). It can be *economically* oriented (WTO, the North American Free Trade Agreement (NAFTA)), *strategic* (NATO), *political* (UN voting

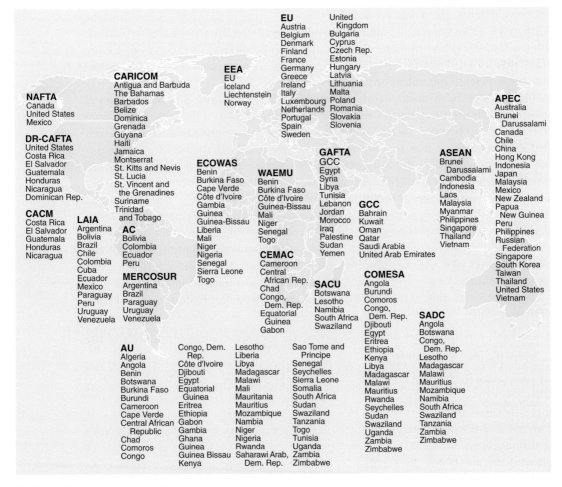

Fig 12.1: Selected supranational integration agreements

*Source:* Updated from World Bank (2002: 155, Figure 6.1)

blocs), *sociocultural* (United Nations Educational, Scientific and Cultural Organization (UNESCO)) or *mixed* (EU, AU) in orientation. We distinguish all these institutions from, for example, the IMF and World Bank, which are not oriented so much towards encouraging integration among states as to regulating state macroeconomic policies and intervening within states to encourage certain kinds of development. In other words, they, like the UN General Assembly and Security Council, represent the global status quo insofar as they are based on a state logic of development even when, as the IMF and World Bank did in the 1970s and 1980s, they give advice and use coercive loans to open up national economies to global competition. They can be thought of as searching for a role for themselves in a world increasingly following a logic of globalization for which they themselves were never designed, dating as they do back to the era immediately after the Second World War.

## THE GATT FRAMEWORK AND THE WTO

Our immediate concern here is with economically oriented integration schemes. Within the capitalist world, these have had to conform to the rules of the General Agreement on Tariffs and Trade (GATT), an international association of most of the world's trading countries formed to promote worldwide free trade and to untangle the complex trade restrictions in the aftermath of the Second World War. The original GATT agreement (in 1947) reduced the average tariff on goods from over 40 per cent to less than 30 per cent. Subsequent rounds of renegotiation have brought the average tariff level down to about 5 per cent (Table 12.1).

Yet the GATT became the victim of its own success. As more countries have joined the agreement and the world economy became increasingly globalized and interdependent, so trade issues have become increasingly complex. The original agreement was written to deal primarily with trade in manufactured goods among developed countries, yet by 1990 and also in 2000 only about 60 per cent of world export earnings came from manufactures. Services accounted for an increasing share of world trade; many of the NICs were not fully subject to GATT rules; and foreign direct investment by TNCs was beyond the scope of the GATT. And although tariffs on manufactured goods were successfully reduced through the GATT, substantial non-tariff barriers (e.g., import quotas, import licences, exchange rate manipulation, government subsidies to domestic industries, special labelling and packaging regulations, etc.) remained a problem. Thus, whereas the early rounds of GATT renegotiation took several months, more recent rounds haven taken several years. The Uruguay Round began in 1986 and was not concluded until December 1993. The chief obstacle was disagreement between the USA and the European Union over non-tariff barriers in the form of various subsidies that both were paying to their farmers. The current Doha Round has so far achieved very little indeed, with major divisions once more between the USA and the EU over trade in services as well as agricultural goods and increasing hostility towards the GATT/WTO process from many of the world's poorer countries whose primary products continue to be excluded from most core country markets by exclusionary tariffs and other restraints on trade. Increased membership and the movement of debate into areas of trade such as services and agriculture long given the status of 'national priorities' by many rich countries suggest that the WTO may be coming up against its political

**Table 12.1** Average tariff levels (per cent) for selected countries, 1988 and 2004–05

|  | 1988 | 2004–05 |
|---|---|---|
| Australia | 15.6 | 4.2 |
| Brazil | 42.2 | 13.1 |
| Canada | 7.7 | 3.7 |
| Chile | 19.9 | 4.9 |
| China | 39.5 | 9.6 |
| European Union | 5.7 | 1.8 |
| Hong Kong | 0.0 | 0.0 |
| India | 79.1 | 28.1 |
| Indonesia | 18.1 | 6.4 |
| Japan | 5.9 | 2.9 |
| Malaysia | 13.6 | 7.4 |
| Mexico | 10.5 | 14.6 |
| New Zealand | 14.9 | 3.7 |
| Philippines | 27.9 | 4.4 |
| Singapore | 0.3 | 0.0 |
| South Korea | 19.2 | 9.3 |
| Taiwan | 12.6 | 5.3 |
| Thailand | 31.2 | 13.3 |
| United States | 5.7 | 3.0 |

*Source:* Based on World Bank (*World Development Indicators Online*, http://devdata.worldbank.org/wdi2006)

limits. For example, unable to persuade the US delegation to cut its incredibly high subsidies to American farmers, the Indian commerce minister spent much of his time at the WTO's Doha Round of talks in July 2006 watching the soccer World Cup.

The crowning achievement of the Uruguay Round in 1993 was the creation of the World Trade Organization (WTO) in 1995 as a replacement for the GATT (which had become labelled by wags as the 'General Agreement to Talk and Talk'). Whereas the GATT had little ability to enforce its decisions, the WTO is a global body with both judicial and regulatory power. Its framework is a series of lengthy agreements that extend beyond trade in manufactured goods to cover investment, services and intellectual property rights. In the words of the organization's former director-general, Renato Ruggiero, the WTO 'is writing the constitution of a single global economy'. A significant step towards this was taken in February 1997 when the 68 original members of the WTO signed an agreement to free up their markets to international competition in telecommunications. By January 2007 the WTO had a membership of 150 countries, including China, with a waiting list of 30 others, including the Russian Federation. Whether the 'constitution' Ruggiero refers to is worth the paper it is written on remains to be seen.

Many of the WTO's agreements are derived from GATT rulings, including the provision that each member state shall extend most-favoured-nation (MFN) treatment to all other member countries. (Thus if, say, the USA were to lower its import duty on textile products from Canada, it would immediately have to extend that same reduced rate to every other WTO member.) There is, however, an exception to this principle for free trade associations and customs unions, members of which may reduce their tariffs against one another without extending such concessions to remaining WTO members. It is this exception that has provided the basis for regional economic integration within the globalizing world economy. To proponents of global free trade it is precisely this exclusion that encourages the substitution of bilateral and regional trading agreements for the multilateral ones that they see as the key to continued globalization. They worry that trading blocs are forming that will merely scale up protectionism from the national to the supranational level.

## INSTITUTIONAL FORMS OF SUPRANATIONAL INTEGRATION

Supranational integration can take a number of different forms. In practice, some of these are also more or less successful in meeting their objectives. As yet many types of integration are relatively limited in both membership and efficacy. In a free trade association, member countries eliminate tariff and quota barriers to trade from other member states, but each individual member continues to charge its regular duties on materials and products coming from outside the association. Membership of the European Free Trade Association (EFTA) dwindled to Iceland, Liechtenstein, Norway and Switzerland when six of the original members left to join the EU (Austria, Denmark, Finland, Portugal, Sweden and the United Kingdom) (Figure 12.1). The Southern African Development Community (SADC) countries signed a free trade agreement in 2000.

Meanwhile, Canada, Mexico and the United States, with over 443 million consumers today, established a trading zone in 1994 with the completion of the North American Free Trade Agreement (NAFTA). This was not only an unprecedented economic integration of core countries and a semi-peripheral country but also the first instrument of economic integration to liberalize trade in services. Since the establishment of NAFTA, trade and investment between Canada, Mexico and the USA has steadily increased. NAFTA's phasing out of tariffs and other trade and investment barriers between these countries over 15 years is leading to a reorganization of the economic geography of North America. Many labour-intensive manufacturing jobs have already been switched from Canada and the USA to Mexico; while the expanding Mexican market is now open to the kinds of product and service in which the USA and Canada have a competitive advantage, such as high-technology products, telecommunications and financial services. Eventually, there will be total access in agricultural markets, which will rewrite the agricultural geography of Mexico and significantly modify agricultural patterns in the southwestern United States. The expected eventual expansion southwards of NAFTA to include countries such as Argentina, Brazil, Chile, Colombia, Paraguay, Peru, Uruguay and Venezuela will lead to a further reorganization of the economic geography of these countries. Currently, however, this possibility meets with considerable opposition in Central and South America not least because the terms of trade are seen to favour US businesses over local business and labour.

A customs union also involves the elimination of tariffs between member states, but has a common protective wall against non-members, as in the case of the Southern African Customs Union (SACU). Where, in addition, internal restrictions on the movement of capital, goods, labour and enterprise are removed, the result is a common market. Most customs unions have gone at least some way towards common market status. Examples include the Central American Common Market (CACM), the Southern Cone Common Market (or Mercado Común Sudamericano (MERCOSUR)), the Andean Common Market (ANCOM) of the Andean Community (AC) (formerly the Andean Pact), the Caribbean Community and Common Market (CARICOM), the Gulf Cooperation Council (GCC), the Economic Community of West African States (ECOWAS) and the Common Market for Eastern and Southern Africa (COMESA). The Arab Free Trade Area (AFTA) is considered an important step towards the ultimate goal of an Arab Common Market (Figure 12.1).

A still higher form of integration is the economic union, which, in addition to the characteristics of a common market, provides for integrated economic policies among member states. The members of WAEMU (the West African Economic and Monetary Union), for example, have moved some way towards economic union with their shared single currency and monetary policy. The Economic and Monetary Community of Central Africa (Communauté Économique et Monétaire de l'Afrique Centrale (CEMAC)) also share a single currency.

The highest form of integration possible involves some form of supranational political union, with a single monetary system and a central bank, a unified fiscal system, a common foreign economic policy and a supranational authority with executive, judicial and legislative branches. Except for the supranational political union of the EU, however, free trade associations and common markets have found it difficult to overcome the obstacles imposed by memberships that include countries at very different levels of development and that involve enormous distances and poorly developed transportation networks. It was in response to such problems that the GATT authorized, in 1971, the waiver of the Article I most-favoured-nation (MFN) provision for developing countries offering concessions to other developing national economies. As a result, Mexico, for example, could offer to reduce its duty on a product from Bolivia without having to extend the same lower rate to the USA. The GATT decision meant that developing countries were free to experiment with a variety of integration models without incorporating internal free trade as a legally binding obligation. The result has been the emergence of a series of trade preference associations such as the Association of Southeast Asian Nations (ASEAN) and the Latin American Integration Association (LAIA).

The increasing globalization of the world economy has broadened and deepened the trend towards regional economic integration. In 1989, for example, the ASEAN countries joined with Australia, Canada, China, Hong Kong, Japan, New Zealand, South Korea, Taiwan and the United States to form the Asia Pacific Economic Cooperation group (APEC), with the objective of promoting the liberalization of trade and promoting cooperation in trade and investment around the Pacific Rim. APEC members have reduced or eliminated some trade and investment barriers as part of voluntary efforts in response to the 1994 Bogor

Declaration (written by the Second Informal APEC Economic Leaders Meeting in Indonesia) and the Information and Technology Agreement that came out of the 1996 WTO Ministerial Conference in Singapore. But, so far, that is about it. In 1992 EFTA and the European Union agreed to establish a unified free trade zone, the European Economic Area (EEA), which has a combined market size today of over 495 million people. (The EEA took effect on 1 January 1993 without the Swiss, whose electorate voted against the agreement.) (See Figure 12.1.)

## 12.3  SPATIAL OUTCOMES OF ECONOMIC INTEGRATION

It follows from the basic principles of economic geography that the enlargement of markets and the removal of artificial barriers to trade will result in a realignment of patterns of economic activity. Two main sets of effects can, in fact, be anticipated. The first relates to patterns of trade. With international integration, the *removal of trade barriers should lead to a more pronounced spatial division of labour*, with each region in the larger association tending to specialize in those activities in which it has the greatest comparative advantage. In effect, production is thereby reallocated from high- to low-cost settings and a great deal of trade is generated within the association. At the same time, lower costs can, theoretically, be passed on to consumers, thus contributing to improved levels of living. These effects of integration are generally referred to as trade creation effects.

Countries that do not belong to the association, however, tend to lose trade: the external tariff wall prevents them from competing effectively with higher cost internal producers whose output is able to circulate duty free within the association. To the extent that the old sources of supply were more efficient producers than the new ones, trade diversion will have taken place, with the result that consumption is shifted away from lower cost external sources to higher cost internal sources, consumers have to pay more for certain goods and levels of living may be depressed.

The extent to which trade creation might outweigh trade diversion depends on several factors, including the degree to which the range of goods produced in member states overlap and the degree of pre-integration reliance on trade with countries outside the association. If integration is successful in the long run in creating trade and accelerating economic growth, it is possible that consequent increases in demand for goods and raw materials will generate 'spread effects', thus creating a positive spillover effect for other economies.

The second set of effects relates to patterns of regional development. Because of the need to exploit new patterns of comparative advantage, a certain amount of relocation of production must take place, with related activities tending to cluster together in the most efficient settings. The corollary is the disinvestments that take place as production is withdrawn from less efficient locations. Given the logic of cumulative causation, the net effect in terms of regional development within the association will clearly be a tendency for *spatial polarization* as a result of 'backwash effects' (see p. 213). Because of the political dimension inherent to integration, this in turn provides a powerful case for a strong *regional policy*.

Meanwhile, integration can also be expected to precipitate other changes in patterns of regional development. A reorganization of patterns of production may occur where changes in patterns of comparative advantage are not sufficient to write off past investment or to prompt relocation, but are sufficient to justify intra-industry specialization. Steel-producing regions, for example, may come to specialize in certain kinds of steel products rather than producing a broad spectrum of steel products for a domestic national market; or agricultural regions may move from mixed farming to a more specialized set of outputs.

Another important consequence of integration is the stimulus that is provided for foreign direct investment. Excluded by high external tariff barriers, foreign suppliers are likely to seek to open branch plants inside the association in order to get access to its market. If successful, this not only makes for a drain of capital when profits are repatriated, it also makes for a degree of external control of some local labour markets. Finally, we must consider the implications of integration for patterns of regional development *outside* the association. The most striking effects in this context will be those related to the dislocations experienced by specialized regions whose exports are no longer competitive within the protected market of the association.

These same principles and tendencies mean that we should expect integration to reinforce the dominant core–periphery patterns in the world's economic landscapes at the macro scale. Patterns of trade between core economies, for instance, are already so strong that integration is able to draw on a good deal of momentum. At the same time, *it is relatively easy for core states to meet the political, social and cultural prerequisites for successful economic integration.* These include:

- similarity in the power of units joining the association
- complementarity of elite value systems
- existence of pluralistic power structures in member countries
- positive perceptions concerning (a) the expected equity of the distribution of benefits from integration and (b) the magnitude of the costs of integration
- compatibility of states' decision-making styles
- adaptability, administrative capacity and flexibility of member states' governments and bureaucracies.

The success of the European Union has dramatized how effective integration between core states can be. Between 1959 and 1971 trade between the six original members – Belgium, France, Italy, Luxembourg, the Netherlands and the former West Germany – increased nearly sixfold; by 2000 the expanded Union of 15 countries accounted for one-fifth of all world trade, excluding intra-Union trade. In 2000 the EU was the world's largest exporter of goods and the second largest importer, after the USA. The EU was the largest importer of commercial services and the second largest exporter, again, after the USA. The enlargement of the EU in 2004 to include a set of semi-peripheral economies in eastern and southern Europe, however, has set the organization on a different course. These 10 countries (plus the addition of Bulgaria and Romania in 2007) all have much lower standards of living that the previous 15 members, many of them were until recently Soviet-style economies and all have serious economic handicaps of one sort or another (political corruption, lack of legal transparency, outdated heavy industries, etc.). But just as the EU helped the economic growth of new members in prior rounds of enlargement, perhaps most notably Spain, Portugal and Greece in their day, so too it will this time with a much larger group of new members. From one viewpoint, enlargement has been the most successful policy of the EU. Politically, its promise has stabilized states while they have been in transition from authoritarian rule and it has offered a broad range of potential economic benefits to countries whose economic growth has long lagged behind their potential, measured in terms of educational levels, adjacency to centres of economic growth and technological sophistication. From another perspective, however, enlargement has undermined the process of 'deepening' the central institutions of the EU by making them more transparent and accountable to the people already under the umbrella of the EU. The failure of Dutch and French referendums on a new European constitution in 2005 can at least, in part, be put down to fears of further expansion to include Turkey and countries in the western Balkans from which new immigrants might come, countries that are even more economically underdeveloped than most countries included in the recent enlargements.

In the case of peripheral economies, by the same token, patterns of trade offer little realistic scope for the reallocation of output following the removal of trade barriers in trade preference organizations, common markets or free trade associations. As we have seen (Chapters 2, 9 and 10), most peripheral countries produce primary commodities that are exported to the core economies rather than to each other and most are so short of capital that even pooled resources are likely to be insufficient to trigger economies of scale of sufficient magnitude to be able to break free from their functional dependency on trade with core economies. Experience has shown, meanwhile, that it is difficult for peripheral and even semi-peripheral states to meet the political, social and cultural preconditions for successful economic integration. Of course, the EU experiment in eastward enlargement and NAFTA suggest that collaboration across the core–semi-periphery divide can meet with some success. How great this is overall and who wins and who loses is something else again. The political strength of the EU and the redistributive policies this currently allows indicates that this may be the difference between these two cases. NAFTA has undoubtedly failed to solve the most pressing of Mexico's economic problems – providing sufficient new jobs for its growing population – and thus one of its main goals, to reduce illegal immigration into the United States, remains unfulfilled. US investment has never compensated for the loss of Mexican investment because of the removal of protective tariffs and increased competition from China in many of its previously most successful manufacturing sectors. Indeed, total manufacturing employment in Mexico has declined since 2000, suggesting that rather than helping Mexican development NAFTA has actually undermined it.

Some efforts at regional integration solely among semi-peripheral states suggest that simply signing up to the organization is never going to be enough to make them a success. ASEAN, for example, despite having generated a growing sense of regional identity, has been unable to progress beyond a preliminary stage of economic regionalism during the last three decades. Regional projects such as the Asian Highway and the Mekong Basin Project have been discussed and only tentative national responsibilities and commitments planned. In the early 1990s ASEAN began working towards the introduction of the ASEAN Free Trade Area (AFTA) and the share of intra-ASEAN trade rose from 20 to almost 25 per cent of total trade as trade in electrical appliances and machinery, mineral products and chemicals increased. A large proportion of intra-ASEAN trade, however, is accounted for by exports that are trans-shipped through Singapore with only marginal value added by processing or packaging. A significant obstacle to significant intra-ASEAN trade growth is that these economies are more complementary to those of

Japan, the United States and western Europe than they are to one another: ASEAN itself cannot absorb all the primary commodities it produces and it is still dependent on the core economies for capital, technology and many consumer goods.

Consequently, as the ASEAN countries have struggled to recover from the Asian financial crisis in the late 1990s, a hot topic of discussion has been increased East Asian trade, not only with Japan, but also with countries such as China and South Korea. But ASEAN's continued commitment to a policy of non-interference in the affairs of other members and to decision-by-consensus continues to hinder progress. Until the political relationship between Japan and the rest of Asia, reflecting the failure of Japanese governments to come to terms with their country's imperial past in Asia, and the increasing military power of China are explicitly addressed, little progress in 'deepening' ASEAN can be expected. This indicates the degree to which successful economic integration has to have at least minimal political foundations.

Even less successful than ASEAN as an example of supranational integration has been the Andean Pact, whose efforts at moving beyond the initial agreement between member states have been truly half-hearted. Members have been unwilling to build integration into their own economic planning and policymaking and have been unable to reach agreement about the harmonization of policies with regard to foreign trade, industrial development or fiscal affairs. Although some progress has been made at diplomatic levels (on pronouncements in favour of human rights in Nicaragua, for instance) and some increase had been achieved in absolute levels of intra-market trade, the negative effects of spatial and socioeconomic polarization, particularly in Bolivia and Ecuador, have led to tensions. Meanwhile, there have been virtually no positive effects in terms of the promotion of new sectors of production or the strengthening of existing regions of production. As a result, the import substitution model was abandoned and a new Andean Community (AC) replaced the Andean Pact in 1997. Beginning with the establishment of an executive body, council of presidents and council of foreign ministers, the AC is moving towards a common market and, in theory, eventually to a supranational political union modelled on the European Union with a parliament directly elected by the more than 96 million citizens of its four member countries, despite the exit of Venezuela (Figure 12.1).

One important response to the problems of development, trade and regional integration within the LDCs has been the so-called 'north–south dialogue'. The most important platform for this dialogue has been the United Nations Conference on Trade and Development (UNCTAD), launched in Geneva in 1964. By the end of the Geneva meetings, a degree of political solidarity had emerged among developing countries. Under the banner of the 'Group of 77' they issued a declaration:

> The unity [of the developing countries in UNCTAD] has sprung out of the fact that facing the basic problems of development they have a common interest in a new policy for international trade and development. The developing countries have a strong conviction that there is a vital need to maintain, and further strengthen, this unity in the years ahead. It is an indispensable instrument for securing the adoption of new attitudes and new approaches in the international economic field.

The Group of 77, which now has more than 130 members, has succeeded in articulating demands for a 'new international economic order' (not to be confused with the new international division of labour). Central to the new order envisioned by the Group of 77 are demands for fundamental changes in the marketing conditions of world trade in primary commodities. These changes would require a variety of measures, including price and production agreements among producer countries, the creation of international buffer stocks of commodities financed by a common fund, multilateral long-term supply contracts and the indexing of prices of primary commodities against the price of manufactured goods. Such changes have been at the centre of discussions in a series of UNCTAD conferences, special sessions of the United Nations General Assembly, meetings of a specially convened Conference on International Economic Cooperation and successive meetings of the heads of state of the British Commonwealth. Throughout these discussions, however, the core countries in general, and the United States in particular, have been reluctant to do more than agree to general statements about the desirability of a new international economic order. As a result, Williams' observation (G. Williams, 1981: 99) remains true, that 'the New International Economic Order is still a dream'.

In practice, therefore, there have been two dominant sets of spatial outcomes of international and supranational economic integration. One has simply been the reinforcement of the dominant core–periphery structure of the world economy because of the relative success of economic integration between core states. The second has been the imprint of this success on particular regions. This imprint can be discerned: (1) in terms of the effects of trade creation, trade diversion, spatial polarization, regional policy and sociospatial tensions within core-based associations such as the EU, and (2) in terms of the dislocations experienced subsequently by non-member states. In the remainder of this chapter we illustrate the importance and complexity of the second of these sets of spatial outcomes – the consequences of the success of economic integration between core states – using the example of the European Union.

## THE IMPRINT OF THE EUROPEAN UNION

The European Union had its origins in pragmatic responses to the changed economic climate of postwar Europe. The main objective was to recapture the core status within the world economy that Europe had forfeited as a result of the war. But there was also a more idealistic impulse to bind countries together so that the wars that had so bitterly divided Europe in the 20th century would never reoccur. This political motivation is important because it has long made the EU more than simply a supranational *economic* organization. Although there was a good deal of popular concern over the dominance of US-based TNCs in Europe's postwar economic recovery, the crux of the problem was that the centre of technological advance had moved to the United States. As a result, 'The real challenge was to ensure that Europe did not remain dependent on imported capital goods and that it began to generate its own research so as to pre-empt the United States in any future technological cycle of production' (George, 1991: 59).

The European Community was formed in 1957 by an amalgamation of three institutions that had been set up in the 1950s in order to promote progressive economic integration along particular lines for six countries (Belgium, France, West Germany, Italy, Luxembourg and the Netherlands): Euratom, the European Coal and Steel Community (ECSC) and the European Economic Community (EEC). This amalgamation fostered the recovery of core status:

[B]y providing favourable conditions for multinational investment, so bringing jobs and prosperity back to Europe; by encouraging the emergence of European multinationals that had cultural reasons for situating their headquarters and research facilities in Europe; by providing the conditions in which capital accumulation could proceed to the point where research and development funds were available for profits; but also by an injection of public funding into the process, through Euratom, and through EEC industrial research programmes.

George (1991: 59)

Having expanded from its six original members to include Denmark, the Republic of Ireland and the United Kingdom in 1972, Greece in 1981, Portugal and Spain in 1984 and Austria, Finland and Sweden in 1995, the European Union (as by then it had been renamed) then boasted a population of nearly 380 million, with a combined GDP in 2000 of over US$7.8 billion (which was nearly 80 per cent of the United States' almost US$9.9 billion). In 2004 Cyprus, the Czech Republic, Estonia, Hungary, Latvia, Lithuania, Malta, Poland, Slovakia and Slovenia joined, with Bulgaria and Romania coming into the fold in 2007. As of 2007 the EU had 490 million people and a 2005 GDP larger than that of the USA, US$10.8 billion compared to the United States at $10.03 billion. The EU has developed into a large, sophisticated and powerful institution with a pervasive influence on patterns of economic and social well-being within its member states and a significant impact on certain aspects of economic development within many non-member countries (Figure 12.2).

The initial cornerstone of the European Community was a compromise worked out between the strongest two of the original six members. The former West Germany wanted a larger but protected market for its industrial goods; France wanted to continue to protect its highly inefficient (but large and politically important) agricultural sector from overseas competition. The result was the creation of a tariff-free market within the Community, a common external tariff and a Common Agricultural Policy (CAP) to bolster the Community's agricultural sector. Given the nature of this compromise, it should be no surprise that the European Community performed very unevenly.

Meanwhile, the rest of the world economy had changed significantly, intensifying the challenge to Europe. By the early 1980s the US and Japanese economies, having accomplished a large measure of restructuring, were becoming increasingly interdependent and prosperous on the basis of globalized producer services and new, high-tech industries. London's once pre-eminent financial services were losing ground to those of New York and Tokyo; and even the former West Germany, with the Community's healthiest economy, faced the prospect of being left behind as a producer of obsolescent capital goods and consumer goods. In response, the European Community re-launched itself, beginning in the mid-1980s with the ratification of the Single European Act 1985, which affirmed the ultimate aim of economic and political harmonization within a single supranational government. The measures to introduce the Single European Market in 1992 with the Treaty of European Union (the 'Maastricht Treaty'), conferred on the Union many of the major functions of a sovereign nation-state, including:

- creation of a single currency, the euro
- coordination, supervision and enforcement of economic policies
- maintenance of a completely free internal market

Fig 12.2: Enlargement of the European Union

- preservation of law and order
- protection of fundamental rights of individual citizens
- maintenance of equity and, where necessary, the redistribution of wealth between regions
- management of a common external policy covering all areas of foreign policy and a common defence policy.

This re-launching represents an impressive achievement, particularly since it had to be undertaken at a time when there were major distractions: having to manage a changing relationship with the United States through GATT renegotiations, having to cope with the reunification of Germany and the break-up of the former Soviet sphere of influence in eastern Europe and, not least, having to cope with a wide-spread resurgence of nationalism (see Chapter 13). Ratification of the Maastricht Treaty was in fact achieved in 1993 only after last-minute manoeuvrings prompted by the concerns of Danish and UK voters over aspects of nation-state sovereignty. Despite such misgivings, however, the economic benefits of EU membership are widely recognized. Croatia, Macedonia and Turkey have opened discussions about future membership, although Turkey's application has long faced considerable hostility because of its economic and political distinctiveness to say nothing of its religious difference (it is a largely Muslim country) and geographical 'distance' from the core of Europe. Other countries, such as Bosnia, Moldova, Montenegro, Serbia and Ukraine are also in the queue for membership at some time in the future. Among existing member states there is something of an 'enlargement fatigue' associated with incorporating existing new members, the failure to make much progress on making the European Commission in Brussels (the main bureaucracy of the EU) more responsive to public opinion or representative of the varying population size of the different member states as the organization expands in membership and the increasingly liberal and less redistributive policies pursued in recent years that seem to augur, at least for some people, the spectre of increased uneven development within the EU as businesses from rich areas search out opportunities such as lower wages and standards of living in the poorer areas. Western contracts and investment have undoubtedly flooded into eastern Europe. The biggest fuel for this boom has been wage costs that are typically still half that of western levels. At the same time there is also concern that membership is also increasingly à la carte with some members committed to all EU policies whereas others continue to opt out on such key issues as a common currency (e.g., Britain, Sweden) and common immigration and travel rules (e.g., Britain). The common currency (now covering 13 member states) has made it impossible for member governments to use monetary policies such as devaluations and interest rate shifts to manipulate their economies but it has boosted trade among them, if less than originally envisaged. The fact that the countries that opted out of the euro – Britain, Denmark and Sweden – have seen equivalent gains to within-EU trade suggests that in the future many one-size-fits-all policies may face increasing pressure for opt-outs from member states.

## TRADE CREATION AND DIVERSION

The economic benefits of EC membership were soon felt. Even by 1970, trade between member countries was 40–50 per cent higher, overall, than it would have been if the Community had not been formed; by 1980 the figure had risen to a gain of between 100 and 125 per cent. While many trade liberalization measures to implement the Single European Market in 1992 have still to take full effect, the most recent analyses by the EU indicate an increase in intra-EU trade of 4 to 5 per cent in 1994, for example, due to the Single Market. The net benefits of these increases are far from clear, however, since it is generally acknowledged that the overall increase in intra-Union trade has been the product of a high degree both of *trade creation* and of *trade diversion*. While it is very difficult to isolate the effects of Union membership from other effects, such as TNC activity, overall increases in intra-Union competition and trade have generated economies of scale for EU producers; these have in turn stimulated further competition and trade, accelerated changes in industrial structure and corporate organizations and brought about efficiency gains in both importing and exporting countries. Owen (1983) estimated that these economic benefits could be more than half as great as the value of trade itself.

## SPATIAL POLARIZATION

It is also clear that these benefits have been associated with a significant amount of regional change within the Union, although once again it is difficult to isolate the effects of supranational political union from others. In overall terms, the removal of internal barriers to labour, capital and trade has worked to the clear disadvantage of peripheral regions within member states and in particular to the disadvantage of those furthest from the European core (see Figure 5.3) that is increasingly the 'centre of gravity' in terms of both production and consumption. At the same time, integration has accelerated and extended the processes of concentration and centralization, creating structural as well as spatial inequalities. As Holland (1980: 8) put it:

> [T]he market of the Community is essentially a capitalist market, uncommon and unequal in the record of who gains what, where, why and when. Its mechanisms have already disintegrated major industries and regions in the Community and threaten to realize an inner and outer Europe of rich and poor countries.

Slower growing member states with economies dominated by inefficient primary or manufacturing industries are, in short, in danger of remaining problem regions within a prosperous EU. Evidence on trends in personal incomes supports this prognosis. Clusters of richer and poorer member states are identifiable in terms of per capita income relative to the EU average. At the top end of the range, with above average incomes, are Austria, Belgium, Denmark, France, Germany, Italy, Luxembourg, the Netherlands and Sweden. Just below the average are Finland, Ireland and the United Kingdom, although the UK's position has fallen during the last 10 years while Ireland's has risen. Per capita incomes in Spain, Portugal and Greece, not to mention most of the most recent new members, have remained consistently well below the EU average. Of course, variations in income persist among the regions *within each member* country, such as between the richer north and poorer south of Italy (see Figure 7.8). Indeed, the enlargement of the EU to include a large number of countries in eastern Europe whose GDPs are much lower than the EU average is rewriting the pattern of spatial polarization within the EU.

## EFFECTS OF THE COMMON AGRICULTURAL POLICY (CAP)

The most striking changes in the regional geography of the EU, however, have been those related to the operation of the CAP. It is the CAP that dominates the EU budget. For a long time, it accounted for more than 70 per cent of the EU's total expenditures, and it still accounts for more than 40 per cent. Its operation has had a significant impact on rural economies, rural landscapes and rural levels of living and has even influenced urban living through its effects on food prices.

The basis of the CAP was a system of support for farmers' incomes that was operated through the artificial support of wholesale prices for agricultural produce. While motivated mainly by political considerations, the CAP provided a relatively risk-free environment in which investment for farm modernization could be encouraged. At the same time, stable, guaranteed prices provided security and continuity of food supplies for consumers. Assured markets also allowed trends in product specialization and concentration by farm, region and country to proceed at a faster rate than might otherwise have occurred, as Bowler (1985) showed in his survey of the geography of agriculture under the CAP. Not all products have been subject to CAP support, however. While regions specializing in crops and livestock subject to price guarantees, intervention and market regulation have been able to intensify their specialization, other regions have been subject to Union-wide competition.

The overall result has been a *realignment of production patterns*, with a general withdrawal from mixed farming. Ireland, the United Kingdom and Denmark, for example, have increased their specialization in the production of wheat, barley, poultry and milk; while France and Germany have increased their specialization in the production of barley, maize and sugar beet. It is at regional and sub-regional scales that these changes have been most striking. CAP support for oilseeds, for example, made rapeseed a profitable break crop in cereal-producing regions of the United Kingdom, with the bright yellow flowers of the crop bringing a remarkable change to the summer landscapes of the countryside.

The reorganization of Europe's agricultural geography under the CAP also brought some *unwanted side-effects*, however, as outlined now:

1 Environmental problems occurred because of the speed and scale of modernization, combined with farmers' desire to capitalize on generous levels of guaranteed prices for arable crops. In particular, moorlands, woodlands, wetlands and hedgerows have come under threat and some 'vernacular' landscapes of small farms have been replaced by the prairie-style settings of specialized agribusiness.

2 Another serious problem with geographical implications concerns the large surpluses fostered by the price support system. These 'mountains' of beef, butter, wheat, sugar and milk powder and 'lakes' of olive oil and wine had to be sold off at a loss to neighbouring countries, dumped on world markets, donated as famine relief or 'denatured' (rendered unfit for human consumption) at a considerable cost.

3 A third set of problems arose from the income transfers caused by CAP policies. Price support mechanisms involve a transfer of income from taxpayers to producers and from consumers to producers. There is plenty of evidence to show that these transfers are regressive within member countries and inequitable between them. Expenditure on food generally accounts for a larger proportion of disposable income in poorer households than in better off households. Producers, contrariwise, benefit from price support policies in proportion to their total production, so that the larger and more prosperous farmers receive a disproportionate share of the benefits. Spatial inequity arises because countries or regions that are major producers of price-supported products receive the major share of the benefits while the costs of price support are shared among member states according to the overall size of their agricultural sector. Furthermore, the CAP pricing system made no concessions for a long time to the variety of agricultural systems practised on farms of different sizes and in different regions. As a result, areas with particularly large and/or intensive or specialized farm units (such as northern France and the Netherlands) benefited most, together with regions specializing in the most strongly supported crops (cereals, sugar beet and dairy products). Effectively, this has meant that the most prosperous agricultural regions have benefited most from the CAP, so that farm income differentials within member countries have been maintained, if not reinforced.

4  In addition to all this, the budgetary cost of the CAP escalated. By 1983 budgetary problems had become acute; but reform of the CAP was hampered by domestic political considerations in member countries that were the biggest beneficiaries of the CAP. The CAP became a source of serious disharmony, particularly in the United Kingdom, where, before EU membership, food policies had been progressive, subsidizing lower income households. Embracing the CAP meant a higher and regressive system of food prices without any compensatory benefits: peasant farming and inefficient agricultural practices had been purged from the UK economy long before.

Meanwhile, EC agricultural subsidies had become a serious issue in GATT and WTO negotiations; and the re-launch of the EC/EU in the mid-1980s required a more open and competitive approach to internal markets in every sector, including agriculture. Together with increasing awareness of the unwanted side-effects of the CAP, these considerations have led to ongoing reforms of the CAP. Since 1992 the guaranteed prices that farmers receive for arable crops, beef, dairy and wine products have been cut gradually. To offset the lower guaranteed prices, direct payments to farmers have been increased, but the member states are now allowed to target these payments to achieve specific national or regional production priorities.

## REGIONAL POLICY

The United Kingdom's accession to the Community in 1972 highlighted the lopsidedness of Community policy in favour of rural interests compared with those of industrial areas. Although the Community had effectively operated 'regional' policies through the ECSC and the European Investment Bank (EIB) for some time, there had been no comprehensive, coordinated framework within which to operate. The ECSC was limited to the 're-adaptation' of workers and the 'conversion' of local economies in depressed coalmining and steel-producing regions. The EIB was a Community banking system designed to reduce intra-Community disparities in economic development by disbursing loans to selected projects in priority regions; but although it was particularly influential in sponsoring projects in marginal, cross border regions, it was simply not equipped to deal with the casualties of regional economic restructuring within an expanding common market.

The entry of the United Kingdom to the Community not only made for a significant increase in the scope and intensity of regional restructuring processes but also brought a legacy of chronic regional problems and, with them, a certain political resolve. Following an examination of the issues (Commission of the European Communities, *Thompson Report*, 1973), the Community launched the structural funds in 1975 with a relatively modest budget.

The addition of Portugal and Spain to the Community in 1984 changed both the nature and intensity of regional problems. The proportion of the EC population living in 'least favoured' regions (those where gross domestic product was under half the EC average) doubled, with most of the increase being accounted for by depressed rural regions. At the same time, the re-launch of the EC, with more open internal markets, brought the probability of intensified spatial polarization. This was recognized by the Single European Act (SEA), which raised 'economic and social cohesion' to the status of a new policy objective within the Community. The SEA doubled the funding – in real terms – for regional development assistance from the structural funds (from 7 billion European currency units (ECUs) to 14 billion ECUs at 1988 prices). This was further reinforced by the budget for 1993–97 (the so-called 'Delors II Package'), which contained a real increase of 30 per cent in the Community budget, including 10 billion ECUs over 5 years for a cohesion fund to help Greece, Ireland, Portugal and Spain achieve comparable levels of economic development to the rest of the Community by financing transportation and environmental infrastructure projects. By 2000 the structural funds accounted for 35 per cent of the overall EU budget.

Meanwhile, the re-launch of the Union, the reform of the CAP and the accessions of 15 new members between 1995 and 2007 (Figure 12.2) provided the impetus for ongoing reforms of EU regional policy objectives. There are now three priority objectives to guide the disbursement of regional development assistance grants from the structural and cohesion funds between 2007 and 2013, as follows:

- *Convergence*: to promote the development of the most disadvantaged regions (with a GDP per capita less than 75 per cent of the EU average) whose development is lagging behind (equivalent to the previous 'Objective 1' regions).
- *Regional competitiveness and employment*: to strengthen the competitiveness, employment and attractiveness of selected regions (other than those which are the most disadvantaged).
- *European territorial cooperation*: to strengthen cross-border and interregional cooperation (based on the previous INTERREG initiative).

A number of funds address these priority objectives. The structural funds comprise the European Regional Development Fund (ERDF) which supports productive investment including transportation and communications infrastructure, and the European Social Fund (ESF) which supports education and training. The cohesion fund is intended to reduce social and economic disparities. The *convergence* and *regional competitiveness and employment* objectives have an explicit regional dimension (Figure 12.3).

These policies clearly represent a serious response to the spatial implications of economic integration. It is difficult to assess how effective they can be in redressing the regional restructuring and spatial polarization that have accompanied the creation and enlargement of the European Union. Yet it is debatable whether regional policies can, in fact, do so, particularly since the new reach and flexibility of TNCs can exploit cost advantages elsewhere in the world that the EU structural funds could never hope to match. What is clear, however, is that the funds are not always put to use. For the period 2000–06, percentages actually used varied from 48 per cent in Portugal to only 16 per cent in the Netherlands. Within countries, usage also varies, seemingly in line with administrative capacity.

## EXTERNAL EFFECTS OF THE EU

Meanwhile, the scale of the EU and its maintenance of a strongly protectionist agricultural policy, as well as a protected EU market, have inevitably had a significant impact on non-member countries: diverting trade and creating complex new layers of interdependence. Much of this complexity relates to the 'pyramid of privilege' that has arisen from the EU's trade agreements with different groups of non-member countries. At the base of the pyramid is a generalized system of preferences negotiated through UNCTAD. This allows access to the EU market for a broad range of products from developing countries. Bilateral trade agreements also exist with some

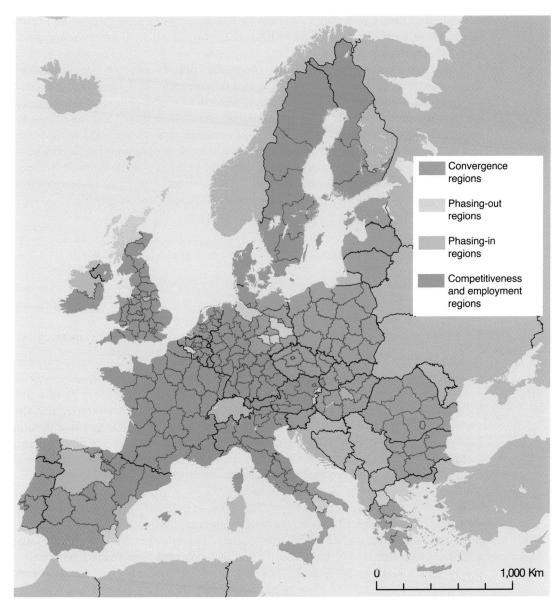

Fig 12.3: Regional policy in the European Union, 2007–2013

*Source:* Adapted from European Union, available at http://ec.europa.eu/regional_policy/atlas2007/fiche_index_en.htm

countries as a result of attempts by the EU to extend and diversify its trading patterns. The most favourable trading privileges are extended to a large group of countries in Africa, the Caribbean and the Pacific (the 'ACP states'), most of them former colonial territories of member states. Originally established as the Youndé Convention in 1963 and later extended at Lomé Conventions in 1975 and 1979, these privileges allow access to the EU market for tropical agricultural products without having to provide reciprocal privileges to EU members or abandon trading agreements with other developing countries. They also involve an export revenue stabilization scheme – STABEX – that covers nearly 50 key primary products and raw materials.

In detail, the mechanics of these privileges are complex and it is very difficult to assess their impact on patterns of trade and development. It is clear, however, that the 'privileges' extended to non-members are essentially designed to enhance the position of the EU rather than to contribute to a 'new international economic order'. 'Sensitive' products (i.e., those that compete directly with EU agricultural and industrial products), for example, are excluded from preferential treatment or are subject to seasonal restrictions. Moreover, the net effect of the Lomé 'privileges' has been to increase the dependency of many countries on exports of a narrow range of primary produce to the EU market. Particular examples include:

- Burundi (coffee)
- Chad (cotton)
- Côte d'Ivoire (groundnuts)
- Ghana (cocoa)
- Senegal (wood, groundnuts)
- Sudan (coffee)
- Tonga (copra)
- Uganda (coffee).

As a result, EU relations with ACP countries have been interpreted as neo-imperialist, effectively extending the core–periphery structure of the world economy.

It is not only peripheral countries that have been affected by the EU, however. The EU represents an outcome of the struggle for economic power within the core and to preserve power in relation to the semi-periphery as much as it is an attempt to consolidate power in relation to the periphery. EU trade relations with the United States have been fractious, while the EU has been forced to mount a 'diplomatic assault' on Japan in an attempt to stem the impact of Japanese direct investment in sophisticated manufacturing industries (automobiles, electronics, etc.) within the EU.

Core and semi-periphery countries have also been directly affected by the trade-diverting effects of the EU's protection of 'temperate' agricultural products. Trade diversion effects are particularly evident where EU subsidies have produced large surpluses for export. For example, EU exports of beef rose from 5 per cent of world trade in 1977 to over 20 per cent in 1980 and in so doing displaced Australian and Argentinian exports to Egypt and Uruguayan exports to Ghana. Of course, the outbreaks of 'mad cow disease' and foot and mouth disease, which caused EU beef exports in 2001 to reach their lowest level for 20 years, created serious disruptions in trade for the EU's primary beef export markets of Egypt and Russia, which, like other countries, put a temporary ban on EU beef.

Other striking cases of trade diversion have occurred as specialist producers of 'temperate' products with strong traditional ties to European markets found themselves largely excluded by the EU's external tariff wall. New Zealand is a good example. The United Kingdom used to take nearly all New Zealand's butter, cheese and lamb, so that after the United Kingdom joined the EU, New Zealand agriculture had to be restructured, new products had to be developed (a notable success here being the kiwi fruit) and new markets had to be penetrated in Latin America, India and Japan – in the face of competition from the subsidized surpluses of dairy produce from the EU.

## Box 12.1 Genetically modified foods and US–EU trade

'Not since the Green Revolution of the 1960s, when high-yielding wheat and rice varieties were developed that increased harvests in Asia two-, five- and even ten-fold, have technological advances had the potential to so affect world agricultural trade.' These optimistic words touting the 'promise of technology' came from James M. Murphy, Assistant US Trade Representative in 1999. The proponents of bioengineered seeds and food – genetically modified through biotechnology – argue that, compared to traditional crops, genetically modified ones require less water and fewer herbicides, produce higher yields and not only can taste better but may also be more nutritious and easily digested. Yet the opponents of genetically modified food for human consumption contend that the technology has not been adequately tested scientifically. They point to the potential for new allergens and toxins to be produced, which could cause mild to potentially deadly allergic reactions or for antibiotic-resistant genes to be transferred to humans, leading to the growth of antibiotic-resistant disease strains.

Since the mid-1990s, genetically modified foods have become a hot-button issue, not only in Europe, but also, increasingly, in the USA. In 1999, Cornell University researchers reported in *Nature* that laboratory tests showed that the use of genetically modified Bt-corn killed not only intended pests such as the corn borer, but also Monarch butterfly larvae. In September 2000 bioengineered food hit the newspaper headlines when Kraft Foods recalled 'tainted' taco shells from supermarket shelves because they contained 'StarLink', a kind of genetically modified corn that was not approved for human consumption by the US Food and Drug Administration (FDA).

In the USA, however, consumer awareness, while growing, remains low. The FDA does not require testing of genetically modified foods and has not indicated that it intends to change its existing voluntary labelling guidelines. US agribusinesses (including Monsanto, the major supplier of genetically modified seeds in the USA) remain staunchly against mandatory labelling of genetically modified foods. Yet polls report that only between about 20 and 30 per cent of those surveyed are aware that genetically modified foods are being sold in US supermarkets. At the same time, over 80 per cent of those surveyed support the mandatory labelling of genetically modified foods and would avoid buying them if they were clearly labelled. It is estimated that between 60 and 70 per cent of the foods eaten by US consumers contain some genetically modified organisms (GMOs).

Europe since the mid-1980s has seen increasingly widespread public support for stricter health safety standards in conjunction with the strengthening of EU environmental and consumer protection standards. More recently, there has been an undermining of public confidence following the highly visible failure of EU and national regulations to respond quickly enough to particular high-profile health and safety crises, most notably the outbreak of 'mad cow disease'. In response to protests and shoppers' objections, some supermarket chains in Britain and other European countries have refused to stock genetically modified foods. A number of companies, including Frito-Lay, Gerber and McDonald's, announced that they would stop using foods that came from genetically altered seeds in their products that are sold in Europe and the USA.

In 2001 the European Commission approved new rules requiring labelling of food or animal feed that contains more than 1 per cent genetically modified ingredients. The rules also establish mechanisms to trace GMOs through production to distribution – 'from farm to table'. While these rules, considered to be the toughest in the world, remain to be approved by EU member countries and the European Parliament, EU decisions such as this are expected to have a major impact on US farmers and producers who export food and animal feed to Europe. The USA produces a significant proportion of the genetically modified food that is marketed throughout the world and is the world's largest exporter of wheat for animal as well as human consumption. More than three-quarters of the US soybean crop and nearly 40 per cent of the corn crop is grown from genetically modified seeds. Agribusiness in the USA has already lost millions of dollars in exports because individual countries (such as Austria, France and Luxembourg) have refused to accept shipments of genetically modified crops and food despite the fact that they were approved for sale by the EU and their actions were in violation of WTO rules against vetoing products without a clear scientific basis. In 2007, however, the EU trade commissioner officially urged member countries to comply with EU rules or face serious countermeasures in the WTO.

Showing greater concern for the food and environmental plight of less developed countries where poor soils and hunger are serious problems, the UN has called for a more balanced approach (UNDP, 2001: 3–4):

> The current debate in Europe and the United States over genetically modified crops mostly ignores the concerns and needs of the developing world. Western consumers who do not face food shortages or nutritional deficiencies or work in fields are more likely to focus on food safety and the potential loss of biodiversity, while farming communities in developing countries are more likely to focus on potentially higher yields and greater nutritional value, and on the reduced need to spray pesticides that can damage soil and sicken families.

## SUMMARY

In this chapter, we have shown how the imprint of international and supranational economic and political integration has begun to affect the world's economic land-scapes as nation-states have responded to the changing economic and geopolitical context of the world economy. This response has resulted in a variety of forms and levels of integration, but, in practice, the basic principles of economic geography have resulted in three main outcomes:

1 reinforcement of the dominant core–periphery structure of the world economy
2 spatial reorganization of production as trade creation and trade diversion affect both member and non-member states
3 creation and intensification of regional polarization as the economies of scale and multiplier effects in regions most favoured by integration create backwash effects elsewhere.

Yet, while it is important to acknowledge international and supranational integra-tion as a response to the globalization of the world economy, it would be unwise to overstate its effects. International and supranational organizations are not about to replace countries and we must recognize their limits as contributors to the constant rewriting of the world's economic landscapes. The further integration of the EU, for example, is seriously hampered by a number of issues that transcend its territory and jurisdiction, including its inability to reduce unemployment and significantly reduce income disparities between the richest and poorest regions. Moreover, as Nairn pointed out, spatial polarization within the EU has:

> [S]ought out and found the buried fault lines of the area ... Nationalism in the real sense is never a historical accident, or a mere invention. It reflects the latent fracture lines of human society under strain.

Nairn (1977: 69)

Indeed, nationalism and localism can be seen to be intensifying, not only in response to the backwash effects of international and supranational integration but also in response to the overall globalization of the economy, the internationalization of culture and society and the insecurity and instability generated by the transition to advanced capitalism.

In the next chapter of the book, therefore, we turn to an examination of decentralist reactions to the changing world economy.

## KEY SOURCES AND SUGGESTED READING

Agnew, J. 2001. How many Europes? The European Union, eastward enlargement and uneven development, *European Urban and Regional Studies*, 8, 29–38.

Artis, M. and Lee, N. (eds) 1994. *The Economics of the European Union*. Oxford: Oxford University Press.

Foster, J.W. 2005. NAFTA after its first decade, in *The USA and Canada 2005*. London: Europa Publications.

Gibb, R. and Michalak, W. (eds) 1994. *Continental Trading Blocs: The Growth of Regionalism in the World Economy*. Chichester: John Wiley & Sons.

Grant, C. 2006. *Europe's Blurred Boundaries: Rethinking Enlargement and Neighbourhood Policy*. London: Centre for European Reform.

Hardy, S., Hart, M., Albrechts, L. and Katos, A. (eds) 1995. *An Enlarged Europe: Regions in Competition?* London: Regional Studies Association.

Hoekman, B.M. and Kostecki, M.M. 1996. *The Political Economy of the World Trading System: From GATT to WTO*. New York: Oxford University Press.

Jacoby, W. 2004. *The Enlargement of the European Union and NATO: Ordering from the Menu in Central Europe*. Cambridge: Cambridge University Press.

Milio, S. 2007. Can administrative capacity explain differences in regional performances? Evidence from structural funds implementation in southern Italy, *Regional Studies*, 41, 429–42.

Peet, R. 2003. *Unholy Trinity: The IMF, World Bank and WTO*. London: Zed Books.

Pinder, D. 1998. *The New Europe*. Chichester: John Wiley & Sons.

Vogel, D. 2001. *The Regulation of GMOs in Europe and the United States: A Case-Study of Contemporary European Regulatory Politics*. Paper prepared for a workshop on trans-Atlantic differences in GMO regulation sponsored by the Council on Foreign Relations.

## RELATED WEBSITES

European Union's Directorate General for Regional Policy: http://europa.eu/pol/reg/index_en.htm
this website provides the latest information on the EU's regions and regional policy

NAFTA Secretariat: http://www.nafta-sec-alena.org/
this website contains public documents on the North American Free Trade Agreement (NAFTA),
including the entire agreement itself

ASEAN: http://www.aseansec.org/
this is ASEAN's official website and contains a wealth of information on the history and activities of
this association of countries in Southeast Asia

APEC: http://www.apecsec.org.sg/
APEC's official website provides comprehensive information on the history and activities of this
association of countries in the Asia?Pacific region

Andean Community: http://www.comunidadandina.org/endex.htm
the official website of the Andean Community contains information on the history and activities of
this association of countries in Latin America

Group of 77: http://www.g77.org/
the official website of the Group of 77 at the United Nations offers the history, aims and activities
of this coalition of LDCs

United Nations: http://www.un.org/
the main website for the United Nations and a rich source of information and hyperlinks for the
UN and its agencies, history, research and activities

Ag BioTech InfoNet: http://www.biotech-info.net/
this website provides information and hyperlinks to articles with a variety of views on issues
related to genetically modified foods

Picture credit: © European Community, 2007

# Chapter 13

# Reassertion of the local in the age of the global: regions and localities within the world economy

A persisting theme of this book is the existence of trends towards ever more powerful states and ever larger corporate structures. In the broader sweep of change within the world economy, these trends can appear to be inexorable and irreversible. Similarly, the increasing prominence of international and supranational institutions and initiatives (such as the EU, NAFTA and the WTO) and transnational corporations (TNCs) can suggest a pervasive bureaucratization of modern life under the control of fewer and fewer organizations and individuals. Yet, while trends toward centralization, homogenization and standardization are real enough, there is also evidence for persisting and even increasing differentiation and decentralization: the peripheral industrialization that has come with the new international division of labour (NIDL) and the growth of the NICs, the apparent reversal of previously depressed or underdeveloped local economies (e.g., the Sunbelt phenomenon in the USA), and the revival or creation of regional–national identities (e.g., Ukraine, Quebec, Scotland, Catalonia, Lombardy, Punjab), for example.

The two sets of phenomena are often related. Thus, for example, it is the centralization of economic power in TNCs that has often led to a decentralization of their productive activities (as noted in Chapters 3, 6 and 10); and it is attempts at political and cultural homogenization through international and supranational political unification that have generated resistance at the local or regional level (as noted in Chapters 3 and 8). The end of the Cold War and the collapse of the former Soviet Union gave an added stimulus to economic decentralization and political fragmentation. It is still too early to say whether this signals for eastern Europe and the former Soviet Union a permanent trend or a temporary hiatus prior to renewed political–economic centralization as evidenced by the accession of a number of east European countries to the EU and Russia's inclusion on the waiting list to become a member of the WTO.

However, a general trend all over the world in the wake of the increased integration of the world economy has been an enhanced differentiation between places. So, even as the world has shrunk in real terms with respect to flows of goods, services and investments, small differences in economic characteristics and cultural practices have taken on greater significance. As a result pressures towards a localizing of political decision-making power and political identities have increased. Three kinds of 'decentralist reaction' have been increasingly common since the 1970s, as described later.

First, national governments have had to satisfy local and regional constituencies that they represent their best interests. When faced by geographically differentiated patterns of economic growth and decline, regional policies and regional devolution have been important responses. Since 1998, for example, certain powers formally vested in the UK's parliament have been devolved to new legislative bodies in Scotland, Wales and Northern Ireland. Under regional devolution, Scotland, Wales and Northern Ireland have gained some measure of self-government, while remaining, with England, constituent parts of the UK and its national institutional framework. In Scotland, the responsibilities of the Scotland Office now include health, education, crime, housing and economic development; the UK government has retained responsibility for a range of other issues for Scotland including employment, fiscal and economic policy, taxation and social security.

Second, many modern countries are internally divided along cultural lines with regional/geographical bases. This has sometimes led to nationalist–separatist movements directed towards achieving autonomy or independence for disaffected regions. Basque nationalist separatists consider seven provinces that straddle the Pyrenees, four in Spain and three in France, to be the Basque country. The almost 3 million people in this region are believed to be the oldest indigenous ethnic group in Europe. During Franco's dictatorship (1939–75), the Basques lost any political autonomy they had previously enjoyed, their culture was suppressed and the use of their language was forbidden. In an effort to accommodate the region's separate national identity, the Spanish government has recognized since the early 1980s three Basque provinces as an autonomous region, with its own parliament, police force and separate language. While the majority of Basques in this region oppose the use of violence, up to 40 per cent continue to support independence from Spain.

Third, and most generally, the growing globalization of the world economy has encouraged decentralization rather than centralization in the location of economic activities; whether in the form of the branch plants of big corporations or the localization and clustering of specialized small firms inherent in industrial districts. In particular, small-scale production has become of increasing importance (batch production, etc., as noted in Chapters 6, 7 and 10). Ideas such as 'basic needs', 'appropriate technology' and 'local control' have become increasingly attractive in this context in framing the basic demands of new political movements calling for economic as well as political democracy. Although usually dismissed as 'Utopian', such ideas have become especially attractive as global resource and pollution problems arising as by-products of constant increases in global production and consumption have attracted more attention.

## 13.1 REGIONALISM AND REGIONAL POLICY

As we have shown in previous chapters, processes of economic growth and decline are not geographically neutral in their impact. In particular, the locational requirements of new profitable manufacturing production under the market-access regime and the growing service industries (such as finance) are likely to differ from those of established production (see Chapters 3, 6 and 10). It is in this context that appeals for governmental action arise to 'help' a particular region or set of regions either 'adjust' to a new economic situation or encourage compensating investment by means of fiscal measures such as tax breaks or relocation allowances.

In the 1950s and 1960s there was widespread acceptance in many core countries of the need to encourage regional 'balance' in economic growth at a time when established regional economies were beginning to experience challenges to their competitive advantage, and 'poorer' regions (such as the Italian south or the US south) were seen as lagging behind other regions. It is no coincidence that this acceptance flourished at a time of relative prosperity: quite simply, affluent societies could afford to indulge in redistributive policies. In some countries this took the form of revitalizing or establishing lower 'regional' tiers of government. Regional governments were viewed as agents for maintaining or attracting private investment. In some countries, such as Italy, Norway and, to a lesser degree, the United Kingdom, regional authorities were introduced to encourage regional economic planning and foster local industrial regeneration. In many countries, especially those with federal political systems (such as the United States, Canada, Australia, Switzerland and Germany), lower tier governments have traditionally played an important role in stimulating economic growth within their territories.

Two questions are especially pertinent with respect to the history of regional policy. One concerns the extent to which regionalism, or explicit commitment to spatial or regional planning, has inspired regional policy. The second involves the impact, if any, of regional and local development policies organized by lower tiers of government.

## REGIONAL PLANNING

With regard to the first, some countries, such as France, Germany and Italy, have long-established traditions of regionalism. In particular, French programmes of 'territorial management' and the Italian 'Cassa del Mezzogiorno' (Southern Development Agency, replaced in 1987 by several smaller agencies) provide well-known examples. The United Kingdom and the United States acquired formal regional policies in the 1930s but in neither case has there been the same political consensus in favour of such policies (or anything that smacks of formal 'planning') as in other countries in Europe and elsewhere (e.g., Japan, Brazil, India). In both cases earlier initiatives have largely been abandoned since the late 1960s in favour of either very localized programmes, such as 'enterprise zones', or lower level government rather than national-level policies.

This reflects, in part, the coming to national power of governments ill disposed on ideological grounds to government intervention in the direction of economic activities to particular places. But it also reflects a negative appraisal of the effects of previous planning activities. If regional unemployment rates can be used as an indicator of regional 'economic well-being', the fact that such rates are highly correlated over time and across countries irrespective of the commitment to regional policies suggests that such policies do not make much difference (Chisholm, 1990: 167–9). Incidentally, however, this also suggests a lack of evidence for the long-run spatial equilibrium in the distribution of economic activities assumed in most static models of regional development (discussed in Chapters 7 and 10) and, hence, for the ideology that has often inspired the abandonment of regional policies.

## REGIONAL AND LOCAL DEVELOPMENT POLICIES

The trend throughout the core countries over the past 30 years has been away from formal regionalism sponsored by national governments and towards the adoption of competitive spatial policies by regional and local governments. This has older roots, particularly in the United States where it dates back to the years immediately after the Second World War when southern states such as Tennessee and Mississippi began 'attracting' firms from the northeast and Midwest with a mix of low production costs and fiscal advantages (especially low taxes). This approach spread widely in the USA with the onset of the massive restructuring of industry in the early 1970s. At the same time the narrow focus on attracting industry shifted to a broader concern with general local economic competitiveness, primarily through improving the overall 'climate' for business and creating a mix of incentives for stimulating 'new' industries with potential multiplier effects.

Individual US states and municipalities have created economic development agencies to attract industry and foster endogenous economic development. Particularly conspicuous have been public–private partnerships and government offices established abroad, in London, Tokyo or Brussels, to entice foreign business to particular locations in the USA. This latter strategy paid off handsomely for some states, such as Ohio and Kentucky, which succeeded in beating off other US states in attracting major Japanese auto-assembly plants to their jurisdictions. Local government intervention of a similar type began to appear in the UK and other European countries in the 1980s, in part taking a leaf out of the American book but also reflecting the availability of EU structural funds for providing grants and cheap loans to prospective employers.

The overall effectiveness of these local development efforts remains in doubt. While 'success stories', such as that of Kentucky in the USA or the local government/small business linkages present in many parts of central and northeast Italy, are well known, evidence for the positive impact of these efforts in general is mixed. Frequently, local programmes of tax abatements and subsidized plant and equipment merely relocate industry from another state or municipality rather than building fresh capacity and employment nationally. Ironically, given the usual association of 'good' business climate with low taxes and limited public services, some evidence suggests that in the USA, state and local education, training and infrastructure expenditures are more beneficial in generating fresh investment and new industry than are subsidies to individual firms. Systematic fiscal reform, in the sense of aiming for low tax rates and broad tax bases, combined with efficient service delivery seems to offer the best formula for successful local development efforts in the USA. Specific tax subsidies to firms (including so-called enterprise zone experiments) seem a much less successful route to job growth and overall economic development in local economies. The theoretical framework outlined in Chapter 3 would suggest that the best local policies would be those that assist clustering by firms so as to increase transactional, learning, work training and other linkages. Otherwise competition between states and localities might encourage a 'race to the bottom' with jurisdictions such as Mississippi becoming the norm against which states with long traditions of active government intervention to regulate workplaces and encourage economic development based on high-quality public services would find themselves at a disadvantage in the scramble to attract inward investment.

## THE BALANCE SHEET ON REGIONAL PLANNING AND COMPETITION POLICIES

A basic dilemma remains unresolved, however. When local policies successfully promote economic development, both the capital and the labour (when educated or skilled) that benefited from the policies will probably act to undermine what the policies initially achieved. Capital will do this through takeovers and moving investment elsewhere; labour by migration to higher wage areas. This is the paradox of planning regional and local initiatives in the context of a world economy that is dynamic and 'placeless' in its orientation to securing improvements in rates of return on investment. Yet, at the same time, rather than 'rooting capital' in weak as well as strong local economies, local policies will, as the model of regional cumulative causation described in Chapter 7 might suggest, produce deepening spatial inequalities. Richer localities will have advantages in revenues and infrastructure that poor ones lack. The end result of this will be greater geographical concentration of productive economic activities.

Whatever the strength of this logic, however, after the downturn of the world economy beginning in the mid-1970s local governments in many countries did became relatively focused on economic development efforts. What they were able to achieve, however, was constrained by their relative autonomy and by the need for national governments to curb public spending and reduce taxation. In the UK until 1994, the absence of a formal regional tier of government could be seen as a particular drawback to local initiative. Localities, such as city governments, are often too small to create effective economic development policies. Their control over physical (landuse) planning is likewise too parochial when the environmental and labour market impacts of 'new' industries extend beyond jurisdictional boundaries. Indeed, from one point of view the UK had the worst of all worlds because of the absence of a regional tier of government: the national government monopolized most controls over economic development and local government exercised control over physical planning. There was no intersection of authority or coordination of powers. This disadvantaged the UK as a whole in a context of increased international competition in which regions elsewhere were able to offer 'packages' of advantages not available in the UK. Partly in response to this and to the difficulties of coordinating the EU's regional programmes and funding from London, the main state departments (employment and education, environment, trade and industry, transportation) were integrated in 1994 to create a regional government office for each region. These regional government offices (for the northeast, northwest, West Midlands, etc.) now attempt to coordinate the economic development activities of the local governments within their regions in their dealings with potential inward investors. But even in Italy, usually presented as a 'showcase' of successful economic regionalism, the regions are relatively weak institutions with limited powers and a low popular profile. The Italian administrative regions have served mainly as spending agencies for national government policies. They also vary substantially in size, competence and legitimacy; with those in the south particularly disadvantaged. Strong 'regional motors' (such as those in central and northern Italy), therefore, do not necessarily generate a parallel strong model of regional or local governance.

One trend that goes against the tendency for enhanced competition between regions and localities is the emergence of 'compacts' or agreements between regions in different countries with respect to technology licensing and plant establishment. Thus, such regions as Baden-Württemberg in Germany and Wales in the United

Kingdom have arranged contacts to encourage the flow of technology and invest-ment from the former to the latter. Of course, such cooperation can be regarded as simply a way of encouraging competitive advantage for the regions concerned rather than something totally different from more typical competitive strategies.

The 'fiscal crises' experienced by many national governments beginning in the 1970s – increasing expenditures on 'entitlements' (social security, healthcare) and defence were not matched by corresponding increases in revenues – led to increased pressure on local governments to provide compensatory spending on education and other public services. This has at one and the same time increased the fiscal problems of local governments, especially apparent in the USA, and reduced their ability to nego-tiate special 'deals' with increasingly mobile businesses. Indeed, a strong case can be made that there has been a rolling back of government in many countries irrespective of the level at which it operates. Regions and localities are as caught up in the pressures of the market-access regime as are national governments. The primacy of market forces leads to an emphasis on entrepreneurialism, the imperative of flexibility and a 'business localism' in which there is little or no popular oversight or control.

Direct central government intervention has still remained an important dimen-sion of regional policy, if in some countries more than others. Substantial regional variations in economic development (especially when they are reflected in high regional unemployment rates) have been widely viewed as creating a national polit-ical problem, threatening the social and economic cohesion of the state itself. As a result, and beginning in the 1930s, national governments have felt it necessary to intervene in the economic geography of their territories by manipulating the costs of production.

The policies adopted have varied over time and by country. Some have sought to reduce the costs of fixed capital in declining regions by undertaking government investment in infrastructure, providing subsidies for private investment, etc. (German and Italian policies, in particular, have emphasized such strategies.) Others have sought to reduce the costs of capital in declining regions through sub-sidies for labour costs in those regions or through artificially increasing costs in 'overheated' regions (in the 1960s French and British policies tended in this direc-tion). The increased globalization of the world economy, however, has challenged the relevance of such conventional regional policies. In the first place, the largest firms no longer choose sites from among a single national set. There is no longer much correspondence between the scale of economic–locational decision making and the spatial scale over which governments can exert their fiscal powers. Indeed, in this context 'the difficulties of guaranteeing full employment nationally mean that the state has increasingly to focus its attention on the national rather than the regional crisis; regional policy is in large part irrelevant' (Johnston, 1986: 274).

In the second place, the cost of subsidies raises government spending and pro-duces a macroeconomic environment that is unattractive to global capital. Regional policy is then viewed as both an expensive luxury and an increasing lia-bility. This was very much the view adopted by the Thatcher/Major governments in the United Kingdom and the Reagan/Bush administrations in the United States. Reducing state spending on regional policy was seen as a necessity for improving national competitiveness in a global economy. In the UK between 1979 and 1985, for example, regional aid was cut from £842 million to £560 million, a cut in real terms of exactly one-third. Moreover, the areas eligible for aid were 'rolled back' considerably (Figure 13.1).

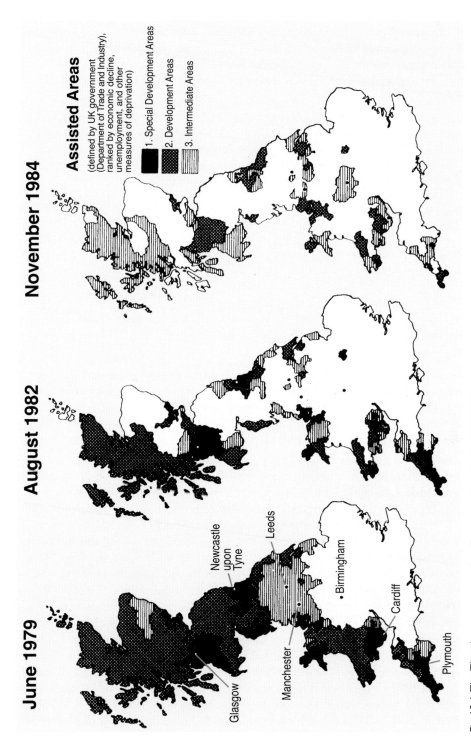

Fig 13.1: The Thatcher government's rolling back of regional aid, 1979–84

Source: Based on Martin (1986: 273, Figure 8.4)

Third, and finally, as Doreen Massey (1984: 298) points out: 'No longer is there really a "regional" problem in the old sense. No longer is there a fairly straightforward twofold division between central prosperous areas and a decaying periphery.' Rather, because 'it is not regions which interrelate, but the social relations of production which take place over space' (1984: 122) a new spatial division of labour based on spatial division of firms' activities has given rise to a new and more localized pattern of spatial inequality. Her summary argument is as follows (1984: 295):

> The old spatial division of labour based on sector, on contrasts between industries, has gone into accelerated decline and in its place has arisen to dominance a spatial division of labour in which a more important component is the inter-regional spatial structuring of production within individual industries. Relations between economic activity in different parts of the country are now a function less of market relations between firms and rather more of planned relations within them.

From this perspective regional policy no longer engages with economic reality. Rather than discrete regional economies in competition with one another: '[A] new spatial division of labour made possible by new information and communication technologies and new non-spatial scale economies has created a localized pattern of restructuring' (Agnew, 1988: 131). In a world in which exogenous links have become central to local development, area-based policies for endogenous development often can appear less and less fruitful.

As decentralist reactions, therefore, regional policy and, especially, regionalism appear increasingly problematic. As Martin and Hodge (1983: 319) have argued with respect to the United Kingdom:

> however much regional policies of the conventional type are strengthened, if they are pursued against a background of continued unfavourable macro-economic conditions, their 'social' role will be largely limited to simply spreading the misery of mass unemployment more 'fairly' around the country while providing little boost to total economic activity or employment.

It may be too early to write off regional policy entirely, even if regionalism, the commitment to planning in a nationally coordinated fashion the economic development of fixed regional units, is largely in retreat. For one thing, to counterbalance its commitment to improving the overall efficiency of European industry in global competition through enhanced European competition, the EU has placed renewed emphasis on regional incentives to compensate for losses of traditional industries and employment (see Chapter 12). After declining steadily from the late 1950s, regional disparities in income increased throughout the EU from the mid-1970s, levelled off and fell slightly during the late 1980s, before rising again since 1990. In response, the European Commission has concentrated its spending on infrastructural projects and vocational training, while its competition policy attempts to restrict the provision of state aids such as grants and subsidies for private firms to within the 'less favoured' regions. Whether these are sufficient to rebalance regional disparities is questionable given the continued high rates of job loss in regions facing structural difficulties or where development is lagging behind. Second, some emerging industries enjoy economies of agglomeration (particularly localization economies). Once established in specific areas such industries have a local dependence that generates competitive advantage. Unfortunately, not everywhere can benefit from this. This has been the problem with proliferating growth poles, trying to mass produce the dynamism associated with initial advantage at great public expense but without much of a return on investment. There can only be a limited number of 'silicon valleys' and 'silicon fens'. Hence, there is an economic return to early organization of specialized complexes. If a national economy is going to share in the potential for national economic development represented by these, then a national government will require a regional policy to encourage early response.

For example, Japanese regional policy is now centrally concerned with creating the conditions for early response in growing sectors such as computing and biotechnology. There is a network of 170 regional centres that channel support for innovation and research into companies with fewer than 300 employees. Three-quarters of the staff of these *kohsetsushi* centres are engineers who carry out applied research, and offer training and advice. The centres encourage small firms to collaborate with one another and with the large firms they often supply with components and services. The regional system provides an organizational framework for Japanese economic innovation. Countries such as the United Kingdom and the United States have suffered from the absence of such government 'priming' of the pump of innovation while waiting for firms to do it themselves. Firms, however, have had no incentive to look beyond their own short-run interests to the interest of the country as a whole. From one point of view, that is what governments are for.

## 13.2 NATIONALIST SEPARATISM

The growth of industrial capitalism in the 19th century was accompanied by promotion of the nation-state and the growth of nationalism. The conviction grew among elites and populations at large that each state should be clearly bounded geographically, it should be organized as an economy, and it should be as linguistically and culturally homogeneous as possible. To many in western Europe, North America and Australasia, the blessings of material abundance and personal freedom became associated with the interrelated development of capitalism and the nation-state.

In the 20th century, however, nationalism was regularly perverted into fascism. Dreadful wars were fought. National independence has been no guarantee of national prosperity. Even in the original or 'founding' states of Europe, such as Spain, France and the UK, political movements rejecting established national claims and asserting political and economic rights for regional and ethnic populations have become widespread.

### STATES VERSUS NATIONS

This last trend reflects the fact that state making and nationalism have never redounded equally to the benefit of all the nominal citizens of a country. In particular, since their earliest formation modern nation-states have contained a diversity of cultural groups within their boundaries. In the social science literature the term 'ethnicity' has come to signify the organization of cultural diversity within modern states. Thus, an ethnic group can be defined as 'a collectivity of people who share some pattern of normative behaviour, or culture, and who form a part of a larger population, interacting within the framework of a common social system' (Cohen, 1974: 92).

Ethnic groups, however, are not simply primordial groupings, even though they usually draw on myths of common ancestry and cultural distinctiveness. They are differentiated from one another and integrated internally through such mechanisms as a cultural division of labour, political favouritism and historically created economic roles. Indeed, ethnicity can be viewed as a mechanism for allocating wealth and power within states that have not inherited or successfully imposed a unifying set of cultural practices and symbols on their populations. A clear example of the use of ethnicity in this way would be Northern Ireland between 1920 and 1972 where a dominant elite of Protestant landowners and businessmen maintained their hegemony over the region through a web of mutual obligations, customs, duties and economic favours that bound Protestant workers and small farmers to them while excluding the Roman Catholic population. This process of ethnic competition for control over the fruits of economic growth and government policy is extremely widespread the world over; the more so the greater the number of ethnic groups and the weaker the alternative means of political mobilization (e.g., social class).

Students of ethnicity have noted that in recent years the level and intensity of conflicts between ethnic groups have been on the increase. Writing of Indonesia, Clifford Geertz (1973: 244–5) has provided a particularly vivid description:

> Up until the third decade of this century, the several ingredient traditions – Indic, Sinitic, Islamic, Christian, Polynesian – were suspended in a kind of half-solution in which contrasting, even opposed styles of life and world outlook managed to coexist, if not wholly without tension, or even without violence, at least in some sort of workable, to-each-his-own sort of arrangement. This modus vivendi began to show signs of strain as early as the mid nineteenth century, but its dissolution got genuinely under way only with the rise, from 1912 on, of nationalism; its collapse, which is still not complete, only in the revolutionary and post-revolutionary periods [1945 on]. For then what had been parallel traditionalisms became competing definitions of the essence of the New Indonesia. What was once, to employ a term I have used elsewhere, a kind of 'cultural balance of power' became an ideological war of a peculiarly implacable sort.

Some, for example Kedourie (1960), have seen this ethnic 'schismogenesis' as a worldwide process associated with the diffusion of the idea of nationalism from Europe along with colonialism. Others have emphasized modernization or industrialization as universal processes laying the material foundations for the politics of nationalism (e.g., Gellner, 1964). In fact, ethnic nationalism seems to have developed in different ways and with different causes in different parts of the world. Rokkan and Urwin (1983), for example, argue that processes of economic, military–administrative and cultural 'system building' have combined in different ways to produce different effects in different European localities. In turn, ethnic nationalism has been accommodated in some settings (such as the Celtic fringe of the UK (Scotland, Wales, Northern Ireland) and the Basque provinces of Spain), and discouraged elsewhere (for example, in Alsace, France and the south Tyrol, Italy).

## ETHNIC CONFLICT AND NATIONALIST SEPARATISM

Whatever its precise origins in particular cases, however, ethnic conflict and nationalist separatism (when ethnic groups are geographically concentrated) have become increasingly marked features of the contemporary world. From Ireland to the former Yugoslavia to Lebanon to India to Sri Lanka to Canada, to name just a few of the best known cases, ethnic groups and ethnic conflict have become major elements in national political life. Three factors seem to be especially important in this trend. One of these is the increased economic–geographical differentiation within states and its relationship to ethnic divisions. It is not that ethnic conflict always involves increasingly poor regions rebelling against more affluent ones. It is difference per se generating a sense of deprivation or exploitation. In Spain, for example, it is the Basque and Catalan regions – the most prosperous in the country – that are the most rebellious. Likewise in the former Yugoslavia, where the relatively well-off Slovenians and Croatians demonstrated their impatience with 'subsidizing' the ethnic groups (Serbs, ethnic Albanians, etc.) that occupy other regions, by agitating for and achieving political independence. Yet within the now Serb-dominated 'rump' of Yugoslavia, it is the poorer ethnic Albanians in the province of Kosovo who have engaged in the most active nationalist separatism efforts.

The break-up of the former Yugoslavia illustrates a second factor of singular importance in the explosion of nationalist separatism in 1989–93: the collapse of the Soviet Union, the exhaustion of state socialism and the end of the Cold War. The demise of strong central governments and the exhaustion of state socialism as an ideology have opened the way for a re-emergence of political identities based on ethnic divisions. Formerly communist states such as Yugoslavia and the Soviet Union were organized administratively around geographical units that reproduced ethnic cleavages. Even though some groups, such as Russians in the Soviet case, are to be found scattered in considerable numbers outside their own 'republics', the dominant identify of particular administrative units remained that of the histori- cally dominant ethnic group.

Within Russia itself the absence of the distinct groups that underpin the political divisions in other countries, such as organized labour or religious traditions, has led to political organization by entrenched vested interests from the bureaucracies and by ethnic group. One of the early results of the break-up of the Soviet Union within Russia was the shift in power from the centre to the regions. Local govern- ments were formerly the instruments of central rule but by 1992 they had become major protagonists in political–economic development. Some of the 27 million non-Russians in Russia have even declared sovereignty within their local govern- ment units. These units have different economies, some are raw materials producers and others are industrial, and thus have different interests in terms of pricing and macroeconomic policies. So there is the possibility within Russia of ethnic and economic differences becoming mutually reinforcing as they did within the former Soviet Union as a whole (Figure 13.2).

At the same time, the 'freezing' of political boundaries that both sides in the Cold War had quietly accepted no longer can be tied to an overriding global con- flict. Each and every territorial dispute is no longer a potential spark for a Third World War. This opens the way for a possible proliferation of nationalist sepa- ratisms (and also expansionist claims by existing states) in all world regions as established political boundaries lose their previous inviolability.

The third factor is the growing globalization of political and economic activity. The shift of power and control over local economies to ever more distant locations provides an incentive for regional counter-mobilization. The development of the EU in Europe may have been one stimulus; the growing importance of TNCs may be another. At the same time the increase in the flow of international migrants, especially into western Europe, introduced new ethnic groups, such as Indians in the United Kingdom, Turks and east Europeans in Germany and Algerians in France, which both stimulate the demands of indigenous ethnic groups and provide additional 'out-groups' for new rounds of ethnic conflict and nationalist politics.

Fig 13.2: Governmental decentralization of Russia, 1993

*Source:* Based on *Economist* (1992c: 25)

With the exception of the former Soviet Union and some parts of eastern Europe (Yugoslavia, Czechoslovakia) outright separatist movements have not met with success, at least as measured in terms of political independence. During the Cold War the world superpowers generally refused to back separatist movements, perhaps for fear of stimulating them at home or within their own spheres of influence. Often, political changes short of outright independence have proved satisfactory responses to regional–ethnic revolt. These include federalism, regional devolution and *consociationalism* (power sharing among ethnic groups as in Switzerland and the Netherlands). What is clear, however, irrespective of the prospects for nationalist separatism as such, is that 'there is little likelihood of an abatement of ethnic nationalism in the near future' (Williams, 1982: 36).

## Box 13.1 International terrorism

One strategy used by some nationalists, following in the path of guerrilla movements in former colonies, has been to use terrorist methods to try to make the 'occupation' of their lands by others intolerable. These tactics have ranged from the bombs planted by IRA (Irish) and ETA (Basque) separatists to fully fledged warfare, as in Chechnya and other territories in the northern Caucasus region of Russia.

Since the late 1990s, however, this largely nationalist terrorism has been supplemented by the growth of a brand of international terrorism interpreted by many, not least by the US administration of G.W. Bush, as a war against the United States and the world economy. Associated with such shadowy groups as the Islamic jihadist *al Qaeda* (which has been linked to the attacks on the World Trade Center in New York on 11 September 2001), this type of terrorism has been seen by some as a violent response to the spread of globalization, particularly by extreme elements in the Arab and Islamic worlds, even as it makes use of the very technologies, such as cell phones and jet aeroplanes, that globalization entails.

Not only has terrorism taken on a global reach, however, it is also apparent that cities have become a preferred location for large-scale terrorist attacks. Even before the terrorist attacks on the World Trade Center in 2001, cities had become the central venues of terrorist attacks. Between 1993 and 2000, for example, there had been over 500 terrorist incidents in more than 250 cities around the world.

There are several reasons for this. First, cities – especially world cities – have considerable symbolic value. They are not only dense agglomerations of people and buildings but also symbols of national prestige and military, political and financial power. A bomb in London's underground or a poison gas release in a Tokyo metro arouses international alarm. This kind of event will be communicated instantly to a world audience. Second, the assets of cities – densely packed and with a large mix of industrial and commercial infrastructure – make them rich targets for terrorists. Third, cities have become nodes in vast international networks of communications. This is a reflection not only of their power, but also of their vulnerability. A well-placed explosion can produce enormous reverberations, paralyze a city and spread fear and economic dislocation. Finally, word gets around more quickly and socialization proceeds more rapidly in high-density localities. These kinds of environment can be an abundant source of recruits for terrorist organizations.

Terrorism takes a toll on cities in a variety of ways. The impacts of the 2001 terrorist attacks on New York City have been significant – and not limited to the death and destruction that was targeted on lower Manhattan. The time and cost of doing business in New York has gone up, even for workers and companies quite distant from the attack site.

In this connection, central London has sought to reduce the threat of terrorist attacks. Physical and increasingly technological approaches to security have been adopted at increasingly expanded scales. In 1993, a security cordon was put into place, securing all entrances to the central financial zone of the City of London (the Square Mile). The 30 entrances to the City were reduced to seven, with roadchecks manned by armed police. Over time the spatial scale of the security cordon was increased to cover 75 per cent of the Square Mile. The security cordon, as a territorial approach to security, was augmented by retrofitting the closed circuit TV (CCTV) system. The police, through its 'CameraWatch' partnership effort, encouraged private companies to install CCTV. At the seven entrances to the security cordon, 24-hour automated number plate recording (ANPR) cameras, linked to police databases, were installed. Within a decade the City of London had been transformed into the most surveilled space in the United Kingdom, and perhaps in the world, with more than 1500 surveillance cameras in operation, many of which are linked to the ANPR system.

Ultimately, the response to international terrorism mirrors the response to the nationalist use of terrorist methods that have been attempted in the past. Although bloody in terms of loss of civilian lives, terrorism of all kinds is rather like the strategic bombing campaigns carried out by air forces during the Second World War: it does not work to intimidate populations into surrender. Although often the seemingly only available 'weapon of the weak', it tends to create increased animosity and violence rather than the political outcomes desired.

## 13.3 GRASSROOTS REACTIONS

### SMALL IS BEAUTIFUL?

A peculiar paradox of the growing globalization of the world economy has been the stimulus it has provided to the destruction of some specialized local/regional economies and the decentralization/ localization of single plants or use of subcontractors at disparate locations. New information and transportation technologies have made it possible to decentralize production operations to 'cheaper' locations (lower wage bills, etc.) or ones with special advantages in terms of access to technology, labour skills or markets at the same time that central corporate control is maintained or enhanced. This process has been brought about by increased competitive pressures on large firms from the appearance of foreign competitors. Many large firms, especially in Europe and the United States, now face a global marketplace far more competitive than the more geographically restricted ones they had known previously. Of course, as argued in general in Chapters 1 and 3, and then repeatedly in subsequent chapters, branch-plant industrialization is only one among a number of strategies for re-establishing firm competitiveness. And, it does not signify that there are not continuing and new pressures for the clustering of production facilities. The point to be made here is more that, today, there are greater incentives and technological possibilities for firms – even small firms – maintaining control over production at a distance than was the case in the past.

Coincidentally, union/management conflicts in established production facilities and changes in market conditions, especially the increased demand in many developed countries for customized rather than mass produced goods, have also encouraged decentralization of production. In Italy, for example, one can see evidence of both causes. Large firms in Piemonte (around Turin) and Lombardia (around Milan) have increasingly contracted out to small firms for parts and services that used to be provided onsite at large factories. Moving production in this way both undermines the power of workers in large factories, where solidarity is more easily achieved than in scattered small factories and protects the large firm from the need to shed labour cyclically. In Emilia-Romagna (around Bologna) and elsewhere in central Italy many small firms provide customized products (both producer and consumer goods) to domestic and export markets that are better served by the flexible response to shifts in fashion that these small firms can provide. Whether they can continue to do so in the face of intense competition from Chinese and other low cost producers in the same sectors remains to be seen. Some Italian firms have already joined the rush to invest in China and eastern Europe to reduce their wage bills once more, this time by foreign outsourcing rather than by relocating or decentralizing production within Italy (see also Box 6.4).

To some commentators, however, the previous development of a highly competitive Third Italy (midway between the old industrial triangle of the northwest and the underdeveloped south) signified a wholehearted shift away from mass to customized production, with local rather than long-distance connections central to the new mode of flexible production. In fact, although local clusters of small firms have been very important to this process, they are strongly tied into the longstanding industrial system and its main urban centres. Thus, in Italy during the 1990s the provinces that had the highest levels of foreign exports all cluster in the vicinity of Milan in the 'traditional' industrial northwest rather than in the Third Italy of central and northeastern Italy (Figure 13.3).

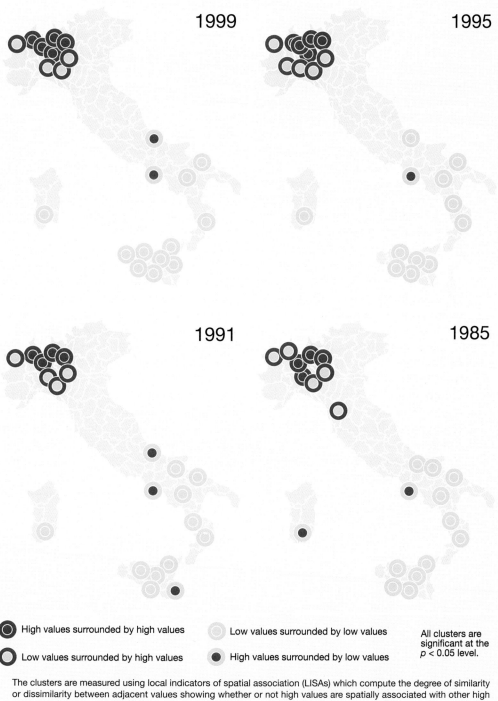

High values surrounded by high values

Low values surrounded by high values

Low values surrounded by low values

High values surrounded by low values

All clusters are significant at the $p < 0.05$ level.

The clusters are measured using local indicators of spatial association (LISAs) which compute the degree of similarity or dissimilarity between adjacent values showing whether or not high values are spatially associated with other high values, high values with low values, low values with low values, or low values with high values, all at a certain pre-selected level of statistical significance.

Fig 13.3: Geographical clustering of export shares in Italy, by province, 1985–1999

*Source:* Adapted from Agnew *et al.* (2005: 96, Figure 4)

In the United States both types of decentralization to small firm clusters – away from large, unionized plants and in the interest of customized production – are also increasingly common, although the small firm as supplier to the plants of a large firm has been most characteristic since the late 1960s. Companies with fewer than 500 workers added 1.2 million jobs in the United States between 1976 and 1984, while larger companies lost 300,000 jobs. By 1999, Census Bureau statistics for US businesses indicate that companies with fewer than 500 workers had risen to 91 per cent of all manufacturing firms and accounted for 41 per cent of manufacturing jobs. Paralleling this, production facilities have also shrunk in size. Plants in the USA during the 1960s had, on average, 30 per cent more workers compared to plants now (Figure 13.4). These data cast doubt on the claim that not much has changed in either the scale of production or the average ownership size in US manufacturing industries. What perhaps has not changed in the USA is the *directing* role of large firms, only now in relation to a variety of production arrangements with other firms rather than solely in terms of vertical integration of all stages of production within one firm (see Chapter 3).

A similar fragmentation of production has been noted in the United Kingdom. Since the late 1970s average employment in plants of firms employing more than 999 people has shrunk and the average number of plants operated by these firms has increased significantly. In 1973 average employment per plant was 459 and there were 12 plants per firm. The comparable figures for 1982 were 338 and 15. Yet, at the same time, there was a decrease in the number of firms in the category of 999+ employees, indicating an increasing concentration of ownership. By 1996, for example, only 0.1 per cent of the manufacturing businesses registered for value-added tax (VAT) in the UK had 999+ employees, while 69.4 per cent of manufacturing firms had between one and nine employees. In the British case, reduction in the size of plants has not involved a reduction in the concentration of ownership of manufacturing industry. However, some of the decrease in the average size of all workplaces (as opposed to just those of the larger firms) is due to the expansion of employment in small firms. Between 1980 and 1991, for example, UK manufacturing firms with fewer than 100 employees were responsible for at

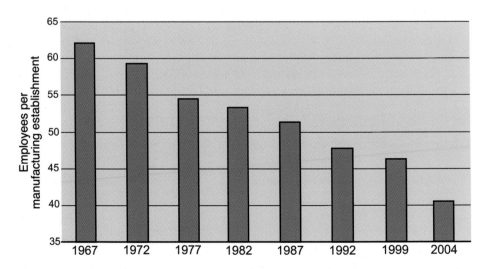

Fig 13.4

least 50 per cent of job creation, while firms with over 100 employees accounted for just over 60 per cent of jobs lost. The expansion of employment in small manufacturing firms in the United Kingdom, however, appears to lag well behind other countries such as Italy, Japan and the United States.

The new 'decentralized economy', however, is incredibly volatile. Patterns of new firm creation/destruction are extremely sensitive to minor cyclical fluctuations in demand from larger firms and final markets. Many firms have tiny inventories and limited equity. Although advantageous financially, this introduces major limitations in terms of employee security and long-term commitment to local economies. In this context, local rather than aggregate national conditions are of increased significance for the welfare of populations. Political parties such as the Labour Party in the United Kingdom have supported the decentralization of some governmental powers over economic development as a reaction (in part, at least) to the increased localization of economic activities. In Italy, the Communist Party (and now that part of it called the Democratic Party of the Left), excluded from national governments on a permanent basis during the Cold War, has been a major sponsor of both economic and political decentralization in the central regions (Emilia-Romagna, Toscana and Umbria) where it dominates local government. Without supportive national government policies, however, local economic initiatives organized on a geographical basis are problematic. Above all, they face the dilemma of protecting current employment while attempting to create local economies that can capture the benefits of 'emerging' industries.

Perhaps local initiative and control or 'small is beautiful' can only work when decision-making power is no longer vested in giant transnational corporations, as it still is even when small firms proliferate to serve them (as is the case even in many industrial districts). For example, the strategy for procuring components used by Ford in Europe involves the increased use of widely scattered and expendable suppliers. This approach is hardly amenable to either government controls or local economic development strategies geared towards long-term stability in employment. The lack of a 'natural evolution' of economies towards greater security of employment and increased participation in the benefits of economic growth has fuelled the revival of thinking about the possibility of wider popular participation in economic decision making. The theme of 'economic democracy' is especially strong in some recent proposals for stimulating the US economy. Economic democracy refers to an egalitarian form of political–economic structure in which a serious attempt is made to democratize the economic sphere in general and workplaces in particular. The major point is to challenge the political and economic position of global capital and the commitment to it and its international role by the major states (the UK, USA, etc.). It builds on the view characteristic of movements for participatory democracy that, to be more than a sham, democracy should be extended beyond episodic political activities such as voting into the economic sphere.

## ECONOMIC DEMOCRACY

Economic democracy differs from democratic capitalism (in both *laissez-faire* and welfare state manifestations), in which democracy is limited to periodic involvement in electoral politics and the means of production are largely privately owned. It also differs from conventional state socialism, especially of the now defunct Soviet variety, in which markets are prohibited (in public), there is little meaningful electoral politics and the means of production are owned by the state.

There are a number of reasons why interest in both the theory and practice of economic democracy has increased in recent years. First, as the heavy 'smokestack' industries in the United States, western Europe and other developed countries have become less profitable there have been numerous attempts by their employees to save their jobs by buying failing factories. Changes in tax laws have also made employee stock option plans (ESOPs) more attractive to businesses. Between 1976 and 2002 the number of ESOPs grew in the United States from fewer than 300 to about 11,000. While owning stock is hardly the same as control, ESOPs do raise the question of where employees' participation should stop. But it is probably the competitive environment for businesses and the prospect for bankruptcy that do most to encourage talk about and proposals for producer cooperatives and worker self-management.

Second, interest in economic democracy reflects consideration of actual practices in a number of countries that have had high levels of economic growth and high standards of living. In Germany, for example, 'codetermination' allocates positions on corporate boards to employees. In addition, the success of several large-scale prototypes has given advocates of economic democracy a ready reply to those who assert that self-management by employees is inherently Utopian. The extensive network of Basque financial, industrial and distribution cooperatives in Spain, 'Mondragon', employs over 60,000 workers and has for many years enjoyed better profitability due in part to higher worker productivity compared to some of its more conventional competitors.

Third, and finally, especially in the LDCs, economic democracy can be seen as an alternative both to American-style corporate capitalism and socialist-style central planning. Under nationalistic pressure to avoid becoming satellites of the major world powers, the rhetoric and sometimes the substance of economic democracy arise; but the pressure is also immediately practical. Considerable evidence suggests that rapid economic growth in LDCs does not necessarily improve the welfare of large numbers of their people. Markets, based on effective demand, which means the given distribution of income, have generally failed to allocate resources to the basic human needs of the poor in many LDCs – mass poverty, unemployment and malnutrition are the consequences. Directing attention to local production for 'basic needs' has been one response, based on the use of indigenous knowledge and traditions of production as opposed to imported ones. Discussions of 'appropriate technology' and 'alternative' development strategies, however, are both inspired by similar concerns. They also reflect increasing concern over the limits to the growth of the world economy. Can the world's natural resources and increasingly fragile physical environment support the levels of production that it would take for the entire population of the world to enjoy American or Swiss levels of consumption?

There is, of course, a range of possible 'grassroots reactions' within the general confines of economic democracy. Among advocates of economic democracy are some who are committed to a vision of large firms with powerful, central councils, while others look to smaller, decentralized firms embedded in non-state networks of social association. Comisso (1979) compared this difference to that between federalists (such as Hamilton) and Jeffersonians at the time of the founding of the United States. To take one example, Hirst (1994) has argued for what he calls 'associative democracy' resting on two major principles: a decentralized economy based on cooperation and mutuality and a system of governance based on self-governing associations of mutual interests. State power is to be weakened through a pluralizing and federalizing of political authority and economic power is to be redistributed to local economies. Hirst draws on the examples of manufacturing success in Italian industrial districts, German regions and Japanese firms to propose an associative regional economy linked into others by federal channels of authority. Hirst claims that such a model would both stimulate economic growth and redistribute its fruits in a more egalitarian fashion than is the case with the present world economy.

One important objection to economic democracy of all types, but especially the more decentralized ones, is that they are Utopian dreams since those in power will not hear of them. The world is now bureaucratized; bureaucracies will not seriously consider participatory democracy. In particular, most states are run by oligarchies determined to fix the best deals for themselves from transnational corporations and the most powerful states. Williams (1981), however, has defended the need for utopias. He argues that:

> [T]he purpose of a radical utopia is to create a tension in our souls ... We must imagine something better. That defines us as people who offer our fellow citizens a meaningful choice about how we can define and live our lives ... Radicals must confront centralized nationalism and internationalism and begin to shake it apart, break it down, and imagine a humane and socially responsible alternative. It simply will not do to define radicalism as changing the guard of the existing system.
>
> W.A. Williams (1981: 95, 98)

In essence, this is what grassroots reactions inspired by a vision of economic democracy are really all about.

A second objection is more by way of a critique of possibilities of successful long-term local development in the absence of a relatively strong state presence in economic regulation. Amin (1996: 309–10), for example, is critical of proponents of local 'associative democracy' (particularly Hirst) for 'failing to distinguish between different forms of state economic intervention and state practice' and for undervaluing 'the strategic and developmental role played by the state in some of the most successful economies in the world'. In a somewhat different vein, Donahue (1997) has claimed that a state defines something of a 'commons' in which externalities across local and regional boundaries are so intense as to vitiate against the possibility of ever successfully separating out groups of people into discrete geographical communities that can be run as if the others did not exist. Federalism is about achieving a balance between the common and the particular. For Donahue (1997: 42), the 'devil in devolution' is that, in the US case, the dominant consensus:

> [I]n favour of letting Washington [the US federal government] fade while the states take the lead is badly timed. The public sector's current trajectory – the devolution of welfare and other programs, legislative and judicial action circumscribing Washington's authority, and the federal government's retreat to domestic role largely defined by writing checks to entitlement claimants, creditors, and state and local governments – would make sense if economic and cultural ties reaching across state lines were *weakening* over time. But state borders are becoming more, not less permeable.

## SUMMARY

In this chapter, three types of decentralist reaction to the impact of the world economy have been described in the context of the trend towards globalization of economic activities.

Regionalism and regional policy under state sponsorship were common up until the 1960s but their relevance has increasingly been questioned in the face of the changed relationship between national and world economies. In many countries, regional and local tiers of government have tended to displace the regionalism carried out under the sponsorship of national governments.

Nationalist separatism challenges existing states, international and supranational organizations, and the existing distribution of economic activities. But most separatist movements will usually settle for something less than complete independence.

Finally, recent trends in the world economy have generated renewed interest in the possibility of economic democracy. Disillusionment with both American-style corporate capitalism and Soviet-style socialism in the face of an increasingly volatile world economy has directed attention to the possibility of people taking control of their economic activities and putting them to work for them.

Whether or not decentralist reactions increase in importance depends in part on whether the world economy recovers from its present problems, especially the debt crisis, the slowing of growth in world trade and the lack of congruence between global production and global consumption, and whether or not the 'free market' ideologies antithetical to many of these reactions and associated for many years with the Reagan/Bush administrations in the USA, and the Thatcher/Major governments in the United Kingdom continue to find support around the world and in international organizations such as the World Bank. Without some dramatic rebalancing of global patterns of production and consumption, and the geographical spread of the benefits of globalization, the trend towards decentralist reactions may prove inexorable as people begin to take their fate into their own hands.

## KEY SOURCES AND SUGGESTED READING

Amin, A. and Thrift, N. 1992. Neo-Marshallian nodes in global networks, *International Journal of Urban and Regional Research*, 16, 571–87.
Brusco, S. and Sabel, C. 1981. Artisan production and economic growth, in F. Wilkinson (ed.) *The Dynamics of Labour Market Segmentation*. London: Academic Press.
Eisenschitz, A. and Gough, J. 1992. *The Politics of Local Economic Policy: The Problems and Possibilities of Local Initiative*. London: Macmillan.
Gause, F.G. 2005. Can democracy stop terrorism?, *Foreign Affairs*, 84/5, 62–76.
Harvie, C. 1994. *The Rise of Regional Europe*. London: Routledge.
Johnston, R.J. 1986. The state, the region, and the division of labor, in A.J. Scott and M. Storper (eds) *Production, Work, Territory: The Geographical Anatomy of Industrial Capitalism*. Boston, MA: Allen & Unwin.
Rokkan, S. and Urwin, D. 1983. *Economy, Territory, Identity: Politics of West European Peripheries*. London: Sage.
Scott, A.J. 1998. *Regions in the World Economy*. Oxford: Oxford University Press.
Shin, M.E., Agnew, J., Breau, S. and Richardson, P. 2006. Place and the geography of Italian export performance, *European Urban and Regional Studies*, 13, 195–208.

## RELATED WEBSITES

Fraser Institute: http://www.fraserinstitute.ca/
this public policy organization focuses on the interaction between the operation of competitive markets and the social and economic prosperity of Canadians, and includes articles on Quebec and devolution

*Guardian*: http://www.guardian.co.uk/
the *Guardian* newspaper's website includes numerous articles on Basque separatism

Her Majesty's Stationery Office: http://www.hmso.gov.uk/acts/acts1998/19980038.htm

HMSO's website provides access to a wealth of United Kingdom government publications, including the Government of Wales Act 1998

Mondragon: http://mondragon.mcc.es/ing/index.asp

this website provides information on the history and activities of this cooperative corporation in Spain

Scotland Office: http://www.scotlandoffice.gov.uk/

this website contains official documents and information on devolution, and the role and activities of the Scotland Office within the United Kingdom government

World Policy Institute: http://www.worldpolicy.org/

this website contains research on globalization and policy issues. Its *Eurasia Project* provides information on the politics and economics of secession (e.g,. in Quebec, Scotland and Catalonia)

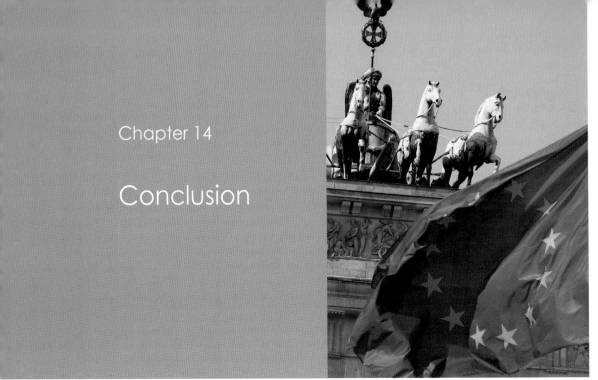

Chapter 14

Conclusion

Picture credit: © European Community, 2007

The task facing economic geography is to make sense of the geographical pattern of economic activities around the world. In this book, the task has been pursued using the geographical metaphor of core and periphery to provide a basic model or way of seeing, against which actual patterns of economic activities at a range of scales can be compared. Even at scales finer than the global or world region like Europe, the core–periphery conceptualization can be useful in thinking about how the core and periphery intersect locationally. The social, economic and locational polarization of migrant workers in world cities like Los Angeles, for example, reflects a kind of periphery or semi-periphery existing within the core. Significant pockets of wealth in some NICs and oil-rich semi-peripheral countries, in contrast, could be viewed as part of the core within the semi-periphery.

In this connection, geographers Stephen Graham and Simon Marvin have identified an important recent tendency in cities – splintering urbanism. Splintering urbanism is characterized by an intense geographical differentiation, with individual cities and parts of cities engaged in different – and rapidly changing – ways in ever broadening and increasingly complex circuits of economic and technological exchange. The uneven evolution of networks of modern information and communications technologies is forging new and dynamic landscapes of innovation, economic development and cultural transformation, while at the same time intensifying social and economic inequalities within and between cities.

In this book, a number of claims about the processes creating and recreating economic landscapes have been investigated using a historical–geographical framework deriving from an evolutionary perspective on the development of the modern world economy. In this short concluding chapter, the key elements in the argument are drawn together as a way of summarizing the perspective and pointing the reader back to the themes of the introductory chapters after reading the detailed empirical studies that form the body of the book. A number of controversial issues at the heart of contemporary debates in economic geography are also introduced to highlight the open-ended and exciting character of the field.

First, the modern world economy is an open system that evolves over time. Although there is an obvious geographical path dependence to its motion, as illustrated by the return to initial advantage produced through increasing returns to scale, there are also locational reversals and shifts in the way it works under different organizational–political and technological conditions. Thus, although the core of the world economy was (by definition) the first to industrialize on a massive scale, some other parts of the world have recently experienced a substantial expansion in industrial and, more recently, service activities. This reflects the shifts in the operation of the world economy detailed in Chapters 4–11, especially the recent slow disintegration of Fordism/organized capitalism that was important in the core for much of the 20th century. The workings and outcomes of the world economy, therefore, are not set in stone but evolve and change over time. In particular, the evolution of the world economy is not best thought of as a cyclical repetition of what has happened previously only with different technologies and countries but with much the same process of capital accumulation and territorial imperialism driving the long-wave cycle. The mechanisms driving the world economy have also changed. Today, for example, it is misleading to suppose, as some scholars still do, that the globalization of production and finance is essentially indistinguishable from the territorialization of production and trade within empires that characterized the world economy in the late 19th and early 20th centuries. These are different processes and should be seen as such (see, for example, Agnew and Grant, 1997).

Second, this dynamic understanding of the world economy allows us to combine a focus on general economic forces with a concern for the local variability that characterizes the world's economic geography. The expansion of the world economy has incorporated regions with distinctive economic histories that are themselves changed in different ways as they engage with the interests and influences emanating from organizations that span ever larger geographical areas. The growth of the world economy has produced difference rather than homogenization. The uniqueness of different places and their economies is the result of interaction over space rather than of a singularity produced by isolation. This approach challenges the assertion that globalization of production and finance portend the demise of uneven development or a progressive reduction of economic differences between places. The 'end of geography' is nowhere in sight. Indeed, recent trends indicate a deepening of differences between regions and localities within countries as well as between countries at a global scale. These reflect not only the impact of decisions by transnational corporations and macroeconomic differences between countries but also the relative success of localities and regions in inserting themselves into and protecting themselves from the circuits of global capitalism (Cox, 1997).

Third, the evolution of the world economy has followed a number of long-term cyclical fluctuations that correlate highly with the emergence of distinctive technological systems. Of particular importance are the so-called Kondratiev cycles describing distinctive epochs of economic and political development since the late 18th century (see Box 3.1). A vital dimension of change bringing about these shifts has been the transformation of the nature of capitalism; more especially, change in its mode of regulation. There have been two phases so far and now the world economy appears to be entering a third. The earliest phase of competitive capitalism lasted from the 18th century until the end of the 19th. The second phase, of organized capitalism based on close coordination between business, government and labour, dominated throughout much of the 20th century. However, recently this mode of political–economic organization has begun to be replaced by a disorganized (advanced) capitalism in which the geographical coincidence between production and consumption that characterized the previous phase has started to unravel. Rather than a sudden shift, however, the transition has been gradual with some 'old' and many more 'emerging' sectors representing most clearly the new modes of organization and production.

The focus on cycles can lead to the overemphasis of sharp breaks or ruptures and the exaggeration of the suddenness of change (see, for example, Sayer and Walker, 1992). The idea of total change is open to doubt, as argued in the latter part of Chapter 3 where the new 'regional motors' of the world economy are placed in the context of a range of locational outcomes depending on the mix of externalities and spatial transaction costs associated with different economic sectors. Mass production is still of great importance, particularly in relation to branch-plant industrialization such as that in manufacturing export processing zones (EPZs). But it is a mistake to identify the continuance of some mass production with the persistence of Fordism or organized capitalism alone (the association of mass production with high mass consumption by workers) or with the absence of *any* break with the past in the essential structure of economic organization. What is also clear, however, is that the present trend towards flexible modes of accumulation by TNCs in the developed countries (see Chapters 3 and 7) does not necessarily portend a stable and irreversible pattern that will extend indefinitely into the future.

Fourth, as the world economy has evolved so have the economic and locational principles that govern its operation. The perfect competition, transportation costs, factor endowments and comparative advantage that were important in the phase of competitive capitalism and, to a lesser degree, with organized capitalism, have faded in relative significance. Today, monopolistic competition (sectors dominated by small numbers of large companies), macroeconomic regulation, the market-access regime of international relations, position in the global urban hierarchy, global financial networks, regional motors, industrial districts, economies of scope and coordination and competitive advantage are all more important (Chapters 3–11). This means that the models of economic activities that identify, for example, transportation costs as *the* key factor in determining location (characteristic of many traditional economic geography textbooks) are potentially misleading in contemporary circumstances. Such static models – based on the presumed eternal significance of this or that factor and so deaf to history and geography – need to be adjusted or supplemented by more dynamic conceptualizations of economic change (in this connection, see Ron Martin's (1999) critique of the 'new economic geography' and the work of economists including Paul Krugman and Michael Porter). And, during the last few years, there have been a number of promising theoretical reorientations in economic geography (including the 'relational turn', as well as attention for the 'cultural economy' (see Chapter 7)).

Fifth, although neglected by economic geographers in the past, the daunting environmental problems associated with such trends as the destruction of tropical rainforests, global warming and increasing air, soil and water pollution are vitally important in understanding world economic geography. Despite the disproportionate use of non-renewal resources by the core countries, most of these threats are greatest in the world's periphery and will intensify the contrasts between rich and poor regions. Environmental problems are inseparable from processes of economic development and human welfare. These issues are alarming not only for the peoples of the affected regions but also for the peoples of DCs; it has become clear that environmental problems are going to be increasingly enmeshed in matters of national security and regional conflict. The main concern is that the continued prosperity of the DCs and the future prosperity of the LDCs may depend on processes of globalization that could be disrupted by large-scale environmental disasters, unmanageable mass migrations or the breakdown of stability in the world-system as a whole.

Sixth, state or political regulation of economic activities is of fundamental importance in understanding world economic geography, yet was typically neglected or ignored in conventional economic geography. The achievement of comparative–competitive advantage by companies and places rests importantly on political organization and coordination. The real world economy is not one of *laissez-faire* economics but of political economy. Macroeconomic policies regulating agriculture, industry and services have significant and often determining impacts on economic landscapes. The rise of different national economies within the world economy both historically and as manifested today by the NICs reflects in large part the organizational and mobilization capabilities of governments. Financial systems are particularly important in mediating between states and the investment decisions of firms that are so important in bringing about patterns of economic location (Chapter 3). Today states face the challenge of coping with trends towards globalization and localization that make economic management much more problematic than it was in the past. One reaction on their part – creating trading blocs such as the European Union (see Chapter 12) – threatens both to undermine the present relatively open world trading system and, through its centralization of decision making in distant seats of power, further stimulate the decentralist politics of various types already under way around the world (see Chapter 13). Success in many sectors of the modern world economy also seems related to certain social and cultural attributes, such as high levels of social trust and well-developed social networks supporting, for example, the links between dominant firms and subcontractors. This strongly suggests that economic geography can no longer remain isolated from consideration of the institutional, sociological and cultural bases of economic activity (see Chapter 7).

As we have tried to show throughout this book, the world economy is a complex and changing intermeshing of institutions and markets producing different effects in different places, rather than a closed global isotropic plain governed by the same invariant determinants everywhere and always. This is the central message we hope you take away from reading this book.

## KEY SOURCES AND SUGGESTED READING

Cox, K.R. (ed.) 1997. *Spaces of Globalization: Reasserting the Power of the Local*. New York: Guilford Press.

Jacobs, J. 2004. *Dark Age Ahead*. New York: Random House.

Lee, R. and Wills, J. (eds) 1997. *Geographies of Economies*. London: Edward Arnold.

# Glossary

**advanced capitalism** (disorganized capitalism, globalized capitalism) Label given to the most recent or advanced phase of capitalism that uses flexible production systems. Under advanced capitalism, relationships between capital, labour and government are more flexible, largely because a great deal of corporate activity has escaped the framework of nation-states and their institutions that still constrain organized labour and most government functions.

**African Union (AU)** The 53 members of the AU, formerly the Organization of African Unity (OAU), represent nearly all African countries. A treaty that entered into force in 1994 put these countries on the road to a continent-wide African Economic Community (AEC).

**agglomeration** Clustering together of functionally related activities. This clustering allows agglomeration economies – cost advantages that accrue to individual firms because of their location among functionally related activities.

**agglomeration economies** Cost advantages that accrue to individual firms because of their location clustered together among functionally related activities.

**agribusiness** An integrated, corporate system, involving all aspects of agriculture, from food production, to processing and distribution. The direct corporate involvement of TNCs in agriculture is an aspect of the new international division of labour (NIDL).

**Asian Tigers** The four Asian Tigers – Hong Kong, Singapore, South Korea, Taiwan – are so called because they adopted an export-driven model of economic development that allowed them to maintain high rates of economic growth and industrialization during the later decades of the 20th century.

**autarky** National economic self-sufficiency and independence.

**back-office functions** Record keeping and analytical functions that do not require frequent personal contact with clients or business associates and so can be located in 'back offices' in lower rent areas instead of the high-rent locations necessary for the front offices of companies, such as banks.

**backwash effects** The negative spillover effects on a region (or regions) of the economic growth of some other region.

**batch production** Manufacturing production involving small batches (rather than continuous mass production) of similar items. Small-batch, just-in-time (JIT) production and distribution systems can allow producers to reduce the costs of raw materials stockpiles, parts inventories and warehousing.

**branch-plant industrialization** The growth of manufacturing employment in declining industrial regions to which companies have moved some or all of their operations in order to take advantage of reserves of skilled manual labour, cheap factory space and an established infrastructure. Branch-plant industrialization proper typically involves activities that require significant inputs of technology and of skilled (or at least experienced) labour and that also require a certain degree of centrality in order to assemble and distribute raw materials and finished products, such as 'light' industries (car batteries, cash registers and cameras to tyres, watches and light engineering), white-collar information processing and wholesaling functions.

**Bretton Woods agreement** An effort to stimulate international trade by stabilizing currency fluctuations between countries. The allies met for a conference in Bretton Woods, New Hampshire, in 1944 in order to make financial arrangements for the postwar period following the anticipated defeat of Germany and Japan. They established a system of fixed exchange rates that lasted until 1971. The US dollar served as the convertible medium of currency with a fixed relationship to the price of gold. The representatives of 44 countries, including the Soviet Union, also agreed to establish the International Bank for Reconstruction and Development (of the World Bank) and the International Monetary Fund (IMF).

**BRICs** In 2003 economists at the US investment bank, Goldman Sachs, predicted that during the following 50 years, Brazil, Russia, India and China – termed the BRIC economies – could become a major force in the world economy, primarily as export-oriented manufacturing centres (particularly in the cases of China and India) but also as major export-oriented resource economies (particularly in the case of Russia and Brazil).

**business process outsourcing (BPO)** BPO is a cost-saving measure which involves the contracting out of business tasks – such as insurance claims processing, billing services, credit card services, telemarketing – to another company either domestically or internationally.

business services A subset of producer services. Business services include legal services, advertising and marketing, public relations, accounting, research and development, personnel training, recruitment, architecture and engineering and consulting.

capital flight The withdrawal of liquid assets from a national economy by domestic and overseas investors or transnational corporations.

capital goods Producer goods that are 'fixed', e.g., machinery and heavy equipment, and used to produce other goods.

capitalization The process whereby capital-intensive inputs such as technology are deployed by large firms and replace labour-intensive methods associated with smaller scale production.

captive outsourcing Captive outsourcing involves 'internal' outsourcing where a company from a country where labour and other costs are high has certain manufacturing or services activities undertaken by an affiliated company in another country where the work can be done more cheaply. *See also* offshore outsourcing, offshoring, outsourcing

carrying capacity Used in the context of food and agriculture, this term refers to the maximum population that can be supported within a given territory on a minimum daily diet, given the quality of local soils and local climatic conditions and assuming the availability of appropriate forms of mechanization.

cartel An organization of independent producers or traders who agree to restrict output, fix prices or divide markets in order to improve the profitability of its members. A well-known international cartel is the Organization of Petroleum Exporting Countries (OPEC).

cash crops Crops grown by farmers for trade or sale (versus subsistence crops where most of what is produced is consumed by the farmers and their families).

Celtic Tiger Comparing Ireland's incredible economic boom to that of the Asian Tigers (Hong Kong, Singapore, South Korea, Taiwan), economist Kevin Gardiner, working for the US investment bank Morgan Stanley, coined this term to describe Ireland's astonishing growth rates of between 5 and 10 per cent of gross domestic product during the 1990s. By the end of the decade unemployment was down to 4.5 per cent, the national debt was down and the country's GDP per capita had outstripped that of the UK and even Germany.

central place systems and central places Central places are urban centres (hamlets, villages, towns, cities) that provide goods and services to their surrounding hinterlands (market areas). A central place system comprises a hierarchy of central places – ranging from a small number of very large central places (cities) that offer higher order goods (expensive and infrequently purchased items, such as designer furniture and jewellery) at the top of the hierarchy, down to a large number of small central places (hamlets) that offer low-order goods (inexpensive, frequently purchased, everyday necessities, such as newspapers and milk).

centralization A trend towards corporate economic integration that involves the ownership of private enterprise by progressively fewer corporations. It is the result of corporate mergers and takeovers and is characterized by diversified, conglomerate, transnational corporations (TNCs).

client states Countries that are dependent, economically or militarily, on larger and more powerful countries.

collectivization of agriculture The creation of communal (collective ownership) farms.

COMECON (also known as the Council for Mutual Economic Assisstance (CMEA)) A communist international organization established in 1949 to reorganize the eastern European economies in the Stalinist mould – even to the point of striving for autarky for individual members, each pursuing independent, centralized plans. This proved unsuccessful, however, and in 1958 COMECON was reorganized by Stalin's successor, Khrushchev. The goal of autarky was abandoned, mutual trade among the Soviet bloc was fostered and some trade with western Europe was permitted. COMECON was disbanded in 1991 because the fall of communism and the shift to democracy and capitalism in eastern Europe made it redundant.

command economy An economy commanded from a central administration, in which the means of production are publicly owned. The central administration plans what and how many goods will be produced and sets prices. Communist countries such as the former Soviet Union, North Korea, Vietnam, and Cuba established command economies; the command economy model was imposed on the countries of eastern Europe that had been liberated from German occupation by Soviet forces.

commodity chain A network of labour and production processes beginning with the extraction or production of raw materials and ending with the delivery of a finished commodity.

common market A form of international economic integration that involves the elimination of tariffs and other trade barriers between members states, the removal of internal restrictions on the movement of factors of production and the creation of a common set of trade agreements with non-member countries.

comparative advantage The principle used to explain patterns of trade and specialization: if each region or country specializes in those economic activities they perform relatively better than others and imports goods for which their own production costs are relatively higher, each is likely to gain (transport costs and terms of trade notwithstanding).

competitive advantage The advantage acquired in economic competition by some locations because of the benefits that accrue from an early start in production of a particular good and the continuing defence of that historic base through superior organization and adaptability. Other locations can suffer from a competitive disadvantage due to the absence of an initial advantage that would have allowed them to develop and maintain an ongoing competitive advantage.

competitive capitalism The early phase of industrial capitalism, lasting until about 1890, characterized by comparatively high levels of free market competition, with many small-scale producers, consumers and workers who acted almost completely independently, and relatively little government intervention.

competitive disadvantage The disadvantage suffered in economic competition by some locations because of the absence of an initial advantage that would have allowed them to develop and maintain an ongoing competitive advantage.

concentration A trend towards the reduced numbers of firms in any given industry or economic sector. It is partly the result of the elimination of smaller weaker firms through competition and partly the result of corporate mergers and takeovers.

consumer durables Goods intended to be used for a number of years, e.g., household appliances.

consumer goods Commodities purchased by individuals or households for final consumption. Consumer goods comprise consumer durables (goods intended to be used for a number of years, e.g., household appliances, automobiles) and consumer non-durables (goods intended for relatively immediate consumption, e.g., fresh fruit, icecream).

consumer services Personal services, including retailing, medical care, personal grooming, leisure and recreation, culture and entertainment.

containerization Automated cranes efficiently load and unload massive standardized containers filled with large amounts of cargo between the ships and the flatbeds of nearby trains and trucks. Before container cargo handling, ships, trains and trucks sat in port while major items of cargo were loaded and unloaded individually by a sizeable intensive workforce. Containerization has improved the operation of cargo shipping and handling by reducing the turnaround time at ports.

cordon sanitaire A chain of independent buffer countries set up to form a barrier (literally, a 'sanitary line') around a country which is considered hostile militarily or dangerous ideologically.

creative destruction The withdrawal of investments from activities (and regions) that yield low rates of profit, in order to reinvest in new activities (and new places).

crossover system of trade A system of multilateral trade established in the late 19th century, which lingered into the 1930s. Europe and North America bought raw materials from less developed countries (LDCs). In return, Britain imported manufactures from and exported capital to Europe and North America. Britain's assets were boosted by the return on foreign investment and the export of manufactured goods to the LDCs (both colonies and independent states).

cultural economy The cultural economy can be defined as a group of sectors (cultural products industries) that produce goods and services – including jewellery, live theatre, music recording, film production – whose symbolic value to consumers is high relative to their practical purpose.

cumulative causation A spiral build-up of advantages that occurs in specific geographic settings as a result of the development of agglomeration economies, external economies of scale and localization economies.

customs union A form of international economic integration that involves the elimination of some (but not necessarily all) trade barriers between member states and the creation of a common set of trade barriers to non-member states.

debt trap The cycle of borrowing that results when the productivity gains from investments undertaken with borrowed capital are insufficient to meet interest repayments. Further loans and debt rescheduling provide temporary relief, but in the long term make it even more difficult to achieve increases in productivity sufficient for self-sustaining growth.

deindustrialization Many authors use this term rather loosely. At the heart of the concept is a *relative* decline in industrial *employment* in a country or region where industry has traditionally been a significant component of the economy. It may be the result of climacteric changes or of secular shifts in an economy that are related to technological change and/or the globalization of the economy. In some instances, such trends may involve not just a relative decline but an *absolute* one; and may involve declining industrial *output* as well as employment.

demographic transition The evolution of vital rates – birth rates and death rates – over time, from high to low levels. The demographic transition model posits improved diets, public health and scientific medicine as causing a steady decline in death rates with increasing levels of economic development over time. Birth rates decline later, and more slowly, as sociocultural practices take time to adjust to these new circumstances. The result is a sharp increase in population growth, until birth rates fall to relatively low levels. This model is based on the experience of DCs and so all LDCs should not be expected to follow this exact demographic path.

dependence or dependency A high level of dependence by a country on foreign enterprises, investment or technology. External dependence for a country can mean that it is highly dependent on levels of demand and the overall economic climate of other countries. Dependency for a LDC, for example, can result in a narrow economic base in which the balancing of national accounts and the generation of foreign exchange are dependent on the export of one or two agricultural or mineral resources.

deskilling A reduction in the range and level of skills within a local labour market that is the result of two trends: increased mechanization and computerization of production processes (including management and management support functions) and the geographic consolidation and localization of higher skilled activities in world cities, major control centres and centres of innovation (which leaves other labour markets with a preponderance of routine jobs in local offices and branch plants).

diagonal integration A form of business organization in which a company tries to diversify its interests by using corporate mergers or acquisitions of firms that are engaged in separate and distinct enterprises, producing different goods or services for different markets. An automobile manufacturer, for example, may buy into energy, advertising or entertainment companies.

differential of contemporaneousness In regional economic development, new technologies, ideas and market conditions may reach different regions at the same time, but they impact the regions in very different ways because they were *differently equipped to respond to them.*

diffuse industrialization The growth of manufacturing employment in rural regions, in which companies decentralize some or all of their activities from established centres of operation, such as a major city, in response to the increasing shortage, cost and militancy of labour there and the availability of reserves of relatively cheap and non-unionized unskilled and semi-skilled labour, less expensive/more available land and lower taxes in rural areas. Typically, diffuse industrialization involves activities in which labour costs are an important part of overall production costs and in which there has been little scope for reducing labour costs through technological change.

digital divide The digital divide refers to the gap in opportunities between individuals, households, businesses and areas at different socioeconomic levels to access advanced information and communication technologies (ICTs) for a variety of activities. The digital divide exists both within countries (for example, between urban and rural areas or between richer and poorer neighbourhoods) and between countries or groups of countries (for example, between the LDCs and the DCs). The primary concern is that lack of access to and development of information, communication and e-commerce technology will prevent many people from benefiting from the new knowledge-based economy.

diminishing returns (law of) The tendency for productivity to decline, after a certain point, with the continued application of capital and/or labour to a given resource base. A simple example is provided by agricultural productivity: a large farm will yield progressively higher levels of output with the addition of more farm hands and more machinery, but there will be a point at which productivity decreases as some of the labour and machinery is underemployed, people get in one another's way and coordination of activities becomes costly.

disorganized capitalism (advanced capitalism) The label given to the most recent or advanced phase of capitalism that uses flexible production systems. Under disorganized capitalism, the relationships between capital, labour and government are more flexible, largely because a great deal of corporate activity has escaped the framework of nation-states and their institutions that still constrain organized labour and most government functions.

ecological footprint The World Wide Fund for Nature's (WWF) measure of the human pressures on the natural environment from the consumption of renewable resources and the production of pollution. The ecological footprint indicates how much space a population needs compared to what is available. It changes in proportion to population size, average consumption per person and the resource intensity of the technology being used. It is measured in 'area units', where one area unit is equivalent to one hectare of biologically productive land with world average productivity. As land varies in productivity, a hectare of highly productive cropland would represent more 'area units' than the same amount of less productive grazing land.

economic union A form of international economic integration that involves the removal of all internal barriers to trade and the movement of factors of production, the creation of a common set of trade barriers and trade agreements with non-member states and the coordination of integrated economic policies within the union.

economies of scale Cost advantages for firms from large-scale production. Economies of scale in production are equivalent to increasing returns to scale. *See also* economies of scope, internal economies of scale

economies of scope Cost advantages from large-scale flexible organization. Economies created by the capacity to provide entirely new products and/or services through the flexible use of the same production or service network.

elasticity of demand The degree to which levels of demand for a product or service change in response to changes in price. Where a relatively small change in price induces a significant change in demand, elasticity is high; where levels of demand remain fairly stable in spite of price changes, demand is said to be inelastic.

encapsulation Howells (2003) notion of service encapsulation of goods and materials illustrates how services are increasingly incorporated into manufactured products. Manufactured products are offered to consumers not in their own right but in terms of their wider service attributes. Either the manufactured product is offered along with closely aligned service products in a single package (e.g., finance, insurance, maintenance warranties with an automobile purchase) or the consumer may not be offered the manufactured product itself in a single one-time purchase, but may be offered the service that the manufactured product offers in a continuing process involving long-term customer contact through service delivery (e.g., automobile lease instead of purchase).

enterprise zone An officially designated economically distressed area where public fiscal and other incentives are available as an inducement to private companies to locate and create jobs there.

entrepôt A port that specializes in the trade of goods for re-export. Entrepôts operate primarily as intermediary trading centres – they receive goods from foreign countries for re-export to other countries. Hong Kong, Singapore and Rotterdam are the world's top three entrepôts.

eurodollars US currency that is held in banks located outside the USA, traditionally mostly in Europe, hence the name. Currently, China holds the largest amount – in the hundreds of billions. It is a pool of currency for which there is a distinctive and independent market, because it conventionally represented a fairly stable, hard currency that is beyond the control of the US government and its financial institutions. At the same time, the strength of the US economy and the value of the dollar affect investor confidence in eurodollars.

export processing zones (EPZs) Small, closely definable areas within which especially favourable investment and trading conditions are created by governments in order to attract export oriented industries, usually foreign owned. These conditions include the absence of foreign exchange controls, the availability of factory space and warehousing at subsidized rents, low tax rates and exemption from tariffs and export duties.

external control The term refers to situations where employment opportunities and decisions about investment and production in a given plant or locality are controlled by corporate managers based in other cities, regions or countries.

external economies of scale The specific benefits that accrue to producers from associating with similar producers in places that offer services that they need.

factors of production The fundamental components of any economic system: land, labour and capital. Land includes not only space or territory but also the associated soils and natural resources. Labour includes not only the size of the available workforce but also its skills, experience and discipline. Capital includes not only money capital but also everything deliberately created for the purpose of production, such as factories and machinery (i.e., 'fixed' capital). A fourth factor, enterprise, is often recognized, although it may be missing from some forms of economic organization (e.g., subsistence economies), while it may legitimately be regarded as one aspect of labour.

'fallow' agriculture or shifting cultivation Involves sowing or planting on scorched land using slash-and-burn methods (cutting down the natural vegetation (e.g., forest) and burning it to release its nutrients into the soil). No special tools are required for such a system, neither is weeding or fertilization necessary, provided that cultivation is shifted in a couple of years to another burned plot after a few crops have been taken from the old one, which is then abandoned (left fallow) for a period of time.

feudalism and feudal systems Forms of economic organization based on a mode of production in which the surplus product (i.e., the outputs of productivity in excess of subsistence levels) is appropriated through a hierarchy of sociopolitical ranks by institutionalized coercion. In classical feudal systems, lords allocate land to vassals in return for military service and/or labour on the lord's estate.

FIRE *See* finance, insurance and real estate services

finance, insurance and real estate (FIRE) A subset of producer services. Finance, insurance and real estate (FIRE) includes commercial and investment banking, insurance of all kinds (property, medical, casualty) and the residential and commercial real estate business.

flexible accumulation A phase of capitalist development (a regime of accumulation, in the terminology of regulation theory) characterized by a set of production technologies, labour practices, inter-firm relations and consumption patterns that have evolved in order to allow greater economic and geographic flexibility in economic affairs. Because it succeeded Fordism, flexible accumulation is also known as post- or neo-Fordism.

flexible production systems and flexible production Various practices whereby manufacturing operations achieve flexibility in what they produce, when they produce it, how they produce it and where they produce it. These practices include the exploitation of various kinds of enabling technologies, greater use of subcontracting, the exploitation of different labour markets, the exploitation of different market niches for products and the development of new labour processes using flexible working hours, part-time workers, etc.

Fordism (Fordist regime of accumulation) A regime of accumulation that centres on the mutual reinforcement of mass production and mass consumption. Named after Henry Ford because of his innovations and philosophy concerning automobile manufacture, it features a highly specialized and differentiated division of labour with assembly line production geared to the provision of standardized, affordable goods for mass markets.

foreign direct investment (FDI) Direct investment in a company or companies in one or a number of foreign countries (e.g., takeovers, new subsidiaries, etc., rather than portfolio investment) in order to achieve managerial and production control.

franchise An business that has a licence to manufacture or sell a product or service under the name of the original company, e.g., a retail outlet that is not owned by Benetton but that has a franchise agreement to use the company's name for the store and to sell the company's products.

free trade association A form of international economic integration that involves the elimination of some (but not necessarily all) trade barriers between member states, but where each member state continues to set its own tariffs and quotas as trade barriers to non-member states.

geographical path dependence The historical relationship between the present economic activities associated with a place and its past experience.

global currencies Currencies used in international transactions. The US dollar is the most important one today, although its use is challenged somewhat by the euro and the Japanese yen.

global sourcing Use of multiple sources in different countries for the components of a particular product that is assembled elsewhere.

globalized capitalism (advanced capitalism or disorganized capitalism) The label given to the most recent or advanced phase of capitalism that uses flexible production systems. Under globalized capitalism, the relationships between capital, labour and government are more flexible, largely because a great deal of corporate activity has escaped the framework of nation-states and their institutions that still constrain organized labour and most government functions.

Green Revolution An agricultural programme in the 1960s and 1970s to tackle hunger in the LDCs by transferring methods of modern agricultural technology to traditional farming regions. A package of measures to improve yields of food crops such as wheat, maize and rice involved the application of greater mechanization, chemical fertilizers and pesticides and irrigation water to genetically improved high-yield seeds. While many Asian and some Latin American countries achieved significantly increased crop yields, the strategy was not embraced to the same extent in Sub-Saharan Africa. The Green Revolution has been criticized for benefiting wealthier farmers at the expense of smaller landowners who cannot afford the costs of initial inputs, especially fertilizers and irrigation water. Production has also levelled out in recent years.

gross domestic product (GDP) When gross national income (GNI) is adjusted to remove the value of profits from overseas investments and the 'leakage' of profits accruing to foreign investors, the result is a measure of gross domestic product (GDP).

gross national income (GNI) Also known as gross national product (GNP), this is a measure of the market value of the production of a given economy in a given period (usually a year). It is based on the market price of finished products and includes the value of subsidies; it includes the value of profits from overseas investments and profits accruing to foreign investors; it does not take into account the costs of replacing fixed capital.

gross national product (GNP) *See* gross national income (GNI)

gross value added (GVA) Gross value added is equal to GDP minus taxes on products plus subsidies on products. In other words, GVA plus taxes on products minus subsidies on products is equal to GDP.

growth pole A growth pole, which can be unplanned or planned, benefits from agglomeration economies and can spread prosperity to nearby regions through spread effects. Examples of efforts to plan growth poles to stimulate regional development by generating spread effects include the industrial complexes located in Taranto and Bari in the Mezzogiorno (south) of Italy or the eight *metropoles d'équilibre* (balancing metropolises) in France, such as Lyon, Marseille and Bordeaux, which were intended also to redirect some economic activity away from Paris and reduce its primacy.

hearth area An area of origin of people, ideas or technologies which then spread to other areas.

hegemony A difficult and controversial concept, hegemony is often applied to the dominance of one country or region or group over others. Greek for leadership, this term was originally applied to the dominance of one Greek city state over others. In addition to military dominance, the hegemonic power must also have economic and cultural dominance to set and enforce the rules of conduct that it prefers.

horizontal integration A form of business organization in which a company tries to capture the market for a single stage of production, a single good or service or an entire industry and achieve economies of scale, by using corporate mergers or acquisitions of firms that formerly competed in the same market(s) with similar goods or services. A successful automobile manufacturer, for example, might buy out other automobile manufacturers.

imperialism The extension of the power of a country through direct or indirect control of the economic and political life of other territories.

import penetration This describes the result of a significant share of domestic markets for a particular product or service being lost by domestic firms in the face of competition from foreign sources.

import substitution Development of domestic firms capable of producing goods or services formerly provided by foreign firms.

increasing returns to scale Cost advantages from large-scale production. Increasing returns to scale in production are equivalent to economies of scale. An increase in inputs (raw materials, labour, etc.) by x per cent results in an increase in output by more than x per cent.

industrial production In addition to manufacturing, industrial production includes mining and power generation.

infant industries Industries at an early stage of development that are protected by tariffs and other trade barriers until they can survive foreign competition without protection.

inflation A decline in the value of money because prices keep rising. A number of economic theories have been formulated to explain why inflation occurs. In the 18th century Hume theorized that prices rise as the supply of money rises. And a reduction in the purchasing power of money can occur when a national government increases the supply of money. Keynes assumed that inflation takes place when demand outstrips the supply of goods and services (resulting in the need for a national government to intervene to control inflation by adjusting spending, tax and interest rate levels). In the cost–push theory, the price–wage spiral causes inflation – worker demands for higher wages necessitate an increase in prices, which result in demands for higher wages, and so on. Structural theory suggests that structural factors can cause a country's currency to lose value so that prices rise, such as when an LDC has poor terms of trade where the price of imports keep rising relative to the price of exports.

informal sector Economic activities which are undertaken without any formal systems of regulation or remuneration. In addition to domestic labour, these activities include strictly illegal activities such as drug peddling and prostitution as well as a wide variety of legal activities such as casual labour in construction crews, on docks or on farms; domestic piece work; street trading; scavenging; and providing personal services such as shoe shining or letter writing.

informational economy A new mode of economic production and management in which productivity and competitiveness rely heavily on generating new knowledge and accessing and processing appropriate information.

initial advantage Advantage acquired in economic competition by some locations because of the benefits that accrue from an early start in production of a particular good.

intermediate goods Producer goods for manufacturing, processing or resale (e.g., raw materials and semi-finished items for use in the production of other goods or services rather than for final consumption), such as shoelaces for shoe manufacturing, hinges for furniture manufacturing and tyres for automobile manufacturing.

intermodal transportation Transportation using more than one means of conveyance, e.g., truck and ship, air and rail, etc.

internal economies of scale The specific benefits that accrue to producers from large-scale production within a company. As a company increases production, the average cost of each product begins to fall for that company.

international division of labour The idea of the organization of spatial divisions of labour, organized principally at the national scale until the late 20th century, in which each country specialized in certain sectors of the economy, such as industry in the UK or agriculture and raw materials in many African countries.

International Monetary Fund (IMF) The IMF is a United Nations affiliate established in 1945 to help encourage international monetary cooperation, to ensure international currency exchange stability, to promote economic and employment growth and, while not a development bank, to provide temporary economic assistance to countries experiencing balance of payment problems. In early 2007 the IMF had about US$28 billion in credit and loans to 74 of its more than 180 member countries. The IMF and the World Bank are different organizations but share the same member countries.

isotropic Homogenous in all respects.

just-in-time (JIT) production 'Lean' production employing vertical disintegration within large formerly functionally integrated firms such as automobile manufacturers in which daily and even hourly deliveries of parts and other supplies from smaller (often non-union) subcontractors and suppliers now arrive 'just in time' to maintain 'last-minute' and 'zero' inventories. A computer system is used to adjust deliveries at short notice to meet changing demand. The goal is to reduce costs by eliminating waste from overproduction and minimizing warehousing.

*keiretsu* Keiretsu is a Japanese form of corporate organization. A keiretsu is a grouping of affiliated companies that form a business network to work towards each other's mutual benefit. The keiretsu system also involves central government setting up favourable trade policies, technology policies and fiscal policies to help Japanese industry compete successfully in the world economy.

Keynesianism Specifically, this refers to a doctrine of macroeconomic management that is closely associated with British economist, John Maynard Keynes, who advocated the use of fiscal policy (e.g., budget deficits) and the exploitation of economic multiplier effects in order to achieve and maintain full employment. The term is also used to denote the mode of regulation associated with the Fordist regime of accumulation.

kin-ordered system (or societies) A system of social organization based on relationships between people who are related either biologically or by other arrangements such as through marriage or adoption.

Kondratiev cycles Cyclical waves of 50–55 years in duration that have characterized the rate of change in price inflation within the capitalist world economy for the past 250 years. Their origins and significance remain controversial, but in recent years they have been widely recognized to be closely tied in to distinctive phases of political–economic development.

Kuznets cycles Business cycles of approximately 25 years in duration that have characterized the pattern of acceleration and deceleration in economic growth. Named after Ukrainian-born economist Simon Kuznets, who established their existence in the 1920s, they are cycles of activity in investment and building.

land tenure A system of land use rights and transfer mechanisms. The major types of land tenure include owner occupation, cash tenancy, share cropping (a form of tenancy in which rent is paid in kind), use rights (where there is no codified legal owner and a person or group establishes a right to the land by using it) and collectivism (in which individual farmers work in cooperatives that own the land).

latifundia Large farms or estates farmed by labourers – found predominantly in Latin America, where they originated as imperial land grants to new settlers.

less developed countries (LDCs) Peripheral and semi-peripheral countries within the world-system, with low economic output and per capita incomes, which tend to have politically weak states and low-wage, labour-intensive production. Since the end of the Cold War and the economic growth of the newly industrializing countries (NICs) and other formerly peripheral countries, the designation of 'Third World' is no longer as useful in distinguishing the LDCs from either the capitalist, economically developed countries such as the USA and the UK (the 'First World') or the former communist countries in what was the Soviet bloc (the 'Second World').

localization economies Cost savings that accrue to firms as the output of their particular industries increase as a result of clustering together at a specific location.

machinofacture A form of organization of industrial production that is capital intensive, with labour tending machines rather than operating them directly. It was the basis for the regime of accumulation that preceded Fordism.

*maquiladoras* Literally, 'mills' in Spanish. These are export processing zones (EPZs) in Mexico, mainly near the US border.

Marshall Plan A US-financed programme that provided almost US$13 billion in economic aid to its war-torn European allies after the Second World War. Conceived as a self-help plan that would foster a healthy world economy, the funds were used to promote economic recovery and political stability in Europe.

Mercantilism The basis of this economic ideology adhered to from the 16th century to the early 18th century in most European countries was that national wealth was to be measured in terms of gold or silver and that the fundamental source of economic growth was a persistently favourable balance of trade. This was the economic 'logic' that justified not only overseas colonization but also the coercion of plantation labour and the prohibition of manufacturing in the colonies. It was also the logic that, on the domestic front, promoted thrift and saving as a means of accumulating capital for overseas investment. It required a high degree of economic regulation, sponsorship and protection by the government.

merchant capitalism The label given to the initial phase of capitalism. As the feudal system disintegrated, it was replaced by an economy that was dominated by market exchange, in which communities came to specialize in the production of the goods and commodities that they could produce most efficiently in comparison with other communities. The key actors in this system were the merchants who supplied the capital required to initiate the flow of trade – hence the label merchant capitalism.

minisystems Local societies with a simple division of labour within a single cultural framework, such as hunter-gatherer and some agricultural societies.

mode of production A fundamental form of economic organization, such as feudalism or capitalism, which has distinctive relationships between the main factors of production (land, labour and capital). The concept is derived from Marxian economics (a body of theory originally derived from the work of Karl Marx) but now has much wider use.

mode of regulation The terminology of regulationist theories for a collection of structural forms (political, economic, social, cultural) and institutional arrangements that define the 'rules of the game' for individual and collective behaviour within a specific regime of accumulation or phase of economic development. The mode of regulation gives expression to, and serves to reproduce, fundamental social relations.

monetarism A doctrine of macroeconomic management that disavows demand management and regards the money supply as the most important determinant of economic stability. Important in the USA and UK in the late 1970s and early 1980s, it reasserted the relevance of price theory and the importance of free markets.

monoculture The agricultural practice in which one crop is grown intensively over a large area of land.

most-favoured-nation (MFN) treatment This non-discrimination principle means that a country treats all trading partners in a manner equal to that accorded to the most favoured nation. This is a method for promoting free trade by ensuring equal trading opportunities among countries, especially as they relate to import duties and freedom of investment. Members of the World Trade Organization (WTO) negotiate this kind of tariff and trade arrangement.

multiplier effects The extra industries, firms, incomes and employment generated by a new activity can be said to result from that activity's multiplier effects. Such effects can be localized and give rise to a growth pole or occur in a more diffuse manner.

nation A group of people with a common identity based on such shared characteristics as origins, history, customs and, frequently, language – a nationality. The terms country, nation, nation-state and state are often used interchangeably.

nation-state A state that corresponds for the most part with the people of only one nation.

nationalism Devotion and loyalty to one's nation. Nationalist feelings and movements, for example, often arose in opposition to colonialism in African and Asian countries in the 20th century based on a desire for national independence.

nationalist separatism A nation or group's autonomy or independence from a larger group or political unit.

neoclassical economics Forms the basis of a particular conceptualization of how economic activity operates in capitalist society. The economy comprises many small producers and consumers. All act rationally, although none is large enough to affect significantly the operation of the market. Firms are seen as atomistic agents with full information in a world of pure markets (with no entry barriers) and all have exactly the same resources, technological capability and market power with deviations regarded as market 'imperfections'. Firms utilize factors of production (land, labour, capital) in order to maximize their profits. Consumers sell their factors of production (especially labour) in order to purchase goods and services that maximize their individual preferences. The market is an abstract space in which firms and consumers set the prices. The forces of supply and demand cause economic resources to be used in the most efficient way possible. Neoclassical economics involves normative model building – constructing simplified versions of how the real world ought to operate.

Neo-Fordism Sometimes referred to as 'post-Fordism' or flexible accumulation, this term identifies the regime of accumulation that has succeeded Fordism within parts of the world's economies. Rather than being predicated on the mutual reinforcement of mass production and mass consumption, it depends on flexible production systems to exploit specific market segments and/or niches.

neoliberalism Neoliberalism involved a shift in the 1970s away from the egalitarian liberalism (and the Keynesian welfare state) that had dominated public policy in DCs like the USA and the UK since the 1930s and a selective return to the ideas of classical liberalism. The process involves 'rollback' neoliberalization (e.g., deregulation of finance and industry, cutbacks in welfare programmes) and 'rollout' neoliberalization (e.g., public–private partnerships, workfare requirements, privatization of government services). The net effect has been to 'hollow out' the capacity of the central governments while forcing local governments to become entrepreneurial in pursuit of jobs and revenues and pro-business in their expenditures. The 'free markets' associated with neoliberalism have intensified uneven relationships among places, the inevitable result being an intensification of economic inequality at every scale, from the neighbourhood to the nation-state.

Neolithic period Literally, the 'New Stone' age, between about 7000 and 5500 BC, characterized by the use of stone tools produced by grinding or polishing, and an agricultural revolution involving the switch from hunting and gathering to food production based on the domestication of plants and animals.

New Deal The domestic program introduced by President Franklin D. Roosevelt in the 1930s to promote economic recovery. Roosevelt promised 'a new deal for the American people' in his acceptance speech for the 1932 presidential nomination. New Deal legislation included the establishment of the Civil Works Administration to address unemployment, the National Recovery Administration to restore industrial production and the Agricultural Adjustment Administration to bolster farm production.

new international division of labour (NIDL) The idea of the reorganization of spatial divisions of labour, formerly organized principally at the national scale, to a global scale based on international production and marketing systems.

newly industrializing countries (NICs) Countries, formerly peripheral within the world-system, that have acquired a significant industrial sector, usually through foreign direct investment (FDI).

non-tariff barriers Policy instruments (other than import taxes) designed to protect domestic industry from foreign competition (e.g., import quotas, import licensing requirements, special standards and regulations, exchange rate manipulation, government subsidies to domestic industries and special labelling and packaging regulations).

offshore financial centres Islands or micro-states that have become specialized nodes in the geography of worldwide financial flows. They are attractive because they provide no- or low-tax settings for savings and are less regulated than financial centres elsewhere.

offshore outsourcing External outsourcing, where a company has certain manufacturing or services activities undertaken by an unaffiliated company in another country where the work can be done more cheaply. *See also* captive outsourcing, offshoring, outsourcing

offshoring Offshoring involves a company having certain manufacturing or services activities undertaken by an affiliated or unaffiliated company in another country where the work can be done more cheaply. *See also* captive outsourcing, offshore outsourcing, outsourcing

Organization for Economic Cooperation and Development (OECD) The OECD is an organization of 30 industrialized countries that include the USA, Canada, Japan, Australia, New Zealand, South Korea and European countries such as the UK, France, Switzerland and the Czech Republic. It was founded in 1961 to stimulate economic growth and world trade (taking over from the Organization for European Economic Cooperation (OEEC), which had been established to administer US and Canadian postwar reconstruction aid in Europe under the Marshall Plan). The OECD defines itself as an international organization of countries that share a commitment to democratic government and the market economy. Its mission is to help governments tackle the economic, social and governance challenges of the global economy. Based in Paris, the OECD is probably best known as a source of economic statistics and publications.

Organization of Petroleum Exporting Countries (OPEC) OPEC is an international cartel of 12 oil-exporting countries. It was created in 1960 to coordinate oil output and fix prices in an effort to improve profitability and reduce market volatility. Its members are all LDCs: Algeria, Angola, Indonesia, Iran, Iraq, Kuwait, Libya, Nigeria, Qatar, Saudi Arabia, UAE and Venezuela. In 2005 OPEC produced nearly 31 million barrels of crude oil each day or almost 43 per cent of the world's output of nearly 72 million daily barrels. OPEC holds more than 78 per cent of the world's estimated proven crude oil reserves of more than 1 trillion barrels.

organized capitalism The later phase of industrial capitalism that was characterized by comparatively highly structured relationships between labour, government and corporate enterprise. These relationships were mediated through legal and legislative instruments, formal agreements and public institutions.

outsourcing In the global economy, outsourcing typically involves a company, often in a DC where labour and other costs are high, having certain manufacturing or services activities undertaken by an unaffiliated company (e.g., an independent subcontractor) either domestically or in another country. *See also* captive outsourcing, offshore outsourcing, offshoring

outsourcing, captive *See* captive outsourcing

overaccumulation A distinctive phase in the long-term dynamics of capitalist economies, characterized by unused or underutilized capital and labour. It is an inevitable outcome of the difficulty of matching supply to demand under changing conditions and it represents a critical moment for the political economy of capitalism. It can be recognized by the appearance of idle productive capacity, excess inventories, gluts of commodities, surplus money capital and high levels of unemployment.

positional goods Consumer goods that are acquired (in part, at least) in order to denote affluence, social status and/or style.

primary commodities *See* primary production

primary production Primary production and its commodities are derived from natural resources, as in agriculture, mining, forestry and fishing.

**primate cities/primacy** A primate city is a country's leading city as evidenced by measures of this primacy including its significantly larger population compared to other cities (being more than twice as large as the country's second largest city) and by other characteristics reflecting the primate city's national importance and influence, such as economic and political activity and power.

**privatization** The sale of government assets (such as key industries) to private owners and the contracting out of services formerly provided by government to private companies in an effort to increase government efficiency and save public money.

**producer goods** Manufactured goods used in the production of other goods and services rather than for final consumption. Producer goods comprise **intermediate goods** (e.g., raw materials and semi-finished items) and fixed **capital goods** (e.g., machinery and heavy equipment).

**producer services** Services that enhance the productivity or efficiency of other firms' activities or that enable them to maintain their specialized roles. Usually subdivided into (a) **business services**, including legal services, advertising and marketing, public relations, accounting, research and development, personnel training, recruitment, architecture and engineering and consulting and (b) **finance, insurance and real estate (FIRE)**, including commercial and investment banking, insurance of all kinds (property, medical, casualty) and the residential and commercial real estate business.

**product lifecycle** Locational requirements for production change as products move from being novel and expensive to being standardized and cheaper. In particular, labour costs can become more important than adjacency to markets.

**public–private partnerships** Coalitions of private sector businesses and/or business leaders and public sector officials and agencies, with others such as unions and chambers of commerce, which seek to promote economic growth and the well-being of an area.

**purchasing power parity (PPP)** When making international comparisons of economic prosperity, it is vital to take into account differences in national price levels. PPP does this by measuring how much of a common 'market basket' of goods and services each country's currency can purchase locally.

**rank redistribution and rank-redistributive societies** A form of economic organization that is dominated by the redistribution of surplus product from one social group to another (e.g., **feudalism**), usually through an institutional framework such as one established by the **state**.

**Reaganomics** The application of **supply-side** economics to the management of the US economy in the 1980s. Supply-side economics is similar to monetarism in its disavowal of demand management; rather, the key to economic stability and well-being is seen to be the enhancement of aggregate supply. Reaganomics consisted of a set of objectives that included tax reduction, deregulation of business, increased government spending on defence and decreased government spending on social welfare.

**regime of accumulation** The terminology of regulationist theories for a particular way of organizing economic production, income distribution, consumption, and public goods and services.

**regional devolution** The transfer of certain powers from national government to one or more regional units of government within a country. Under devolution, the region or regions remain part of the country while gaining some measure of self-government within the overall national institutional framework (in contrast to independence where the regions would no longer be constituent parts of the country).

**regionalism** The commitment to planning in a nationally coordinated fashion the economic development of fixed regional units that are designated as the basis for allocating economic activities by central government. Regionalism also refers to the ideology of political movements.

**returns to scale, increasing** *See* **increasing returns to scale**

**sexual divisions of labour** The division, specialization and different rewards between occupations predominantly occupied by either men or women.

**share cropping** A type of farming in which the rent for the land that tenants pay to the landowner is in agricultural produce rather than in cash. Landlords often provide inputs such as seeds and fertilizer in return for a fixed percentage of what is produced.

**shifting cultivation or 'fallow' agriculture** Involves sowing or planting on scorched land using slash-and-burn methods (cutting down the natural vegetation (e.g., forest) and burning it to release its nutrients into the soil). No special tools are required for such a system, neither is weeding or fertilization necessary, provided that cultivation is shifted in a couple of years to another burned plot after a few crops have been taken from the old one, which is then abandoned (left fallow) for a period of time.

**socialism** A system of social and economic organization where private property and income distribution are subject to social control. In state socialism, or statism, the central government has responsibility for social control. In the former Soviet Union, for example, markets were prohibited (in public), there was little meaningful electoral politics and the means of production were owned by the state.

**sovereignty** Sovereignty is a notion that is interrelated with other concepts, such as state, government, independence, democracy, nation-state and nationalism, to name a few. Sovereignty in government is the ultimate and independent authority – the absolute right to govern – as held or claimed by a state or nation. It involves the international independence of a state or nation – the right and authority to regulate its internal affairs without outside interference.

**space–process relationship** The idea that different types of firm activity are carried out at different locations within a hierarchy of places, from world cities to various peripheries.

**spatial division of labour** Regional economic specialization, based on the distribution of resources and markets and on the exploitation of agglomeration economies, economies of scale and localization economies.

**spread effects** The positive spillover effects on a region (or regions) of the economic growth of some other region.

**stagflation** Episodes of economic recession accompanied by comparatively high rates of price inflation.

**state** Political organization of society (requiring a state bureaucracy, a state religion, a judicial apparatus, a military establishment and a police force) with a defined territory over which it has complete sovereignty to use the rule of law to maintain order and security on behalf of the nation or nations inhabiting that territory.

**strategic alliances** Commercial agreements between transnational corporations, usually involving shared technologies, marketing networks, market research or product development.

**structural adjustment programme** Structural adjustment programmes involve policy changes that are stipulations for getting new loans from the International Monetary Fund (IMF) or the World Bank or for obtaining lower interest rates on existing loans. Structural adjustment programmes were created with the primary goal of reducing the borrowing country's macroeconomic imbalances. In general, loans from both the World Bank and the IMF are designed to promote economic growth, to generate income and to pay off the debt which the countries have accumulated. Structural adjustment programmes are based on fiscal and monetary restraint, combined with deregulation and liberalization of national markets. They have been criticized for exacerbating the hardships experienced by ordinary citizens during the structural adjustments.

**subsistence economies** An economic system, usually of farming, in which the producers (farmers), and their families, consume most of what is produced, leaving little surplus for trade or sale.

**supply-side** Related to the economic theory that increasing the availability (supply) of capital for investment in an economic system by reducing marginal tax rates will promote long-term growth by providing the incentive necessary to increase overall economic activity, productivity and income.

**supranational political union** A form of international economic integration that extends beyond economic union to a unified fiscal and monetary system controlled by a supranational authority with executive, judicial and legislative powers.

**sustainable development** A pattern of resource use and economic development that does not jeopardize non-renewable resources, damage existing ecosystems or harm individual species.

**tariffs** The schedules of duties or taxes imposed by a government on exported or, more typically, imported goods and services.

**Taylorism** The name given (after analyst F.W. Taylor) to forms of organization in manufacturing industries wherein the planning and control of work are given over entirely to management, leaving production workers to be allocated specialized tasks that are subject to careful analysis – 'scientific management' using techniques such as time-and-motion studies.

**technology systems** Distinctive 'packages' of technologies, energy sources, and political–economic structures that represent the most efficient means for the organization of production at any given phase of economic development. Based on key sets of interdependent technologies, they represent the underpinnings of successive modes of regulation and regimes of accumulation.

**technopole** A planned development, within a concentrated area, for technologically innovative, industrial-related production. Technopoles include science parks, science cities and other high-tech industrial complexes.

**terms of trade** The ratio of the prices at which exports and imports are exchanged. When the price of exports rises relative to the price of imports, the terms of trade reflect an improvement for the exporting country.

**time–space compression** The reduction in barriers to decision making and action as a result of transportation and communications improvements that have allowed the pace of life to accelerate. Increasingly, key economic activities, such as the circulation of capital and goods, can occur more rapidly. Time–space compression involves more than the traditional notion of *time–space convergence*, which identified how new systems of transportation and communications, such as the railway replacing the stagecoach, while not changing absolute distance over space, made places closer when distance is measured in time.

trade creation effects The positive effects of international economic integration, resulting from the free movement of factors of production and free trade, which allows each country or region to specialize according to its comparative advantage, thus leading to a greater overall productivity and internal trade.

trade diversion The displacement of pre-existing trade flows as a result of international and supranational economic integration.

trade preference associations Loose forms of international economic integration that involve reduced trade barriers between member states.

trading blocs Groups of countries with formalized systems of trading agreements.

transnational corporations (TNCs) Also known as multinational corporations (MNCs), these companies operate in a number of countries. Many of the headquarters of the largest TNCs are concentrated in the world cities of London, New York and Tokyo. Production is carried out at a global scale in such a way as to maximize profits. For example, as part of a global assembly system, a low-skill labour-intensive stage of the production process may be located in a less developed country where wages and unionization levels are low.

unequal exchange Biases in the international trade system promote the unequal exchange of commodities between countries, which results in some countries gaining more and others less. Goods produced in peripheral countries (especially agricultural products), for example, command low prices on the international market compared to the amount of intensive labour that went into producing them, thereby transferring value from peripheral countries to core countries.

uneven development The spatial outcome, within and between countries, of the continuous see-sawing of capital from one set of opportunities to another on the basis of particular local mixes of skills and resources. Capital is invested unevenly over time and across space because, whenever possible, development will occur wherever businesses judge that their investment will yield the highest return. When businesses try to exploit differences between places, they create a continuously variable geometry of labour, capital, production, markets and management.

vertical disintegration A form of business organization in which specialized firms are created and operate as part of a network of subcontractors and suppliers within industries formerly dominated by large, functionally integrated firms. As part of a flexible production system, an automobile manufacturer, for example, may subcontract parts and other supplies to smaller specialized firms.

vertical integration A form of business organization in which a company tries to control all aspects of the same industry or enterprise and capture a greater proportion of the final selling price by using corporate mergers or acquisitions of firms that were formerly engaged in different stages of the same industry or enterprise (from production to sale). A car manufacturer, for example, may take over companies that make specialized components like engines or car navigation systems or that distribute or sell automobiles.

wage labour When people work in exchange for monetary payment rather than bartered goods, military protection or as a result of enslavement.

World Bank The World Bank (and its main component, the International Bank for Reconstruction and Development) is a United Nations affiliate established in 1948 to finance productive projects that further the economic development of its more than 180 member countries from Afghanistan to Uganda. In fiscal year 2005, the World Bank loaned US$22.3 billion to less developed countries for 278 projects.

world city One of the cities that dominate world finance and serve as headquarters to transnational corporations. Typically, London, New York and Tokyo are identified as the leading tier of world cities, although other cities such as Chicago, Frankfurt, Paris, Los Angeles and Zurich also have important global roles.

world-system Any spatially extensive economic system that has a single division of labour but multiple cultural systems.

xenophobia 'Xenos' and 'phobos' are the Greek words for stranger and fear: xenophobia is a rejection of strangers or foreigners or of anything that is foreign or unknown based on feelings of fear or hatred.

# Bibliography

Aarebrot, F.H. 1982. On the structural basis of regional mobilization in Europe, in B. De Marchi and A.M. Boileau (eds) *Boundaries and Minorities in Western Europe*. Milan: Franco Angeli.

Achebe, C. 1975. *Morning Yet on Creation Day*. London: Faber.

Adelman, I. 1984. Beyond export-led growth, *World Development*, 12, 937–49.

Agnew, J.A. 1987. *The United States in the World Economy: A Regional Geography*. Cambridge: Cambridge University Press.

Agnew, J.A. 1988. Beyond core and periphery: the myth of regional political–economic restructuring and a new sectionalism in American politics, *Political Geography Quarterly*, 7, 127–39.

Agnew, J.A. 1992. The United States and American hegemony, in P.J. Taylor (ed.) *The Political Geography of the Twentieth Century*. London: Belhaven Press.

Agnew, J.A. 1993. Trading blocs or a world that knows no boundaries?, in C.H. Williams (ed.) *The Political Geography of the New World Order*. London: Belhaven Press.

Agnew, J.A. and Corbridge, S. 1995. *Mastering Space: Hegemony, Territory and International Political Economy*. London: Routledge.

Agnew, J.A. and Grant, R.J. 1997. Falling out of the world economy? Theorizing 'Africa' in world trade, in R. Lee and J. Wills (eds) *Geographies of Economies*. London: Edward Arnold.

Agnew, J.A., Shin, M. and Richardson, P. 2005. The saga of the 'Second Industrial Divide' and the history of the 'Third Italy': Evidence from export data, *Scottish Geographical Journal*, 121, 83–101.

Albrechts, L. and Swyngedouw, E. 1989. The challenges for regional policy under a flexible regime of accumulation, in L. Albrechts, F. Moulaert, R. Roberts and E. Swyngedouw (eds) *Regional Policy at the Crossroads*. London: Jessica Kingsley.

Allen, J. 1988. Fragmented firms, disorganised labour?, in J. Allen and D. Massey (eds) *Restructuring Britain: The Economy in Question*. London: Sage.

Amin, A. (ed.) 1994. *Post-Fordism. A Reader*. Cambridge, MA: Blackwell.

Amin A. 1996. Beyond associative democracy, *New Political Economy*, 1, 309–33.

Amin, A. and Robins, K. 1990. The re-emergence of regional economies? The mythical geography of flexible accumulation, *Society and Space*, 8, 7–34.

Amin, A. and Thrift, N. 1992. Neo-Marshallian nodes in global networks, *International Journal of Urban and Regional Research*, 16, 571–87.

Amin, A. and Thrift, N. (eds) 1994. *Globalization, Institutions, and Regional Development in Europe*. Oxford: Oxford University Press.

Amiti, M. and Wei, S.-J. 2005. Fear of service outsourcing: is it justified?, *Economic Policy*, 42, 307–47, available at http://www.oecd.org/dataoecd/44/24/35333668.pdf.

Amsden, A. 1989. *Asia's Next Giant: South Korea and Late Industrialization*. New York: Oxford University Press.

Anderson, A.B. 1990. Smokestacks in the rainforest: industrial development and deforestation in the Amazon Basin, *World Development*, 18, 1191–205.

Andrews, J. 1992. A change of face: a survey of Taiwan, *Economist*, 10 October.

Aoyama, Y. 2000. Networks, keiretsu, and locations of the Japanese electronics industry in Asia, *Environment and Planning A*, 32, Pion Limited, London, 223–44.

Armstrong, W. and McGee, T. 1986. *Theatres of Accumulation: Studies in Asian and Latin American Urbanization*. London: Methuen.

Arthur, W.B. 1989. Competing technologies, increasing returns, and lock-in by historical events, *Economic Journal*, 99, 116–31.

Artis, M. and Lee, N. (eds) 1994. *The Economics of the European Union*. Oxford: Oxford University Press.

Aryeetey-Attoh, S. (ed.) 1997. *Geography of Sub-Saharan Africa*. Upper Saddle River, NJ: Prentice Hall.

Auty, R.M. 1991. Third world response to global processes: the mineral economies, *Professional Geographer*, 43, 68–76.

Baer, W., da Fonseca, M.A.R. and Guilhoto, J.J.M. 1987. Structural changes in Brazil's industrial economy, 1960–80, *World Development*, 15, 275–86.

Bagchi-Sen, S. and Sen, J. 1997. The current state of knowledge in international business in producer services, *Environment and Planning A*, 39, 1153–74.

Bain, J.S. 1959. *Industrial Organization*. New York: John Wiley & Sons.

Bairoch, P. 1982. International industrialization levels from 1750 to 1980, *European Journal of Economic History*, 11, 269–333.

Balassa, B. 1979. *The Changing International Division of Labor in Manufactured Goods*. Washington, DC: World Bank, Working Paper 329.

Baldwin, R.E. 1994. *Towards an Integrated Europe*. London: Centre for Economic Policy Research.

Barff, R. 1995. It's gotta be da shoes, *Environment and Planning A*, 27, 55–79.

Barnes, M. and Haskel, J. 2001. *Job Creation, Job Destruction and Small Firms: Evidence from the UK.* Queen Mary, University of London Research Paper.

Barnet, R.J. and Cavanagh, J. 1994. *Global Dreams. Imperial Corporations and the New World Order.* New York: Simon & Schuster.

Barratt Brown, M. 1993. *Fair Trade: Reform and Realities in the International Trading System.* London: Zed Books.

Bates, R.H. 1983. *Essays on the Political Economy of Rural Africa*. Cambridge: Cambridge University Press.

Bayoumi, T. 1989. *Saving-Investment Correlations*. Washington, DC: IMF Working Paper 89/66.

Bayoumi, T. and Lipworth, G. 1997. Japanese foreign direct investment and regional trade, *Finance & Development*, September, 11–13.

Beenstock, M. 1983. *The World Economy in Transition*. London: Allen & Unwin.

Belderbos, R. and Zou, J. 2006. Foreign investment, divestment and relocation by Japanese electronics firms in East Asia, *Asian Economic Journal*, 20, 1–27.

Bellini, N. 1996. Regional economic policies and the non-linearity of history, *European Planning Studies*, 4, 63–73.

Belussi, F. 1996. Local systems, industrial districts and institutional networks: towards a new evolutionary paradigm of industrial economics?, *European Planning Studies*, 4, 5–26.

Beneria, L. 1981. Conceptualising the labour force: the underestimation of women's activities, *Journal of Development Studies*, 17, 10–27.

Benko, G. and Dunford, M. (eds) 1991. *Industrial Change and Regional Development: The Transformation of New Industrial Spaces*. London: Belhaven Press.

Berg, E.J. 1965. The development of the labor force in sub-Saharan Africa, *Economic Development and Cultural Change*, 13, 394–412.

Berry, B.J.L. 1991. *Long Wave Rhythms in Economic Development and Political Behavior*. Baltimore, MD: Johns Hopkins University Press.

Berry, B.J.L., Conkling, E.C. and Ray, D.M. 1976. *The Geography of Economic Systems*. Englewood Cliffs, NJ: Prentice Hall.

Beyon, J. and Dunkerley, D. (eds) 2000. *Globalization: The Reader*. New York: Routledge.

Biersteker, T.J. 1995. The 'triumph' of liberal economic ideas in the developing world, in B. Stallings (ed.) *Global Change, Regional Response: The New International Context of Development.* Cambridge: Cambridge University Press.

Bingham, R.D. and Hill, E.W. (eds) 1997. *Global Perspectives on Economic Development*. New Brunswick, NJ: Center for Urban Policy Research.

Birch, D.L. 1979. *The Job Generation Process*. Cambridge, MA: MIT Program on Neighborhood and Regional Change.

BISNIS (Business Information Service for the Newly Independent States) 2001. *Russia: Fact Sheet, July 2001*, available at http://www.bisnis.doc.gov/bisnis/country/RussiaFactsheet–2001.htm.

Blinder, Alan S. 2006. 'Offshoring: the next industrial revolution?', *Foreign Affairs*, March/April.

Bluestone, B. and Harrison, B. 1982. *The Deindustrialization of America*. New York: Basic Books.

Boggs, J.S. and Rantisi, N.M. 2003. The 'relational turn' in economic geography, *Journal of Economic Geography*, 3, 109–16.

Bonacich, E., Chen, L., Chinchilla, N., Hamilton, N. and Ong, P. 1994. *Global Production: The Apparel Industry in the Pacific Rim*. Philadelphia, PA: Temple University Press.

Borchert, J.R. 1967. American metropolitan evolution, *Geographical Review*, 57, 301–32.

Borchert, J.R. 1978. Major control points in American economic geography, *Annals of the Association of American Geographers*, 68, 214–32.

Boserup, E. 1981. *Population and Technology*. Oxford: Blackwell.

Bourgin, F. 1989. *The Great Challenge: The Myth of Laissez-Faire in the Early Republic*. New York: Geoge Braziller.

Bowler, I. 1985. *Agriculture under the Common Agricultural Policy*. Manchester: Manchester University Press.

Boyte, H. 1980. *The Backyard Revolution: Understanding the New Citizen Movement*. Philadelphia, PA: Temple University Press.

Bradford, C.I. 1987. Trade and structural change: NICs and next-tier NICs as transitional economies, *World Development*, 15, 299–316.

Bradley, P.N. and Carter, S.E. 1989. Food production and distribution – and hunger, in R.J. Johnston and P.J. Taylor (eds) *A World in Crisis?* 2nd edn. Oxford: Blackwell.

Bradshaw, M. 1991. *The Soviet Union: A New Regional Geography?* London: Belhaven Press.

Braudel, F. 1972. *The Mediterranean and the Mediterranean World in the Age of Phillip II* (trans. S. Reynolds). New York: Harper & Row.

Brenner, R. 1977. The origins of capitalist development: a critique of neo-Smithian Marxism, *New Left Review*, 104, 25–91.

Brockett, C.D. 1988. *Land, Power, and Poverty: Agrarian Transformation and Political Conflict in Central America*. Boston, MA: Unwin Hyman.

Brundenius, C. 1984. *Revolutionary Cuba: The Challenge of Economic Growth with Equity*. Boulder, CO: Westview.

Brunn, S. (ed.) 2006. *Wal-Mart World: The World's Biggest Corporation in the Global Economy*. New York and London: Routledge.

Brusco, S. and Sabel, C. 1981. Artisan production and economic growth, in F. Wilkinson (ed.) *The Dynamics of Labour Market Segmentation*. London: Academic Press.

Bryson, J.R., Daniels, P.W. Henry, N. and Pollard, J. (eds) 2000. *Knowledge, Space, Economy*. London: Routledge.

Bryson, J.R., Daniels, P.W. and Warf, B. 2004. *Service Worlds: People, Organisations, Technologies*. London and New York: Routledge.

Bryson, J.R., Henry, N., Keeble, D. and Martin, R. (eds) 1999. *The Economic Geography Reader*. New York: John Wiley & Sons.

Buchanan, K. 1972. *The Geography of Empire*. London: Spokesman Books.

Burbach, R. and Flynn, P. 1980. *Agribusiness in the Americas*. New York: Monthly Review Press.

Busse, M. 2002. *Competition Intensity, Potential Competition and Transaction Cost Economics*, HWWA Discussion Paper 183. Hamburg: Hamburg Institute of International Economics.

Buzzetti, L. 1996. Efforts to reorganize the state within the new international framework, in A. Vallega, R.C. de Azevedo, L. Buzzetti, A. Celant, P. Landini, B. Cardinale, F. Salvatori, G. Massimi, F. Martinelli, A. Montanari and G. Spinelli (eds) *The Geography of Disequilibrium: Global Issues and Restructuring in Italy*. Rome: Societa Geografica Italiana.

Cameron, R. 1973. The logistics of European economic growth: a note on historical periodization, *Journal of European Economic History*, 2, 145–58.

Carter, H. 1983. *An Introduction to Urban Historical Geography*. London: Edward Arnold.

Castells, M. 1988. High technology and urban dynamics in the United States, in M. Dogan and J. Kasarda (eds) *The Metropolis Era. Vol. 1: A World of Giant Cities*. Newbury Park, CA: Sage.

Castells, M. 2000. *The Information Age: Economy, Society and Culture: Volume I, The Rise of the Network Society* 2nd edn. Oxford: Blackwell.

Castells, M. and Hall, P. 1994. *Technopoles of the World. The Making of 21st Century Industrial Complexes*. London: Routledge.

Celant, A. 1996. Italy's foreign trade: economic and territorial characteristics, in A. Vallega, R.C. de Azevedo, L. Buzzetti, A. Celant, P. Landini, B. Cardinale, F. Salvatori, G. Massimi, F. Martinelli, A. Montanari and G. Spinelli (eds) *The Geography of Disequilibrium: Global Issues and Restructuring in Italy*. Rome: Societa Geografica Italiana.

Champion, A.G. and Townsend, A.R. 1990. *Contemporary Britain*. London: Edward Arnold.

Chandler, A.D. 1992. Organizational capabilities and the economic history of the industrial enterprise, *Journal of Economic Perspectives*, 6, 79–100.

Chaunu, P. 1969. *L'expression européenne du XIIIe au XVe siècle*. Collection Nouvelle Clio 26. Paris: Presses Universitaires de France.

Chernesky, R.J. 2006. *Strategic Alliances*. Dayton, OH: Chernesky, Heyman & Kress PLL.

Cheshire, P.C., D'Arcy, E. and Giussani, B. 1992. Purpose built for failure? Local, regional and national government in Britain, *Environment and Planning C: Government and Policy*, 10, 355–69.

Childe, V.G. 1950. The urban revolution, *Town Planning Review*, 21, 3–17.

Chisholm, M. 1982. *Modern World Development*. Totowa, NJ: Barnes & Noble.

Chisholm, M. 1990. *Regions in Recession and Resurgence*. London: Unwin Hyman.

Christopher, A.J. 1984. *Colonial Africa*. Beckenham: Croom Helm.

Christopherson, S. 1989. Flexibility in the US service economy and the emerging spatial division of labour, *Transactions of the Institute of British Geographers*, 14, 131–43.

Christopherson, S. 1995. Changing women's status in a global economy, in R.J. Johnston, P.J. Taylor and M.J. Watts (eds) *Geographies of Global Change*. Oxford: Blackwell.

CIA (US Central Intelligence Agency) 1999. *Handbook of International Economic Statistics*. Washington, DC: Directorate of Intelligence.

CIA 2001. *World Factbook 2001*. Washington, DC: Directorate of Intelligence, available at http://www.cia.gov.

Cipolla, C. 1981. *Before the Industrial Revolution. European Society and Economy, 1000–1700* 2nd edn. London: Methuen.

Claessens, S. and Jansen, M. (eds) 2000. *The Internationalization of Financial Services: Issues and Lessons for Developing Countries*. London: Kluwer Law International.

Claessens, S., Glaessner, T. and Klingebiel, D. 2002. *Electronic Finance: A New Approach to Financial Sector Development?* World Bank Discussion Paper No. 431. Washington, DC: World Bank.

Clark, C. 1977. *World Prehistory in New Perspective*. Cambridge: Cambridge University Press.

Clark, G.L. 1993. Global interdependence and regional development: business linkages and corporate governance in a world of financial risk, *Transactions of the Institute of British Geographers*, 18, 309–25.

Clark, G., Feldman, M. and Gertler, M.S. (eds) 2000. *The Oxford Handbook of Economic Geography*. New York: Oxford University Press.

Cline, W.R. 1982. Can the East Asian model of development be generalized?, *World Development*, 10, 81–90.

Coaffee, J. 2004. Rings of steel, rings of concrete and rings of confidence: designing out terrorism in Central London pre and post September 11th, *International Journal of Urban and Regional Research*, 28, 201–11.

Coffey, W.J. 2000. The geographies of producer services [progress report], *Urban Geography*, 21, 170–83.

Coghlan, A. 1993. Dying for innovation, *New Scientist*, 137, 12–14.

Cohen, A. 1974. *Two-Dimensional Man: An Essay on the Anthropology of Power and Symbolism in Complex Society*. Berkeley, CA: University of California Press.

Cohen, R.B. 1981. The new international division of labor, multinational corporations and the urban hierarchy, in M. Dear and A.J. Scott (eds) *Urbanization and Urban Planning in Capitalist Society*. London: Methuen.

Cohen, S.B. 1982. A new map of global geopolitical equilibrium: a developmental approach, *Political Geography Quarterly*, 1, 233–41.

Cohen, S.S. and Zysman, J. 1987. *Manufacturing Matters: The Myth of the Post-Industrial Economy*. New York: Basic Books.

Comisso, E. 1979. *Workers' Control under Plan and Market*. New Haven, CT: Yale University Press.

Commission of the European Communities 1973. *Report on the Regional Problem in the Enlarged Community (Thompson Report)*. Brussels: Commission of the European Communities.

Conzen, M.P. 1981. The American urban system in the nineteenth century, in D.T. Herbert and R.J. Johnston (eds) *Geography and the Urban Environment: Progress in Research and Applications, Volume IV*, Chichester: John Wiley & Sons.

Cook, P. and Kirkpatrick, C. 1997. Globalization, regionalization and third world development, *Regional Studies*, 31, 55–66.

Cooke, P. 1988. Flexible integration, scope economies, and strategic alliances: social and spatial mediations, *Society and Space*, 6, 281–300.

Cooke, P. 1992. Regional innovation systems: competitive regulation in the new Europe, *Geoforum*, 23, 65–82.

Cooper, F. 1980. *From Slaves to Squatters: Plantation Labour and Agriculture in Zanzibar and Coastal Kenya, 1890–1925*. New Haven, CT: Yale University Press.

Corbridge, S. 1982. Urban bias, rural bias, and industrialisation: an appraisal of the work of Michael Lipton and Terry Byres, in J. Harriss (ed.) *Rural Development: Theories of Peasant Economic and Agrarian Change*. London: Hutchinson.

Corbridge, S. 1986. *Capitalist World Development: A Critique of Radical Development Geography*. London: Macmillan.

Corbridge, S. 1993. *Debt and Development*. Oxford: Blackwell.

Corbridge, S.E. and Agnew, J.A. 1991. The US trade and budget deficits in global perspective: an essay in geopolitical economy, *Society and Space*, 9, 71–90.

Cornford, A. 2004. *The WTO Negotiations on Financial Services: Current Issues and Future Directions*. Geneva: UNCTAD.

CorpTech 2000. *CorpTech Directory of Technology Companies* 15th US edn. Woburn, MA: Corporate Technology Information Services.

Council of Economic Advisors 1991. *Economic Report of the President*. Washington, DC: US Government Printing Office.

Cowhey, P.F. and Aronson, J.D. 1993. *Managing the World Economy: The Consequences of Corporate Alliances*. New York: Council on Foreign Relations Press.

Cox, K.R. (ed.) 1997. *Spaces of Globalization: Reasserting the Power of the Local*. New York: Guilford Press.

CRIC 2006. *Innovation in Services*. CRIC Briefing No. 2. Manchester, Centre for Research on Innovation and Competition, University of Manchester.

Crook, C. 1991. Sisters in the wood: a survey of the IMF and the World Bank, *Economist*, 12 October.

Crossley, J.C. 1983. The River Plate countries, in H. Blakemore and C.T. Smith (eds) *Latin America: Geographical Perspectives* 2nd edn. London: Methuen.

Crow, B. and Thomas, A. 1985. *Third World Atlas*. Milton Keynes: Open University Press.

Cuadrado-Roura, J.R., Rubalcaba-Bermejo, L. and Bryson, J.R. (eds) 2002. *Trading Services in the Global Economy*. Cheltenham: Edward Elgar.

Cumings, B. 1984. The origins and development of the Northeast Asian political economy: industrial sectors, product cycles and political consequences, *International Organization*, 38, 1–40.

Cunningham, S. 1986. Multinationals and restructuring in Latin America, in C.J. Dixon, D.W. Drakakis-Smith and H.D. Watts (eds) *Multinational Corporations and the Third World*. Boulder, CO: Westview.

Currah, A. and Wrigley, N. 2004. Networks of organizational learning and adaptation in retail TNCs, *Global Networks*, 4, 1–23.

Curtin, P., Feierman, S., Thompson, L. and Vansina, J. 1978. *African History*. Boston, MA: Little, Brown.

Dalton, D.H. and Serapio, M.G. 1999. *Globalizing Industrial Research and Development*. Washington, DC: US Department of Commerce, Technology Administration Office of Technology Policy.

Daniels, P.W. 1985. *Service Industries: Growth and Location*. London: Methuen.

Daniels, P.W. 1991. A world of services?, *Geoforum*, 22, 359–76.

Daniels, P.W. and Bryson, J.R. 2002. Manufacturing services and servicing manufacturing: Knowledge-based cities and changing forms of production, *Urban Studies*, 39, 977–91.

Daniels, P. and Lever, W.F. (eds) 1996. *The Global Economy in Transition*. New York: Addison Wesley Longman.

Dawson, A.H. 1993. *A Geography of European Integration*. London: Belhaven Press.

Day, G. and Rees, G. (eds) 1991. *Regions, Nations, and European Integration: Remaking the Celtic Periphery*. Cardiff: University of Wales Press.

De Janvry, A. 1984. The role of land reform in economic development: policies and politics, in C.K. Eicher and J.M. Staatz (eds) *Agricultural Development in the Third World*. Baltimore, MD: Johns Hopkins University Press.

De Vries, J. 1976. *Economy of Europe in an Age of Crisis, 1600–1750*. Cambridge: Cambridge University Press.

De Vroey, M. 1984. A regulation approach to interpretation of the present crisis, *Capital and Class*, 23, 45–66.

DeGeer, S. 1927. The American manufacturing belt, *Geografiska Annaler*, 9, 233–359.

Destler, I.M. 1992. *American Trade Politics* 2nd edn. Washington, DC: Institute for International Economics.

Deudney, D. and Ikenberry, G.J. 1991/92. The international sources of Soviet change, *International Security*, 16, 74–118.

Diakosavvas, D. and Scandizzo, P. 1991. Trends in the terms of trade of primary commodities, 1900–1982: the controversy and its origins, *Economic Development and Cultural Change*, 39, 231–64.

Diamond, J. 1997. *Guns, Germs, and Steel*. New York: W.W. Norton.

Dicken, P. 1992. International production in a volatile regulatory environment: the influence of national regulatory policies on the spatial strategies of transnational corporations, *Geoforum*, 23, 303–16.

Dicken, P. 1994. Global-local tensions: firms and states in the global space-economy, *Economic Geography*, 70, 101–27.

Dicken, P. 1998. *Global Shift: Transforming the World Economy* 3rd edn. New York and London: Guilford Press.

Dicken, P. and Thrift, N. 1992. The organization of production and the production of organization: why business enterprises matter in the study of geographical industrialization, *Transactions of the Institute of British Geographers*, 17, 279–91.

Dobb, M. 1963. *Studies in the Development of Capitalism*. London: Routledge & Kegan Paul.

Donahue, J.D. 1997. The devil in devolution, *American Prospect*, 32, 42–7.

Dosi, G. 1988. Sources, procedure and microeconomic effects of innovation, *Journal of Economic Literature*, 26, 1–12.

Duignan, P. and Gann, L.H. 1985. *The United States and Africa: A History*. Cambridge: Cambridge University Press.

Duncan, K. and Rutledge, I. 1977. Introduction: patterns of agrarian capitalism in Latin America, in K. Duncan and I. Rutledge (eds) *Land and Labour in Latin America*. Cambridge: Cambridge University Press.

Dunford, M. 1990. Theories of regulation, *Society and Space*, 8, 297–321.

Dunford, M. 2002. *Cohesion and Enlargement*, paper presented at a Round Table on European Regional Disparities and the Cohesion and Structural EU Policy, Jean Monnet Graduate School in European Law and Economics, Belvedere di San Leucio, San Leucio, Caserta, Italy, 8 May.

Dunford, M. and Kafkalas, G. 1992. The global-local interplay, corporate geographies and spatial development strategies in Europe, in M. Dunford and G. Kafkalas (eds) *Cities and Regions in the New Europe*. London: Belhaven Press.

Dunford, M. and Perrons, D. 1983. *The Arena of Capital*. London: Macmillan.

Dunford, M. and Smith, A. 2000. Catching up or falling behind? Economic performance and regional trajectories in the 'New Europe', *Economic Geography*, 76, 169–95.

Dunning, J.H. 1979. Explaining changing patterns of international production: in defence of the eclectic theory, *Oxford Bulletin of Economics and Statistics*, 41, 269–96.

Dunning, J.H. 1983. Changes in the level and structure of international production: the last one hundred years, in M. Casson (ed.) *The Growth of International Business*. London: Allen & Unwin.

Dunning, J.H. (ed.) 1997. *Governments, Globalization, and International Business*. New York: Oxford University Press.

Dunning, J.H. and Norman, G. 1987. The location choice of offices of international companies, *Environment & Planning A*, 19, 613–31.

Durham, K.F. 1977. *Expansion of Agricultural Settlement in the Peruvian Rainforest: The Role of the Market and the Role of the State*, paper presented at the Latin American Studies Association, Houston, TX, 2–5 November.

*Economist* 1983. Hard pounding this, gentlemen: a survey of the world economy, 24 September.

*Economist* 1987. The rag trade: on the road to Mandalay, 27 June, 67–8.

*Economist* 1992a. Net financial flows to developing countries, 14 September, 120.

*Economist* 1992b. Zero inflation: how low is low enough?, 7 November, 23–6.

*Economist* 1992c. Survey: Russian reborn, 24 September, 25.

*Economist* 1993a. The global firm: RIP, 6 February, 69.

*Economist* 1993b. The final frontier, 20 February, 63.

*Economist* 1996a. Getting together, 29 June, 42–3.

*Economist* 1996b. How poor is China?, 12 October, 35–6.

*Economist* 1996c. The buying and selling of Brazil Inc., 9 November, 83–4.

*Economist* 1997. The last Emperor, 22 February, 21–5.

*Economist* 2001. The technology industry: big is beautiful again, 21 July, 51–2.

*Economist* 2005. Industrial metamorphosis, 29 September, 81–2.

*Economist* 2006. The euro and trade, 24 June, 90.

Edquist, C. 1985. *Capitalism, Socialism, and Technology: A Comparative Study of Cuba and Jamaica*. London: Zed Books.

Edwards, C. 1985. *The Fragmented World: Competing Perspectives on Trade, Money and Crisis*. London: Methuen.

Eichengreen, B. 1996. *Globalizing Capital: A History of the International Monetary System*. Princeton, NJ: Princeton University Press.

Eicher, C.K. 1984. Facing up to Africa's food crisis, in C.K. Eicher and J.M. Staatz (eds) *Agricultural Development in the Third World*. Baltimore, MD: Johns Hopkins University Press.

Eisenschitz, A. and Gough, J. 1992. *The Politics of Local Economic Policy: The Problems and Possibilities of Local Initiative*. London: Macmillan.

Eisenschitz, A. and Gough, J. 1996. The contradictions of neo-Keynesian local economic strategy, *Review of International Political Economy*, 3, 434–58.

Eisold, E. 1984. *Young Women Workers in Export Industries: The Case of the Semiconductor Industry in South East Asia*. Geneva: Working Paper, ILO World Employment Programme.

Elbaum, B. 1990. Cumulative or comparative advantage? British competitiveness in the early 20th century, *World Development*, 18, 1255–72.

Emmanuel, A. 1972. *Unequal Exchange: A Study of the Imperialism of Trade.* London: New Left Books.

Epstein, G. 1992. Political economy and comparative central banking, *Review of Radical Political Economics*, 24, 1–30.

Esser, S. 2001. Globalizing the board of directors, *Corporate Board*, 22, 1–5.

Ettlinger, N. 1991. The roots of competitive advantage in California and Japan, *Annals of the Association of American Geographers*, 81, 391–407.

Ettlinger, N. 1997. An assessment of the small-firm debate in the United States, *Environment and Planning A*, 29, 419–42.

Eurostat 2007. *News Release: Regional GDP per inhabitant in the EU27.* Luxembourg: Eurostat, available at http://epp.eurostat.ec.europa.eu/pls/portal/docs/PAGE/PGP_PRD_CAT_PREREL/ PGE_CAT_PREREL_YEAR_2007/PGE_CAT_PREREL_YEAR_2007_MONTH_02/1-19022007-EN-AP.PDF.

Evans, D. and Alizadeh, P. 1984. Trade, industrialization and the visible hand, in R. Kaplinsky (ed.) *Third World Industrialisation in the 1980s: Open Economies in a Closing World.* London: Cass.

Evans, P. 1979. *Dependent Development: The Alliance of Multinational, State, and Local Capitalism in Brazil.* Princeton, NJ: Princeton University Press.

Evans, P. 1987. Dependency and the state in recent Korean development: some comparisons with Latin American NICs, in K.D. Kim (ed.) *Dependency Issues in Korean Development: Comparative Perspectives.* Seoul: Seoul National University Press.

Evenson, R.E. 1984. Benefits and obstacles in developing appropriate agricultural technology, in C.K. Eicher and J.M. Staatz (eds) *Agricultural Development in the Third World.* Baltimore, MD: Johns Hopkins University Press.

FAO (Food and Agricultural Organization of the United Nations) 1992. *World Food Conference: Report.* Rome: FAO.

FAO 1995. *World Agriculture: Towards 2010.* Rome: FAO, available at http://www.fao.org/ inpho/ vlibrary/u8480e/U8480E0e.htm.

FAO 2000. *The State of Food Insecurity in the World, 2000.* Rome: FAO.

FAO 2001. *The State of Food Insecurity in the World, 2001.* Rome: FAO.

FAO 2004. *The State of Agricultural Commodity Markets.* Rome: FAO.

FAO 2005. *Summary of World Food and Agricultural Statistics.* Rome: FAO.

Farrell, D. (ed.) 2005. *The Emerging Global Labor Market.* San Francisco: The McKinsey Global Institute.

Feder, E. 1978. *Strawberry Imperialism.* Mexico City: Editorial Campesina.

Fiala, R. and Kamens, D. 1986. Urban growth and the world polity in the nineteenth and twentieth centuries: a research agenda, *Studies in Comparative International Development*, 21, 23 *The Emerging Global Labor Market* 35.

Fine, B. 1994. Towards a political economy of food, *Review of International Political Economy*, 3, 519–45.

Fisher, P.S. and Peters, A.S. 1997. Tax and spending incentives and enterprise zones, *New England Economic Review*, March/April, 109–30.

Fisher, R.C. 1997. The effects of state and local services on economic development, *New England Economic Review*, March/April, 53–67.

Flannery, K.V. 1969. Origin and ecological effects of early domestication, in P.J. Ucko and G.W. Dimbleby (eds) *The Domestication and Exploitation of Plants and Animals.* London: Duckworth.

Florida, R. and Smith, D.F. Jr 1993. Venture capital formation, investment and regional industrialization, *Annals of the Association of American Geographers*, 83, 434–51.

Forbes, D. and Thrift, N. 1987. International impacts on the urbanization process in the Asian region: a review, in R.J. Fuchs, G.W. Jones and E.M. Pernia (eds) *Urbanization and Urban Policies in Pacific Asia.* Boulder, CO: Westview.

*Fortune* 2002. *Fortune* magazine's Global 500 in 2000 (the world's largest corporations), available at http://www.fortune.com.

Fothergill, S. and Guy, J. 1990. *Retreat from the Regions: Corporate Change and the Closure of Factories.* London: Regional Studies Association.

Frank, A.G. 1967. *Capitalism and Underdevelopment in Latin America.* New York: Monthly Review Press.

Frankman, M.T. 1974. Sectoral policy preferences of the Peruvian government, 1946–1968, *Journal of Latin American Studies*, 6, 289–300.

Fridell, G. 2006. Fair trade and neoliberalism: Assessing emerging perspectives, *Latin American Perspectives*, 33, 8–28.

Friedman, B. 1989. *Day of Reckoning: The Consequences of American Economic Policy*. New York: Random House.

Friedmann, H. 1991. Changes in the international division of labor: agro-food complexes and export agriculture, in W.H. Friedland, L. Busch, F.H. Buttel and A.P. Rudy (eds) *Towards a New Political Economy of Agriculture*. Boulder, CO: Westview.

Friedmann, J. 1956. Locational aspects of economic development, *Land Economics*, 32, 213–27.

Friedmann, J. 1986. The world city hypothesis, *Development and Change*, 17, 69–84.

Friedmann, J. 1995. Where we stand: a decade of world city research, in P.L. Knox and P.J. Taylor (eds) *World Cities in a World-system*. Cambridge: Cambridge University Press.

Friedmann, J. and Weaver, C. 1979. *Territory and Function*. Berkeley, CA: University of California Press.

Fröbel, F., Heinrichs, J. and Kreye, O. 1977. *Die Neue Internationale Arbeitsteilung*. Reinbeck: Rowhohlt.

Fuchs, R.J. and Pernia, E.M. 1987. External economic forces and national spatial development: Japanese direct investment in Pacific Asia, in R.J. Fuchs, G.W. Jones and E.M. Pernia (eds) *Urbanization and Urban Policies in Pacific Asia*. Boulder, CO: Westview.

Galbraith, J.K. 1977. *The Affluent Society*. Boston: Houghton-Mifflin.

Galbraith, R. 2001. Leaner, more innovative, Italian footwear springs back to fore, *International Herald Tribune*, 27 June.

Galor, O. and Weil, D. 2000. Population, technology, and growth: from Malthusian stagnation to the demographic transition and beyond, *American Economic Review*, 90, 806–28.

Gann, L.H. and Duignan, P. 1978. *The Rulers of British Africa, 1870–1914*. Stanford, CA: Stanford University Press.

Geertz, C. 1973. *The Interpretation of Cultures*. New York: Basic Books.

Gellner, E. 1964. *Thought and Change*. London: Weidenfeld & Nicolson.

George, S. 1991. European political cooperation: a world-systems perspective, in M. Holland (ed.) *The Future of European Political Cooperation. Essays on Theory and Practice*. New York: St Martin's Press.

George, S. 1992. *The Debt Boomerang: How Third World Debt Harms Us All*. London: Pluto Press.

Gereffi, G. 1995. Global production systems and third world development, in B. Stallings (ed.) *Global Change, Regional Response: The New International Context of Development*. Cambridge: Cambridge University Press.

Gereffi, G. 1999. *A Commodity Chains Framework for Analyzing Global Industries*. Durham, NC: Duke University.

Gereffi, G. 2001. Shifting governance structures in global commodity chains, with special reference to the internet, *American Behavioural Scientist*, 44, 1616–37.

Gereffi, G. and Korzeniewicz, M. (eds) 1993. *Commodity Chains and Global Capitalism*. Westport, CT: Greenwood Press.

Gertler, M.S. 1986. Discontinuities in regional development, *Society and Space*, 4, 71–84.

Gertler, M.S. 1992. Flexibility revisited: districts, nation-states, and the forces of production, *Transactions of the Institute of British Geographers*, 17, 259–78.

Gibb, R. and Michalak, W. (eds) 1994. *Continental Trading Blocs: The Growth of Regionalism in the World Economy*. Chichester: John Wiley & Sons.

Gibson, M.L. and Ward, M.D. 1992. Export orientation: pathway or artifact?, *International Studies Quarterly*, 36, 331–44.

Gifford, P. and Louis, W.R. (eds) 1971. *France and Britain in Africa: Imperial Rivalry and Colonial Rule*. New Haven, CT: Yale University Press.

Gill, S. 1990. *American Hegemony and the Trilateral Commission*. Cambridge: Cambridge University Press.

Glasmeier, A. 1990. The role of merchant wholesalers in industrial agglomeration formation, *Annals of the Association of American Geographers*, 80, 394–417.

Glyn, A., Hughes, A., Lipietz, A. and Singh, A. 1990. The rise and fall of the Golden Age, in S.A. Marglin and J.B. Schor (eds) *The Golden Age of Capitalism: Reinterpreting the Postwar Experience*. Oxford: Clarendon Press.

Goldberg, M. 1987. *The Chinese Connection: Getting Plugged in to the Pacific Rim Real Estate, Trade and Capital Markets*. Vancouver: University of British Columbia Press.

Goldman Sachs 2003. *Dreaming with the BRICs: The Path to 2050*. Global Economics Paper No. 99. New York: Goldman Sachs, available at https://www.gs.com.

Goldsbrough, D. 1985. Foreign direct investment in developing countries: trends, policy issues, and prospects, *Finance and Development*, 22, 31–4.

Gomes, C. and Perez, A. 1979. The process of modernization in Latin American agriculture, *CEPAL Review*, 8, 55–74.

Goodman, M.K. 2004. Reading fair trade: political ecological imaginary and the moral economy of fair trade foods, *Political Geography*, 23, 891–915.

Gordon, D.M. 1979. *The Working Poor: Toward a State Agenda*. Washington, DC: Council of State Planning Agencies.

Gordon, D. 1988. The global economy: new edifice or crumbling foundations?, *New Left Review*, 68, 24–64.

Gordon, L. 2001. *Brazil's Second Chance: En Route toward the First World*. Washington, DC: Brookings Institution Press.

Gore, C. 1984. *Regions in Question: Space, Development Theory and Regional Policy*. London: Methuen.

Gough, J. 1996. Not flexible accumulation – contradictions of value in contemporary economic geography: 1. Workplace and interfirm relations, *Environment and Planning A*, 28, 2063–79.

Graham, S. and Marvin, S. 2001. *Splintering Urbanism*. New York: Routledge.

Grant, R.J. and Agnew, J.A. 1996. Representing Africa: the geography of Africa in world trade, 1960–1992, *Annals of the Association of American Geographers*, 86, 729–44.

Grant, R.J., Papadakis, M.C. and Richardson, J.D. 1993. Global trade flows: old structures, new issues, empirical evidence, in C.F. Bergsten and M. Noland (eds) *Pacific Dynamism and the International Economic System*. Washington, DC: Institute for International Economics.

Green, A.E. 1988. The north–south divide in Great Britain: an examination of the evidence, *Transactions of the Institute of British Geographers*, 13, 178–98.

Griffin, K. 1974. *The Political Economy of Agrarian Change*. Cambridge, MA: Harvard University Press.

Griffith-Jones, S. 1980. The growth of multinational banking, the Eurocurrency markets and their effects on the developing countries, *Journal of Development Studies*, 16, 96–109.

Griffith-Jones, S. and Rodriguez, E. 1984. Private international finance and industrialization in LDCs, in R. Kaplinsky (ed.) *Third World Industrialization in the 1980s: Open Economies in a Closing World*. London: Cass.

Griffith-Jones, S. and Stallings, B. 1995. New global financial trends: implications for development, in B. Stallings (ed.) *Global Change, Regional Response: The New International Context of Development*. Cambridge: Cambridge University Press.

Grindle, M.S. 1986. *State and Countryside: Development Policy and Agrarian Politics in Latin America*. Baltimore, MD: Johns Hopkins University Press.

Grote, M.H. and Täube, F.A. 2006. Offshoring the financial services industry: implications for the evolution of Indian IT clusters, *Environment and Planning A*, 38, 1287–305.

Gugler, J. 1980. A minimum of urbanism and a maximum of ruralism: the Cuban experience, *International Journal of Urban and Regional Research*, 4, 516–36.

Gugler, J. and Flanagan, W.G. 1978. *Urbanization and Social Change in West Africa*. Cambridge: Cambridge University Press.

Haggett, P. 1983. *Geography: A Modern Synthesis* 3rd edn. London: Harper & Row.

Hall, D. and Danta, D. (eds) 2000. *Europe Goes East: EU Enlargement, Diversity and Uncertainty*. London: The Stationery Office.

Hall, P. 1981. The geography of the fifth Kondratieff cycle, *New Society*, 55, 535–6.

Hall, T.D. 1986. Incorporation in the world-system: toward a critique, *American Sociological Review*, 51, 390–402.

Hamilton, C. 1983. Capitalist industrialisation in the four little tigers of East Asia, in P. Limqueco and B. McFarlane (eds) *Neo-Marxist Theories of Development*. Beckenham: Croom Helm.

Hamilton, F.E.I. 1978. Multinational enterprise and the European Economic Community, in F.E.I. Hamilton (ed.) *Industrial Change: International Experience and Public Policy*. London: Longman.

Hamilton, F.E.I. 1984. Industrial restructuring: an international problem, *Geoforum*, 15, 349–64.

Hammond, R. 1994. A geography of overseas aid, *Geography*, 79, 210–21.

Hancock, M.D., Logue, J. and Schiller, B. 1991. *Managing Modern Capitalism: Industrial Renewal and Workplace Democracy in the United States and Europe*. Westport, CT: Praeger.

Hansen, G. and Prescott, E. 2002. Malthus to Solow, *American Economic Review*, 94(2), 1205–17.

Hansen, N. 1981. Mexico's border industry and the international division of labor, *Annals of Regional Science*, 15, 1–12.

Hansson, K. 1952. A general theory of the system of multilateral trade, *American Economic Review*, 42, 59–88.

Hardy, S., Hart, M., Albrechts, L. and Katos, A. (eds) 1995. *An Enlarged Europe: Regions in Competition?* London: Regional Studies Association.

Hargittai, E. and Centeno, M.A. 2001. Introduction: defining a global geography. *American Behavioral Scientist*, 44, 1545–60.

Harrigan, J. and Martin, P. 2002. Terrorism and the resilience of cities, *Economic Policy Review*, 8, 97–116.

Harris, C. 1982. The urban and industrial transformation of Japan, *Geographical Review*, 72, 50–89.

Harris, N. 1978. *The Mandate of Heaven: Marx and Mao in Modern China*. London: Quartet.

Harris, N. 1986. *The End of the Third World: Newly Industrialising Countries and Decline of an Ideology*. London: I.B. Taurus.

Harris, N. 1996. *The New Untouchables: Immigration and the New World Worker*. London: Penguin.

Harrison, B. 1992. Industrial districts: old wine in new bottles?, *Regional Studies*, 26, 469–83.

Harrison, B. 1994. *Lean and Mean: The Changing Landscape of Corporate Power in the Age of Flexibility*. New York: Basic Books.

Harrison, B. 1997. Comments on 'The effects of state and local public policies on economic development', *New England Economic Review*, March/April, 140–1.

Harrison, B. and Bluestone, B. 1990. Wage polarization in the US and the 'flexibility' debate, *Cambridge Journal of Economics*, 14, 351–73.

Hart, K. 1982. *The Political Economy of Agriculture in West Africa*. Cambridge: Cambridge University Press.

Harvey, D. 1990. *The Condition of Postmodernity*. Oxford: Blackwell.

Harvey, D.W. 1988. The geographical and geopolitical consequences of the transition from Fordist to flexible accumulation, in G. Sternlieb and J.W. Hughes (eds) *America's New Market Geography: Nation, Region, and Metropolis*. New Brunswick, NJ: Center for Urban Policy Research.

Harvie, C. 1994. *The Rise of Regional Europe*. London: Routledge.

Hauchler, I. and Kennedy, P.M. 1994. *Global Trends*. New York: Continuum.

Hayami, Y. 1984. Assessment of the Green Revolution, in C.K. Eicher and J.M. Staatz (eds) *Agricultural Development in the Third World*. Baltimore, MD: Johns Hopkins University Press.

Hayes, S.L. and Hubbard, P.M. 1990. *Investment Banking: A Tale of Three Cities*. Cambridge, MA: Harvard Business School Press.

Haywood, J. 1998. *Historical Atlas of the 19th Century World 1783–1914*. New York: Barnes & Noble.

Heim, C.E. 1991. *Dimensions of Decline: Industrial Regions in Europe, the US, and Japan in the 1970s and 1980s*, paper presented at the Social Science History Association, Annual Meeting, New Orleans, November.

Held, D. and McGrew, A. (eds) 2000. *The Global Transformations Reader*. Malden, MA: Blackwell.

Henderson, J. 1989. *The Globalization of High Technology Production: Society, Space and Semiconductors in the Restructuring of the Modern World*. London: Routledge.

Henry, N. and Pinch, S. 2000. (The) industrial agglomeration (of Motor Sport Valley): a knowledge, space, economy approach, in J.R. Bryson, P.W. Daniels, N. Henry and J. Pollard (eds) *Knowledge, Space, Economy*. London: Routledge.

Hepworth, M. 1992. *Geography of the Information Economy*. London: Belhaven.

Herzog, H.W. and Schlottmann, A.M. (eds) 1991. *Industry Location and Public Policy*. Knoxville, TN: University of Tennessee Press.

Hewett, E.A. and Gaddy, C.G. 1992. *Open for Business: Russia's Return to the Global Economy*. Washington, DC: Brookings Institution.

Hicks, J.R. 1959. *Essays in World Economics*. Oxford: Oxford University Press.

Hill, P. 1986. *Development Economics on Trial: The Anthropological Case for the Prosecution*. Cambridge: Cambridge University Press.

Hirschman, A.O. 1958. *The Strategy of Economic Development*. New Haven, CT: Yale University Press.

Hirschman, A. 1992. Industrialization and its manifold discontents: west, east and south, *World Development*, 20, 1225–32.

Hirst, P. 1994. *Associative Democracy*. Cambridge: Polity Press.

Hirst, P. and Zeitlin, J. (ed.) 1989. *Reversing Economic Decline: Industrial Structure and Policy in Britain and Her Competitors*. Oxford: Berg.

Hobsbawm, E.J. 1968. *Industry and Empire*. New York: Pantheon.

Hoekman, B.M. and Kostecki, M.M. 1996. *The Political Economy of the World Trading System: From GATT to WTO*. New York: Oxford University Press.

Holland, S. 1980. *UnCommon Market*. London: Macmillan.

Holloway, S.R. and Pandit, K. 1992. The disparity between the level of economic development and human welfare, *Professional Geographer*, 44, 57–71.

Hopkins, A.G. 1973. *An Economic History of West Africa*. London: Longman.

Hopkins, M. 1983. Employment trends in developing countries, 1960–80 and beyond, *International Labour Review*, 122, 461–78.

Hopkins, T.K. and Wallerstein, I. 1979. Cyclical rhythms and secular trends of the capitalist world-economy, *Review*, 2, 483–500.

Hossain, M. 1982. Agrarian reform in Asia – a review of recent experience in selected countries, in S. Jones, M. Murmis and C. Joshi (eds) *Rural Poverty and Agrarian Reform*. New Delhi: Allied.

Howells, J. 2003. *Innovation, Consumption and Knowledge: Services and Encapsulation*. CRIC Discussion Paper No. 62. Manchester: University of Manchester, Centre for Research on Innovation and Competition.

Howells, J. and Wood, M. 1993. *The Globalisation of Production and Technology*. London: Belhaven Press.

Hsu, R.C. 1982. Agricultural financial policies in China, 1949–80, *Asian Survey*, 22, 638–58.

Hudson, R. 1983. Regional labour reserves and industrialization in the EEC, *Area*, 15, 223–30.

Hugill, P. 1993. *World Trade Since 1431. Geography, Technology, and Capitalism*. Baltimore, MD: Johns Hopkins University Press.

Hugill, P. 1999. *Global Communications since 1844: Geography, Technology, and Capitalism*. Baltimore, MD: Johns Hopkins University Press.

Hutton, W. 1995. *The State We're In*. London: Jonathan Cape.

Hutton, W. and Giddens, A. (eds) 2000. *Global Capitalism*. New York: New Press.

Hymer, S. 1972. The multinational corporation and the law of uneven development, in J.N. Bhagwati (ed.) *Economics and World Order*. London: Macmillan.

IFAD (International Fund for Agricultural Development) 2001. *Rural Poverty Report 2001: The Challenge of Ending Rural Poverty*. Rome: IFAD.

IFAD 2002. *Regional Strategy Paper: IFAD Strategy for Rural Poverty Reduction in Asia and the Pacific*. Rome: IFAD.

ILO (International Labour Office) 2000. *HIV/AIDS: A Threat to Decent Work, Productivity and Development*. Geneva: ILO.

ILO 2000. *Yearbook of Labour Statistics*. Geneva: ILO.

ILO 2004. *World Employment Report 2004–05*. Geneva: ILO.

ILO 2007. *Global Employment Trends*. January Brief. Geneva: ILO.

IMF (International Monetary Fund) 1991. *World Imports and Exports*. Washington, DC: International Monetary Fund.

IMF 2001. *World Economic Outlook: The Information Technology Revolution*. Washington, DC: IMF Publication Services.

Independent Commission on International Development Issues 1980. *North–South: A Programme for Survival (The Brandt Report)*. Oxford: Oxford University Press.

Independent Commission on International Development Issues 1983. *Common Crisis: North–South Cooperation for World Recovery (Brandt II)*. London: Pan Books.

Jackson, R.H. 1986. Conclusion, in P. Duignan and R.H. Jackson (eds) *Politics and Government in African States, 1960–1985*. Beckenham: Croom Helm.

Jackson, R.H. 1990. *Quasi-States*. Cambridge: Cambridge University Press.

Jacobs, J. 1969. *The Economy of Cities*. New York: Random House.

Jacobs, J. 1984. Cities and the wealth of nations, *Atlantic Monthly*, March, 41–66.

Jacquemin, A. 1987. *The New Industrial Organization*. Oxford: Clarendon Press.

Jenkins, R.O. 1988. *Transnational Corporations and Uneven Development: The Internationalization of Capital and the Third World*. London: Methuen.

Jessop, B. 1992. Post-Fordism and flexible specialization. Incommensurable, contradictory, or just plain different perspectives?, in H. Ernste and V. Meier (eds) *Regional Development and Contemporary Industrial Response*. London: Belhaven.

Joekes, S.P. 1987. *Women in the World Economy*. New York: Oxford University Press.

Johnson, A.W. and Earle, T. 1987. *The Evolution of Human Societies: From Foraging Group to Agrarian State*. Stanford, CA: Stanford University Press.

Johnston, R.J. 1980. *City and Society*. Harmondsworth: Penguin.

Johnston, R.J. 1984. The world is our oyster, *Transactions of the Institute of British Geographers*, 9, 443–59.

Johnston, R.J. 1986. The state, the region, and the division of labor, in A.J. Scott and M. Storper (eds) *Production, Work, Territory: The Geographical Anatomy of Industrial Capitalism*. Boston, MA: Allen & Unwin.

Johnston, R.J. 1992. The rise and decline of the corporate-welfare state: a comparative analysis in global context, in P.J. Taylor (ed.) *The Political Geography of the Twentieth Century*. London: Belhaven Press.

Johnston, R.J., Taylor, P.J. and Watts, M. (eds) 2002. *Geographies of Global Change: Remapping the World* 2nd edn. Cambridge, MA: Blackwell.

Jones, R.S., King, R.E. and Klein, M. 1993. Economic integration between Hong Kong, Taiwan and the coastal provinces of China, *OECD Economic Studies*, 20, 115–44.

Jones, S. 1982. Introduction, in S. Jones, M. Murmis and C. Joshi (eds) *Rural Poverty and Agrarian Reform*. New Delhi: Allied.

Jones, S., Murmis, M. and Joshi, C. (eds) 1982. *Rural Poverty and Agrarian Reform*. New Delhi: Allied.

Kaimowitz, D. 1995. *Livestock and Deforestation in Central America in the 1980s and 1990s: A Policy Perspective*. EPTD Discussion Paper No. 9. Washington, DC: Environment and Production Technology Division, International Food Policy Research Institute.

Kai-Sun, K, Leung-Chuen, C., Lui, F.T. and Qiu, L.D. 2001. *Industrial Development in Singapore, Taiwan, and South Korea*. River Edge, NJ: World Scientific.

Kaplinsky, R. 1984. *Automation: The Technology and Society*. London: Longman.

Kapur, D. and Ramamurti, R. 2001. India's emerging competitive advantage in services, *The Academy of Management Executive*, 15, 20–32.

Karmarkar, U. 2004. Will you survive the services revolution?, *Harvard Business Review*, 82, 101–7.

Katouzian, H. 1983. Shi'ism and Islamic economics: Sadr and Bani Sadr, in N.R. Keddie (ed.) *Religion and Politics in Iran: Shi'ism from Quietism to Revolution*. New Haven, CT: Yale University Press.

Kedourie, E. 1960. *Nationalism*. London: Hutchinson.

Kirchner, J. 1983. Supercomputing seen as key to economic success, *Computerworld*, 3 October, 8.

Knox, P.L. 1984. *The Geography of Western Europe: A Socio-Economic Survey*. Beckenham: Croom Helm.

Knox, P.L. 1994. *Urbanization: An Introduction to Urban Geography*. Englewood Cliffs, NJ: Prentice Hall.

Knox, P.L. 1995. World cities in a world-system, in P.L. Knox and P.J. Taylor (eds) *World Cities in a World-System*. Cambridge: Cambridge University Press.

Knox, P.L., Bartels, E.H., Bohland, J.R., Holcomb, B. and Johnston, R.J. 1988. *The US: A Contemporary Human Geography*. London: Longman.

Knox, P.L. and Taylor, P.J. (eds) 1995. *World Cities in a World-System*. Cambridge: Cambridge University Press.

Kopytoff, I. 1987. *The African Frontier: The Reproduction of Traditional African Societies*. Bloomington, IN: Indiana University Press.

Kornhauser, D. 1989. *Japan: Geographical Background to Urban and Industrial Development* 2nd edn. London: Longman.

Kosters, M.H. 1992. *Workers and Their Wages*. Washington, DC: American Enterprise Institute.

Krebs, G. 1982. Regional inequalities during the process of national economic development: a critical approach, *Geoforum*, 13, 71–81.

Krueger, A. 1978. Alternative trade strategies and employment in developing countries, *American Economic Review*, 68, 523–36.

Krugman, P. 1990. *The Age of Diminished Expectations: US Economic Policy in the 1990s*. Cambridge, MA: MIT Press.

Krugman, P. 1991. *Geography and Trade*. Cambridge, MA: MIT Press.

Krugman, P. 1994. The myth of Asia's miracle, *Foreign Affairs*, 73, 62–78.

Krugman, P. 1995. The localization of the world economy, *New Perspectives Quarterly*, Winter, 34–8.

Laird, S. and Yeats, A. 1990. Trends in non-tariff barriers of developed countries, 1966–1986, *Weltwirtschaftliches Archiv. Review of World Economies*, 126, 299–325.

Landes, D.S. 1999. *The Wealth and Poverty of Nations*. New York: W.W. Norton.

Landsberger, H.A. 1969. *Latin American Peasant Movements*. Ithaca, NY: Cornell University Press.

Langley, L.D. 1983. *The Banana Wars: An Inner History of American Empire, 1900–1934*. Lexington, KY: University Press of Kentucky.

Lanvin, B. 1991. Services and new industrial strategies: what is at stake for developing countries?, in P.W. Daniels and F. Moulaert (eds) *The Changing Geography of Advanced Producer Services: Theoretical and Empirical Perspectives*. London: Belhaven.

Lardy, N.R. 1984. Prices, markets, and the Chinese peasant, in C.K. Eicher and J.M. Staatz (eds) *Agricultural Development in the Third World*. Baltimore, MD: Johns Hopkins University Press.

Lash, S. and Urry, J. 1987. *The End of Organized Capitalism*. Cambridge: Polity Press.

Latham, A.J.H. 1978. *The International Economy and the Undeveloped World, 1865–1914*. Beckenham: Croom Helm.

Lavrov, S.B. and Sdasnyk, G.V. 1982. The growth pole concept and the regional planning experience of developing countries, *Development Dialogue*, 3, 15–27.

Lechner, F.J. and Boli, J. (eds) 2000. *The Globalization Reader*. Malden: Blackwell.

Lee, R. and Wills, J. (eds) 1997. *Geographies of Economies*. London: Edward Arnold.

Lele, U. 1984. Rural Africa: modernization, equity, and long term development, in C.K. Eicher and J.M. Staatz (eds) *Agricultural Development in the Third World*. Baltimore, MD: Johns Hopkins University Press.

Lessard, D.R. and Williamson, J. 1987. *Capital Flight and Third World Debt*. Washington, DC: Institute for International Economics.

Lesser, A. 1961. Social fields and the evolution of society, *Southwestern Journal of Anthropology*, 17, 40–8.

Leung, C.K. and Chin, S.S.K. (eds) 1983. *China in Readjustment*. Hong Kong: Centre for Asian Studies, University of Hong Kong.

Levy, F. and Murnane, R.J. 1992. US earnings levels and earnings inequality: a review of recent trends and proposed explanations, *Journal of Economic Literature*, 30, 1333–81.

Levy, F. and Murnane, R.J. 2004. *The New Division of Labor: How Computers are Creating the Next Job Market*. New York: Russell Sage Foundation.

Lewis, P. 1988. Third World funds: wrong way flow. *New York Times*, 11 February, D1, D9.

Lewis, W.A. 1978. *Growth and Fluctuations 1870–1913*. London: Allen & Unwin.

Leyshon, A. and Thrift, N. 1997. *Money/Space: Geographies of Monetary Transformation*. London: Routledge.

Light, I. 1983. *Cities in World Perspective*. New York: Macmillan.

Linge, G.J.R. and Hamilton, F.E.I. 1983. Industrial systems, in F.E.I. Hamilton and G.J.R. Linge (eds) *Spatial Analysis, Industry and the Industrial Environment*. Chichester: John Wiley & Sons.

Lipietz, A. 1986. Behind the crisis: the exhaustion of a regime of accumulation. A 'regulation school' perspective on some French empirical works, *Review of Radical Political Economics*, 18, 13–32.

Little, I. 1982. *Economic Development: Theory, Policy, and International Relations*. New York: Basic Books.

Lloyd, P. and Meegan, R. 1996. Contested governance: European exposure in the English regions, *European Planning Studies*, 4, 75–97.

Locatelli, R.L. 1985. *Industrializacao, Crescimento e Empregno: Uma Avaliacao da Experiencia Brasileira*. Rio de Janeiro: IPEA/INPES.

Lonsdale, J. 1985. The European scramble and conquest in African history, in R. Oliver and G.N. Sanderson (eds) *The Cambridge History of Africa: Vol. 6, From 1870 to 1905*. Cambridge: Cambridge University Press.

Loup, J. 1983. *Can the Third World Survive?* Baltimore, MD: Johns Hopkins University Press.

Lu, M., Fan, J., Liu, S. and Yan, Y. 2002. Employment restructuring during China's economic transition, *Monthly Labor Review*, August, 25–31.

MacFarquhar, R. 1992. Deng's last campaign, *New York Review of Books*, 17 December, 22–8.

MacLaughlin, J.G. and Agnew, J.A. 1986. Hegemony and the regional question: the political geography of regional industrial policy in Northern Ireland 1945–1972, *Annals of the Association of American Geographers*, 76, 247–61.

Maddison, A. 1983. A comparison of levels of GDP per capita in developed and developing countries, 1700–1980, *Journal of Economic History*, 43, 27–41.

Maddison, A. 2001. *The World Economy: A Millennial Perspective*. Paris: OECD Development Centre Studies.

Malassis, L. 1975. *Agriculture and the Development Process*. Paris: UNESCO.

Malecki, E. 1979. Locational trends in R&D by large US corporations, 1965–1976, *Economic Geography*, 55, 308–23.

Malecki, E. 1991. *Technology and Economic Development. The Dynamics of Local, Regional and National Change*. London: Longman.

Malmberg, A. and Maskell, P. 1997. Towards an explanation of regional specialization and industry agglomeration. *European Planning Studies*, 5, 25–41.

Mankiw, N.G. and Swagel, P. 2006. *The Politics and Economics of Outsourcing*. Working Paper 12398. Cambridge, MA: National Bureau of Economic Research.

Marks, S. and Rathbone, R. (ed.) 1982. *Industrialization and Social Change in South Africa*. London: Longman.

Markusen, A. 1983. High tech jobs, markets, and economic development prospects, *Built Environment*, 9, 18–27.

Marshall, A. 1920. *Principles of Economics*. London: Macmillan.

Marston, S.A., Knox, P.L. and Liverman, D.M. 2008. *World Regions in Global Context: Peoples, Places, and Environments* 3rd edn. Upper Saddle River, NJ: Pearson Education.

Martin, R.L. 1986. Thatcherism and Britain's industrial landscape, in R.L. Martin and B. Rowthorne (eds) *The Geography of Deindustrialization*. London: Methuen.

Martin, R.L. 1988. The political economy of Britain's north–south divide, *Transactions of the Institute of British Geographers*, 13, 389–418.

Martin, R.L. 1999. The new 'geographical turn' in economics: some critical reflections, *Cambridge Journal of Economics*, 23, 65–91.

Martin, R.L. and Hodge, J.S.C. 1983. The reconstruction of Britain's regional policy, 2: towards a new agenda, *Environment and Planning C: Government and Policy*, 1, 317–40.

Martin, R.L. and Rowthorn, B. (eds) 1986. *The Geography of De-Industrialisation*. London: Macmillan.

Mason, M. 1992. *American Multinationals and Japan: The Political Economy of Japanese Capital Controls, 1899–1980*. Cambridge, MA: Harvard University Press.

Massey, D. 1984. *Spatial Divisions of Labour*. London: Methuen.

Massey, D. 2005. *For Space*. London: Sage.

Massey, D. and Meegan, R. 1989. Spatial divisions of labour in Britain, in D. Gregory and R. Walford (eds) *Horizons in Human Geography*. Totowa, NJ: Barnes & Noble.

Mattera, P. 1985. *Off the Books: The Rise of the Underground Economy*. New York: St Martin's Press.

McCarthy, L. 2000. European integration, urban economic change, and public policy responses, *Professional Geographer*, 52, 191–205.

McDowell, L. 1991. Life without father or Ford: the new gender order of post-Fordism, *Transactions of the Institute of British Geographers*, 16, 400–19.

McGowan, K. 2001. Lessons from around the world, *American Demographics*, 23, 50–3.

McGranahan, D.V., Richard-Proust, C., Sovani, N.V. and Subramanian, M. 1970. *Content and Measurement of Socio-Economic Development*. Geneva: UNRISD.

McMichael, P. 1994. Agro-food restructuring in the Pacific Rim: a comparative-international perspective on Japan, South Korea, the United States, Australia, and Thailand, in R.A. Palat (ed.) *Pacific-Asia and the Future of the World-system*. Westport, CT: Greenwood Press.

McMichael, P. 1996. *Development and Social Change: A Global Perspective*. Thousand Oaks, CA: Pine Forge Press.

McMichael, P., Petras, J. and Rhodes, R. 1974. Imperialism and the contradictions of development, *New Left Review*, 85, 83–104.

Meadows, D.H., Meadows, D.L., Randers, J. and Behrens, W.W. 1972. *The Limits to Growth*. London: Earth Island.

Meier, G.M. and Baldwin, R.E. 1957. *Economic Development*. New York: John Wiley & Sons.

Menzel, U. and Senghaas, D. 1987. NICs defined: a proposal for indicators evaluating threshold countries, in K.D. Kim (ed.) *Dependency Issues in Korean Development: Comparative Perspectives*. Seoul: Seoul National University Press.

Metcalf, D. 1969. *The Economics of Agriculture*. Harmondsworth: Penguin.

METI 2001. *White Paper on International Trade 2001: External Economic Policy Challenges in the 21st Century*. Tokyo: Ministry of Economy, Trade and Industry.

Meyer, D.R. 1983. Emergence of the manufacturing belt: an interpretation, *Journal of Historical Geography*, 9, 145–74.

Mintz, S. 1985. *Sweetness and Power: The Place of Sugar in Modern History*. New York: Viking.

Mishra, P. 2007. Impasse in India, *New York Review of Books*, 28 June, 48–51.

Mittelman, J.H. 2000. *The Globalization Syndrome: Transformation and Resistance*. Princeton, NJ: Princeton University Press.

Morello, T. 1983. Sweatshops in the sun?, *Far Eastern Economic Review*, 15, September, 88–9.

Morris, M.D. 1980. *Measuring the Condition of the World's Poor*. New York: Pergamon.

Moudoud, E. 1986. *The Rise and Fall of the Growth Pole Approach*, Department of Geography Discussion Paper No. 89. Syracuse, NY: Syracuse University.

Murata, K. 1980. *An Industrial Geography of Japan*. London: Bell & Hyman.

Murphey, R. 1980. *The Fading of the Maoist Vision*. London: Methuen.

Myrdal, G. 1957. *Economic Theory and Underdeveloped Regions*. London: Duckworth.

Nairn, A. 1981. Guatemala, *Multinational Monitor*, 2, 12–14.

Nairn, T. 1977. Super-power or failure?, in T. Nairn (ed.) *Atlantic Europe?* Amsterdam: Transnational Institute.

Nakane, C. 1970. *Japanese Society*. London: Weidenfeld & Nicolson.

Nau, H.R. 1990. *The Myth of America's Decline: Leading the World Economy into the 1990s*. New York: Oxford University Press.

Nelson, R. 1995. Recent evolutionary theorizing about economic change, *Journal of Economic Literature*, 33, 1089–98.

Nelson, R. and Winter, S. 1982. *An Evolutionary Theory of Economic Change*. Cambridge, MA: Belknap Press of the Harvard University Press.

Neuman, S.G. 1984. International stratification and third world military industries, *International Organization*, 38, 167–98.

Newby, H. 1980. Rural sociology, *Current Sociology*, 28, 1–141.

Nolan, P. 1983. De-collectivization of agriculture in China, 1979–82: a long-term perspective, *Cambridge Journal of Economics*, 7, 381–403.

O'Brien, P. 1982. European economic development: the contribution of the periphery, *Economic History Review*, 35, 1–18.

O'Brien, R. 1992. *Global Financial Integration: The End of Geography*. New York: Council on Foreign Relations Press.

O'Connor, A.M. 1978. *The Geography of Tropical African Development: A Study of Spatial Patterns of Economic Change since Independence* 2nd edn. Oxford: Pergamon.

O'Farrell, P.N. and Wood, P.A. 1998. Internationalisation by business service firms: towards a new regionally based conceptual framework, *Environment and Planning A*, 30, 109–28.

O hUallacháin, B. 1996. Vertical integration in American manufacturing: evidence for the 1980s, *Professional Geographer*, 48, 343–56.

O'Loughlin, J. 1989. World power competition and local conflicts in the third world, in R.J. Johnston and P.J. Taylor (eds) *A World in Crisis? Geographical Perspectives* 2nd edn. Oxford: Blackwell.

O'Meara, P., Mehlinger, H.D. and Krain, M. (eds) 2000. *Globalization and the Challenges of a New Century*. Bloomington, IN: Indiana University Press.

ODCCP (United Nations Office for Drug Control and Crime Prevention) 2000. *Global Illicit Drug Trends 2000*. Vienna: ODCCP.

OECD (Organization for Economic Cooperation and Development) 1979. *The Impact of the NICs on Production and Trade in Manufactures*. Paris: Organization for Economic Cooperation and Development.

OECD 1996. *The Knowledge-Based Economy*. Paris: OECD.

OECD 2001a. *OECD in Figures, 2001: Statistics on the Member Countries*. Paris: OECD Observer.

OECD 2001b. *Understanding the Digital Divide*. Paris: OECD.

OECD 2006. *OECD in Figures, 2006–07 Edition: Statistics on the Member Countries*. Paris: OECD Observer.

Orwell, G. 1962 (1937). *The Road to Wigan Pier*. Harmondsworth: Penguin.

Owen, N. 1983. *Economies of Scale, Competitiveness, and Trade Patterns within the European Community*. Oxford: Clarendon Press.

Oxfam 2002. *Rigged Rules and Double Standards: Trade, Globalisation, and the Fight against Poverty*. Oxford: Oxfam International.

Oxfam 2004. *Trading Away our Rights: Women Working in Global Supply Chains*. Oxford: Oxfam International.

Parboni, R. 1988. US economic strategies against western Europe: from Nixon to Reagan, *Geoforum*, 19, 45–54.

Parker, J. 1992. Survey: Russia reborn, *Economist*, 5 December, 58.

Pauly, L.W. and Reich, S. 1997. National structures and multinational corporate behavior: enduring differences in the age of globalisation, *International Organization*, 51, 1–30.

Payer, C. 1974. *The Debt Trap*. Harmondsworth: Penguin.

Pearse, A. 1975. *The Latin American Peasant*. London: Cass.

Pearse, A. 1979. *Seeds of Plenty, Seeds of Want*. London: Oxford University Press.

Peck, J. and Tickell, A. 2002. 'Neoliberalizing space', in N. Brenner and N. Theodore (eds) *Spaces of Neoliberalism. Urban Restructuring in North America and Western Europe*. Oxford: Blackwell.

Peet, R. 1987. Industrial devolution, underconsumption and the third world debt crisis, *World Development*, 15, 777–88.

Peet, R. 1991. *Global Capitalism: Theories of Societal Development*. New York: Routledge.

Perez, C. 1983. Structural change and assimilation of new technologies in economic-social systems, *Futures*, 10, 357–75.

Perkins, D. and Yusuf, S. 1984. *Rural Development in China*. Baltimore, MD: Johns Hopkins University Press.

Perroux, F. 1955. Note sur la notion de pole de croissance, in I. Livingstone (ed.) 1979, *Development Economics and Policy: Selected Readings*. London: Allen & Unwin, 182–7.

Perroux, F. 1961. La firme motrice dans la région et la région motrice, *Thorie et Politique de la Expansion Regionale*. Liège: Université de Liège.

Petras, J. 1984. Toward a theory of industrial development in the third world, *Journal of Contemporary Asia*, 14, 182–203.

Picciotto, S. 1991. The internationalization of the state *Review of Radical Political Economics*, 22, 28–44.

Pinder, D. 1998. *The New Europe*. Chichester: John Wiley & Sons.

Piore, M. and Sabel, C. 1984. *The Second Industrial Divide*. New York: Basic Books.

Plant, R. 1998. *Indigenous Peoples and Poverty Reduction: A Case Study of Guatemala*. Washington, DC: Inter-American Development Bank.

Polanyi, K. 1957. The place of economies in societies, in K. Polanyi, C. Maynadier Arensberg and H.W. Pearson (eds) *Trade and Markets in the Early Empires*. Glencoe, IL: Free Press.

Pollard, S. 1981. *Peaceful Conquest: The Industrialization of Europe, 1760–1970*. Oxford: Oxford University Press.

Popke, J. 2006. Geography and ethics: Everyday mediations through care and consumption, *Progress in Human Geography*, 30, 504–12.

Porter, M.E. (ed.) 1986. *Competition in Global Industries*. Cambridge, MA: Harvard Business School Press.

Porter, M.E. 1990. *The Competitive Advantage of Nations*. New York: Free Press.

Powell, A. 1991. Commodity and developing country terms of trade: what does the long run show?, *Economic Journal*, 101, 1485–96.

Puyana de Palacios, A. 1982. *Economic Integration among Unequal Partners: The Case of the Andean Group*. New York: Pergamon.

Quinn, J.B. 1987. The impacts of technology in the service sector, in B.R. Guile and H. Brooks (eds) *Technology and Global Industry: Companies and Nations in the World Economy*. Washington, DC: National Academy Press.

Rada, J. 1984. *International Division of Labor and Technology*. Geneva: ILO.

Ranger, T. 1976. From humanism to the science of man: colonialism in Africa and the understanding of alien societies, *Transactions of the Royal Historical Society*, 26, 115–41.

Reardon, T., Timmer, C.P., Barrett, C.B. and Berdegué, J. 2003. The rise of supermarkets in Africa, Asia and Latin America, *American Journal of Agricultural Economics*, 85, 1140–6.

Reich, R. 1991. *The Work of Nations: Preparing Ourselves for 21st Century Capitalism*. New York: Vintage Books.

Reid, M. 1996. Mercosur: remapping South America, *Economist*, 12 October.

Reitsma, H.A. and Kleinpenning, J.M.G. 1985. *The Third World in Perspective*. Totowa, NJ: Rowman & Allanheld.

Reynolds, R. 1961. *Europe Emerges. Transition Toward an Industrial World-Wide Society*. Madison, WI: University of Wisconsin Press.

Richardson, R. and Belt, V. 2001. Saved by the bell? Call centres and economic development in less favoured regions, *Economic and Industrial Democracy*, 22, 67–98.

Roberts, S. 1994. Fictitious capital, fictitious spaces: the geography of offshore financial flows, in S. Corbridge, R. Martin and N. Thrift (eds) *Money, Power, and Space*. Oxford: Blackwell.

Rodriguez, E. and Griffith-Jones, S. (eds) 1992. *Cross-Conditionality, Banking Regulation and Third World Debt*. London: Macmillan.

Rogoff, K. 1992. Dealing with developing country debt in the 1990s, *The World Economy*, 15, 475–92.

Rokkan, S. 1980. Territories, centres and peripheries, in J. Gottmann (ed.) *Centre and Periphery*. London: Sage.

Rokkan, S. and Urwin, D. 1983. *Economy, Territory, Identity: Politics of West European Peripheries*. London: Sage.

Rondinelli, D.A. 1983. Dynamics of growth of secondary cities in developing countries, *Geographical Review*, 73, 42–57.

Roosevelt, A.C. 1992. Secrets of the forest: an archaeologist appraises the past – and the future – of Amazonia, *The Sciences*, November/December, 22–8.

Rose, R. 1984. *Understanding Big Government*. London: Sage.

Ross, R. 1982. Regional illusion, capitalist reality, *Democracy*, 2, 93–9.

Rowher, J. 1992. When China wakes: a survey, *Economist*, 28 November.

Rowher, J. 1993. A billion consumers: a survey of Asia, *Economist*, 30 October.

Rubenstein, J.M. 2005. *The Cultural Landscape: An Introduction to Human Geography* 8th edn. Upper Saddle River, NJ: Pearson/Prentice Hall.

Rudolph, L.I. and Rudolph, S.H. 1987. In *Pursuit of Lakshmi: The Political Economy of the Indian State*. Chicago, IL: University of Chicago Press.

Ruggie, J.G. 1983. International regimes, transactions and change: embedded liberalism in the postwar economic order, in S.D. Krasner (ed.) *International Regimes*. Ithaca, NY: Cornell University Press.

Sabel, C.F. 1982. *Work and Politics: The Division of Labor in Industry*. New York: Cambridge University Press.

Sachar, A. and Öberg, S. (eds) 1990. *The World Economy and the Spatial Organization of Power*. Brookfield, VT: Gower.

Sadler, D. 1992a. Industrial policy of the European Community: strategic deficits and regional dilemmas, *Environment & Planning A*, 24, 1711–30.

Sadler, D. 1992b. *The Global Region*. Tarrytown, NY: Pergamon.

Samuelson, P. 1964. *Economics*. New York: McGraw-Hill.

Sanders, R. 1987. Towards a geography of informal activity, *Socio-Economic Planning Sciences*, 21, 229–37.

Santiago, C.E. 1987. The impact of foreign direct investment on employment structure and employment generation, *World Development*, 15, 317–28.

Sassen, S. 2001. *The Global City: New York, London, Tokyo* rev. edn. Princeton, NJ: Princeton University Press.

Savitch, H.V. and Ardashev, G. 2001. Does terror have an urban future?, *Urban Studies*, 38, 2515–33.

Saxenian, A. 1994. *Regional Advantage: Culture and Competition in Silicon Valley and Route 128*. Cambridge, MA: Harvard University Press.

Sayer, A. 1985. Industry and space: a sympathetic critique of radical research, *Society and Space*, 3, 3–29.

Sayer, A. and Walker, R. 1992. *The New Social Economy: Reworking the Division of Labor*. Cambridge, MA: Blackwell.

Schejtman, A. 1982. Land reform and entrepreneurial structure in rural Mexico, in S. Jones, M. Murmis and C. Joshi (eds) *Rural Poverty and Agrarian Reform*. New Delhi: Allied.

Schiffer, J. 1981. The changing post-war pattern of development: the accumulated wisdom of Samir Amin, *World Development*, 9, 515–37.

Schoenberger, E. 1990. US manufacturing investments in western Europe: markets, corporate strategy, and the competitive environment, *Annals of the Association of American Geographers*, 80, 379–93.

Scott, A.J. 1986. Industrial organization and location: division of labor, the firm, and spatial process, *Economic Geography*, 62, 215–31.

Scott, A.J. 1987. The semi-conductor industry in Southeast Asia: organization, location, and the international division of labour, *Regional Studies*, 21, 143–60.

Scott, A.J. 1988a. Flexible production systems and regional development. The rise of new industrial spaces in Europe and North America, *International Journal of Urban and Regional Research*, 12, 171–86.

Scott, A.J. 1988b. *New Industrial Spaces*. London: Pion.

Scott, A.J. 1992. The role of large producers in industrial districts: a case study of high technology systems houses in southern California, *Regional Studies*, 26, 265–75.

Scott, A.J. 1993. *Technopolis: High-Technology Industry and Regional Development in Southern California*. Berkeley and Los Angeles: University of California Press.

Scott, A.J. 1996. Regional motors of the global economy, *Futures*, 28, 391–411.

Scott, A.J. 1998. *Regions in the World Economy*. Oxford: Oxford University Press.

Scott, A.J. 2000. *The Cultural Economy of Cities: Essays on the Geography of Image-Producing Industries*. London: Sage.

Scott, A.J. 2001. *Global City-Regions: Trends, Theory, Policy*. New York: Oxford University Press.

Scott, A.J. 2005. *On Hollywood: The Place, The Industry*. Princeton, NJ: Princeton University Press.

Scott, A.J. and Storper, M.J. (eds) 1986. *Production, Work, Territory*. London: Allen & Unwin.

Seers, D. 1979. The periphery of Europe, in D. Seers, B. Schaeffer, M.-L. Kiljunen (eds) *Underdeveloped Europe: Studies in Core-Periphery Relations*. Hassocks: Harvester Press.

Segal, G. 1999. Does China matter?, *Foreign Affairs*, 78, 24–36.

Seiber, M.J. 1982. *International Borrowing by Developing Countries*. New York: Pergamon.

Sen, A. 1981a. *Poverty and Famines: An Essay on Entitlement and Deprivation*. Oxford: Clarendon Press.

Sen, A. 1981b. Public action and the quality of life in developing countries, *Oxford Bulletin of Economics and Statistics*, 43, 111–23.

Sender, J. and Smith, S. 1986. *The Development of Capitalism in Africa*. London: Methuen.

Shaw, D. 1999. *Russia in the Modern World* 2nd edn. Oxford: Blackwell.

Shiba, T. and Shimotami, M. (eds) 1997. *Beyond the Firm: Business Groups in International and Historical Perspective*. New York: Oxford University Press.

Shunzan, Y. 1987. Urban policies and urban housing programs in China, in R.J. Fuchs, G.W. Jones and E.M. Pernia (eds) *Urbanization and Urban Policies in Pacific Asia*. Boulder, CO: Westview.

Shutt, J. and Whittington, R. 1987. Fragmentation strategies and the rise of small units: cases from the north west, *Regional Studies*, 21, 13–23.

SIA 2007. Global chip sales hit record $247.7 billion in 2006, Semiconductor Industry Association 2 February, available at http://www.sia-online.org/pre_release.cfm?ID=426.

Sirbu, M.A. Jr, Treitel, R., Yorsz, W. and Roberts, E.B. 1976. *The Formation of a Technology-Oriented Complex*. Cambridge, MA: MIT Center for Policy Alternatives.

Skocpol, T. 1976. France, Russia, China: a structural theory of social revolution, *Comparative Studies in Society and History*, 18, 181–96.

Slater, D. 1992. On the borders of social theory: learning from other regions, *Society and Space*, 10, 307–27.

Smeeding, T., O'Higgins, M. and Rainwater, L. (eds) 1990. *Poverty, Inequality, and Income Distribution in Comparative Perspective: The Luxembourg Income Study*. London: Harvester Wheatsheaf.

Smith, D. 1979. *Where the Grass is Greener*. Harmondsworth: Penguin.

Smith, I. 1979. The effects of external takeover and manufacturing employment change in the northern region, 1963–1973, *Regional Studies*, 13, 421–36.

Smith, R. and Walter, I. 1996. *Global Banking*. New York: Oxford University Press.

Smith, T. 1979. The underdevelopment of development literature: the case of dependency theory, *World Politics*, 31, 247–88.

Smith, T. 1981. *The Pattern of Imperialism: The United States, Great Britain, and the Late-Industrializing World since 1815*. Cambridge: Cambridge University Press.

South, R.B. 1990. Transnational 'maquiladora' location, *Annals of the Association of American Geographers*, 80, 549–70.

Stallings, B. 1990. The role of foreign capital in economic development, in G. Gereffi and D.L. Wyman (eds) *Manufacturing Miracles: Paths of Industrialization in Latin America and East Asia*. Princeton, NJ: Princeton University Press.

Stein, A.A. 1984. The hegemon's dilemma: Great Britain, the United States, and the international economic order, *International Organization*, 38, 355–86.

Stokes, E. 1959. *The English Utilitarians and India*. London: Oxford University Press.

Storper, M. 1987. The new industrial geography, *Urban Geography*, 8, 585–98.

Storper, M.J. and Harrison, B. 1991. Flexibility, hierarchy and regional development: the changing structure of industrial production systems and their forms of governance in the 1990s, *Research Policy*, 20, 407–22.

Storper, M.J. and Scott, A.J. (eds) 1992. *Pathways to Industrialization and Regional Development*. London: Routledge.

Streeten, P. 1968. A poor nation's guide to getting aid, *New Society*, 18, 154–6.

Stutz, F.P. and Warf, B. 2007. *The World Economy: Resources, Location, Trade and Development* 5th edn. Upper Saddle River, NJ: Pearson Education.

Suhartono, F.X. 1987. *Growth Centers in the Context of Indonesia's Urban and Regional Development Program*. MA thesis, Social Science Program, Syracuse University.

Sukhotin, I. 1994. Stabilization of the economy and social contrasts, *Problems of Economic Transition*, November, 44–61.

Sutcliffe, R.B. 1971. *Industry and Underdevelopment*. London: Addison-Wesley.

Sutcliffe, R.B. 1984. Industry and Underdevelopment re-examined, in R. Kaplinsky (ed.) *Third World Industrialization in the 1980s: Open Economies in a Closing World*. London: Cass.

Svedberg, P. 1991. The export performance of sub-Saharan Africa, *Economic Development and Cultural Change*, 39, 549–66.

Swindell, K. 1985. *Farm Labour*. Cambridge: Cambridge University Press.

Sylvester, D. 2001. Recession seen as painful cure for excesses of dot.com era, *Mercury News*, 1 October.

Szczepanik, E. 1969. The size and efficiency of agricultural investment in selected developing countries. *FAO Monthly Bulletin of Agricultural Economics and Statistics*, December, 2.

Tata, R.J. and Schultz, R.R. 1988. World variation in human welfare: a new index of development status, *Annals of the Association of American Geographers*, 78, 580–93.

Taussig, M. 1978. Peasant economies and the development of capitalist agriculture in the Cauca Valley, Colombia, *Latin American Perspectives*, 18, 62–91.

Taylor, A. 2000. Bumpy roads for global automakers, *Fortune*, 18 December.

Taylor, M.J. and Thrift, N.J. 1983. Business organisation, segmentation and location, *Regional Studies*, 17, 445–65.

Taylor, P.J. (ed.) 1992. *Political Geography of the Twentieth Century: A Global Analysis*. Harlow: Pearson Education.

Taylor, P.J. 2000. *Political Geography: World-Economy, Nation-State, and Locality* 4th edn. London: Longman.

Taylor, P.J. 2004. *World City Network: A Global Urban Analysis*. London: Routledge.

Taylor, P.J. 2007. Cities within spaces of flows: theses for a materialist understanding of the external relations of cities, in P.J. Taylor, B. Derudder, P. Saey and F. Witlox (eds) *Cities in Globalization: Practices, Policies and Theories*. London: Routledge.

Taylor, P.J., Derudder, B., Saey, P. and Witlox, F. (eds) 2007. *Cities in Globalization: Practices, Policies and Theories*. London: Routledge.

Tempest, R. 1996. Barbie and the world economy, *Los Angeles Times*, 22 September, A1, A12.

Terlouw, C.P. 1989. World-system theory and regional geography, *Tijdschrift voor Economische en Sociale Geografie*, 80, 206–21.

Terlouw, C.P. 1992. *The Regional Geography of the World-System: External Arena, Periphery, Semiperiphery, Core*. Utrecht: Netherlands Geographical Studies, No. 144.

Thiesenhusen, A. 1989. *Searching for Agrarian Reform in Latin America*. Boston, MA: Unwin Hyman.

Thomas, T. 1996. Africa for the Africans, *Economist*, 7 September.

Thrift, N. 1989. The geography of international economic disorder, in R.J. Johnston and P.J. Taylor (eds) *A World in Crisis?* 2nd edn. Oxford: Blackwell.

Thrift, N.J. 2002. A hyperactive world, in R.J. Johnston, P.J. Taylor and M. Watts (eds) *Geographies of Global Change: Remapping the World* 2nd edn. Oxford: Blackwell.

Thurow, L. 1993. *Head to Head: The Coming Economic Battle Among Japan, Europe, and America*. New York: Warner Books.

Tickell, A. 1999; 2001; 2002. *Progress in Human Geography* progress reports on the geography of services, 23, 633–9; 25, 283–92; 26, 791–801.

Tickell, A. and Peck, J.A. 1992. Accumulation, regulation and the geographies of post-Fordism, *Progress in Human Geography*, 16, 190–218.

Tilly, C. (ed.) 1975. *The Formation of National States in Western Europe*. Princeton, NJ: Princeton University Press.

Tilly, C. 1992. *Coercion, Capital, and European States*. Cambridge, MA: Blackwell.

Timmer, C.P. and Falcon, W.P. 1975. The political economy of rice production and trade in Asia, in L.G. Reynolds (ed.) *Agriculture in Development Theory*. New Haven: Yale University Press.

Tosh, J. 1980. The cash crop revolution in Africa: an agricultural reappraisal, *African Affairs*, 79, 79–94.

Toyota 2001. *Corporate Profile 2001*, Tokyo: Toyota, available at http://toyota.irweb.jp/IRweb/corp_info/datacenter/2001/2001databook.pdf.

Tunstall, J. 1986. *Communications Deregulation*. Oxford: Blackwell.

Tuong, H.D. and Yeats, A.J. 1981. Market disruption, the new protectionism, and developing countries: a note on empirical evidence from the US, *The Developing Economies*, 19, 107–18.

Turits, R. 1987. Trade, debt, and the Cuban economy, *World Development*, 15, 163–80.

Turnock, D. 1984. Postwar studies on the human geography of eastern Europe, *Progress in Human Geography*, 8, 315–45.

Turnock, D. (ed.) 2001. *East Central Europe and the Former Soviet Union: Environment and Society*. London: Arnold.

Turton, A. 1982. Poverty, reform and class struggle in rural Thailand, in S. Jones, M. Murmis and C. Joshi (eds) *Rural Poverty and Agrarian Reform*. New Delhi: Allied.

Tylecote, A. 1992. *The Long Wave in the World Economy: The Current Crisis in Historical Perspective*. London: Routledge.

Tyler, W.G. 1976. Manufactured exports and employment creation in developing countries: some empirical evidence, *Economic Development and Cultural Change*, 24, 355–73.

Tyler, W.G. 1981. Growth and export expansion in developing countries: some empirical evidence, *Journal of Development Economics*, 9, 121–30.

Tyler, W.G. 1986. Stabilization, external adjustment, and recession in Brazil: perspectives on the mid-1980s, *Studies in Comparative International Development*, 21, 5–33.

Tyson, L.D. 1992. *Who's Bashing Whom? Trade Conflict in High Technology Industries*. Washington, DC: Institute for International Economics.

UK Office of the Deputy Prime Minister 2004. *The English Indices of Deprivation 2004 (revised)*. London: HMSO, available at http://www.viral.info/iod/iodpdf/odpm_urbpol_029534.pdf.

UN (United Nations) 2000. *Economic Vulnerability Index: Explanatory Note*. New York: UN Committee for Development Policy, available at http://www.un.org/esa/analysis/devplan/cdp00p21.pdf.

UN 2001a. *2001 Report on the World Social Situation*. New York: Economic and Social Council.

UN 2001b. *World Economic and Social Survey 2001: Trends and Policies in the World Economy*. New York: UN Department of Economic and Social Affairs.

UN Centre for Human Settlements (Habitat) 2001. *Cities in a Globalizing World: Global Report on Human Settlements 2001*. Nairobi: UN.

UN Economic Commission for Europe 1972. *Economic Survey of Europe in 1971*. New York: United Nations.

UN Economic Commission for Europe 1979. *The European Economy in 1978*. New York: United Nations.

UN Economic Commission for Europe 1989. *Economic Survey of Europe in 1988–89*. New York: United Nations.

UNAIDS (Joint United Nations Programme on HIV/AIDS) 1999. *The UNAIDS Report*. Geneva: UNAIDS.

UNCTAD (United Nations Conference on Trade and Development) 1987. *Commodity Yearbook*. Geneva: UNCTAD.

UNCTAD 1994. *Commodity Yearbook*. Geneva and New York: UNCTAD.

UNCTAD 2000. *Handbook of Statistics*. New York and Geneva: UN.

UNCTAD 2001. *Economic Development in Africa: Performance, Prospects and Policy Issues*. New York and Geneva: UN (UNCTAD/GDS/AFRICA/1TB/B/48/12).

UNCTAD 2001. *World Investment Report 2001*. New York and Geneva: United Nations.

UNCTAD 2003. *E-Commerce and Development Report 2003*. New York and Geneva: United Nations.

UNCTAD 2004. *World Investment Report 2004: The Shift towards Services*. New York and Geneva: United Nations.

UNCTAD 2006. *World Investment Report 2006: FDI from Developing and Transition Economies: Implications for Development*. New York and Geneva: United Nations.

UNDP (United Nations Development Programme) 2001. *Human Development Report 2001: Making New Technologies Work for Human Development*. New York and Oxford: Oxford University Press.

UNDP 2005. *Human Development Report 2005: International Cooperation at a Crossroads*. New York: UNDP.

UNDP 2006. *Human Development Report 2006: Beyond Scarcity: Power, Poverty and the Global Water Crisis*. New York and Oxford: Oxford University Press.

UNEP (United Nations Environment Programme) 2002. *Vital Water Graphics: An Overview of the State of the World's Fresh and Marine Waters*. New York: UNEP, available at http://www.unep.org/vitalwater.

UNFPA (United Nations Population Fund) 2001. *The State of World Population 2001*. New York: UNFPA.

UNIDO (United Nations Industrial Development Organization). Various issues. *Industrial Development: Global Report*. Oxford: Oxford University Press.

UNIDO 1981. *A Statistical Review of the World Industrial Situation, 1980*. Vienna: United Nations Industrial Development Organization.

UNIDO 2000. *UNIDO Round Table – Marginalization versus Prosperity*. Vienna: UNIDO.

Urry, J. 1985. Social relations, space and time, in D. Gregory and J. Urry (eds) *Social Relations and Spatial Structures*. London: Macmillan.

US Census Bureau 1999. *Statistics of US Businesses: 1999, Manufacturing*. Washington, DC: US Department of Commerce, available at http://www.census.gov/epcd/susb/1999/ us/US31.HTM.

US Census Bureau 2007. *International Data Base*. Washington, DC: US Department of Commerce, available at http://www.census.gov/.

US Department of Agriculture (USDA) 2002. *Agricultural Outlook*. AGO-293, August. Washington, DC: USDA Economic Research Service.

US Department of Commerce, Bureau of Economic Analysis 1999. *Preliminary Results from 1999 Foreign Direct Investment in the United States: Operations of US Affiliates of Foreign Companies*. Washington, DC: BEA.

US Department of Commerce 2000. *Digital Economy 2000*. Washington, DC: Economics and Statistics Administration.

US Department of Housing and Urban Development 1982. *The President's National Urban Policy Report 1982*. Washington, DC: US Government Printing Office.

US Department of Labor 2001a. *International Comparisons of Hourly Compensation Costs for Production Workers in Manufacturing, 2000*. Washington, DC: Bureau of Labor Statistics.

US Department of Labor 2001b. *International Comparisons of Manufacturing Productivity and Unit Labor Cost Trends, 2000*. Washington, DC: Bureau of Labor Statistics.

US Department of Labor 2002. *Comparative Civilian Labor Force Statistics, Ten Countries, 1959–2001*. Washington, DC: Bureau of Labor Statistics.

Vance, J. Jr 1970. *The Merchant's World: The Geography of Wholesaling*. Englewood Cliffs, NJ: Prentice Hall.

Venables, A.J. 2006. Shifts in economic geography and their causes, *Federal Reserve Bank of Kansas City Economic Review*, 31, 61–85.

Verhulst, A. 1999. *The Rise of Cities in North-West Europe*. Cambridge: Cambridge University Press.

Vernon, R. 1966. International investment and international trade in the product cycle, *Quarterly Journal of Economics*, 80, 190–207.

Vogel, D. 2001. *The Regulation of GMOs in Europe and the United States: A Case-Study of Contemporary European Regulatory Politics*, paper prepared for a workshop on trans-Atlantic differences in GMO regulation sponsored by the Council on Foreign Relations.

Vogel, E. 1980. *Japan as Number 1: Lessons for America*. New York: Harper & Row.

Wachtel, H.M. 1987. Currency without a country: the global funny money game, *The Nation*, 245, 26 December, 784–90.

Walker, R. 1988. The geographical organization of production-systems, *Society and Space*, 6, 377–408.

Wallerstein, I. 1974. *The Modern World-System: Capitalist Agriculture and the Origins of the European World-Economy in the Sixteenth Century*. New York: Academic Press.

Wallerstein, I. 1979a. *The Capitalist World-Economy*. Cambridge: Cambridge University Press.

Wallerstein, I. 1979b. Underdevelopment and Phase-B, in W. Woldfrank (ed.) *The World-System of Capitalism: Past and Present*. Beverly Hills, CA: Sage.

Wallerstein, I. 1980. *The Modern World-System II: Mercantilism and the Consolidation of the World-Economy 1600–1750*. London: Academic Press.

Wallerstein, I. 1984. *The Politics of the World-Economy*. Cambridge: Cambridge University Press.

Wallerstein, I. 1991. *Geopolitics and Geoculture. Essays on the Changing World-System*. Cambridge: Cambridge University Press.

Warf, B. 1990. US employment in foreign-owned high-technology firms, *Professional Geographer*, 42, 421–32.

Warf, B. 1995. Telecommunications and the changing geographies of knowledge transmission in the late 20th century, *Urban Studies*, 32, 361–78.

Warf, B. 2001. Segueways into cyberspace: multiple geographies of the digital divide, *Environment and Planning B: Planning and Design*, 28, 3–19.

Warf, B. 2007. Embodied information, actor-networks, and global value-added services, in J. Bryson and P. Daniels (eds) *The Handbook of Service Industries*. London: Edward Elgar.

Warman, A. 1980. *'We Come to Object': The Peasants of Morelos and the National State*. Baltimore, MD: Johns Hopkins University Press.

Warren, B. 1980. *Imperialism, Pioneer of Capitalism*. London: Verso.

Wasylenko, M. 1991. Empirical evidence on interregional business location decisions and the role of fiscal incentives in economic development, in H.W. Herzog and A.W. Schlottmann (eds) *Industry Location and Public Policy*. Knoxville, TN: University of Tennessee Press.

Wasylenko, M. 1997. Taxation and economic development: the state of the economic literature, *New England Economic Review*, March/April, 37–52.

Watts, M. 1994. Life under contract: contract farming, agrarian restructuring and flexible accumulation, in P.D. Little and M.J. Watts (eds) *Living Under Contract: Contract Farming and Agrarian Transformation in Sub-Saharan Africa*. Madison, WI: University of Wisconsin Press.

Webb, M.C. 1991. International economic structures, government interests, and international coordination of macroeconomic adjustment policies, *International Organization*, 45, 309–42.

Webber, M.J. and Rigby, D.L. 1996. *The Golden Age Illusion: Rethinking Postwar Capitalism*. New York: Guilford Press.

Wei, Y.D. 2000. *Regional Development in China: States, Globalization, and Inequality*. London and New York: Routledge.

Wells, L.T. 1972. International trade: the product lifecycle approach, in L.T. Wells (ed.) *The Product life-cycle and International Trade*. Boston, MA: Harvard University Press.

Wells, P. and Rawlinson, M. 1992. New procurement regimes and the spatial distribution of suppliers: the case of Ford in Europe, *Area*, 24, 380–90.

White, G. 1987. Cuban planning in the mid-1980s: centralization, decentralization and participation, *World Development*, 15, 153–61.

Wigen, K. 1992. The geographic imagination in early modern Japanese history, *Journal of Asian Studies*, 51, 3–29.

Williams, A.M. 1994. *The European Community* 2nd edn. Oxford: Blackwell.

Williams, C.H. (ed.) 1982. *National Separatism*. Cardiff: University of Wales Press.

Williams, D.E. 1992. Motives for retailer internationalisation: their impact, structure and implications, *Journal of Marketing Management*, 8, 269–85.

Williams, G. 1981. *Third World Political Organizations*. Montclair, NJ: Allenheld, Osmun.

Williams, K., Cutler, T., Williams, J. and Haslam, C. 1987. The end of mass production?, *Economy and Society*, 16, 405–39.

Williams, R. 1983. *The Year 2000: A Radical Look at the Future and What We Can Do to Change It*. New York: Pantheon.

Williams, R.G. 1986. *Export Agriculture and the Crisis in Central America*. Chapel Hill, NC: University of North Carolina Press.

Williams, W.A. 1981. Radicals and regionalism, *Democracy*, 1, 87–98.

Williamson, J.G. 1965. Regional inequality and the process of national development, *Economic Development & Cultural Change*, 13, 3–45.

Williamson, O.E. 1985. *The Economic Institutions of Capitalism*. New York: Free Press.

Wise, M. and Gibb, R. 1993. *Single Market to Social Europe*. London: Longman.

Wolf, E.R. 1968. *Peasant Wars of the Twentieth Century*. New York: Harper & Row.

Wolf, E.R. 1982. *Europe and the People without History*. Berkeley, CA: University of California Press.

Wong, K.Y. 1987. China's special economic zone experiment: an appraisal, *Geografiska Annaler, B*, 69, 27–40.

Woolley, L. 1963. The urbanisation of society, in J. Hawkes and L. Woolley (eds) *History of Mankind, Vol. 1, Part 2: The Beginnings of Civilisation*. Paris: UNESCO.

World Bank 1979. *World Trade and Output of Manufactures*. Staff Working Paper, January.

World Bank 1982. *World Development Report 1982*. New York: Oxford University Press.

World Bank 1983. *World Development Report 1983*. New York: Oxford University Press.

World Bank 1991. *World Development Report 1991*. New York: Oxford University Press.

World Bank 1992. *World Development Report 1992*. New York: Oxford University Press.

World Bank 1995. *World Development Report 1995: Workers in an Integrating World*. Oxford: Oxford University Press.

World Bank 1996. *World Development Report 1996: From Plan to Market*. New York: Oxford University Press.

World Bank 1998. *MIGA: The First Ten Years*. Washington, DC: Multilateral Investment Guarantee Agency.

World Bank 2000. *World Development Report 2000/2001: Attacking Poverty*. Oxford: Oxford University Press.

World Bank 2001a. *A Study of Alternative Special and Differential Arrangements for Small Economies*. Washington, DC: World Bank.

World Bank 2001b. *Global Development Finance 2001*. Washington, DC: World Bank.

World Bank 2001c. *World Development Indicators 2001*. Washington, DC: World Bank.

World Bank 2001d. *World Development Report 2001*. Washington, DC: World Bank.

World Bank 2002. *Globalization, Growth, and Poverty: Building an Inclusive World Economy*. New York: Oxford University Press.

World Bank 2006. *World Development Indicators 2006*. Washington, DC: World Bank.

World Commission on Environment and Development 1987. *Our Common Future*. New York: Oxford University Press.

World Resources Institute 1996. *World Resources 1996–97*. New York: Oxford University Press.

World Resources Institute 2000. *World Resources 2000–2001: People and Ecosystems: The Fraying Web of Life*. Oxford: Elsevier Science and World Resources Institute, available at http://www.wri.org/ wr2000/.

World Trade Organization (WTO) 2001. *International Trade Statistics 2001*. Geneva: WTO.

WTO 2004. *Developing Countries in the WTO Services Negotiations*. Staff working paper ERSD-2004-06. Geneva: Economic Research and Statistics Division.

WTO 2006. *World Trade Report 2006: Exploring the Links between Subsidies, Trade and the WTO*. Geneva: WTO, available at http://www.wto.org/english/res_e/booksp_e/anrep_e/world_trade_report06_e.pdf.

World Wildlife Fund (WWF) 2000. *Living Planet Report 2000*. Gland, Switzerland: WWF, available at http://www.panda.org/livingplanet/lpr00/.

WWF 2006. *LivingPlanet Report 2006*. Gland, Switzerland: WWF, available at http://assets.panda.org/downloads/living_planet_report.pdf.

Wortman, S. and Cummings, R.W. 1978. *To Feed This World*. Baltimore. MD: Johns Hopkins University Press.

Yang, D. 1994. Reform and the restructuring of central-local relations, in D.S.G. Goodman and G. Segal (eds) *China Deconstructs: Politics, Trade and Regionalism*. London: Routledge.

Yang, F. 2004. Services and metropolitan development in China: the case of Guangzhou, *Progress in Planning*, 61, 181–209.

Yapa, L. 1979. Ecopolitical economy of the Green Revolution, *Professional Geographer*, 31, 371–6.

Yapa, L. 1980. The concept of the basic goods theory, in R.L. Singh and R.P.B. Singh (eds) *Rural Habitat Transformation in World Frontiers*. Varanasi: National Geographical Society of India.

Yates, R.L. 1959. *Forty Years of Foreign Trade*. London: Allen & Unwin.

Yusuf, F. 2001. The East Asian miracle at the millennium, in J.E. Stiglitz and S. Yusuf (eds) *Rethinking the East Asian Miracle*. Washington, DC and New York: World Bank and Oxford University Press.

Ziegler, C. 2007. *Favored Flowers: Culture and Economy in a Global System*. Durham, NC: Duke University Press.

Zimbalist, A. 1987. Cuban industrial growth, 1965–84, *World Development*, 15, 83–93.

Zimbalist, A. and Eckstein, S. 1987. Patterns of Cuban development, *World Development*, 15, 5–22.

Zinnov 2005. *Outsourcing: Product Innovation from India*, available at RealInnovation.com.

Zysman, J. 1983. *Government, Markets and Growth: Financial Systems and the Politics of Industrial Change*. Ithaca, NY: Cornell University Press.

# Index